COMPANY MEETINGS

Law, Practice and Procedure

COMPANY MEETINGS

Law, Practice and Procedure

Leslie Kosmin QC
Catherine Roberts

OXFORD
UNIVERSITY PRESS

OXFORD
UNIVERSITY PRESS

Great Clarendon Street, Oxford OX2 6DP

Oxford University Press is a department of the University of Oxford.
It furthers the University's objective of excellence in research, scholarship,
and education by publishing worldwide in

Oxford New York

Auckland Cape Town Dar es Salaam Hong Kong Karachi
Kuala Lumpur Madrid Melbourne Mexico City Nairobi
New Delhi Shanghai Taipei Toronto

With offices in

Argentina Austria Brazil Chile Czech Republic France Greece
Guatemala Hungary Italy Japan Poland Portugal Singapore
South Korea Switzerland Thailand Turkey Ukraine Vietnam

Published in the United States
by Oxford University Press Inc., New York

First published 2008

British Library Cataloguing in Publication Data
Data available

Library of Congress Cataloging in Publication Data
Data available

Typeset by Cepha Imaging Private Ltd, Bangalore, India
Printed in Great Britain
on acid-free paper by
CPI Antony Rowe, Chippenham

ISBN 978-0-19-921454-9

1 3 5 7 9 10 8 6 4 2

ὅτι μὲν τοίνυν ἀνάγκη νομοθέτην αὐτὸν εἶναι, δῆλον, καὶ κεῖσθαι νόμους, ἀλλὰ μὴ κυρίους ᾗ παρεκβαίνουσιν, ἐπεὶ περὶ τῶν γ' ἄλλων εἶναι δεῖ κυρίους· ὅσα δὲ μὴ δυνατὸν τὸν νόμον κρίνειν ἢ ὅλως ἢ εὖ, πότερον ἕνα τὸν ἄριστον δεῖ ἄρχειν ἢ πάντας; καὶ γὰρ νῦν συνιόντες δικάζουσι καὶ βουλεύονται καὶ κρίνουσιν, αὗται δ' αἱ κρίσεις εἰσὶ πᾶσαι περὶ τῶν καθ' ἕκαστον. καθ' ἕνα μὲν οὖν συμβαλλόμενος ὁστισοῦν ἴσως χείρων· ἀλλ' ἐστὶν ἡ πόλις ἐκ πολλῶν, ὥσπερ ἑστίασις συμφορητὸς καλλίων μιᾶς καὶ ἁπλῆς· διὰ τοῦτο καὶ κρίνει ἄμεινον ὄχλος πολλὰ ἢ εἷς ὁστισοῦν.

The best man, then, must legislate, and laws must be passed, but these laws will have no authority when they miss the mark, though in all other cases retaining their authority. But when the law cannot determine a point at all, or not well, should the one best man or should all decide? According to our present practice Assemblies meet, sit in judgment, deliberate, and decide, and their judgments all relate to individual cases. Now any member of the Assembly, taken separately, is certainly inferior to the wise man. But the state is made up of many individuals. And as a feast to which all the guests contribute is better than a banquet furnished by a single man, so a multitude is a better judge of many things than any individual.

Aristotle, *Politics* 1286a 22–31

Νῦν οὖν ἀτεχνῶς ἥκω παρεσκευασμένος βοᾶν, ὑποκρούειν, λοιδορεῖν τοὺς ῥήτορας.

Now, indeed, I have come to the Assembly, fully prepared to brawl, interrupt and abuse the speakers.

Aristophanes, *Acharnians* 37–8

PREFACE

Legislation regulating the affairs of companies has formed part of the legal landscape since the mid-nineteenth century. It is fair to observe that as the years have gone by such legislation has grown in detail, length and complexity. This statement is well illustrated by the most recent legislation, the Companies Act 2006, which received the Royal Assent on 8 November 2006. This is primary legislation on a grand and expansive scale, comprising 47 different Parts, 1,300 sections and 16 schedules, not to mention detailed explanatory notes and a seemingly constant supply of associated statutory instruments.

Notwithstanding the vast and record-breaking length of the legislation it is sad to note that there are no glittering prizes for the implementation of this legislative leviathan, which has proved to be both piecemeal and protracted. Even today, more than a year and a half since receiving the Royal Assent, not all of the legislative provisions have been brought into legal force. As a consequence, practitioners and others who are concerned with the administration of companies and, most importantly, those whose conduct is directly affected by the legislation, have to grapple with an array of complex commencement orders some of which make significant amendments to the primary legislation. Those who are engaged in law reform often assert that it is their intention to clarify and simplify the law. Surely this laudable aim is defeated or at the least very seriously undermined, when the implementation of important legislative changes is the subject of a seemingly endless stream of delegated legislation of labyrinthine complexity.

The Companies Act 2006, in common with its statutory predecessors, makes provision for the regulation of company meetings. Most of the legislative provisions are directed at meetings of members. The section numbers of the provisions contained in the Companies Act 1985 that regulate meetings and that are familiar to established practitioners will have to be re-learned and substituted for those that are found in Part 13 of the Companies Act 2006. Part 13 comprises sections 281 to 361.

This book is concerned with the law, practice and procedure of meetings of solvent companies (both public and private) at both shareholder and board levels. The book is divided into four parts. Part 1 (Chapters 1 to 18) deals with the regulation and procedure applicable to general meetings of members. Part 2 (Chapters 19 to 22) is concerned with meetings of directors. Part 3 contains an annotation of the underlying legislative regime that is found in Part 13 of the Companies Act 2006 which came into force on 1 October 2007. In Part 4 those provisions of the 1985 Table A that relate to meetings of members and directors are set out and commented upon. In the Appendix there is an annotation of the Draft Model Articles which are scheduled to come into force on 1 October 2009. We hope that this will serve as a useful primer for those wishing to prepare in advance for when the new Model Articles are law. Several versions of the Draft Model Articles have been published and the Department for Business Enterprise and Regulatory Reform intends to publish the final version in December 2008.

The text of this book does not deal with European Directive 2007/36/EC on the exercise of certain rights of shareholders in listed companies. This Directive was promulgated on 11 July 2007 and requires Member States of the European Union to bring into force requisite laws, regulations and administrative provisions by no later than 3 August 2009 reflecting its terms. The Directive, which forms part of European Law, establishes minimum standards in relation to the exercise of certain shareholder rights of public listed companies relating to information, participation and voting at general meetings. It seems inevitable that implementation of the Directive will necessitate changes to the provisions of Part 13 of the Companies Act 2006, the precise details of which have yet to be formulated. Readers are accordingly forewarned that the process of legislative change introduced by the Companies Act 2006 is not complete and that further new legislation must be expected.

Companies, whether large or small, will from time to time hold meetings of their members. Such meetings have to be convened, held and conducted in a regular and orderly manner, otherwise such meetings may become reminiscent of some Hobbesian vision of being 'nasty, brutish and short'. The annual general meeting of a listed public company is a most significant event in its calendar and its conduct contains an element of theatre. The element of theatre may descend into drama when unexpected events and difficult situations arise. Consequently, it is clear that advance planning and good organization for general meetings are indispensable and invaluable. In most companies meetings of directors will be held on a much more regular basis than meetings of shareholders. Even in this milieu issues may arise as to how they should be convened and conducted. No book can be a panacea in such circumstances, but we hope that those who involve and concern themselves with the conduct of such meetings will find the text informative, useful and practical.

Writing a text when engaged in legal practice is not an exercise that can be undertaken lightly and time estimates, no doubt in the best traditions of the Chancery Bar, can become somewhat imprecise and extended. It is therefore only right that we record our sincere thanks to our editorial and production team at Oxford University Press for the patience and support that they have shown to us while waiting for the manuscript to be completed and for all their industry and commitment in preparing the text for publication.

Whilst we have taken all reasonable care in the preparation of this text and made every effort to state the law on company meetings as it exists at 30 June 2008, we do not accept any responsibility for any errors or omissions that may be in the text or for any loss that may be sustained by any person relying upon its contents. This book is a guide and nothing more.

LGK
CR
Erskine Chambers
London
July 2008

CONTENTS—SUMMARY

CONTENTS

PART 2: MEETINGS OF DIRECTORS

PART 3: COMMENTARY ON THE PROVISIONS OF THE COMPANIES ACT 2006, PART 13, SECTIONS 281 TO 361

PART 4: ANNOTATION OF 1985 TABLE A REGULATIONS RELATING TO MEETINGS OF MEMBERS AND PROCEEDINGS OF DIRECTORS

TABLE OF CASES

AUSTRALIA

BERMUDA

CANADA

HONG KONG

IRELAND

NEW ZEALAND

UNITED KINGDOM

TABLE OF STATUTES

Statutory Instruments

Part 1

MEETINGS OF MEMBERS

1

THE CONCEPT OF A MEETING AND QUORUM

Introduction

The need to hold a meeting will arise in many different and diverse situations. All meetings are subject to procedural rules and regulations of the particular institution that has convened the meeting. The reason why there are rules and regulations is so that the participants at a duly convened meeting can transact business in a lawful manner and so that they will be able to debate and discuss issues in an orderly fashion. This book is concerned with the meetings of solvent companies that are registered and incorporated under the statutory provisions regulating companies. The reason for the requirement for meetings under the Companies Act 2006 (CA 2006) is so that the members can attend either in person or by proxy in order to debate and vote on matters affecting the affairs of a company. There are a number of procedures, some that are derived from the common law and others that are the creation of statute that have to be observed in order for a meeting of a company to transact business in a lawful and regular manner. **1.01**

What is a Meeting?

1.02 As a general rule a meeting usually means a coming together of more than one person. This basic proposition is illustrated by the important decision of the Court of Appeal in *Sharp v Dawes*.[1] This case concerned the legitimacy of a meeting purportedly held by a Cornish cost-book mining company called the Great Caradon Mine. The legislation governing the company was the Stannaries Act 1869, for tin mining companies were unincorporated entities and governed by special statutes. A meeting of the mining company was convened for the purpose of making a call on the shares.[2] Only one member holding 25 shares, a Mr RH Silversides, attended the meeting and he took the chair. Also, in attendance at the meeting was the secretary of the mining company, who was not a member. Proceedings were purportedly transacted at the meeting attended only by Mr Silversides. Following the meeting a notice was sent by the secretary of the company to the members, recording that a general meeting of the shareholders had been held at 2, Gresham Building, Basinghall Street, London EC on Wednesday, 30 December 1874 and that five resolutions had been passed. It stated that among other things, a resolution had been passed that a call of four shillings and sixpence per share be made and be payable to the secretary, and that a discount of 5% be allowed if the call was paid by a certain date. The notice sent to the members recorded that at the conclusion of the meeting Mr Silversides had proposed and passed a vote of thanks to himself as chairman.

1.03 The over-confidence of Mr Silversides evidenced by the self-congratulatory resolution of thanks was short-lived. In due course one member, Mr Dawes, refused to pay the call. Proceedings were taken in the name of the secretary of the company, Mr Granville Sharp, against Mr Dawes to enforce the payment of the call. The Court of Appeal held that as the meeting had been attended by only one person, it was invalid, as the attendance of Mr Silversides alone could not constitute a meeting. Consequently, the meeting was a nullity and the call was invalid. In the course of his judgment Lord Coleridge CJ said:[3]

> … the [Stannaries] Act [1869] says that a call may be made at a meeting of a company with special notice, and we must ascertain what within the meaning of the Act is a meeting, and whether one person alone can constitute such a meeting. It is said that the requirements of the Act are satisfied by a single shareholder going to the place appointed and professing to pass resolutions. The sixth and seventh sections of the Act show conclusively that there must be more than one person present; and the word 'meeting' prima facie means a coming together of more than one person. It is,

[1] (1876) 2 QBD 26 (CA).

[2] A call is a procedure for demanding payment of the unpaid proportion of share capital.

[3] (1876) 2 QBD 26 at 28–9 (CA).

of course, possible to show that the word 'meeting' has a meaning different from the ordinary meaning, but there is nothing here to show this to be the case. It appears therefore to me that this call was not made at a meeting of the company within the meaning of the Act.

The general rule that a meeting is comprised of more than one person

The important decision of the Court of Appeal in *Sharp v Dawes*[4] establishes the conventional legal meaning of the word 'meeting' in the context of shareholders as an assembly or the coming together of two or more such persons. The decision in *Sharp v Dawes*[5] was followed and applied in *Re Sanitary Carbon Co*.[6] In this case a sole shareholder, named Mr Worswick, was the only person present at a meeting and he also held proxies for all the other three shareholders. Mr Worswick voted himself into the chair, proposed a resolution to wind up the company voluntarily, declared the resolution passed and appointed a liquidator. The purported passing of a resolution to wind up the company was set aside because on the facts there had been no meeting and a compulsory winding up order was made. **1.04**

The importance of the decision in *Sharp v Dawes*[7] is illustrated by the fact that it has been followed and applied in many subsequent cases including *James Prain & Sons, Petitioners*,[8] *Re London Flats Ltd*,[9] *In re MJ Shanley Contracting Ltd*,[10] *New Cedos Engineering Co Ltd*[11] and most recently in *Re Altitutde Scaffolding Ltd*; *Re T & N Ltd*.[12] **1.05**

In *Re London Flats Ltd*[13] a meeting of shareholders was called to consider a resolution to appoint a successor to a liquidator who had died. One of the only two shareholders present proposed an amendment to substitute his own name, at which point the other shareholder left the meeting which the remaining shareholder purported to continue alone. The remaining shareholder then purported to appoint himself as liquidator. When the appointment was challenged the court held that the appointment was invalid for the reason that the applicant had left the meeting and that from that moment there was only one member present and therefore no meeting. Plowman J acknowledged that there were exceptional cases prescribed in the statute which enabled one member of a company to constitute a meeting. However, those exceptional cases had no application to the facts **1.06**

4 Op. cit.
5 Op. cit.
6 [1877] WN 223.
7 Op. cit.
8 1947 SC 325.
9 [1969] 1 WLR 711 (Plowman J).
10 (1980) 124 Sol Jo 239.
11 [1994] 1 BCLC 797 at 813–14 (Oliver J).
12 [2007] 1 BCLC 199 (David Richards J).
13 Op. cit.

before Plowman J. The purported appointment of the liquidator was a nullity as the meeting was invalid from the moment the quorum ceased to exist.

The strength of the conventional position

1.07 The nineteenth-century authority of *Sharp v Dawes* on the basic concept of a meeting is a fundamental tenet of company law, and although there are exceptions[14] to this principle that have become well established, a court will be reluctant, and rightly so, to condone any radical departure from the conventional position. This is illustrated by the recent decision of David Richards J in *Re Altitude Scaffolding Ltd; Re T&N Ltd*,[15] in the context of scheme meetings convened by the court for the purposes of considering schemes of arrangement under the Companies Act 1985 (CA 1985), s 425.[16] The issue before the court in this case was whether the attendance in person or by proxy of one member of a class of creditors at the time and place fixed for a meeting convened to consider a scheme of arrangement under CA 1985, s 425 would constitute a meeting of the class for the purposes of that section.

1.08 In a carefully reasoned judgment containing a detailed review of the relevant authorities, David Richards J held that unless the conditions in CA 1985, s 425 were satisfied, there was no jurisdiction to sanction the scheme so as to be binding on the class in question, and CA 1985, s 425 required that a meeting be summoned and held. David Richards J held that the submissions made on behalf of the applicant companies that only one member of the class present could constitute a sufficient quorum for a meeting involved not an exception to the ordinary meaning of the term 'meeting', but its complete replacement. He held further that as Parliament had used the word 'meeting' in the statute there was no real basis for concluding that it had been intended to have any but its ordinary legal meaning, save for the exceptional case of the single member of the class or perhaps the case where it was established that it had been impossible for any other member of the class to attend in person or by proxy.

1.09 The court accepted that it was inevitable from the need where appropriate to divide members or creditors into different classes for the purposes of a scheme of arrangement, that a class might in some cases comprise a single person; to deny that such a situation can and often does arise would be unrealistic. In the case of a class comprised of a single member, it was not essential to convene a meeting of that class, because it was well established that a member or creditor might by his individual consent agree to be bound by a scheme of arrangement.

---

[14] The exceptions are considered at paras 1.11 *et seq*.
[15] [2007] 1 BCLC 199.
[16] See further Ch 14.

However, on the facts of the case there was no evidence before the court that there was only one creditor in any particular class. As a result, the limited qualification to the ordinary meaning of the word 'meeting' that had been applied in established authorities did not apply. The ordinary meaning of the word 'meeting', as a coming together of two or more persons, was well established in the context of companies. The case of the single member of the class had been treated in the authorities as exceptional, resulting in what the legislature or other framers of the document in question would have intended to be an extended meaning to cover that case. The court concluded that it had no jurisdiction to sanction the scheme in the case of Altitude Scaffolding Ltd, and that the direction sought by the administrators of T&N Ltd in advance of their meetings, namely that the attendance of one creditor alone should constitute a meeting, would not be made.

Modern technology and the concept of a meeting

The older authorities such as *Sharp v Dawes*[17] and *In Re Sanitary Carbon Co*[18] **1.10** considered the concept of a meeting in terms of members being physically present in order to debate and vote on matters. The advances in modern technology now mean that debate and discussion can take place without the need to be physically present in the same venue. Adequate audio-visual links in order to enable all those in different locations to see and be seen, to hear and be heard in the meeting will be accepted as constituting a valid meeting.[19] The use of modern technology in relation to meetings was not universally accepted. In the Canadian case of *Re Associated Color Laboratories Ltd*[20] it was held that two persons were unable to hold a meeting by telephone. The decision failed to appreciate that the fundamental nature of a meeting is the ability of all those who are present to be able to participate in the proceedings of the meeting. The effect of the decision was reversed in respect of meetings of directors by subsequent legislation in Canada. It is now well established that a meeting can be held with participants at more than one venue where there is two-way, real time communication between the participants. But what if communications fail? If technology is used for a meeting of members it would be sensible to check throughout the course of the meeting that the ability of the members to see, be seen, hear and be heard remains active.

Exceptions to the general rule

Over the years a limited number of exceptions to the general rule that more than **1.11** one person must be present in order to constitute a valid members' meeting

[17] Op. cit.
[18] Op. cit.
[19] See *Byng v London Life Association Ltd* [1990] Ch 170 (CA).
[20] (1970) 12 DLR (3d) 388.

have arisen. In certain circumstances it is possible for a valid meeting to take place that is attended by only one person. Each of these exceptions will be considered in turn.

Single member companies

1.12 A fundamental change to the orthodox position of companies being comprised of more than one person was introduced to the legislation in 1992. On 15 July 1992 with the advent of the Companies (Single Member Private Limited Companies) Regulations 1992[21] it became possible to incorporate and register a private company with a single member under CA 1985, s 1(3A). The provisions in these regulations implemented changes to CA 1985 and 1985 Table A to reflect the fact that a company could come into existence with a sole member. In particular a new section, CA 1985, s 370A, was introduced which provided:

> Notwithstanding any provision to the contrary in the articles of a private company limited by shares or limited by guarantee having only one member, one person present in person or by proxy shall be a quorum.

1.13 Single member companies are permitted under CA 2006, s 38, which provides that any enactment or rule of law applicable to companies formed with two or more persons or having two or more members applies with necessary modifications to a company formed by one person and having only one person as a member.

CA 2006, s 318

1.14 Provision for single member companies is now to be found in CA 2006, s 318, which provides that in the case of a company limited by shares or guarantee and having only one member, one qualifying person present at a meeting is a quorum and thus a valid meeting.[22] In all other cases two qualifying people must be present, subject to the proviso that they must not both represent the same member.[23]

1.15 Where a meeting is held in relation to a company that has only one qualifying member there can be evidential problems with regard to what was done at the meeting. In order to address such issues CA 2006, s 357 imposes a requirement on a single member company to take the decision in the form of a written resolution, or for the single member to provide the company with a written record of the decision. This requirement under CA 2006, s 357 is not a complete answer to the practical problems of a single qualifying member proving what decisions have been taken and failure to comply with s 357 does not invalidate the decision.[24]

---

21 SI 1992/1699.

22 A qualifying person is defined in CA 2006, s 318(3).

23 See the commentary on s 318 at paras 22.231–22.237 below.

24 See the commentary on s 357 at paras 22.433–22.434 below.

A situation can arise where a single person becomes the only enfranchised shareholder in a company, for example where in a 'two-man' company one of the members dies and no steps are taken to administer the estate of that deceased person. In such a case the register of members would record the names of two shareholders and the commonplace articles of association would reflect the usual rule of two persons being necessary for a quorum at a general meeting. The only shares capable of being voted at a general meeting would be those of the surviving member. In such a situation it is to be doubted whether a meeting attended by the single surviving shareholder would be valid and capable of transacting lawful business. In such circumstances it is plain that it would be impracticable to hold a meeting as it will be impossible to form a quorum. The remedy is provided by way of an application to the court under CA 2006, s 306.[25] 1.16

Single member holding all the shares of a particular class

If a single member holds all the shares of a particular class, for example all of a class of preference shares, the assent of that single shareholder will be valid. The case of *East v Bennett Bros*[26] concerned the requirement in the memorandum and articles of association of a company for approval for an issue of new shares to be given by a resolution passed at a separate meeting of the preference shareholders. On the facts there was only one preference shareholder. Warrington J identified the relevant question as whether: 1.17

> [O]n the construction of this particular memorandum and the particular part of it, can there be such a thing as a meeting of one shareholder? It is not a question of there being several shareholders, and one shareholder only attending the so-called meeting, but where there is only one shareholder, so that a meeting in the sense of an assembly of persons is impossible. The object of the provisions in the memorandum is quite plain. It is to obtain, before the issue of new shares, the assent in a binding and formal manner of the person or persons whose rights are affected.

Warrington J went on to state, referring to *Sharp v Dawes* and *In re Sanitary Carbon Co* that, 'In an ordinary case I think it is quite clear that a meeting must consist of more than one person' but, in circumstances where there was only one member of the class, he held that 'meeting' included the case of a single shareholder. Warrington J said:[27] 1.18

> But now what I have to consider is whether this is not one of the cases referred to by Lord Coleridge CJ as one in which it may be possible to show that the word 'meeting' has a meaning different from the ordinary meaning. For that purpose I think I am entitled to see what is the object of the provision in the memorandum of association. Plainly, as I have already said, that object is that before affecting the rights of the preference shareholders it shall be necessary to obtain and record in a formal manner

---

[25] See Ch 6 and the commentary at paras 22.164–22.167 for an analysis of CA 2006, s 306.
[26] [1911] 1 Ch 163 (Warrington J).
[27] [1911] 1 Ch 163 at 169–70.

> the assent of the preference shareholders to that course. I think I may take it also that the persons who framed this document may have had, and must be taken to have had, in their minds the possibility at all events that this particular class of shares might fall into the hands of one person. There is nothing to prevent it in the constitution of the company. One must regard the memorandum as far as possible as providing for circumstances which in the ordinary course may arise. That being so, I think I may very fairly say that where one person only is the holder of all the shares of a particular class, and as that person cannot meet himself, or form a meeting with himself in the ordinary sense, the persons who framed this memorandum having such a position in contemplation must be taken to have used the word 'meeting', not in the strict sense in which it is usually used, but as including the case of one single shareholder. There is, of course, no difficulty in treating the formally expressed assent of Bennett as a resolution. The only question is the purely technical difficulty arising from the use of the word 'meeting' in the memorandum.
>
> I think on the whole that I may give effect to obvious common sense by holding that in this particular case, where there is only one shareholder of the class, on the true construction of the memorandum, the expression 'meeting' may be held to include that case.

1.19 This approach has been adopted in other contexts. For example, in *Re RMCA Reinsurance Ltd*[28] Morritt J held, on an application under CA 1985, s 425(1) to convene meetings of creditors to consider a scheme of arrangement, that where one class comprised only one creditor, a meeting attended by that creditor would satisfy the statutory requirements for a meeting. Morritt J followed the decision of Warrington J in *East v Bennett Brothers Ltd*[29] and a decision of the Supreme Court of New South Wales in *Re Hastings Deering Pty Ltd*,[30] which had been decided on the equivalent provision in the legislation in New South Wales. In that case Kearney J referred to the 'general rule that a plurality of persons is required to constitute a meeting' and, after referring to *East v Bennett Brothers Ltd* said:[31]

> In the present case, by reason of the difference in interests between the single individual shareholders and the general body of shareholders, such individual shareholder is, in my view, properly regarded as constituting a class of the members of the company. It follows that in order to fulfil the requirements of subsection (4) a meeting of such class must be convened.

Quorum

1.20 In order to transact lawful business at any general meeting of the shareholders of a company it must be quorate, that is to say a quorum of members must be present.[32] A meeting that is inquorate has no jurisdiction to transact lawful

28 [1994] BCC 378.
29 Op. cit.
30 (1985) 3 ACLC 474.
31 (1985) 3 ACLC 474 at 475.
32 The quorum requirements of meetings of directors are discussed in Ch 19.

business and cannot even start. A meeting that purports to transact lawful business when it is inquorate is irregular and the business will be a nullity. The constitution of a company or the companies legislation will stipulate the minimum number of members who are required to constitute a quorum. Those who are involved in the conduct of a meeting of members must therefore ensure that before it proceeds to do business it is quorate, and this important fact must be noted in the minutes.[33] This is a primary responsibility of the chairman.[34]

Definition

The word 'quorum' is Latin for 'of whom'. It denotes the minimum number of members of a company whose presence at a meeting of the members is required in order to make the proceedings of the meeting valid. The Shorter Oxford English Dictionary[35] indicates that the origin of the word 'quorum' was that it was used in the wording of commissions for members of bodies or committees, usually justices of the peace, in which particular people were designated as members of a body and whose presence was necessary to constitute a deciding body. **1.21**

General quorum provision in a company's articles

For companies registered and incorporated under the Companies Acts the general rule is that two persons is the minimum number required to constitute a valid meeting. This rule also applies to a meeting that is adjourned. This usual requirement will be found in a company's articles of association and, by way of example, regs 40 and 41 of the 1985 Table A provide as follows: **1.22**

> 40. No business shall be transacted at any meeting unless a quorum is present. Two persons entitled to vote upon the business to be transacted, each being a member or a proxy for a member or a duly authorised representative of a corporation, shall be a quorum.
>
> 41. If such a quorum is not present within half an hour from the time appointed for the meeting, or if during a meeting a quorum ceases to be present, the meeting shall stand adjourned to the same day in the next week at the same time and place or such time and place as the directors may determine.

Regulation 41 contemplates that there may be a period of delay of 30 minutes in starting the meeting from the time specified in the notice of the meeting. It is sensible and practical to have such an express provision in a company's articles of association in order to allow for some latitude in starting a general meeting where circumstances make this necessary, such as transport delays in inclement weather. Even if the articles were silent on the point it is suggested that the chairman of a **1.23**

---

[33] See Ch 16.
[34] See Ch 7.
[35] Vol 2, (5th edn, 2002) 2442.

meeting would have an inherent power to delay the start of a meeting for a few minutes in order to allow shareholders who had travelled to the venue to take their places in the meeting room.[36]

1.24 Under the quorum formulation in the 1985 Table A cited at para 1.22 above, it is to be noted that reg 41 requires a quorum of members to be present throughout the entirety of the meeting. In practice, in the context of a large public company this presents no problem at all, but in relation to a small private company such a requirement can prove to be troublesome and impractical. Under reg 53 of the 1948 Table A it was sufficient that there was a quorum of members at the beginning of the meeting. In *Re Hartley Baird Ltd*[37] the articles of association of the company fixed the quorum at ten. Wynn-Parry J held that if a quorum was present at the beginning of the meeting the subsequent departure of a member reducing the number of members below the number required by the articles for the quorum did not invalidate the proceedings of the meeting after the departure of that one member.

Continuing quorum

1.25 Regulation 41 of the 1985 Table A requires a continuing quorum, which is obviously highly desirable if not essential as a matter of law. Private companies which wish not to adopt such a provision in order to avoid the practical difficulties that may ensue if during the meeting the departure of a member renders the meeting inquorate, should ensure that reg 41 of the 1985 Table A is disapplied. However, at all times at least two persons must be present for the meeting to continue.

1.26 In the absence of any provision to the contrary, presence at a meeting of members for the purposes of a quorum, means presence in person and not by proxy.[38] A Scottish case[39] concerning the provisions of CA 1985, s 370(4) has held that a member present in two capacities, for example, as a member and as a trustee, counts as two members personally present. However, this decision is to be doubted. The better rule is that where the quorum is two members present and proxies are counted, the presence of only one member who holds proxies for several others will not be sufficient to constitute a quorum. This rule was laid down in the well-known nineteenth-century case of *Re Sanitary Carbon*.[40] In Australia it has been

---

[36] See *John v Rees* [1970] Ch 345 at 382–3 (Megarry J).

[37] [1955] Ch 143. In this case Wynn-Parry J declined to follow the earlier Scottish decision of *Henderson v James Louttit & Co Ltd* (1894) 21 Rettie 674 where the Lord President expressed the view that it would be highly inconvenient to hold that all that was necessary was that a quorum should be present at the earliest stage of the meeting but that after the real business of the meeting had started the quorum might go away.

[38] See *M Harris Ltd* 1956 SC 207.

[39] See *Neil MacLeod & Sons, Petitioners* 1967 SC 16.

[40] [1877] WN 223, and see para 1.04 above.

expressly held that one member cannot turn himself into two members by appointing two proxies, each of which is deemed to be a member, and thereby constitute a quorum.[41]

In relation to the important issue of constituting a quorum it is important to note that under the provisions of what is now CA 2006, s 323 a corporation which is a member of a company, and which has authorized a person to act as its representative at a duly convened meeting, is regarded as personally present and not present by proxy.[42] This principle is illustrated by the decision of Astbury J in *In Re Kelantan Cocoa Estates Limited.* The company's articles of association provided that 'two members personally shall be a quorum'. At a meeting held to pass a special resolution for a reduction of share capital there were present one member of the company and one representative appointed to represent a corporate shareholder. In deciding that the special resolution to reduce the company's share capital had been duly passed, Astbury J held that the meeting attended by one member and one duly appointed corporate representative had been duly constituted. **1.27**

Statutory default provisions under CA 2006

CA 2006, s 318, which is derived from CA 1985, ss 370(4) and 370A, now regulates the requirement of a quorum for a meeting of members where a company's articles of association do not make express provision. Section 318 sets out certain basic rules with regard to the quorum at meetings. The section introduces a new concept of a 'qualifying person'.[43] Such a person is defined as (a) an individual who is a member of the company, (b) a person authorized as a company representative under s 323, or (c) a person appointed as a proxy of a member in relation to the meeting. By s 318(1) in the case of a company limited by shares or by guarantee and having only one member, one qualifying person present at a meeting is a quorum. In any other case, the quorum must comprise two qualifying persons present. However, this will not suffice if both those persons are representatives of the same corporate member or proxies of the same member. These provisions apply subject to the provisions of the company's articles. **1.28**

Special quorum in legislation—variation of class rights

Sometimes the legislation regulating companies imposes special provisions with regard to a requisite quorum for a particular decision. CA 1985, s 125(6) stipulated that a class meeting to propose a variation of class rights required a quorum of two persons holding or representing by proxy at least one-third in nominal value of the **1.29**

[41] *Donrob Enterprises Pty Ltd v Queensland Petroleum Management Ltd* (1988) 14 ACLR 307 (Supreme Court of Queensland).

[42] See *In re Kelantan Cocoa Nut Estates Ltd* [1920] WN 274 (Astbury J).

[43] See CA 2006, s 318(3).

issued shares of the class in question.[44] In practice this requirement could prove to be onerous and the prescribed quorum was sometimes difficult, or indeed impossible, to obtain. If the stipulated statutory requirement relating to the quorum was not obtained, the class meeting would be adjourned. It was provided in CA 1985, s 125(6)(a) that at an adjourned meeting the quorum was one person either in person or by proxy holding shares of the relevant class.

CA 2006, s 334

1.30 The CA 2006 largely reproduces the pre-existing law. CA 2006, s 334 contains the new provisions governing the procedure to be applied for what is now defined as a 'variation of class rights meeting'. Section 334(3) expressly provides that the quorum requirements of s 318 do not apply to such a meeting. Equally s 321, dealing with a member's right to demand a poll, does not apply. In place of these provisions s 334(4) provides that for a class meeting other than an adjourned meeting, two persons present holding at least one-third in nominal value of the issued shares of the class in question (leaving aside any shares of that class held as treasury shares) shall be a quorum. For the purposes of this subsection, where a person is present by proxy or proxies, he is treated as holding only the shares in respect of which these proxies are authorized to exercise voting rights. As regards an adjourned meeting, one person alone present and holding shares of the class constitutes a quorum. As to demanding a poll, s 334(6) states that at a variation of class rights meeting, any holder of shares of the class in question present may demand a poll.

1.31 CA 2006, s 335 applies a separate set of rules to class meetings of a company without a share capital. Once again, the quorum requirements of ss 318 and 321, dealing with a member's right to demand a poll, do not apply. Instead, s 335(4) provides that for a meeting other than an adjourned meeting two members of the class present in person and by proxy who together represent at least one-third of the total voting rights of the class constitute a quorum. For an adjourned meeting, one member of the class present in person or by proxy is sufficient for a quorum. By s 335(5) at a variation of class rights meeting any member present in person or by proxy may demand a poll.

Special quorum provision contained in the articles of association

1.32 Articles of association sometimes provide a very particular requirement for a valid quorum for a general meeting. For example, where the issued share capital of a company is divided into shares of different classes, the articles may stipulate that a general meeting cannot be held unless it is attended by two members, at least one member representing each class of shares. Plainly, when general meetings

---

[44] Excluding any shares of that class that are held as treasury shares.

are held and such a provision regulates the quorum, the stipulated requirement must be observed. Thus, in such a situation the non-attendance of say, a 'B' shareholder renders the meeting inquorate and unable to proceed to transact lawful business. In such a situation the members not holding 'B' shares will not be permitted to override the class rights of the 'B' shareholder by the expedient of applying for, and obtaining an order under CA 2006, s 306, formerly CA 1985, s 371.[45]

Meetings ordered by the court

Under the provisions of CA 2006, s 306[46] in circumstances where it is established that it is impracticable to hold a meeting the court has jurisdiction to order the holding of a meeting, and may impose conditions under which such a meeting shall be convened and conducted. This is a statutory exception to the general rule that one person cannot constitute a lawful and valid meeting of members. Where, in a two-person company, the minority shareholder refuses to attend a general meeting of members thereby rendering it inquorate and incapable of transacting business, the court may make an order under CA 2006, s 306(2) whereby a valid meeting can be held and conducted. Section 306(3) expressly authorizes the court to make a direction that one member of a company present at the meeting will be deemed to constitute a quorum.[47] This deeming provision and that in s 306(5) indicate that, in the context of companies, the ordinary meaning of the word 'meeting' is well established as a coming together of two or more persons.[48] It is clear from the authorities on the statutory predecessor of s 306 that a minority shareholder will not be permitted by the court to turn his non-attendance at a duly convened general meeting of a company into a power of veto, not commensurate with his shareholding, over the stipulated quorum provision in the articles of association. Under CA 2006, s 306(4) the court has express jurisdiction to make a direction that one member of the company present at the meeting can constitute a quorum. **1.33**

This issue is discussed in detail in Chapter 6 where it will be seen that the jurisdiction of the court to order a meeting under CA 2006, s 306 is not unfettered. The Court of Appeal has restricted its use if the effect of an order would be to break an intentional deadlock of members or where the articles of association have conferred on a member class rights affecting the quorum required for general meetings.[49] **1.34**

---

45 See *Harman v BML Group Ltd* [1994] 1 BCLC 674 (CA) and Ch 6.
46 Formerly CA 1985, s 371.
47 See *Re El Sombrero Ltd* [1958] Ch 900; *Re Opera Photographic Ltd* [1989] 1 WLR and Ch 6.
48 See *Re Altitude Scaffolding Ltd; Re T & N Ltd* [2007] 1 BCLC 199 (David Richards J).
49 See *Harman v BMLGroup Ltd* [1994] 1 BCLC 674 (CA).

Meetings ordered by the Secretary of State under CA 1985

1.35 CA 1985, s 367 conferred a power on the Secretary of State to convene a meeting where there had been default on the part of a company in complying with the provisions of CA 1985, s 366 in relation to the calling of an annual general meeting. Pursuant to CA 1985, s 367(2) the Secretary of State could give directions for the calling of an annual general meeting and such directions could include a direction that one member of the company present in person or by proxy should be deemed to constitute a valid meeting. Again, the use of the word 'deemed' in the legislation is not unimportant as it is both a recognition and reinforcement of the conventional and long-standing principle that usually one person cannot constitute a meeting.

1.36 CA 1985, s 367 has been repealed and is not replaced by any provision in CA 2006.[50] Accordingly, there is no longer any power vested in the Secretary of State to convene a general meeting or to direct the size of the quorum.

[50] Under CA 2006 only public companies remain under a duty to hold an annual general meeting—see further Ch 4.

2

NOTICE OF MEETINGS OF MEMBERS

Introduction

2.01 In order to convene a general meeting in a lawful manner a valid and regular notice of the general meeting must be issued to all of the members who are entitled to receive notice. There are a number of fundamental requirements of a valid notice. A valid notice of a general meeting must:

(a) state the correct date and time of the meeting;[1]
(b) state the place of the meeting;[2]
(c) state accurately the purpose of the meeting;
(d) give notice of any special business;
(e) comply with all legal rules and statutory requirements, for example, explain the right of a member to appoint a proxy or multiple proxies; [3]
(f) be clear and explicit in its contents;
(g) be given with due and proper authority;
(h) be given in the prescribed manner;
(i) allow the correct period of time between service and the date that is set for the meeting;
(j) be sent to all those persons who are entitled to receive it.

Date and time of the meeting

2.02 It is plain that a notice of a meeting must state clearly and accurately where and when the meeting is to take place. In most circumstances[4] the directors have a discretion as to the choice of the date and timing of the meeting. However, such discretion must not be abused or used to serve the directors' own purposes. Accordingly, directors ought to select a date and time that permits the largest possible attendance of members. It is arguably a breach of fiduciary duty for them to convene

[1] See CA 2006, s 311(1)(a).
[2] See CA 2006, s 311(1)(b).
[3] See CA 2006, ss 324 and 325.
[4] If directors are responding to a request for a meeting under CA 2006, s 303 the time for the holding of the meeting is prescribed by CA 2006, s 304.

a meeting on a date or for a time that is manifestly inconvenient for the majority of shareholders. The convenience of the directors is merely one factor to be taken into account when convening the meeting. However, this factor should not assume an undue importance when fixing the date and time of a general meeting.

If a board of directors convene a meeting on a date or at a time that would prevent certain members from attending, a court may restrain the directors from proceeding with the meeting as they had planned. In *Cannon v Trask*[5] the articles of association of a company stipulated that the ordinary general meeting of the shareholders[6] had to be held in the month of August. The facts disclosed that historically a meeting had never been held before the third or fourth Monday in August. The plaintiff was a substantial shareholder in the company who was in dispute with the board of directors concerning the management of the company. The board convened a meeting for 3 August. On this date the plaintiff would have been unable to exercise all of the votes in respect of his shareholding, some of which had been acquired in recent transactions. The court granted an injunction preventing the holding of the meeting before 13 August, by which date the plaintiff would have been enfranchised in respect of the totality of his shareholding in the company. **2.03**

CA 2006, s 311

CA 2006, s 311(1)(a) provides that the notice of a general meeting must state the time and date of the meeting. This provision does no more than state what is the obvious and a matter of best practice. It must be assumed that the existing case law will continue to apply to the choice of time and date for the meeting. **2.04**

Good practice dictates that the notice should also state the day of the week on which the meeting is to be held. Of course care must be taken to state the correct day of the week. If the day is incorrectly stated the notice will generate confusion and the notice may be regarded as invalid. **2.05**

Sometimes it is impossible to convene a meeting for a fixed time. This occurs where a second general meeting is scheduled to take place after another meeting, for example, the annual general meeting.[7] A notice for such a meeting is valid if, after giving the date and time, it contains the words: '. . . or so soon thereafter as the [annual general meeting] of the company convened to be held at the same place and on the same day shall have been concluded or adjourned'. Members **2.06**

---

[5] (1875) 20 Eq 669.

[6] This was the previous name for an annual general meeting.

[7] The CA 2006 requires an annual general meeting only for public companies: see CA 2006, s 336. See Ch 4.

receiving such notice are thereby made aware that the second meeting will take place immediately after the preceding meeting has been concluded or adjourned.

Geographical location

2.07 Selection of the place of meeting is entirely at the discretion of the directors.[8] However, once again the decision as to the location of the general meeting involves an exercise of the directors' powers of management which must be exercised for proper purposes and not for any collateral or ulterior motive. Accordingly, it would be a breach of fiduciary duty for the directors deliberately to select as a venue a place where they know that some members will be unable to attend in order to stifle debate on controversial matters. A long history of holding meetings at one location might call into question the decision of a board to hold a meeting at a new venue, when what is to be debated is highly contentious and is strongly opposed by a group of shareholders. For example, it would be improper for a company based in England to choose to hold a general meeting abroad, in say Stockholm, if the purpose of selecting this location was simply for the purpose of reducing the numbers of members who might be able to attend.

Challenge to the location

2.08 Whether a shareholder will be successful in preventing a general meeting from being held in a particular location that is different from the customary place where meetings have been held in the past will depend on all of the relevant facts. It is likely that a meeting to discuss uncontroversial business at a different location will not be capable of successful challenge. In *Martin v Walker*[9] an ordinary general meeting of the Hearts of Oak Life and General Insurance Co Ltd was convened to take place in Liverpool in circumstances where the facts disclosed that the majority of previous meetings had been held in London. A dissident challenged this decision on behalf of himself and the other shareholders, arguing that it would be more convenient to hold the meeting in London where more shareholders would be able to attend. The court declined to intervene in the absence of evidence of misconduct.

2.09 CA 2006, s 311(1)(b) provides that the notice of a general meeting must state the place of the meeting. Again, this is an obvious requirement which does not alter the existing law. It reflects part of the content of reg 38 of the 1985 Table A. In relation to public companies the notice of an annual general meeting will usually contain a detailed map of the location and give relevant information in relation to access to that location by different forms of transport.

---

[8] *Martin v Walker* (1918) 145 LT Jo 377.

[9] (1918) 145 LT Jo 377.

Venue

2.10 The choice of venue is an important issue, particularly for large companies with many thousands of registered members. A number of basic questions must be examined in relation to the choice of a suitable venue for a meeting:

(a) Is the venue large enough to accommodate all of the potential attendees?
(b) Is the accommodation suitable in terms of access, seating and general facilities, such as heating and lighting and public address system?
(c) Is the venue accessible to the physically disabled or the visually impaired or those who are hard of hearing?
(d) Is the public address system sufficient for those with hearing difficulties?
(e) Is the venue convenient for members arriving by public transport?
(f) Is there convenient car parking in the vicinity?
(g) Is there an adequate platform for speakers?
(h) Are stewards required?
(i) Are there any security issues that need to be addressed?
(j) What is the cost of the hire of the venue?

Capacity of the venue

2.11 The capacity of the selected venue is a matter of great importance which should be considered carefully by the board. If the board chooses to hold a meeting at a location which cannot accommodate the total number of members wishing to attend, there is great risk that the meeting will be declared to be invalid. This occurred in the well-known case of *Byng v London Life Association Ltd.*[10] In that case notice had been given of an extraordinary general meeting of the company to be held at 12 noon at Cinema 1 at the Barbican Centre in London. The sole purpose of the meeting was to consider a special resolution amending the company's memorandum of association so that the company could finalize negotiations for the transfer of its long-term insurance business. The company expected a large attendance of its members and in advance had arranged for other rooms and the cinema foyer to be available with audio-visual links to Cinema 1. As an extra precaution the Café Royal in Piccadilly was booked from 1.30pm to 5pm. On the day of the meeting approximately 800 members attended in person, but there were no audio-visual links connecting the various rooms and because of difficulties in registering members to vote the meeting did not start before 12.30pm. At the time the meeting opened many members were still registering to vote. Some members proposed that the meeting should be abandoned and others that it should be adjourned sine die. At about 12.45pm the chairman indicated that he was adjourning the meeting to 2.30pm at the Café Royal, despite the fact that

10 [1990] Ch 170 (CA).

a number of members said that they would not be able to attend if the meeting was adjourned. The adjourned meeting at the Café Royal was attended by about 600 people, who included only 335 of the 468 members who had registered at the Barbican Centre.

Do all the members have to be in the same room?

2.12 In *Byng v London Life Association Ltd*[11] the plaintiff challenged the validity of the meetings, arguing that a meeting for the purpose of CA 1985 requires that everyone should be physically present in the same room or space. The Court of Appeal rejected this submission. Sir Nicolas Browne-Wilkinson V-C stated that the rationale behind the requirement for meetings in the legislation was that the members should be able to attend in person or by proxy so as to debate and vote on matters affecting the company. Modern technology had made it possible to have a meeting where the members were not physically present in the same room but were joined by electronic means, and could hear and be heard, be seen and see what was going on.

2.13 Accordingly, in cases where the original venue proves to be inadequate to accommodate all those members who wish to attend, a valid general meeting can be held using overflow rooms provided, first, that all due steps are taken to direct to the overflow rooms those unable to get in to the main meeting, and secondly, that there are adequate audio-visual links to enable those in all the rooms to see and hear what is going on in the other rooms. In *Byng v London Life Association Ltd*[12] the audio-visual links to the main meeting in the cinema had not worked with the result that those in the foyer and in the overflow rooms were excluded from effective participation. The meeting in the cinema was therefore incapable of transacting any business.[13]

The purpose of the meeting

2.14 In order for a notice to be valid it must state the purpose of the meeting, that is to say, it must specify the general nature of the business to be transacted.[14] A notice that is general and non-specific will be insufficient. CA 2006, s 311(2) provides that notice of a general meeting of a company must state the general nature of the business to be dealt with at the meeting. This subsection has effect subject to any provision of the company's articles of association.

2.15 In *Normandy v Ind Coope Co*[15] a notice convening a general meeting for the purposes of altering the company's articles of association was held to be insufficient

[11] Op. cit.

[12] Op. cit.

[13] See also *Re Abbey National plc* [2005] 2 BCLC 15 (Evans Lombe J) (in the context of CA 1985, s 425 and the power to adjourn). See further Ch 12 and Ch 14.

[14] See reg 38, 1985 Table A.

[15] [1908] 1 Ch 84 (Kekewich J).

because it did not specify the nature of the proposed alterations to the articles. By reason of its omission to refer to matters of importance to the shareholders (the changes included the introduction of a power for the board to grant pensions and increased remuneration for the directors) it was held that the notice did not sufficiently state the general nature of the business of the meeting as required by the articles. It was further held that it made no difference that copies of the new articles of association were available for inspection at the offices of the company. The resolutions were therefore invalid.

In *Choppington Collieries Ltd v Johnson*[16] the notice of an annual general meeting stated that the purpose of the meeting included 'To elect directors'. On a fresh line there appeared a statement that a named director retired and, being eligible, offered himself for re-election. He was the only director retiring from office. At the meeting the retiring director was proposed for re-election but an amendment was moved that three other persons should be elected as directors. The amendment was rejected by the chairman of the meeting as being out of order. The chairman also rejected a substantive motion that the three persons in question be elected as directors. It was held by Uthwatt J and the Court of Appeal that the notice of the meeting was sufficient in that it sufficiently specified the general nature of the business to enable the meeting to elect directors up to the number permitted by the articles. The chairman was held to have been wrong in rejecting both the amendment and in refusing to put the substantive motion to the meeting. **2.16**

Whether or not the notice for a meeting is sufficient is a question of fact. It is of cardinal importance that the notice contains sufficient information to enable the recipient to decide for himself whether or not he should attend the meeting, or appoint a proxy, or whether he is content to abide by what is decided at the meeting without any participation on his part.[17] **2.17**

Special business

Where the articles of association of a company contain reference to 'special business' a notice convening a meeting at which special business is to be transacted must state the general nature of that business, otherwise the notice will be defective. Under reg 52 of the 1948 Table A all business to be transacted at an extraordinary general meeting was deemed to be special business. In addition, all business to be transacted at an annual general meeting with the exception of declaring a dividend, the consideration of the accounts, balance sheets and reports of the directors and auditors, the election of directors in place of those retiring and the appointment of, and fixing the remuneration of, the auditors, was deemed to be special business. **2.18**

---

[16] [1944] 1 All ER 762 (Uthwatt J and CA).

[17] This subject is discussed in Ch 3 where the relevant case law is analysed.

2.19 A new approach to special business was taken by the provisions of the 1985 Table A. Regulation 38 of the 1985 Table A dealing with notices of general meetings did not contain any similar provision to the 1948 Table A. It stated simply that notice of any meeting should specify the time and place of the meeting and the general nature of the business to be transacted and, in the case of an annual general meeting, should specify the meeting as such.

2.20 Notwithstanding the introduction of CA 2006 it remains the case that it is to the articles of association of a company that reference should be made when formulating the contents of a notice of a meeting. The articles of association will continue to govern the nature and extent of the notice that must be given of the business to be transacted at any general meeting.

Compliance with statutory and legal obligations

2.21 A member of a company is entitled to expect and indeed can require that the affairs of the company are conducted in accordance with the company's articles of association. This is particularly relevant in the context of company meetings where enfranchised shareholders are permitted to take part in the conduct of the affairs of the company. Subject to the provisions of CA 2006, a company and its members can agree whatever they see fit in relation to the content of the articles of association. The supervisory jurisdiction of the courts in this area of the law is very important and it cannot be ousted by a provision in articles of association which provides that a central committee or other body is to be the only entity that is competent to interpret the articles.[18] Such a provision would be contrary to public policy and void. Companies are the creation of statute and the rights of members are protected by the courts.

Notice to whom?

2.22 In order for the meeting to be valid and lawful, due notice must be given to all persons who are entitled to receive notice. The category of those persons has been expanded by the provisions of CA 2006. This has therefore become an area of practice requiring close attention to detail.

2.23 Most articles of association will stipulate the persons who are entitled to receive notice. If reg 38 of the 1985 Table A applies, then, subject to the articles and to any restrictions imposed on the shares, the notice shall be given to all members[19] and to those who are entitled to a share as a consequence of death or bankruptcy of a member and to the directors and to the auditors.

---

[18] See *Baker v Jones* [1954] 1 WLR 1005 (Lynskey J) (albeit a decision in relation to an unincorporated association).

[19] See CA 2006, s 112 for a definition of the word 'member'.

CA 1985, s 370

Default provisions were contained in CA 1985, s 370. Where the articles of association of a company did not make any provision for the identity of the recipient of a notice, s 370(2) provided that the notice of a meeting of the company must be given to all the members in the manner in which notices are required to be served under Table A. **2.24**

CA 2006, s 310

CA 2006, s 310 contains new default provisions which are more extensive than those contained in the previous legislation. These provisions are subject to any enactment and to the provisions of the company's articles of association. By s 310(1) notice of a general meeting must be given to every member of the company and to every director. By s 310(2) the reference to members includes any person who is entitled to a share in consequence of the death or bankruptcy of a member,[20] if the company has been notified of their entitlement.[21] It follows that if no notification has been given, such person would not be entitled to the notice.[22] **2.25**

It is believed that the impact of s 310 being subject to any provision of the company's articles of association is that it is open to a company to provide in the articles that the company need no longer provide notice of a meeting to a member for whom the company has no valid address. **2.26**

A company must also give notice of any general meeting to its auditor under CA 2006, s 502.[23] **2.27**

Persons exercising members' rights

Under CA 2006, Part 9[24] provision can be made in a company's articles of association to enable a member to nominate another person or persons as entitled to enjoy or exercise all or any specified rights of membership of the company. Amongst those rights is the right under s 310 to receive notice of general meetings.[25] By s 145(2) the company is required to treat the nominated person or persons as if he were a member of the company. This right is enforceable against the company only by the member. **2.28**

[20] Or the equivalent in Scottish law—see CA 2006, s 310(3).

[21] CA 2006, s 310(2).

[22] CA 2006, s 310(3) states that the reference to the bankruptcy of a member includes the sequestration of the estate of a member and a member's estate being the subject of a protected trust deed within the meaning of the Bankruptcy (Scotland) Act 1985.

[23] See further para 2.42 below.

[24] CA 2006, ss 145–53. See Ch 10.

[25] See CA 2006, s 145(1) and (3)(d), and Ch 10.

2.29 CA 2006, s 146, which applies only to traded companies,[26] operates where shares are held by a member on behalf of another person. That member may nominate that person to enjoy various rights which are defined in the section as 'information rights'. Among these rights is the right to receive a copy of all communications that the company sends to its members generally or to any class of its members. Section 149 deals with the case where the company sends a copy of a notice of meeting to a person nominated under s 146. In that case the copy of the notice of meeting must be accompanied by a statement that the nominated person may have a right under an agreement between him and the member who appointed him to be appointed, or to have someone else appointed as a proxy for the meeting, and if he has no such right or does not wish to exercise it, that he may have a right under such an agreement to give instructions to the member as to exercise of voting rights.[27] The inclusion of this statement is an additional burden on listed companies with regard to sending notice of meetings.

Notice to deceased or bankrupt members

2.30 The 1985 Table A made provision for the sending of notices to persons who had become entitled to a share following the death or bankruptcy of a member. Regulation 116 of the 1985 Table A provided as follows:

> A notice may be given by the company to the persons entitled to a share in consequence of the death or bankruptcy of a member by sending or delivering it, in any manner authorised by the articles for the giving of notice to a member, addressed to them by name, or by the title of the representatives of the deceased, or trustee of the bankrupt or by any like description at the address, if any, within the United Kingdom supplied for that purpose by the persons claiming to be entitled. Until such an address has been supplied, a notice may be given in any manner in which it might have been given if the death or bankruptcy had not occurred.

2.31 Provisions in articles of association in the form that is cited above are commonplace. Another form of article in common usage does not contain any specific reference to the service of notices in the case of a deceased member. Such a provision will provide that notices of meetings have to be served on members personally or by sending them by prepaid post to the member's registered address. In *Allen v Gold Reefs of West Africa*[28] it was held that in the case of a deceased member whose death was known to the company, it was not necessary to send a notice addressed to the deceased member at his registered address or to serve a notice on his legal personal representatives unless they had themselves become registered as members of the company. Lindley MR held that under the articles notice had to be given only to members and the executors were not members.

---

[26] That is, companies whose shares are admitted to trading on a regulated market—listed companies.

[27] CA 2006, s 149 is discussed further in Ch 9.

[28] [1900] 1 Ch 656, 670 (CA).

Under most articles of association where a person becomes entitled to a share in a company as a result of death or bankruptcy of the registered member that person may, upon the provision of proper evidence of their entitlement being produced to the directors, elect to be registered as the holder of the share or to have some other person nominated by him as the transferee. The person who becomes entitled to the share as a consequence of death or bankruptcy of a member has the rights to which he would be entitled if he were the holder of the share, save that he cannot vote at any meeting of the company until he has become registered as a member. **2.32**

It is apparent from the decision in *Morgan v Gray*[29] that unless the articles of association provide to the contrary, the bankrupt member cannot be prevented from attending at a general meeting of the company for so long as he remains the registered member and is entitled to exercise the votes which are attributable to that status as member, notwithstanding that he no longer has any beneficial interest in the shares. However, he must exercise his votes in accordance with the wishes of his trustee in bankruptcy, as the beneficial interest will have vested in the trustee. **2.33**

CA 2006, Sch 5, Part 6, para 17, which deals with communications by a company, contains provisions dealing with the case of the death or bankruptcy of the holder of shares. These provisions have effect subject to any provisions in the company's articles of association. The provisions apply to documents or information required or authorized to be sent or supplied to the member, including notices of meetings. By para 17(2) it is provided that such documents or information may be supplied to the persons claiming to be entitled to the shares in consequence of the death or bankruptcy. They may be supplied by name or by the title of the representatives of the deceased or trustee of the bankrupt or by any similar description and must be sent to the address in the United Kingdom supplied by those claiming to hold those respective positions. Until such an address has been supplied to the company the notice of meeting (or any other document or information) may be sent or supplied in any manner in which it might have been despatched if the death or bankruptcy had not occurred. The provisions of Sch 5 are examined in more detail below.[30] **2.34**

Notice to members who are joint holders

Very often shares may be owned legally by more than one person. Where shares are owned by two or more joint holders their names will be listed in the register of members. Regulation 112 of the 1985 Table A provides that where there are joint holders of shares all notices for meetings of members shall be given to the joint holder whose name stands first in the list in the register of members in respect **2.35**

29 See *Morgan v Gray* [1953] Ch 83 (Danckwerts J).
30 See paras [2.100]–[2.104] below.

of the joint holding. Once notice has been given to the first-named joint holder the company has discharged its obligation of notifying all of the joint holders of the tranche of shares. It is imprudent for a company to do anything other than send notice of the meeting to the first-named joint holder, but it is suggested that a company should properly provide a notice to any named joint holder if such a person makes a request to receive a notice.

2.36 CA 2006, Sch 5, Part 6, para 16, which governs communications by a company, contains certain specific provisions relating to joint holders of shares and their entitlement to receive notice. These rules have effect subject to anything in a company's articles of association and are therefore default provisions. Paragraph 16(2) of Sch 5 provides that anything to be agreed or specified by the holder must be agreed or specified by all of the joint holders. This provision has material significance in relation to any agreement to accept communications from a company in electronic form or by means of a website. The provisions of Sch 5 are examined in more detail below. Of equal importance is Sch 5, para 16(3) which provides that anything authorized or required to be sent or supplied to the holder may be sent or supplied either to each of the joint holders or to the holder whose name appears first in the company's register of members. This new provision therefore provides the company with a choice of either sending a notice to each of the joint holders or merely to the first-named of the joint holders.

Notice to members who are outside the United Kingdom

2.37 Since the nineteenth century the general rule has been that if a shareholder is overseas he need not be given notice of a meeting.[31] This rule is reflected in reg 112 of the 1985 Table A which provides that a company need not give notice to a member whose registered address is not within the United Kingdom and who has not given the company an address within the United Kingdom for the purpose of giving notices to him or an email address.[32] In the light of modern communications a provision excluding a requirement to send notice to members whose registered address is outside the United Kingdom appears to be out-moded and probably inappropriate.

Notice to a transferee of shares?

2.38 The core requirement for a company is to give notice to its members of all meetings. A member is defined in CA 2006, s 112 as a subscriber to the company's memorandum of association on its registration and every other person who agrees to become a member of a company and whose name is entered in the register

---

[31] *Re Union Hill Silver Co* (1870) 22 LT 400.
[32] See *Parkstone Ltd v Gulf Guarantee Bank plc* [1990] BCLC 850 (Warner J).

of members. If a person's name is entered in the register of members after a notice of meeting has been sent out, prima facie he is not entitled to receive that notice. However, reg 114 of the 1985 Table A provides that every person who becomes entitled to a share shall be bound by any notice in respect of that share, which before his name was entered in the register of members, had been duly given to a person from whom he derives his title.

Members who may be excluded from receiving notice

The articles of association of a company may exclude certain categories of members from any entitlement to receive notice of meetings, or to attend or to vote thereat. This is a quite common situation with regard to classes of preference shares and deferred shares. Such restrictions are legitimate and are a concomitant of an issued share capital being divided into different classes of shares. The category may be extended for example to any member for whom the company does not have a valid address. It is permissible to incorporate such a provision is the articles.[33] **2.39**

Notice to the auditors

The auditor of a company has the right to receive notice of meetings of members.[34] This right was enshrined previously in statute by CA 1985, s 390 which provided that the auditors of the company had the right to receive notice of all general meetings and other communications relating to such meetings which the members are entitled to receive. In addition, the auditors have the right to attend any general meeting of the company and to be heard on any part of the business of the meeting which concerns them as auditors. **2.40**

Auditors who were removed from office before the expiry of their term of office had additional rights. Such auditors were entitled to notice of the meeting at which their term of office would have expired or of any meeting at which the company proposed to fill the vacancy created by their removal.[35] **2.41**

CA 2006, s 502(2)

The statutory entitlement of an auditor to receive all notices of, and other communications relating to, any general meeting which a member is entitled to receive is re-enacted in CA 2006, s 502(2)(a) without alteration. The auditor has the right to attend any general meeting of the company.[36] He is also entitled to be heard **2.42**

[33] See CA 2006, s 310(4) which applies subject to any provision of a company's articles of association.

[34] See reg 38, 1985 Table A.

[35] See CA 1985, s 391(4).

[36] See CA 2006, s 502(2)(b).

at any meeting which he attends on any point if the business of the meeting concerns him as auditor. In this respect the law is unchanged.

Notice of special resolutions under CA 1985

2.43 CA 1985, s 378(2) provided that a resolution was a special resolution when it had been passed by such majority as was required for the passing of an extraordinary resolution at a general meeting of members of which not less that 21 days' notice, stating the intention to propose the resolution as a special resolution, had been given. That majority was one which was not less than 75% of the members who, being entitled to vote in person or by proxy at a general meeting, vote to pass the resolution. The intention to consider and, if thought fit, pass a resolution as a special resolution had to be set out in the notice of the meeting and the exact words of the special resolution had to be set out.

Notice of special resolutions under CA 2006

2.44 One of the major changes introduced by CA 2006 is the abolition of the traditional requirement that not less than 21 days' notice be given of a general meeting at which a special resolution is to be considered and voted upon. Under the new legislation a special resolution is defined in s 283(1) as a resolution passed by a majority of not less than 75%.[37] However, and most importantly for these purposes, a resolution passed at a meeting will not be a special resolution unless the notice of the meeting included the text of the resolution and specified the intention to propose the resolution as a special resolution.[38] Under CA 2006 the requirement of 21 days' notice is preserved only for the annual general meeting of a public company. All other meetings may be called by notice of at least 14 days, regardless of whether the business to be transacted includes the consideration of a special resolution.

'Special notice' provisions under CA 1985, s 379

2.45 Under the provisions of CA 1985, s 379 there were situations where 'special notice', usually of not less than 28 days before the meeting at which the resolution was to be moved, had to be given *to* the company in order for a resolution to be proposed at the meeting to be effective. Resolutions requiring special notice were as follows:

(a) to remove a director from office under CA 1985, s 303;[39]
(b) to appoint a person in place of a director removed under CA 1985, s 303;[40]
(c) to appoint or approve the appointment of a director over the age of 70;[41]

37 See also CA 2006, s 283(4) and (5) and Ch 11.
38 CA 2006, s 283(6).
39 CA 1985, s 303(1).
40 CA 1985, s 303(2).
41 CA 1985, s 293(5).

(d) to fill a casual vacancy in the office of auditor;[42]
(e) to reappoint a retiring auditor who was appointed by the directors to fill a casual vacancy;[43]
(f) to remove an auditor from office before the end of his term of office;[44]
(g) appointing another person as auditor in place of a retiring auditor.[45]

CA 1985, s 379(1) stipulated that if special notice was required for a resolution, the resolution would not be effective unless notice of the intention to move it had been given to the company at least 28 days before the meeting at which it was intended to be moved. The company was required to give members notice of the resolutions listed in para 2.45 above at the same time and in the same way as giving notice of the meeting. If this was not possible then the company was obliged to give notice to its members either by way of an advertisement in a newspaper with the appropriate circulation or in any other way permitted by its articles of association, at least 21 days before the meeting.[46] **2.46**

'Special notice' under CA 2006, s 312

CA 2006, s 312 introduces few changes to this legislation. It provides that where by any provision of the statutes 'special notice' is required of a resolution, the resolution will not be effective unless notice of the intention to move it has been given to the company at least 28 days before the meeting at which it is moved. The obligation is then on the company, where practicable, to give notice of any such resolution to its members in the same manner and at the same time as it gives notice of the meeting.[47] No assistance is provided as to what is meant by 'practicable' in this context but it must be assumed that common sense will dictate the outcome. **2.47**

By CA 2006, s 312(3), where giving notice in that manner and at that time is not practicable, the company must give its members notice at least 14 days before the meeting either by an advertisement in a newspaper 'having an appropriate circulation' or in any other manner allowed by the company's articles. The requirement of notice in this form under CA 1985 is therefore reduced from 21 days to 14 days. It is considered that where the company is a public company with a wide body of shareholders the newspaper used would need to be a national newspaper. If, after notice of the intention to move such a resolution has been given to the company, a meeting is called for a date 28 days or less after the notice has been given, **2.48**

---

42 CA 1985, s 388(3).
43 CA 1985, s 388(3).
44 CA 1985, s 391A.
45 CA 1985, s 391A.
46 CA 1985, s 379(2).
47 CA 2006, s 312(2).

the notice is deemed to have been properly given, though not given within the time required.[48]

Clarity of the notice

2.49 The notice must be unambiguous, intelligible and written in language that is precise, clear and readily understood. In *Kaye v Croydon Tramways Co*[49] the notice of meeting was held to fail the clarity test in circumstances where it was for the purpose of authorizing the sale of the undertaking of one company to another, but nothing at all had been mentioned in the notice of the fact that substantial compensation was to be paid to the directors of the vendor company by way of compensation for loss of office.

2.50 Where there is vagueness or ambiguity in a notice the result will be that the notice is not definite in its terms and such a notice will be insufficient to convene a valid meeting. This proposition is well illustrated by the decision in *Alexander v Simpson*.[50] In this case a notice for an extraordinary general meeting to be held on 12 July 1889 for the passing of certain identified resolutions concluded with the statement that if the resolutions should be passed '... the same will be submitted for confirmation ... to a subsequent extraordinary general meeting which will be held on Monday 29 July 1889 ...'. The court held that the notice of the second meeting was defective when it was sent. In addition, the validity of the subsequent meeting for the end of July 1889 could not be saved by the shareholders finding out whether the resolutions had been passed at the first meeting.

2.51 It is important to note that in certain circumstances a single notice may convene two valid meetings. In *Re Espuela Land Cattle Co*[51] the notice convening the second of two meetings was held to be valid where the composite notice stated that 'should the resolution not be passed by the requisite majority at [the first meeting] due notice would be given to shareholders that [the second meeting] will not be held'.

2.52 Very often business that will be transacted at a meeting will depend on some prior event. The practice in such circumstances is for due notice to be given of the meeting, but a particular resolution that is proposed may have wording to the effect that subject to and conditionally upon some prior event that such and such a resolution will be proposed to be passed by the meeting. If the aforementioned event does not take place the second meeting must be held but the chairman will have to explain why in all the circumstances the resolution cannot be put before the members. After such an explanation the meeting will be declared to be closed.

[48] CA 2006, s 312(4) and the Transitional Provisions referred to in the Commentary in Part 3.
[49] [1898] 1 Ch 358 (CA). See Ch 3.
[50] [1890] 43 ChD 139 (CA, affirming Chitty J).
[51] (1900) 48 WR 684.

Mistakes in notices may give rise to ambiguity

Experience shows that the use of the word processor to 'cut and paste' text from out-of-date notices is a hazardous exercise when it comes to the drafting of notice of meetings. If a notice states that a meeting will be convened for Monday, 11 April in a year when 11 April in fact falls on a Tuesday, then the notice of the general meeting will be defective. On the other hand if the error in the notice is an obvious typographical error then the notice may be held to be valid. For example, where notice is given for the 2006 annual general meeting but the date is incorrectly stated as 'Monday, 26 June 2005' it is suggested that the notice would be effective as the error is plain and obvious. Where there is a minor error in the stated address of the venue this would also not invalidate the notice of the meeting. In such a case effective steps must be taken to ensure that all persons arriving at say, 30 Chancery Lane, are redirected to 33 Chancery Lane. **2.53**

It is suggested that where the directors become aware of an error in the notice of a meeting they should take immediate steps to correct the error and circulate a notice in correct form. In the case of public companies such a corrective notice should be inserted on the company's website and should be the subject of a public announcement including, where appropriate, an advertisement in the financial press. For a listed company the matter should be notified to the UK Listing Authorities for their guidance and agreement. **2.54**

The purpose of the notice is to give 'fair warning' of the business that is to be dealt with at the meeting. It must disclose all the facts necessary to enable a shareholder receiving it to determine, in his own interests, whether or not he ought to attend the meeting.[52] *Tiessen v Henderson* is authority for the proposition that the notice will be construed together with any accompanying circular in order to assess whether the notice given to shareholders is a fair and valid one.[53] This approach was also applied by Slade J in *Re Moorgate Mercantile Holdings Ltd*[54] and by Neuberger J in *Re RAC Motoring Services Ltd, Royal Automobile Club Ltd.*[55] **2.55**

If a notice is misleading the court will intervene at the instigation of shareholders and may by injunction restrain the meeting from considering the matters in the notice. This matter is considered in more detail in Chapter 3. **2.56**

Due authority to convene the meeting

In order to have a valid meeting it must be summoned with due and proper authority. A well-drafted notice of meeting will indicate on the face of that **2.57**

52 *Tiessen v Henderson* [1899] 1 Ch 861 (Kekewich J), following *Kaye v Croydon Tramways Co* [1898] 1 Ch 358 (CA).

53 *Tiessen v Henderson* [1899] 1 Ch 861 at 866.

54 [1980] 1 WLR 227 at 242 (Slade J).

55 [2000] 1 BCLC 307 at 327 (Neuberger J).

document on whose authority it has been issued. It is usual, at least in the case of a public company, for the document that is sent to members to be signed by the company secretary. The omission of the signature of the secretary on the document will not invalidate the notice of meeting, provided that in all other respects the notice is valid and that it shows on whose authority it has been issued.

Notice where members convene a meeting under s 305

2.58 Where members have convened the meeting for themselves, having served a request on the board pursuant to CA 2006, s 303 and the directors have failed to respond in accordance with s 304,[56] the notice to the other shareholders should be issued in the names of the members who have requested the meeting. Where the request received by the company included the text of a resolution intended to be moved at the meeting, the notice of the meeting must include notice of the resolution.[57]

Notice of court ordered meetings under s 306

2.59 Where a court makes an order that a meeting be called under CA 2006, s 306[58] the notice of the meeting should record that it is issued in accordance with the provisions of the relevant court order and comply with such directions as the court has imposed under s 306(3). It is suggested that as a matter of good practice it may be sensible to enclose with the notice of meeting a copy of the court order that has been obtained.

Ratification of authority

2.60 If a notice of meeting is issued on behalf of a company without proper authority from the board of directors it can be made good by subsequent ratification and approval by the board of directors. This mechanism is a vital legal protection for companies and avoids the meeting being declared to be invalid. In *Hooper v Kerr Stewart and Co*[59] the secretary of a company summoned an extraordinary general meeting in response to a request from members who wished to remove some of the directors from office. An action was started for an injunction to prevent the meeting being held, on the ground that it had not been lawfully summoned. Prior to the date fixed for the meeting the directors held a board meeting and ratified the secretary's action in relation to the meeting. The court held that the notice of the extraordinary general meeting was valid in view of the ratification by the board of directors. In the absence of an act of ratification by a board of directors a notice

[56] See Ch 5.
[57] See CA 2006, s 305(2).
[58] Formerly CA 1985, s 371. See Ch 6.
[59] (1900) 83 LT 729.

issued without proper authority will be invalid and the meeting, if it takes place, will be of no effect.[60]

Prescribed form of the notice

It is important that the notice of the meeting is in the proper form set out in the company's articles of association. The standard form provision in the 1985 Table A provides that any notice given to any person pursuant to the articles of association shall be in writing.[61] Since the advent of the Companies Act 1985 (Electronic Communications) Order 2000[62] it has been permissible to give notice by electronic means. The CA 2006 now incorporates express provisions dealing with the form of notice and the means by which notices may be served on members by the company. The company communications provisions in CA 2006, ss 1143–1148 and Schs 4 and 5 also govern the supply of documents to and by a company. These provisions are considered in detail in Chapter 17. **2.61**

CA 2006, s 308

CA 2006, s 308 provides that notice of a general meeting must be given (a) in hard copy form[63] or (b) in electronic form[64] or (c) by means of a website[65] (having regard to s 309) or partly by one such means and partly by another. The incorporation into English law of notice of meeting by a website is a provision which first appeared in the Companies Act 1985 (Electronic Communications) Order 2000, Art 18[66] which came into force on 22 December 2000. Section 308 is cast in mandatory terms and would appear to invalidate any article which provides an alternative method of giving notice, for example, by means of an advertisement in a newspaper in the event of a postal strike. **2.62**

CA 2006, s 309

CA 2006, s 309 is written in negative terms, in that it provides that notice of a meeting is not validly given by a company by means of a website unless it is given in accordance with this section. The requirements of the section are that the company must notify the member of the presence of the notice of meeting on the website. That notification must state that it concerns a notice of a company meeting, specify the place, date and time of the meeting, and in the case of a public company, state whether the meeting will be an annual general meeting. In addition, **2.63**

---

60 See *Re State of Wyoming Syndicate* [1901] 2 Ch 431 (Wright J).
61 See reg 111, 1985 Table A.
62 SI 2000/3373.
63 See CA 2006, s 1168(2), (6) and (7).
64 See CA 2006, s 1168(3)–(7).
65 See CA 2006, s 309 and the Commentary in Part 3.
66 SI 2000/3373.

by s 309(2) the notice of meeting must be available on the website throughout the period beginning with the date of that notification and ending with the conclusion of the meeting.

Accidental omission to give notice

2.64 It is of course the duty and responsibility of the company to send out a notice to all the members entitled to receive such a notice. Failure to comply with this basic obligation may render the proceedings at the meeting invalid. Standard form articles offer a company a modicum of protection in the form of reg 39 of the 1985 Table A which provides:

> The accidental omission to give notice of a meeting to, or the non-receipt of notice of a meeting by, any person entitled to receive notice shall not invalidate the proceedings at the meeting.

2.65 The relief that is offered to a company by such a provision must not be taken by a company as a method of circumventing the overriding duty to give due and proper notice to all members entitled to receive notice of a meeting. It is axiomatic that where the omission to give notice is deliberate, the protection afforded to a company for an accidental omission to send a notice will not apply.[67] The facts of each particular case will have to be examined in order to ascertain the true reason why there has been a failure to give due notice of a general meeting. The person who alleges that the omission to give due notice was accidental, normally the company, will have to discharge the burden of proof.[68] Where the relevant facts disclose that the omission to give notice was based on a deliberate decision, notwithstanding the fact that this was based on a mistaken assumption, the provision will not apply.[69] For example, if a notice of meeting was sent only to voting members rather than all the members of a company entitled to receive such notice, it is suggested that that omission would not be accidental.

2.66 The inadvertent failure to give notice to a large block of members whose names were entered on the register of members after an acquisition may not be protected by an article based on the wording of reg 39 of the 1985 Table A. In *Re West Canadian Collieries Ltd*[70] the registrar of a company failed by accident to give notice to nine shareholders who held in total 101 shares out of a total issued share

---

[67] See *Re Acquisition and Development Ltd* [1995] BCC 338 at 341 and 342; *Re West Canadian Collieries Ltd* [1962] Ch 370 (Plowman J); *Re Peninsula Oriental Steam Navigation Co* [2006] EWHC 389 (Ch), [2006] All ER (D) 36 (Mar) at [86]–[106] (Warren J), affirmed at [2006] EWCA Civ 432 at [44]–[58] (CA).

[68] *POW Services Ltd v Claire* [1995] BCLC 435 at 450 (Jacob J).

[69] See *Musselwhite v Musselwhite (CH) Sons* [1962] Ch 964 (Russell J).

[70] [1962] Ch 370 (Plowman J).

capital of 692,718 shares. This omission was excused by the court and the meeting was held to have been valid.

In *Re Peninsula Oriental Steam Navigation Co*[71] the company and its solicitors had issued instructions to the registrars to proceed to convene a meeting in the correct manner laid down in the company's articles but those instructions were inadvertently not carried out. It was held that the error of the registrars in failing to give effect to the company's express and proper instruction was not to be attributed to the company. As a result, so far as the company was concerned, the error of the registrars was properly to be characterized as an accidental omission. **2.67**

Accidental omission to give notice under CA 2006

CA 2006, s 313 introduces into the legislation a provision dealing with the accidental failure by a company to give notice to one or more persons. It covers such failure in relation to a notice of a general meeting or of a resolution intended to be moved at such meeting. It provides that in that event such accidental failure shall be disregarded for the purpose of determining whether notice of the meeting or of the resolution is duly given. This section has effect subject to any provision of the company's articles, except in relation to (a) the notice of a meeting called by directors under s 304 following a request from members under s 303,[72] (b) a notice given by members themselves under s 305 where the directors fail to meet a request for a meeting given under s 303,[73] and (c) a notice of a members' resolution for an annual general meeting of a public company given by the company under s 339.[74] These are all excluded. **2.68**

It is noteworthy that the new section again refers only to the concept of 'accidental omission'. It will not cover an inadvertent failure to give notice where the failure has been the consequence of a deliberate, albeit misguided, decision not to give proper notice. It is likely therefore that the section will be of limited application. **2.69**

No notice because of circumstances beyond the control of the company

There may be situations where, for external reasons beyond the control of the company, it is not possible in practice to give members notice of a meeting. In an age of electronic and almost instantaneous communication such situations will be exceptional and rare. If a company was prevented from sending notices to members with a registered address situated in an enemy territory, the company would be able to continue to carry on its business without giving notices to such members.[75] **2.70**

---

[71] Op. cit.
[72] See Ch 5.
[73] See Ch 5.
[74] See Ch 4.
[75] *Re Anglo-International Bank* [1943] Ch 233 (CA).

2.71 If a postal strike delays the receipt by members of the notice and agenda of a meeting a company may have to use alternative methods of sending out notices of meetings to members, but in such circumstances the holding of the meeting may be restrained by an order of the court. In *Bradman v Trinity Estates plc*[76] a shareholder sought an injunction to restrain the holding of a general meeting on the basis that owing to a postal strike some shareholders had not received notice of the meeting. The evidence showed that shareholders within the London area had been sent their circulars by courier but those with addresses outside London had been sent their notices in unsealed letter-boxes. Some of these documents had only arrived some 10 days later and others had not been delivered at all. Under the company's articles delivery of a notice sent by post was deemed to be effected 24 hours after it was posted. The company therefore argued that the shareholders outside London had been properly served. The court held that from a practical point of view it would be wrong to allow the meeting to proceed.[77]

2.72 It is not uncommon to find in articles of association a provision which permits the company in question to give notice of a meeting by means of an advertisement in a newspaper in the event of a postal strike. However, the mandatory wording of CA 2006, s 308 renders nugatory the efficacy of such a provision.

Length of the notice under CA 1985

2.73 Correctly calculating the length of notice that must be given for a meeting is a most important requirement and one that can give rise to problems in practice. If the requisite period of notice is not given the meeting will be invalid.[78] Under CA 1985, s 369 various periods of notice were prescribed for notices of meetings of members. In the case of an annual general meeting the period of notice that had to be given was 21 days' notice in writing. In respect of meetings other than an annual general meeting or a meeting convened for the passing of a special resolution notice of only 14 days was required.[79]

2.74 Articles of association could stipulate a longer period of notice but could not require a shorter period of notice than that provided for in CA 1985, s 369. CA 1985, s 369(2) stipulated the statutory periods of notice if the articles of association made no provision for the length of notice that had to be given for meetings.

2.75 Unsurprisingly the provisions contained in Regulation 38 of the 1985 Table A reflect the statutory requirements relating to length of notice and also make

---

[76] (1989) 5 BCC 33 (Hoffmann J).

[77] The effect of this decision was to encourage public companies to include in their articles provisions for alternative methods of service of notices in the event of a postal strike or other serious industrial action. Such provisions are now commonplace.

[78] *Woolf v East Niger Gold Mining Co Ltd* (1905) 98 LT 225.

[79] Seven days' notice in the case of an unlimited company: see CA 1985, s 369(1)(b)(i).

provision for shareholders to give their consent to short notice. Under reg 38, at least 21 clear days' notice must be given for an annual general meeting and for an extraordinary general meeting called for the passing of a special resolution. All other extraordinary general meetings must be called by at least 14 clear days' notice. The definitions in reg 1 of the 1985 Act Table A make it clear that 'clear days' means the period excluding the day when the notice was given or deemed to be given and the day for which the notice is given or on which it is to take effect. Where articles of association do not specify that the notice must be a certain number of clear days there is authority for the proposition that the words mean 'clear days' notice'.[80]

Length of the notice under CA 2006

Under the new legislation the minimum length of notice for general meetings of a company has changed. The changes reflect a desire to simplify the law as to the length of notice required. Section 307 replaces CA 1985, s 369. It provides that for both public and private companies the minimum period of notice shall be 14 days, except in the case of the annual general meeting of a public company where the requirement of at least 21 days' notice remains. These provisions are subject to anything in the company's articles of association which may require a longer period of notice. Most importantly, it is to be noted that the previous rule requiring at least 21 days' notice for a general meeting at which a special resolution is to be proposed has been abolished. **2.76**

CA 2006, s 306

CA 2006, s 306 introduces rules for the purposes of calculating the requisite period of notice under s 307. The section sets out what is known as the 'clear day rule'. This states that any reference in s 307 (or in any of the other statutory provisions listed) to a period of notice is to be calculated by excluding (a) the date of the meeting and (b) the day on which the notice is given. **2.77**

Calculating the number of days' notice required for a meeting, especially when a number of clear days is required, is an essential and sometimes daunting task for the company secretary and the company's legal advisers. For the reasons stated above the consequences of miscalculating this may be very serious and may lead to substantial additional expense. In the circumstances, companies are recommended where possible to give more than the minimum period of notice of meetings so as to ensure that the problem and consequences of inadequate notice do not arise. **2.78**

---

[80] See *Mercantile Investments and General Trust Co v International Company of Mexico* [1893] 1 Ch 484 (CA) and *Re Hector Whaling Ltd* [1936] 208 (Bennett J).

Consent to short notice under CA 1985

2.79 CA 1985, s 369(3) made provision for a valid meeting to be called by shorter notice than that required by CA 1985, s 369(2) or by a company's articles of association, provided that there was unanimous consent of the members in the case of an annual general meeting, or by the requisite majority of members in respect of all other meetings. The requisite majority in this case was a majority in number of members having the right to attend and vote at the meeting, being a majority holding not less than 95% in nominal value of the shares.[81] CA 1985, s 369 only identified 'members' as the group of people who had to give such consent.

Consent to short notice under CA 2006

2.80 CA 2006, s 307 contains new provisions enabling a company to give shorter notice of a general meeting than that generally required by the statute. These provisions do not apply in the case of an annual general meeting.[82] A distinction is made in CA 2006 between the rules relating to public companies and those affecting private companies.

2.81 **Consent to short notice—private companies** For a private company the shorter notice must be agreed to by a majority in number of the members having a right to attend and vote at the meeting who together hold not less than 90% (or such higher percentage not exceeding 95% as may be specified in the company's articles) in nominal value of the shares having the right to attend and vote at the meeting. In making this calculation it is necessary to exclude any shares held by the company as treasury shares.

2.82 **Consent to short notice—public companies** In the case of a public company the shorter notice must be agreed to by a majority in number of the members having a right to attend and vote at the meeting who together hold not less than 95% in nominal value of the shares having the right to attend and vote at the meeting.

2.83 In the case of an annual general meeting, where the legislation now applies only in respect of public companies, CA 2006, s 337(2) provides that the meeting may be called by shorter notice than the period of at least 21 days allowed for in s 307(2) or by the company's articles, as the case may be, if *all* the members entitled to attend and vote at the meeting agree to the shorter notice. This does not change the existing law. The provision is unlikely to be used very often as it is usually impossible to obtain the unanimous consent of the large number of members of a public company.

[81] In the case of a company not having a share capital the requisite majority was members together representing not less than 95% of the total voting rights.

[82] See CA 2006, s 307(7). CA 2006, s 337(2) applies to annual general meetings (public companies only).

Consent to short notice—companies not having a share capital In the case of a company not having a share capital, the shorter notice must be agreed to by a majority in number of the members having a right to attend and vote at the meeting, being a majority who together represent not less than the requisite percentages stated above of the total voting rights at that meeting of all the members. **2.84**

Consent to short notice can be given in a number of ways. It is essential that there is certainty as to whether the members of a company have given such consent and their consent should therefore be recorded carefully in the minutes of the meeting. Invariably a written form of consent is produced for signature and retained with the company's records. **2.85**

Transitional provisions

There are transitional provisions that are applicable to the introduction of CA 2006, s 307 which are set out in the Third Commencement Order, Sch 3, paras 26 and 26A. These transitional provisions are discussed in the commentary to CA 2006, ss 307 and 311 at paras 22.169 to 22.174 and 22.187 to 22.193 below. **2.86**

Informality: A possible remedy for the failure to give proper notice?

If a company fails to give to its members the requisite period of notice for a general meeting of its members, the meeting will not be able to transact any lawful business. The reported cases show that in certain circumstances this infelicitous and stark consequence can be avoided. In *Re Express Engineering Works Ltd*[83] it was noted that if all of the members of the company were present at the meeting then all the requirements for a valid meeting had been observed. In that case there was a total of five members of the company and all of them met in a board meeting as directors. Thereafter, and without sending out any form of notice, they met as shareholders and passed a resolution to issue debentures. In these circumstances the court held that as the members had resolved to do something that was within the capacity of the company, all the members of the company were able to waive the formalities with regard to notice and as a result the resolution was as valid as if the meeting had been held with the requisite and formal period of notice. **2.87**

Another example of this principle is the decision in *Re Oxted Motor Co*[84] where there were only two members of a company. These individuals met and agreed that the company should be wound up. A minute of this unanimous decision of the members was drawn up and signed by all of the members. At no time had any notice of the intention to propose the resolution as an extraordinary resolution been given. Again, it was decided that as there was unanimous agreement of the **2.88**

[83] [1920] 1 Ch 466 (CA).
[84] [1921] 3 KB 32 (Divisional Court).

members of the company to waive the formalities with regard to notice, the resolution passed to wind up the company was valid as an extraordinary resolution. A similar result occurred in the cases of *Re Horsley Weight Ltd*,[85] and *Re M J Shanley Contracting Ltd (in voluntary liquidation)*.[86]

2.89 The cases cited above illustrate the proposition that the unanimous consent of the members to waive a procedural requirement will produce the same result as a valid notice.[87] Such a situation is possible in the case of a small private company with only a few members, but it is unlikely to apply in relation to a large public company with many thousands of members on its register of members.

2.90 In *Re Pearce Duff & Co*[88] a company sent to its members a notice of an extraordinary general meeting containing one resolution, but failed to give the required period of 21 days' notice. The company wished to add another resolution for consideration at the extraordinary general meeting. At the meeting the shareholders signed a consent to short notice relating to the second resolution alone. The company obtained the consent of all of the members to both of the resolutions. It was held that for a valid consent to short notice for the statutory provision the members had to realize that the resolution in question was being passed on short notice and to agree to the passing of the resolution with that fact in their minds. On the facts of the case it was established those members who had signed the consent to short notice for the second resolution did not have it in mind that there was a basic defect in the notice for the first resolution. Accordingly, there was no consent from the members to cure the matter. However, because of the later unanimous consent from the members to both of the resolutions, it was not possible for any of the members to contend successfully that the resolutions had not been passed.

Manner of service of a notice of meeting under CA 1985

2.91 Until CA 1985 the articles of association of any company governed the manner in which notice to members had to be given. In the absence of any express provision in the articles of association CA 1985, s 370(2) stipulated that notice had to be served on every member in the manner in which notices had to be served by the Table A that was currently in force. There were four regulations in the 1985 Table A that were relevant. These provisions were reg 111, 112, 113 and 115 which provided as follows:

> 111. Any notice to be given to or by any person pursuant to the articles (other than a notice calling a meeting of the directors) shall be in writing or shall be given using electronic communication to an address for the time being notified for that purpose to the person giving the notice.

85 [1982] Ch 442 (CA).
86 (1980) 124 SJ 239.
87 See *Re Duomatic Ltd* [1969] 2 Ch 365 (Buckley J).
88 [1960] 1 WLR 1014 (Buckley J).

In this regulation, 'address', in relation to electronic communications, includes any number or address used for the purposes of such communications.

112. The company may give any notice to a member either personally on by sending it by post or in a prepaid envelope addressed to the member at his registered address or by leaving it at that address or by giving it using electronic communications to an address for the time being notified to the company by the member. In the case of joint holders of a share, all notices shall be given to the joint holder whose name stands first in the register of members in respect of the joint holding and notice so given shall be sufficient notice to all the joint holders. A member whose registered address is not within the United Kingdom and who gives to the company an address within the United Kingdom at which notices may be give to him or an address to which notices may be sent using electronic communications, shall be entitled to have notices given to him at that address, but otherwise no such member shall be entitled to receive any notice from the company.

In this regulation and the next, 'address', in relation to electronic communications, includes any number or address used for the purposes of such communications.

113. A member present, either in person or by proxy, at any meeting of the company or of the holders of any class of shares in the company, shall be deemed to have received notice of the meeting and, where requisite, of the purposes for which it was called.

...

115. Proof that an envelope containing a notice was properly addressed, prepaid and posted shall be conclusive evidence that the notice was given. Proof that the notice contained in an electronic communication was sent in accordance with the guidance issued by the Institute of Chartered Secretaries and Administrators shall be conclusive evidence that the notice was given. A notice shall be deemed to be given at the expiry of 48 hours after the envelope containing it was posted or, in the case of a notice contained in an electronic communication, at the expiration of 48 hours after the time it was sent.[89]

The address for service will be the address that appears in the company's register **2.92** of members, for it is that important document that is prima facie evidence of matters which are directed to be contained in it.[90]

The term 'posted' means the placing of the envelope in the post, or the delivery to **2.93** an authorized official of the Post Office. In view of the vagaries of the postal system those responsible for the administration of company meetings will be well advised to obtain compelling evidence, sometimes in the form of a certificate of posting, of the posting of notices of meetings. In private companies with small numbers of members it is sometimes advisable to send a notice of meeting by registered or special delivery post. Such methods of posting require a signature on delivery from the recipient and can be tracked by the sender.

---

89 See paras 2.95–2.98 below.

90 See CA 2006, s 127, formerly CA 1985, s 361.

Manner of service of a notice of meeting under CA 2006

2.94 As stated above the new legislation in s 308 expressly provides that notice of a general meeting of a company must be given (a) in hard copy form, (b) in electronic form or (c) by means of a website or partly by one such means and partly by another. As part of the aim of increasing the use of electronic communications, CA 2006 incorporates in ss 1144–1148 and Schs 4 and 5 new provisions governing all communications made to and from companies. These are known as the 'companies communication provisions'[91] and are dealt with below in Chapter 17. These important provisions apply to communications by a company with its shareholders and therefore govern the service of notices of meetings. Section 1147 will be considered first, before examining the key provisions of Sch 5.

CA 2006, s 1147

2.95 Section 1147 sets out a number of rules governing the deemed delivery of documents sent or supplied by a company. So far as members of a company are concerned this section has effect subject to any contrary provision contained in a company's articles of association.[92] So far as debenture holders of a company are concerned this section has effect subject to any contrary provision contained in the instrument constituting the debenture.[93] In relation to documents sent or supplied by a company to a person otherwise than in their capacity as a member or as a debenture holder (for example, a director who is not also a member), the provision takes effect subject to any contrary contained in an agreement between the company and that person articles of association.[94]

2.96 Where a document, such as a notice, is sent by post, whether in hard copy or electronic form to an address in the United Kingdom and the company is able to show that it was properly addressed, prepaid and posted it is deemed to have been received by the intended recipient 48 hours after it was posted.[95] It is understood that a document will be sent by post in electronic form within the meaning of the section if the company's letter encloses a computer disc containing the notice of meeting.

2.97 Where the document is sent or supplied to a member by electronic means and the company is able to show that it was properly addressed it is deemed to have been received by the intended recipient 48 hours after it was sent.[96]

[91] See CA 2006, s 1143.
[92] See CA 2006, s 1147(6)(a).
[93] See CA 2006, s 1147(6)(b).
[94] See CA 2006, s 1147(6)(c).
[95] See CA 2006, s 1147(2).
[96] See CA 2006, s 1147(3).

Where the document is sent or supplied by means of a website, it is deemed to have been received by the intended recipient (a) when the material was first made available on the website or (b) if later, when the recipient received (or is deemed to have received)[97] notice of the fact that the material was available on the website. This provision ties in with CA 2006, s 309 governing the publication of the notice of a general meeting on a website. The company is required to notify the member of the presence of the notice of the general meeting. So far as members of a company are concerned this section has effect subject to any contrary provision contained in a company's articles of association.[98] The notice of general meeting on the website and the notification must state that it concerns the notice of a company meeting, specify the place, date and time of the meeting and, in the case of a public company, state whether the meeting will be an annual general meeting. The notice of the meeting must be available on the website throughout the period beginning with the date of that notification and ending with the conclusion of the meeting. **2.98**

Calculating the period of time

For the purposes of CA 2006, s 1147 and in calculating a period of hours under that provision, s 1147(5) provides that no account shall be taken of any part of a day that is not a working day. This means that the 48-hour period for deemed service under s 1147(2) and (3) cannot include any part of a weekend (Saturday or Sunday), Christmas Day, Good Friday or any day that is a bank holiday in the part of the United Kingdom where the company is registered.[99] **2.99**

CA 2006, Sch 5

Documents to be sent by a company, including notices of a meeting, must be sent or supplied in accordance with the provisions of Sch 5. That schedule deals separately with communications in hard copy form (Part 2), communications in electronic form (Part 3) and communications by means of a website (Part 4). For an analysis of this schedule see Chapter 17. **2.100**

Notices—hard copy form

It is important to note in this context that a member of a company can insist on his continuing to require the company to send to him a version of any document or any other relevant information in hard copy form.[100] Where a notice of meeting **2.101**

---

[97] See CA 2006, s 1147(4).

[98] See CA 2006, s 1147(6)(a).

[99] For the definition of 'working day' see s 1173(1). It should be noted that there are different bank holidays in different parts of the United Kingdom.

[100] See CA 2006, s 1145(1).

is sent in hard copy form it may continue to be sent by post to one of several possible addresses. Those addresses are:[101]

(a) the address specified for the purpose by the intended recipient;
(b) in the case of a company, its registered office;
(c) to a person in his capacity as a member of the company to the address shown in the company's register of members;
(d) to a person in his capacity as a director of the company to the address shown for that director in the company's register of directors;
(e) where the company is unable to obtain an address falling within any of the above categories the notice may be sent or supplied to the intended recipient's last address that is known to the company.

Notices—electronic form

2.102 Schedule 5, Part 3 deals with communications by a company in electronic form. Most importantly a notice of a general meeting may only be sent or supplied by a company in electronic form to a person who has agreed, either generally or specifically, that the notice may be sent or supplied in that form and that agreement has not been revoked. It is anticipated that as a result of this provision large numbers of public companies will continue to seek the agreement of their members to accept notices of meetings in electronic form. A notice of a meeting that is sent by electronic means must be supplied to the address specified for the purpose by the intended recipient, ie to the correct email address as notified to the company.[102] In addition where the notice is supplied in electronic form by post it must be sent to an address to which it could have been validly sent if it were in hard copy form.[103]

Notices—website

2.103 Schedule 5, Part 4 contains detailed provisions regulating communications by means of a website—see further Chapter 17. The most important aspect of these provisions is that a company is only entitled to give notice by means of a website if the shareholder has agreed, either generally or specifically, that notice may be supplied in that manner or is taken to have so agreed under the provisions of Part 4, para 10 and has not revoked that agreement. The three conditions that must be met for this purpose are:

(1) the members of the company must have resolved that documents be sent or supplied to members by making them available on a website or the company's articles of association must contain a provision to that effect;

101 See Sch 5, Part 2, para 4.
102 Sch 5, Part 3, para 7.
103 Sch 5, Part 3, para 7(2)(b).

(2) the person must have been asked individually by the company to agree to the use of the website; and
(3) the company has not received a response within the period of 28 days beginning with the date on which its request was sent.

The request from a company must state clearly what the effect of a failure to respond will be. If it fails to do so, the member will not be taken to have so agreed. The request may be made at 12-monthly intervals. If the request is sent less than 12 months after a previous request no agreement can be deemed to have been made.

Schedule 5, Part 4, para 13 requires the company to notify intended recipients on each occasion that a notice or other document is published on a website. Such notification must state: **2.104**

(a) the presence of the notice on the website;
(b) the address of the website;
(c) the place on the website where it may be accessed; and
(d) how to access the document or information.

The document or information is taken to be sent on the date on which the required notification is sent by the company, or if later, on the date on which the document or information first appears on the website after that notification is sent. Once again care must be taken to ensure that the company also complies with the requirements of s 309, namely that the notification must, if it concerns a notice of a company meeting, specify the place, date and time of the meeting, and in the case of a public company state whether the meeting will be an annual general meeting.[104]

The receipt of notice by a non-shareholder director

One consequence of the introduction of the new requirement in CA 2006, s 310 that directors must be given notice of all general meetings is that it may no longer be possible, even with the consent of all the shareholders, to hold an immediate general meeting to transact business. If one particular director, who is not also the holder of shares, is not present at the time the proposed general meeting is to be called at short notice he will have had no notice at all and the meeting will be invalid under s 310. If he is a shareholder the problem does not arise as the statute permits in s 307 the requisite percentage of members to agree to short notice of the meeting but he must of course have some notice. **2.105**

However, a non-shareholder director must receive proper notice in accordance with s 310(1)(b). CA 2006, s 1147 (deemed delivery of documents and information) provides in subs (2)(b) that where the company is able to show that a document, **2.106**

[104] See para 2.63 above.

such as a notice of meeting, was sent by pre-paid post and was correctly addressed it is deemed to have been received by the addressee 48 hours after posting. There is a similar deeming provision in relation to documents or information sent by electronic means in s 1147(3). Where a website is used the document is deemed to have been received by the intended recipient when the material is first made available on the website, or if later, when he received or is deemed to have received notice of the fact that the material was on the website.

2.107 All of s 1147 takes effect subject to subs (6). In relation to a company's members s 1147(6)(a) permits a derogation from the 48-hour deeming period by a contrary provision in the articles. In relation to documents sent or supplied to a person who is not a member, such as the non-shareholding director, s 1147(6)(c) provides that in order to derogate from the 48-hour period for deemed receipt there must be a contrary provision in an agreement between the company and that person.

2.108 Accordingly, consideration should be given to including a provision in the articles reducing the period of deemed delivery from 48 hours to a lesser period. In relation to non-shareholding directors it is necessary to make a separate agreement to this effect.

2.109 The impact of s 310 is therefore extensive. A director, like a member, is entitled to be given notice of every general meeting and he must receive or be deemed to have received the notice before any meeting can be held at short notice.

Notice of an adjourned meeting

2.110 Where a meeting is adjourned in accordance with the proper procedure the adjournment constitutes a continuation of the meeting and the notice that was given for the original meeting endures for and is valid for all other meetings that are dependant on the first meeting. This principle is subject to any provision in the company's articles which requires a further notice to be supplied by the company in the event that the meeting is adjourned for longer than a few days. If a meeting is adjourned 'sine die' ie without giving a specific date and time for the holding of the adjourned meeting, a new notice will have to be given to the members in respect of the adjourned meeting. These issues are examined in more detail in Chapter 12.

Challenges to the validity of a notice of meeting

2.111 In relation to this issue three very important principles should be noted. First, a person who is present, whether in person or by proxy, at a meeting and takes an active part in the meeting will not be able to make an effective challenge to the validity of a notice of a meeting.[105] This principle is often incorporated in the company's articles of association. For example, reg 113 of the 1985 Table A provides:

> A member present, either in person or by proxy, at any meeting of the company or of the holders of any class of shares in the company shall be deemed to have received notice of the meeting and, where requisite, of the purposes for which it was called.

Secondly, any challenge to the validity of a notice of a meeting must be made promptly.[106] The longer the matter is left the greater may be the reluctance on the part of a court to intervene. **2.112**

Thirdly, a court may not interfere where there is a challenge to minor irregularities in a notice of meeting. The court will only intervene if the challenge to the notice is one of substance. This principle reflects the reluctance of the court to become involved in factional disputes between shareholders and the principle that if a defect can be rectified easily there is no logical basis for an intervention by the courts.[107] **2.113**

Set against these three principles it has to be remembered that a shareholder in a company is entitled to have the affairs of the company conducted in accordance with the company's articles of association. A serious procedural irregularity in the convening of a meeting of members may be capable of challenge either in a normal personal action or under the provisions of CA 1985, s 459. If such a challenge is made the shareholder must establish that the conduct that he impugns is both unfair and prejudicial to his interests as a member. **2.114**

If, on a proper consideration of all the relevant evidence before it, a court comes to the conclusion that a defect in the notice could be remedied by the issuing of another notice and that a majority of members support the resolution that has been passed at the meeting, the court may be reluctant to make an order restraining persons from acting on the resolution.[108] **2.115**

European Directive

It should be noted that the provisions of the CA 2006 dealing with the length of notice of meetings are likely to be amended in so far as they relate to general meetings of listed companies to reflect Directive 2007/36/EC. Article 5.1 of that Directive will require 21 days' prior notice to be given of a general meeting of a listed company, which period can be reduced to 14 days for a meeting other than an annual general meeting where the company offers the facility for shareholders to vote by electronic means. **2.116**

---

105 See *Re British Sugar Refining Co* (1857) 3 K & J 408.
106 See *Southern Counties Deposit Bank Limited v Kirkwood* (1892) 11 TLR 563.
107 See *Re Legal Costs Negotiators Ltd* [1999] 1 BCLC 171 (CA).
108 See *Bentley-Stevens v Jones* [1974] 1 WLR 638 (Plowman J).

3

CIRCULARS TO MEMBERS AND MEMBERS' STATEMENTS

Circulars

The purpose of a circular

Very often when a meeting of members of a company is convened the notice of the meeting will be accompanied by a circular that is addressed to all of the members. Such a circular for distribution to members will be prepared by the board of directors, usually in consultation with relevant appropriate professional advisers. The purpose of sending a circular to members is to appraise them of the reason for, **3.01** and purpose of, the resolutions that are proposed to be considered at the forthcoming general meeting, and to provide pertinent information to shareholders in order to enable them to take an informed decision as to whether or not to attend the meeting[1] and as to how they will cast their votes.[2] A board of directors must ensure that a circular to members contains an accurate summary of all of the relevant information relating to the proposals upon which the members have been asked to vote at the forthcoming general meeting.

Members' statements

3.02 It is to be noted that the first part of this chapter deals with the requirements of a circular to be sent to the members of the company by the board of directors. Another form of communication is a members' statement which the company may be required to circulate in accordance with the provisions of CA 2006, ss 314–317 (inclusive).[3] These provisions are considered separately at paras 3.48–3.62 below.

A summary of relevant facts

3.03 It is well recognized that a circular to members is a summary of the facts and matters that are germane to the forthcoming general meeting. The document is drafted by or on behalf of the board of directors which has access to all the relevant information. Were it to be the case that a circular had to set out all of the details of a transaction in infinitesimal detail that would defeat the object and purpose of a circular to members, namely to summarize the matters at issue. This obvious and sensible point was acknowledged by Maugham J in *Re Dorman, Long and Company*[4] in the context of a complex scheme of arrangement where a circular had been sent to members. In this case Maugham J observed that:

> The practice being to send out an explanatory circular in such a case, it is, in my opinion, the duty of the Court very carefully to scrutinize the circular when the matters involved are matters of considerable difficulty and doubt. In a case of great

---

[1] See *Tiessen v Henderson* [1899] 1 Ch 861 (Kekewich J) following *Kaye v Croydon Tramways* [1898] 1 Ch 358. This latter case was followed in *Clarkson v Davies* [1923] AC 100 (PC).

[2] See *Re Smiths of Smithfield Ltd* [2003] All ER (D) 325 (Mar) at para 46 where the Deputy Judge of the High Court said in his judgment: 'It is long established that the directors of a Company have a duty in equity to give shareholders sufficient information for them to make an informed decision about proposals to be put to them at a Company meeting. Where the contents of a circular to shareholders are challenged the court will take into account the impact of any lack of information or alleged misrepresentation on the decision of shareholders'—see *Residues Treatment and Trading Co. Ltd v Southern Resources Ltd* (1998) 14 ACLR 375 at 377–378 (Supreme Court of Australia), cited with approval by Neuberger J in *Re RAC Motoring Services Ltd* [2000] 1 BCLC 307 at 307a–d.

[3] These provisions came into force on 1 October 2007—see Third Commencement Order.

[4] [1934] Ch 635 at 665–6 (Maugham J).

> complexity it is true that not every relevant fact can be stated. I apprehend that if the circular were to assume such a length as to state all the relevant facts in Dormans' petition it would be so lengthy as to defeat its own object.

In a more recent decision[5] the court recognized that information contained in a circular to members may not be completely full but it must be sufficient to enable a member to make further enquiries if he so wishes. The law recognizes the importance of circulars as the primary method of communicating information to shareholders. Nowadays only a very small minority of shareholders or those persons interested in the equity of a company will attend any general meeting. Members determine how they should vote or indeed whether they should attend a general meeting in the light of the contents of a company's circular. **3.04**

When a circular comes to be examined with the benefit of hindsight it can probably always be said that something further could, or should, have been contained in the text of the document, or that a more capable author might have expressed an issue in clearer language. However, a court adopts a practical and commonsense approach and will only condemn a circular as inadequate if there is compelling evidence that some recipients have been misled. The principles applied by the court are referred to in detail at para 3.22 below. **3.05**

The aim of the author of a circular must be to give an accurate precis of all of the relevant details in a manner that is readily understandable. The particular form and content of every circular document to members will depend on the circumstances in which a company is communicating with its members. Whether individual shareholders will understand for themselves the contents of a circular that relates to a complex commercial transaction is a moot point. However, it is incumbent on the company to impart the relevant information to the members in a clear and unambiguous manner. Thereafter it is for the members to seek relevant professional advice if they do not understand the document or if they are uncertain about what action to take. Sometimes members of a company who have received a circular may write to the chairman or the company secretary seeking further information. It is not possible to state how companies should react to all such communications but where the request is reasonable it is suggested that it may be unwise to ignore the enquiry from a shareholder. **3.06**

Directors must take very great care in the preparation of a circular addressed to members as it is they who will have to take the legal responsibility for its contents and the consequences that flow from any defects and shortcomings. It is most important for a board of directors to summarize the information that is pertinent **3.07**

---

[5] See *Re RAC Motoring Services Ltd; Re Royal Automobile Club Ltd* [2000] BCLC 307 (Neuberger J); *Buttonwood Nominees Pty Ltd v Sundowner Minerals NL* (1986) 10 ACLR 360 (Supreme Court of New South Wales, Equity Division, Young J).

to the proposed resolutions in a clear, accurate, unambiguous and understandable manner. The reason for this is so that the members of the company can not only understand the issue upon which they have been asked to vote, but also have access to all relevant information, or sources of such information, and can make an informed decision about the proposals. Where the issues for a general meeting of members are very complex the circular that is sent to members will inevitably become a much more detailed and lengthy document.[6] In many cases the circular will include the advice received by the board from the company's professional advisers or institutions such as merchant bankers or corporate financiers. It is the board of directors who have to take ultimate legal responsibility for the accuracy and contents of the published circular.

No prescribed statutory format

3.08 There is no standard or prescribed statutory format for a circular which a board of directors is compelled by law to use and there is no formal statutory requirement under CA 2006 to issue a circular to members prior to a general meeting. However, in relation to public listed companies circulars are required to comply with the Listing Rules, the details of which will be considered below. It is to be noted that under CA 2006, s 239, which enables a company to seek ratification from shareholders in respect of the conduct of a director that amounts to negligence, default, breach of duty or breach of trust in relation to a company, such ratification must be obtained by means of a duly passed resolution of the members of a company.[7] In circumstances where some form of explanation to the members could be considered as an indispensable prerequisite to obtaining the informed approval of the shareholders, it is surprising that the legislation makes no provision for the company to send an explanatory circular to members. It is suggested that it would be imprudent for a board of directors, and might expose them to justifiable criticism, to seek approval from the members under CA 2006, s 239, without having sent an explanatory circular to members.

Circulars issued by private companies and unlisted public companies

3.09 In the context of a private company with a small number of members, the necessity for a board of directors to send an explanatory circular to members may arise on rare and infrequent occasions. Such a circular will be a more frequent occurrence for an unlisted public company. Circulars will frequently be sent to members in respect of general meetings held to consider an ordinary resolution to remove

---

[6] When Abbey National plc was the subject of a takeover by Banco Santander in 2004 the circular that was sent to members of Abbey National plc seeking their approval resembled in size a small telephone directory.

[7] See CA 2006, s 239 (1) and (2).

a director under CA 2006, s 168 or to pass a special resolution to approve the terms of a contract for the purchase of its own shares under CA 2006, s 694 or where directors propose to make extensive amendments to a company's articles of association pursuant to CA 2006, s 21. An explanatory circular to members summarizing and explaining proposed amendments to articles of association or the factual background that gives rise to a need for any other resolution of the members may be regarded as a hallmark of good corporate governance. Such a circular should fully and fairly inform the shareholders of what is proposed to be done.[8]

In some instances a circular to the members of an unlisted company may be no more than a detailed letter from the chairman of the board that is addressed to all of the shareholders. Such a letter would explain and summarize the proposals that are to be considered by the members, and may take the opportunity to encourage the members to vote in favour of the resolutions that have been proposed. **3.10**

Circulars issued by public listed companies

As is to be expected a much more formal regime applies in relation to circulars that are issued by listed companies. The board of directors of a public listed company may come under an obligation imposed by reason of the Listing Rules to issue an explanatory circular to members, for example, where a transaction constitutes a related party transaction,[9] or where there is to be a significant disposal of assets[10] and thus the transaction in question becomes conditional upon the members of the company passing resolutions authorizing the transaction. **3.11**

In general, the circulars of such institutions come under the aegis of the Financial Services Authority (FSA),[11] which was given statutory powers by the Financial Services and Markets Act 2000. The FSA is financed by the financial services industry and the board of the FSA is appointed by HM Treasury. The Financial Services and Markets Act 2000 conferred four statutory regulatory objectives on the FSA:[12] **3.12**

(1) market confidence: maintaining confidence in the financial system;
(2) public awareness: promoting public understanding of the financial system;
(3) consumer protection: securing the appropriate degree of protection for consumers; and
(4) the reduction of financial crime: reducing the extent to which it is possible for a business to be used for a purpose connected with financial crime.

---

8 *Bancorp Investments Ltd v Primac Holdings Ltd* (1984) 9 ACLR 263.

9 See, for example, the circular sent to members of International Power plc in May 2007 when that public company was proposing a new joint venture with Mitsui & Co, Ltd.

10 See, for example, the circular sent to members of Luminar plc in December 2006 seeking the approval of members to the proposed disposal of its entertainment division and non-core assets.

11 The FSA is constituted as a company limited by guarantee.

12 See Financial Services and Markets Act 2000, ss 3–6.

3.13 The FSA has been given a wide range of rule-making, investigatory and enforcement powers in order to meet its four statutory objectives. In meeting those statutory objectives the FSA is obliged to have regard to the principles of good corporate governance.[13] The FSA summarizes its statutory objectives and principles of good regulation in three strategic aims:

(1) promoting efficient, orderly and fair markets;
(2) helping retail consumers achieve a fair deal; and
(3) improving the UK's business capability and effectiveness.

FSA Handbook

3.14 The FSA produces a Handbook which sets out all of the FSA's rules made under the statutory powers given to the FSA by the Financial Services and Markets Act 2000. Included in the FSA's Handbook are the Listing Rules. Chapter 13 of the Listing Rules prescribes detailed rules for the contents of circulars that are issued by listed companies. The FSA Handbook is amended and updated from time to time and can be viewed on the website of the FSA.

Definition of the term 'circular'

3.15 For the purposes of the Listing Rules a circular is defined as 'any document issued to holders of listed securities including notices of meetings but excluding prospectuses, listing particulars, annual reports and accounts, interim reports, proxy cards and dividend or interest vouchers'.[14]

Chapter 13 of the Listing Rules

3.16 Chapter 13 of the Listing Rules, which is entitled 'Contents of circulars' governs circulars that are issued by public listed companies, that is to say a company that has any class of its securities listed. A listed company must ensure that any circular it issues to holders of its listed equity securities complies with the requirements of Chapter 13 of the Listing Rules. Detailed consideration of the requirements of Listing Rules is outside the scope of this work.

3.17 It is no surprise that under the Listing Rules a public company has to comply with certain fundamental principles in relation to circulars. For example a circular that is issued by a listed public company must:

(1) provide a clear and adequate explanation of its subject matter giving due prominence to its essential characteristics, benefits and risks;
(2) state why the security holder is being asked to vote or, if no vote is required, why the circular is being sent;

---

[13] See Financial Services and Markets Act 2000, s 7.
[14] See FSA Handbook—Glossary section.

(3) if voting or other action is required, contain all information necessary to allow the security holders to make a properly informed decision;
(4) if voting or other action is required, contain a heading drawing attention to the document's importance and advising security holders who are in any doubt as to what action to take to consult appropriate independent advisers;
(5) if voting is required, contain a recommendation from the board as to the voting action security holders should take for all resolutions proposed, indicating whether or not the proposal described in the circular is, in the board's opinion, in the best interests of security holders as a whole;
(6) state that if all the securities have been sold or transferred by the addressee the circular and any other relevant documents should be passed to the person through whom the sale or transfer was effected for transmission to the purchaser or transferee;
(7) if new securities are being issued in substitution for existing securities, explain what will happen to existing documents of title.

The information that is specified in items (1) to (3) in para 3.17 above are requirements that would be applicable to any well-drawn circular of any company whether or not it fell within the jurisdiction of the Listing Rules. It is as a result of the specific requirements of the Listing Rules that circulars issued by public listed companies seeking the approval of shareholders to a particular transaction contain a '[health] warning' to members in the following terms: **3.18**

> THIS DOCUMENT IS IMPORTANT AND REQUIRES YOUR IMMEDIATE ATTENTION. If you are in any doubt as to what action you should take, you are recommended to seek immediately your own financial advice from your stockbroker, bank manager, solicitor, accountant or other independent financial adviser duly authorised under the Financial Services and Markets Act 2000 if you are resident in the United Kingdom or, if you reside elsewhere, another appropriately authorised independent financial adviser.
>
> If you have sold or otherwise transferred all of your shares in [XYZ plc], please forward this document, together with the accompanying form of proxy as soon as possible to the purchaser or transferee, or to the stockbroker, bank or other agent through whom the sale or transfer was effected, for transmission to the purchaser or transferee. If you have sold or otherwise transferred only part of your holding you should retain this document.

Consequences of a public listed company's failure to comply with Listing Rules in relation to a circular

A listed public company's failure to comply with the Listing Rules in relation to the requirements regulating circulars is a very serious matter as is illustrated by the decision in May 2000 of the Quotations Committee of the UK Listing Authority in relation to a circular sent to members of Leicester City plc. At issue in this case was the publication by Leicester City plc of a circular to its shareholders on **3.19**

29 November 1999.[15] The Quotations Committee decided that the Listing Rules had been breached and that the company should be publicly censured. The evidence before the Quotations Committee disclosed that Leicester City plc had acted in breached of paras 14.1, 14.2 and 14.4 of the then applicable Listing Rules. These rules required public listed companies to seek the prior approval of the UK Listing Authority for all circulars of a non-routine nature that were issued to shareholders. In 1999, in breach of the then applicable Listing Rules, Leicester City plc committed three breaches of the rules in that it failed to obtain the approval of the UK Listing Authority for its circular before sending it to shareholders, it failed to include the prescribed information in the circular, and it failed to lodge copies of the circular at the Company Announcements Office of the Stock Exchange. These breaches of the rules were admitted by Leicester City plc and by way of excuse it was stated that the breaches had taken place during a period of uncertainty on the board of directors. The Quotations Committee regarded the requirements of Chapter 14 of the Listing Rules as of prime importance for the protection of shareholders and the particular circumstances relating to the breaches that had been committed by Leicester City plc were held not to be an acceptable excuse.

3.20 Under the current regulatory regime the FSA can impose a penalty on, or publicly censure, a listed company and its directors for breaches of the Listing Rules, including those relating to the form and content of circulars. The FSA publishes a statement of its policy on the imposition of penalties and sanctions.

Challenges to Circulars

3.21 In the event that the resolutions are passed by the requisite majority of members at the duly convened general meeting of a company, there may be dissenting members who feel aggrieved that the proposals of the board of directors have received approval from the other shareholders. In situations such as these the dissenting members may seek to make a legal challenge to the basis on which an affirmative vote of the majority of members has been procured at the meeting. To this end such shareholders may contend that the circular to members that was issued by the board of directors was 'tricky'[16] or 'misleading' and/or 'inadequate' to obtain the informed consent of the members to the proposals. Shareholders who make such serious allegations must take care that they are made on the basis

[15] The Listing Rules applicable at the time of the breaches committed by Leicester City plc were those published in January 1999.

[16] A word that derives from the important decision of the Court of Appeal in *Kaye v Croydon Tramways* [1898] 1 Ch 358 (CA).

of adequate and cogent evidence. It is not surprising that such allegations are relatively infrequent, and when they are made the result is not always favourable to the complaining shareholders. Shareholders of a company may challenge the efficacy and validity of a circular by means of a petition under CA 2006, s 994 or by means of a derivative action brought under the provisions of CA 2006, Part 11.

Principles

The principles that will be applied by the court when a challenge is made to a circular are as follows: **3.22**

(1) a circular to shareholders must give a fair, candid, and reasonably full explanation of the purpose for which the meeting is called;[17]
(2) any circular must contain a fair and reasonably full statement of the facts upon which the directors are asking the shareholders to vote;[18]
(3) a statement which is not frank, not open, not clear and not candid may be challenged;[19]
(4) a circular must not be framed in a manner so as to mislead the shareholders;[20]
(5) a circular must not conceal from shareholders material facts and matters which are relevant to the matter that is to be considered at the forthcoming general meeting;[21]
(6) in essence the shareholders must receive fair warning of what is to be submitted to the meeting;[22]
(7) the language that is used in the circular must be unambiguous and capable of being understood by ordinary people;[23]
(8) the court must ask itself what effect the information provided will have on the ordinary shareholder who scans or reads the document quickly, not as a lawyer, but as an ordinary man or woman in commerce or as an ordinary investor. One asks, viewed in such a way, will the information fully and fairly inform and instruct the shareholder about the matter upon which he or she will have to vote?[24]
(9) the company must give a fair, candid and reasonable explanation of the purposes for which the general meeting has been convened;[25]

---

17 *Baillie v Oriental Telephone and Electric Company Limited* [1915] 1Ch 5503 at 514 (Cozens-Hardy MR).

18 ibid.

19 ibid.

20 *Kaye v Croydon Tramways Co* [1898] 358 at 369–70 per Lindley MR.

21 ibid; *Clarkson v Davies* [1923] AC 100 (PC).

22 *Tiessen v Henderson* [1899] 1 Ch 861 at 866–7 (Kekewich J).

23 Op. cit. 358 at 372–3 per Rigby LJ.

24 *Devereaux Holdings Pty Ltd v Pelsart Resources Pty Ltd (No 2)* (1985) 9 ACLR 956 at 958–9 (Supreme Court of New South Wales, Equity Division, Young J).

25 *CAS Nominees v Nottingham Forest FC plc* [2002] 1 BCLC 613 at para [72].

(10) where there is more than one purpose for a meeting each purpose must be fairly disclosed; [26]

(11) when a circular is challenged the question is not whether the circular might not have been differently framed, but whether there is any reasonable ground for supposing that such imperfections as may be found in the circular have had, with or without other circumstances, the result that the majority (who have approved the proposal placed before them) have done so under some serious misapprehension of the position;[27]

(12) sufficiency of information is a matter of fact and degree. Directors have a duty in equity to give shareholders sufficient information for them to make an informed decision about proposals to be put to them at meetings. However, it is not necessary to give to shareholders every piece of information which might conceivably affect their voting. The essence of the duty is the requirement of reasonableness or fairness in the circumstances, having regard to the interests of the company as a whole. A surfeit of information may well obscure the purpose of a resolution. A lack of information may constitute misrepresentation by omission. It is a matter of sensible judgment by the directors in each case and ultimately by the court if complaint is made to it. [28]

3.23 The cases that are discussed below illustrate the approach that the court takes to such allegations. Explaining a complex transaction to members of a company may well test the literary skills of a board of directors and those advising them in drafting a circular that is clear, accurate, unambiguous and provides sufficient details to members of the company. The complexity of the transaction cannot serve as a valid excuse to frame a circular in a misleading or tricky manner.

Kaye v Croydon Tramways

3.24 In *Kaye v Croydon Tramways*[29] an action was brought by Major-General GF Kaye, who was the holder of ordinary stock in the tramways company which was incorporated by the Croydon Tramways Act 1889, a piece of legislation which incorporated the Companies Clauses Act 1845 and Parts II and III of the Tramways Act 1870. The plaintiff brought the action on behalf of himself and all the other members of the Croydon Tramways Company except the defendants,[30] against the company and its directors for a declaration that an agreement dated

---

[26] Op. cit. 358 at 372–4 per Rigby LJ.

[27] *Re Imperial Chemical Industries Ltd* [1936] Ch 587 at 618 (Lord Wright MR, Romer LJ and Clauson J).

[28] *Residues Treatment & Trading Co Ltd v Southern Resources Ltd* (1988) 14 ACLR 375 at 377–8 (Full Court of the Supreme Court of South Australia, White J).

[29] [1898] 1 Ch 358 (CA).

[30] That is, a derivative claim under what is now CA 2006, Part 11.

25 November 1897 that had been made under the Tramways Act 1870, s 44 between the Croydon Tramways Company and the British Electric Traction Company Limited, for the sale of the undertaking of the tramways company to the traction company, and a resolution approving the agreement, which had been purportedly passed at a meeting of the shareholders of the tramways company held on 14 December 1897 were ultra vires and ought to be set aside. In addition, the plaintiff applied for an injunction to restrain the defendants from carrying out the agreement. Clause 1 of the agreement provided for the purchase of the undertaking of the tramways company by the traction company, and the taking over by the traction company of all liabilities affecting the undertaking. Clause 2 of the agreement made provision for the payment of a sum of money by the traction company to the tramways company on completion. In addition, this clause stipulated that the traction company had to pay the sum of £500 to the secretary and to each of the present directors, other than a Mr WJ Carruthers Wain to whom the sum of £1,250 had to be paid as compensation for loss of office. The sums payable to the directors and secretary of the tramways company under clause 2 of the agreement amounted in the aggregate to £3,250—a not inconsiderable sum of money in 1897. Clause 6 of the agreement provided that all the terms of the agreement were conditional upon the same being adopted by the shareholders of the tramways company and if the agreement was not so adopted it would be lawful for the traction company, by notice in writing to the tramways company, to determine this agreement. By Clause 7 of the agreement a meeting of the tramways company was to be convened and held forthwith in order to consider the terms of the agreement.

On 26 November 1897 the tramways company gave notice of an extraordinary **3.25**
general meeting of the shareholders of the company, to be held on 14 December 1897. The notice stated that the purpose of the meeting was '. . . considering, and if thought advisable of approving, the terms of an agreement to be made between the Croydon Tramways Company of the one part and the British Electric Traction Company, Limited, of the other part, being an agreement for sale of the undertaking and assets of the Croydon Tramways Company to the British Electric Traction Company, Limited'. On 1 December 1897 the secretary of the tramways company sent out a circular to the members of the company enclosing the notice dated 26 November 1897 and also a form of proxy. The circular to members stated that:

> The object of the agreement is to carry out a sale of the undertaking and assets of the company to the British Electric Traction Company, Limited, at a price which will pay off the preference capital at par, and will return 60 per cent. to the holders of the ordinary stock. The traction company in addition assume the responsibility for the debentures and other liabilities of the company, and, as they are desirous of having the management in their own hands, the directors and the secretary have agreed to retire on being paid a lump sum as compensation for their loss of office. The near approach of the period at which the lines will become purchasable by the local

authority, and the heavy expenditure which is inevitable on the reconstruction and equipment of the lines for electrical traction, which the directors understand the local authorities make a condition precedent to any extension of the term, has led your directors to believe that the shareholders will be wise in accepting the present offer, and securing now for themselves what may be considered fairly satisfactory terms.

3.26 The circular concluded with a statement reminding members that the enclosed form of proxy might be filled in and signed and returned to the secretary if members were not able to attend the extraordinary general meeting. On the receipt of the circular, the plaintiff (Major-General Kaye) sent a letter to the secretary requesting further information as to the terms of the agreement, particularly with regard to the sums of money which were to be paid to the directors and to the secretary. The plaintiff also asked the secretary in person to provide this information. However, none of the requested information was provided to the plaintiff. At the meeting of the shareholders held on 14 December 1897 the chairman called attention to certain of the terms of the agreement, but did not read it, and a resolution approving the agreement was passed by a large majority of the members, notwithstanding the opposition of the plaintiff.

3.27 The plaintiff objected to the agreement on the ground that the provision for the compensation payable to the directors and to the secretary was illegal, that both the notice and circular did not fairly disclose to the members the nature of the agreement, and that the price was grossly inadequate. The managing director of the traction company stated in an affidavit that was filed in opposition to the plaintiff's application that the price was agreed upon before making any arrangement with the directors of the tramways company as to their remuneration; that even if no remuneration were to be given, the traction company would give no greater price for the undertaking; that it was originally proposed to take over the direction of the tramways company, but that the traction company preferred to be unfettered, and so made a compensation to the directors and secretary.

3.28 At first instance the application of the plaintiff was heard by Kekewich J who granted the injunction and held that the notice of the meeting was not a sufficient compliance with the Companies Clauses Act 1845, s 71 and secondly, that the agreement could not be upheld against a dissentient shareholder, as it authorized payments for the compensation of the directors from which the company could derive no benefit. The defendant appealed and in the Court of Appeal it was held that the provision for compensation in favour of the directors did not render the agreement ultra vires, but that the notice of the meeting, by reason of its omission to refer to this provision, did not fairly disclose the purpose for which the meeting was convened. Lindley MR referred to the circular, which he considered had been sent out in order to get proxies just as much as to give additional information to the shareholders who should attend the meeting and stated that the circular did not contain a full and fair disclosure of what was proposed to be done by the company.

Baillie v Oriental Telephone and Electric Co Limited

An inadequate circular was at the core of the facts that were considered by the Court of Appeal in *Baillie v Oriental Telephone and Electric Co Limited*.[31] The plaintiff was a shareholder in the defendant company and brought a derivative action on behalf of himself and all other shareholders of the defendant company against the company and its directors seeking the following relief: **3.29**

(i) a declaration that certain special resolutions purportedly passed and confirmed at extraordinary general meetings of the company held in June and July 1914 were not binding upon the company;
(ii) an injunction so as to restrain the directors from acting on the purported special resolutions;
(iii) an account of all sums received by the directors as remuneration for acting as directors of the Telephone Company of Egypt, Limited, since the year 1913 in excess of remuneration at the rate of £800 per year;
(iv) a declaration that the defendant directors were jointly and severally liable to repay to the defendant company the sums found to have been received by the defendant directors on taking such account; an order for and payment of such sums to the defendant company accordingly.

The defendant company had been incorporated in 1894 to take over and acquire the undertaking, property, assets, and business of a former company having the same name which had been incorporated in 1880. The defendant directors were also directors of certain subsidiary companies including one called the Telephone Company of Egypt, Limited (the Egyptian company). The defendant company held the majority of the issued share capital of the Egyptian company. Prior to 1903 the remuneration of the directors of the Egyptian company had been £800 per annum. By a special resolution of the Egyptian company passed and confirmed at extraordinary general meetings held respectively on 12 August and 27 August 1903 a new article had been substituted for the existing article which had fixed the directors' remuneration at £800 per annum. Under the terms of the new article the annual remuneration of the directors was £2,500 per annum to be divided as the directors thought fit. **3.30**

By a special resolution of the Egyptian company passed and confirmed at extraordinary general meetings of that company held respectively on 2 August **3.31**

[31] [1915] 1 Ch 503 (CA).

and 22 October 1907, a further amendment was made to the article which had been substituted in 1903. The 1907 amendment to the articles provided:

> The remuneration of the directors shall be the sum of 2500l. per annum, and in addition thereto in each year a sum equal to 20 per cent. of the balance of the net profits arising from the carrying on of the business of the company during such year remaining over, after carrying such sums to reserve or sinking fund as the directors think proper, and after payment of a dividend of 10 per cent. for such year upon the amount paid up on the issued ordinary share capital of the company. Such additional remuneration shall be divisible amongst the directors as they shall determine.

3.32 These resolutions of the Egyptian company were passed by the directors in exercise of the voting power of the defendant company as shareholders in the Egyptian company. The evidence before the court disclosed that the profits of the Egyptian company had been large. Between 1907 and 1914, relying on the amendment to the articles that had been made in 1907, the directors had taken remuneration amounting to £44,876. A further sum of £7,100 to which the directors were entitled under the 1907 articles was undrawn.

3.33 The auditors of the defendant company in auditing the accounts of the defendant company for the year 1913 drew attention to the fact that the directors were receiving remuneration in the capacity of directors of subsidiary companies and that such remuneration should be authorized by the shareholders of the defendant company. In order to secure the authorization of the shareholders on 15 June 1914 the directors of the defendant company caused a circular to be sent to members in the following terms:

> Dear Sir (or Madam),
>
> It will be in your recollection that in the auditors' certificate attached to the report and accounts for the year 1913 a paragraph was inserted by the auditors as follows:-
>
> > 'The directors of the company who are directors of subsidiary companies receive remuneration in the latter capacity which should be authorised by the shareholders of this company.'
>
> The directors were unable to submit a resolution to the shareholders at the annual general meeting, but in accordance with the promise made at that meeting the directors are now convening a meeting for the purpose of complying with the auditors' certificate.
>
> The remarks of the auditors apply only to the cases of the Telephone Company of Egypt, Limited, and the China and Japan Telephone and Electric Company, Limited. All the directors of your company with the exception of Mr. Charles P. Ackers are directors of the former company, while in the case of the China and Japan Telephone and Electric Company, Limited, the directors are Mr. Henry Grewing, Mr. H. Johnstone Grewing and Mr. T. Lloyd.
>
> The article dealing with the directors' remuneration in the articles of association of the Telephone Company of Egypt, Limited, is article 58, which is as follows:-
>
> > 'The remuneration of the directors shall be the sum of 2500l. per annum, and in addition thereto in each year a sum equal to 20 per cent. of the balance of the net profits arising from the carrying on of the business of the company during such year remaining

> over, after carrying such sums to reserve or sinking fund as the directors think proper, and after payment of a dividend of 10 per cent. for such year upon the amount paid up on the issued ordinary share capital of the company. Such additional remuneration shall be divisible amongst the directors as they shall determine.'
>
> In the case of the China and Japan Telephone and Electric Company, Limited, which for its articles of association adopted what is now the old Table 'H', the remuneration is such as is voted by the shareholders at the annual general meeting; the amount voted at the last annual general meeting being 525l.
>
> Some of the shareholders will no doubt recollect that for many years your company was unsuccessful, but under the management of the present board its fortunes have revived, and for several years has paid substantial and increasing dividends.
>
> In 1907 the articles of association of your company were altered so as to increase the remuneration of the directors, and your directors, believing that it was in accordance with the wishes of the shareholders, provided at the same time for a similar alteration being made in the articles of association of the Telephone Company of Egypt, Limited. It should, however, be stated that the directors have on no occasion availed themselves of the full remuneration to which under the articles of association of the Telephone Company of Egypt, Limited, they are entitled, the amount actually received by them by way of remuneration being 1500l. per annum, plus 20 per cent. of the balance of net profits.
>
> The notice convening the extraordinary general meeting is herewith enclosed, the day fixed, the 24th June, being the earliest date for which it could be arranged.

The meeting of which notice was thus given was duly held. The chairman gave no detailed information as to the directors' remuneration in respect of the Egyptian company, but merely stated that the directors' fees had averaged since 1881 the sum of £320 per annum for each director. The resolutions were duly passed as special resolutions and were confirmed at a subsequent meeting convened for that purpose. **3.34**

The plaintiff brought an action and moved the court at first instance (Astbury J) for an interim injunction. In his affidavit in support of the application for injunctive relief the plaintiff stated that he had attended the meeting held on 24 June 1914, and voted against the proposed resolutions. At that meeting the chairman did not state the amount of the sums the payment of which was proposed to be confirmed by the resolutions. Two other shareholders, one of them having previously written to the directors complaining that no full disclosure had been made, made objections and asked for information. The true amount of the remuneration asked to be voted upon at the meeting was concealed and obfuscated so much that no one knew what it really was. The chairman did not disclose the figures for remuneration, but informed the meeting that he had sufficient proxies to carry the resolutions and proceeded to put them to the meeting. The plaintiff had also attended the confirmatory meeting of 15 July 1914, when he stated that he had been advised that the resolutions were irregular as the notice had not disclosed material facts, and he therefore protested against them altogether and declined to vote. **3.35**

3.36 On procedural grounds Astbury J, without expressing any opinion as to the validity or otherwise of the resolutions, dismissed the plaintiff's application. Against this background the plaintiff appealed to the Court of Appeal where it was held that the notice did not give a sufficiently full and frank disclosure to the shareholders of the facts upon which they were asked to vote; and that the resolutions were invalid and not binding upon the company. The important statement made by Lord Cozens-Hardy MR[32] about how directors should approach the task of obtaining consent from members of their company is still applicable today:

> . . . I am very clear in my own mind that if any attempt is to be made by the directors to get the sanction of the shareholders it must be made on a fair and reasonably full statement of the facts upon which the directors are asking the shareholders to vote. *This notice coupled with the circular, and I think also with the statements made by the chairman at the meeting, seems to me to be not frank, not open, not clear, and not in any way satisfactory*. That being so, assuming that the notice is, by its suppression as well as by what it states, not satisfactory or, to use Lindley L.J.'s word, 'tricky', what are the consequences? The Court of Appeal in Kaye v. Croydon Tramways Co . . . which in all that is material is almost a replica of the present case, decided that in such a case the Court could say that when there was a special resolution passed by what was a 'tricky' notice it could not be supported. As the special resolutions were obtained by means of a notice and circular which did not substantially put the shareholders in the position to know what they were voting about they could not be supported, and the companies could not act upon them.
>
> (emphasis added)

Re Imperial Chemical Industries Ltd

3.37 In *Re Imperial Chemical Industries Ltd*[33] the eponymous company Imperial Chemical Industries Ltd (ICI) presented a petition for the confirmation by the court of a reduction of capital involving conversion of deferred shares into ordinary shares. The conversion had been approved by large majorities of the shareholders in general meeting and of the holders of ordinary and deferred shares. For present purposes the precise details of the scheme to reduce the share capital of ICI are not relevant. The proposed reduction was supported by the directors, not on the ground of any loss of capital (of which there was no evidence), but in order to simplify the capital structure of the company. The object of the scheme was to abolish the class of deferred shares by exchanging them, at the proposed ratio, into ordinary shares. The memorandum and articles of ICI provided that the special rights attached to any class of shares should not be affected or abrogated without the sanction of a separate meeting of the holders of shares of the class.

---

[32] [1915] 1 Ch 503 at 514.

[33] [1936] 1 Ch 587 (Eve J and CA).

A circular explaining the details of the scheme was sent by the board of directors to all shareholders and meetings to obtain the shareholders' approval were convened and held on 1 May 1935. The first such meeting was an extraordinary meeting of all shareholders. At this meeting the chairman made a speech commending the scheme to members. This speech was proposed by the chairman and intended to be treated as a speech in relation to the first meeting and the two subsequent class meetings. A poll was taken at the conclusion of the first meeting, and afterwards meetings purporting to be separate class meetings, first of the ordinary shareholders and then of the deferred shareholders, were held. At the meeting of the deferred shareholders the resolution was defeated on a show of hands, but carried by the requisite majority on a vote that was taken on a poll. No measures were taken to prevent shareholders, other than those of the particular class concerned, being present in the hall during the holding of the two class meetings, but there was no evidence that any shareholder voted out of his own class. **3.38**

The petition seeking the court's confirmation of the reduction of capital was opposed by some of the deferred shareholders who contended for various reasons that the scheme involved in the reduction was unfair to that class and was not such as an ordinary business man would approve, and ought not therefore to be confirmed by the court. Both the judge at first instance (Eve J) and the Court of Appeal held that the presence at a separate meeting of the holders of one class of shares of other shareholders of a different class, not voting at it either by show of hands or on a poll, did not invalidate the meeting as a separate class meeting, or affect the validity of the poll taken thereat and that the circular issued to the shareholders contained a full and fair explanation of the scheme free from ambiguity. In addition the Court did not consider that the directors were under a duty to the shareholders to disclose to them in the circular explaining the scheme their holdings or respective proportional interests in ordinary and deferred shares. Against this background it was clear that the scheme had been fully and properly explained to the shareholders without concealment of any relevant facts, and as it had been approved on a poll being taken by the requisite majorities of each class of member, the reduction of capital ought properly to be confirmed by the Court. **3.39**

In the course of his judgment Eve J stated that in the circular signed by the secretary of the company a successful attempt was made to explain to the recipients the nature and effect of the proposals on which they were being invited to use their votes: **3.40**

> I cannot recall any criticism directed to any ambiguity to be found in this circular. It has been freely criticized, and amongst other complaints made was one to the effect that the phraseology is in places complicated. The same might be said of the scheme itself, but in my opinion the circular is so composed as to convey to the recipients not only all the information necessary to enable them to realize what the proposals of the board were, but also the grounds upon which the policy underlying the proposals

was based. No one has come forward to say that he did not understand the circular or was misled thereby.[34]

3.41 In the Court of Appeal it was stated explicitly that in settling the terms of the circular the board of directors of ICI had acted to the best of their ability in attempting fully to explain the whole position. However, the circular was criticized as being inadequate because attention was not drawn to the fact that the subsidiary companies had in their balance sheets what was described as 'obsolescence reserve funds' which were said to amount to about £3m and that attention was not drawn to the fact that there was some £6m of capital invested in what was called the 'Billingham undertaking', a venture which was likely to become revenue-producing in the near future. Complaint was also made that the circular did not state the holding of the directors in the various classes of share capital. In relation to the first two complaints that had been levelled at the circular the Court held that although the two matters in question were not specifically mentioned in the circular their omission did not arise from any desire on the part of the board of directors to conceal them or to discount them.

3.42 The Court of Appeal stated:

> ...Where the matter is one of difficulty, the Court will always scrutinize such a circular very carefully; but where, as in this case, there is no suggestion that the directors were doing otherwise than honestly putting forward to the best of their skill and ability a fair picture of the company's position, the question is not whether the circular might not have been differently framed, but whether there is any reasonable ground for supposing that such imperfections as may be found in the circular have had, with or without other circumstances, the result that the majority (who have approved the proposal placed before them) have done so under some serious misapprehension of the position . . . .[35]

CAS Nominees v Nottingham Forest FC plc

3.43 A petition alleging unfair prejudice under CA 1985, s 459[36] was the means used by disaffected members of a public company to challenge, inter alia, the contents of a circular in *CAS Nominees v Nottingham Forest FC plc*.[37] Nottingham Forest plc, (the company) was a public company the shares of which were quoted on Alternative Investment Market (AIM) and it was the owner of all of the issued share capital in a private company called Nottingham Forest Football Club Ltd (the club). Since 1982 the club had operated the football team known as Nottingham Forest. The company was the corporate entity through which

[34] [1936] 1 Ch 587 at 599. Evidence from members that they did not understand the circular and that they were misled by it is of central importance.

[35] [1936] 1 Ch 587 at 618 (Clauson J giving the judgment of the Court of Appeal).

[36] Now CA 2006, s 994.

[37] [2002] 1 BCLC 613 (Hart J). The allegation of the petitioners in this case that the circular was tricky and misleading failed—see para 3.47 below.

a consortium of investors had acquired the share capital of the club in 1997 for some £16m. Members of the consortium became directors of the company. Later in 1997 the company was floated on AIM, and about 3.7m shares were subscribed for at 70 pence. The business relationship between individuals on the board of the company became strained. The members of the consortium had invested in the company on the basis that an economic profit could be earned in the medium term by their investment, but by 1999 the prospects had changed and the possibility of profits looked remote. The club made a poor start to the 1998–99 football season with the consequence that it seemed likely that the club would be relegated from the Premier League. In about May 1999 an outside investor was found who was interested in investing a substantial sum in the company, but only on the basis that his investment would give him control.

The mechanics of the transaction required to secure the investment necessitated the passing of a special resolution under CA 1985, s 95(1) authorizing a subscription by the new investor for the necessary number of new shares for cash. Such a special resolution could not be passed if the trustees of two shareholders voted against it. In the face of the inability to pass a special resolution the proposed investment by the outside investor was restructured with the result that the company would procure that the club issued shares to the outside investor in return for two tranches of much needed finance. The result of this arrangement was that the company was left as a holding company with a 49% minority shareholding in the club, and the outside investor obtained a controlling 51% shareholding in the club, subject to a shareholders' agreement. This arrangement was put in place, the board of directors of the club was replaced and the shareholders in the company were sent a circular which set out details of the board's proposals. At a duly convened extraordinary general meeting of the members of the company approval was given to the proposal by means of an ordinary resolution. **3.44**

In October 1999 the petitioners who were members of the company presented a petition under CA 1985, s 459 claiming that in setting the structure of and implementing the transaction which the shareholders approved at the extraordinary general meeting the board acted for an ulterior purpose, namely enabling the outside investor to acquire control of the assets of the company while circumventing protections given to members by the company's articles of association and CA 1985. Further, the petitioners contended that the ordinary resolution passed at the extraordinary general meeting did not have the effect of curing the abuse of power that had allegedly been committed by the board of directors, and that the ordinary resolution was in any event flawed by serious shortcomings in the circular which the board had caused to be sent to the shareholders. **3.45**

The petitioners alleged that circular was tricky in five ways. First, that the circular gave undue emphasis to the outside investor as the only possible investor in the **3.46** club, and did not inform shareholders of another possible source of funds. Secondly, that the circular failed to explain to shareholders the true rationale of the proposal, namely the wish to avoid putting a special resolution to shareholders. Thirdly that the circular failed to disclose the true contemplation of the board and of the outside investor that the latter would in due course become a shareholder in the company instead of the club. Fourthly, that the circular concealed from shareholders the true nature of the interests of two directors in the shares which they were proposing to vote in favour of the transaction. Finally, it was alleged that the circular was also deficient in various respects relating to the amount of financial information and analysis provided to shareholders.

3.47 The petition failed because having heard the evidence the court found that at no stage had the board of directors acted in breach of any provisions of the company's articles of association. Further, the court rejected the allegations that the circular to members was in any way defective. At paragraph 72 of his carefully reasoned judgment Hart J said:

> *A circular to shareholders must give a fair, candid, and reasonably full explanation of the purpose for which the meeting is called.* In *Kaye v Croydon Tramways Co* [1898] 1 Ch 358 at 369 Lindley MR used the word 'tricky' to describe a document which had, as he found, 'been most artfully framed to mislead the shareholders'. This circular did not, in my judgment, suffer from that vice. *The question is 'not whether the circular might not have been differently framed, but whether there is any reasonable ground for supposing that such imperfections as may be found in the circular have had, with or without other circumstances, the result that the majority (who have approved the proposal placed before them) have done so under some serious misapprehension of the position'* (see per Lord Wright MR, Romer LJ and Clauson J in *Re Imperial Chemical Industries Ltd* [1936] Ch 587 at 618). In answering that question in the present case, I take into account the fact that there is no evidence that any shareholder was in fact misled[38] by any of the alleged imperfections in the circular, whether taken singly or cumulatively (cf per Lord Maugham LC in *Carruth v Imperial Chemical Industries Ltd* [1937] 2 All ER 422 at 461, [1937] AC 707 at 769).
>
> (emphasis added)

Members' Statements

3.48 Under CA 1985, ss 376 and 377, it was possible for members of both public and private companies to have a statement of up to one thousand words circulated by the company to all of the other members. This important right of members has been retained in CA 2006, ss 314 and 315.

[38] A number of shareholders had adduced evidence that they had attended the meeting and voted in favour of the resolution and had not been misled by the contents of the circular.

Changes under the new law

Three significant changes have been made in the new legislation. The first difference when compared with the old provisions under CA 1985 is that where the statement relates to a resolution or other matter which will be dealt with at an annual general meeting of a public company and the statement is received before the end of the public company's financial year, the shareholders who require the statement to be circulated are not required to cover the public company's costs of the circulation process.[39] The second change is that the shares of members that are relied upon in order to utilize the right to have a statement circulated must have a right to vote on the relevant resolution, rather than have rights to vote at the meeting in general.[40] The third change is that the members may make their request in electronic form as well as in hard copy form.[41] **3.49**

The members have the right to require the company to circulate a statement with respect to a matter referred to in a proposed resolution to be dealt with at the meeting or some other business that is to come before that meeting.[42] The wording in CA 2006, s 314 permits members to circulate a statement through the company in respect of resolutions or general business that is to come before a meeting of whatever kind. It is not the case that a company has to circulate whatever the members produce because the length of the statement is subject to an express limitation of one thousand words.[43] Implicit in this restriction on the length of a members' statement is the ability of the company to reject a statement that exceeds 1,000 words in length. It may be unwise to reject a members' statement that is only a few words over the prescribed statutory limit, but where the length of the proposed statement is vastly in excess of that limitation, a company will be justified in rejecting it on grounds of excessive length and thus for non-compliance with the legislative requirements. **3.50**

The number of members required for s 314

Section 314 (2) and (3) imposes a limitation on the number of members required for the regular exercise of the statutory right. A request must be supported by members representing at least 5% of the total voting rights of all the members having a relevant right to vote[44] or by at least 100 members who have a relevant right to vote and hold shares in the company on which there has been paid an **3.51**

39 See CA 2006, s 316(1).
40 See CA 2006, s 314(2)(a) and (3).
41 See CA 2006, s 314(4)(a).
42 See CA 2006, s 314(1)(a) and (b).
43 See CA 2006, s 314(1).
44 See CA 2006, s 314(3).

average sum per member of at least £100.[45] The required limit in s 314(2)(b) may be difficult to achieve in circumstances where the share capital of the company is divided into shares of a small nominal value as at least £10,000 in the aggregate of paid up share capital is required. Section 314(2) makes reference to CA 2006, s 153 which governs the exercise of rights where shares are held on behalf of others.[46] It is to be noted that s 314 is the first of the four sections to which the rights in s 153 apply.[47]

Form and timing of request

3.52 By CA 2006, s 314(4) the form of the request for the circulation of a members' statement may be in hard copy or electronic form. It would appear that s 314(4)(b) requires the statement that is to be circulated to be included with the request. The document must be authenticated[48] within the meaning of CA 2006, s 1146 and to be effective the members' request must be received at least one week before the general meeting to which the request relates.[49] This prescribed time period of one week is short and may give rise to serious practical difficulties. For example, there may be insufficient time for the company to circulate the statement to members and to receive back from the members a valid form of proxy. Members would be well advised to serve on the company their statement well in advance of the meeting and not to rely on the prescribed period of one week.

Obligation to circulate members' statement

3.53 Section 315 is based on the remainder of CA 1985, ss 376 and 377. The purpose of s 315 is to make provision for the action to be taken by a company in circumstances where it is required to circulate a members' statement. Under CA 2006, s 315(1) where a company has received a valid request to circulate a statement made under s 314, it becomes under a duty to send a copy of the statement to all the other members of the company who are entitled to receive due and proper notice of the meeting. The obligation on the company is to circulate the statement in the same way as circulating the notice of a meeting and at the same time, or as soon as reasonably practicable, after the company has given notice of the meeting. As a result of this provision the members' statement will in the majority of cases form part of the company's circular sent to the members prior to a general meeting.

---

[45] See CA 2006, s 314(2)(b).

[46] See Ch 10.

[47] The others are ss 338 (public companies: power to require circulation of a resolution for an AGM), 342 (power to require independent report on a poll) and 527 (power to require a website publication of audit concerns).

[48] See CA 2006, s 314(4)(c).

[49] See CA 2006, s 314(4)(d).

Qualifications to the duty to circulate—CA 2006, s 315(2)

The duty of the company is not absolute because CA 2006, s 315(2) provides that the company's obligation to circulate a statement is qualified by the provisions of CA 2006, s 316(2) concerning the deposit or tender of the requisite funds to meet the expense of circulation. The duty is also qualified by the ability of the company to make an application to court under CA 2006, s 317.[50] This provision confers jurisdiction on the court to grant a company relief from the statutory duty if circumstances disclose that the members' right to require the circulation of a statement is being abused. **3.54**

Consequences of a breach of CA 2006, s 315

If a company fails to comply with the requirements of CA 2006, s 315 every officer who is in default will have committed a criminal offence created by s 315(3) and penalties are prescribed in s 315(4). **3.55**

Expenses of circulating a members' statement

The costs of, and incidental to, the circulation of a members' statement may be considerable in the context of a public company and in particular for a listed public company. CA 2006, s 316 deals with the expenses of the circulation of a members' statement. Where the circumstances fall within the scope of s 316(1) the members need not pay the expenses of circulating a statement. These are if the meeting to which the valid request relates is the annual general meeting of a public company and sufficient numbers of valid requests are received before the financial year-end of the public company in question. **3.56**

If the requirements of CA 2006, s 316(1) do not apply, the expenses of the company will have to be paid by the members who have requested the circulation of the statement. This means that the members requesting the circulation of the statement must deposit with, or tender to the company, a sum of money that is '... reasonably sufficient ...' to meet the costs of circulating the statement. This sum of money must be deposited or tendered to the company not later than one week before the relevant meeting.[51] This rule will apply unless the company resolves otherwise. The statute does not state whether it is the resolution of the company in general meeting, or the resolution of the board of directors that can release the members from the obligation to provide a reasonable sum in respect of the expenses of circulation. It seems that in default of a clear statement of statutory intention the resolution removing the requirement to provide a reasonable sum in respect **3.57**

---

50 See para 3.59 below.
51 See CA 2006, s 316(2)(b).

of the expenses may be passed by either the shareholders in general meeting or by the board of directors. It is also arguable that an appropriate provision may be inserted in a company's articles of association. The adoption of such a provision in a company's articles of association will constitute a resolution of a company within the meaning of CA 2006, s 316(2)(b).

3.58 CA 2006, s 315(2) is of importance in that it makes the company's compliance with the request to circulate a members' statement under s 314 dependant upon compliance by the relevant members with the terms of s 316(2)(b). A company is not bound to comply with CA 2006, ss 314 and 315 unless it has received by way of deposit or has had tendered to it, not later than one week before the meeting, a sum that is reasonably sufficient to meet its expenses of compliance with the obligation to circulate a members' statement. It is suggested that in order to avoid such problems an officer of the company should write to the relevant members upon receipt of their request made under s 314, explaining to them the probable amount of the company's expenses and their composition. At the same time a request should be made of the members for the deposit or tender of the estimated sum within the statutory timetable. It is hoped that if such a procedure is adopted the scope for uncertainty will be diminished.

Application to court for an order not to circulate a members' statement

3.59 CA 2006, s 317 is based on CA 1985, s 377(3). The court is given jurisdiction to grant relief from the statutory duty to circulate a members' statement if the court reaches the view that the members' right to require circulation of a statement is being abused. There is no statutory definition or listed criteria as to when the members of a company will be held to be abusing their rights under CA 2006, s 314; this will be a question of fact in each case.

Standing to apply

3.60 An application under CA 2006, s 317 may be made by the company or by another person (being a legal person) who claims to be aggrieved. Obviously, the court hearing any such application has to strike a fair balance between the interests of the members on the one hand, and the interests of the company on the other hand. In order to bring an application in the capacity of a person who claims to be aggrieved such an applicant must show a sufficient connection with the proposed members' statement. For example, a person who is named in the proposed statement might apply to the court in order to prevent the circulation of defamatory matter, or where the statement contains material that is misleading or inaccurate. However, in practical terms this right will be of little value as it can only be utilized by someone who knows the contents of the proposed statement.

Costs

If a company's application under s 317 is successful, the court has jurisdiction to make an adverse order for costs against the members concerned, even if they do not appear before the court on the hearing of the company's application or even if they are not parties to the application. **3.61**

Transitional provisions

CA 2006, ss 314–317 came into force on 1 October 2007. The Third Commencement Order provides that the sections apply only to requests made on or after 1 October 2007. CA 1985, ss 376 and 377 continue to apply to requests made before that date.[52] **3.62**

[52] See Sch 3, para 29.

4

THE ANNUAL GENERAL MEETING

Practice

The annual general meeting of a company has been an established part of the corporate landscape since the passing of the first Companies Act in 1862.[1] The annual general meeting provides shareholders with the opportunity to consider the contents of the company's annual financial statements, the reports of the directors and auditors, chooses the composition of the board of directors of the company and questions the management about their conduct of the company's affairs in the previous year.[1a] It is the forum at which the shareholders, in companies both large and small, have the opportunity to 'have their say'. If the concept of shareholder 4.01

[1] CA 1862, s 49.

[1a] Directive 2007/36/EC article 9 provides that every shareholder shall have the right to ask questions related to the items on the agenda of the general meeting of a listed company and the company shall answer the questions put to it by shareholders.

democracy means anything, it is reflected in the obligation of companies to hold an annual general meeting for their shareholders.

4.02 Modern companies, especially quoted public companies whose securities are listed on a recognized stock exchange, make enormous efforts to prepare for their annual general meetings. It is frequently the role of the company secretary and the company's solicitors to brief the Chairman, Chief Executive and other senior executive directors in relation to the questions that may arise at the meeting, to arrange for the appointment of scrutineers in the event of a poll, and nowadays to organize the elaborate security arrangements which are often thought to be necessary. Annual general meetings of large public companies have in a sense become public events attracting a great deal of media interest. If the company concerned has a high public profile or is involved in matters of public or political controversy arrangements may also have to be made to accommodate the media, including radio and television, as well as the press. However, there is no legal requirement to admit representatives of the press or other media. It should be noted that the entitlement to attend an annual general meeting is reserved to the members alone. The attendance of other persons who do not fall within the definition of a 'member' is a matter for the discretion of the Chairman.[2] Nevertheless, many companies go to great lengths to project a concerned and popular image, sensitive to the views of both their shareholders and the wider public. The handling of the publicity surrounding an annual general meeting is therefore a matter of considerable significance.

4.03 As will be seen below, CA 2006 has adopted an entirely different approach to annual general meetings so far as private companies are concerned. Such meetings are no longer required by the statute and steps have been taken to encourage companies only to hold such meetings if they so wish. The long-term ramifications of such an approach are uncertain. If minority shareholders are deprived of the opportunity on a regular annual basis to question those in control of their company about the conduct of its affairs and the contents of its accounts the consequences for them may be adverse. This may prove to be a real and substantial setback for small shareholders, who will otherwise be left with having to formally request a general meeting under CA 2006, s 306, if necessary with the support of others.[3]

4.04 As a result of the new legislative changes this chapter inevitably concentrates on the concept of annual general meeting for a public company but, where appropriate, mention is made of the pre-existing law and the important transitional provisions

---

[2] See Ch 7.
[3] See Ch 5.

that have been introduced. These topics are also covered in Part 3 of this work, commenting on the specific provisions of CA 2006, Part 13.

The Law under CA 1985

Under CA 1985 every company (public or private) was obliged to hold an annual general meeting once in every calendar year, in addition to any other meetings in that year.[4] The only exception was in the first year of the company's existence when it was permissible to hold the first annual general meeting within 18 months of its incorporation.[5] Not more than 15 months were allowed to elapse between the date of one annual general meeting and that of the next.[6] In the event of the failure of the board to convene an annual general meeting the company and every officer who was in default was liable to a fine.[7] **4.05**

In addition, in the event of the failure of the board to convene an annual general meeting, it was open to the member to apply to the Secretary of State at the Department of Trade and Industry to call or direct the calling of an annual general meeting.[8] The Secretary of State was given the power to make such ancillary or consequential directions as he or she thought expedient, including directions modifying or supplementing, in relation to the calling, holding and conduct of the meeting, the operation of the company's articles. The directions might include a direction to the effect that one member of the company present in person or by proxy might be deemed to constitute the meeting.[9] This would enable the meeting to be held notwithstanding the determined opposition of other members and the risk of their refusing to attend in the hope of preventing there being a quorum of members present. **4.06**

Companies Act 1989—Elective Resolution Dispensing with the Annual General Meeting

The Companies Act 1989 introduced a new s 366A which permitted a private company by 'elective resolution' passed in accordance with s 379A to elect to dispense with the holding of annual general meetings. The section provided that the **4.07**

[4] CA 1985, s 366(1).
[5] CA 1985, s 366(2).
[6] CA 1985, s 366(3).
[7] CA 1985, s 366(4).
[8] CA 1985, s 367(1).
[9] CA 1985, s 367(2), going against the well-established position in relation to company law that two persons are required to constitute a meeting; see further Ch 1.

election had effect for the year in which it was made and subsequent years, but did not affect any liability already incurred by reason of default in holding an annual general meeting. The company could, however, only opt out of holding an annual general meeting if there was unanimity. The section therefore provided that in any calendar year a member might write to the company or send an electronic communication and give notice not later than three months before the end of the year, requiring an annual general meeting to be held.[10] In the event of there being less than three months from the year end when the election ceased to have effect, the company would not be obliged by s 366 to hold the annual general meeting in that year. Thus, if one member did not agree to the dispensing with annual general meetings the meetings would have to be held.

4.08 Following the Company Law Review, the government White Paper entitled 'Modernising Company Law'[11] adopted the view that for most private companies the annual general meeting was an unnecessary formality that carried out no business of substance. Accordingly, the White Paper undertook that the proposed new legislation would remove the requirement for private companies to hold annual general meetings, as well as the requirements to lay the accounts and re-appoint the auditors annually at a general meeting of the members.

CA 2006

4.09 This permissive regime for private companies is now adopted wholesale by CA 2006. CA 2006 makes the most radical changes to this area of the law since 1862. CA 2006, Part 13, Chapter 4 (ss 336–340)[12] contains provisions dealing with the annual general meetings of public companies.[13] Private companies are no longer required to hold annual general meetings. In this regard the provisions of CA 2006 are confined just to public companies.

CA 2006, s 366

4.10 A public company is required by s 336(1) to hold a general meeting as its annual general meeting in each period of six months beginning with the day following the company's accounting reference date, in addition to any other meetings held during that period. Thus, a public company with an accounting reference date

[10] CA 1985, s 366A(3).

[11] Cm 5553-I (July 2002) paras 2.10–2.19.

[12] All of CA 2006, Part 13, Chapter 4 came into legal force on 1 October 2007 by reason of provisions in the Third Commencement Order.

[13] A public company is defined in CA 2006, s 4(2).

and financial year end of 30 April would need to have held its annual general meeting by 31 October in the same calendar year. In the event of the company having specified a new accounting reference date and shortening the current accounting reference period or the previous accounting reference period it is to be treated as having complied with the requirements of s 336(1) if it holds a general meeting as its annual general meeting within three months of giving notice to that effect under s 392.

If a public company fails to comply with s 336(3) an offence is committed by every officer of the company who is in default. No liability will rest on the company. A person guilty of an offence under this section is liable on conviction on indictment to a fine, and on summary conviction, to a fine not exceeding the statutory maximum.[14] **4.11**

The timing of the annual general meeting is therefore now linked even more obviously to the company's annual reporting cycle. The effect of CA 2006 is to require an annual general meeting within six months of the end of the company's financial year. While the company's accounts are typically laid for approval at the annual general meeting, it should be noted that the timing requirement applies independently of the laying of the accounts. Accordingly, an annual general meeting of a public company must be held within the period even if the annual accounts have not yet been provided to the shareholders. **4.12**

Notice of annual general meeting

A notice calling an annual general meeting of a public company must state that the meeting is to be an annual general meeting.[15] At least 21 days' notice must be given in the case of an annual general meeting,[16] although the company's articles may specify a longer period.[17] While most general meetings may be called at shorter notice than that required by the statute or under the articles if the requisite proportion of members entitled to attend and vote at the meeting agrees to the shorter notice,[18] this provision does not apply to an annual general meeting of a public company.[19] By s 337(2) an annual general meeting of a public company can be called at short notice only if all the members entitled to attend and vote at the meeting agree to the shorter notice period. This is a severe requirement. In reality, in the case of a large public company with a substantial number of shareholders, in **4.13**

---

14 CA 2006, s 336(3),(4).
15 CA 2006, s 337(1).
16 CA 2006, s 307(2)(a).
17 CA 2006, s 307(3).
18 The shorter notice must be agreed by a majority in number of the members having the right to attend and vote, who together hold not less than 90% in nominal value of the voting shares of the members in the case of a private company and 95% in the case of a public company— see CA 2006, s 307(4), (5) and (6). See also the Transitional Provisions to CA 2006, s 307 in Part 3 of this book.
19 CA 2006, s 307(7).

particular a listed company, at least 21 days' notice will always be required for the holding of an annual general meeting.

Private companies

4.14 With regard to private companies,[20] CA 2006 makes no reference at all to the holding of annual general meetings. It is therefore a matter for the judgment of the directors as to whether a general meeting should be held in any year as the annual general meeting. It must be supposed that many private companies which in the past have held annual general meetings will now dispense with holding them. However, it is anticipated that others, especially private companies with a large number of shareholders, will continue to hold such meetings for a variety of reasons, in particular in order to remain in touch with their shareholders and to provide an opportunity for them to question the board over the conduct of the company's affairs.

4.15 The articles of association of nearly all existing private companies refer expressly to annual general meetings.[21] These provisions will continue to apply unless and until they are deleted by amendment. The new legislation provides no short cut mechanism for the removal of these constitutional provisions relating to annual general meetings. Indeed, the directors of a private company which has a provision in its articles requiring the holding of an annual general meeting will be acting in breach of duty if they neglect to call an annual general meeting. In addition, where directors are required to retire by rotation at the annual general meeting in accordance with reg 73 of the 1985 Table A the failure to hold an annual general meeting can lead to the automatic removal of directors as from 31 December in any year where an annual general meeting is not held.[22] In such circumstances, where no attempt is made to alter the company's articles, the effect of the new statute will merely be to remove the criminal sanction for default in calling an annual general meeting. The ability of a member to seek redress by an application to the Secretary of State no longer exists under the CA 2006.[23]

Transitional Provisions

4.16 The Third Commencement Order contains extensive transitional provisions governing the implementation of CA 2006, ss 336–340 and the subject of annual general meetings. These transitional provisions are set out and commented upon

[20] A private company is defined in CA 2006, s 4(1).

[21] See 1985 Table A regs 36, 38 and 73, which are considered in Part 4 of this book.

[22] *Re Consolidated Nickel Mines Ltd* [1914] 1 Ch 883 (Sargant J); *Cane v Jones* [1980] 1 WLR 1451 at 1462 Michael Wheeler QC.

[23] CA 1985, s 367 has been repealed and has not been replaced.

in Part 3 of this book.[24] Schedule 3, para 32 provides that the repeal of CA 1985, s 366, containing the duty to hold annual general meetings, does not affect any provision of a private company's memorandum or articles that expressly requires the company to hold an annual general meeting. Any such provision continues to have such effect as it had immediately before the coming into force of CA 2006, Part 13 on 1 October 2007. However, the paragraph adds, for the purpose of avoiding uncertainty, that a provision in a company's articles specifying that one or more directors is to retire at an annual general meeting is not a provision expressly requiring the company to hold an annual general meeting.

Schedule 5, para 2(6) to the Fifth Commencement Order also deals with existing private companies whose articles of association require them to hold an annual general meeting. This paragraph amends para 32 of the Third Commencement Order, which brought into force CA 2006, Part 13. Paragraph 32(4) now provides that a private company does not have to hold annual general meetings, even if its articles expressly state that annual general meetings must be held, if an elective resolution under CA 1985, s 366A (dispensing with the need to hold annual general meetings) was in force immediately prior to 1 October 2007. All elective resolutions (except those under CA 1985, s 80A) fell away on 1 October 2007 leading to uncertainty as to whether companies in this position needed to hold annual general meetings or amend their articles to remove the requirement to hold annual general meetings. Schedule 5, para 2(6) to the Fifth Commencement Order now clarifies the position with the effect that any relevant elective resolution remains operative. However, this dispensation only applies where an elective resolution was passed prior to the operation of the new legislation. It therefore does not exempt an existing company from complying with any requirement in its articles for the calling of an annual general meeting. **4.17**

Schedule 3, para 33 to the Third Commencement Order provides that the repeal of the default power of the Secretary of State to call an annual general meeting in CA 1985, s 367 has effect in relation to a private company as from 1 October 2007 even if an application has been made to the Secretary of State before that date, or the Secretary of State has called or directed the calling of an annual general meeting under that section before that date. However, Sch 3, para 36 provides that the repeal of CA 1985, s 367 does not affect the operation of that section in relation to a public company where an application was made before 1 October 2007. This provision illustrates the different treatment of private and public companies in relation to annual general meetings. **4.18**

[24] The transitional provisions relating to annual general meetings are to be found in the commentary in Part 3 of this book following CA 2006, s 340.

Power of Members to Require Circulation of Resolutions for Annual General Meetings

4.19 Under CA 1985, s 376 a member or several members representing not less than one twentieth of the total voting rights of all members or not less than 100 members holding shares in the company on which there had been paid up an average sum of not less than £100 were empowered to requisition the company to give notice to members of a resolution which might properly be moved and which was intended to move at the next annual general meeting. The right also included an obligation on the company to circulate to members a statement of not more than 1,000 words with respect to the matter referred to in any proposed resolution or the business to be dealt with at that meeting. Unless the company resolved otherwise the cost of the notice and circular to members had to be borne by the requisitionists.

4.20 However, by CA 1985, s 377 the company was not bound to comply with the section unless a copy of the requisition, signed by the requisitionists was deposited at the registered office. In the case of a requisition requiring notice of a resolution the notice had to be deposited not less than six weeks before the meeting.[25] In any other case the notice had to be given not less than one week before the meeting. In both cases the requisition had to be accompanied by a deposit or tender of a sum 'reasonably sufficient' to meet the company's expenses in giving effect to it. This was an essential requirement which if not met relieved the company of the obligation to give notice of the proposed resolution or to circulate the statement.

4.21 The only other means by which the company could escape from the requirement to circulate a statement submitted in accordance with s 377(1) was provided by s 377(3). Either the company or another person claiming to be aggrieved could apply to the court for release of the company from this obligation if the court was satisfied that the rights conferred by the section were being abused to secure needless publicity for defamatory matter. It will be seen that if the company was of the view that the member was abusing the statutory process, it had only a very narrow and rather difficult ground on which to rely to avoid compliance with the section.

CA 2006, ss 338–340

4.22 CA 2006 revises and adapts these provisions in three sections—ss 338–340. These provisions only apply to an annual general meeting of a public company. The sections operate in respect of requests that are made on or after 1 October 2007.[26]

[25] This requirement was reduced by CA 1985, s 377(2), where an annual general meeting was called for a date six weeks or less after the deposit of the requisition.

[26] See Sch 3, para 38, Third Commencement Order.

Under s 338 the members of a public company may require the company to give, to members entitled to receive notice of the next annual general meeting, notice of a resolution which may properly be moved and is intended to be moved at that meeting. CA 2006 assumes that a resolution may properly be moved unless:

(a) it would, if passed, be ineffective (whether by reason of inconsistency with any enactment or the company's constitution or otherwise), or
(b) it is defamatory of any person, or
(c) it is frivolous or vexatious.

The terms set out above are wider than those found in CA 1985, s 377(3). The reference to a resolution being 'ineffective' is a welcome addition to the legislation as it is not infrequently the case that members try to introduce an ordinary resolution which interferes with the discretion of the board and their right under the articles to manage the affairs of the company. Such a resolution is legally ineffective as it would amount to a de facto alteration of the articles, which can only be achieved by the passing of a special resolution. In addition, the reference to defamatory matter is wider than under CA 1985, s 377(3) as that required proof that the rights under the section were being abused in order to secure '. . . needless publicity for defamatory matter . . .'. That test no longer has to be met. It is now sufficient if the resolution is defamatory of any person. 4.23

Lastly, the new legislation introduces a third category for objection, namely that the resolution is 'frivolous or vexatious'. This is potentially a very wide provision. There is no guidance in CA 2006 as to what these terms mean in this legislative context. [27] It is suggested that a resolution will be frivolous or vexatious if it is instituted amongst other things with insufficient reason and as a device for causing embarrassment or annoyance to the company, or for no legitimate purpose connected with the company or its business, or is repetitive of previously attempted and failed resolutions that have been decisively rejected in the past. 4.24

Number of members

Once again, the threshold for requiring the company to give notice of a resolution of a member is that the request is supported by members representing at least 5% of the total voting rights of members who have the right to vote on the resolution at the annual general meeting to which the requests relate[28] or at least 100 members who have the right to vote on the resolution at the annual general meeting and hold shares on which there has been paid up an average sum per member of at least £100.[29] 4.25

[27] Reference may perhaps be made to the use of this phrase in other contexts, such as cases under the Rules of the Supreme Court 1965, Ord 18, r 19, dealing with the striking out of legal proceedings.
[28] Excluding any rights attached to any shares in the company held as treasury shares.
[29] CA 2006, s 338(3).

Form of request

4.26 CA 2006 states that the request for the resolution may be in hard copy form or in electronic form,[30] thereby recognizing the increasing use of electronic communications, in particular the use of email. It must identify the resolution of which notice is to be given and be 'authenticated' by the person or persons making it.[31] The meaning of the term 'authenticated' and the statutory requirements of authentication are set out in s 1146. In the government White Paper of July 2002 entitled 'Modernising Company Law—Draft Clauses'[32] the draft of this provision provided that the requisition notice for the circulation of a statement be 'signed' by the requisitionists. It is not apparent why the new legislation has dropped the use of such clear and intelligible wording in favour of the more obscure word 'authenticate'.

4.27 By s 1146(2) a document sent or supplied to a company in hard copy form is sufficiently authenticated if it is signed by the person sending or supplying it. For a document sent or supplied in electronic form there are different requirements in s 1146(3). The document is sufficiently authenticated if the identity of the sender is confirmed in a manner specified by the company, or in the absence of such a provision, if the communication contains or is accompanied by a statement of the identity of the sender and the company has no reason to doubt the truth of that statement. Where a document is sent or supplied on behalf of someone else it is open to the company to require reasonable evidence of the first person's authority to act on behalf of the other. It is therefore open to a public company to make its own rules in respect of documents or information supplied to it in an electronic form. Section 1146(3) merely contains a default provision which will apply in the absence of specific regulations in the company's articles of association.

Timing under s 338

4.28 As to timing, CA 2006, s 338(4) requires that the request be received by the company not later than six weeks before the annual general meeting to which it relates or, if later, not later than the time at which notice is given of that meeting.[33] This provision must be strictly complied with for an effective use of s 338 by a member.

---

[30] CA 2006, s 338(4)(a).
[31] CA 2006, s 338(4)(b) and (c).
[32] Cm 5553-2 (July 2002).
[33] CA 2006, s 338(4)(d).

Duty to circulate

Section 339 specifies the company's duty to circulate the members' resolutions provided under s 338. A copy of the resolution must be given by the company to each member of the company entitled to receive notice of the annual general meeting in the same manner as the notice of the meeting and at the same time as, or as soon as reasonably practicable after, it gives notice of the meeting. This provision is designed to ensure that the shareholders have ample time to consider the contents of the members' resolution before the meeting. The duty to circulate is made expressly subject to s 340(2) which deals with the members' obligation to meet the expenses involved in this procedure. **4.29**

Offence

Failure by the company to comply with s 339 will result in the commission of an offence by any officer who is in default. That person will be liable on conviction on indictment to a fine (of unlimited amount), or on summary conviction to a fine not exceeding the statutory maximum. **4.30**

Expenses of circulation

Expenses are dealt with in s 340. Under s 340(1) the expenses of the company in complying with s 339 need not be paid by the members who requested the circulation of the resolution if requests sufficient to require the public company to circulate it are received before the end of the financial year preceding the meeting.[34] This provision is clearly designed to encourage members who wish to utilize their rights under ss 338 and 339 to do so promptly, giving adequate notice to the public company, well in advance of the annual general meeting. In any other case, the expenses of the public company must be paid by the members who request the circulation of the resolution unless the company resolves otherwise. **4.31**

Unless the public company has so resolved previously, it is not bound to comply with the duty to circulate under the section unless the members deposit with the company or tender to it a sum reasonably sufficient to meet its expenses in complying with it. This sum must be so deposited or tendered not later than six weeks before the annual general meeting or, if later, not later than the time at which notice is given of that meeting.[35] CA 2006 does not give any guidance as to what sum will be reasonably sufficient to meet the public company's expenses in complying with the duty to circulate. This issue will be a question of fact in each case. **4.32**

---

[34] For the definition of a company's financial year see CA 2006, s 390.

[35] CA 2006, s 340(2). For a more detailed discussion of the problems posed by s 340, see the commentary on this section in Part 3 of this book.

Members' Statements at an Annual General Meeting

4.33 It is to be noted that the previous statutory right of members to require the circulation of a statement relating to the business to be dealt with at a general meeting is now to be found in CA 2006, ss 314–317 (inclusive) of the CA 2006. Those provisions apply to both public and private companies but may be used by members who serve a request for the circulation of a resolution for the annual general meeting of a public company under CA 2006, s 338.

4.34 The members may require the public company to circulate to members of the company entitled to receive notice of the annual general meeting a statement of not more than 1,000 words with respect to the matter referred to in the proposed resolution or other business to be dealt with at the annual general meeting. The company is required to circulate the statement once it has received requests to do so from, again, members representing at least 5% of the total voting rights of members who have the right to vote on the resolution at the annual general meeting to which the requests relate[36] or at least 100 members who have the right to vote on the resolution at the annual general meeting and hold shares on which there has been paid up an average sum per member of at least £100.[37]

4.35 The request for the circulation of the statement may be made in hard copy form or in electronic form.[38] The request must identify the statement which is to be circulated and must be 'authenticated' by the person or persons making it.[39] The meaning of the term authenticated is once again to be found in s 1146.[40] As to timing, CA 2006 requires that the request be received by the company at least one week before the annual general meeting to which it relates.[41]

4.36 Any statement relating to a matter in issue should, as a practical matter, be delivered to the company for circulation to the members under s 314 as soon as reasonably practicable. This is necessary in order to ensure that the statement is despatched by the company to the members and received by them in advance of the date on which they return to the company their forms of proxy for the forthcoming annual general meeting. The vagaries and unreliability of the post, and the requirements of the articles of association with regard to the timing of receipt of proxies in advance of the meeting[42] mean that in most cases it would be very unwise for

---

36 Excluding any rights attached to any shares in the company held as treasury shares.
37 CA 2006, s 314(2), (3).
38 CA 2006, s 314(4)(a).
39 CA 2006, s 314(4)(b) and (c).
40 See para 4.27 above.
41 CA 2006, s 314(4)(d).
42 By reg 62 of the 1985 Table A a proxy must be received by the company or its agent not less than 48 hours before the time for holding the meeting. See also CA 2006, s 327(2).

a member to rely upon the strict terms of s 314(4). A request to circulate a statement should in general be supplied to the company not merely 'at least one week before the meeting' but well in advance of that date.

The public company must circulate the members' statement in accordance with s 315 by sending a copy to each member entitled to receive notice of the annual general meeting. This must done in the same way as giving notice of the annual general meeting and, with regard to timing, must be done at the same time as or as soon as reasonably practicable after it gives notice of the annual general meeting. However, the members' right to require circulation of the statement is not absolute. The duty of the company is expressed to be subject to the requirement of the members to deposit or tender a sum of money in respect of the company's expenses in accordance with s 316 and the outcome of any application to the court that may be made under the provisions of s 317.[43] **4.37**

Expenses of circulation of a members' statement

Section 316, dealing with expenses, provides that the expenses of the company need not be paid by the members requesting the circulation of the statement if the meeting is an annual general meeting of a public company and requests sufficient to require the company to circulate the statement are received before the end of the financial year preceding the annual general meeting.[44] The combined effect of these requirements makes it highly unlikely that members will be exempt from the requirement to pay the company's expenses for the circulation of the statement. Members will surely wish any statement prepared by them for circulation by the company at an annual general meeting to be up to date and relevant to the then prevailing situation of the company. **4.38**

In every other situation the expenses of the company in complying with s 315 must be paid by the members who requested the circulation of the statement, unless the company resolves otherwise. Unless the company has previously so resolved, it is not bound to comply with s 315 unless the members deposit with the company or tender to it a sum reasonably sufficient to meet its expenses in complying with it. This sum must be so deposited or tendered not later than one week before the annual general meeting. **4.39**

These provisions (like CA 2006, ss 338–340) may leave the public company in something of a dilemma and vulnerable to the risk of sending out a members' statement at its own expense with the notice of meeting, only to discover that the promised sum in payment of those expenses is not forthcoming. It will be appreciated **4.40**

[43] CA 2006, s 315(2). For a more detailed discussion of the problems posed by s 316, see Part 3 of this book.

[44] CA 2006, s 316(1)(a) and (b).

that if the sum of money in respect of the expenses is not deposited or tendered at the same time as the request and well in advance of the meeting the company will be well advised to wait until the actual sum has been provided (by way of deposit or tender), rather than send the statement with the company's own papers. Unfortunately, the legislation does not require the deposit or tender of expenses to accompany the request, a requirement which would have avoided these problems.

4.41 The failure of the company to comply with CA 2006, s 315 may have very serious consequences for the directors of a public company. Failure to comply amounts to a criminal offence by every officer of the company who is in default, under s 315(3). The offence is punishable on indictment by a fine (of unlimited amount) and on summary conviction by a fine not exceeding the statutory maximum.[45]

Application to the court not to circulate the members' statement

4.42 CA 2006, s 317 permits the company or another person who claims to be aggrieved to apply to the court for an order that the company be relieved from the requirement to circulate the members' statement under s 315. The court must be satisfied that the rights conferred by ss 314 and 315 are being abused. No guidance is provided as to what amounts to an 'abuse' in this context. Equally, CA 2006 does not identify the criteria to be applied in order for a person to have standing as 'a person aggrieved'. Such a person must surely be someone mentioned in the statement or directly or indirectly affected by the contents of the statement and whose rights or interests have been or are likely to be injured or wronged by the contents.[46]

4.43 The onus of showing that the rights under ss 314 and 315 are being abused will be on the applicant. In those circumstances, and in the light of the importance of the statutory right conferred on members by these sections, it likely that a statement will only be characterized as abusive if it is manifestly improper. Such impropriety may take the form of the use of defamatory words or a statement which is scurrilous or vexatious. It is to be noted that if the statement is in excess of 1,000 words long there is in any event no obligation on the company to circulate it to the members.[47]

4.44 Section 317(2) provides for the costs of the court application for an order under s 317(1) to be paid by the members requesting the circulation of the abusive statement, even if they are not parties to the application. The court will only make this

[45] The same is the case in the event of a failure to comply with the duty to circulate a members' resolution for an annual general meeting under s 339(4) and (5)—see para 4.29 above.

[46] Somewhat similar language was used in CA 1985, s 653.

[47] See CA 2006, s 314(1). If a statement exceeded the limit of 1,000 words by a few words only it is suggested that it would be unwise to reject it on that ground alone.

type of costs order in an appropriate case, where such an order would be fair and just. In practice, the relevant members ought to be joined to the company's application under s 317. CA 2006 therefore envisages the possibility of an application being made by the company without notice to the relevant members. It is suggested that such an application would be extraordinary and, save in exceptional circumstances, would be likely to be met with some judicial resistance.

The Business of an Annual General Meeting

The articles of association of many existing companies specify that notice must be given of the general nature of the business to be transacted at any general meeting with the exception that specific notice need not be given of certain matters which are dealt with regularly at an annual general meeting. Among those matters are the consideration of the company's accounts, the reports of the directors and auditors, the declaration of dividends, the election of directors in place of those retiring and the appointment of, and the fixing of the remuneration of, the company's auditors. Where the company's articles contain such a provision the business of the meeting may include these matters even if no notice of those items has been given. In practice, it is recommended that notice should always be given of these matters in order to avoid confusion and uncertainty and to ensure that the shareholders are aware of the business which is to be transacted at the meeting. This issue is discussed in Chapter 2. **4.45**

Accounts and reports under CA 1985

One of the key items discussed at any annual general meeting is the company's accounts and reports. By CA 1985, s 241 the directors were required in respect of each financial year to lay before the company in general meeting copies of the company's accounts, the directors' report, in the case of a quoted company the Directors' Remuneration Report, and the auditors' report on those accounts and reports. In practice, members are entitled to put questions about the form and content of the accounts and reports not only to the chairman but also to the company's auditor. Indeed, the chairman should take personal responsibility to ensure that the relevant audit partner is present to answer questions and that a reasonable opportunity is given to the members to pose questions. **4.46**

It is customary, but not an essential legal requirement, that the meeting be asked to adopt the reports and accounts at the end of the discussion. If the meeting declines to do so and there is a majority against such adoption, the accounts are still valid and must be filed with the registrar of companies. However, the vote will amount to one of no confidence in the board and may lead to the resignation of the finance director or other serious internal repercussions for the company. **4.47**

Members' approval of the Directors' Remuneration Report

4.48 CA 1985, s 241A, which was inserted with effect from 1 August 2002 in relation to financial years ending on or after 31 December 2002, introduced special requirements for the consideration of the Directors' Remuneration Report of quoted companies. Prior to CA 2006 this was a report prepared by the directors in accordance with the requirements of CA 1985, ss 234B and 234C.[48] Notice had to be given to members prior to the meeting at which the accounts were considered (invariably the annual general meeting) of the intention at the meeting to move an ordinary resolution approving the Directors' Remuneration Report for that financial year. This had then to be dealt with as part of the business of the meeting and the directors were under a statutory duty to ensure that the resolution was put to the vote. The requirement that this form part of the business of the meeting applied notwithstanding any failure to give notice or anything in the company's articles of association. If this provision was not complied with by the company and the resolution was not put to the vote of the meeting, each existing director (meaning anyone who was a director immediately before the meeting) was guilty of an offence.

CA 2006—accounts and reports

4.49 The provisions of the legislation with regard to the consideration and approval of the company's accounts and reports are substantially amended by CA 2006 as a result of the fact that it is not anticipated by the draftsman that private companies will continue to hold an annual general meeting at which the accounts and reports will be reviewed by the members. CA 2006, ss 437 and 438 which comprise Part 15, Chapter 8, dealing with Accounts and Reports, retain the requirement that the directors of a public company must lay before the company in general meeting copies of its annual accounts and reports. These sections came into force on 6 April 2008 by reason of provisions in the Fifth Commencement Order.[49]

4.50 Section 437(3) creates the concept of an 'accounts meeting' in relation to a public company, meaning a general meeting at which the company's annual accounts and reports are laid in accordance with the section.

4.51 If the requirements of CA 2006, s 437 are not complied with before the end of the period, every person who immediately before the end of that period was a director of the company commits an offence under s 438(1). However, it is a defence for a person charged to prove that he took all reasonable steps for securing that those

---

[48] These sections were introduced by the Directors Remuneration Report Regulations 2002, SI 2002/1986, reg 3. The report must comply with CA 1985, Sch 7A.

[49] See Art 3(1)(d), Fifth Commencement Order, SI 2007/3495.

requirements would be complied with before the end of that period.[50] On the other hand it is not a defence to prove that the documents in question were not in fact prepared as required by CA 2006, Part 15.[51]

By s 423 every company must send a copy of its annual accounts and reports for each financial year to every member, every debenture-holder and every person entitled to notice of general meetings. By s 424(3), in the case of a public company, this obligation under s 423 must be complied with at least 21 days before the date of the relevant accounts meeting. This is a reference to the accounts meeting at which the accounts and reports are to be laid. There is no similar requirement for a private company.[52] **4.52**

Section 439 reproduces CA 1985, s 241A. It provides that a quoted company must, prior to the accounts meeting, give to the members of the company entitled to be sent notice of the meeting notice of the intention to move at the meeting as an ordinary resolution a resolution approving the directors' remuneration report for the financial year. Once again, if the resolution required by s 439 is not put to the vote of the accounts meeting, an offence is committed by each existing director.[53] It is a defence for a director to show that he or she took all reasonable steps for securing that the resolution was put to the vote of the meeting.[54] **4.53**

Record date—European Directive

For the purposes of organizing the voting by shareholders and their rights to participate at an annual general meeting (as well as the payment of dividends) it is common for listed companies to resolve that there should be a particular date, known as the record date, as of which the persons who are registered as shareholders shall be entitled to any notice, information, document or circular, receipt of any dividend or other distribution or allotment. This will invariably be a fixed date prior to the general meeting of the company. Article 7.3 of Directive 2007/36/EC requires each Member State to ensure that a single record date applies to all listed companies, which shall not lie more than 30 days before the date of the general meeting to which it applies. **4.54**

---

50 See CA 2006, s 438(2).

51 See CA 2006, s 438(3).

52 A private company must comply with s 423 not later than the end of the period for filing accounts and reports, or if earlier, the date on which it actually delivers its accounts and reports to the registrar: see s 424(2).

53 See CA 2006, s 440(2).

54 See CA 2006, s 440(3).

5

MEETINGS REQUESTED BY MEMBERS

Introduction

In accordance with their general powers of management the board of directors of a company are empowered to convene general meetings of members whenever they consider it to be in the best interests of the company to do so and whenever it is necessary. Prior to CA 2006 such meetings were known as extraordinary general meetings so as to distinguish them from the annual general meeting which used to be compulsory for both public and private companies.[1] Under CA 2006 the term 'extraordinary general meeting' is no longer used. It is replaced by the generic term 'general meeting'. The power to convene a meeting is to be found in the articles of association and appears in reg 37 of the 1985 Table A.[2] **5.01**

[1] Under CA 2006 only public companies are required to hold annual general meetings— see Ch 4.

[2] So far as material, reg 37 of the 1985 Table A provides as follows: 'The directors may call general meetings and, on the requisition of members pursuant to the provisions of the Act, shall forthwith proceed to convene an extraordinary general meeting for a date not later than eight weeks after receipt of the requisition.' This regulation is commented on in Part 4 of this book.

5.02 The circumstances in which a general meeting of this type may be called are almost limitless. For instance, there are many matters upon which directors are obliged to obtain the informed consent of the members. Such consent will have to be obtained from the members at a duly convened meeting. This power to convene general meetings is an aspect of management and enables the board to direct the affairs of the company as they consider appropriate.

5.03 However, in addition to meetings of members that were convened at the behest of the board of directors there has for over a century been a power vested in the members of a company to requisition a general meeting of shareholders. Such a power is a valuable one when it is used correctly by members. Under CA 1985 this power was found in s 368, which derives from the Companies Act 1900, s 13.[3]

5.04 Requisition notices issued in accordance with CA 1985, s 368 were used very often in the context of attempts by shareholders to change the composition of the board of directors of a company by means of initiating the consideration and subsequent passing of an ordinary resolution under CA 1985, s 303.[4] The service of the requisition notice ensured that a general meeting could take place to consider this issue whatever the reluctance or objections of the board.

5.05 Under CA 1985, s 368 the directors were under a duty 'forthwith' to convene a meeting of the members of a company if a valid requisition notice had been deposited at the registered office of the company. Following the decision in *Re Windward Islands Enterprises (UK) Ltd*[5] the word 'forthwith' in this statutory context was held to mean 'as soon as reasonably practicable'. If the directors failed to convene the meeting that had been requisitioned validly by the requisitionists, then the requisitionists themselves could proceed to convene the meeting.

The Support Required for a Requisition

5.06 In the case of a company having a share capital a valid requisition notice had to be made by members holding not less than one-tenth of the paid-up share capital[6] that, as at the date of the deposit of the requisition notice, carries the right of

[3] Such a provision is commonplace in the legislation of former and existing Commonwealth countries: see eg Hong Kong Companies Ordinance (Cap 32), s 113.

[4] This power is now found in CA 2006, s 168.

[5] [1983] BCLC 293 at 295 (Nourse J).

[6] The section was amended with effect from 1 December 2003 by the introduction of s 368(2A) which provides that for the purposes of s 368(2)(a) any of a company's paid up capital held as treasury shares must be disregarded.

voting at a general meeting.[7] In the case of a company not having an issued share capital, the requisitionists had to be members representing not less then one-tenth of the total voting rights of all of the members who at the date of the deposit of the requisition notice are enfranchised. The ability for a shareholder with the requisite 10% of voting rights to requisition a general meeting was something of real value, as it enabled that shareholder to have influence over the conduct of the company's business, if only by calling the directors to account at an occasional general meeting.

Single member holding sufficient shares

Although the language of CA 1985, s 368(1) referred to 'members' in the plural it is clear that a single shareholder holding the qualifying number of shares had standing to use the procedure under section 368.[8] Originally, where the qualifying shares were registered in the name of more than one person, all of the registered shareholders were required to sign the requisition notice in order to make it a valid notice.[9] By s 368(3) the requisition notice could consist of several documents in like form each signed by one or more of the requisitionists. **5.07**

The statutory right conferred on members by CA 1985, s 368 was not capable of being abrogated or overridden by any provision contained in the articles of association of a company. However, the articles might permit a smaller number of members to requisition a meeting; such a provision (say, requiring not less than one-twentieth of the total voting rights) is valid and effective. **5.08**

The Form of the Requisition

CA 1985, s 368 contained no express statutory requirement for the requisition notice to set out the precise format of the proposed resolution that was to be considered at the meeting. In order to be valid the requisition notice merely had to (a) state the purpose of the meeting, (b) be signed by all of the requisitionists, and (c) be deposited at the registered office of the company. **5.09**

A requisition notice was valid if it was comprised in more than one document provided that document was signed by one or more of the requisitionists.[10] Where more than one document was used the documents had to be 'in like form'. **5.10**

---

[7] CA 1985, s 368(1).
[8] See Interpretation Act 1978, s 6.
[9] See *Patent Wood Keg Syndicate v Pearse* [1906] WN 164 at 165 (Buckley J).
[10] See CA 1985, s 368(3).

In *Fruit and Vegetable Growers Association Ltd v Kekewich*[11] the requisitionists signed a number of separate documents, not all identical in their terms. One document called for the meeting for the purpose of considering the reconstitution of the board and resolutions concerning the directors and officers of the company. The other form was in the same language but with the addition of the words 'in addition to the affairs of the company in general'. Warrington J held that notwithstanding the inclusion of these additional words the requisitions were in 'like form' within the meaning of the statute, as the extra words used in the second version made no difference to the general purpose of the requisition. It was a requisition to the directors to call a meeting for the purpose of considering the reconstitution of the board and it was the duty of the directors to convene a meeting for that purpose.

An Ineffective Requisition

5.11 If a resolution proposed in a requisition notice is not capable of having legal effect if it were to be passed by the members in general meeting, then the directors are under no obligation to convene a meeting to consider it.[12] As a matter of commercial common sense the board is not required to convene a general meeting if the only purpose is to pass an ineffective resolution. This was first made clear by Fry LJ in *Isle of White Railway Co v Tahourdin*.[13] If the object of a requisition to call a meeting were such that by no manner and by no machinery could it be legally carried into effect, the directors would be justified in refusing to act upon it.

5.12 It was important for the requisitionists to serve a valid requisition notice under CA 1985, s 368 because they were not entitled at the subsequent meeting to attempt to cure any defects by substituting a different resolution or resolutions for that originally specified in the requisition notice.[14] At the same time it appears from the decision in *Rose v McGivern*[15] that if the requisition notice stated the objects of the meeting, rather than set out specific resolutions, and by some lawful means the objects could be carried into effect, the directors were under a duty to call a meeting. Generally, it was and remains the case that it is ill-advised for directors to take fine and pedantic points upon the form and content of a requisition

[11] [1912] 2 Ch 52 (Warrington J).

[12] *Rose v McGivern* [1998] 2 BCLC 593 (Neuberger J).

[13] *Isle of Wight Rlwy v Tahourdin* (1883) 25 Ch D 320 (CA).

[14] See *Rose v McGivern* [1998] 2 BCLC 593 (Neuberger J).

[15] Op. cit. at 610–12 where Neuberger J considered the cases of *Isle of Wight Railway Co v Tahourdin* (1883) 25 Ch D 320 (CA) and *Fruit and Vegetable Growers' Association Ltd v Kekewich* [1912] 2 Ch 52 at 59 (Warrington J).

notice, as the court has tended to favour a finding that a requisition notice is valid.[16]

Where a requisition fails on technical grounds it may nevertheless be appropriate for the board of directors to consider convening an extraordinary general meeting themselves, in order to take up the suggestion of the shareholders. Where the board so decides, they are acting independently of the failed requisition by the members, in that they are acting under their general power to call meetings of the company as they think fit under reg 37 of the 1985 Table A or an equivalent article of the company.[17] This general approach remains unchanged notwithstanding the implementation of CA 2006. **5.13**

Deposit of the Requisition

It was arguable that the phrase '. . . deposited at the registered office. . .' in CA 1985, s 368 connoted the delivery of a physical document at the company's registered address. No doubt when the same phrase appeared in the Companies Act 1900, s 13, physical delivery of the document to the registered office was the sole means of complying with the terms of the then prevailing legislation. In an era where the use of electronic communication is widespread and ever expanding, the phrase '. . . deposited at the registered office . . .' came to be construed so as to cover the many different ways in which a document may be delivered to an addressee. This was made very clear in the decision of Morritt V-C in *PNC Telecom plc v Thomas*.[18] Prior to this decision it was commonplace for shareholders using the requisition process to avoid the use of facsimile as a means of sending in a requisition notice, in order to avoid a challenge to the efficacy of it. This authority settled that matter once and for all in favour of a constructive and modern approach to the provision. **5.14**

If the requisitionists knew that the company in question had a trading address in addition to, and different from its registered office address, they would be well advised to send[19] the requisition notice to this address, in addition to sending it to the registered office address. The reason for this is that the object of serving the requisition notice is to bring the contents of their demand for a meeting to the attention of the board of directors. If a valid requisition notice contains a special **5.15**

16 See *Isle of Wight Railway v Tahourdin* (1883) 25 Ch D 320 (CA).

17 See *Currie v Cowdenbeath Football Club Ltd* [1992] BCLC 1029 (Lord Penrose, Court of Session (Outer House)).

18 [2004] 1 BCLC 88 (Morritt V-C).

19 It was always good practice in view of the sometimes unreliable state of the postal system to send a requisition notice by registered or special delivery post so that the requisitionists would have some credible and verifiable evidence that the requisition notice had been received safely at its intended destination.

resolution the board of directors would have to comply with the provisions of CA 1985, s 378(2) concerning the requisite period of notice.[20]

Timing of the Meeting

5.16 The requirement of CA 1985, s 368 was for the directors duly to proceed to convene an extraordinary general meeting 'forthwith' on receipt of the requisition. Under s 368(4) the directors were given a time limit of 21 days from the date of the deposit of the requisition notice at the company's registered office to proceed to convene a meeting of the members.

5.17 The meeting convened in response to a valid requisition notice had to be convened by the directors sitting as a board and it would be irregular if it was convened merely by the company secretary without the consent of all the individual directors.[21] The secretary has no power to call a general meeting upon receipt of such a requisition notice. The power to convene meetings is vested in the directors, whose duty is to respond to the requisition from the members.[22] Nevertheless, a notice of meeting that is circulated by the secretary without board approval can be subsequently ratified by the board of directors. However, if there is no ratification the meeting will be invalid and the business transacted is of no effect.

5.18 In *Hooper v Kerr, Stuart & Co Limited*[23] following the service of a requisition the company sent out a notice convening a meeting. The notice purported to be issued 'by order of the board'. The facts disclosed that no meeting of directors had been held after the receipt of the requisition and the notice of the meeting had been sent by the company secretary without any authority. A meeting of directors was held before the date of the general meeting, at which it was resolved by the board to adopt, ratify and confirm the action of the company secretary in issuing the notice convening the meeting of members. In these circumstances Cozens-Hardy J held that on ratification, the notice of meeting became good for all purposes.

5.19 For many years a common reaction of directors to an unwelcome requisition for a meeting was to employ delaying tactics in order to try to fix the meeting for as far ahead as possible. No doubt by this means such directors hoped to give themselves time to build up support with a view to frustrating the intentions of the requisitionists. Eventually, the Companies Act 1989 (CA 1989) attempted to deal with this problem by introducing a new subs (8) to s 368. Under CA 1985, s 368(4) directors were deemed

[20] See CA 1985, s 368(7).

[21] See *Re Haycroft Gold Reduction and Mining Co* [1900] 2 Ch 230 (Cozens-Hardy J).

[22] See *Re State of Wyoming Syndicate* [1901] 2 Ch 431 (Wright J), following *Re Haycroft Gold Reduction and Mining Co* [1900] 2 Ch 230 (Cozens-Hardy J).

[23] (1900) 83 LT 729 (Cozens-Hardy J).

not to have duly convened a general meeting if they convened the meeting for a date which was more than 28 days after the date of the notice convening the meeting.[24] Section 368(8), which was a recommendation of the Jenkins Committee in 1962, came into force on 1 March 1990.[25] Where the directors failed to convene the meeting within the time period, or for a date which is more than 28 days ahead, the requisitionists were able to convene a meeting themselves under s 368(4).[26]

Prior to the enactment of CA 1985, s 368(8), it had been held that a meeting convened by the directors did not have to be held either within 21 days from the deposit of the requisition or within three months from that date.[27] This decision in *Re Windward Islands Enterprises (UK) Ltd* was doubted, and in a later decision it was suggested that for the purposes of CA 1985, s 368 a meeting would only be validly convened by the directors if it was not only convened within the 21-day period but also held within that period as well.[28] In *McGuinness v Bremner plc*,[29] the decision in *Re Windward Islands Enterprises (UK) Ltd* was followed as to the construction of the section and quite properly it was noted that shareholders who exercised their constitutional rights under the section were entitled to expect that a meeting would be held within 'a reasonable period'. Accordingly, if directors were misguided enough to convene a meeting for a date which involved a long period of delay, such conduct could be held to be 'unfairly prejudicial' within the meaning of CA 1985, s 459 (now CA 2006, s 994). **5.20**

A Meeting Convened by the Requisitionists

If the directors failed to discharge the statutory duty imposed upon them by CA 1985, s 368 then the requisitionists themselves, or any of them representing more than one half of the total voting rights of all of them, were empowered to convene the meeting. The requisitionists had to take care not to convene the meeting for a date more than three months from the date of the deposit of their requisition notice, for such a meeting would be invalid.[30] **5.21**

---

24 See CA 1985, s 368(8).

25 This was added by CA 1989, s 145, Sch 19, para 9 and was based on a recommendation contained in the Report of the Company Law Committee (Cmnd 1749, 1962), para 458.

26 Interestingly CA 1989 did not amend reg 37 of the 1985 Table A which permits the directors to convene an extraordinary general meeting for a date not later than eight weeks after receipt of the requisition. This is a trap, since if the meeting is convened for more than 28 days ahead it will be ineffective under s 368(8).

27 See *Re Windward Islands Enterprises (UK) Ltd* [1983] BCLC 293 (Nourse J).

28 See *Niltan Carson Ltd (Joint Receivers and Managers) v Hawthorne* [1988] BCLC 298 at 322–4 (QBD, Hodgson J), differing from the approach of Nourse J in *Re Windward Islands Enterprises (UK) Ltd* (op. cit.). The views of Nourse J on the construction of s 368 are to be preferred.

29 [1988] BCLC 673 at 677– 8 (Court of Session, Outer House).

30 See CA 1985, s 368(4).

5.22 Where the requisitionists convened a meeting under CA 1985, s 368(4) they were required to do so in the same manner, so far as possible, as the way in which meetings were convened by the board of directors. Notices of the meeting had to be sent out in good time before the meeting to all the members who were entitled to receive notice of a company meeting in accordance with the company's articles of association. Where the requisitionists themselves convened the meeting, it has been held in Australia that they are under no obligation to inform the directors that they have issued a notice of meeting.[31] Under English law the directors will of course receive notice of a general meeting, as notices must be sent to every member of the company and every director.[32]

5.23 If a valid requisition notice contained a resolution that required the giving of special notice to the company, such as a resolution seeking the removal of a director under CA 1985, s 303, then the requisitionists also had to comply with the provisions of CA 1985, s 379 by giving at least 28 days' notice to the company of their intention to move the resolution.

Costs and expenses

5.24 Plainly, requisitionists would incur some expense, sometimes of a significant amount in the case of a company with a large number of members, in convening the meeting for themselves. Requisitionists were therefore well advised to keep a careful record of their expenditure incurred in connection with and incidental to the convening of the meeting. Section 368(6) provided that any reasonable expenses so incurred by reason of the directors' failure to convene the meeting were to be repaid to the requisitionists by the company. As a sanction on the unwilling directors the subsection also provided that any sum so repaid to the requisitionists should be retained by the company out of any sums due or to become due from the company by way of fees or other remuneration in respect of their services to such of the directors as were in default. Quite how this provision, which was meant to avoid the requisitioning members themselves paying in part for the default of the directors, was to be enforced was not explained. In practice, there were relatively few instances of directors failing to discharge their statutory duty under CA 1985, s 368.

Practical difficulties

5.25 As the issues discussed above in relation to the statutory requirements of CA 1985, s 368 make clear, it was generally unwise to underestimate the difficulties faced by requisitionists seeking to convene a meeting of their company under s 368. In companies with many shareholders unless some of the larger shareholders

[31] See *Browne v Panga Mines Pty Ltd* (1995) 17 ACSR 75.

[32] See CA 2006, s 310(1)(b), and Ch 2.

are willing to co-operate, it is often very difficult for an individual shareholder to enlist the support of a sufficient number of his fellow members to be able to requisition a meeting. Where the requisitioning shareholders face the prospect of having to convene the meeting themselves, they suffer from the additional burden of setting up the meeting and giving adequate notice to all of the members. Inevitably, the requisitionists do not have access to the administrative and company secretarial resources of the company. However, the efficacy of CA 1985, s 368 in the context of a private company with very few members, even if that company amounts in law to a quasi-partnership, is not to be underestimated.

Meetings Called under CA 2006, ss 303–305

CA 2006 has retained the important statutory right of shareholders with the requisite number of shares to require the board of directors to convene a general meeting of members. Such a meeting is no longer to be called an extraordinary general meeting. It is interesting to note that whereas under CA 1985 only one statutory provision was required to set out the requirements of this important right, CA 2006 deals with this matter in ss 303–305 (inclusive). **5.26**

There are some significant changes set out in the new legislation. In particular, the threshold required for what is now a meeting request has been changed. For private companies the threshold is 5% or 10% of the paid-up capital (or for companies with no share capital, 5% or 10% of the total voting rights) depending on when there was last a meeting of the company in advance of which members had the right to circulate a resolution. The lower threshold applies if there has been no such meeting within the last 12 months. There is no equivalent change for public companies. **5.27**

The new legislation relies heavily for its substance upon the provisions contained in CA 1985, s 368. Such reliance is to be welcomed, for in the main the provisions contained in the previous enactment have worked well in practice and have enabled shareholders to compel directors to convene a general meeting in circumstances where it is considered necessary to discuss matters of importance to the members. CA 2006 has abandoned the use of the word 'requisition' and instead uses the word 'request'. As the word 'request' is a synonym for the word 'requisition'[33] it is suggested that it must be the case that in practice there is no change in the substance of what has to be done. **5.28**

[33] See *Oxford Thesaurus of English* (2nd edn, 2004) at 803.

The support required to request a meeting

5.29 Section 303(1) provides that the members of the company (as defined in s 112) can require the directors of the company to call a general meeting. In order for members to have standing to use this provision they must be members who hold the 'required percentage' of shares in the company's paid up share capital carrying the right to vote at general meetings.[34] If a single member holds the requisite percentage of shares or voting rights that will be sufficient to make a valid request. Section 303(3) stipulates as a general rule that the required percentage is 10% of the paid-up share capital as carries the right to vote at a general meeting of the company (excluding any paid-up capital held as treasury shares). In relation to a company that does not have a share capital, the required number of shareholders who can request a meeting is that comprising members with 10% of the total voting rights of all the members having a right to vote at meetings.

5.30 For private companies only there is a derogation from the requirement of 10% to only 5% in circumstances where more than 12 months have elapsed since the end of the last general meeting, which was either called in pursuance of a requirement under s 303, or in relation to which any members of the company had rights with respect to the circulation of a resolution 'no less extensive than they would have had if the meeting had been so called at their request'. It is very unclear as to what this exception is meant to cover. The wording is obscure and the Parliamentary debates on the subject are equally uninformative.

The contents of a meeting request

5.31 Section 303(4) stipulates that the request must state the general nature of the business to be dealt with at the intended meeting and it may include the actual text of the resolution intended to be moved at the meeting. However, the precise format of the resolution that may properly be moved does not have to appear in the request. A general description of the nature of the business to be dealt with at the meeting is sufficient for a valid request. Nevertheless, experience shows that the request will be more effective and less open to manipulation by the board if the precise terms of the proposed resolutions are incorporated in the document.

Invalid request

5.32 There has always been an attempt in the legislation regulating members' rights to convene a meeting to offer some protection to companies from the activities of what might be described as 'the lunatic fringe', that is to say, those individuals

[34] CA 2006, s 303(2). The subsection excludes any paid-up capital held as treasury shares.

whether alone or in concert with others, who wish to abuse the requisition process as a means of causing trouble, or making themselves a nuisance or trying to obtain the oxygen of publicity for causes that are only indirectly associated with the business and affairs of the company. There has been an increasing trend in recent years for groups of activists for particular causes to buy small shareholdings (sometimes only a single share) in companies (especially listed public companies) in order to be able to attend general meetings of the company and to have access to information that a shareholder is entitled to receive.

The limited protection offered to companies is re-enacted in s 303(5) which provides that a resolution may properly be moved at a meeting unless it would, if passed, be ineffective, or it is defamatory of any person or it is frivolous or vexatious. The new legislation does not give any indication as to what will be covered by the phrase 'frivolous or vexatious'.[35] **5.33**

The form of the request

Section 303(6) makes it clear that a request for a meeting can be made in hard copy or in electronic form. Documents to be sent to a company must be sent or supplied in accordance with the provisions of CA 2006, Sch 4. This schedule is discussed in Chapter 17. Section 303 leaves no room for any doubt that a request can be sent by facsimile or by email. The old language of CA 1985, s 368, namely that the requisition notice had to be '. . . deposited at the registered office . . .' has been omitted. Plainly, members making a request for a meeting must send the request to the directors of the company at the address or addresses which will ensure that the notice comes to the attention of the board. **5.34**

The request for a meeting from the members must be 'authenticated' by the person or persons making it. The requirements of authentication are dealt with in CA 2006, s 1146. By s 1146(2), a document sent in hard copy form is sufficiently authenticated if it is signed by the person sending or supplying it. However, if it is sent or supplied in electronic form then it will be sufficiently authenticated only if the identity of the sender is confirmed in a manner specified by the company (presumably in its articles of association) or, where no such manner has been specified, if the communication contains or is accompanied by a statement of the identity of the sender and the company has no reason to doubt the truth of that statement. Section 1146(4) adds that if a document is sent by one person on behalf of another nothing in the section affects any provision of the company's articles that may require the person to produce evidence of authority to act. **5.35**

---

[35] See Part 3 of this book for further analysis of s 303(5) and the meaning of this phrase.

Timing of the meeting

5.36 In common with earlier enactments concerning this area of the law the new legislation stipulates that the directors have a duty to call a meeting that has been duly requested by members. Under s 304(1)(a) the directors must call the meeting within 21 days from the date on which they become subject to the requirement. By s 304(1)(b) the meeting must be held on a date not more than 28 days after the date of the notice convening the meeting. The old trick of convening the meeting for several weeks or months in advance is thereby ruled out.

5.37 It is to be noted that under CA 1985, s 368 all the time periods for the subsequent actions to be taken by the directors in relation to a valid requisition notice were measured from the time of the deposit of the requisition notice at the registered office. In general the occurrence of this event was quite easy to identify. The new legislation uses a more imprecise phrase to describe the starting point for actions in relation to the request to the directors, that is to say, the date on which they become subject to the requirement. In practice this ought usually to be the date of receipt by the company of the request. However, where there are numerous requests, not all received by the company at the same time, the requirement will arise when the company has received sufficient requests from the required percentage of members for the purposes of s 303(2).

The notice of meeting

5.38 Very often members who wish to requisition a meeting are able to employ the services of lawyers who will be able to draft the precise text of the resolution or resolutions that are intended to be moved at the general meeting. If such resolutions are included in the request then they must be included in the notice of the meeting which the directors are required to send out to members.[36] Where the request includes the text of a special resolution the directors must take care to give the notice that is required by CA 2006, s 283. This provision replaces CA 1985, s 368(7). The notice must include the text of the resolution and specify the intention to propose the resolution as a special resolution.[37]

Power of the members to call the meeting

5.39 Ever since the power to requisition a general meeting was conferred upon registered members the legislation has always made provision for the circumstances where the directors in default of their duty to convene the meeting, and s 305

[36] See CA 2006, s 304(3).

[37] See CA 2006, s 266(6). 21 days' notice of a meeting at which a special resolution is to be proposed is no longer required.

continues this sound practice. Under s 305(1) where the directors default in their statutory duty to call the meeting, the members who requested the meeting, or any of them representing more than one half of the total voting rights of all of them, may themselves call the meeting. It must be called in the same manner as nearly as possible as meetings are called for by the board.[38] The meeting must be called for a date not more than three months after the date on which the directors become subject to the requirement to call the meeting.[39]

Once again, the statute provides a fine-sounding statement of principle but in practice it has to be remembered that the members who request the meeting will not have the same administrative and company secretarial support as is available to the company. Accordingly, other than in a small private company with few members, the practical difficulties facing members who request a meeting should not be underestimated. Experience shows that there is no substitute for thorough forward-planning for the eventualities that may occur when a meeting has been requested under what is now CA 2006, s 303. **5.40**

Costs and expenses

The ability of members to have their reasonable expenses reimbursed by the company is retained by s 305(6), which provides that their reasonable expenses incurred by the failure of the directors duly to call the meeting must be reimbursed by the company. Care must be taken by the requesting members to keep an accurate and contemporaneous account of their expenses and to avoid unnecessary expense for which they may not obtain reimbursement. The legislation casts no light on what constitutes reasonable expenses. In each case it will be a question of fact and degree. In addition, it should be noted that provision is made in s 305(7) to enable the company to recoup these expenses from the defaulting directors. **5.41**

Transitional provisions

The transitional provisions relating to ss 303–305 are to be found in the Third Commencement Order, Sch 3, para 25. From these provisions it is apparent that the new legislation applies only to requests from members that are made on or after 1 October 2007.[40] **5.42**

[38] See CA 2006, s 305(4). This is the procedure to employ rather that an application to the court under CA 2006, s 306. If it became 'impracticable' for the members to convene a general meeting, an application would have to be made under CA 2006, s 306.

[39] See CA 2006, s 305(3).

[40] The transitional provisions that are applicable to these sections are set out below in Part 3 of this book.

Conclusion

5.43 The reformulation of the shareholder's statutory right to request the calling of a meeting of members into three sections of the new legislation with certain amendments and modifications is to be welcomed. The new sections use simpler language but otherwise make few changes to the existing law. In these circumstances it is suggested that the existing jurisprudence will be of use in the interpretation and application of the new legislation. A request for a meeting will remain a useful weapon for minority shareholders, to be deployed in circumstances where they wish to raise concerns amongst the shareholders in relation to important matters concerning the affairs of the company. In the light of the removal of the requirement for annual general meetings in relation to private companies, it is considered likely that general meetings called pursuant to these new sections may grow in both number and importance.

6

MEETINGS OF MEMBERS ORDERED BY THE COURT

Introduction

The two key organs of a company are the board of directors and the members of the company exercising their constitutional rights in a general meeting. Company law attaches great significance to the due convening of general meetings of shareholders. The general meeting is the forum for considering many of the essential matters relating to the company's affairs including increasing or reducing the share capital of the company, changes to the memorandum or articles of association, alterations to the composition of the board of directors, considering the content of the company's financial statements and approving dividends. **6.01**

Under reg 37 of the 1985 Table A the board of directors is empowered to call general meetings of the company at any time they consider it to be appropriate. This general power is now reflected in CA 2006, s 302.[1] In exercising this power, which is one of the important management functions of the directors, the board **6.02**

[1] See the commentary on CA 2006, s 302 in Part 3 of this work.

has control over the agenda for the meeting, subject only to the limited rights of members to have a resolution placed before the meeting for consideration.[2]

6.03 In addition, as has been discussed in Chapter 5, since 1900 the shareholders of a company have had a statutory right to require the directors of a company to convene a meeting of the company. The directors must react in a positive fashion to a lawful and valid request that they receive from members, and in default of such action fulfilling their statutory duty as directors, the members themselves may convene a general meeting of the company. However, the question arises as to what happens in the event that it is not possible for either the board of directors or the members of the company to convene a meeting or for a meeting that is duly convened to be conducted. This chapter considers the separate statutory power of the court to order a meeting of members in cases where the normal mechanism for convening and conducting general meetings has broken down, or has ceased to or cannot operate.

Court-ordered Meetings

6.04 In order to counter the possibility of such an undesirable impasse the Court has jurisdiction to convene a meeting of members if for any reason it is impracticable to hold a general meeting. If an order is made by the court it has jurisdiction to do so on such terms as it thinks fit. It is to be noted that the jurisdiction of the court extends only to meetings of members of a company and it has no application to meetings of directors. A meeting can also be convened by the court under CA 2006, s 896 in circumstances where a compromise or scheme of arrangement is being proposed between a company and its members or class of members and creditors or class of creditors. This is a separate topic which is dealt with in Chapter 14.

CA 1985, s 371

6.05 Prior to the enactment of CA 2006 the discretionary jurisdiction of the court to order the holding of a general meeting of members was found in CA 1985, s 371. This section provided as follows:

> Power of the court to order a meeting
> (1) If for any reason it is impracticable to call a meeting of a company in any manner in which meetings of that company may be called, or to call a meeting in the manner prescribed by the articles or this Act, the court may, either of its own motion or on the application
> (a) of any director of the company, or

2 See Ch 2 and Ch 5.

(b) of any member of the company who would be entitled to attend and vote at the meeting,

order a meeting to be called, held and conducted in any manner in which the court thinks fit.

(2) Where such an order is made the court may give such ancillary or consequential direction as it thinks expedient; and these may include a direction that one member of the company present in person or by proxy be deemed to constitute a member.

(3) A meeting called, held and conducted in accordance with an order under sub-section (1) is deemed for all purposes to be a meeting of the company duly called, held and conducted.

An application for an order under s 371 could be made by the company itself, or a shareholder or even by the court acting on its own initiative, although examples of the last mentioned form of application were rare. **6.06**

CA 1985, s 371 was a procedural section which was designed to enable company business which needed to be transacted at a general meeting to be conducted. In general terms it is right that a company should be permitted to get on with managing its legitimate corporate affairs without being frustrated by any form of impracticability in relation to calling and conducting general meetings in accordance with its articles of association or with the provisions of CA 1985.[3] **6.07**

CA 1985, s 371 conferred on the court a discretionary power which had to be exercised properly having regard to all of the relevant circumstances. Accordingly, in relation to an application where the court had jurisdiction, that is to say because on the facts it was impracticable to hold a meeting, the court was not bound to make an order under CA 1985, s 371.[4] This proposition of law was made clear by Brightman J in *Re H. R. Paul & Son Ltd*[5] where he held that the quorum provisions in a company's articles of association requiring the attendance of two members at a general meeting could not be regarded as conferring upon a minority member a right of veto not commensurate with his shareholding. The point was reiterated by Morritt J in *Re Opera Photographic Ltd*.[6] **6.08**

[3] See *Vectone Entertainment Holding Ltd v South Entertainment Ltd and others* [2004] 2 BCLC 224 (Richard Sheldon QC, sitting as a Deputy Judge of the High Court).

[4] See *Monnington v Easier plc* [2006] 2 BCLC 283 (Rimer J) where it was held that the court had no jurisdiction to make an order because on the evidence it had not been established that it was 'impracticable' to hold a meeting.

[5] (1974) 118 SJ 166 (Brightman J).

[6] [1989] 1 WLR 634 (Morritt J).

CA 2006, s 306

6.09 The new legislation has retained the discretionary jurisdiction of the court in CA 2006, s 306.[7] The wording of s 306 is in substance identical to that which was found in CA 1985, s 371. In the circumstances it must be presumed that the existing case law will continue to apply and to be of relevance to the exercise by the court of its discretion under the new statutory provision. The section remains a powerful and effective tool for the protection of shareholders, in particular majority shareholders, whose wishes would otherwise be frustrated by the abuse of the quorum provisions in a company's articles of association.

'Impracticable'

6.10 In order for the court to have jurisdiction to make an order under CA 2006, s 306 it has to be alleged and proved by the applicant that it is 'impracticable' to hold a meeting of the company. An applicant for an order under CA 1985, s 306 has to establish either that it was 'impracticable' to call a meeting of the company in any manner in which meetings might be called and/or that it is 'impracticable' to conduct a meeting in a manner that was prescribed by the articles of association or by the provisions of the legislation regulating companies. If neither condition is satisfied on the evidence as in the case of *Monnington v Easier plc*,[8] then the court does not have any jurisdiction to make an order.

6.11 Following the decision of Wynn Parry J in *Re El Sombrero Ltd*[9] it is apparent that the proper approach to the section is to examine the circumstances of the case and to ask the question, whether as a practical matter, the desired meeting of the company could be conducted. Wynn Parry J dismissed the suggestion that the language of the section indicated that the jurisdiction could only be invoked if there was no opposition to the application. He held that there was nothing to prevent the court from intervening in an apposite case and where the application was opposed by other shareholders.

6.12 A court must examine carefully all the relevant facts of a case in order to test the contention made by an applicant for an order under CA 2006, s 306 that it is 'impracticable' to hold a meeting in accordance with a company's articles of association. Such a careful examination of the salient facts is illustrated by the case of *Might SA v Redbus Interhouse plc*[10] where the applicant for an order under

---

[7] This section is set out in full in Part 3 of this work where there is a commentary on the section. CA 2006, s 306 applies to general meetings only and has no application to class meetings or to meetings of directors.

[8] [2006] 2 BCLC 283 (Rimer J).

[9] [1958] Ch 900 at 904 (Wynn-Parry J).

[10] [2004] 2 BCLC 449 (Lindsay J).

CA 1985, s 371 held 28.5% of the shares in a public company called Redbus Interhouse. The articles of association of the company provided that the chairman, if any, of the board of directors was to preside as chairman at general meetings of the company and if there was no chairman the directors present were to select one of their number to be chairman of the meeting. The applicant had requested that an extraordinary general meeting of Redbus Interhouse be convened to consider resolutions put forward by it for the removal of all five directors[11] of the company and for the appointment of three new directors. Redbus Interhouse had no formally appointed chairman and the applicant applied to the court for an order restraining any of the existing five directors from acting as chairman of the extraordinary general meeting. It was the applicant's contention that it was 'impracticable' to call a meeting of Redbus Interhouse because the existing directors would be faced with a conflict of interest if they were to act as chairman as they had a vested interest in remaining as directors. In these circumstances it was submitted that the court ought to exercise its powers under what was then CA 1985, s 371 to order the meeting to be called, held and conducted in such manner as the court thought fit.

The application for an order under CA 1985, s 371 was refused by Lindsay J. He held that as there was no requirement in CA 1985 or the articles of association of Redbus Interhouse that the chairman of a general meeting had to be neutral, the fiduciary position of a director of the company did not prevent him from assuming the position of chairman of a general meeting of the company, even though that might put him in a position of conflict between his individual position and his fiduciary duty. The mere fact that there might be such a conflict between duty and interest was not sufficient to render it 'impracticable' to call a meeting of the company. **6.13**

Categories of impracticability are not closed

There can be many and diverse reasons why it may be impracticable to hold a meeting of the members of a company. For instance, there may be no board of directors, or there may be real uncertainty as to the identity of the members of the company through the loss or destruction of a company's register of members. In addition, it may not be possible to summon a meeting with the required quorum if a member declines to attend and the meeting cannot proceed to transact lawful business. However the authorities provide that where there are quorum provisions requiring two members' attendance that will not in itself be sufficient to prevent the court from making an order under s 306. This is the case even where the applicant is seeking to pass a resolution to remove or appoint a director, something **6.14**

---

[11] Under CA 1985, s 303, now CA 2006, s 168.

which a majority shareholder would have the legal right to procure in normal circumstances. The authorities show that the contractual provision in relation to the quorum for a general meeting between the members created by the articles of association can be overridden by the court's ordering the holding of a meeting under s 306 at which the quorum provision in the articles ceases to apply.[12]

Re El Sombrero Ltd

6.15 From the inclusion of this statutory provision in the Companies Act 1862 reported decisions on the exercise of the jurisdiction were rare. In England and Wales the first reported case was the decision in 1958 of Wynn-Parry J in *Re El Sombrero Ltd.*[13] In this case there were three shareholders in a private company: the applicant holding 900 shares and the two respondents, who were the directors of the company each holding 50 shares. No general meetings of the company had ever been held. Under the articles of association of the company the quorum required for a valid and lawful meeting was two members present in person or by proxy. The applicant shareholder applied to the court under a statutory predecessor of CA 2006, s 306,[14] but this was opposed by the respondent directors. The court exercised the jurisdiction conferred on it and made an order for the holding of a meeting on the basis that if it declined to make the order it would have prevented the applicant, as the majority shareholder, from exercising his rights as such to remove the directors from office. It is also of note that a relevant factor in the exercise of the court's discretion was that the respondent directors had failed in their statutory duty to convene an annual general meeting.

6.16 Most of the reported cases concern applications made by a majority shareholder in a private limited company where there has been a breakdown in normal communications between the shareholders and a refusal on the part of one or more minority shareholders to attend a general meeting at which changes are sought to be made to either the articles of association or the composition of the board of directors. Nevertheless, the jurisdiction can be used in relation to private or public companies, though it is axiomatic that an effective exercise of the jurisdiction will be very rare in the context of a listed public company.

---

[12] *Union Music Ltd v Watson* [2003] 1 BCLC 458 at paras 33–6 (CA).

[13] [1958] Ch 900. There was an earlier decision in 1934 in Scotland in the case of *Re Edinburgh Workman's Houses Improvement Co Ltd* [1934] SLT 513. In this case the company's constitution stipulated a quorum of 13 members. On the facts it was not possible to have such a quorum, and the court ordered the holding of a meeting with a quorum of five shareholders personally present.

[14] CA 1948, s 135.

Quorum problems

As has been discussed in Chapter 1, the quorum provision in a company's articles of association is the constitutional mechanism to ensure that there is a valid meeting of a company. In small private companies, for example with only two registered members, the absence of one of the shareholders would mean that a meeting could not proceed to transact any lawful business. It is plain that in such a two-person company a situation could arise where one member might refuse to attend a meeting, thereby frustrating the possibility of a lawful meeting taking place. It is now clear that in cases where there is only one class of shares the quorum provision cannot be regarded as a right vested in a minority shareholder to prevent the majority from exercising rights that are attached to their shares.[15] In *Re Opera Photographic Ltd* an order was made under CA 1985, s 371 where the shares were held as between the applicant and respondent in the proportion 51:49. The majority shareholder in this case wished to pass a resolution under CA 1985, s 303 removing the other director, who also held 49% of the shares, from office as a director. The applicant requisitioned a meeting and used the power under CA 1985, s 368(4) to call the meeting himself because a regular board meeting could not be held. Resolute opposition continued from the holder of the 49% of the issued share capital and he refused to attend a meeting of the two members. His absence rendered the meeting inquorate and thus unable to proceed to transact lawful business. In the circumstances it was held that it was impracticable to hold a general meeting and the court granted the application under CA 1985, s 371. **6.17**

Interaction with CA 2006, s 994

The existence or possibility of a petition under CA 2006, s 994[16] is not a bar to an order being made under s 306. It is a factor that may be considered by the court when exercising its discretion under the statutory jurisdiction. In *Re Sticky Fingers Restaurant Ltd*[17] W, one of two directors and shareholders in a successful private company, applied to the court for an order under s 371 in circumstances where no effective meetings of the board or the company could be held because of the quorum provisions in the company's articles and the refusal of M, the respondent, to attend any such meetings. Board meetings were needed to deal with the accounts, statutory returns and VAT. M had presented a petition under CA 1985, s 459 (the predecessor of CA 2006, s 994) seeking an order that W purchase his shares. In the application W sought an order convening a meeting, at which one member would constitute a quorum, for the purpose of considering the appointment of two **6.18**

[15] See *Re Opera Photographic Ltd* [1989] 1 WLR 634 (Morritt J) and *Re Whitchurch Insurance Consultants Ltd* [1993] BCLC 1359 (Harman J).

[16] Re-enacted as CA 2006, s 994.

[17] [1992] BCLC 84 (Mervyn Davies J).

additional directors. The court considered that the company required an effective board of directors to deal with its affairs. At the same time, pending the trial of the s 459 petition, the court ordered that any new director appointed at the meeting should be restrained from acting as such director unless and until he had provided an undertaking to M's solicitors that he would not at any meeting vote to dismiss M, or interfere with his day-to-day conduct of the business or effect any change in the constitution or capital of the company.

6.19 The decision in *Re Opera Photographic Ltd* has been followed in *Re Whitchurch Insurance Consultants Ltd*[18] and more recently in *Re Woven Rugs Limited.*[19] There can be no doubt that the court will uphold the right of a majority shareholder to remove a director under CA 2006, s 168 where that director is also a minority shareholder and is trying to make his non-attendance at a general meeting tantamount to a power of veto over the constitutional rights of the majority shareholder.

New situations

6.20 The discretionary jurisdiction of the court under s 306 is flexible and can be adapted to meet new and sometimes difficult situations. The necessity to control the disruption caused by so-called activist members of the British Union for the Abolition of Vivisectionists (BUAV) resulted in a novel, but most valuable exercise of the court's discretion under s 371 in 1995.[20] In this case the BUAV was a company that was limited by guarantee. Under the terms of its constitution the votes of members had to be given in person and there was no ability on the part of a member of the BUAV to have a proxy. At the annual general meeting of the BUAV, which was held in July 1994, a small group of members of the BUAV was intent on disrupting the meeting to the maximum extent that they could achieve. The officers of the BUAV therefore convened an extraordinary general meeting in November 1994 for the purpose of considering and voting upon an important constitutional change, namely the introduction of voting by proxy. Regrettably, the extraordinary general meeting was disrupted by disorderly conduct and the police closed down the meeting. There was little point in convening another meeting, and no doubt serious risk of disruption and disorder.

6.21 In these circumstances the court was requested by eight members of the executive committee of the BUAV to make an order under s 371 to convene a general meeting to consider and to vote upon a special resolution to amend the articles of association to introduce the ability of a member to vote by proxy. The order sought

[18] [1993] BCLC 1359 (Harman J).

[19] [2002] BCLC 324 (Anthony Mann QC, sitting as a Deputy Judge of the High Court).

[20] *Re British Union for the Abolition of Vivisection* [1995] 2 BCLC 1 (Rimer J).

was that the persons entitled to attend in person at the meeting should be restricted to the members of the BUAV executive committee; the other members of the company were to be permitted to vote only by way of a postal ballot. This proposal dispensed with the requirement of personal attendance as provided for in the articles. The court acceded to the application in the light of the previous conduct of the minority at the annual general meeting and extraordinary general meeting, which had generated a fear that such conduct would be repeated at any future meeting convened in accordance with the company's constitution.

Class rights

There has sometimes been a different outcome where the shareholder who has declined to co-operate in the convening of a valid meeting has done so in reliance on his class rights. Articles of association and shareholders' agreements sometimes provide that a valid quorum can only exist with the attendance of a shareholder who holds a share of a specific class. In *Harman v BML Group Ltd*[21] there were five shareholders in the private company, one of whom, B, held all of the 'B' shares. All of the shareholders were directors and there was in place a shareholders' agreement. Under that agreement B, whose shareholding amounted to 38% of the issued share capital of the company, was entitled to remain a director of the company for so long as he held 'B' shares, and a general meeting would not be quorate unless a B shareholder or his duly authorized proxy was present. B became concerned that two directors who between them controlled 52% of the company's issued share capital were taking money from the company to which they were not entitled. These two directors were removed from office as directors by a vote on a show of hands. The majority shareholders then attempted to requisition a meeting of members but B refused to attend. At first instance[22] His Honour Judge Paul Baker QC, sitting as a Deputy Judge of the High Court, held that it was impracticable to hold a meeting and exercised the jurisdiction under CA 1985, s 371. He ordered that a meeting be held at which any two members, not necessarily including the holder of the 'B' shares, would constitute a quorum. **6.22**

The company appealed to the Court of Appeal where the leading judgment was given by Dillon LJ, who pointed out that it was entirely novel to use CA 1985, s 371 to override class rights conferred on a member in a shareholders' agreement. Dillon LJ held that it was not right to use the section to override class rights which had been deliberately imposed for the protection of the holders of those shares, although those shareholders were in a minority. Class rights have to be respected and the right of B to be present in the quorum was a class right for his protection, **6.23**

21 [1994] 1 WLR 893 (CA).
22 [1994] BCC 502.

which would not be overridden by the machinery of CA 1985, s 371. It was not for the court to make a new shareholders' agreement and impose its terms on the parties.

Equal shareholders

6.24 Sometimes the shares in a company are held on a 50:50 basis as between the members and this situation has been deliberately created by the incorporators. In such circumstances the company can become deadlocked. It is now well established that an order under s 371 cannot be made in circumstances where the court is being asked to resolve a deadlock. Where there is no deadlock the court will usually make an order under s 371. However, in the event that the court is being asked to resolve a deadlock between two *equal* shareholders, the court will refuse to exercise its discretion to the make the order requested.

6.25 In *Ross v Telford*[23] a husband and wife were the only two directors of each of two companies. The circumstances arose in the context of an acrimonious divorce case, where both companies were deadlocked. They were equal shareholders in one company and the shareholders of a second company were the husband and the first company. Legal proceedings had been brought by the first company against a bank, which proceedings had been instigated by the husband. The husband applied to have a meeting to be called under CA 1985, s 371 in order to ratify the second company's action. The Court of Appeal held that the authorities did not support the proposition that s 371 enabled the court to break a deadlock between two equal shareholders. The court could not make an order so as to allow a 50% shareholder to override the wishes of the other 50% shareholder.

Destroyed or missing register of members

6.26 In order to convene and hold a valid meeting of a company due and proper notice must be given to all members who are entitled to receive such a notice. A company's register of members is the document that contains a record of the current members, and it is by reference to this document that a board of directors will notify members of a proposed meeting. Where a company's register of members is destroyed or is missing, recourse can be made to the jurisdiction of the court under CA 2006, s 306 in order to assist with the convening of a valid meeting. In circumstances where a company does not know the names and addresses of all of its members the court may order the holding of a meeting to be convened by a notice in the usual way to known members and by public advertisement to those members who names and addresses are unknown. Such an order was made by Vaisey J in

[23] [1998] 1 BCLC 82 (CA).

Payne v Coe,[24] but not under the statutory predecessor of CA 1985, s 371 as this was a decision that concerned the Pall Mall Building Society, and thus the order was made under the Building Societies Act 1884.

Summary of principles

It is suggested that for the purposes of CA 2006, s 306 the following principles can be derived from the decisions cited above: **6.27**

(a) The quorum provision in articles of association is not be regarded as conferring a power of veto on a minority shareholder, so as to enable him to impede the proper running of a company in accordance with its agreed constitution by the simple expedient of not attending a meeting of members.
(b) The court should uphold the contractually binding effect of a company's articles of association where those impose special class rights on certain shares and the effect of an order convening a meeting with a modified quorum under CA 2006, s 306 would be to infringe those class rights.
(c) The court will not allow the section to be used as an alternative to a petition on grounds of unfair prejudice under CA 2006, s 994 in cases of deadlock but the existence of such a petition is not a bar to an order.
(d) The court has a wide discretionary jurisdiction which it will seek to exercise whenever a meeting should properly be permitted to take place.
(e) The court has the jurisdiction to impose conditions or other restrictions when making an order under CA 2006, if it is necessary to do so in order to achieve justice in the case.

Procedure

Applications for an order under s 306 are usually made by way of an application under CPR Part 8. The application must be supported by credible testimony that it is impracticable to hold a meeting in accordance with the company's articles of association or the provisions of the Companies Act. In most cases the application will be heard without the makers of the witness statements being cross-examined on their evidence. However, the court may order cross-examination if the circumstances of the case justify such an order for the proper disposal of the matter.[25] **6.28**

Alternatively, the court may consider the case to be appropriate for summary determination under CPR Part 24 on the basis that the respondent has no real prospect of successfully defending the application and there is no other **6.29**

---

[24] [1947] 1 All ER 841 (Vaisey J).

[25] Cross-examination was ordered and did take place in *Re Woven Rugs Ltd* [2002] BCLC 324.

compelling reason why the application should be disposed of at a trial.[26] Such an application was made but rejected in *Alvone Developments Ltd v Manhatten Loft Corporation (AC) Ltd*.[27]

Costs consequences

6.30 Where an application has to be made under s 306 because a minority shareholder is abusing the quorum provisions in a company's articles by refusing to attend a meeting thereby rendering it inquorate, the application for an order becomes necessary because of a stubborn and unjustified refusal on the part of one shareholder to attend a meeting. Such conduct is regarded as an improper attempt to exercise a power of veto over the business to be transacted at a company's general meeting. In such circumstances the recalcitrant member may be vulnerable to an adverse costs order against him.

[26] See CPR Part 24.2.
[27] [2005] All ER (D) 252 (Peter Smith J).

7

THE ROLE OF THE CHAIRMAN

Introduction

For there to be an effective general meeting of members of a company someone has to perform the role of chairman and be appointed to that position. In the absence of a person exercising procedural control over the affairs of the general meeting it may be unable to proceed to transact business in an orderly manner. At a shareholders' meeting that person is often the chairman of the board of directors of the particular company but this is not always the case. The chairman is the person who conducts the meeting and leads it through the business on the agenda which is to be transacted. A vast array of skills are required in order to discharge this important role in an efficient and effective manner. In carrying out this task **7.01** the chairman must have regard not only to the interests and concerns of the majority present but also the rights of the minorities.

7.02 In relation to any company the essential function of the chairman of a general meeting is to preside at the meeting, to control procedural aspects of the general meeting and to maintain good order. If the chairman steers a safe course through these potentially turbulent waters a general meeting will be able to proceed to transact business in an orderly manner and after debate has taken place in a controlled, rational and reasonable atmosphere. The chairman is the person who is in charge of the agenda and his main function is to ensure that the business of the meeting is conducted in an efficient, fair and competent manner. A chairman may have to take many decisions regarding procedure, for example, deciding who may be present at the meeting, selecting the persons to speak on any issue, and exercising powers in relation to voting procedures and adjournments. In general terms the chairman must always act in good faith, must act reasonably and must apply the procedures laid down in the articles. In addition, he must seek to ascertain 'the sense of the meeting', that is, the general consensus among the participants.

Appointment

7.03 Usually the articles of association of a company contain detailed provisions for the appointment of the chairman at a general meeting. The appointment is made either in advance of the meeting, by the automatic selection of the chairman of the board or one of the directors or by the meeting itself. By statute the election of the chairman of the meeting is one of only two matters where the articles may exclude the right to demand a poll.[1]

Articles of association relating to appointment

7.04 Regulations 42 and 43 of the 1985 Table A provide as follows:

> 42 The chairman, if any, of the board of directors or in his absence some other director nominated by the directors shall preside as chairman of the meeting, but if neither the chairman nor such other director (if any) be present within fifteen minutes after the time appointed for holding the meeting and willing to act, the directors present shall elect one of their number to be the chairman and, if there is only one director present and willing to act, he shall be chairman.

[1] See CA 2006, s 321(1). The other matter is the adjournment of the meeting.

> 43 If no director is willing to act as chairman, or if no director is present within fifteen minutes after the time appointed for holding the meeting, the members present and entitled to vote shall choose one of their number to be chairman.[2]

The effect of provisions in the form cited above is to place the role of chairman primarily in the hands of a member of the board, so that either the board chairman presides at the meeting or some other director chosen in advance or selected on the day by the other directors is placed in control of the general meeting. Under these provisions it is only when the board chairman is absent and no director is prepared to act as chairman or is not present within 15 minutes of the start time that the members present who are entitled to vote have the right to choose the chairman. **7.05**

CA 2006, s 319

In the absence of express provision in the articles the legislation contains certain default provisions. Under CA 1985, s 370(5) it was provided that any member elected by the members present at a meeting was able to be chairman of the meeting. This provision has been re-enacted in CA 2006, s 319 which provides:[3] **7.06**

> (1) A member may be elected to be the chairman of a general meeting by a resolution of the company passed at the meeting.
> (2) Subsection (1) is subject to any provision of the company's articles that states who may or may not be chairman.

A company should give very careful consideration to the issue of whether it is desirable that a member who is not also a director should have the capacity to act as the chairman of a general meeting. It is legitimate for a company's articles to make express provision for who is and who is not capable of holding office as chairman. It is suggested that an express provision regulating this important matter is appropriate and prudent. Where there are no directors an express provision in the articles of association stating that a member of the board can act as chairman cannot operate because there is no person who is eligible to act as chairman. In such circumstances the default position provided for in the legislation becomes operative, and it may be of use in avoiding a situation where otherwise there would be uncertainty as to how a chairman would be appointed.[4] **7.07**

Proxy can be elected as chairman

In addition, it is to be noted that by CA 2006, s 328 a proxy (who may not be a member of the company) may be elected to act as the chairman[5] of a general meeting. This is a new statutory entitlement for a duly appointed proxy. Again, this is not **7.08**

[2] See the commentary on these regulations in Part 4.
[3] See the commentary on s 319 in Part 3.
[4] See *Re Brick and Stone Co* [1878] WN 140.
[5] See the commentary on CA 2006, s 328 in Part 3.

an absolute statutory right as it may be removed by an express provision in a company's articles of association.

Re Bradford Investments Ltd

7.09 It is to be noted that in every case where the chairman is selected by the general meeting that individual must be a member of the company. This requirement itself has on occasion led to confusion and difficulty. In *Re Bradford Investments Ltd*[6] a company had no directors and an extraordinary general meeting was convened to consider appointments to the board. At the start of the meeting there was therefore no chairman of an existing board available to take the chair and, in addition, there was a dispute as to whether the holders of the ordinary or preference shares were entitled to vote at the meeting. [7] At the beginning of the meeting the solicitor for the persons eventually appointed directors assumed the position of 'temporary chairman' in order to supervise the selection of a proper chairman for the meeting. The solicitor was not a member of the company. In his capacity as 'temporary chairman' he ruled that under the articles the ordinary shareholders were not entitled to vote, but that the preference shareholders could vote. As a result of this decision, the nominee of the preference shareholders was appointed as chairman of the meeting, at which point the ordinary shareholders walked out. The preference shareholders then elected four new directors. Subsequently, the ordinary shareholders applied to the court for a declaration that the resolutions passed at the meeting were invalid and of no effect.

7.10 Hoffmann J expressed the view that it would be wrong to give the articles of the company an interpretation which made the outcome of the meeting dependant upon who was sufficiently forceful to assume control as temporary chairman. In the circumstances the correct position was to hold that the election of the chairman was entrusted to the members present, in person or by proxy, who were entitled to vote and that any ruling by the self-appointed chairman at the time would be subject to review and legal challenge in later proceedings.[8] Nevertheless, the position of a 'temporary chairman', self-appointed solely for the purpose of electing a chairman of the meeting, derives some support from this decision.

---

[6] [1991] BCLC 224 (Hoffmann J).

[7] This dispute centred on whether the dividend payable on the preference shares was in arrears and whether there were sums presently payable to the company by the ordinary shareholders, the shares having been allotted to them for the transfer of a business without the consideration having been independently valued as required by CA 1985, s 103.

[8] Given the finding by the court that only the preference shareholders had the right to vote, they could have passed the necessary resolutions informally with unanimous consent in accordance with the principle laid down in *Re Duomatic Ltd* [1969] 2 Ch 365 at 373 (Buckley J).

The Role of the Chairman

Nowadays, the position of the company chairman has importance even outside meetings. However, there is no doubt that the role of the chairman will vary from company to company. In the context of a private unquoted company there may be no need to have a company chairman at all. On the other hand, in respect of a public listed company the position of the chairman will be indispensable. In many instances the chairman of a listed public company will act as the 'public face' of the company and will have the annual duty to take the chair at that annual general meeting[9] and take control of all other important general meetings with potentially a large number of members present. For public companies the annual general meeting will be the regular occasion on which the board of directors and others who are charged with the management of the affairs of such a company will be answerable in public to the shareholders.[10] Whether members of public companies take up the opportunity that is afforded to them in this regard will be a matter for each individual shareholder. **7.11**

Preparations for the meeting

In practice, a great deal of time is taken up with the planning of company meetings. This is something to be welcomed, as it ensures the smooth running of the meeting and, on occasion, it may avoid a descent into procedural chaos. In the case of large public companies the annual general meeting is a very important date in the company's year. Depending on what events have taken place in the intervening time since the last annual general meeting there may be a great deal of interest, not just from the company's shareholders but from the public and the media in general, in the forthcoming annual general meeting. Of course, it is not possible to anticipate everything that may occur at a general meeting but it has become very common for the legal advisers to companies to prepare in advance of a meeting what is in effect a script for the chairman. The script often contains not only the chairman's opening and closing remarks but also a series of directions, explaining how important procedural matters should be dealt with. It is usual for the legal advisers to run through the script with the chairman before the meeting, so as to ensure that he understands the extent of the discretionary and other powers available to him and the various procedural issues that may arise for decision. **7.12**

---

[9] Under the deregulation policy of CA 2006 a private company is no longer under a statutory duty to hold an annual general meeting—see Ch 4.

[10] See Ch 4.

7.13 In advance of the meeting the chairman should, in any event and as a matter of general practice, familiarize himself with the provisions of the company's articles of association relating to the conduct of the meeting so that he is well prepared for any difficulties that may arise. The more controversial the business of the meeting, the greater the responsibility on the chairman to be well prepared. He must therefore also familiarize himself with the agenda and the business to be transacted, so that he is aware of the significance of each item. Another important matter to be considered by the chairman in advance of the meeting is the minutes of the last meeting. The approval of the minutes of the last meeting will almost certainly be the first item on the agenda. The evidential importance attached to the minutes of a general meeting is explained in Chapter 16. The minutes should be read and understood by the chairman.

7.14 It is axiomatic that before a general meeting of any company is held a great deal of careful planning and advance preparation will have taken place. More often than not a listed public company will be required to prepare and issue to its members a circular in accordance with the Listing Rules in relation to the business that is proposed to be transacted at a general meeting.[11] Advance preparation should try to anticipate and take due account of potential difficulties, in terms of issues such as procedure and presentation. Contentious issues may arise at a general meeting in relation to many items including:

(a) who may have access to the meeting, for example, whether non-members such as the press can attend the meeting;
(b) whether to delay the start of a meeting in order to let all members gain access to the venue;
(c) whether the meeting has to be adjourned;
(d) resolving any issues on the existence of a quorum;
(e) changing the order of business on the agenda;
(f) dealing with points of order that may be raised by members;
(g) deciding who can speak on a matter;
(h) deciding how long debate can go on for in relation to a particular resolution;
(i) deciding which member of the board will answer particular questions from members;
(j) dealing with amendments to proposed resolutions;
(k) dealing with an objection raised in relation to a member's right to vote;
(l) deciding how a vote on a resolution is to be taken;
(m) deciding whether to demand a poll on a vote;

[11] See Ch 3.

(n) deciding whether to use any casting vote that he may have under the constitution of the company;[12]
(o) declaring the result of a vote that is taken on a show of hands;
(p) deciding whether attendees who are acting in a disorderly manner should be removed from the meeting; and
(q) deciding when to close the meeting.

In dealing with the issues that will arise in relation to the matters that are listed above a chairman will require a good command of, and where necessary, legal advice on the relevant procedure that is applicable to the company, together with sound judgment and adept presentational skills. **7.15**

The Duties of the Chairman

It is the duty of the chairman to preside over the general meeting with a view to ensuring it is conducted in a well-regulated, lawful and efficient manner in accordance with the general law and the constitution of the company. The chairman must ensure, so far as is reasonably practicable, that those who are in lawful attendance at the general meeting obtain a fair hearing. The chairman is in a fiduciary position and as such must remember that he is the delegated individual who has been charged by the company to conduct the business of the general meeting. The chairman is not running the general meeting for his own benefit, but for the benefit of the company as a whole. **7.16**

Certain powers that are entrusted to the chairman, that are necessary for the proper regulation of business, will be capable of lawful exercise only with the consent of the meeting. These include, in particular, the power to adjourn the meeting.[13] Other powers, such as the right to demand a poll on a vote, are capable of being exercised by the chairman by reason of the fact that he holds that office.[14] **7.17**

The test of reasonableness

When exercising any of his powers and discretions the chairman must take into account only those matters which are relevant to his decision and must not take into account any matters which are irrelevant to his decision. This rule, which is derived from the *Wednesbury* principles[15] applied in administrative law, was introduced into this area of the law in the decision of the Court of Appeal in **7.18**

---

[12] At common law there is no right to a casting vote: see *Nell v Longbottom* [1894] 1 QB 767 (Div Court).
[13] See Ch 12.
[14] See Ch 9.
[15] See *Associated Provincial Picture Houses Ltd v Wednesbury Corporation* [1948] 1 KB 223 (CA).

Byng v London Life Association Ltd,[16] a case which concerned the chairman's power to adjourn a meeting where the chosen venue for the meeting proved to be inadequate.[17] However, the judgment of Uthwatt J in *The Second Consolidated Trust Ltd v Ceylon Amalgamated Tea & Rubber Estates Ltd*[18] provides an earlier application of the rule, where he held that the decision of a chairman not to demand a poll at a meeting was invalid on the grounds that he had failed to take into account a relevant factor, namely the scale of opposition to the resolution of those members who had voted by proxy.

7.19 The clear guidance of the Court of Appeal in *Byng v London Life Association Ltd* is that a court will not declare the decision of a chairman to be invalid unless, on the facts which he knew or ought to have known, he failed to take into account all the relevant factors, took into account irrelevant factors or reached a conclusion which no reasonable chairman, properly directing himself to his duties, could have reached.[19]

Who can be admitted to the meeting?

7.20 A chairman may be faced with the question of who can attend a general meeting of a company. There will be categories of persons who have an absolute right to attend a general meeting but there may be others who seek permission to attend. Members of a company and their duly authorized proxies, and in the case of corporate members, duly authorized corporate representatives, have a legal right to attend a general meeting of a company. The auditor of a company has a legal right to attend a company's general meeting.[20] Directors of a company must be given notice of general meetings under CA 2006, s 310, and if the articles of association adopt an article in the form of reg 44 of the 1985 Table A directors also have the right to attend and speak at any general meeting.

7.21 Prima facie a company has the right to exclude non-members from a general meeting. With the consent of members at the meeting, the chairman has to make the decision as to whether non-members should be admitted.[21] There are no definitive rules regulating the admission of non-members to a general meeting. Clearly, the size of the venue for the general meeting will be a relevant and important factor and priority of admission must be given to those with the legal right to attend. The admission of bona fide financial journalists may be of benefit to the company and the exclusion of such persons completely could be detrimental. As

---

[16] [1990] Ch 170 (CA).

[17] See the detailed facts of this case set out in Ch 12.

[18] [1943] 2 All ER 567 (Uthwatt J).

[19] [1990] Ch 170,189B-D per Sir Nicolas Browne-Wilkinson V-C.

[20] See CA 2006, s 502. Auditors are entitled to speak only on business which concerns them as auditors and they are not entitled to vote.

[21] *Carruth v ICI* [1937] AC 707 (HL).

a general rule, non-members who seek admission but who are perceived to have the potential to cause disruption to the general meeting should not be admitted.

Is a quorum present?

As has been discussed in Chapter 1, a meeting must be quorate in order for it to be able to proceed to transact lawful business. The chairman must therefore ensure as his first task that the requisite quorum is present and, where necessary, remains present for the duration of the meeting. Under CA 2006, s 318 the statutory default position is that two qualifying persons present constitute a quorum.[22] In practice this will not be an onerous task in the case of a large company with many members and where the members of the board of directors also hold shares. If the quorum is not present within the time prescribed by the articles of association the chairman will have to adjourn the meeting to another day, time and venue.[23] **7.22**

Decision to delay the start of the meeting

The notice of a general meeting must state the time at which the meeting is to start.[24] Where many shareholders are eligible to attend a meeting circumstances can arise that at the time appointed for the start of the meeting significant numbers have still not been admitted to the meeting room. Proper procedures for the registration and admission of members should obviate this problem. If at the time appointed for the start of the meeting it is plain that there are still members waiting to gain access to the venue, the chairman may have to delay the start of the meeting for a short period of time. Where this situation does arise, the chairman should open the meeting at the time that is appointed in the notice but delay moving to the formal business of the meeting until all of the members waiting to enter the venue have been admitted. **7.23**

Changing the order of business on the agenda

If the agenda is a long one and he wishes to change the order in which matters on the agenda will be considered, the chairman should do so only with the consent of the meeting. He should obtain this by announcing his intention to deal with matters in a different order, explain his reasons and ask if anyone objects. In respect of the exercise of his functions the chairman should at all times endeavour to act in an impartial and fair manner. **7.24**

---

[22] See further Ch 1, and the commentary on CA 2006, s 318 in Part 3.
[23] See Ch 12 and the commentary on reg 41, 1985 Table A in Part 4.
[24] See Ch 2.

Amendments to resolutions

7.25 Members of a company must be given due notice of a general meeting.[25] It is the chairman who will have to deal with the difficult issue of whether amendments should be permitted to resolutions that have been proposed to be considered at a general meeting. This important issue is considered in detail in Chapter 11.

Points of order

7.26 A chairman will have to consider points of order that may be raised by members during the course of a general meeting. A shareholder may consider that there has been an infringement of the company's articles that regulate the conduct of meetings or may question a decision that has been taken on an aspect of procedure. If a point of order on a procedural issue is raised the chairman should deal with it immediately[26] and his decision thereon is final.

Regulating debate

7.27 A general meeting of a company, whether it is convened by the board of directors,[27] the members themselves[28] or by the court,[29] is the forum in which members of a company are entitled to air their views on the subject matter of the resolutions that are contained in the notice of the meeting. Although the chairman has a duty to maintain order at the meeting so that debate can proceed in a rational and measured manner, he must let members articulate their views on the resolutions that come up for debate and consideration. However, it is legitimate for the chairman to require members to desist from interrupting other members when the latter are speaking, or from talking amongst themselves while another member is speaking. It is to be hoped that members themselves would appreciate the lack of politeness in such conduct, but where they do not it is correct for the chairman to intervene so as to ensure that the general meeting is conducted in an orderly fashion. The manner of such intervention from the chairman is important and the key is for the chairman to demonstrate consistent, polite and impartial conduct when maintaining good order at the meeting. Members who deviate from the subject matter of the resolutions and digress on to irrelevant issues should be called to order by the chairman. The chairman should also take decisive action in relation to improper language and disorderly behaviour.

---

25 See Ch 2.

26 See *Re Indian Zoedene Co* (1884) 26 ChD 70, (CA).

27 See CA 2006, s 302; see the commentary in Part 3.

28 See CA 2006, s 303; see the commentary in Part 3.

29 See CA 2006, s 306; see the commentary in Part 3.

Selecting speakers

Shareholders should be afforded a reasonable opportunity to express their views on resolutions that are to be put to the general meeting. The chairman's conduct in relation to this important area must be, and must appear to be, fair and impartial. The chairman must try to ascertain the views of the meeting on the resolutions that are comprised in the notice of the general meeting. It would be an improper exercise of the chairman's discretion to refuse any debate at all. However, the chairman is permitted to keep debate within reasonable and acceptable bounds. What are reasonable bounds of debate will be a question of fact and degree in each case and ultimately will be a matter for the judgment of the chairman. There are no definitive rules in this regard but it is legitimate for the chairman to: **7.28**

(a) permit debate on one issue at a time;
(b) limit the time for which members speak on a particular resolution; and
(c) decline to take questions on other issues while a particular matter is being debated.

The decision to bring discussions to an end

The chairman is under a duty to provide a reasonable opportunity for the members present at the meeting (and their duly appointed proxies) to participate in the debate on any resolution or amendment or other matter. The chairman must ensure, so far as is practicable, that there is a fair opportunity for different points of view to be expressed by members. Eventually, the chairman must make a decision to bring the discussion on a matter to an end. This is a question for the exercise of the chairman's discretion, acting in good faith and in the interests of the company, with the assent of the members present. In this context, the interests of the company really means the interest of having a fair debate over a reasonable period of time, while enabling a conclusion to be reached within that reasonable time frame. The decision to close debate can be challenged by legal proceedings, but normally the court will be very reluctant to interfere with the exercise by the chairman of his discretion in this sphere. **7.29**

National Dwellings Society v Sykes

However, in *National Dwellings Society v Sykes*[30] the court indicated its willingness to intervene in an extreme case. The annual general meeting of a company was attended by some 35 members. When the chairman moved a resolution to adopt the report and accounts an amendment was put forward that a committee of investigation should be established to ascertain the financial position of the company. **7.30**

[30] [1894] 3 Ch 159 (Chitty J).

The chairman ruled the amendment out of order on the basis that no special notice had been given and refused, on legal advice, to put the amendment to the meeting. Ultimately, he put the resolution to approve the report and accounts, which was heavily defeated. The chairman then immediately dissolved the meeting, left the chair and walked out of the room, together with his supporters. The resolutions to elect the directors and auditors, which formed part of the business of the annual general meeting, had not been dealt with. The shareholders remaining elected one of their number as chairman and thereafter dealt with the rest of the business on the agenda. They concluded by adjourning the meeting for six weeks. Their actions were later challenged in proceedings. Chitty J held that the original chairman had not acted correctly. While it was his duty to preserve order, he had to have regard to the sense of the meeting. He had no power to adjourn at will or to dissolve it. The meeting was entitled to continue in his absence after he left the chair in order to deal with the business for which it had been convened. For that purpose the meeting was also entitled to elect a replacement chairman to conduct the remainder of the meeting.

Wall v London and Northern Assets Corporation

7.31 On the other hand in *Wall v London and Northern Assets Corporation*[31] Lord Lindley MR held that discussion at a meeting can be brought to an end by the chairman so that the question may be put to the vote, with the sanction of a majority vote of the meeting and provided that the views of the minority have been heard and the matter has been reasonably debated. His view was supported by Chitty LJ, who stated that on the facts of that case there was nothing arbitrary or vexatious on the part of the chairman or the majority which justified the intervention of the court.

7.32 In *Carruth v Imperial Chemical Industries Ltd*[32] Lord Maugham expressed similar views, emphasizing that the conduct of a meeting was a matter largely in the hands of the chairman, with the assent of the persons properly present. He held that it is open to a meeting to decide either 'that an untiring speaker shall no longer be heard, or that a much debated question shall be put to the vote without further discussion'.

Deciding how a vote is to be taken

7.33 Voting on resolutions at general meetings can be taken by way of a vote on a show of hands, that is to say one member one vote, or by means of a vote on a poll, a distributive form of voting where the number of shares actually held by the

[31] [1898] 2 Ch 469 (CA).
[32] [1937] AC 707 at 760–2 (HL).

member becomes of significance.[33] Under CA 2006, s 321 a member or members who satisfy the threshold requirements may demand to have a vote on a resolution taken by way of a vote on a poll.[34] If a poll is so demanded it is the responsibility of the chairman to regulate the holding of the poll in accordance with the provisions contained in the company's articles.

The decision to hold a poll

A resolution put to a meeting must usually be decided on a show of hands unless a poll is duly demanded in accordance with the articles. Articles of association invariably provide that one of the persons who may demand a poll is the chairman.[35] Indeed, it has been held that the chairman of a meeting has the right and, on occasion, the duty at common law to demand a poll. **7.34**

This principle was established in *The Second Consolidated Trust Ltd v Ceylon Amalgamated Tea & Rubber Estates Ltd*[36] where the outcome of a meeting convened to alter the conditions attached to debenture stock was dependant upon the holding of a poll. The trust deed stated that on a show of hands a stockholder present only by proxy should have no vote. All 14 persons present in person were in favour of the resolution but they did not constitute a quorum unless the proxies were counted in. If a poll was demanded, the proxies were such that the resolution could not be passed. The chairman was aware of these facts but did not demand a poll. Uthwatt J held that, so far as the person giving the proxy was concerned, it was contemplated that the vote so authorized to be given would be used, and in the way it was required by him to be used. The duty of the chairman of a meeting is to ascertain the sense of the meeting upon any resolution properly coming before the meeting. The right to demand a poll is not a personal right to be exercised according to the fancy of the chairman and he does not have an unlimited discretion as to the manner in which he may exercise that power. Uthwatt J concluded: **7.35**

> It appears to me that the power to demand a poll is a power possessed by the chairman which is to be exercised or not exercised according to his decision whether it is necessary to exercise the power in order to ascertain the sense of the meeting upon the matter before them; in other words, it is a power directed towards enabling him to carry on the meeting for the purpose for which it is convened.

On the facts the chairman was under a duty to demand a poll and to exercise the proxies in accordance with the instructions they contained, as he was aware of the

---

[33] See CA 2006, s 322 and the commentary in Part 3.

[34] See Ch 9.

[35] See reg 46, 1985 Table A.

[36] *The Second Consolidated Trust Ltd v Ceylon Amalgamated Tea & Rubber Estates Ltd* [1943] 2 All ER 567 (Uthwatt J).

fact that the result on the poll would be different from that recorded on the show of hands.

7.36 The chairman will direct how the poll should be conducted and, where the articles so permit, he may appoint scrutineers for this purpose.[37] In exercising this discretion the chairman must act in good faith and in what he considers to be the best interests of the company. Articles may exclude the right to demand a poll only on the questions of the election of the chairman of the meeting or the adjournment of a meeting.[38]

Any objection to a person's right to vote

7.37 Articles of association usually contain a provision that no objection may be taken to a person's qualification to vote at a general meeting except at the meeting itself or at any adjourned meeting at which the vote objected to is tendered. The article then provides that the matter should be referred to the chairman whose decision shall be final and conclusive.[39] Once again, this important decision must be made by the chairman, acting in good faith and in the interests of the company.

CA 2006, s 287

7.38 The right of a company to require an objection to a person's entitlement to vote on a resolution to be made in accordance with the express provisions contained in a company's articles of association and for the determination of any objection to be final and conclusive is reinforced by CA 2006, s 287.[40] The purpose of this section is to put onto a statutory basis the effect of provisions in the form of reg 58 of the 1985 Table A. Such provisions are eminently sensible and are designed to achieve certainty in the conduct of a meeting when an issue arises in relation to a member's entitlement to vote on a resolution.

7.39 In addition, nothing in CA 2006, Part 13, Chapter 1 affects the grounds upon which such a determination of any objection may be questioned in legal proceedings. Section 287 therefore preserves the existing case law.

The chairman's casting vote

7.40 Under most articles of association the chairman of a general meeting is granted a casting vote in the event of an equality of valid votes cast on any resolution.[41]

---

37 See Ch 9. CA 2006, s 342 contains a new right to require the directors of a quoted company to appoint an independent assessor to produce a report on any poll. See the commentary on this section in Part 3.

38 See CA 2006, s 321(1) and the commentary in Part 3.

39 See reg 58, 1985 Table A. See further the commentary in Part 4.

40 There was no such provision in CA 1985.

41 See reg 50, 1985 Table A. See further the commentary in Part 4.

A provision equivalent to reg 50 of the 1985 Table A has existed in Table A since the middle of the nineteenth century. The reason why it is sensible to have such a provision is so that a deadlocked resolution can be resolved one way or the other.[42] It is difficult to know how frequently a chairman has had to exercise the power to use a casting vote, but the ability to resolve a tied vote in a simple and efficacious manner is both important and practical for the proper administration of a company.

In the absence of express provision in the articles for a casting vote the chairman does not have one.[43] This is not a personal right that is conferred on the individual who happens to be the chairman, but it is a concomitant of the office of chairman. Accordingly, the power to use a casting vote is a fiduciary power and must be exercised for proper purposes in the interests of the company and not for motives that are collateral or improper. The chairman will exercise this vote after the show of hands or poll has taken place and he has announced the result of the voting. **7.41**

As will be discussed in Chapter 11, a problem has recently arisen in relation to the very common provision for a chairman's casting vote. This is the result of the new statutory definition of an ordinary resolution contained in CA 2006, s 282. Section 282 states that an ordinary resolution of the members or of a class of members means a resolution which is passed by a simple majority by reference to persons holding a simple majority of the total voting rights of members. Attention should also be paid to s 284 which provides that a member has one vote in relation to each share held (subject to any special rights provided by the articles). As a consequence there has been concern as to the potential invalidity of ordinary resolutions passed on the basis of the chairman's casting vote. Such a provision exists in the articles of most modern companies.[44] **7.42**

Queries from practitioners on the effect of CA 2006, s 282 on a provision (such as reg 50 of the 1985 Table A) conferring a casting vote on a chairman were raised with the Department for Business, Enterprise and Regulatory Reform (BERR). The initial response of BERR as published on its website under the heading 'frequently asked questions' confirmed that the effect of the new provision requiring a simple majority of members' votes to pass an ordinary resolution under s 282 would override any casting vote provisions in the articles. This was an unintended result of the new legislation. As a consequence a provision has been included in the Companies Act 2006 (Commencement No 5, Transitional **7.43**

---

[42] The casting vote provision may be excluded in certain circumstances: for example where a joint venture company is established and it is intended that the company should be a 'deadlocked' company.

[43] See *Nell v Longbottom* (op. cit.).

[44] Reference should be made to the commentary on ss 282 and 284 and the subsequent provisions in Part 3 of this book.

Provisions and Savings) Order 2007 (the Fifth Commencement Order)[45] relating to the casting vote of a chairman. This states that companies whose articles made provision for a chairman's casting vote immediately before 1 October 2007 may continue to rely on the relevant article notwithstanding CA 2006 and any such company which had amended its articles to remove the casting vote may reinstate the provision and continue to rely on it.[46]

7.44 However, it appears that other companies, including any incorporated on or after 1 October 2007, cannot rely on the validity of the chairman's casting vote provided for in their articles, save in the absence of very careful drafting where the chairman is a member in his own right and has a vote as such. Accordingly, in practical terms, in such a case it is essential that the person acting as the chairman of any general meeting is himself a member of the company.

7.45 The website of BERR now contains the following explanatory statement in relation to the efficacy of a chairman's casting vote under the new legislation:

> **Can Chairman still use a Casting Vote?**
> Sections 281 and 282 of the 2006 Act have the effect of making void a resolution passed at a company meeting by use of a casting vote of the chairman. The Fifth Commencement Order (**Schedule 5, paragraph 2**(5)) includes a saving provision for the Chairman's casting vote to allow those companies who previously had such a provision in their articles to continue with it. The saving also allows companies who have removed such a provision since 1 October 2007 to revert to it, should they wish to do so.[47]

7.46 It should also be noted that the 1985 Table A has been amended for new companies incorporated since CA 2006, Part 13 came into force on 1 October 2007. The new form of the 1985 Table A does not contain reg 50, thereby ensuring that the chairmen of new companies which adopt that version of the 1985 Table A do not have a casting vote.[48]

The chairman as proxy

7.47 It is customary for forms of proxy to be drafted in such a manner as to appoint the chairman of the meeting, or some other person whose name must be inserted, as the proxy for a member. A proxy will frequently be able to exercise his discretion as to how to vote on the matters before the meeting, alternatively he must act as directed by his principal. Accordingly, it is commonplace for the chairman to attend the meeting with knowledge that he has in his hands the votes of numerous members for whom he has been appointed proxy. In practice, this usually enables

---

[45] SI 2007/3495.

[46] Fifth Commencement Order (Sch 5, para 2(5) which amends Sch 3 of The Third Commencement Order).

[47] BERR website: FAQs Fifth Commencement Order.

[48] See the commentary on the 1985 Table A in Part 4.

the chairman to conduct the business of the meeting with some confidence as to the outcome on any contentious issue. This matter is considered further in Chapter 9. The chairman must exercise the votes given to him as proxy if that would materially affect the outcome of the meeting.[49]

The power to adjourn

The chairman's power at common law to adjourn a general meeting is linked to his duty to maintain order.[50] The chairman also has the power at common law to adjourn the meeting where it is apparent that not all the persons who wish to take part can properly participate in the meeting.[51] The general power to adjourn a meeting is considered in detail in Chapter 12. **7.48**

Declaring the result of voting

It is important for members to know what has happened when a resolution has been put to a vote. It is for the chairman to declare the result of a vote on a resolution which has been taken by means of a vote on a show of hands. This power is conferred by CA 2006, s 320 which in turn is based on CA 1985, s 378, although this latter provision was confined to declarations in relation to special and extraordinary resolutions. Section 320 also derives from reg 47 of the 1985 Table A which regulates ordinary resolutions. In the absence of fraud the declaration of the chairman that a special resolution has been carried on a show of hands (no poll having been demanded) is conclusive. In *Re Caratal (New) Mines Ltd*,[52] the articles of association of the eponymous company provided, inter alia that '. . . at any general meeting, unless a poll is demanded by at least five members personally present, a declaration by the chairman that a resolution has been carried, and an entry to that effect in the book of proceedings of the company, shall be sufficient evidence of the fact without proof of the number or proportion of the votes recorded in favour of or against such resolution'. Meetings were convened to pass and confirm resolutions relating to the reconstruction of the company by means of the voluntarily winding up of the company and the appointment of a liquidator. After debate and discussion the resolutions were proposed and seconded, and after an amendment had been rejected, the chairman put the resolutions for the reconstruction of the company to the vote. A vote on a show of hands took place and the chairman said, 'Those in favour 6; those against 23; but there are 200 voting by proxy, and I declare the resolutions carried **7.49**

[49] *The Second Consolidated Trust Ltd v Ceylon Amalgamated Tea & Rubber Estates Ltd* [1943] 2 All ER 567 (Uthwatt J).

[50] See also Ch 12.

[51] *Byng v London Life Association Ltd* [1990] Ch 170 (CA).

[52] [1902] 2 Ch 499 (Buckley J).

as required by Act of Parliament.' The facts disclosed that no poll was taken or demanded. The declaration of the result of the vote by the chairman was not sustained by the court. In the course of his judgment Buckley J said:[53]

> It has been held that, if the chairman by his declaration affirms erroneously or without sufficiently ascertaining the facts but bonâ fide that a resolution has been carried, the Court cannot go behind that declaration. Two cases establish that proposition—namely, *In re Hadleigh Castle Gold Mines, Limited*, and *Arnot v. United African Lands, Limited*. In the latter case there was confusion at the meeting, but the Court came to the conclusion that the chairman had put the resolutions to the meeting properly and had declared them carried, and therefore declined to enter on an investigation as to what numbers voted for and against the resolutions. In the former case the meeting was a stormy one, and there was a considerable conflict of evidence as to what took place, and the Court refused to entertain the question whether the resolution was carried by the requisite majority. But those decisions do not apply to a case where the chairman by his declaration finds the figures and erroneously in point of law holds that the resolution has been duly passed. That is what the chairman has done in the present case. He had no right to count the 200 votes by proxy, and his declaration is not conclusive. If a poll had been demanded and the 200 votes had been available, other people might have given proxies, and the resolution might have been negatived. It is sufficient here for me to say that, on the face of the declaration, it is shewn that the resolution has not been passed by the majority required by the statute.

7.50 The authorities in this area show that it is very difficult to persuade a court to go behind the chairman's declaration of the result on a show of hands.[54] However, if the chairman's declaration demonstrates clearly that the requisite majority has not been obtained, his declaration that the resolution has been carried is not conclusive.[55]

The power to exclude people from the meeting

7.51 Sometimes the sphere of business that is carried on by a company, particularly a listed public company, may court controversy. Such companies can be targeted by activists who purchase a small shareholding or act as a proxy for an existing member in order to gain access to the company's general meetings. Such members have the potential to cause disruption at general meetings.

7.52 The power of the chairman to exclude persons from a meeting may be set out in the company's articles.[56] Where that is the case the power and any conditions that

---

[53] Op. cit. at 500–1.

[54] See *Arnot v United African Lands* [1901] 1 Ch 518 (CA), following *Re Hadleigh Castle Gold Mines Ltd* [1900] 2 Ch 419 (Cozens-Hardy); see also *Kerr v John Mottram Ltd* [1940] Ch 657 (Simonds J); *Re Brynmawr Coal and Iron Co* [1877] WN 45; and *Wall v London and Northern Assets Corpn* [1899] 1 Ch 550 (North J).

[55] See *Re Caratal (New) Mines Ltd* [1902] 2 Ch 498 (Buckley J). See also Ch 9.

[56] There is no such express power in the 1985 Table A.

are imposed on its exercise must be strictly observed. In the absence of such an express power the chairman has the power to request that troublemakers causing a disturbance leave the meeting. This is part of his responsibility for maintaining order at the meeting. This power must be handled with politeness, caution and great care. On no account should the power be used to stifle a frank exchange of views and fair and vigorous debate. An effective chairman may be able to placate disruptive attendees at meetings by offering such persons the opportunity to discuss their grievances at an alternative meeting or after the meeting has concluded. Where attempts to pacify disruptive attendees come to nothing such a persons should be asked to leave the meeting voluntarily. If such a person refuses to leave at the request of the chairman then it may be the case that he will have to be ejected from the meeting, but only with reasonable and minimal force. It for this purpose that large public companies often employ groups of stewards or security staff to attend their general meetings.

Challenges to the Chairman's Conduct

It is possible for members and other who have been in legitimate attendance at a general meeting to challenge in legal proceedings the conduct of the chairman after the conclusion of the meeting. Clearly, such a challenge must be done promptly and without undue delay. If a member establishes that he was disenfranchised or deprived of some other legal right in relation to the conduct of the meeting, the validity of what was resolved upon by the meeting may be impeached.[57] However, a minority shareholder who has an insufficient number of shares to prevent the passing of a particular resolution may find it very difficult to obtain any effective relief unless he can show serious prejudice to his rights as a member and the possibility that the outcome of the meeting might have been different had his rights been recognized. As stated in Chapter 12[58] the courts are very reluctant to become involved in the minutiae of the conduct of meetings and generally prefer to leave matters to the chairman's discretion provided that there is no evidence of bad faith. **7.53**

---

[57] See *Henderson v Bank of Australasia* (1890) 45 Ch D 330.

[58] See Ch 12, para 12.32.

8

PROXIES AND CORPORATE REPRESENTATIVES

Introduction

An individual shareholder may attend a company meeting either in person or by proxy. A corporation, whether a company within the meaning of CA 2006 **8.01** or otherwise,[1] may attend a meeting by its duly appointed corporate representative or by proxy. The purpose of this chapter is to examine the law on the appointment of proxies and corporate representatives and to consider the rights and powers which they possess. CA 2006 has extended the right of proxies in respect of both public and private companies. Members of public and private companies have the right to appoint more than one proxy and all lawfully appointed proxies can attend, speak and vote at general meetings both on a show of hands and on a poll.

Proxies

Appointment of proxies

8.02 A proxy is a person who is duly authorized to attend, speak and vote on behalf of a member at a general meeting. For there to be a valid appointment what is required is an instrument of proxy, which document is frequently, and confusingly, also referred to as a proxy. In the text which follows the document will be referred to as a proxy form. A duly appointed proxy is the agent for the member and the contract between them is governed by the general law of agency. That contract is only of limited interest to the company, which is more concerned with the effectiveness of any appointment, the possibility of revocation and the lodging of the proxy form in good time before the general meeting.

The form of proxy

8.03 A company's articles of association will usually regulate the form of any proxy to be used at a meeting of the company[2] (other than a court meeting convened for the purposes of considering a compromise or arrangement under CA 2006, Part 26).[3] A company whose shares are listed on the UK Stock Exchange plc must send a proxy form to its shareholders in respect of every general meeting with the notice convening the meeting. The proxy form must be of the 'two-way' sort, allowing the member to indicate whether or not he supports each resolution to be transacted except in relation to procedural resolutions. It must state that the member is entitled to appoint a proxy of his own choice and leave room for the insertion of that person's name. The form must state that if it is returned without an indication as to how the proxy is to exercise his vote on a particular matter, the proxy will exercise his discretion as to whether, and if so how, to vote.

---

[1] eg a corporation sole.

[2] See regs 60 and 61 of the 1985 Table A; see the commentary in Part 4.

[3] See Ch 14.

The basic right of appointment

There is no right at common law to appoint a proxy.[4] The entitlement of any member to make such an appointment originally depended entirely on the rules contained in the company's articles of association. However, the position has been regularized by statute since the Companies Act 1947. CA 2006, ss 324–331 (inclusive) contain a series of basic, default provisions governing the appointment of proxies, their powers and rights.[5] These provisions replace CA 1985, s 372 and make several alterations to the existing law, by extending the rights of proxies. In addition, CA 2006, s 331 makes it clear that nothing in ss 324–330 prevents a company's articles from conferring more extensive rights on members or proxies than are conferred by those sections. **8.04**

Right to appoint a proxy

Under CA 2006, s 324(1) a member of a company is entitled to appoint another person as his proxy to exercise all or any of his rights to attend and speak and vote at a meeting of the company.[6] Prior to the enactment of this provision a proxy appointed in a public company had no right to speak at the meeting except to demand or join in demanding a poll, unless the company's articles otherwise provided. However, in a public company there was a right to appoint more than one person. At the same time the proxy in a public company was not entitled to vote except on a poll unless the articles otherwise provided.[7] **8.05**

CA 2006, s 324(2) now provides that in the case of a company having a share capital, a member may appoint more than one proxy in relation to a meeting, provided that each proxy is appointed to exercise the rights attached to a different share or shares held by him. The effect of this provision is that multiple appointments of proxies are now possible in every type of company having a share capital. This is an important change in the law with regard to private companies. Under CA 1985, s 372(2)(b), unless the articles provided otherwise, a member of a private company was not entitled to appoint more than one proxy to attend on the same occasion. **8.06**

Notification of the right to appoint a proxy

By CA 2006, s 325(1), which replaces CA 1985, s 372(3) and (4) every notice convening a general meeting must contain a statement informing the members of **8.07**

---

[4] See *Harben v Phillips* (1883) 23 Ch D 14 at 22 (Chitty J).

[5] See the commentary on ss 324–331 (inclusive) in Part 3.

[6] This is a change in the law for companies which do not have a share capital. Under CA 1985, s 372(2)(a) there was no such entitlement unless the articles of association so provided.

[7] See CA 1985, s 372(1) and (2).

their rights to appoint a proxy under s 324 and of any more extensive rights conferred by the company's articles to appoint more than one proxy. The statement of the members' rights must appear '. . . with reasonable prominence . . .' in the notice of the general meeting. By CA 2006, s 352(2) and (3), failure to comply with the section does not invalidate the meeting or any business that is transacted at the meeting, but it does amount to an offence by every officer of the company who is in default. This provision is directed in particular to the company secretary and others concerned with the administration of the company.

8.08 A proxy card for the annual general meeting of a public company should include notes containing the following information:

(a) the address where the form of proxy should be deposited;
(b) the time period (not later than 48 hours) by which the form of proxy has to be lodged at the relevant address;
(c) in the case of joint holders of shares that the vote of the senior who tenders a vote will be taken to the exclusion of all others;
(d) in the case of a corporation that the proxy form should be under the common seal of the corporation or under the hand of a duly authorized officer or attorney;
(e) that if the shareholder wishes to appoint someone other than the chairman of the meeting to act as his proxy, the name and address of that other person should be inserted in the blank place provided on the form and that the reference to the chairman should be deleted and initialled;
(f) that a proxy need not be a member of the company;
(g) that a proxy can attend, speak and vote at the general meeting;
(h) that if the proxy is appointed in relation to less than the member's full voting entitlement this fact should be recorded on the form by indicating the number of shares in relation to which they are authorized to act as the member's proxy;
(i) that if more that one proxy is appointed the proxy form should be photocopied or state where additional forms can be obtained;
(j) that in the case of the appointment of multiple proxies the number of shares in relation to which each proxy is authorized;
(k) that in the case of multiple proxies all of the forms should be signed and returned in the same envelope;
(l) that the lodgement of a proxy will not preclude the member from attending the general meeting;
(m) that if the member completes the proxy form in relation to a resolution by ticking the 'vote withheld' column such a situation enables the member to instruct the proxy not to vote on a particular resolution but that such an indication will not be included in the calculation of the proportion of votes cast 'for' or 'against' a resolution.

Company-sponsored invitations to appoint proxies

CA 2006, s 326 permits a company to issue express invitations to members to appoint a proxy.[8] This is common practice in relation to meetings of companies. However, if invitations are issued to members at the company's expense to appoint as proxy a specified person or a number of specified persons (such as the chairman of the meeting) the invitations must be issued to all members entitled to vote at the meeting. This provision is designed to avoid the partial canvassing of support for the company. **8.09**

There is an exception to the rule in CA 2006, s 326(1). The rule does not apply where a form of appointment naming the proxy or a list of persons willing to act as a proxy is issued to a member at his request, and the form or list is available on request to all members entitled to vote at the meeting. **8.10**

Joint holders of shares

Shares can be registered in the name of more than one member and the issue can arise as to whether more than one registered joint shareholder can vote by proxy. This question is usually dealt with by a provision in a company's articles of association to the effect that only one of the joint shareholders may vote in person or by proxy and that the person whose name appears first in the register of members will be the person so enfranchised to the exclusion of all of the other joint holders.[9] This situation is now covered by statute in CA 2006, s 286. Subject to any provisions of a company's articles, in the case of joint holders of shares only the vote of the senior who votes, and any proxies that are duly authorized by him, may be counted by the company. The senior holder of a share is determined by the order in which the names of the joint holders appear in the company's register of members.[10] **8.11**

The effect of s 286 is that the company must accept only the proxy that has been duly authorized by the senior holder, to the exclusion of the votes of the other joint holders. Section 286(1) refers to '. . . the senior holder who votes . . .'. It would seem that this need not be the first named holder of the shares in the register of members but could be the most senior member who in fact votes, or authorizes a proxy. **8.12**

Personal representatives of a deceased member

Shares will devolve by operation of law to the legal personal representatives of a deceased shareholder. A company's articles of association will usually make provision for the enfranchisement of personal representatives.[11] Unless and until the **8.13**

---

[8] This section derives from CA 1985, s 372(6).
[9] Regulation 55, 1985 Table A is to this effect.
[10] See CA 2006, s 286(2).
[11] See reg 31, 1985 Table A.

personal representatives become registered members in respect of a deceased member's shares they have no entitlement to attend and vote at a meeting of members. Accordingly, a personal representative will not be able to sign a valid form of proxy until he has been registered as a member of the company.

Lodging of proxy forms—time limits

8.14 For reasons of efficiency companies have stipulated in their articles of association a limited time period within which a proxy form must be delivered to the company in advance of the relevant meeting. Any proxy that is lodged outside that prescribed time period has to be treated as invalid and of no effect. Indeed, it has been held by Street J in the Supreme Court of New South Wales in the decision of *Armstrong v Landmark Corp Ltd*[12] that all of the members of a company are entitled to have such invalid votes excluded from being counted when motions are placed before a meeting and each shareholder is entitled to have the provisions of the articles faithfully observed in relation to the regulation of the rights to cast votes at meetings.

8.15 The inclusion of such time limits for the lodging of proxies in company articles has led on occasion to abuse, with the result that the Companies Acts have intervened by invalidating provisions which are considered by Parliament to be over-harsh, burdensome or unreasonable to members. The current basic rules are contained in CA 2006, s 327 which replaces CA 1985, s 372(5). The new statutory provision introduces several important changes. In particular, it should be noted that the new section covers the receipt of documents in relation to polls not taken immediately as well as meetings and adjourned meetings.

8.16 CA 2006, s 327 operates by invalidating any provision in a company's articles insofar as it would have the effect of requiring an appointment of a proxy or related document to be received by the company or another person (this being a reference perhaps to the company's registrars in the case of a public company) earlier than 48 hours before the time for holding a company meeting or adjourned meeting.[13] In the case of a poll taken more than 48 hours after it was demanded the time limit must not be less than 24 hours before the time appointed for the taking of the poll.[14]

8.17 Section 327 came into force on 1 October 2007 with the exception of s 327(2)(c).[15] That subparagraph invalidates any provision in a company's articles which would require the proxy documents to be received by the company or another person

[12] (1966) 85 WN (Pt 1) NSW 238.

[13] See CA 2006, s 327(2)(a).

[14] See CA 2006, s 327(2)(b).

[15] See Third Commencement Order, para 2(1)(f). Section 327(2)(c) will not be commenced and can be ignored.

earlier than, in the case of a poll taken not more than 48 hours after it was demanded, the time at which it was so demanded. The effect of this provision would be to validate the late delivery and receipt of any proxy brought along to the meeting by a member if a poll were to be successfully demanded and directed to be taken within 48 hours of the demand, for example 24 hours later. In practice, the vast majority of polls at meetings are taken forthwith but this provision, if brought into force, would encourage a delay for up to 48 hours in order to enable late proxies to be counted in the poll. That would be most unfair to those members who had complied with the regulations. Not surprisingly, the Secretary of State has chosen to delay, if not abandon, the implementation of this provision and it has been deliberately excluded from the ambit of the Third Commencement Order.

Calculation of time periods

In calculating the time periods in CA 2006, s 327 no account must be taken of any **8.18** part of any day that is not a working day. A working day is defined in CA 2006, s 1173(1) as a day that is not a Saturday or Sunday, Christmas Day or Good Friday or any bank holiday in the part of the UK where the company is registered. The important effect of this provision is that in the case of a company meeting called for 11 am on a Tuesday after a bank holiday, proxies must be delivered and received by the company or its registrars by, at the latest, 11 am on the previous Thursday. Under CA 1985 the latest time for service of the documents would have been 11 am on the previous Sunday. It should be noted that under this provision of CA 2006, in the case of Easter, where Good Friday must be excluded as well as the bank holiday falling on Easter Monday, the latest time for receipt by the company or the registrars for a meeting starting at 11 am on the following Tuesday would be 11 am on the previous Wednesday.

Proxies in electronic form

The Companies Act 1985 (Electronic Communications) Order 2000[16] intro- **8.19** duced a statutory right for a member to serve a proxy by means of an electronic communication, notwithstanding any provision to the contrary in the company's articles. This provision was inserted in CA 1985, s 372, subss (2A), (2B) and (6A). CA 2006 contains similar provisions in s 333, which applies whenever the company has given an electronic address in the notice calling the meeting. An 'electronic address' is an address or number used for the purposes of sending or receiving documents or information by electronic means.[17] This means both an email address and a fax number. In relation to any proxy form sent by the company

---

16 SI 2000/3373.
17 See CA 2006, s 333(4). See also the commentary on this section in Part 3.

or invitation to appoint a proxy sent out by the company in relation to a meeting, the company is deemed to have agreed that any document or information relating to proxies for that meeting may be sent by electronic means to that address. The documents referred to are the appointment of a proxy, any document necessary to show the validity of the appointment and any notice of termination of the proxy.[18] This section came into force on 20 January 2007 by virtue of the First Commencement Order.[19]

8.20 Most listed companies now permit proxies to be appointed by electronic means. Where they do so the notice of general meeting and proxy form must refer to this entitlement. Such a statement will usually take the form of a note to the notice of general meeting, or to the form of proxy explaining to members how to lodge their proxy form using the internet via the company's website. The address of the website must be stated on the notice.

Limitations on CA 2006, s 333

8.21 The right to send a proxy form in by electronic means under CA 2006, s 333(1) is expressly made subject to any condition or limitation that may be specified in the notice of meeting. In order to ensure that the proxy form is valid it is customary to insist upon the proxy form and the power of attorney or other authority under which it is signed, or a copy of such authority certified notarially or in some other way that has been approved by the board, be deposited with the company (usually not less than 48 hours before the time of the general meeting). However, it is open to a company to require that any power of attorney or other authority relating to an appointment of a proxy cannot be submitted electronically but must be deposited in hard copy format for the appointment to be valid. In the absence of such an express limitation in the notice of the general meeting s 333 permits such supporting documents to be sent to the company by electronic means.

Right to inspect proxy forms that have been lodged

8.22 One practical reason for the requirement to lodge proxies within a stipulated time before the start of the meeting is in order to facilitate the voting at the meeting and the checking of the proxies against the company's register of members. Proxies invariably appoint the chairman of the meeting as the proxy and he will wish to know in advance of the meeting how many votes he has at his disposal for the purposes of the business to be transacted at the meeting.

8.23 In Australia it has been held that any director is entitled to inspect the proxy forms that have been lodged prior to a meeting, provided that this does not unreasonably

[18] See CA 2006, s 333(3).

[19] See First Commencement Order, Art 3(1)(b): SI 2006/3428.

interfere with the required preparations for the meeting.[20] The basis for this decision is that it is within the province of any director to interest himself in the question of whether the individual rights of shareholders to have the articles faithfully observed in relation to voting are being properly respected. A director therefore has the right to inspect such documents as may cast light directly upon the observance or otherwise by the company and its officers of the individual rights of shareholders.[21] It is suggested that a similar reasoning should apply in the UK to the right of a director to inspect proxy forms that have been lodged.

The right of a proxy to be elected as chairman

Subject to any contrary provision in the articles of a company, CA 2006, s 328 provides that a proxy may be elected as the chairman of the meeting by a resolution passed at the meeting itself.[22] This right was first recognized at common law by Hoffmann J in *Re Bradford Investments plc*[23] where the court had to consider articles which provided that the members present at a meeting should choose one of their number to be the chairman. The articles also provided that a proxy was entitled to vote but was not entitled to speak. Nevertheless a proxy was to be taken into account for the purposes of deciding whether there was a quorum. Hoffmann J held that it would be strange if a meeting could be quorate because two persons were present by proxy but neither of them was entitled to be the chairman. **8.24**

The right of a proxy to demand a poll

CA 2006, s 329[24] makes it clear that the appointment of a proxy to vote on a matter at a meeting authorizes the proxy to demand, or join in demanding, a poll on any matter. This provision is linked to CA 2006, s 321, which sets certain minimum standards in articles in relation to the right to demand a poll. **8.25**

Proxies appointed by more than one member

In the event that more than one member appoints the same person to act as a proxy, the appointed proxy has only one vote on a vote that is taken on a show of hands. The proxy appointed by more than one member does not have one vote for each member by whom he has been appointed.[25] **8.26**

---

[20] See *Re Coles Myer Ltd* (2002) 43 ACSR 432 (Hansen J), citing the earlier decision of Street J in *Armstrong v Landmark Corp Ltd* (1966) 85 WN (Pt 1) NSW 238.

[21] See *Armstrong v Landmark Corp Ltd* (1966) 85 WN (Pt 1) NSW 238 at 239–40.

[22] There was no equivalent statutory right in CA 1985.

[23] [1990] BCC 740 at 745C (Hoffmann J). See also Ch 7.

[24] This section derives from CA 1985, s 373(2). See the commentary on s 329 in Part 3.

[25] See CA 2006, s 284(2). Where such appointments are made the difficult question is how should that one proxy vote on a show of hands on a resolution where respective appointors have given him different instructions. Suppose member A has instructed the proxy to vote 'for' resolution 1

Duties of the proxy-holder

8.27 As a matter of law a proxy is the agent of the member. When a shareholder appoints another person to act as his proxy it is the duty of the proxy-holder to carry out the business that he has been appointed to undertake. If the duly appointed proxy cannot undertake the business that he has been asked to perform he should inform his appointor as expeditiously as possible of this fact. The proxy-holder must vote in accordance with his instructions as set out in the completed proxy form and should vote all of the proxies. Where a proxy-holder fails to comply with the instructions of his appointor he may become liable to his appointor in damages for any loss arising from the breach of contract.

How should a proxy-holder vote on an amendment to a resolution?

8.28 Where an amendment to an ordinary resolution[26] comes before a company meeting the issue arises as to how the proxy-holder should vote in relation to this issue. This is a difficult question and a definitive answer is not possible. Where the chairman of the meeting holds proxies for members he will be the agent for all of those members who have seen fit to appoint him as their proxy. A chairman in such a position should vote the proxies in the manner he considers to be in accordance with the wishes of his appointors. If time permits, for example in relation to a vote on a poll, where the chairman has been appointed as proxy for a large tranche of shares, he may be well advised to consult with his appointor. These principles necessarily apply to any proxy-holder, not merely to the chairman. A proxy-holder could vote in favour of an amendment to an ordinary resolution in circumstances where he held 'yes' proxies if the consequence of the amendment to the ordinary resolution was to strengthen the impact of the resolution on the company. However, where a proxy-holder holds 'no' proxies, voting on a proposed amendment to an ordinary resolution is more troublesome. In these circumstances it may be difficult for the holder of the proxy to discern the attitude or wishes of his appointor to the proposed amendment which may be designed to improve or clarify the proposed ordinary resolution. In such circumstances, a proxy-holder may be well advised to abstain on an amendment resolution. Of course, the correct approach will depend on the particular facts and issues arising in each situation.

8.29 If the proxy takes the form of an 'at discretion' type the proxy-holder will not be placed in this dilemma as he will be entitled to exercise his own judgment as to how to vote on any amendment resolution. Plainly, the power must exercised by the

---

but member B has instructed the proxy to vote against resolution 1. No decided case governs this invidious situation for the proxy. It is suggested that the appropriate solution is for the proxy to demand a poll so that he can register his differing votes.

[26] It is not possible to amend the substance of a special resolution: see *Re Moorgate Mercantile Holdings Ltd* [1980] 1 WLR 222 (Slade J) and Ch 11.

proxy-holder in good faith and in what he reasonably perceives to be the interests of the appointing member.

How should a proxy-holder vote on a resolution to adjourn a meeting?

Where a resolution to adjourn a meeting is put to the vote, the issue arises as to whether the proxy-holder should exercise the power to vote on behalf of the appointing member. The issue of voting on an adjournment resolution is considered in detail in Chapter 12. This issue has frequently arisen in the context of company meetings in general and, in particular, in relation to meetings that have been convened to consider schemes of arrangement under CA 1985, s 425 and its statutory predecessors, now CA 2006, s 896. **8.30**

It is clear that proxy votes may be utilized on a motion to adjourn both at a normal general meeting of a company and at a meeting convened by the court for the purposes of considering a scheme under CA 2006, s 896.[27] Once again, the duty of the proxy-holder is to ascertain, so far as is possible, how to act in accordance with the actual or perceived wishes of the appointing member. For that reason in *Re Waxed Papers Ltd*[28] the Court of Appeal held that where proxies had been lodged on behalf of members who opposed a scheme they should be tendered by the proxy in favour of a resolution to adjourn the meeting, whereas proxies that had been lodged on behalf of supporters of the scheme should be used by the proxy in voting against any resolution to adjourn the meeting. A proxy necessarily confers a power to vote on all procedural matters that are incidental or ancillary to the specified business of the meeting. The power necessarily enables the proxy to vote for or against any resolution for the adjournment of the meeting. **8.31**

Adjourned meetings and proxies

It is often the case and indeed good practice, that where a meeting is adjourned, members may be invited to lodge a further proxy for the adjourned meeting if that is more than a few days ahead. If that is not done the proxies lodged in due time for the original meeting will remain valid for use at the adjourned meeting. However, a proxy that is not lodged in good time for the original meeting cannot be used as valid for the adjourned meeting unless the wording of the relevant articles expressly admits this. **8.32**

In *McLaren v Thomson*[29] the articles of the company provided that: **8.33**

> The instrument appointing a proxy shall be deposited at the registered office of the company not less than two clear days before the day for holding the meeting at which the person named in such instrument proposes to vote.

---

27 See Ch 14.
28 [1937] 2 All E R 481 (CA).
29 [1917] 2 Ch 261 (CA).

Proxies were lodged after the date of the original meeting but more than two clear days before the day fixed for an adjournment of the original meeting. The Court of Appeal held that because the adjourned meeting was to be treated as a continuation of the original meeting, those proxies could not be used for the purpose of voting at the adjourned meeting as they had not been lodged in time for the original meeting. However, the prohibition derived from this decision will not operate if the articles expressly provide for the lodging of proxies not less than a fixed period (say 48 hours) before either the time for holding the original meeting or an adjourned meeting.[30]

Termination of a proxy—CA 2006, s 330[31]

8.34 The authority of a proxy to attend and vote at a meeting can be revoked by the appointing member before it is exercised by the proxy. Unless the company receives notice of termination of a person's authority to act as a proxy before the start of the meeting, such termination does not affect whether that person counts in deciding whether there is a quorum, the validity of anything he does as chairman or the validity of a poll demanded by him at the meeting.[32] Similar provision is made in respect of the validity of a vote given by that person unless the company receives notice of the revocation before the start of the meeting or adjourned meeting at which the vote is given or, in the case of a poll taken more than 48 hours after it is demanded, before the time appointed for the poll.[33] The statute reflects the decision of Russell J in *Spiller v Mayo (Rhodesia) Development Co (1908) Ltd*.[34]

8.35 The provisions of s 330(2) and (3) are subject to any requirement of the company's articles which has the effect of requiring notice of termination to be received earlier than specified by the statute. However, CA 2006 imposes certain basic requirements by means of s 330(6) which invalidates any provision of the company's articles which has the effect of requiring the notice of termination to be received earlier than 48 hours before the time for holding the meeting or adjourned meeting as the case may be, or, in the case of a poll taken more than 48 hours after it was demanded, earlier than 24 hours before the time fixed for taking the poll.[35]

---

30 See eg reg 69, 1948 Table A and reg 62, 1985 Table A.
31 See also the commentary on this section in Part 3.
32 See CA 2006, s 330(2); this provision is based on reg 63, 1985 Table A.
33 See CA 2006, s 330(3).
34 [1926] WN 78 (Russell J).
35 See CA 2006, s 330(6)(a) and (b).

CA 2006, s 330(6)(c)

CA 2006, s 330(6) also contains a sub-para (c) which declares to be void any provision of the company's articles which states that in relation to a poll taken not more than 48 hours after it was demanded the notice of termination of the proxy must be received earlier than the time at which the poll was demanded. Like CA 2006, s 327(2)(c) this sub-paragraph has been the subject of criticism and was omitted from the Third Commencement Order. It was not brought into operation on 1 October 2007 along with the rest of the section. It would seem unlikely that the provision will be brought into force. **8.36**

Calculation of time periods

In relation to the time periods fixed by CA 2006, s 330 for the receipt by the company of the notice of termination of any proxy, s 330(7) applies the same rule as found in s 327, dealing with the notice required of the appointment of a proxy. In calculating the time periods in CA 2006, s 330, no account must be taken of any part of any day that is not a working day. A working day is defined in s 1173(1) as a day that is not a Saturday or Sunday, Christmas Day or Good Friday or any bank holiday in the part of the UK where the company is registered. **8.37**

These new statutory provisions are clearly designed to reduce uncertainty. Their effect is to place the onus on the member revoking his proxy to give due notice to the company well before the start of the meeting. **8.38**

Revocation of a proxy by the personal attendance by the member

At common law it has been held that the attendance and voting of the member himself at a meeting constitutes a revocation of the proxy's right to vote. In *Cousins v International Brick Co*[36] a legal challenge was made to the decision of the chairman of the meeting to reject certain proxy votes on the grounds that a number of shareholders who had previously given proxies had voted personally at the meeting, although they had not given notice of revocation of their proxies. It was argued that a proxy once given for a meeting could not be revoked except by notice in writing received before the meeting within the timetable laid down by the articles. At first instance Luxmoore J held that there is no contract binding the shareholders vis-à-vis the company to exercise the option to vote either in person or by proxy at any time before the actual moment when the vote is to be given.[37] A shareholder who has lodged a proxy may still elect to exercise his right to vote in person. In those circumstances any votes tendered by the proxy must be rejected. **8.39**

---

[36] [1931] 2 Ch 90 (Luxmoore J and CA).
[37] Op. cit. at 95.

8.40 The Court of Appeal upheld this view. Lord Hanworth MR concluded that on the construction of an article which stated that 'votes may be given in person or by proxy' the personal right to vote of the member was not taken away by the appointment of a proxy. The shareholders were entitled to attend and give their own votes at the meeting and the proxy had no right to prevent it.[38] Lawrence LJ stated that every proxy is subject to an implied condition that it should only be used if the shareholder is unable or finds it inconvenient to attend the meeting. The proxy is merely the agent of the shareholder and is not entitled to act contrary to the instructions of the latter. Romer LJ considered that when a shareholder appoints a proxy but himself attends the meeting and says he prefers to vote in person, he is not revoking the proxy but doing an act which does away with the necessity of the proxy ever being exercised at all.[39]

The right to speak

8.41 The decision in *Cousins v International Brick Co* does not cover the right of a member to speak at a meeting in circumstances where the member, who has appointed a proxy to attend a meeting on his behalf, later decides to attend that meeting in person. It is suggested that where a member attends a meeting in addition to his duly appointed proxy and asserts his right as a member to address the meeting a similar principle should be applied. Where the member has exercised his right to attend and speak, the proxy's right to speak should be treated as abrogated. If this is not the case, the member will in fact exercise more than one right to speak on a given issue.

8.42 Under CA 2006, s 324(1) a member may appoint another person as his proxy to exercise all or any of his rights to attend and to speak and vote at a meeting. Support for the application of the principle in *Cousins v International Brick Co* is to be derived from the use in the section of the phrase '. . . to speak and vote. . .'. Under the statute the two actions are indivisible and therefore the principle in *Cousins v International Brick Co* should apply to both.

8.43 If the proxy is the person who speaks first, different considerations may apply as at this stage the member will not have exercised his own right to speak. It is of course a serious matter to deprive a member of his right to speak at a meeting, but if a member rises to speak after the proxy has spoken and the proxy had been appointed in respect of the member's entire holding, it would surely be a matter for the chairman's discretion as to whether the member should be permitted to speak in addition to his proxy. The chairman would be entitled to disallow the member from speaking in these circumstances provided that he acted in good

[38] Op. cit. at 101.
[39] Op. cit. at 103.

faith and in what he considered to be the best interests of the meeting. Although the matter is far from clear, it is suggested that the chairman's discretion to deny the member the right to address the meeting would not arise if the proxy had been appointed in respect of part only of the member's shareholding.

The effect of multiple proxies

CA 2006, s 324 empowers the member to appoint more than one proxy for a meeting provided that each proxy represents a different share. The effects of multiple appointments of proxies will further complicate this issue. When several proxies appointed by the same member in respect of different shares are present at a meeting, it would seem that each has the separate right to speak and later to vote in respect of his particular tranche of shares, unless the member himself has already spoken. In those circumstances it would be open to the chairman of the meeting to decline to hear from a proxy as well as from the member. **8.44**

Revocation by the death of the member

Articles usually provide that the death of the appointing member will revoke the proxy if notice of such death has reached the company before the start of the meeting or adjourned meeting at which the proxy is to be used.[40] If no notice has been received by the company any vote given subsequent to the death of the appointing member will be valid. Where, as is sometimes the case, there is a rumour as to the death of a member but no certainty, the company secretary should take immediate steps to investigate the truth of the rumour, as it is potentially embarrassing for the chairman to have to question a proxy-holder at the meeting as to the possible demise of the appointing member. Where such investigations do not confirm the accuracy of the rumour, it is suggested that the vote of the proxy should be admitted. **8.45**

The same rule applies to any poll demanded by a proxy. Such a demand will be valid notwithstanding the death of the appointing member unless notice of the determination of authority was received by the company before the start of the meeting or adjourned meeting at which the poll was demanded or, in the case of a poll taken later than that day, the time fixed for taking the poll.[41] **8.46**

Proxies appointed by a corporate member

There is no reason why a company which is a shareholder of another company cannot appoint a proxy in the same way as other members. Such a proxy must be lodged in accordance with the articles and the holder of the proxy will enjoy the **8.47**

40 See eg reg 73, 1948 Table A.
41 See reg 63, 1985 Table A.

same rights as the proxies appointed by any other member. There is a clear legal distinction between such a proxy appointed by a company and a company's corporate representative. The rights of a corporate representative are examined below.

Irregularity in proxy forms

8.48 One of the most difficult tasks facing a company chairman may arise in relation to questions concerning the validity of proxies. The member completing the proxy form must ensure that he complies with the strict requirements of the form as set out in the articles. If such requirements are not met, the proxy form may be the subject of a challenge and be invalidated. This issue is discussed in detail in Chapter 9.

8.49 A minor but obvious error or misprint in the proxy form may not entitle the company to reject the proxy, for example describing an extraordinary general meeting as an annual general meeting when the facts show that there is only one meeting taking place. In *Oliver v Dalgleish*[42] Buckley J was faced with a challenge based on such a misdescription of the meeting recorded on several proxies, although the date of the meeting was accurately stated. When the proxies were shown to the chairman by the scrutineers he ruled that the votes were all invalid. The proxies were in the form set out in reg 70 of the 1948 Table A (which was repeated in reg 60 of the 1985 Table A). Buckley J held that an article requiring a proxy to be in that form could not mean that if there was some misprint or quite innocuous error in the document it had to be treated as invalid. A palpable or obvious error on the face of the document did not entitle the company to refuse to accept the proxy.

Corporate Representatives

The appointment of a corporate representative

8.50 CA 2006, s 323 deals with the representation of corporate shareholders at general meetings. Shares, particularly those held by institutional investors may be registered in the names of nominee companies. If a corporation is a member of a company it may by resolution of its directors or other governing body authorize a person or persons to act as its representative or representatives at any meeting of the company. The rights that are conferred by s 323 cannot be negated by provisions

42 [1963] 1 WLR 1274 (Buckley J).

in a company's articles. CA 2006 does not provide in express terms that more extensive rights may be conferred by a company's articles.[43]

The ability to appoint a corporate representative may prove useful where the timetable for appointing a proxy has expired, or where the corporate investor has changed its mind in relation to voting on a particular issue or where intervening circumstances need to be addressed at a general meeting. **8.51**

This new section replaces CA 1985, s 375 and is somewhat wider in its terms. By the use of the plural it makes it clear that a corporate shareholder may appoint more than one representative for a general meeting. In that sense the situation is now analogous with the appointment of more than one proxy under CA 2006, s 324. **8.52**

One corporate representative

Where only one representative is appointed he is entitled by CA 2006, s 323(2) to exercise the same rights on behalf of his appointor as the corporation could exercise if it were an individual member of the company. The corporate representative may therefore attend, speak and vote at any general or class meeting of a company, may demand a poll or join in such a demand, question the directors or the chairman and generally act as if he were an individual member. **8.53**

A corporate representative must also be counted as if he were a member for the purposes of meeting the quorum requirements contained in the company's articles. This principle was established by the decision of Astbury J in *Re Kelantin Coco Nut Estates Limited*[44] where the company's articles stated that 'two members personally present shall be a quorum'. The two persons present at a meeting were one individual shareholder and one corporate representative appointed[45] to represent Eastern Development Corporation Ltd, which was a shareholder in the company. The meeting was held to be duly constituted for the purposes of passing a special resolution to reduce the share capital of the company. **8.54**

More than one corporate representative

Having granted the right to a corporate member to appoint more than one representative the section has had to tackle the practical impact of such an appointment. CA 2006, s 323(3) provides that where more than one is appointed, any one of them is entitled to exercise the same powers on behalf of the corporation as it could have exercised if it were an individual member. However, problems **8.55**

---

[43] Compare with CA 2006, s 331 in relation to proxies, which states that more extensive rights may be included in the articles.

[44] [1920] WN 274 (Astbury J).

[45] The appointment was made under the Companies (Consolidation) Act 1908, s 68.

will arise if all the representatives do not agree on the strategy to follow at the meeting.

8.56 Under CA 2006, s 323(4) if the representatives do not purport to exercise a power in the same way, the power is to be treated as not exercised. This means that if there is a disagreement about how votes should be exercised among several corporate representatives, including abstention from voting, none of the votes of that corporate member should be accepted by the company. This may give rise to practical problems for a company. Unless there is a form of internal poll before the meeting the chairman will not know whether there has been a disagreement among the several corporate representatives. This may lead to confusion. However, CA 2006, s 323 is declaratory of the law and cannot be abrogated or overridden by the company's articles.

8.57 As discussed in the Commentary on Part 3 in relation to CA 2006, s 323(4)(b) there has been a considerable difference of opinion as to the correct interpretation of this section. It has been common practice for many years for separate corporate representatives to be appointed by financial institutions, thereby treating each beneficial owner as though he were a separate shareholder. Section 323(4)(b) renders this practice ineffective if there is a difference of view between the corporate representatives as to how votes should be exercised on a particular resolution. The practical solution to this problem is for the financial institution to appoint proxies for differing blocks of shares wherever this is practical.

'Designated corporate representative'

8.58 The Commentary in Part 3 on CA 2006, s 323 discusses in detail an alternative procedure that has been recommended[46] as a solution to the problem of multiple corporate representatives with different voting intentions. That is for the chairman of the general meeting to put in place arrangements for him to be appointed as the corporate representative of a corporate shareholder with instructions to vote on a poll in accordance with the directions of all of the other corporate representatives for that corporate shareholder at the meeting. Alternatively, the designated corporate representative may be nominated from among the multiple corporate representatives of that corporate shareholder who attend the general meeting. That nominated person will then vote on a poll in accordance with the voting directions given to him in his capacity as the designated corporate representative.

[46] See ICSA: Guidance on Proxies and Corporate Representatives at General Meetings (January 2008): This document contains a specimen form of representation letter if the chairman is to be appointed as the designated corporate representative.

Proof of appointment

The company's articles will usually include requirements for proving the representative's appointment on behalf of the corporate member. Invariably, the articles will require a copy of the appointing resolution to be brought to the meeting. However, the right to vote and otherwise participate at the meeting as if the corporation was an individual member depends not on the quality of the proof, but on the actual passing of the appropriate valid resolution by the board or other governing body of the appointing corporation.[47] Accordingly, a vote given by the representative of a company under a resolution passed in accordance with s 323 can properly be admitted by the chairman on the evidence afforded by a copy of such resolution. **8.59**

It has even been known for a resolution proffered at a general meeting as proof of authority to be forged. In *Ting v Borrelli*[48] proxies were lodged in good time on behalf of two corporate shareholders but they were rejected by the chairman before the meeting commenced because they did not comply with the authentication requirements imposed by the court for what was a meeting to consider a scheme of arrangement. The proxies were merely signed on behalf of the two corporate shareholders, contrary to the printed directions on the proxy forms that they had either to be executed by the corporate shareholder under its common seal or 'under the hand of an officer or attorney duly authorized'. Subsequently, during the course of the meeting, board resolutions of the two corporate shareholders, dated the same day as the proxies, were delivered to the meeting bearing the signature of the chairman of the board of each shareholder company. The resolutions were an attempt to validate the proxies. In the subsequent legal proceedings, after hearing the evidence of a handwriting expert, the Supreme Court of Bermuda held on the facts that the signatures on the two resolutions were forgeries in that they were not executed by the chairman of the two corporate shareholders but were done by someone else imitating his handwriting with intent to deceive people into believing that they were genuine signatures. The chairman of the meeting had therefore acted correctly in refusing to admit the votes of these two shareholders at the scheme meeting. Fortunately, incidents of this nature are extremely rare in practice. **8.60**

---

47 See *Colonial Gold Reef Ltd v Free State Rand Ltd* [1914] 1 Ch 382.
48 [2007] Bda LR 73, Supreme Court of Bermuda (Ground CJ).

9

VOTING

Introduction

This purpose of this chapter is to examine the right of a member to vote at general meetings of a company. When a general meeting of a company has been duly convened and proceeds to transact the business contained in the notice, enfranchised members of the company will be required to vote on the particular resolutions. There are two basic methods by which votes may be cast by members at a general meeting. A vote at a general meeting may be taken on a show of hands, or alternatively, **9.01** a vote may be conducted by means of a poll. These two well-known methods of voting in relation to companies will be considered in this chapter.

9.02 The voting rights attached to shares are contained in the company's articles of association which form part of the company's constitution. CA 1985 contained a default provision to the effect that, in the rare event that the articles did not make any alternative provision, in the case of a company originally having a share capital every member has one vote in respect of each share or each £10 of stock held by him, and in any other case every member has one vote.[1] This provision is reproduced in CA 2006, s 284(3) (in relation to a vote on a resolution on a poll taken at a meeting) and s 284(1) (in relation to a vote on a written resolution).[2]

9.03 However, it is almost unheard of for articles of association to fail to set out the voting rights attached to the shares of various classes. For example, reg 54 of the 1985 Table A provides as follows:

> Subject to any rights or restrictions attached to any shares, on a show of hands every member who (being an individual) is present in person or (being a corporation) is present by a duly authorised representative, not being himself a member entitled to vote, shall have one vote and on a poll every member shall have one vote for every share of which he is the holder.[3]

9.04 A company's articles are supplemented by the provisions of CA 2006, Part 13 dealing with voting rights. The new statutory provisions re-state the law in relation to voting on a show of hands, voting on a poll, the appointment of proxies and corporate representatives. The law relating to the appointment of proxies and corporate representatives is dealt with in Chapter 8 to which reference should be made.

9.05 As will be seen, safeguarding the right of members to vote at a general meeting is one of the most important functions of the chairman of the meeting. All members must be given a fair opportunity to exercise their votes, following which the chairman will declare the result of the vote.

Voting on a Show of Hands

9.06 A vote that is conducted on a show of hands is the oldest and simplest form of voting at a meeting. On a vote by show of hands on any resolution the chairman will ask those persons present to raise a hand in favour of resolution. Once those hands

---

[1] See CA 1985, s 370(6).

[2] See also the commentary on these sections in Part 3. The written resolution procedure in Chapter 13, Part 2 (ss 288–300) applies only to private companies. See further Ch 15. A resolution of the members or a class of members of a public company must be passed at a meeting—see CA 2006, s 281(2).

[3] See the commentary on reg 54 in Part 4.

have been counted he will request those opposing the resolution to raise a hand and those votes will then be counted. If there is a very large number of persons present at the meeting and counting the hands is a formidable task, the chairman will be entitled to ask another person present, usually the secretary or another board member, to help him count the votes. When the counting has been completed the chairman will declare the result.

In *Ernest v Loma Gold Mines Limited*[4] Chitty J described the operation of a show of hands in the following terms: **9.07**

> What is the essence of voting by a show of hands? It is that the hands—one hand for every member present—are held up, the number of hands counted for the resolution, and the number of hands counted against, and the one subtracted from the other. In that way there is the decision by a show of hands. It is the eye that is called upon to decide when this method is resorted to, with the simple process of making a calculation of the result.

CA 2006, s 320 intervenes at this stage and sets out certain legal presumptions based upon the decision by a show of hands. First, a declaration by the chairman that the resolution has or has not been passed or has been passed with a particular majority is conclusive evidence of that fact. There is no need for proof of the number or proportion of the votes recorded in favour or against the resolution.[5] **9.08**

CA 2006, s 320 also states that the entry of such a declaration in the minutes of the meeting, recorded in accordance with CA 2006, s 355, is also conclusive evidence of the outcome of the vote without any further proof required. Section 355 requires the company to keep records comprising the minutes of its meeting for a period of at least 10 years from the date of the resolution or meeting.[6] However, s 320 does not apply where a poll has been demanded and not withdrawn. Accordingly, if a demand for a poll is made but is withdrawn the chairman's declaration of the result will be conclusive. **9.09**

CA 2006, s 284(2) and the problem of multiple proxies

CA 2006, s 284(2) also contains certain new general rules governing the holding of a vote by means of a show of hands. The section provides that on a vote by show of hands at a meeting every member present in person has one vote and every proxy present who has been duly appointed by a member entitled to vote on the resolution has one vote. [7] This seemingly innocuous provision does however give rise to a variety of problems. The reason for this is that CA 2006, s 324(2) permits **9.10**

4 See the first instance judgment of Chitty J at [1896] 2 Ch 572.
5 See CA 2006, s 320(1).
6 See Ch 16.
7 See CA 2006, s 284(2)(b).

a member to appoint more than one proxy to attend a general meeting on his behalf and therefore to vote on a show of hands.

9.11 CA 2006, s 324(1) provides that a member of a company is entitled to appoint another person as his proxy to exercise all or any of his rights to attend and vote at a meeting of the company. Section 324(2) extends that right in the case of a company having a share capital to the appointment by a member of multiple proxies. The section merely requires that each proxy is appointed to exercise the rights attached to a different share or shares held by that member, or to a different £10 or multiple of £10, of stock held by him.

9.12 The combined effect of ss 284(2)(b) and 324 is that at a vote on a show of hands at a general meeting a single member who has appointed more than one proxy can exercise multiple votes, as each proxy will have a separate vote. It may perhaps be doubted that this was the intention of the draftsman of the section but there is no reasonable alternative construction that may be applied to the section. The only saving grace for companies, and in particular large public companies, is that the provisions of s 284 take effect subject to any provision in the company's articles of association. The need for an article avoiding such a potentially absurd outcome is obvious.

CA 2006, s 285(1): specific requirements

9.13 The impact of s 284(2)(b) is made even more extraordinary by CA 2006, s 285(1) which invalidates any provision in a company's articles which would provide that a proxy has fewer votes on a resolution on a show of hands taken at a meeting than the member himself would have had if he were present in person. Such a provision in a company's articles must be extremely rare. In such a case the proxy must have the same number of votes as the member present would have had. Section 285(2) states that where, in a company with articles of this nature, a member entitled to vote on a resolution has appointed more than one proxy, subs (1) applies as if the references to the proxy were references to the proxies taken together.

9.14 The effect of this wording is that only if a company's articles of association contain the rare type of article caught by s 285(1) must the votes cast by the proxies on a show of hands be treated as the one vote of the individual member. It is to be noted that s 285(2) does not apply generally but only where the special type of article is to be found. In any other case, absent a specific restriction in the company's articles, the votes of multiple proxies must be counted on a show of hands, even though the member present in person will only have a single vote. This part of the new legislation makes little sense and requires urgent review.

One human being—one vote on a show of hands

9.15 More generally, it should be noted that on a show of hands each human being present has one vote and no more. This common law rule applies both to members and to their proxies. In *Ernst v Loma Gold Mines*[8] the Court of Appeal expressly rejected the argument that on a show of hands a proxy representing more than one member could be counted for each member that he represented. Lindley LJ held that absent members who vote by one and the same proxy when no poll is demanded, vote not separately, as if they were individually present, but as an aggregate. Their proxy is entitled to only one vote, however many members he represents. The Court held that to suggest that on a show of hands a proxy has more than one vote would be to introduce a mode of voting never heard of in practice and not recognized by law.

Advantages of a vote taken on a show of hands

The advantages of conducting a vote at a general meeting by means of a vote that is taken on a show of hands include: **9.16**

(1) the vote is taken relatively quickly;
(2) the outcome of the vote can be ascertained without undue delay;
(3) the company is not put to the expense and delay that may be associated with a vote that is taken on a poll;
(4) the administration of the general meeting is not made unduly complicated;
(5) members who are present in person or by proxy at the general meeting actively participate in the decision-making process.

In the context of a company with a large number of enfranchised members some of the perceived advantages of voting at a general meeting on a show of hands that are listed above may be less apparent. It would be unwise for those involved in the administration of a general meeting to assume that voting on a resolution will always be conducted by way of a vote taken on a show of hands. Adequate measures should always be put in place before the meeting to be able to deal with a demand for a vote to be taken on a poll. **9.17**

Disadvantages to a vote taken on a show of hands

There are some disadvantages to the taking of a vote on a show of hands. These include: **9.18**

(1) a shareholder with a substantial number of shares will not be able to reflect the true extent of his voting power;
(2) a group of 'activist' shareholders with relatively small numbers of voting shares may be able to have a disproportionate influence on the outcome of a vote;

[8] [1897] 1 Ch 1 (CA).

(3) poor attendance at general meetings by enfranchised shareholders gives those who attend and vote on a show of hands an inconsistent degree of power over the affairs of the company;
(4) the result of voting by such a method is more random and uncertain.

It is for these reasons that the leading financial institutions in the UK always prefer that any resolution of any significance that is proposed at a general meeting of a public company is decided upon by a poll.

Voting on a Poll

9.19 Owing to the fact that the proportion of members who attend in person at general meetings is very low, voting by show of hands is frequently regarded as unsatisfactory. For this reason it has been common practice for articles of association to permit voting by means of a poll. A poll is a vote in writing with the precise number of votes exercised being recorded on a piece of paper. A poll is not a new meeting but a method of ascertaining the sense of the meeting, which is continued for that purpose.[9]

9.20 A company's articles of association determine the number of votes permitted for each member on a poll, how votes may be cast on a poll, who may demand or join in a demand for a poll, and when and how a poll should be taken. A company's articles of association may also specify certain issues where a poll must be taken immediately.

Advantages of voting by means of a poll

9.21 When resolutions at a general meeting are voted on by means of a vote taken on a poll, the result of voting is extremely precise in the sense that it will show exactly how many shares were voted in favour of or against the particular proposal. A shareholder who had a substantial block of shares will be able to use the entirety of that shareholding and can vote in a manner that is directly proportionate to the number of shares he holds in the company. A poll also avoids any risk of a resolution falling foul of some of the technical problems concerning voting that have arisen as the result of the introduction of CA 2006.[10]

Disadvantages of voting on a poll

9.22 The main disadvantages to a vote on a resolution being conducted by means of a vote on a poll are that more time will usually be taken to determine the outcome of a vote and that the administration of the general meeting may become more

---

[9] See *R v Wimbledon Local Board* (1882) 8 QBD 459 at 464 (Brett LJ) and 465 (Cotton LJ).

[10] See paras 9.10–9.12 above; Ch 11 at paras 11.11–11.12 and the commentary relating to reg 50 of the 1985 Table A in Part 4.

complex and costly. In the case of a company with a vast number of shareholders there may be a significant period of delay in calculating the result of a vote that has been taken on a poll.

However, some large public companies in the UK have in recent times adopted a form of electronic voting at meetings, using hand-held electronic voting devices. Each shareholder or proxy present at the meeting is presented on arrival at registration with one of these devices, into which is inserted a plastic card containing details of their name and the number of shares held or represented by them. When a poll is announced during the course of the meeting the chairman invites those members in favour of the resolution to press 'button 1', those against to press 'button 2' and those wishing neither to support nor oppose the resolution to press 'button 3'. Within a very short time the results of the voting on the poll are then displayed on a screen above the platform, with details of the percentages in favour or against the proposed resolution. This system, which makes use of the most up-to-date technology is much to be preferred over the traditional methods of voting on a poll. However, precautions must be taken in case the system fails and it is necessary to conduct a vote on a poll by the traditional methods. **9.23**

Preparations for a poll

As members have a right to demand a poll, those concerned in the administration of a general meeting must be prepared for such a demand so that if such a demand is made at a general meeting the conduct of the poll can be as efficient as possible. In order to be prepared for a vote on a poll consideration should be given to issues such as: **9.24**

(1) checking the articles of association for any relevant provisions in relation to the conduct of a vote on a poll;
(2) making provision in the chairman's script for voting on a poll;
(3) ensuring that a suitable form of poll card is available;
(4) deciding how poll cards are to be distributed to members;
(5) deciding how poll cards are to be collected from members once they have cast their votes;
(6) deciding who is to be responsible for the counting of votes;
(7) deciding how the result of the vote on the poll is to be announced.

A company may decide to have votes on all resolutions that are proposed at a general meeting determined by way of a vote on a poll. This is the preferred policy of many of the UK's major institutions. However, such a policy may serve to operate as yet another disincentive for shareholders with small numbers of shares to attend general meetings. In these circumstances it may be prudent to inform shareholders of the company's intention prior to the general meeting so as to avoid **9.25** complaints from members who hold only a few shares and who may prefer to vote by way of a show of hands.

9.26 A member who is entitled on a poll to more than one vote need not use all of his votes in the same way on the poll.[11] This provision enables an institutional shareholder representing many account holders to reflect the differences of view that may exist amongst the underlying beneficial holders.

The right to demand a poll

9.27 In order to facilitate the holding of a poll the legislation has prescribed minimum standards as to the right to demand a poll. These are now to be found in CA 2006, s 321 which is derived from CA 1985, s 373.

9.28 Section 321(2) provides that any provision in a company's articles is void insofar as it would have the effect of 'making ineffective' a demand for a poll which is made in three specified cases. First, a demand made by not less than five members who have the right to vote on the resolution. Secondly, a demand made by a member or members representing not less than 10% of the total voting rights of all enfranchised members (excluding any voting rights to shares held as treasury shares). Thirdly, a demand made by a member or members holding shares conferring a right to vote on the resolution which comprise 10% of the total paid up share capital conferring the right to vote (again, excluding shares which are held as treasury shares).

9.29 It is frequently the case that articles of association contain more generous provisions for demanding a poll than those that are described above. For example reg 46 of the 1985 Table A provides that a poll may be demanded:

(a) by the chairman; or
(b) by at least two members having the right to vote at the meeting; or
(c) by a member or members representing not less than 10% of the total voting rights; or
(d) by a member holding shares conferring the right to vote on which there has been paid up 10% of the total sum paid up on all shares conferring that right.

9.30 By CA 2006, s 329(1) the appointment of a proxy to vote on a matter at a general meeting authorizes the proxy to demand a poll, or to join in a demand for a poll. The demand for a poll by a proxy is equivalent to the demand for a poll by a member for the purposes of CA 2006, s 321(2).[12]

[11] See CA 2006, s 322.
[12] See generally CA 2006, s 329(2). See the commentary on this section in Part 3.

Restrictions on taking a poll

From time to time articles of association have attempted to exclude the right to demand a poll. By virtue of CA 2006, s 321(1) articles may exclude the right to a poll on two specified matters, namely, the election of the chairman of a meeting or on the adjournment of the general meeting. Such a provision is designed to facilitate the commencement of the meeting and the efficient and orderly transaction of business. The taking of a poll may sometimes lead to a period of some considerable delay. **9.31**

By CA 2006, s 321(1) any attempt by a company to exclude the right to demand a poll on any question other than the election of the chairman or the adjournment of the general meeting is void and of no effect. **9.32**

When can a poll be demanded?

A poll can be demanded at any time during the course of a general meeting. It is often the case that the articles of association of a company provide for matters including resolutions to be decided first on a show of hands, unless a poll is duly demanded before the declaration of the result by the chairman.[13] In such circumstances, a poll can be seen to be an alternative and more formal method of voting on resolutions at general meetings. **9.33**

As a practical matter, if a member desires to have a poll he should make his request to the chairman of the meeting in a prompt manner in order to prevent the completion of an effective vote by a show of hands. **9.34**

The withdrawal of a demand for a poll

Articles of association invariably contain provisions regulating the withdrawal of a demand for a poll.[14] Sometimes the demand for a poll may only be withdrawn with the consent of the chairman, and a demand so withdrawn is said not to have invalidated the result of a vote on a show of hands declared before the demand was made. **9.35**

A poll demanded by the chairman

The articles of association commonly provide that the chairman of the meeting has authority himself to demand a poll.[15] The chairman may exercise this power where he considers that a poll will be the best method of determining the sense of the meeting, including the views of members who have voted by proxy. The power to order a poll is vested in the chairman for the purposes of enabling him to carry out his fiduciary duties as chairman of the general meeting and the power must **9.36**

---

13 See reg 46 of 1985 Table A. See also Ch 7.
14 See reg 48, 1985 Table A.
15 See reg 46, 1985 Table A.

not be used in order for the chairman or the board to procure some advantage. It must therefore be exercised in good faith in what he genuinely considers to be the interests of the company.[16]

9.37 In an appropriate case the chairman is under a positive duty himself to demand a poll and then order the poll to take place in accordance with the articles.[17] The decision of Uthwatt J in *The Second Consolidated Trust Ltd v Ceylon Amalgamated Tea & Rubber Estates Ltd*[18] is authority for the proposition that it is improper for a chairman to refuse to demand a poll in circumstances where he knows that the outcome of the poll will differ from a vote on a show of hands.

The mode and timing of taking the poll

9.38 The articles will determine the manner and timing of taking the poll. They will invariably stipulate that the poll shall be conducted in such manner and at such time and place as the chairman directs.[19] Again, this is a fiduciary power, to be exercised by the chairman in good faith and in the interests of the company. A voting method beyond the scope of the articles will not be permitted even though it has been directed by the chairman.[20]

9.39 Voting on a poll will often be in writing but electronic voting is now possible.[21] The number of votes cast by each shareholder should be recorded in writing or on computer. The outcome of the poll and how members cast their votes has been held not to be confidential, and may be disclosed for the purpose of checking the validity of the voting.[22]

9.40 Timing of a poll that has been duly demanded is a matter for the chairman's discretion unless the articles otherwise provide. For example, reg 51 of the 1985 Table A requires a poll demanded on the election of a chairman or on a question of adjournment to be taken forthwith. Any other poll may be taken either forthwith, or at a later time during the same day or at a later date being not more than 30 days after the poll is demanded. There are no legislative restrictions on timing.

---

16 See *The Second Consolidated Trust Ltd v Ceylon Amalgamated Tea & Rubber Estates Ltd* [1943] 2 All ER 567 at 569 (Uthwatt J).

17 See also Ch 7.

18 [1943] 2 All ER 567 at 569H–570A.

19 See reg 49, 1985 Table A.

20 See *Mcmillan v Le Roi Mining Company Limited* [1906] 1 Ch 331 (Joyce J).

21 See para 9.23 above.

22 See *Haarhaus & Co GmbH v Law Debenture Trust Corporation plc* [1988] BCLC 640 (Hirst J). This is a decision concerning a poll vote of noteholders governed by the terms of a trust deed.

The appointment of scrutineers

Articles of association, in particular those of a public company, frequently entitle the chairman to appoint scrutineers to assist in ascertaining the result of a vote taken on a poll.[23] CA 2006, ss 342–351 contain new statutory provisions applicable to quoted companies where an independent report is required on a poll. **9.41**

CA 2006, ss 342–351—independent report on a poll

CA 2006 confers on the members of a quoted company (only) the right to require the directors to obtain an independent report on any poll that has been taken or is to be taken at a general meeting of the company. The purpose of these new provisions is to ensure that voting on a poll is conducted properly and regularly and that the outcome of the vote on the poll is capable of independent verification.[24] There follows a summary of the effect of these new provisions. Reference should also be made to the detailed commentary on these statutory provisions in Part 3 below. **9.42**

The threshold for making a request

The right conferred by CA 2006, s 342 may be exercised only if the directors receive requests from either members representing not less than 5% of the total voting rights of all the members entitled to vote on the resolution to which the poll relates, or a request from not less than 100 members who have a right to vote and who hold shares in the company on which there has been paid up an average sum of not less than £100. By virtue of s 342(3) where a request relates to more than one vote taken on a poll the threshold requirement relating to the requests must be satisfied in relation to each poll. **9.43**

Timing of the request

Any request made by members must be made promptly as such a request must be received by the company not later than one week after the date on which the poll has been taken.[25] **9.44**

Form of the request

The request for an independent report may be made in hard copy or electronic form. It must identify the poll or polls to which it relates. In addition, it must be authenticated by the person or persons making the request within the meaning of CA 2006, s 1146. Under that section a request made in hard copy form must be signed by the person sending or supplying it. Where the request is made electronically **9.45**

---

[23] See reg 49,1985 Table A.
[24] See CA 2006, s 342.
[25] See CA 2006, s 342(4)(d).

it is sufficiently authenticated if the identity of the sender is confirmed in a manner specified by the company or, in the absence of any such rule, if the communication contains or is accompanied by a statement of the identity of the sender and, further, that the company has no reason to doubt the truth of that statement.

Appointment

9.46 When the board is faced with a request for an independent report on a poll the directors are required by s 343 to appoint 'a person they consider to be appropriate' to prepare a report for the company. This appointment must be made within one week after the company is requested to make the report. The person appointed must meet the requirements of independence set out in CA 2006, s 344.

Requirement of independence

9.47 The requirements of independence set out in s 344 are extensive and are elaborated in s 345 to incorporate a wide class of persons defined as 'associates' for the purposes of s 344. The effect of a partnership is dealt with in s 346. Most importantly, a person cannot be appointed an independent assessor under these provisions if he is an officer or employee of the company, the partner or employee of such a person or a partnership of which such a person is a partner. These restrictions extend to officers or employees of a parent or subsidiary undertaking of the company.[26] However, the company's auditor is not regarded as either an officer or employee for the purposes of s 344.[27]

The assessor's report

9.48 The report of the independent assessor is governed by the provisions of s 347. The report is required to state the opinion of the assessor as to whether the procedures adopted in connection with the poll were adequate, whether the votes cast (including proxies) were fairly and accurately recorded, whether the validity of members' appointments of proxies were fairly assessed, and whether the notice of meeting complied with ss 325 and 326. The report must contain reasons for the opinions reached. Where he is unable to form an opinion on any of the stipulated matters the report must record that fact and give reasons. The report must of course name the independent assessor.

---

[26] See CA 2006, s 344(1)(b) and (3).

[27] See CA 2006, s 344(2).

Assessor's right to attend meetings

The new legislation envisages that an independent assessor may be appointed even before the meeting takes place. By s 348(1) the assessor is entitled to attend the meeting at which the poll may be taken and any subsequent proceedings in connection with the poll. 9.49

Assessor's right to information

By s 349 the assessor is entitled to access to the company's records relating to the poll and in relation to the relevant meeting. He has a right to require information from directors, the secretary, employees of the company, anyone holding or accountable for the records (such as a registrar), a member or any company agent, including a banker or solicitor. The section does not make it clear how the independent assessor is to obtain this information from the identified persons. 9.50

Information to be made available on the website

CA 2006, s 351 requires the company to make available on a website the fact of the appointment of the independent assessor, his identity, the text of the relevant resolution or a description of the subject matter of the poll and a copy of the assessor's report. The website used for this purpose must meet the requirements of s 353.[28] 9.51

Class meetings

The new statutory provisions for the appointment of an independent assessor also cover meetings of the holders of a class of shares in a quoted company in connection with a variation or abrogation of the rights attached to that class. This is provided for in CA 2006, s 352, which applies ss 341–351 with any necessary modifications. In the result it will be possible for members, provided they meet the minimum threshold, to request the company to appoint an independent assessor of a poll at a class meeting and the results of that poll must be available on the website in accordance with s 341. 9.52

Announcing the results of a poll

Where a poll is taken forthwith the result of the poll will be announced by the chairman at the meeting. The result of the poll is deemed to be the resolution of the meeting at which the resolution is demanded. Where a poll is taken subsequent to the meeting the same rule will apply but it will be necessary for the company to notify members of the outcome. CA 2006 is silent as to how 9.53

[28] See CA 2006, s 351(2).

the company should so notify its members, with the exception of quoted companies.

CA 2006, s 341—results to be made available on a website

9.54 In the case of a quoted company, s 341 imposes a new statutory requirement that the results of the poll be made available on the company's website. By virtue of s 353(2) that website must be maintained by or on behalf of the company and must identify the company. The information relating to the poll must be made available as soon as reasonably practicable, and kept available for a period of the next two years. Access to the information on the website and the ability to obtain a hard copy of the information must not be conditional on the payment of a fee or otherwise restricted.

9.55 The information that is required by CA 2006, s 341(1) to be disclosed on the website comprises:

(1) the date of the meeting;
(2) the text of the resolution or a description of the subject matter of the poll;
(3) the number of votes that are cast in favour;
(4) the number of votes that are cast against.

9.56 The failure of a company to comply with the requirements of CA 2006, ss 341 and 353 does not affect the validity of the poll or the resolution or other business to which the poll related. Sections 341 and 353 came into force on 1 October 2007 by Article 2 of the Third Commencement Order.[29]

When does a poll take effect?

9.57 The result of the poll does not have to be announced before the resolution passed by the poll will take effect. On the contrary, a resolution passed on a poll takes effect on the date on which the result of the poll is determined and not later. The ascertainment of the result is the crucial time. The meeting is treated as continuing until the result of voting on the poll is ascertained.

9.58 This principle is illustrated by the decision of the Court of Appeal in *Holmes v Keyes*[30] where a general meeting took place on 23 December 1957 and a poll was taken on resolutions concerning the election of certain directors. The voting on the poll was completed on 23 December but the counting did not take place until the following day when the company was informed by the scrutineers that the directors had been elected. The company's articles required that the shareholding qualification of a director should be 500 shares and should be obtained within two

[29] Article 2(1)(f), SI 2007/2194.
[30] [1959] 1 Ch 199 (Dankwerts J).

months after his appointment. The names of the newly appointed directors were not entered in the register of members until 24 February 1958. A claim was brought by two shareholders to restrain the newly appointed directors from acting, contending that, as the directors had been elected on 23 December, the period of two months had expired before they became shareholders and their names were registered as such. At first instance Dankwerts J acceded to the claim and granted an injunction. The Court of Appeal reversed this decision, holding that the meeting should be treated as continuing until the result on the poll was ascertained. There could be no effective appointment of a director until that time. As a consequence the election of the new directors took place on 24 December when the result of the poll had been ascertained, and the registration made on 24 February 1958 was within time. A poll cannot be said to be taken until the proxies have been examined, the votes finally determined and counted and the result ascertained.

Challenges to a Vote

Articles of association routinely contain a provision regulating the manner in which an objection may be taken to a person's entitlement to vote at a general meeting. The 1948 Table A[31] and the 1985 Table A contained such an article. Regulation 58 of the 1985 Table A provides that no objection shall be taken to the qualification of any voter except at the meeting or the adjourned meeting at which that vote was tendered. Every vote that is not disallowed at the meeting is declared to be valid. This provision applies both to voting on a show of hands and to a vote that is taken on a poll and in relation to voting in person and by proxy. **9.59**

Any objection that is made in due time must be referred to the chairman, whose decision on the matter is described as '… final and conclusive'. Plainly, the chairman must act in good faith and in what he considers to be the best interests of the company. Such an article is designed to provide certainty in order for the meeting to be properly conducted and a final result achieved. However, this is at a cost in the sense that a legitimate objection may be overruled by the chairman who may make an error which in the absence of fraud cannot be overturned. **9.60**

CA 2006, s 287

CA 2006, s 287 preserves the existing law. This section provide that nothing in CA 2006, Part 13, Chapter 1 affects any provision of a company's articles requiring an objection to a person's entitlement to vote on a resolution to be made in **9.61**

[31] Regulation 66.

accordance with the procedure in the articles, and for the determination of any such objection to be final and conclusive. In *Marx v Estates and General Investments Ltd*[32] the company's articles contained a provision that no objection should be raised as to the admissibility of any vote except at the meeting at which it was tendered and '... every vote not disallowed at such meeting shall be valid for all purposes'. A poll was demanded at a meeting held on 16 July and adjourned to 30 July. On 4 August when the count was almost concluded objections were raised as to the validity of certain proxy forms which had been accepted by the company and no objection had been raised at the meeting. Brightman J held that by virtue of the provision in the articles the objection that was raised several days after the meeting at which the votes were tendered was made too late to invalidate them. Brightman J observed that there was much 'sense' in an article in this form, and this pertinent observation still holds good today. A company has plenty of time to examine proxy forms, which have to be lodged with the company 48 hours in advance of the meeting. Where an objection is taken at the meeting at least the voter against whom the objection is made may have the opportunity to provide an answer to the objection. Objections taken later might cause considerable injustice to the voter concerned.

[32] [1976] 1 WLR 380 (Brightman J).

10

EXERCISE OF MEMBERS' RIGHTS

Background

One of the most noteworthy features of modern commerce in the twentieth and twenty-first centuries has been the emergence of the nominee shareholding in large, and in particular, public listed companies. Partly for ease of administration, the clients of banks, brokers and other financial institutions are encouraged to have their share portfolios held on their behalf by nominee companies of the financial institutions. The impact of this structure is such that the nominee company, which may provide a similar service for literally thousands of clients, is the 'member' of the company concerned and, under conventional company law and procedure, is the only person entitled to represent the interests of its clients at any general meeting. **10.01**

Traditional companies legislation has always assumed that the owners of the company are the registered members, whose names appear in the statutory register maintained for that purpose.[1] However, nowadays the registered member is often **10.02**

[1] See CA 2006, s 113, formerly CA 1985, s 356.

not the beneficial owner of the shares, in particular in cases where the shares are actively traded. For example, the effective administration of PEPs and ISAs relies on the use of corporate nominees. As a result, investors, whether large or small, have to rely on separate contractual arrangements to ensure that their nominee passes on to them all necessary shareholder information and acts with regard to the company concerned in accordance with their instructions. For many years anxiety was expressed about the unwieldy nature of this legal structure and the additional expense that it inevitably generated.

10.03 In its 2002 White Paper,[2] the government acknowledged the seriousness of these problems. The White Paper expressed the view that it is crucial to effective corporate governance that the owners of a company hold the directors to account for the company's performance. This means that the owners need to have appropriate information, and be able to express their views through voting and, if necessary, requisitioning resolutions and meetings. The White Paper accepted that the law should be amended so as to reflect modern conditions and make it clear that companies are able to recognize, if they wish, the rights of the holders of beneficial interests in shares at the request of the registered member.

10.04 During the course of the passage of CA 2006 through Parliament a number of attempts were made to insert appropriate wording in the legislation to incorporate these intentions. The aim of making it easier for investors to exercise their governance rights fully and responsibly was widely shared, but the language of the new provisions proved difficult to draft. At one stage the Companies Bill involved the grant of enhanced proxy rights to enable investors, acting as proxy of the registered holder, to exercise all the meeting participation rights that would have remained with the registered member. However, the final wording of these new provisions is more complex and requires detailed consideration.

Non-member Rights Before 1 October 2007

10.05 Prior to 1 October 2007, CA 1985 recognized registered members as the persons who had the legal right to exercise their rights in the company. This general rule was subject to the following exceptions:

(a) a member, whether an individual or a company, who had the right to attend and vote at a general meeting was permitted by CA 1985, s 372 to appoint a proxy to attend and vote in his or its place; and

[2] 'Modernising Company Law' (July 2002) Cm 5553-I paras 2.37–2.41.

(b) where a shareholder was a corporation,[3] it could duly appoint an authorized corporate representative under the provisions of CA 1985, s 375.

CA 1985, ss 372(1) and 375 were repealed with effect from 1 October 2007. The replacement of these sections is now found in CA 2006, Part 9 on the exercise of members' rights and Part 13 in respect of resolutions and meetings. The rights of a member to appoint a proxy and/or, where relevant, a corporate representative remain valuable rights and are considered in Chapter 8. **10.06**

CA 2006, Part 9

This chapter deals with the new provisions contained in CA 2006, Part 9 which is entitled 'Exercise of Members' Rights' and which came into force on 1 October 2007.[4] CA 2006, Part 9 is divided into nine sections, the first (s 145) dealing with the effect of provisions contained in a company's articles of association, the next six (ss 146–151) incorporating what are called 'information rights', and the final two (ss 152 and 153) setting out the rules relating to the exercise of rights where shares are held on behalf of others. **10.07**

Effect of provisions in company articles

A number of FTSE 100 companies, especially those with a large proportion of investors resident in the USA, have already adopted in their articles mechanisms to allow direct participation by persons who are not registered members. CA 2006, s 145 now covers this situation and applies where provision is made by a company's articles enabling a member to nominate another person or persons as entitled to enjoy or exercise all or any specified rights of the member in relation to the company.[5] The section provides that, so far as is necessary to give effect to that provision, anything required or authorized by any provision of the Companies Acts[6] to be done by or in relation to the member shall instead be done, or (as the case may be) may instead be done, by or in relation to the nominated person (or each of them) as if he were a member of the company. **10.08**

The impact of the wording of CA 2006, s 145 is very wide. It gives real power to the nominated person to carry out the steps required of a member under the company's articles. Interestingly, the section, although worded in general terms, **10.09**

[3] CA 1985, s 375 is replaced by CA 2006, s 323, which covers a corporation whether or not it is a company within the meaning of the Act.

[4] See Third Commencement Order—SI 2007/2194.

[5] CA 2006, s 145(1).

[6] See the definition of this term in CA 2006, s 2.

then proceeds in subs (3) to list the statutory rights to which it applies. The eight particular rights are those conferred by the following provisions:

(a) sections 291 and 293 (the right of an eligible member (as defined in s 289) of a private company to be sent a copy of a written resolution proposed by the directors or by the members respectively);[7]
(b) section 292 (the right of members of a private company to require the circulation by the company of a written resolution);[8]
(c) section 303 (the right of members of any company to require the directors to call a general meeting of the company);[9]
(d) section 310 (the right of every member of a company to be sent notice of a general meeting);[10]
(e) section 314 (the right of members of a company to require the circulation to members of a statement of not more than 1,000 words);[11]
(f) section 324 (the right of a member of a company to appoint another person as his proxy to exercise all or any of his rights to attend and to speak and vote at a meeting of the company);[12]
(g) section 338 (the right of members of a public company to require the circulation to members entitled to receive notice of the next annual general meeting, of notice of a resolution which may properly be moved and is intended to be moved at that annual general meeting);[13] and
(h) section 423 (the right of every member to be sent by the company a copy of the annual accounts and reports for each financial year).[14]

10.10 CA 2006, s 145(4) adds two very significant caveats to these provisions. The first is that neither the section nor any such provision in the company's articles referred to in subs (1) confers rights enforceable against the company by anyone other than the member. This has the important effect that if the statutory rights listed in para 10.09 (above) are interfered with or ignored by the company, the only person who can enforce them against the company will be the registered member.[15]

10.11 The second limitation is that neither CA 2006, s 145 nor any such provision in the company's articles of association affects the requirements for an effective transfer or other disposition of the whole or part of a member's interest in the company.

[7] See Ch 15.
[8] See Ch 15.
[9] See Ch 5.
[10] See Ch 2.
[11] See Ch 3.
[12] See Ch 8.
[13] See Ch 4.
[14] The nature of the company's legal duty to circulate copies of its annual accounts and reports is strictly beyond the scope of this book.
[15] See CA 2006, s 145(4)(a).

Accordingly, the law remains that only the registered holder is able to transfer legal title to the shares. This enables shares to be readily traded without complication.

'Information rights'

CA 2006, ss 146–151 confer new statutory rights to information on investors in shares which are admitted to trading on a regulated market.[16] 'Information rights' are defined in CA 2006, s 146(3) as meaning the right to receive a copy of all communications that the company sends to its members generally (including the company's annual reports and accounts)[17] or to any class of its members that includes the person making the nomination. In addition, the term 'information rights' includes the rights conferred by ss 431[18] or 432[19] to require copies of the company's last annual accounts and reports (directors' and auditors') and by s 1145 to require a hard copy version of a document or information supplied in another form.[20] **10.12**

It is to be noted that there is a further important information right relating to company accounts contained in CA 2006, s 426. That section permits a company which complies with certain regulations specified by the Secretary of State to provide a summary financial statement instead of copies of the accounts and reports required to be sent to members by CA 2006, ss 423. By s 146(4) and s 426(5), this provision applies not only to members but also to any person nominated to enjoy information rights. **10.13**

Nomination under s 146

A member of a company whose shares are traded on a regulated market and who holds shares on behalf of another person may nominate that person to 'enjoy information rights'.[21] The nomination must be in respect of *all* these rights and a company is expressly permitted not to act on a nomination purporting to relate to certain information rights only.[22] Clearly, this provision is to avoid both duplication and confusion for the company. **10.14**

[16] CA 2006, s 146(1).
[17] CA 2006, s 146(4).
[18] In respect of unquoted companies these reports comprise the last directors' report and the auditors' report on those accounts.
[19] In respect of quoted companies these reports comprise the last directors' remuneration report, the last directors' report and the auditors' report on those accounts (including the report on the directors' remuneration report and on the directors' report).
[20] CA 2006, s 146(3)(b).
[21] CA 2006, s 146(2).
[22] CA 2006, s 146(5).

The form in which copies are to be provided to a person enjoying information rights

10.15 CA 2006, s 147 establishes the form in which copies of documents and information are to be provided to the person nominated under s 146. If the person to be nominated wishes to receive hard copy documents he must, *before* the nomination is made, request the person making the nomination to notify the company of that fact and provide an address to which the copies may be sent.[23] The notification of these details to the company will establish the right of the nominated person to receive hard copy communications.[24] If no such notification is given (or no address provided) the nominated person is taken to have agreed that documents or information may be sent or supplied to him by the company by means of a website. The timing of a request for hard copy documents is therefore crucial.

Notices of meeting and voting rights

10.16 CA 2006, s 149 (information as to possible rights in relating to voting) deals expressly with the sending of a copy of notice of a general meeting by the company to a person nominated under s 146. The copy of the notice of the general meeting must be accompanied by a statement by the company reminding the person that he may have a right under an agreement between him and the member by whom he was nominated to be appointed, or to have someone else appointed, as his proxy for the meeting. Alternatively, the statement must point out that if he has no such right or does not wish to exercise it, he may have a right under such an agreement to give instructions to the member as to the exercise of voting rights. It is permissible for the statement that is required by the provisions of CA 2006, s 149 (2) (a) and (b) to be contained in the notes that are annexed to the notice of the general meeting.

10.17 This statutory requirement in CA 2006, s 149(3) is in lieu of that contained in s 325 of the 2006 Act, which requires a notice of meeting to contain a statement informing the member of his right to appoint a proxy. Section 325 does not apply to the copy of the notice that is sent to the nominated person and the company must either omit the notice required by that section or include it but state that it does not apply to the nominated person.[25] The choice to be followed is a matter for the company concerned. However, the scope for possible confusion will be large and the operation of these provisions will require careful administration by the company.

---

[23] CA 2006, s 147(2).

[24] CA 2006, s 147(3). This right is subject to the company's entitlement under Sch 5, Parts 3 and 4 to take steps to enable it to communicate in electronic form or by means of a website.

[25] CA 2006, s 149(3).

Status of information rights

CA 2006, s 150 sets out the legal status of these new statutory rights. As was foreseen in the White Paper the legislation provides that enjoyment by the nominated person of the rights conferred by nomination is enforceable against the company by the member as if they were rights conferred by the company's articles. It may be assumed therefore that the rights are to be treated as personal to the member and capable of enforcement by injunction and other legal proceedings through the courts. **10.18**

It is noteworthy that the rights are not stated to be enforceable by the nominated person. It would seem that he must rely upon the willingness of the person nominating him to take action to enforce his information rights. In that sense the new provisions reflect the traditional approach of legislation in England and Wales regulating companies. This conclusion is reinforced by s 150(5) which states in general terms that the rights conferred by the nomination are in addition to the rights of the member himself and do not affect any rights exercisable by virtue of any such provision of the articles of the company as is mentioned in s 145.[26] **10.19**

The failure of the company to respect the information and other rights of a nominated person will have a limited immediate impact on the company's actions. Indeed, CA 2006, s 150(6) expressly provides that a failure to give effect to the rights conferred by the nomination (namely the information rights conferred by s 146(3), the right to hard copy communications conferred by s 147(3) and the information as to possible voting rights required by s 149), does not affect the validity of anything done by or on behalf of the company.[27] However, it may be supposed that the repeated failure of a company to respect these statutory information rights may result in legal action initiated by the member who made the nomination. Repeated and serious failure of compliance by a company may form part of a member's allegations under a petition presented under CA 2006, s 994 on the grounds of unfairly prejudicial conduct. **10.20**

The termination or suspension of a nomination

By CA 2006, s 148 a nomination under section 146 may be terminated either at the request of the member or at the request of the nominated person.[28] Nomination also ceases on the death or bankruptcy of an individual or, in the case of a body corporate, on the dissolution or the making of an order for its winding up otherwise than for the purposes of a reconstruction.[29] The references to bankruptcy and **10.21**

[26] CA 2006, s 145 applies where provision is made in the articles enabling a member to nominate another person or persons as entitled to the enjoyment or exercise of specified rights of the member.

[27] See CA 2006, s 150(7).

[28] CA 2006, s 148(2).

[29] CA 2006, s 148(3).

winding up are extended to similar provisions in Scottish law and to Northern Ireland. Winding up also includes any corresponding provision under the law of a country or territory outside the United Kingdom.[30]

10.22 The remaining parts of CA 2006, s 148 contain certain safeguards to prevent abuse of the member's right to nominate a person to enjoy the information rights. First, the effect of any nomination is suspended under s 148(5) when there are more nominated persons than a member has shares in the company.[31] Secondly, where a member has different shares with different information rights and there are more nominated persons than he has shares conferring a particular right, the effect of any nominations made by him is suspended to the extent that they confer that right.[32] This obscurely worded provision applies to the situation where there are shares of different classes.

10.23 Unfortunately, it is not clear how both these subsections will operate in practice. It may perhaps be assumed that where the effective maximum number of nominations is exceeded, all the nominations of that member are suspended from operation and not merely the excess over the number of shares. If this is the correct interpretation, confusion may be avoided and the company will be relieved from policing the nomination procedures because there will be a total suspension of the nominations. This is to be preferred over the alternative construction of just suspending the most recently made nominations, which may conflict with the true intentions of the member making the nominations and lead to a more uncertain outcome.

10.24 For the avoidance of doubt CA 2006, s 148(8) provides that the termination or suspension of a nomination means that the company is not required to act on it. It does not prevent the company from continuing to do so, to such extent or for such period as it thinks fit. In other words the company cannot be held to account if its administrative procedures erroneously continue to supply information and documents to a person previously nominated by a member whose rights to receive that information have ceased or been suspended.

Company enquiries

10.25 CA 2006, s 148(7) empowers the company to make regular checks on the persons receiving information rights. The company may make such an enquiry of the nominated person once in any period of 12 months. The company may ask the nominated person whether he wishes to retain information rights, and if it does not receive a response (meaning a positive response) within 28 days of the date

30 CA 2006, s 148(4).
31 CA 2006, s 148(5).
32 CA 2006, s 148(6).

on which the enquiry was sent, the nomination will cease to have effect at the end of that period. The aim of this provision is to keep the list of nominated persons entitled to enjoy information rights up to date. However, it represents yet another administrative task for the company secretary if the company decides to operate such a process.

Statutory power to amend information rights

Precisely how these provisions will operate in practice is a matter for speculation. Accordingly, the statute makes provision in CA 2006, s 151 for the Secretary of State to issue regulations amending ss 146–150 so as to extend or restrict the classes of company to which s 146 applies, to alter the circumstances in which a nomination may be made under that section or to extend or restrict the rights conferred by such nomination. To date no such regulations have been proposed. **10.26**

Exercise of rights where shares are held on behalf of others

The final two sections of CA 2006, Part 9 (ss 152 and 153) deal with the related topic of the exercise of rights where shares are held on behalf of other persons. The first of these sections, s 152, inserts a new provision to try to deal with the great degree of confusion that can sometimes occur when a registered member, which is acting as the nominee for several persons and not merely for one person, seeks to exercise in different ways its rights attached to the shares or the rights under any enactment exercisable by virtue of holding the shares. **10.27**

The section provides at first that where such a member holds shares on behalf of more than one person those rights need not all be exercised and, if exercised, need not all be exercised in the same way.[33] That is no more than a clarification of the existing law. The section thus enables the votes attached to various shares to be cast in different ways. **10.28**

However, CA 2006, s 152 goes on to provide that a member who exercises such rights but does not exercise all his rights, must inform the company to what extent he is exercising the rights.[34] If he exercises the rights in different ways he must inform the company of the ways in which he is exercising them and to what extent they are exercised in each way.[35] This will presumably be apparent **10.29**

[33] CA 2006, s 152(1). This is a more sophisticated version of CA 1985, s 374 which dealt with voting on a poll.

[34] CA 2006, s 152(2).

[35] CA 2006, s 152(3).

from any voting slip or proxy form submitted to the company at or before a general meeting.

10.30 CA 2006, s 152(4) states that in the event that a member exercises such rights without informing the company that he is not exercising all his rights or that he is exercising his rights in different ways, the company is entitled to assume that he is exercising all his rights and is exercising them in the same way. This provision appears to be designed to protect the company from criticism, and the process from possible invalidity, if the company misunderstands how the member sought to utilize his various rights.

10.31 Regrettably, it is most unclear how this provision, which is worded in extraordinarily wide terms, will operate in practice. It must be feared that in its attempt to simplify the formidable task frequently faced by company registrars at a general meeting of a quoted company where there are ranks of nominee shareholders, Parliament may have introduced a provision which will only add substantially to the level of legal uncertainty surrounding this area of the law.

Section 153: members' requests

10.32 CA 2006, s 153 deals with a quite separate issue. It is designed to enable indirect investors to exercise their rights though the registered member and to participate in the various request procedures set out in the new legislation. There are four different provisions of CA 2006 in which a member is empowered to require the company to carry out certain tasks. These are:

(1) Section 314—the power to require the circulation to members of a statement of not more than 1,000 words with respect to a proposed resolution to be dealt with at a general meeting or other business to be dealt with there.
(2) Section 338—the power to require a public company to give to members entitled to receive notice of the next annual general meeting, notice of a resolution which may be properly moved and is intended to be moved at that meeting.
(3) Section 342—the power to require the directors of a quoted company to obtain an independent report on any poll taken or to be taken at a general meeting.
(4) Section 527—the power to require the directors of a quoted company to publish on a website a statement of audit concerns that members propose to raise at the next accounts meeting of the company.[36]

10.33 CA 2006, s 153(2) extends the scope of each of these provisions to requests made by at least 100 persons whether they are or are not members of the company,

[36] The process for approving company accounts is beyond the scope of this book.

provided that certain express conditions are satisfied. The conditions are lengthy and complicated and require close analysis.

The accompanying statement

In the case of persons who are not members the request to the company under any of these four sections must be accompanied by a statement containing the following information: **10.34**

(a) the full name and address of the member who holds the shares on that person's behalf;
(b) that the member is holding the shares in the course of a business (ie that the member is a professional nominee);
(c) the number of shares held by the member on behalf of that person;
(d) the total amount paid up on those shares;
(e) that those shares are not held on behalf of anyone else or, if they are, that the other person or persons are not among the others making the request;
(f) the voting rights attached to those shares; and
(g) that the person has the right to instruct the member how to exercise those rights.

Particular care must be taken to clarify whether the shares are held on behalf of any other person and that the other person is not also making the request. This is once again to avoid double counting and confusion.[37]

In circumstances where any of the 100 persons are members of the company the section requires that the request should be accompanied by a statement that the member holds the shares otherwise than on behalf of another person (ie that he holds the shares on his own behalf) or that he holds the shares for one or more other persons but they are not among the other persons making the request. Again, this is a provision to avoid double counting. The company can, within reasonable bounds, require evidence of the matters raised in these statements.[38] **10.35**

The required support

Most importantly, the request must be supported by at least 100 persons, being non-members or members, with shares on which at least an average of £100 has been paid up. The section reaches this conclusion by imposing the condition that the total amount of the sums paid up on the shares divided by the number of persons making the request must be not less than £100. **10.36**

---

[37] See CA 2006, s 153(2)(c)(v).
[38] See CA 2006, s 153(2)(e).

General compliance

10.37 The final condition is, needless to say, that the request must comply with any other requirements of the four sections as to contents, timing and otherwise.[39]

10.38 At the time of writing it remains uncertain how much use will be made of CA 2006, s 153 and its extension of each of the four named sections relating to members' requests. The requirement that it only applies in the case of professional nominee shareholders may place some limitation on its application. It undoubtedly introduces a new concept of participation by indirect investors, enabling them to count towards the total required to activate the four sections. The conditions are however quite stringent, as they are designed to ensure that the sections are used only by genuine investors and that the same shares cannot be counted twice. The other important restriction is the condition that the investor's contract with the registered member must permit the investor to give voting instructions. Where that is not the case, the section will not apply.

Transitional provisions

10.39 CA 2006, Part 9 in common with most of the provisions of CA 2006, is the subject of transitional provisions. In respect of CA 2006, Part 9, the applicable transitional provisions are found in Sch 3, para 3 of the Third Commencement Order.

10.40 CA 2006, s 145 (effect of provisions of articles as to enjoyment or exercise of members' rights) applies in relation to things required or authorized to be done on or after 1 October 2007.

10.41 Nominations of persons to enjoy information rights under CA 2006, s 146 may be made at any time on or after 1 October 2007. It is to be noted that companies had a grace period until 1 January 2008 in that they were not required to act on a nomination before that date. However, if the company elects to act on a nomination before 1 October 2008, CA 2006, ss 147–150 will apply.

10.42 Section 152 of the 2006 Act (exercise of rights where shares held on behalf of others: exercise in different ways) applies in relation to the exercise of rights on or after 1 October 2007.

10.43 Members' requests may be made under CA 2006, s 153 at any time on or after 1 October 2007.

[39] See CA 2006, s 153(2)(g).

11

RESOLUTIONS AND AMENDMENTS

Introduction

This chapter considers the different types of resolutions that may be considered either at a company meeting or, in the case of a private company, by written resolution. Shareholders make their decisions by the passing of resolutions. Such resolutions take various forms, the type of which depends upon the size of the required majority for the resolution to be treated as effective. The form and content of company resolutions is now determined by the provisions of CA 2006. Each of these new statutory requirements will be considered in this chapter. In addition, this chapter examines the procedures that must be followed if it is desired to amend a draft resolution before it is voted upon at a general meeting. As will be seen, for special resolutions the possibilities for amendment are much restricted. **11.01**

CA 2006, Part 13, Chapter 1 sets out a number of general provisions concerning resolutions. Whereas ss 284–287 deal with the general rules relating to voting requirements,[1] ss 281–283 concern the different forms of resolution that may be **11.02**

[1] See Ch 9.

passed by the members of a company under the new legislation. In contrast to CA 1985, where the legislation assumed that decisions of shareholders would be taken in general meetings, CA 2006 operates on the basis that in future private companies will take many of their decisions by means of a written resolution in accordance with the procedure that is set out in Part 13, Chapter 2.[2]

CA 2006, s 301

11.03 This section, which is found at the start of Part 13, Chapter 3, introduces a form of statutory presumption and sets out the general principle governing resolutions at general meetings under the new legislation. It provides that a resolution of the members of a company is validly passed at a general meeting if both the notice of the meeting and the resolution is given and the meeting is held and conducted in accordance with the provisions of Chapter 3 (ss 301–335) and, where relevant Chapter 4 (ss 336–340), and the company's articles.

CA 2006, s 281

11.04 CA 2006, s 281 contains a number of general statements concerning the form of resolutions that may be passed by a private company and by a public company. Section 281(1) provides that a resolution of the members or of a class of the members of a private company must be in the form of either a written resolution in accordance with the provisions of Part 13, Chapter 2, or a resolution passed at a meeting of the members in accordance with the provisions of Part 13, Chapter 3. It follows that a private company has two choices: whether to take a decision by means of a written resolution or by means of a resolution of the members of the company in general meeting.

Public companies

11.05 In marked contrast to the position for private companies a resolution of the members of a public company, or of a class of members of such a company, can only be passed at a duly convened meeting of the members.[3] Such a meeting must be held in accordance with the provisions of Part 13, Chapter 3[4] and, in the case of an annual general meeting, in accordance with the provisions of Part 13, Chapter 4.[5]

11.06 Accordingly, it will be seen that it is no longer possible for a public company to pass a written resolution, which it was able to do under the regime in CA 1985

---

2 See Ch 15.

3 CA 2006, s 281(2).

4 CA 2006, ss 301–305.

5 CA 2006, ss 336–340.

if permitted to do so by its articles of association or if they took the form of reg 53 of the 1985 Table A. This is a significant change in the law which will have particular effect on public companies with a small number of members. It is acknowledged that for larger public companies with many members it will make little practical difference. Such companies were never able to use reg 53 of the 1985 Table A which required the consent of every member.

Section 281(3) provides that where a resolution of a company, or of the members or of a class of the members is required by any provision of the Companies Acts[6] and the type of resolution that is required is not specified, what is required is an ordinary resolution, unless the articles of association of the company require a greater majority than the simple majority that is required for the passing of an ordinary resolution, or unanimity. Accordingly, it follows that where a statutory provision stipulates that only an ordinary resolution is required for the taking of a particular decision, a company's articles of association cannot prescribe a higher majority. **11.07**

Preservation of existing law

Section 281(4) expressly provides that nothing in CA 2006, Part 13 invalidates things that may be done otherwise than by the passing of a resolution. This provision preserves the well-established rules of law concerning the validity of matters that have been decided by the unanimous informal consent of the members of a company. This is a preservation of the well-known rule in *Re Duomatic Ltd.*[7] Equally nothing in CA 2006, Part 13 affects any enactment[8] or rule of law as to the circumstances in which a resolution is or is not treated as having been passed. This again preserves the existing case law dealing with the circumstances in which a resolution may be set aside, for example, on the grounds that it was procured by a misleading or 'tricky' circular.[9] In addition, s 281(4)(c) preserves the existing law dealing with the circumstances in which a person is precluded from alleging that a resolution has not been passed. An example of such a case is where a member has attended at a meeting and has failed to object to the questionable exercise of voting rights by another person. **11.08**

Transitional provisions

The Third Commencement Order[10] preserves the existing law under the provisions of CA 1985 with regard to resolutions of which notice was given before **11.09**

6 See CA 2006, s 2 for the statutory definition of this term.
7 [1969] 2 Ch 365 (Buckley J).
8 See CA 2006, s 1293 for the definition of the word 'enactment'.
9 See further Ch 3.
10 See Sch 3, para 22 to the Third Commencement Order (SI 2007/2194).

1 October 2007 or which were proposed at a meeting of which notice was given before that date.

11.10 For a private company an ordinary resolution may take the form of a written resolution if it is passed by members representing a simple majority of 'eligible members'.[11]

Ordinary Resolution

11.11 An ordinary resolution of the members is the standard form of resolution that is passed by a company. A resolution passed at a meeting on a show of hands is passed by a 'simple majority' if it is passed by a simple majority of the members who (a) are entitled to vote and (b) who do so either in person on the resolution or as duly appointed proxies of members entitled to vote.[12] Where a vote is taken by means of a poll at a meeting it is passed by a simple majority if it is adopted by members representing a simple majority of the total voting rights voting in person or by proxy.

11.12 Somewhat surprisingly, CA 2006, s 282 has generated a great deal of controversy, largely as the result of its definition of what constitutes a simple majority in subs (3). Unfortunately, the draftsman of the section appears to have overlooked the fact that the articles of most companies contain a provision that at a general meeting the chairman has a second or casting vote, which may be used in the event of an equality of votes. In addition, the chairman may sometimes not be a member of the company. The reference in the section to 'a simple majority of the members, who, being entitled to vote, vote in person on the resolution' does not take account of the use of the chairman's casting vote or of the chairman not being a member. As a result of this the new form of Table A introduced in October 2007 has removed reg 50 from the Table A of all new companies, both private and public.[13] This does not however affect existing companies which must exercise special care if an ordinary resolution is carried only on the casting vote of the chairman. On any basis, this is a most unfortunate and unexpected development.[14]

Passing the wrong form of resolution

11.13 It is sometimes the case that in error the directors of a company propose that the company pass a special resolution in circumstances where only an ordinary resolution is required. This may occur when, out of an abundance of caution, the

[11] See CA 2006, s 289 and Ch 15.
[12] CA 2006, s 282(3).
[13] See the Companies (Tables A to F) (Amendment) (No 2) Regulations 2007 (SI 2007/2826).
[14] For a detailed discussion of this issue see the commentary on reg 50 of the 1985 Table A in Part 4.

board of directors considers that a decision will be less open to effective legal challenge if it is approved by means of a special resolution. Such a decision does not offend against the provisions of the statute, which expressly provides in s 282(5) that anything that may be done by ordinary resolution may also be done by special resolution. The principle is that the greater may also include the lesser. This is a helpful provision which spells out the legal consequences of passing a special resolution in a situation where only an ordinary resolution is strictly required. By way of example, a company may at any time by ordinary resolution at a meeting remove a director from office under the provisions of CA 2006, s 168. Where such a resolution is passed in the form of a special resolution it is equally valid.[15]

Special Resolution

CA 2006, s 283 defines a special resolution of the members or a class of members **11.14**
as one which is passed by a majority of not less than 75%. The definition covers a special resolution whether passed at a meeting or as a written resolution of a private company. In the latter case, a written resolution is passed by a majority of not less than 75% if it is passed by members representing not less than 75% of the total voting rights of eligible members.[16]

Notice requirements for a special resolution and the problems of amendment

In a similar way to CA 1985, s 378(2), s 283 preserves the rule that the notice of **11.15**
an intention to propose a resolution as a special resolution must be included in the notice of the meeting. Section 283(6)(a) further provides that the notice of the meeting must include 'the text of the resolution'. If either of these requirements is omitted the resolution in question will not constitute a special resolution. However, if the notice of the meeting does comply with these requirements, the proposed resolution may *only* be passed as a special resolution.[17]

The new legislation is arguably more restrictive than the common law rules set in **11.16**
the landmark judgment of Slade J in *Re Moorgate Mercantile Holdings Ltd*[18] as it requires the precise text to be included in the notice. In that case it was held that for a special resolution to be valid the notice of the meeting had to specify either

[15] In the event that a company elects to remove a director from office by means of a special resolutions (ie by not adopting the prescribed statutory procedure under s 168) it may be able to circumvent the specific protections afforded to a director to protest at his removal that are set out in CA 2006, s 169.

[16] CA 2006, s 283(2).

[17] CA 2006, s 283(6)(b).

[18] [1980] 1 WLR 227 (Slade J).

the entire text or the substance of the resolution which was intended to be proposed. The resolution as passed had to be the same resolution as that identified in the preceding notice. In the case of a special resolution the addition of the words 'with such amendments and alterations as shall be determined upon at such meeting' was therefore meaningless. However, the resolution as passed could be regarded as the resolution identified in the notice even though (a) it departed in some respects from the text set out in the notice—for example, by correcting grammatical or clerical errors, or by reducing the words to more formal language—or (b) it was reduced into the form of a new text, which was not included in the notice, provided that in either case there was no departure whatever from the substance.

11.17 At the same time the court insisted that in deciding whether there was a complete identity between the substance of the resolution as passed and the substance of an intended resolution as notified, there was no room for any de minimis principle or a 'limit of tolerance'. The substance had to be identical. Accordingly, it necessarily followed that an amendment to the previously circulated text of a special resolution could properly be put to and voted on at a meeting if, but only if, the amendment involved no departure from the substance of the circulated text. Slade J added that where a notice is accompanied by a circular the notices and circular can and should ordinarily be treated as one document for the purposes of applying these principles.[19]

11.18 The facts in *Re Moorgate Mercantile Holdings Ltd*[20] themselves provide an interesting example of the application of these principles and the scope for a severe outcome in the event of a drafting error in a special resolution. This was an application by a company by petition for an order confirming the reduction of its share premium account. The account stood at £1,356,579.31 until 12 March 1979 when, following a small share issue, it was increased by £321.17. On the basis that the share premium account had been lost, notices convening an extraordinary general meeting were sent to shareholders, with an accompanying circular, containing a proposed special resolution 'that the share premium account of the company amounting to £1,356,900.48 be cancelled'. The draftsman of the resolution had overlooked the recent share issue and credit to the account of £321.17. At the extraordinary general meeting the chairman of the meeting, having received advice that this sum could not be regarded as having been lost, proposed a resolution 'that the share premium account of the company amounting to £1,356,900.48 be reduced to £321.17'. That amended version of the special resolution was passed on a show of hands. However, Slade J held, applying the principles of law set out

[19] [1980] 1 WLR 227 at 242A–G.
[20] [1980] 1 WLR 227.

above, that the resolution as passed at the extraordinary general meeting was not the same either in form or substance as the text that had been circulated to shareholders. Accordingly, it had not been properly passed and the court had no jurisdiction to confirm the reduction of the share premium account.[21]

If, as is suggested, the new s 283(6) narrows even further the limited possibilities for rescuing a drafting error set out in the judgment of Slade J in *Re Moorgate Mercantile Holdings Ltd*, this will represent a most unfortunate step backwards in the development of English company law in this area. There can be no doubt that, on its facts, the decision in *Re Moorgate Mercantile Holdings Ltd* would be decided that same way under CA 2006. **11.19**

Timing requirements for notice of a special resolution[22]

Under CA 1985, s 378(2), not less than 21 days' notice was required of the intention to propose a special resolution at a general meeting. That has now changed. Under CA 2006 a special resolution may be proposed at a meeting of which only 14 days' notice has been given, in accordance with s 307. The only circumstance in which at least 21 days' notice must now be given of a special resolution is where the meeting concerned is the annual general meeting of a public company.[23] **11.20**

Extraordinary Resolution

One important change that has been introduced by CA 2006 is that the concept of an 'extraordinary resolution' has now disappeared from the law. Under CA 1985, s 378(1) an extraordinary resolution was one which had been passed by a majority of not less than three-fourths of the vote of the members entitled to vote in person or by proxy. Where an extraordinary resolution was to be proposed at a meeting notice was required specifying the intention to propose the resolution as an extraordinary resolution. It is to be noted that Sch 3, para 23 to the **11.21**

---

[21] This decision is to be contrasted with that of the Court of Appeal in *Re Willaire Systems plc* 1987 [BCLC] 67 where it was held that the Court had jurisdiction to confirm a reduction of capital where the special resolution which had been passed by the members contained an obvious error of such an insignificant character that no one could be thought to be prejudiced by its correction. The Court held that the paragraph in the special resolution had to be read and treated as having taken effect as applying to all of the issued shares whatever their number. It is to be noted that no attempt was made to amend the special resolution at the meeting. See also *Re Fenner plc* (11 June 1990, unreported, Scott J).

[22] For a detailed analysis of this issue see Ch 2.

[23] See CA 2006, s 307(2)(a), which applies in relation to meetings of which notice is given on or after 1 October 2007—see Third Commencement Order, Sch,3 para 26(1).

Third Commencement Order[24] provides that any reference to an extraordinary resolution in a provision in the memorandum or articles of association of a company or of a contract continues to have effect and must be construed in accordance with CA 1985, s 378 as if that section had not been repealed. The effect of this provision is that extraordinary resolutions will continue in existence for so long as such articles of association (or any such contract) remain unamended. This is a transitional provision of considerable importance which should not be overlooked.

How to Amend an Ordinary Resolution

11.22 CA 2006, s 311(2) requires that the notice of a general meeting of a company must state the general nature of the business that is to be dealt with at that meeting.[25] Whereas CA 2006, s 283(6)(a) provides that in the case of a special resolution the text of the resolution must be included in the notice of the meeting, there is no similar requirement in relation to an ordinary resolution beyond that stated in CA 2006, s 311(2). Accordingly, an ordinary resolution proposed at a general meeting may be the subject of an amendment proposed at the meeting.

11.23 Where an amendment is proposed which alters the wording of an ordinary resolution, it must be considered by the meeting and, if necessary, voted upon before the resolution itself is considered by the meeting. This is to ensure that if the proposed amendment is passed the meeting can then proceed to consider the resolution in its then amended form.

11.24 It is best practice for any proposed amendment to an ordinary resolution to be submitted to the chairman of the meeting in writing so that there is no uncertainty or misunderstanding as to what is proposed by way of amendment.

Whether a proposed amendment is permissible

11.25 The chairman of the meeting has a discretion as to whether to reject a proposed amendment. In the exercise of this discretion the chairman must act with particular care, as his decision may be open to legal challenge.

11.26 In *Henderson v Bank of Australasia*[26] Chitty J held that any member wishing to insist upon his right to move an amendment to a resolution ought to formulate it and put before the chairman the terms of the proposed amendment. He also considered that he should warn the chairman that his decision would be challenged. He held on the facts in that case that there had been sufficient uncertainty to justify

[24] SI/2007/2194.
[25] See Ch 2, para 2.14 and the commentary on that section in Part 3.
[26] (1890) 45 ChD 330 (Chitty J).

the chairman in not putting the proposed amendment to the meeting. However, the Court of Appeal,[27] reversing the decision on the facts, held that the chairman was entirely wrong in refusing to put the amendment to the meeting, and that as a consequence the resolutions that were passed could not be allowed to stand. There was also no obligation to warn the chairman that his decision might be challenged or any duty on the dissentient member to leave the meeting; such a member is entitled to remain and cast his vote on the unamended resolution if he so wishes.

It follows from this decision that there is no rule of law that an amendment must be put in writing or notified in advance of the meeting. However, for an amendment to be effective it must be expressed in clear and unambiguous terms so that it is understood and be put to the meeting. Best practice remains that amendments should be formulated in writing. **11.27**

Grounds for the rejection of an amendment

A proposed amendment may be rejected by the chairman on one or more of the following grounds: **11.28**

(1) Where the subject matter of the proposed amendment contradicts the wording of the proposed resolution and would render it nugatory or ineffective. The proposer should be told by the chairman that in these circumstances his proper course is to vote against the resolution rather than pursue an amendment.
(2) Where the proposed amendment is inconsistent with an amendment which has already been debated and voted upon. There is no right to insist upon duplication of debate at a general meeting.
(3) Where the proposed amendment is irrelevant in the sense of raising matters which are unrelated to the proposed resolution.
(4) Where the proposed amendment appears to be designed to prevent the meeting coming to a decision on the matter in issue, for instance by delaying or postponing discussion on the topic but not adjourning the meeting.
(5) Where the proposed amendment is outside the scope of the notice of meeting or the matter being debated.[28] This is an important consideration for the chairman as the purpose of proper notice is to forewarn the shareholder of the business to be considered at the meeting. The chairman must therefore have regard to the impact that such a proposed amendment might have had on shareholders who are not present and who are unrepresented.
(6) Where the proposed amendment would be legally ineffective if passed, such as an attempt to amend a special resolution or alter an existing contract of the company.

---

27 Op. cit. 330 at 346 (Cotton LJ).
28 *Betts & Co Limited v Macnaghten* [1910] 1 Ch 430 (Eve J).

(7) Where an amendment takes the form of giving a direction to the board in circumstances in which the management of the company is entrusted to the board, subject only to directions made by special (as opposed to an ordinary) resolution. This objection is the one that most commonly arises. It is not open to a company meeting to direct how to conduct and manage the affairs of the company where there is the usual delegation of management powers to the board.[29] This objection is in substance merely an example of category (6).

11.29 It is sometimes suggested, on the basis of the decision at first instance in *In re London and Mediterranean Bank Ltd, Wright's Case*[30], that a further ground for the rejection of a proposed amendment to an ordinary resolution is that the amendment will place a greater burden on the company or adds onerous conditions to a resolution proposing the approval of a contract. This suggestion appears to have very little legal foundation. *Wright's Case* concerns the formulation of a list of contributories in a winding up and does not provide support for this proposition. It involved an early attempt to cancel an allotment of shares and return capital to a member. The case at best is authority for the proposition that notices of meetings are not to be construed with excessive strictness if they give reasonable notice of the business which is proposed to be done by way of ordinary resolution. It goes no further.

11.30 Faced with an amendment of the questionable type described above the chairman will have to rule that the amendment is out of order and cannot be put to the meeting. The chairman should only take this drastic step if the point is clear. He should err on the side of caution in exercising his discretion in order to avoid the consequences of a legal challenge to his decision. A wise chairman will invariably seek legal advice from the company's solicitors (and where appropriate, counsel) before doing so. At all times when exercising this important discretion he must act in good faith and in the interests of the proper conduct of the meeting.

A protective provision in the articles

11.31 Some public companies have specific provisions in their articles which set out the framework within which the chairman must exercise his discretion to accept or reject a proposed amendment. The articles sometimes provide that if an amendment is proposed to an ordinary resolution the chairman may, acting in good faith, either admit it for debate and consideration by the meeting or rule it out of order. In the event that it is subsequently found that the chairman was mistaken as a matter of law in ruling the amendment out of order, it is permissible for an

[29] *Automatic Self-Cleansing Filter Syndicate Co Ltd v Cuninghame* [1906] 2 Ch 34 (Warrington J and CA).

[30] (1871) LR 12 Eq 331, at 335.

article to provide that the erroneous decision of the chairman shall be final and conclusive and shall not invalidate the proceedings on the substantive resolution. However, the legal effect of such an article, which attempts to reverse the common law position, has yet to be tested by the courts.

It is permissible for a company, in an attempt to avoid being taken by surprise by **11.32** an amendment proposed to an ordinary resolution at a general meeting, to include in its articles a provision requiring that any proposed amendment to a resolution of which notice has been given to members be submitted in writing no later than a prescribed period of time before the start of the meeting. Such a period might be 48 hours in advance. It is suggested such an article might be worded so as to state that 'No amendment may be put to any ordinary resolution, except at the discretion of the chairman, unless it is filed with the company at its registered office not less than 48 hours prior to the time fixed for the meeting.'

Even where no such article exists it is always sensible for a shareholder seeking to **11.33** propose an amendment to a company resolution to give informal notice to the company of his or her intention to do so in advance of the meeting. This avoids anyone being taken by surprise and enables the chairman to consider the scope and nature of what is proposed and plan for full debate at the meeting. The cause of shareholder democracy is generally not facilitated by proposing late amendments for which no one is prepared. Indeed, a shareholder who is properly advised, will usually be told to give the company adequate notice (perhaps of a few days) of a proposed amendment.

Debate on a proposed amendment

Where an amendment is proposed at a meeting a debate will then ensue on **11.34** that proposal. As a matter of good practice the chairman of the meeting should ensure that any discussion is confined to dealing with the amendment. Occasionally the proposed amendment will generate a formal vote of the members and, especially in the case of a public company, a demand for a vote to be taken on a poll. Such a poll ought, if possible, to be taken forthwith in order that the meeting can deal with the business for which it has been convened. However, inevitably the meeting may need to be suspended by the chairman for a time while the poll is conducted and the votes are counted. In the case of a company with a very large number of members the counting of the votes cast on the poll may take several hours.[31] In such circumstances it is necessary that the chairman of the

[31] This may be the case for listed companies which must ensure that adequate resources are available in terms of manpower to count the votes. However, some public companies have recently adopted the use of hand-held electronic voting devices for voting purposes. This development is discussed further in Ch 9.

meeting should ensure that members are informed as to when in the day the meeting will resume. If a chairman decides that a poll will be held at a later time the outcome of the proposed amendment and of the resolution will remain uncertain and the meeting will need to be formally adjourned. As a matter of good practice, proposed amendments ought to be considered separately and therefore no other amendments to the substantive resolution ought to be considered in the meantime.

11.35 If and when the proposed amendment is adopted, the chairman should then put to the meeting the resolution in its amended form. If the amendment is unsuccessful, the chairman must put to the meeting the resolution in its original form.

Voting by proxy on a proposed amendment

11.36 Proxy votes may of course be utilized on a motion to amend a proposed ordinary resolution. The chairman as proxy for absent members may exercise his discretion to vote on such a motion. As proxy-holder, he should vote in accordance with what he believes to be the wishes of the shareholders who appointed him. In general terms, if a chairman holds proxies in favour of a particular resolution he may assume that the shareholders wish him to vote in favour of the existing resolution without amendment. In such circumstances, he may vote the proxies against any amendment, in particular any proposal which seeks to alter or undermine the proposed resolution or its effectiveness.

11.37 On the other hand, if the chairman holds proxies on behalf of shareholders who have indicated their opposition to the proposed resolution, or who have abstained on the resolution, the chairman may be uncertain as to how the shareholders would have wished him to vote on any motion to amend the resolution. In such circumstances the chairman as proxy has a discretion. It is suggested that best practice is to abstain on any amendment where the shareholder has abstained on the substantive resolution. Where the shareholder has voted against the proposed resolution, the proxy may either support an amendment which modifies it or abstain on the amendment and vote against the substantive resolution when it is later put to the vote.[32]

---

[32] See further *Re Waxed Papers Ltd* [1937] 2 All ER 481 (CA); Ch 8 and Ch 14.

12

ADJOURNMENT

Introduction

It is frequently the case that a properly convened general meeting of a company has to be adjourned, in the sense of its proceedings being postponed or deferred to a later time, either on the same day or to a date in the future or indefinitely. The reasons for seeking an adjournment are many and varied and may range from a desire to give more time for consideration of an important matter on the agenda, to a preference for postponing a decision until further facts or information are available for shareholders. **12.01**

Adjournments frequently arise, in the case of listed companies, where new outline proposals that may evolve into a general offer to shareholders or an offer to the company to acquire some or the whole of its business, are made shortly before a meeting is held to consider and approve an existing proposal from another party. In such circumstances the board may consider that, in accordance with its duty to act in the best interests of the company, it has no option but to give more time for **12.02** consideration before a decision is taken by the company in general meeting on the original proposals. For this reason many of the decided cases concerning adjournments have arisen in the context of schemes of arrangement under CA 1985, s 425 and its statutory predecessors (now CA 2006, Part 26, ss 895–899).

12.03 This chapter considers the issues that arise in relation to the question of the adjournment of general meetings including:

(1) What is the procedure for adjourning a meeting?
(2) Who may authorize an adjournment?
(3) What are the grounds for an adjournment?
(4) What is the effect of an adjournment?
(5) Is it necessary to give new notice of an adjourned meeting, and if so, what type of notice?
(6) What business may be discussed at the adjourned meeting?

12.04 The company's regulations governing adjournments of general meetings are invariably contained in its articles of association and the power to adjourn a meeting is invariably afforded to the chairman of the meeting. The articles of association of many public companies contain what are almost standard form provisions, granting the power to adjourn the meeting to the chairman 'with the consent of the meeting'. In addition, following the important decision of the Court of Appeal in *Byng v London Life Association Ltd*,[1] provisions were introduced into the articles of association of many large companies permitting the chairman to adjourn the meeting if it became physically impossible to hold it. These provisions will be considered in more detail below.

Common Law

12.05 Under the common law a meeting was held to be entitled to adjourn its proceedings provided that this power was used for a legitimate purpose connected with the transaction of business and not merely to prevent the meeting from reaching a decision. For example, at common law a meeting could be adjourned where it was not possible to conclude all the business on the agenda without adjourning. The decision to adjourn lay with the meeting itself, which by a simple majority could pass a resolution to adjourn.[2]

12.06 It is important to note that at common law, in the absence of such a provision, a meeting cannot be stopped or adjourned by the chairman at his own will

[1] [1990] Ch 170 (CA).
[2] See *Kerr v Wilkie* (1860) 6 Jur NS 383.

and pleasure.[3] This principle was laid down by Chitty J in *National Dwellings Society v Sykes*[4] where he stated:

> Unquestionably it is the duty of the chairman, and his function, to preserve order, and to take care that the proceedings are conducted in a proper manner, and that the sense of the meeting is properly ascertained with regard to any question which is properly before the meeting. But, in my opinion, the power which has been contended for is not within the scope of the authority of the chairman—namely, to stop the meeting at his own will and pleasure. The meeting is called for the particular purposes of the company. According to the constitution of the company a certain officer has to preside. He presides with reference to the business which is there to be transacted. In my opinion, he cannot say, after that business has been opened, 'I will have no more to do with it; I will not let this meeting proceed; I will stop it; I declare the meeting dissolved, and I will leave the chair.' In my opinion that is not within his power. The meeting by itself . . . can resolve to go on with the business for which it has been convened, and appoint a chairman to conduct the business which the other chairman, forgetful of his duty or violating his duty, has tried to stop because the proceedings have taken a turn which he himself does not like.

This principle was upheld by the Court of Appeal in *Byng v London Life Association Ltd*.[5] It is matched by the rule that, in the absence of a special provision for postponement in the articles, the directors cannot postpone a meeting which has been properly convened. Such a power is not to be implied from the provision in the articles that the directors may fix the time and place at which the meeting is to be held. **12.07**

Adjournment caused by disruptive behaviour

However, it is clearly established at common law that a chairman has a power to adjourn where unruly conduct prevents the meeting from continuing,[6] a point made by Chitty J in the passage cited above and reiterated by Megarry J in *John v Rees*.[7] This power arises from the fact that one of the important functions of the chairman is to preserve order. Where there is disorder it is often impossible for the meeting to consider and pass a resolution for an adjournment, hence the inherent power of the chairman to adjourn a meeting for a short period of time, such as 15 minutes, taking due steps to ensure so far as is possible that all members present know of the adjournment. **12.08**

In *John v Rees*[8] Megarry J expressed the view that the greater the violence the less prolonged need be the chairman's efforts to restore order before adjourning the meeting. **12.09**

---

[3] See Ch 7.
[4] [1894] 3 Ch 159 (Chitty J).
[5] [1990] Ch 170, 186A–E (CA).
[6] See *John v Rees* [1970] 345 at 379 (Meggary J).
[7] Op. cit.
[8] Op. cit.

Indeed, Megarry J considered that the chairman has not merely a power, but a duty to declare an adjournment in this way in the interests of those who fear for their safety.[9] The chairman's inherent power and duty must be exercised bona fide for the purpose of forwarding and facilitating the meeting and not for the purpose of interruption or procrastination. In addition, the adjournment on this ground must be for no longer than is reasonably necessary for the restitution of order. This is a judgment that has to be made by the chairman, having regard to the substantial inconvenience that may be caused to members if the meeting is adjourned to another day when a short adjournment might be sufficient for the restoration of good order.

Poll on motion to adjourn

12.10 When, in an orderly meeting, a poll is demanded on a motion to adjourn and such poll cannot be taken forthwith, the chairman has the residual power to suspend the meeting with a view to its continuance at a later date after the result of the poll is known.[10] This principle was established in *Jackson v Hamlyn*[11] where Upjohn J held that the provision in a company's articles of association that a poll on any question of adjournment should be taken immediately meant that it had to be taken as soon as practicable in all the circumstances. This is the case if, owing to the number of shareholders or proxies or for some other reason, it is impossible then and there to go on with the meeting. In effect the meeting would be suspended until the result of the poll was announced, when there would (if appropriate) be a continuation of the existing meeting.

12.11 Similarly, in *Byng v London Life Association Ltd*[12] Sir Nicholas Browne-Wilkinson V-C held that a chairman would at common law have the power to adjourn a meeting in circumstances where the inadequacy of the space available rendered it impossible for all those entitled to attend to take part in the debate and to vote, and where a motion for adjournment could not be put to the meeting as many members who would be entitled to vote on the motion were excluded. The Court of Appeal held that this was a part of the fundamental common law duty of the chairman to regulate the proceedings at the meeting.

12.12 Most importantly, the Court of Appeal held that the proper test to be applied to the exercise of the chairman's discretion in this type of case were the *Wednesbury* principles derived from administrative law.[13] The chairman's decision will not be declared invalid unless on the facts which he knew or ought to have known he

---

[9] [1970] Ch 345 at 382 B–G.

[10] See *R v D'Oyley* (1840) 12 A & E 139; 113 ER 763; *Jackson v Hamlyn* [1953] Ch 577 (Upjohn J); *Byng v London Life Association Ltd* [1990] Ch 170, at 186 D (CA).

[11] Op. cit.

[12] Op. cit. at 187 B–C.

[13] See *Associated Provincial Picture Houses Ltd v Wednesbury Corporation* [1948] 1 KB 223 (CA).

failed to take into account all the relevant factors, took into account irrelevant factors or reached a conclusion which no reasonable chairman, properly directing himself to his duties, could have reached.[14]

The Power to Adjourn Contained in Articles of Association

The provisions of the company's articles of association are designed to avoid these difficulties by providing an express power to adjourn a meeting with the consent of the meeting. Such a power should be found in all well-drafted articles. Regulation 45 of the 1985 Table A[15] for example, provides as follows: **12.13**

> The chairman may, with the consent of the meeting at which a quorum is present (and shall if so directed by the meeting), adjourn the meeting from time to time and from place to place, but no business shall be transacted at an adjourned meeting other than business which might properly have been transacted at the meeting had the adjournment not taken place. When a meeting is adjourned for 14 days[16] or more, at least 7 clear days' notice shall be given specifying the time and place of the adjourned meeting and the general nature of the business to be transacted. Otherwise it shall not be necessary to give any such notice.

The power conferred on the chairman by an article in the form of reg 45 of the 1985 Table A is a concomitant of the office of chairman and as such it is a fiduciary power. Accordingly, the exercise of the power to adjourn must be exercised in good faith and for proper purposes and not for any collateral motives. **12.14**

Notice of an adjourned meeting to accord with the articles

Where the articles prescribe that notice is required where a meeting is adjourned for 14 days or more, such a provision is a compulsory requirement and the notice of the adjourned meeting will be defective if less time is given. This principle is illustrated by the decision of Romer J in *Robert Batcheller & Sons v Batcheller*.[17] In that case Robert Batcheller & Sons Ltd, a private company limited by shares, held its annual general meeting in August 1943. Item 3 on the agenda for that meeting provided for the re-election of the retiring directors, RA Batcheller and HG Batcheller and item 4 provided for the election of Mrs WW Andrews and PE Dormer to fill the vacancies caused by the retirement of RA Batcheller and HG Batcheller. A vote was taken on a show of hands and the result of that vote was that the resolution for the re-election of the retiring directors was lost. HG Batcheller demanded a poll, and it was decided that the poll should be taken on 28 October 1943. It was also agreed **12.15**

---

[14] See Ch 7.
[15] See the commentary on this regulation in Part 4.
[16] In the corresponding provision in the 1948 Table A the time period was 30 days.
[17] See *Robert Batcheller & Sons v Batcheller* [1945] Ch 169 at 171 (Romer J).

that item 4 of the agenda should be dealt with on the same day. A document, dated 23 September 1943, was sent to the shareholders which stated:

> I have to remind you that the poll on the election of directors will be taken on Thursday, 28th October, 1943, at 2.30 p.m., at the offices of the company at 'Allington', Yeoman Lane, Bearsted. For Robert Batcheller & Sons, Ld. Thomas R. S. Batcheller, Secretary.

12.16 At the resumed meeting held on 28 October 1943 the votes cast were 10,860 for, and 10,979 against, the re-election of RA Batcheller and HG Batcheller. Nevertheless, the chairman of the meeting declared them re-elected under article 93 of the company's articles of association. In doing so he relied on article 93 of the company's articles which stated as follows:

> Subject as herein provided, if at any meeting at which an election of directors ought to take place, the places of the retiring directors, or some of them, are not filled up, the retiring directors, or such of them as have not had their places filled up, shall, if willing to act, be deemed to have been re-elected.

12.17 The shareholders present at the meeting went on to consider item 4 of the agenda, and purported to elect Mrs Andrews and PE Dormer to be directors in their place. An action was commenced by the company against RA Batcheller and HG Batcheller, claiming that neither of them was a director of the company, and that Mrs Andrews and PE Dormer had been duly elected directors on 28 October 1943. By their counterclaim RA Batcheller and HG Batcheller claimed a declaration that they were, and at all material times since 28 October 1943 had been, directors of the company, and that neither Mrs Andrews nor PE Dormer were, or had been, directors at any time since that date.

12.18 In the course of his judgment in relation to the adequacy of the notice of the adjourned meeting Romer J said:

> I am satisfied that, at the [annual general] meeting on August 25, 1943, it was understood and agreed by those present, and not least by the chairman himself, that item 4 on the agenda should stand over and be dealt with at the meeting on October 28, and that it was in fact so adjourned, and I now turn to the question whether a sufficient notice was given of the adjourned meeting. Article 62 of the company's articles provides that 'Whenever a meeting is adjourned for ten days or more, notice of the adjourned meeting shall be given in the same manner as in the case of an original meeting.' That means, and can in my judgment only mean, that where a meeting is adjourned for ten days or more a like notice of the adjourned meeting is required as is necessary in the case of an original meeting under art. 55. That article is peremptory in form and provides that: 'Seven days' notice at the least, specifying the place, the day and the hour of meeting, and in the case of special business the general nature of such business, shall be given in manner hereinafter mentioned to such members as are under the provisions of these articles entitled to receive notices from the company.'
>
> I am unable, therefore, to accept the contention that art. 62 is in this regard merely directory; it is, in my judgment, mandatory, and must be complied with. On its face

> the document of September 23, 1943, the only document sent out to shareholders which could be treated as a notice, does not profess to be a notice of a meeting at all; it purports to be merely a 'reminder'—unnecessary perhaps but intelligible—of the taking on a particular day, and at a specified time and place, of a poll; and a poll on a particular topic, namely, the election of directors. Such a poll, and on such a topic, had been demanded at the August meeting, and prima facie the 'reminder' can only fairly be read as referring to that poll and to nothing else. In my judgment it is not possible to relate it to a resolution which had never been voted on by a show of hands, on which no poll, accordingly, had already been or could have been demanded and which indeed might never become the subject of such a demand.
>
> I am of opinion, therefore, that that document was not a sufficient notice of an adjourned meeting within the meaning of art. 62, and that it was, therefore, not open to the meeting of shareholders, on October 28, 1943, to deal with anything except the taking of the poll. It follows that the purported appointment, at the meeting on October 28, 1943, of Mrs. Andrews and P. E. Dormer to be directors in the place of R. A. Batcheller and H. G. Batcheller was of no effect.

Automatic Adjournment

Most articles of association provide that in the event that a quorum is not present at the start of a meeting, after waiting for a limited period of time the meeting is automatically adjourned, usually to the same day and time and venue in the following week. Such a provision was found in reg 54 of the 1948 Table A which provided as follows: **12.19**

> If within half an hour from the time appointed for the meeting a quorum is not present, the meeting, if convened upon the requisition of members, shall be dissolved; in any other case it shall stand adjourned to the same day in the next week, at the same time and place or to such other day and at such other time and place as the directors may determine.

That is the provision that applied to companies registered on or after 22 December 1980, when CA 1980 came into force, and before the 1985 Table A became operable. For companies registered before that date the following additional words were added at the end of the paragraph:

> and if at such adjourned meeting a quorum is not present within half an hour from the time appointed for the meeting, the members present shall be a quorum.

Regulation 41 of the 1985 Table A adopted a somewhat simpler form while at the same time dealing with the problems caused by the loss of a quorum during the meeting. It states: **12.20**

> If such a quorum is not present within half an hour from the time appointed for the meeting, or if during a meeting such a quorum ceases to be present, the meeting shall stand adjourned to the same day in the next week at the same time and place or such time and place as the directors may determine.

What is the Procedure for Adjourning a Meeting?

12.21 The precise procedure for obtaining an adjournment will usually be set out in the company's articles. Typically, the articles provide that the meeting can only be adjourned by the chairman with the consent of the meeting. The procedure involves a resolution being put to the meeting either by the chairman or by a member from the floor. The resolution must be clearly formulated to reflect the provision of the articles. Usually the resolution will state the duration of the proposed adjournment. This resolution is an ordinary resolution, which will be passed by a simple majority of the members, voting in person or by proxy. The resolution may be decided on either by a show of hands or on a poll. Regulation 51 of the 1985 Table A, like its predecessor reg 61 of the 1948 Table A, requires that a poll on the question of an adjournment shall be taken forthwith. Business efficacy must be given to this provision, so this means that the poll must be taken as soon as practicable in all the relevant circumstances.[18] For that reason it is highly desirable in the case of a listed company that adequate preparation is made in advance for the taking of a poll if there is thought to be any possibility of a member seeking an adjournment. Such preparation will include the appointment of an adequate number of scrutineers.[19]

12.22 A resolution to adjourn should be put to the meeting straight away, and if a poll is successfully demanded or granted, the meeting will be suspended while the counting of the votes cast on the poll takes place. In the case of a large, listed company with thousands of shareholders, it is sometimes the case that the suspension will take many hours. When the votes have been counted the meeting will resume for the announcement by the chairman of the outcome of the voting. If the motion to adjourn is carried, the meeting will be adjourned. If it fails, the meeting will then proceed to business. The resumed meeting is the same meeting.[20]

12.23 If, as is sometimes the case, the articles provide the chairman with a power to adjourn the meeting with the consent of the members present at the meeting, the chairman is not obliged to exercise that right. He may, in the exercise of his discretion, prefer to carry on with the business of the meeting. In that event the members present cannot compel him to exercise his power, even though they form a majority of the meeting. In *Salisbury Gold Mining Co Ltd v Hathorn*[21] the Privy Council held that the chairman of a company with articles in this form was not bound to adjourn the meeting, even though a majority of those present desired

---

18 See *Jackson v Hamlyn* [1953] Ch 577 at 589 (Upjohn J).
19 See Ch 9.
20 See *Jackson v Hamlyn* op. cit.
21 [1897] AC 268 (PC, on appeal from the Supreme Court of Natal).

the adjournment. In this event, it is the chairman who may adjourn the meeting; it is his act and not that of the meeting or of those present at it. Admittedly he cannot adjourn the meeting of his own motion, but the terms in which the members present are given the controlling voice strengthens the view that the adjournment is to be the act of the chairman.

On the other hand, such a provision does not permit the chairman to adjourn the meeting against the wishes of the majority of members. This is apparent from the decision of Chitty J in *National Dwellings Society v Sykes*.[22] Where a resolution to adjourn is defeated the meeting must continue and proceed to business. **12.24**

Voting on an adjournment resolution

One of the key issues which has arisen over the years is whether a proxy given to the chairman of a meeting includes a power and a direction to vote on a resolution to adjourn. In cases where meetings are convened to consider schemes of arrangement under CA 1985, s 425 and its statutory predecessors[23] the courts have held that to vote for a resolution proposing the adjournment of a scheme for a short or long period is to oppose the scheme. Accordingly, as a general rule, proxies lodged on behalf of persons who oppose a scheme should be tendered by the chairman in favour of a resolution to adjourn, and those lodged on behalf of opponents of the scheme should be used in voting against such a resolution. **12.25**

Re Waxed Papers Ltd

This principle was first laid down by the Court of Appeal in *Re Waxed Papers Ltd*.[24] That case concerned a meeting held to approve a scheme of arrangement at which a member who objected to the scheme moved an amendment to the effect that further consideration of the scheme should be adjourned. On a show of hands there was a majority in favour of the adjournment, but the chairman of the meeting demanded a poll. He then used the proxies given to him to secure a majority to defeat that amendment. The substantive resolution was then put to the meeting and with the votes, including the proxies, there was a very large majority in favour of the scheme of arrangement. **12.26**

The Court of Appeal held that the form of proxy given to the chairman of the meeting on its proper construction authorized the holder of the proxy to vote on a motion for an adjournment of the meeting, as the proxy was entitled to vote upon any incidental matter or question that needed to be decided in the course of the meeting before the meeting came to consider the substantive resolution. Slesser LJ **12.27**

22 Op. cit.
23 See now CA 2006, Part 26, ss 895–899.
24 [1937] 2 All ER 481 (CA).

propounded the principle set out in para 25 (above) and held that the motion to adjourn was merely incidental or ancillary to arriving at a final result. Romer LJ agreed and held that where a proxy was given to vote in favour of a scheme at 'such meeting or any adjournment thereof' the power was necessarily implied in the proxy to vote for or against any resolution for an adjournment of the meeting.

12.28 The decision in *Re Waxed Papers Ltd*[25] has been expressly followed more recently in *Re BTR plc*[26] and *Re Abbey National plc*, both cases involving the question of the adjournment of a scheme meeting.[27] Nowadays proxies give the chairman a discretion as to how to vote on such a matter as an adjournment resolution. The chairman of the meeting, if appointed a proxy, is bound to exercise this discretion in accordance with reasonable principles along the lines stated above.

What are the grounds for an adjournment?

12.29 The articles usually permit an adjournment to be sought for any reason whatsoever. However, where the consent of the members is required, the person moving the resolution will be required to explain his reasons for seeking the adjournment. This will particularly be the case if it is the chairman or the board which is seeking the adjournment. Members will have come to the meeting expecting it to proceed to transact the business set out in the notice of meeting. Some members may be angry to think that an important decision may be postponed, and it is commonly the case that such members (often the smaller shareholders) will strongly oppose the proposed adjournment. When proposing an adjournment the chairman must therefore show a large degree of tact and understanding for the possible inconvenience caused to members.

What is the effect of an adjournment?

12.30 The effect of an adjournment is to suspend the further transaction of business at the meeting and postpone it until the adjourned meeting. At common law the adjourned meeting is treated in law as a continuation of the original meeting.[28] This is especially the case where the meeting is suspended solely for the purposes of taking a poll, which strictly speaking is not an adjournment in the full sense.[29]

---

25 Op. cit.

26 [2000] 1 BCLC 740 (CA).

27 [2005] 2 BCLC 15 (Evans Lombe J).

28 See *McLaren v Thomson* [1917] 2 Ch 261 (CA); *Neuschild v British Equatorial Oil Company Limited* [1925] Ch 346 (Astbury J).

29 See *Jackson v Hamlyn* (op. cit.); *Shaw v Tati Concessions Ltd* [1913] 1 Ch 292 (Swinfen Eady J).

However, statute has intervened in this area.[30] CA 1985, s 381 expressly provided that where a resolution is passed at an adjourned meeting (whether a general meeting of a company, or a class meeting or a meeting of the directors) the resolution is for all purposes to be treated as having been passed on the date on which it was in fact passed, and is not to be deemed passed on any earlier date. This provision is re-enacted in CA 2006, s 332 with regard to an adjourned meeting of a company, and applies to class meetings by virtue of CA 2006, s 334(1).

Is a new notice of an adjourned meeting necessary, and if so, what type of notice?

12.31 The articles of companies will differ as to whether it is necessary to give a new notice of an adjourned meeting. Usually this depends upon the length of the adjournment. As can be seen above, reg 45 of the 1985 Table A requires at least seven clear days' notice to be given, specifying the time and place of the adjourned meeting and the general nature of the business to be transacted, when a meeting is adjourned for 14 days or more. The logic of this provision is clearly understood. Only a small proportion of the members may be present in person at the original meeting and an announcement to them of the date of the adjourned meeting will not assist the members who are absent. A similar provision was contained in reg 57 of the 1948 Table A and applies when a meeting is adjourned for 30 days or more.

12.32 As the adjourned meeting is to be regarded as a continuation of the original meeting it is not strictly necessary to send out new forms of proxy for the adjourned meeting. However, care should be taken to ensure that there is no special provision in the company's articles imposing such a requirement.

Directors Have No Power to Postpone a Meeting

12.33 In view of the periods of notice that have to be given for general meetings[31] circumstances may arise where a board of directors may wish to postpone the holding of a meeting. It is important to note that in the absence of an express provision in a company's articles directors do not have power to postpone a duly convened general meeting of shareholders.[32] In the event that the directors purport to postpone such a meeting it is open to the shareholders of the company to hold the general meeting as envisaged by the notice and to transact the business

30 The section was first introduced as CA 1929, s 119.

31 See Ch 2.

32 See *Smith v Paringa Mines* [1906] Ch 193 (Kekewich J).

comprised in that notice. The correct course of action for directors who wish to postpone a meeting is to open the meeting at the time and place specified in the notice and then attempt to persuade the members to pass a resolution agreeing to an adjournment to the date wanted by the directors. If time permits the directors can send a circular to members in which they set out their reasons for seeking an adjournment. Such action may increase the prospects of achieving the consent of the members to a proposed adjournment.

Court's Power to Adjourn

12.34 In an appropriate case the court may be asked to intervene by injunction to restrain the holding of a meeting where allegations are made of some irregularity in the calling of the meeting or of some other default.[33] In such circumstances it is frequently the case that, applying the normal principles for the grant of an interim injunction[34] the court may make an order that the directors do adjourn the meeting for a limited period of time. The effect of the order of the court will be to postpone the business of the meeting to a later date, usually after there has been time for any legal claim to be properly formulated and the matter resolved by a hearing in court. Under the Civil Procedure Rules such an application may be made in proceedings commenced by claim form or as part of the relief sought in a petition for relief on grounds of unfairly prejudicial conduct pursuant to CA 2006, s 994.

12.35 One of the greatest concerns of the applicant for such an injunction will be the cross-undertaking in damages that will have to be given as the 'price' of the injunction. If vital company business is held up the company may suffer considerable loss, and if the outcome of the proceedings is a finding by the court that the injunction was unjustified and should not have been granted, the applicant may face a massive claim for compensation. Accordingly, proposed applications to a court for injunctive relief must always be handled with caution.

12.36 The courts are wary of this type of application. In *Re Piccadilly Radio plc*[35] an application was made to the court for injunctions to restrain certain shareholders from voting their shares at an extraordinary general meeting held to consider a contested takeover offer. The application was made in the context of a petition brought under what is now CA 2006, s 994 on the grounds that the petitioners had been unfairly prejudiced by the registration of the respondents as shareholders, their shares having been allegedly transferred to them in breach of the

[33] See *Northern Counties Securities Ltd v Jackson and Steeple Ltd* [1974] 1 WLR 1133 (Walton J); *Paringa Mining & Exploration Co plc v North Flinders Mines Ltd* (1988) 14 ACLR 587.

[34] See *American Cyanamid Co v Ethicon* [1975] AC 396 (HL).

[35] [1989] BCLC 683 (Millett J).

company's pre-emption articles. Millett J deplored what he described as '. . . a regrettable tendency for contestants in modern takeover battles to try to enlist the aid of the Court'. Millett J dismissed the application and refused an injunction on the grounds that, on the facts, there was no prospect of the applicants obtaining an order to reverse the transfers. Costs were awarded against the applicants on an indemnity basis. This case serves as a warning to future applicants of the need to ensure that they have cogent and compelling grounds before making any court application to restrain a company meeting, in particular when involved in a contested takeover bid or in a similar struggle for control of a company.

13

CLASS MEETINGS AND CLASS CONSENTS

Introduction

It is legitimate for the issued share capital of a company to be divided into shares of different classes, for example, the share capital may include deferred shares, preference shares or redeemable shares as well as ordinary shares. The reasons for such a subdivision of a company's share capital may be many and arise in a variety of different situations. Where the issued share capital of a company is so divided it may be necessary from time to time to convene separate class meetings when such a course is required by statute or under the terms of a company's articles of association. Provided that there is due and proper compliance with the legislation and with any applicable provisions in a company's articles or shareholders' agreement it is possible for members of a company to vary[1] the rights that may be attached to a particular class of shares.[2] This power must not be abused and the court has specific jurisdiction under CA 2006, s 633[3] to protect a minority of the members of a class **13.01**

[1] See *House of Fraser plc v ACGE Investments Ltd* [1987] AC 387 (HL)—variation does not include the situation where shares are cancelled as this involves the fulfilment or satisfaction of the contractual rights of shareholders. Variation of a right presupposes the existence of the right, the variation of the right, and the subsequent continued existence of the right as varied. See also *Re Northern Engineering Industries plc* [1994] BCC 618 (CA).

[2] See *Rights & Issues Investment Trust Ltd v Stylo Shoes Ltd* [1965] Ch 250 (Pennycuick J).

[3] Formerly CA 1985, s 127.

of shares provided that they constitute not less than 15% of the issued shares of the class. Such persons may apply to the court to have the variation cancelled.

13.02 A class meeting is a meeting of the holders of shares of a particular class. Such meetings are one of the two methods of providing the consent of the holders of shares of that class in circumstances where the consent of that class is required. The most frequent reason for calling a class meeting is where a company is considering any variation or abrogation of the rights attached to a class of shares. According to CA 2006, shares are of one class if the rights attached to them are in all respects uniform.[4] Class rights may cover such matters as the right to attend at meetings of the company, the right to vote, rights to receive dividends or to a return of capital on a winding up and related matters.

13.03 CA 1980, s 32 first introduced a statutory code for dealing with the variation of class rights, which provisions were re-enacted in CA 1985, ss 125–129. CA 2006, Part 17, Chapter 9 largely reproduces these provisions in more modern, simplified language. Whereas CA 1985 dealt only with the variation of the rights attached to any class of shares in a company whose share capital was divided into shares of different classes, CA 2006 extends the protections afforded by the statute to companies without a share capital, including companies limited by guarantee.[5]

13.04 The purpose of this chapter is to explain the new procedures for the holding of class meetings and the provision of class consents under CA 2006. It is beyond the scope of this work to consider in any detail the nature of class rights and the circumstances in which such rights are held to have been varied or abrogated.

Procedures under CA 2006

13.05 The articles of association of most modern companies contain provisions for the variation of the rights attached to different classes of shares.[6] These provisions are paramount and must be followed at all times. It is to be noted that such provisions in a company's articles of association may be more liberal than the statutory scheme described below and may impose a less demanding procedure for such variations, including approval by an ordinary resolution of the particular class (ie by a simple majority). By CA 2006, s 630(5) any amendment of a provision contained in a company's articles for the variation of the rights attached to a class

[4] See CA 2006, s 629(1) which came into force for certain purposes on 1 October 2007—see Third Commencement Order, SI 2007/2194, art 2, para (3)(g).

[5] See CA 2006, s 631.

[6] See reg 4 of the 1948 Table A and CA 2006, s 630(2)(a).

of shares, or the insertion of any such provision into the articles, is itself to be treated as a variation of those rights.

Under CA 2006, s 630, where the company's articles of association contain no provision with respect to the variation of those rights the rights may only be varied if the holders of shares of that class consent to the variation in accordance with the section. Such consent must be provided either in writing from the holders of at least three-quarters in nominal value of the issued shares of that class[7] or by a special resolution passed at a separate general meeting of the holders of that class sanctioning the variation.[8] **13.06**

Section 630 differs from its predecessor, CA 1985, s 125(2)(b), which referred to an extraordinary resolution rather than a special resolution. Extraordinary resolutions, which required the support of a majority of not less than three-fourths of the members entitled to vote at a general meeting of which notice specifying the intention to propose the resolution as an extraordinary resolution had been duly given, have been abolished by CA 2006. However, the articles of very many existing companies and many shareholders' agreements and other contracts contain references to extraordinary resolutions of the holders of classes of shares. These provisions continue to have full legal effect. This has been achieved by the implementation of an important transitional provision. Schedule 3, para 23 to the Third Commencement Order provides that any reference to an extraordinary resolution in a provision in the memorandum or articles of a company or of a contract continues to have effect and must be construed in accordance with CA 1985, s 378 as if that section had not been repealed. **13.07**

CA 2006, s 630(3) preserves any other restrictions on the variation of rights. Accordingly, if the articles of association of a company have a more rigorous regime for the variation of class rights than those contained in CA 2006 those provisions must be followed. These may include a requirement for a higher percentage of support for a proposed variation of rights. In this context it should be noted that CA 2006 allows a company to entrench class rights by making what are defined as 'provisions for entrenchment' in accordance with CA 2006, s 22. Such provisions may specify that certain articles of association may be amended or repealed only if certain conditions or procedures are complied with, and such conditions may be more restrictive than a special resolution. Such a provision may only be introduced into the company's articles of association on formation or by an amendment to the articles agreed to by all the members. A provision for entrenchment does not prevent an amendment to the company's articles with the unanimous agreement of the members or by order of the court. **13.08**

---

[7] Excluding any shares held as treasury shares.

[8] See CA 2006, s 630(4)(b).

13.09 CA 2006, s 631 applies similar rules to the variation of the rights of members of a company which does not have a share capital. This provision is new. The rights of a class of members may only be varied in accordance with any provision in the company's articles of association or, where there is no such provision, if the members consent in accordance with s 631(4). The articles may make provision for a less onerous regime than that contained in the section. Under the section, such consent must either be in writing from at least three-quarters of the members of the class or by a special resolution passed at a separate general meeting of the members of the class sanctioning the variation. Once again, CA 2006, s 631 is without prejudice to any other restrictions on the variation of the rights of members. It is therefore open to the company to adopt a more onerous regime for modification of rights and s 22 (dealing with provisions for entrenchment) also applies to this type of company.

Class meetings of companies with a share capital

13.10 CA 2006, s 334, which came into legal force on 1 October 2007[9] and is derived from CA 1985, s 125(6) applies the provisions of CA 2006, Part 13, Chapter 3, namely ss 301–333 (inclusive), to class meetings in the same way as they apply to general meetings but with necessary modifications. These modifications include some express exceptions which are discussed below. It should be noted that the applicable provisions include ss 314–317, by which members may require the company to circulate a statement of not more than 1,000 words to the members entitled to receive notice of the class meeting. These provisions replace CA 1985, s 125(6).[10]

CA 2006, ss 303–305 not applicable to class meetings

13.11 By CA 2006, s 334(2), the power given to members to require the directors to call a general meeting in ss 303–305 does not apply to a class meeting. A class meeting therefore cannot be requested and, if need be, called by members under the statute and can only be called by the directors under s 302.

CA 2006, s 306 not applicable to class meetings

13.12 It is important to note that by CA 2006, s 334(2), the discretionary jurisdiction conferred on the court by CA 2006, s 306 to order the holding of a general meeting of a company[11] in circumstances where for any reason it is impracticable to

---

[9] See Third Commencement Order: SI 2007/2194, art 2(1)(f).
[10] See more generally Ch 3.
[11] See Ch 6.

hold a general meeting, does not extend to class meetings. Accordingly, the court has no power to order a class meeting.[12]

CA 2006, s 334(3) and (4)

Where a meeting has been called to consider the variation of the rights attached to a class of shares (which the statute defines as a 'variation of class rights meeting') the quorum provisions of s 318 do not apply but are instead replaced by the provisions of CA 2006, s 334(4).[13] That section repeats the substance of CA 1985, s 125(6) and provides that for a meeting other than an adjourned meeting two persons holding at least one-third in nominal value of the issued shares of the class (excluding any treasury shares) constitute a quorum. In respect of an adjourned meeting the quorum is formed by one person holding shares of the class in question. A gloss is placed on subs (4) by s 334(5) which states that for the purposes of this provision, where a person is present by proxy or proxies he is treated as holding only the shares in respect of which those proxies are authorized to vote. **13.13**

CA 2006, s 334(3) also disapplies CA 2006, s 321, dealing with the right to demand a poll of a minimum number of members or of a member or members representing a minimum proportion of the total voting rights of all the members having the right to vote. Under s 334(6) at a variation of class rights meeting any holder of shares of the class may demand a poll. **13.14**

Class meetings of companies without a share capital

CA 2006, s 335 makes similar modifications to the provisions of CA 2006, Part 13, Chapter 3 in relation to meetings of a class of members of a company without a share capital. Subject to those exceptions the same provisions apply to such class meetings. The excluded provisions are ss 303–305 (members' power to require directors to call a general meeting), s 306 (the court's power to order a meeting), s 318 (quorum) and s 321 (the right to demand a poll). In respect of a variation of class rights meeting two members of the class, present in person or by proxy, who together represent one-third of the voting rights of the class make a quorum.[14] At an adjourned meeting only one member of the class present in person or by proxy is required.[15] In addition, at such a meeting any member present, in person or by proxy, may demand a poll.[16] **13.15**

---

[12] It is arguable that a class meeting may be ordered by the court under the powers contained in CA 2006, s 996 where the court is satisfied that a petition on grounds of unfair prejudice under s 994 is well founded.

[13] See CA 2006, s 334(3)(a).

[14] CA 2006, s 335(4)(a).

[15] CA 2006, s 335(4)(b).

[16] CA 2006, s 335(5).

Written class consents

13.16 The concept of written resolutions of a class of members of a company is a well-established feature of company law. It has been standard practice for many years for well-drafted articles of association to provide in terms for the consent in writing of a fixed proportion of the issued shares of a class to any variation of class rights.[17] The need to obtain a class consent is, however, not confined to the area of variation of rights. For example, the consent of a particular class of members may sometimes be required under a company's articles of association in relation to any proposed expansion in the limits on the borrowing powers of directors.

13.17 The new provisions in CA 2006, Part 13, Chapter 2 dealing with written resolutions of private companies contain certain declaratory provisions as to the effectiveness of such written resolutions in the context of the making of decisions by classes of shareholders in private companies. Section 288(4) provides that references in 'enactments'[18] passed or made before CA 2006, Part 13, Chapter 2 comes into force to a resolution of a meeting of a class of members of the company, have effect as if they included references to a written resolution of the class of members. In addition, by CA 2006, s 288(5) a written resolution of a private company, proposed and passed in accordance with Chapter 2, has effect as if passed by the company in general meeting or by a meeting of a class of members of the company, and references in any statute passed or made before this section comes into force to a meeting at which a resolution is passed or to members voting in favour of a resolution must be construed accordingly.

13.18 Written resolutions of a class of members of a private company can therefore be passed under the new statutory code in place of a resolution of the members of that class passed at a separate general meeting of that class. This is also apparent from the definition of 'eligible members' in s 289(1), who are defined as the members who would have been entitled to vote on the resolution on the circulation date as defined in s 290. The subsequent provisions of Chapter 2, namely ss 289–300, deal with the new statutory written resolution procedure. For a detailed analysis of these provisions reference should be made to Chapter 15 and to the commentary in Part 3.

13.19 The impact of the application of the new written resolution procedure to private companies could be significant. Members of a class of shares will now be able

[17] See CA 2006, s 630(4)(a) (formerly CA 1985, s 125(2)).

[18] The word 'enactment' is defined in CA 2006, s 1293 as including, unless the context otherwise requires, an enactment contained in subordinated legislation within the Interpretation Act 1978, an enactment of the Scottish Parliament or contained in Northern Ireland legislation.

themselves to initiate a class resolution under CA 2006, s 292 and require the company to circulate such a proposal. The requisite percentage for triggering this process is 5% of the members entitled to vote on the resolution or such lesser percentage as may be specified in the company's articles of association. Interestingly, the members of a class may not request a separate general meeting of the class under s 303 (which applies a general threshold of 10% support) because that right is expressly excluded in relation to class meetings by CA 2006, s 334(2)(a).

Class meetings of quoted companies

CA 2006, s 352 stipulates that the provisions of ss 341–351 (inclusive) apply to class meetings of quoted companies where such class meetings are dealing with variation or abrogation of class rights. As a result of s 352 the result of any vote taken or a poll at a class meeting of a quoted company must be made available on a website under CA 2006, s 341. Further, the requisite number of members of a class of shares of a quoted company have a statutory right to require the appointment of an independent assessor to report on a poll taken at a class meeting in accordance with the elaborate procedure set out in CA 2006, ss 342–351. These statutory provisions are examined in Chapter 9 and in the detailed commentary in Part 3. **13.20**

Schemes of arrangement

Notwithstanding the broad wording of CA 2006, s 288(5) it would seem that the new procedure for obtaining a written resolution of the members of a class does not apply to a scheme of arrangement under CA 2006, Part 26.[19] The reason for this is that the procedure for the sanction of a scheme of arrangement requires the court under s 896(1) to order 'a meeting' of the members of the company or class of members to be summoned. The jurisdiction of the court under s 899(1) to sanction the scheme only arises if a majority in number representing 75% in value of the members or class of members present and voting either in person or by proxy at 'the meeting summoned under section 896' agree the compromise or arrangement. In the light of this wording, it appears that there is no scope for the use of the written resolution procedure in CA 2006, Part 13, Chapter 2 in relation to a scheme of arrangement. Class meetings in the traditional sense will continue to be required for schemes of arrangement.[20] **13.21**

[19] See ss 895–901 (inclusive).
[20] For further discussion of this topic see Ch 14.

Transitional provisions

13.22 CA 2006, ss 334 and 335 came into force on 1 October 2007. The sections are subject to transitional provisions that are to be found in para 31 of the Third Commencement Order. The provisions of CA 1985, s 125(6) continue to apply in relation to meetings of which notice was given prior to 1 October 2007 and where notice of a meeting is given over more than one day it is treated for the purposes of para 31(2) as given on the first of those days.

14

MEETINGS FOR THE PURPOSES OF SCHEMES OF ARRANGEMENT

Introduction

14.01 A scheme of compromise or arrangement may consist of a compromise or arrangement between a company and its creditors or any class of them, or between a company and its members, or any class of them.[1] CA 2006, Part 26, ss 896–901 (inclusive), entitled 'Arrangements and Reconstructions', substantially reproduces CA 1985, ss 425–427 with certain minor modifications to which reference will be made below. The statute applies the term 'arrangement' to include a reorganization of the company's share capital by the consolidation of different classes of shares or by the division of shares into shares of different classes.[2] CA 2006, Part 27, ss 902–941 (inclusive), deals separately with the provisions enabling the merger or division of a public company, previously contained in CA 1985, s 427A and Sch 15B. The detailed practice and procedures governing applications for schemes of arrangement under

---

1 See CA 2006, s 896(1).
2 See CA 2006, s 896(2).

Parts 26 and 27 are beyond the scope of this book and are referred to in this chapter only by way of summary.[3]

14.02 For a scheme of arrangement under Part 26 to take effect the following five key steps must be taken:

(1) a scheme of compromise or arrangement must be formulated;
(2) an application must be made to the court under CA 2006, s 896 to order a meeting of the creditors or class of creditors, or the members or class of members as the case may be, to be summoned in such manner as the court directs;
(3) the scheme of compromise or arrangement must be approved by the meetings summoned as directed by the court by the requisite statutory majority, being a majority in number representing 75% in value of the creditors or class of creditors or members or class of members, as the case may be, present and voting in person or by proxy at the meeting summoned under CA 2006, s 896;
(4) the scheme of compromise or arrangement must receive the sanction of the court under CA 2006, s 899(1); and
(5) a copy of the court's order must be delivered to the Registrar under CA 2006, s 899(4).

14.03 The purpose of this chapter is to examine the special rules governing the meetings of creditors or members summoned by the court under s 896. These special rules have been developed by the courts over many years when exercising the statutory discretion to sanction the compromise or arrangement. One of the most significant tasks facing the persons formulating any scheme is to ascertain the correct classes of creditors or members, so that application may be made to the court for an appropriate order that meetings may be summoned. It is at this stage that a decision needs to be taken as to whether or not to summon more than one meeting and, if so, who should be summoned to which meeting. If an error is made in formulating the correct classes involved, the scheme may be refused sanction by the court and costs will be wasted.[4]

14.04 In an effort to deal with the practical consequences of this problem, in April 2002 Sir Andrew Morritt, the Vice-Chancellor of the Chancery Division of the High Court, issued a Practice Statement[5] in respect of schemes of arrangement between a company and its creditors so as to avoid the waste of costs and court time as illustrated by the facts in *Re Hawk Insurance Co Ltd.*[6]

---

[3] Readers are referred to leading practitioners' textbooks on company law such as *Buckley on the Companies Acts* and *Gore-Browne on Companies* for such analysis.

[4] See eg *Re Hellenic & General Trust Ltd* [1976] 1 WLR 123 (Templeman J); *Re Hawk Insurance Co Ltd* [2001] 2 BCLC 480 (Arden J and CA); *Re Telewest Communications plc (No 1)*; *Re Telewest Finance (Jersey) Ltd (No 1)* [2005] 1 BCLC 752 (David Richards J) at [14].

[5] *Practice Statement (Companies: Schemes of Arrangement)* [2002] 1 WLR 1345.

[6] [2001] 2 BCLC 480 (CA) per Chadwick LJ at [11]–[22].

The 2002 Practice Statement[7]

The Practice Statement is directed to the practice on applications pursuant to what was CA 1985, s 425, now CA 2006, s 896, seeking the sanction of the court to a scheme of arrangement between a company and its creditors. (It makes no mention of members' schemes where similar problems rarely arise.) The purpose is to enable issues concerning the composition of classes of creditor and the summoning of meetings to be identified and, if appropriate, resolved early in the proceedings. The Practice Statement makes it clear that it is the responsibility of the applicant to determine whether more than one meeting of creditors is required by a scheme and, if so, to ensure that those meetings are properly constituted. Each meeting must consist of creditors whose rights against the company are 'not so dissimilar as to make it impossible for them to consult together with a view to their common interest'. **14.05**

It is the responsibility of the applicant by evidence to the court to draw attention as soon as possible to any issues which may arise as to the constitution of meetings of creditors or which otherwise affect the conduct of those meetings. The applicant is obliged to take all steps reasonably open to it to notify any person affected by the scheme that it is being promoted, the purpose which the scheme is designed to achieve, the meetings of creditors which the applicant considers will be required and their composition. **14.06**

When considering whether or not to order meetings of creditors the court will consider whether one or more meetings of creditors is required and, if so, what is the appropriate composition of those meetings. Where an issue arises as to the constitution of the meetings and this has been drawn to the attention of the court, it will also consider whether to give directions for the resolution of that issue, including, where necessary, directions for the postponement of meetings of creditors until the issue is resolved. The aim is that issues over the composition of the meetings are raised at an early stage. **14.07**

The court may give directions for anyone affected by a meetings order to apply to vary or discharge the order within a limited time, with the creditors' meetings to take place in default of such an application within the time prescribed. Creditors who consider that they have been unfairly treated are nevertheless still able to appear and raise objections on the hearing of the application to sanction the scheme, but the court expects them to show good reason why they did not object earlier. **14.08**

The practical consequences of the Practice Statement were considered in *Re Telewest Communications plc (No 1); Re Telewest Finance (Jersey) Ltd (No 1)*, **14.09**

---

7 [2002] 1 WLR 1345.

where David Richards J stated that the procedure is designed to enable, so far as possible, the determination of all issues in relation to the composition of the class or classes of creditors or members for the purposes of the scheme to take place at the hearing of the application for leave to convene meetings. These issues go to the court's jurisdiction to sanction a scheme, rather than the exercise of its discretion to grant or withhold its sanction. In that particular case the hearing of the applications was advertised in a number of newspapers and creditors were invited to make representations to the court if they objected to the class or classes proposed by the companies.

14.10 In *Re British Aviation Insurance Co Ltd*[8] Lewison J followed the decision in *Re Telewest Communications plc (No 1)* and stated that the extent of the notification of the application to the court at the first stage need not be as extensive as the notification that the court may order on the application at that stage. He noted that the requirement of notification is not absolute and applies 'unless there are good reasons for not doing so'. In his view, time and expense were capable of being good reasons for not notifying persons affected by the proposed scheme. The first stage application is purely procedural and regulates the manner in which the scheme is to be presented for approval. Although it is desirable for points about separate classes to be taken at that stage, it is not essential.

Court meetings generally

14.11 It is important to note at the outset that any meeting summoned by the court to consider a proposed compromise or arrangement is not a general meeting of the company in the normal sense but a meeting convened pursuant to an order of the court under CA 2006, s 896. For this reason it is the court which gives directions as to how the meeting should be conducted and the meeting is not governed by the company's articles of association. Notwithstanding the fact that s 896 itself does not refer to methods of voting and procedure, it has been held that the court has an inherent power to decide the mode in which meetings should be held and the methods of voting, including the appointment of proxies.[9]

The application for a meeting

14.12 An application to the court for an order that a meeting of members or creditors may be summoned ('a meetings order') may be made either by the company itself, or by a creditor or member or, in the case of a company that is being wound up or in administration, by the liquidator or administrator.[10]

[8] [2006] 1 BCLC 665 at [56].

[9] See *Re English, Scottish and Australian Chartered Bank* [1893] 3 Ch 385 at 395–6 (CA).

[10] See CA 2006, s 896(2).

An application for an order convening a meeting may therefore be made without the approval or support of the company. However, in such a case, the court has a discretion as to whether to order a meeting under s 896 without the consent of the company. It will not do so if this would serve no useful purpose. This principle was established in the decision made in *Re Savoy Hotel Limited*[11] during the course of the famous takeover battle. The applicant, Trust House Forte Ltd, was a shareholder in the Savoy company who wished to gain control of London's Savoy Hotel. The company had two classes of shares with differential voting rights. Having made takeover proposals to the board of the company, which, unsurprisingly, had been rejected, the applicant applied to the court for an order seeking liberty to convene separate meetings of the A and B shareholders and for consequential directions. The company vigorously opposed the application. **14.13**

Nourse J held that the approval of the company to the scheme was essential and that the court has no jurisdiction to sanction an arrangement under the statute which does not have the approval of the company either through the board or by means of a simple majority of the members in general meeting. In the circumstances, the court would not order meetings of the members to be convened as the scheme did not have board approval and did not provide for the approval of the company in general meeting. As there was no reasonable probability that the meetings would serve a useful purpose, and no real prospect that the meetings would achieve anything, the court would not convene them. The application was dismissed. **14.14**

The application under s 896 for an order that meetings be summoned is quite separate from the later application under CA 2006, s 899 to sanction the scheme. This was emphasized by the court in *Re Telewest Communications plc*,[12] a case which concerned a creditors' scheme. The application for a meetings order is not a hearing to consider the merits or fairness of the scheme. The matters for consideration at this stage concern the jurisdiction of the court to sanction the scheme if it proceeds, being principally the composition of the classes of creditors. David Richards J held that there is no point in the court convening meetings to consider the scheme if it can be seen at this stage that it will lack the jurisdiction to sanction it later. **14.15**

Classes

Usually creditors or members opposing a scheme will argue for separate classes because they wish to vote against the scheme but without a separate class meeting will be outvoted by those with different rights.[13] The scheme will be binding on **14.16**

[11] [1981] Ch 351 (Nourse J). See also *Re MytravelGroup plc* [2005] 1 WLR 2365 (Mann J).

[12] *Re Telewest Communications plc (No 1); Re Telewest Finance (Jersey) Ltd (No1)* [2005] 1 BCLC 752 at [13]–[15] (David Richards J).

[13] ibid at [17].

dissentient minorities and therefore the importance of separate meetings at which the rights of different classes may be considered is crucial. In recent years there have been a number of decided cases in which the court has had to consider the composition of classes for the purposes of the predecessor to CA 2006, s 896, namely CA 1985, s 425. The law on this subject is complex and beyond the scope of this book but it is hoped that the following summary, derived in substantial part from the landmark decision of Lord Millett in the Court of Final Appeal of Hong Kong in *Re UDL Holdings Limited*,[14] may act as a guide to the key principles involved:

16.1 It is differences in legal rights against the company, not the similarity or dissimilarity of interests, which are relevant to the composition of classes.

16.2 A class is confined to those persons whose rights are not so dissimilar as to make it impossible for them to consult together with a view to their common interest. They should be summoned to a single meeting. The rights need not be identical and a broad view should be taken of the meaning of 'class'.[15]

16.3 Where the rights of persons are so dissimilar that the holders cannot sensibly consult together they must be given separate meetings.

16.4 Whether or not a particular group constitutes a separate class must depend on the particular facts of the case and on the nature of the differences said to exist between the alleged classes and the relevant terms of the particular scheme.[16]

16.5 The question is whether the rights which are to be released or varied under the scheme or the new rights which the scheme gives in their place are so different that the scheme must be treated as a compromise or arrangement with more than one class.[17]

16.6 The Court must have regard to the danger that if separate meetings are ordered where persons enjoy similar rights, that may give an unjustified veto to a minority group which might become an instrument of oppression by the minority.[18]

16.7 A member or creditor who falls within two classes is properly a member of each class and must be treated accordingly.[19]

The necessity for there to be a meeting

14.17 It is essential to note that the procedure for the sanction of a scheme of arrangement requires the court under CA 2006, s 896(1) to order 'a meeting' of the members of the company or class of members to be summoned. The jurisdiction of

[14] [2002] 1 HKC 172; see also *Sovereign Life Assurance v Dodd* [1892] 2 QB 573 (CA); and *Re Sovereign Marine and General Insurance Co Ltd* [2007] 1 BCLC 228 at [72]–[93] (Warren J).

[15] See *Re Hawk Insurance Co Ltd* [2001] 2 BCLC 480 (CA) at [62] per Pill LJ.

[16] See *Re Anglo American Insurance Ltd* [2001] 1 BCLC 755, 764 (Neuberger J).

[17] See *Re Equitable Life Assurance Society* [2002] 2 BCLC 510 at [43]–[48] (Lloyd J).

[18] See *Re Hawk Insurance Co Ltd* [2001] 2 BCLC 480 (CA) at [32] and [33] per Chadwick LJ, citing Lush J in *Nordic Bank plc v International Harvester Australia Ltd* [1982] 2 VR 298 at 301.

[19] See *Re Alabama, New Orleans, Texas and Pacific Junction Railway Co* [1891] 1 Ch 213 (CA).

the court under s 899(1) to sanction the scheme only arises if a majority in number representing 75% in value of the creditors or class of creditors or members or class of members present and voting either in person or by proxy at 'the meeting summoned under section 896' agrees the compromise or arrangement. In the light of this wording, there is no scope for the use of the written resolution procedure in CA 2006, Part 13, Chapter 2 in relation to a scheme of arrangement. Class meetings in the traditional sense therefore continue to be required for schemes of arrangement. The only exception to the necessity of a meeting is where the class comprises only one member.[20]

The importance of separate class meetings in relation to a creditors' scheme was re-stated by David Richards J in the recent decision of *Re Altitude Scaffolding Ltd; Re T & N Ltd.*[21] In that case the question arose as to whether the attendance in person or by proxy of only one member of a class of creditors at the time and place fixed for a meeting convened to consider a scheme of arrangement under what was then CA 1985, s 425 constituted a meeting of the class for the purposes of the section. On the first petition there was evidence that only one creditor had attended each class meeting. On the second petition the applicant administrators anticipated that only one creditor might attend the meetings of one or more companies. They therefore sought a direction that the attendance of only one creditor would nevertheless constitute a meeting. **14.18**

After a careful review of the relevant authorities on what constituted a meeting[22] David Richards J concluded that a 'meeting' denoted a coming together of two or more persons.[23] Parliament had intended the word 'meeting' in the section to have its ordinary meaning except where there was only one member of a class.[24] A meeting of each class was the means by which the formal consent of creditors was to be obtained under the statute. Accordingly, a meeting was required to be attended by more than one person and it followed that the court had no jurisdiction to sanction a scheme if no proper meeting had taken place. Equally, the court would not give a direction that the attendance of only one creditor would constitute a meeting for the purposes of the section. David Richards J held: **14.19**

> Section 425 requires approval by the stated majorities to be given at a meeting, rather than for example in writing. The purpose would seem to be to enable each class to debate the merits of the scheme among themselves and, if given the opportunity, to question the scheme's proponents. It is to be noted that in the classic definition of

[20] See *East v Bennett Brothers Limited* [1911] 1 Ch 163 (Warrington J); *Re RMCA Reinsurance Ltd* [1994] BCC 378 (Morritt J).

[21] [2007] 1 BCLC 199 (David Richards J).

[22] See *Sharp v Dawes* (1876) 2 QBD 26; *Re Sanitary Carbon Co* [1877] WN 223; *Re London Flats Ltd* [1969] 1 WLR 711 (Plowman J) and *Re MJ Shanley Contracting Ltd* (1980) 124 Sol Jo 239.

[23] See also Ch 1.

[24] See *Re RMCA Reinsurance Ltd* [1994] BCC 378 (Morritt J).

a class given by Bowen LJ in *Sovereign Life Assurance Co v Dodd* [1892] 2 QB 573 at 583, the fact that a meeting of each class was to be called was a central consideration.[25]

14.20 In the exceptional case where a class of members or creditors comprises only one person the court has jurisdiction to direct a class meeting to be held even though only one person will be present.[26] In fact, it is probably not necessary to ask the court to convene a meeting under CA 2006, s 896(1) in such a case because it is well established that a member or creditor may, by his individual consent, agree to be bound by a scheme.[27]

The court's directions—how to hold the meeting

14.21 Application is made to the court for a meetings order by way of a Claim Form issued under CPR Part 8. In giving its directions under a meetings order the court will give liberty to the company to convene the meetings (often referred to as 'court meetings'), stipulate the manner in which the meetings must be convened, the form of the notice of meeting, the forms of the proxy that must be used and the appointment of the chairman. The meetings order directs the chairman to report to the court on the outcome of the meetings and the chairman's report always forms an important part of the evidence to the court at the hearing of the later application under s 899 to sanction the scheme. Each of these important items must now be considered.

The notice and the explanatory statement

14.22 Section 897 prescribes the information which is to be sent to the members or creditors when a meeting is summoned under s 896. The court will order that every notice summoning the meeting that is sent to a creditor or member be accompanied by a statement complying with CA 2006, s 897 explaining the effect of the compromise or arrangement and stating any material interests of the directors of the company and the effect on those interests of the compromise or arrangement, insofar as it is different from the effect on the like interests of other persons.[28]

14.23 The court order will also make provision for notice to be given by advertisement, to be placed in a national newspaper. Section 897(1)(b) requires that every notice given by advertisement must either include the statement complying with s 897 or state where and how creditors or members entitled to attend the meeting may obtain copies of the statement. The court will invariably order the advertisement

[25] [2007] 1 BCLC 199 at [7].
[26] See *Re RMCA Reinsurance Ltd* [1994] BCC 378 (Morritt J).
[27] See *Re Altitude Scaffolding Ltd; Re T & N Ltd* (op. cit.) at [13].
[28] See CA 2006, s 897(1)(a) and (2) (previously CA 1985, s 426(1)).

to state that copies of the scheme of arrangement, the forms of proxy and copies of the statement required to be furnished pursuant to s 897 may be obtained at the company's registered office.[29]

The court order will provide for a notice convening the meeting to be given, enclosing a copy of the scheme of arrangement, a copy of the statement required under s 897 and a form of proxy in the form initialled by the court to be served personally on or sent by pre-paid first class letter post or airmail as appropriate addressed to each member as appearing in the company's register of members on a record date not more than 15 days before the date of posting (or, in the case of joint holders, to the first named member in the company's register of members) at their registered or last known address. **14.24**

Care should be taken to ensure that the court order includes provision that the accidental omission to serve any holder of shares or any creditor with notice of the meeting, or the non-receipt by any such member or creditor, as the case may be, of the notice of the meeting, will not invalidate the proceedings at the meeting. If such a provision is not included in the order, it may later be necessary at the hearing to sanction the scheme under CA 2006, s 899 to fall back on the court's inherent power to waive non-compliance with its directions as to the convening of the meeting (see below).[30] **14.25**

The forms of proxy

The court will direct that forms of proxy be used and circulated for the purposes of the court meetings of creditors or members as the case may be, along with the notice of the meetings.[31] The proxy form, which will be approved by the court at the hearing of the application for directions, will appoint the chairman of the meeting or some other person whose name must be inserted as the holder's proxy to attend the meeting and vote on his behalf. The proxy is for use at the court meeting or 'at any adjourned meeting'. The language of the proxy therefore correctly assumes that the court meeting may be adjourned. In *Re Waxed Papers Ltd*[32] Slesser LJ held that the form of proxy extended to authorize the holder, the chairman of the particular meeting in that case, to vote on any incidental matter that might arise at the meeting, including a motion for an adjournment.[33] **14.26**

---

[29] See CA 2006, s 897(1)(b) (formerly CA 1985, s 426(3)).
[30] See *Re Anglo-Spanish Tatar Refineries Ltd* [1924] WN 222 (Romer J).
[31] See *Re Dorman Long & Co Ltd* [1934] 1 Ch 635 (Maugham J).
[32] [1937] 2 All ER 481 (CA).
[33] Cited by Jonathan Parker J in *Re BTR plc* [1999] 2 BCLC 675 at 683.

Security

14.27 For a court meeting of a public company it is often sensible for arrangements to be made for security and provision to this effect may be included in the court order. This may be incorporated in the court order by reference to an existing power in the company's articles of association, which of course otherwise do not apply to the court meeting.

The chairman of the meeting

14.28 The chairman of the court meeting has a vital role to play. He and at least one alternative will be named in the court order. He will also be ordered to report to the court the result of the meeting. In case any objection is taken at a later stage to any proxies the report should state the number of proxies voted, the number determined to be invalid and the number supplied to the chairman at the meeting.

14.29 In relation to a creditors' scheme, the chairman is sometimes required by the terms of the meetings order to place a value on a person's claim. The notion of a chairman valuing a claim means that he is required to ascribe a genuine value to it. In *Re British Aviation Insurance Co*[34] Lewison J held that the chairman does not have the luxury of saying that he does not know what the value is and placing an arbitrary notional sum on the claim. To disallow claims because they are uncertain or unreliable is not to value them at all and is a serious matter as it amounts to non-compliance with the court's directions.

The quorum

14.30 CA 2006, s 896, like its predecessor in CA 1985, does not impose any requirement as to the necessary quorum for the court meetings. However, it is apparent from the judgment of David Richards J in *Re Altitude Scaffolding Ltd; Re T & N Ltd*[35] that at least two persons present in person or by proxy are required for an effective meeting.

Liberty to apply

14.31 It is customary to insert in the meetings order a provision for liberty to apply, thereby enabling the applicant to return to the court for further directions as matters evolve. This is a useful and essential device which enables the applicant to keep the court informed as to any change of circumstances that may threaten the outcome of the meeting. It permits additional directions as to the conduct of the meeting to be provided by the court as required.

[34] [2006] 1 BCLC 665 at [107] (Lewison J).
[35] [2007]1 BCLC 199.

Adjournments

By reason of the fact that the court meetings are not convened under the company's constitution and that the regulations contained in the company's articles of association as regards meetings do not generally apply, there is no express power for the meetings to be adjourned unless such a power is included within the meetings order. Where an adjournment is likely but no such power is included in the meetings order, it may be sensible for the applicant to return to the court under the liberty to apply for a further direction, giving the chairman of the meeting a power to order an adjournment where he considers it to be appropriate in the interests of the company. If the chairman goes ahead and adjourns the court meeting without such an express power in the order, he runs the risk that the court might subsequently refuse to sanction the scheme because of some unfairness arising from the adjournment or the manner of reconvening the meeting.[36] **14.32**

As mentioned above, proxy votes may be utilized on a motion to adjourn.[37] In *Re Waxed Papers Ltd* the Court of Appeal held that to vote for a resolution proposing an adjournment of a scheme for a short or long period was to oppose the scheme. Accordingly, proxies on behalf of persons who oppose a scheme should be tendered by the chairman in favour of the resolution to adjourn and those on behalf of supporters of the scheme should be used in voting against a resolution to adjourn.[38] **14.33**

Additional directions

The court may be prepared to include in the meetings order any appropriate direction which will enable an effective meeting to take place. This may include liberty for a person appointed a proxy to vote on a show of hands, provisions for demanding a poll, provisions for the time for holding any poll and a power enabling any person appointed a proxy in relation to a particular meeting to speak at that meeting. **14.34**

The court's power to waive defects

The court has jurisdiction at the hearing of the application to sanction the scheme under s 899 to waive any errors that may have arisen in the procedures ordered to be undertaken in convening the court meetings. This principle is derived from the **14.35**

---

[36] See the remarks of Warren J in *Re Peninsular and Oriental Steam Navigation Company* [2006] EWHC 389 at [54]; [2006] All ER (D) 36 (Mar).

[37] See *Re Waxed Papers Ltd* [1937] 2 All ER 481 (CA) and *Re BTR plc* [1999] 2 BCLC 675 at 683 (Jonathan Parker J).

[38] See *Re BTR plc* [1999] 2 BCLC 675 at 683–4 and *Re Abbey National plc* [2005] 2 BCLC 15 at [8] (Evans Lombe J). See also Ch 12 at paras 12.19 and 12.20.

decision of Romer J in *Re Anglo-Spanish Tatar Refineries Limited*[39] where the company failed to comply with a direction that the court meetings of ordinary and deferred shareholders be advertised in three newspapers at least 14 clear days before the date of the meetings. Through a mistake by the company's solicitors none of the advertisements appeared, although this was not discovered until after the meetings had been held. The company was able to prove that out of 31 shareholders some 30 had received the notices, and the holders of 139,400 of the 140,000 ordinary shares and 199,275 out of 200,000 deferred shares were accounted for at the meetings. On the evidence that was before the Court Romer J held that the meetings had been 'in substance' summoned in the manner prescribed by the court order, the object of which was to secure that every shareholder received notice of the meetings. That appeared to be the case with one exception. In the circumstances the court waived the defect and did not require further meetings to be convened.

14.36 The court's power to waive defects in compliance with its directions may, for example, be used to waive the late service of documents, if such service has caused no prejudice. Equally the court may exercise its discretion to absolve the company where there has been an accidental omission to serve any creditor or class of creditor or member or class of member with notice of the meeting, or the non-receipt by any holder of notice of the meeting. In such a case the court will have regard to the circumstances in which the error occurred, the numbers of persons affected and the possibility of any practical difference to the outcome.[40]

14.37 Finally, it should be noted that from 14 January 2008 Appendix 7 to the Takeover Code applies to takeovers structured as schemes of arrangement under sections 895 to 899 of the CA 2006. Appendix 7 was introduced by the Code Committee of the Takeover Panel by way of an Instrument under s 944 of the CA 2006—Instrument 2007/1—Schemes of arrangement. This provides that the court meeting must normally be convened for a date which is at least 21 days after the date of the scheme circular. It is not clear in what circumstances the Panel may be prepared to waive this requirement.

[39] [1924] WN 222 (Romer J).

[40] For a recent decision containing detailed consideration of the circumstances where proper service of notice is not achieved and the court's power to waive defects see *Re Peninsular and Oriental Steam Navigation Company* [2006] EWHC 389 [2006]; All ER (D) 36 (Mar) (Warren J) and [2006] EWCA Civ 432 (Court of Appeal, Lloyd LJ); see also *Re Alliance Assurance Co Ltd; Re British Engine Insurance Ltd and other companies* [2006] All ER (D) 196 (Oct).

15

WRITTEN RESOLUTIONS OF PRIVATE COMPANIES

Introduction

15.01 The important subject of written resolutions of private companies is dealt with in CA 2006, Part 13, Chapter 2, which comprises ss 288–300.[1] These individual sections are analysed in detail in the commentary in Part 3. These new provisions mark a considerable extension of the statutory code previously contained in CA 1985, ss 381A–381C and Sch 15A. These latter provisions were incorporated into CA 1985 by CA 1989 with effect from 1 April 1990.

Procedure under CA 1985

15.02 Under CA 1985 (as amended) it was permissible for a private company to authorize matters to be done without a meeting and without any previous notice by means of a resolution in writing signed by on or behalf of all the members of the company who at the date of the resolution would have been entitled to attend and vote at such meeting.[2] In order to pass a valid written resolution, a copy of the resolution had to be signed by or on behalf of all members of the company. The relevant signatures did not need to be on a single document for the written resolution to be validly passed.[3]

General meetings and class meetings

15.03 The written resolution procedure of CA 1985 was applicable both to resolutions of the company in general meeting and to a resolution of a class meeting of members. The key requirement under the regime of CA 1985 for a valid written resolution was that it was consented to by *all* of the members of the company, or of the members of a relevant class of members. The requirement of the consent of all of the members resulted in the efficacy of the written resolution procedure of CA 1985 being workable only in the context of companies with very few members or single member companies. There were however, certain restrictions on the scope of these procedures.

Not of universal application

15.04 By CA 1985, Sch 15A, para 1, the written resolution procedure of s 381A did not apply either to a resolution under CA 1985, s 303 to remove a director from office before the expiration of his term of office or to a resolution under CA 1985, s 391

---

[1] Part 13, Chapter 2 came into force on 1 October 2007.
[2] See CA 1985, s 381A.
[3] See CA 1985, s 381(A)(2).

removing an auditor from office. In addition, CA 1985, Sch 15A, Part II incorporated certain procedural modifications to the use of the procedure in relation to a number of significant statutory provisions.[4]

Notification to the auditors

Under the procedure of CA 1985 the auditors had to be notified of the resolution either before or at the same time as the written resolution was sent to shareholders.[5] **15.05**

Effect of written resolution

By CA 1985, s 381A(4), once filed with the Registrar of Companies, a written resolution had the same effect as if passed at an extraordinary general meeting of the company. **15.06**

CA 1985, ss 381A–381C were repealed on 1 October 2007 and replaced by the provisions of CA 2006 concerning written resolutions. **15.07**

CA 2006 Procedure for Written Resolutions

The new legislation is designed to greatly increase the usage of written resolutions by private companies, thereby recognizing the widespread informality in business procedures that is commonly found in smaller unquoted private companies. This deregulatory measure goes in tandem with the position under CA 2006 that private companies no longer need to hold annual general meetings. **15.08**

Unanimity no longer required

The most important change introduced by the new legislation is that a written resolution no longer requires the unanimous consent of the members. Instead written resolutions under CA 2006 will be passed, and will take effect when supported by a simple majority in the case of an ordinary resolution[6] or a three-quarters majority of eligible members in the case of a special resolution,[7] that is, **15.09**

[4] These adaptations applied to s 95, (a resolution for the disapplication of pre-emption rights), s 155 (a resolution approving financial assistance for the purchase of its own shares or those of its holding company), ss 164, 165, 167 (a resolution giving authority for an off-market purchase or contingent purchase contract of a company's own shares), s 173 (a resolution to approve a redemption or purchase of a company's own shares out of capital), s 319 (a resolution approving a director's service contract for more than five years) and s 337 (a resolution approving the funding of a director's expenditure in performing his duties).

[5] See CA 1985, s 381B.

[6] See CA 2006, s 282(1).

[7] See CA 2006, s 283(3).

if it is passed by members representing not less than 75% of the total voting rights of eligible members.

Definition of 'eligible members'

15.10 CA 2006, s 289(1) defines the term 'eligible members' as '. . . the members who would have been entitled to vote on the resolution on the circulation date of the resolution . . .'.

Definition of written resolution in CA 2006

15.11 Section 288 defines a written resolution for the purposes of CA 2006 as '. . . a resolution of a private company proposed and passed in accordance with this Chapter [2]'. Where a private company complies with the procedure that is specified the written resolution takes effect as if it had been passed at a general meeting or at a class meeting.[8]

Private companies only

15.12 The new statutory procedure for written resolutions applies only to private companies. In that respect there is no change from CA 1985. CA 2006 makes no reference to written resolutions passed by a public company, where all matters must be decided by resolutions passed at a general meeting of the members.[9] The vast numbers of members of quoted public companies dictate that such a procedure would be impractical for such companies. Equally, private companies with a large number of members will have to exercise great care when employing the prescribed procedure in relation to written resolutions.

What types of resolutions?

15.13 CA 2006, s 288 provides that 'resolutions', without specifying what type of resolutions, may be passed by a private company by means of the written resolution procedure contained in CA 2006, Part 13, Chapter 2. Under CA 2006 there are only two types of resolution, ordinary and special resolutions, as the law has abandoned the concept of extraordinary resolutions. It is also important to note that there are additional procedural requirements necessary for a valid special resolution under the new written resolution procedure. These requirements are found in CA 2006, s 283.[10]

---

[8] See CA 2006, s 288(5).

[9] See CA 2006, s 281(2) (though in theory a public company could rely on the principle in *Re Duomatic Ltd* [1969] 2 Ch 365 (Buckley J)).

[10] This section is in CA 2006, Part 13, Chapter 1.

Special resolution

By CA 2006, s 283(3) where a resolution is passed as a written resolution, it is not a special resolution unless it is stated that it was proposed as a special resolution. Any resolution that is proposed as a special resolution may only be passed as a special resolution.[11] A written resolution passed by a majority of 75% will not be effective unless it is stated that it was proposed as a special resolution. In this respect, the new procedure differs from the previous statutory procedure. In *Kinlan v Crimmin*[12] a special resolution was required for the purchase by a company of its own shares under CA 1985, s 164, and a written resolution which had complied with the substantive terms of CA 1985, s 381 had been passed. It was held that the fact that a resolution had been labelled as an 'ordinary resolution' did not matter and did not affect the resolution. It was legitimate for the shareholders acting informally but unanimously to waive strict compliance with the statutory provisions. The facts of this case would very likely lead to a different result under the new provisions of CA 2006 regulating written resolutions. **15.14**

Informal consent—at common law

CA 2006, s 281(4) expressly provides that nothing in CA 2006, Part 13 affects any enactment or rule of law as to things that may be done otherwise than by the passing of a resolution, or the circumstances in which a resolution is, or is not treated as having been passed. It similarly preserves cases in which a person is precluded from alleging that a resolution has not been duly passed.[13] A trilogy of cases that were decided in the 1920s, *Re Express Engineering Works Ltd*,[14] *Re Oxted Motor Co Ltd*[15] and *Parker & Cooper Ltd v Reading*[16] are authority for the proposition that where it can be shown that all of the members of a company have agreed to a matter which it was competent for the general meeting to implement, the agreement of all of those members would be binding like a duly passed resolution at a general meeting. This principle is often referred to as the rule in *Re Duomatic Ltd*[17] and CA 2006 preserves the principle of the decision in *Re Duomatic Ltd* (and earlier authorities) which provides that if all the shareholders of a company with the right to vote have given their consent to a proposal, it is not necessary that the company should hold a formal meeting. This important principle has been held to extend to the alteration of articles of association by **15.15**

---

11 See CA 2006, s 283(3).
12 [2007] 2 BCLC 67 (Philip Sales, sitting as a deputy judge of the High Court).
13 See, for example, reg 113, 1985 Table A.
14 [1920] 1 Ch 466 (CA).
15 [1921] 3 KB 32 (Divisional Court).
16 [1926] Ch 975 (Astbury J).
17 [1969] 2 Ch 365 (Buckley J); see also *Atlas Wright (Europe) Ltd v Wright* [1999] 2 BCLC 301 at 311 (CA).

unanimous agreement in the absence of a special resolution.[18] The principle also applies in respect of provisions contained in a shareholders' agreement where a prescribed procedural regulation may be altered or ignored with unanimous consent.[19]

15.16 In *Euro Brokers Holdings Ltd v Monecor* Mummery LJ at para [62] succinctly summarized the principles:

> I see nothing in the circumstances of the present case to exclude the *Duomatic* principle. It is a sound and sensible principle of company law allowing the members of the company to reach an agreement without the need for strict compliance with formal procedures, where they exist only for the benefit of those who have agreed not [to] comply with them. What matters is the unanimous assent of those who ultimately exercise power over the affairs of the company through their right to attend and vote at a general meeting. It does not matter whether the formal procedures in question are stipulated for in the articles of association, in the Companies Acts or in a separate contract between the members of the company concerned. What matters is that all the members have reached an agreement. If they have, they cannot be heard to say that they are not bound by it because the formal procedure was not followed. The position is treated in the same way as if the agreed formal procedure had been followed. The particular context for the application of the principle in this case is that cl 11(2) of the shareholders' agreement requires the notice to be issued by the board. That is a formal corporate procedure. It is irrelevant that the requirement is in a separate agreement entered into by the shareholders in EBFL, rather than in the articles. The shareholders entered into that agreement for the very same purpose as the contract between them constituted by the articles, namely to regulate the relationship between the shareholders in the governance of EBFL. As Neuberger J said in *Re Torvale Group Ltd* [1999] 2 BCLC 605 at 617:
>
> > 'The articles constitute a contract, and if the parties to that contract, or if the parties for whom the benefit of a particular term has been included in that contract, are happy unanimously to waive or vary the prescribed procedure for a particular purpose, then . . . it seems to me that there is no good reason why it should not be capable of applying.'

These common law principles are preserved by the new legislation.

Limitations on the written resolution procedure

15.17 It is not possible for all types of resolutions of a private company to be passed by means of the new written resolution regime. CA 2006, s 288(2)(a) provides that a resolution to remove a director from office before the expiration of his term of office under CA 2006, s 168 cannot be passed as a written resolution. This means that even in the case of a small private company it will continue to be necessary to convene a general meeting to remove a director from office before the expiry of

---

[18] See *Cane v Jones* [1980] 1 WLR 1451 (Michael Wheeler QC sitting as a deputy judge of the High Court).

[19] See *Re Euro Brokers Holdings v Monecor (London) Ltd* [2003] 1 BCLC 506 (Leslie Kosmin QC (sitting as a deputy judge of the High Court) and CA).

his term if the procedure stipulated in CA 2006, s 168 is used.[20] A similar restriction exists in respect of a resolution under CA 2006, s 510 to remove an auditor from office before the expiration of his term of office.[21] Both resolutions under CA 2006, ss 168 and 510 contain statutory procedural protections for the persons who are the subject of such resolutions, and in these circumstances Parliament has decreed that the scope of the written resolution procedure does not extend into these areas. It can thus be seen that CA 2006 reproduces the same restrictions on the availability of written resolutions that existed under CA 1985, s 381A and Sch 15A, para 1.[22]

Formal Requirements for a Written Resolution

Who may propose a written resolution?

As the board of directors is the organ of a company that is charged with responsibility for the conduct of the management of the affairs of a company, it is unsurprising that the legislation confers authority on the board of directors of a private company to propose a written resolution. Where a written resolution is proposed by a board of directors under CA 2006, s 288(3)(a) there must also be due compliance with the provisions of CA 2006, s 291. Alternatively, a written resolution may also be proposed by the members of a private company under s 288(3)(b) and subject to ss 292–295. Each of these procedures will be considered in turn. **15.18**

Circulation of a written resolution proposed by directors

Under CA 2006, s 291(2) where the directors of a private company propose a resolution to be passed as a written resolution the company concerned must send a copy of the resolution to every 'eligible member'.[23] Where the term 'circulation date of a written resolution' is used in Part 13, Chapter 2 it is taken to be the date on which copies of the resolution are sent or submitted to members or, where copies are sent or submitted on different days, the first of those days.[24] **15.19**

By CA 2006, s 291(3) the private company is required to circulate a copy of the resolution either by sending copies at the same time to all eligible members in hard **15.20**

[20] It is only a removal of a director under CA 2006, s 168 that cannot be effected by a written resolution. It is permissible for a company's articles of association to provide a mechanism for the removal of directors and such a procedure could be implemented by means of the written resolution procedure. Indeed, articles can be amended by special resolution in the form of a written resolution to introduce such a procedure.

[21] See CA 2006, s 288(2)(b).

[22] See para 15.04 above.

[23] As defined in CA 2006, s 289(1).

[24] See CA 2006, s 290.

copy form, or in electronic form or by means of a website. This is not an absolute obligation in that the obligation to send out copies at the same time is declared to be '. . . so far as is reasonably practicable'. Alternatively, if it is possible to do so without undue delay, the company must submit the same copy to each eligible member in turn, or different copies to a number of eligible members in turn. Either or both methods of circulation may be used.

CA 2006, s 298

15.21 Section 298 covers the sending of documents relating to written resolutions by electronic means. By s 298(1) where a company has given an electronic address in any document containing or accompanying a proposed written resolution, it is deemed to have agreed that any document or information relating to that resolution may be sent by electronic means to that address, subject to any conditions or limitations specified in the document. This means that if the company has given details of its electronic address a member may send back his consent to the resolution to the company at that address.

Information as to how a member should signify agreement to a written resolution proposed by directors

15.22 By s 291(4) the copy of the resolution must be accompanied by a statement from the company informing the members how to signify their agreement to the resolution in accordance with the provisions of CA 2006, s 296,[25] and as to the date by which the resolution must be passed if it is not to lapse under the terms of CA 2006, s 297. This is essential information if the written resolution procedure is to operate smoothly.

Consequences of failure to comply with s 291

15.23 If the private company fails to comply with the provisions of s 291 an offence is committed by every officer who is in default, and this statutory offence is punishable by a fine.

15.24 However, CA 2006, s 291(7) expressly provides that the validity of a resolution if passed by the requisite majority of eligible members is not affected by a failure to comply with the requirements of the section. This last subsection must have been introduced for the purposes of certainty and does not permit a procedural irregularity (such as a failure by a company to provide the statement of guidance required by s 291(4)) to invalidate the private company's decision-making process. It reinforces the impact of the new legislation in that a written resolution will be valid

[25] See para 15.39 below.

and effective provided that the necessary majority is obtained, even if other members cannot properly take part in the process due to an administrative error.

Written resolution proposed by members—circulation

In accordance with CA 2006, ss 288(3)(b) and 292 the members of a private company may require the circulation of a written resolution. This is a new statutory right which matches the right of members to request a general meeting under CA 2006, s 303.[26] **15.25**

Restrictions on members' resolutions

Where a resolution is proposed by the members of a private company the resolution is confined to one that may properly be moved as a written resolution. Accordingly, if the resolution if passed would be ineffective or it is defamatory of any person, or it is frivolous or vexatious, the resolution may not be moved.[27] In addition, members are under the same restriction as directors in that they may not pass resolutions under CA 2006, ss 168 and 510 by means of the written resolution procedure. **15.26**

'Requisite threshold' for a member's request to circulate resolution

A company is required to circulate the resolution and any accompanying statement once it has received requests to do so from 5% of members representing the total voting rights of all members entitled to vote on the resolution.[28] The requisite percentage may be lower than 5% if the articles of association of a company so provide. It is unlikely that many companies will wish to adopt articles of association that introduce a lower threshold figure than that provided for in the legislation for fear of generating unnecessary shareholder unrest and possible abuse. **15.27**

The form of the member's request

A request may either be in hard copy form or electronic form[29] and must identify the resolution and any accompanying statement. The request must also be authenticated by the person or persons making it within the requirements of CA 2006, s 1146. A document sent or supplied in hard copy form is sufficiently authenticated if it is signed by the person sending or supplying it. Where a document is sent or supplied in electronic form, it is sufficiently authenticated **15.28**

---

26 Formerly CA 1985, s 368.
27 See CA 2006, s 292(2).
28 See CA 2006, s 292(4) and (5).
29 See CA 2006, s 292(6).

if the identity of the sender is confirmed by a manner specified by the company or, in the absence thereof, if the communication contains or is accompanied by a statement of the identity of the sender, and the company has no reason to doubt the truth of that statement.

Accompanying statement from members

15.29 Where members require a private company to circulate a written resolution, by CA 2006, s 292(3) they may also require the company to circulate with it a statement of not more than 1,000 words on the subject matter of the resolution. The members' statement is not an opportunity for members to discuss matters other than the subject matter of the resolution and should be confined to arguments in favour of the proposed resolution. The company should take steps to ensure that there is due compliance with this restriction.

15.30 A company that is required to circulate a resolution must send a copy or submit a copy of the resolution and a copy of any accompanying statement to every eligible member. This obligation is subject to the members' compliance with the requirements of s 294 as to expenses, and to s 295 where an application is made to the court that the company is not required to circulate the statement.

15.31 As to the payment by members of the company's expenses in carrying out the circulation of the resolution, those expenses must be paid by the members who requested the circulation unless the company has previously so resolved that members in such a situation need not pay. The expenses to be borne by the members must be a sum that is reasonably sufficient to meet the proper expenses of the company.[30]

Application to the court not to circulate a members' statement

15.32 Under s 295(1) a company is not required to circulate a members' statement under s 293 if the court is satisfied that the rights conferred by ss 292 and 293 are being abused. The application may be made by the company or by a 'person aggrieved'. The term 'person aggrieved' is not defined in the legislation but it is suggested that such a person must have a sufficient nexus to the application. The categories of persons who may be aggrieved and thus have locus standi to apply to the court are not closed and the status of such an applicant will be examined in each individual case. Such a person could be someone whose conduct is attacked in the proposed members' statement.

15.33 It is suggested that recourse by a company or anyone else to s 295 will be rare and will only arise in exceptional cases. The court is given power under s 295(2) to order the members who requested the circulation of the written resolution to pay

---

[30] For further analysis see the commentary in Part 3.

all or part of the company's costs of such an application. The jurisdiction of the court to make such an order for costs may act to curb the enthusiasm of members who attempt to misuse the statutory right to have a statement circulated. The company will always be a necessary party to such an application. The section is almost identical in its wording to CA 2006, s 317 which applies in relation to court applications to permit a company not to circulate a members' statement in respect of a general meeting.[31]

Method of circulation of a written resolution proposed by members

Section 293(2) provides, with regard to the circulation of a written resolution provided by members, that the company must either send copies of the statement at the same time, so far as reasonably practicable, to all eligible members in one of the following forms, namely, in hard copy form, by electronic form or by means of the company's website, or by a combination of these methods. In the alternative, the company could submit the same copy of the written resolution to each eligible member in turn, but only if this does not result in undue delay. What constitutes delay will be a question of fact in each case. The section clearly permits the circulation of a single document or a number of identical documents. **15.34**

A written resolution and the accompanying statement may be sent by means of a website. For this purpose Sch 5, Part 4 (paras 8–14) applies to all communications from a company by means of a website.[32] By s 299(2) it will not be validly sent in this way unless the resolution is available on the website throughout the period beginning with 'the circulation date' and ending on the date on which the resolution lapses under s 297. By s 290 the circulation date is the date on which copies of the resolution are sent or submitted to members in accordance with Part 13, Chapter 2. If copies are sent or submitted on different days, the circulation date is the first of those days. **15.35**

Timing of circulation of a written resolution proposed by members

By s 293(3) the company is under an obligation to send or submit to the eligible members a copy of the proposed members' written resolution not more than 21 days after it has become required to do so in accordance with s 292. If the written resolution is circulated to members on different days, the statute requires that the first copy to be despatched must be sent not more than 21 days after the request. This is a strict time limit, failure to comply being an offence enforceable by a fine. However, it should be noted that there is no method by which the members **15.36**

[31] See Ch 3.
[32] See Ch 17.

themselves may circulate the proposed written resolution in the event of default by the directors (ie there is no equivalent to s 305 relating to the members' power to call a meeting where the board fails to do so under s 304).[33]

15.37 As documents should only be circulated on behalf of a company to its members with the authority of the board it is necessary for the company's directors to resolve to circulate the resolution proposed by the members. If the secretary were to act on his own authority, without express board approval, his actions could subsequently be ratified by the directors and thereby be rendered valid and effective. However, board consideration of any members' request is essential.

Information as to how a member should signify agreement to a written resolution proposed by members

15.38 By s 293(4) the copy of the resolution must be accompanied by what is described as 'guidance', namely a statement informing the member how to signify his agreement to the resolution in accordance with the provisions of CA 2006, s 296, and the date by which the resolution must be passed if it is not to lapse under the terms of CA 2006, s 297. It is interesting to note the use of the term 'guidance' in s 293(4), in contrast to the accompanying statement informing a member of how to proceed in s 291(4), where the written resolution is one proposed by the directors. However, both documents should take a similar form.

Procedure for showing agreement to any written resolution

15.39 By CA 2006, s 296 a member signifies his agreement to a written resolution, whether proposed by the directors or the members, when the company receives from him or someone acting on his behalf an authenticated document identifying the resolution and indicating his agreement.[34] This may be supplied to the company either in hard copy form or in electronic form. Most importantly, once a member has accepted a written resolution he cannot change his mind and revoke his agreement.[35] Again, this is to avoid confusion. Members and their advisers therefore need to take great care when considering a proposed written resolution of the company as there is no room for second thoughts.

Time for agreement—general

15.40 By CA 2006, s 297 a written resolution, whether proposed by the directors or by members, will lapse if it is not agreed to by sufficient numbers of eligible members

---

[33] See Ch 5.

[34] An authenticated document must meet the requirements of CA 2006, s 1146—see para 15.28 above.

[35] CA 2006, s 296(3).

within the period specified in a company's articles of association. If no period of time for agreement is specified in the articles of association s 297 stipulates a period of 28 days.[36] In practice this should prove to be an adequate period of time. The aim of this provision is to put a finite time limit on the circulation of written resolutions and to avoid unnecessary confusion. There is no leeway for tardy agreement to a written resolution, as any agreement signified after the expiry of the prescribed period will be ineffective.[37]

How and when a written resolution takes effect

By CA 2006, s 296(4) a written resolution is passed when the requisite majority of members have signified their agreement to it. This far-reaching provision represents a major change to the law. It means that as soon as the minimum number needed for an ordinary resolution or a special resolution has signed up the resolution is deemed to have been passed and takes effect. There is no requirement to wait for a particular period or until all members have exercised their right to participate. As soon as the majority has been obtained the resolution is passed. **15.41**

The impact of this provision is such that members may have to make regular checks with the company to see what has happened to a proposed written resolution. If it has been passed by the necessary majority it will be in effect before many members are aware of that fact. **15.42**

Notification of written resolution to auditors

CA 2006, s 502(1)[38] (auditors' rights in relation to resolutions and meetings) came into force on 6 April 2008. By this provision the auditors of a company will continue to have a statutory entitlement to receive copies of written resolutions proposed to be agreed by members. **15.43**

General impact of the statutory scheme

By s 300 any provision of a company's articles will be void insofar as it seeks to restrict the company from using the written resolution procedure in relation to any statutory procedure where the statute permits the use of such a resolution. The somewhat awkward wording of this provision is to be regretted. **15.44**

---

36 See CA 2006, s 297(1)(b).

37 See CA 2006, s 298(2).

38 This section came into force on 6 April 2008 (although CA 1985, s 390(2) was amended for a transitional period from 1 October 2007 until 6 April 2008 to reflect the provisions of s 502(1)).

Transitional provisions

15.45 The Third Commencement Order contains a number of complex transitional provisions relating to the written resolution procedure under CA 2006, Part 13, Chapter 2.

15.46 Sections 288–300 of the 2006 Act apply to all written resolutions for which the circulation date (as defined in s 290) is on or after 1 October 2007.

15.47 CA 1985, ss 381A–381C, and Sch 15A continue to apply to resolutions sent to any relevant member before 1 October 2007.

15.48 In the list of resolutions that may not be passed as a written resolution in the 2006 Act, an amendment has been made by the Third Commencement Order to add to the list, a resolution passed under s 80A of the 1985 Act revoking, varying or renewing the authority of the directors to allot securities. Section 80A of the 1985 Act will not be repealed until 1 October 2009.

15.49 New sections have been added[39] to CA 2006 to apply the procedural requirements for passing written resolutions under the 2006 Act where provisions of CA 1985 relate to share capital and, as such, will not be repealed until 1 October 2008 or 1 October 2009. These are:

(1) CA 2006, s 300A—the disapplication of pre-emption rights by written resolution under CA 1985, s 95(2);
(2) CA 2006, s 300B—financial assistance for the purchase of a company's own shares by written resolution under CA 1985, s 155(4) or (5);
(3) CA 2006, s 300C—authority for off-market or contingent purchase of a company's own shares by written resolution under CA 1985, s 164(2); and
(4) CA 2006, s 300D—approval for payment out of capital by written resolution under CA 1985, s 173(2).

Transitional provisions—notice to auditors

15.50 From 1 October 2007, CA 1985, s 390(2) (entitlement of company's auditors to receive written resolutions) was amended by Sch 4, para 4 to the Third Commencement Order so as to effectively replicate CA 2006, s 502(1). CA 2006, s 502(1) came into force on 6 April 2008 when s 390(2) of the 1985 Act (as amended) was repealed.[40]

---

[39] See Sch 1, para 13, Third Commencement Order.

[40] See article 3 (1) (e) and Part 1, Sch 2, the Companies Act 2006 (Commencement No 5, Transitional Provisions and Savings) Order 2007 (Fifth Commencement Order).

It is to be noted that in contrast to CA 1985, s 381B, neither CA 2006, s 502 nor the amended CA 1985, s 390 provide that directors are liable to be fined for breach of the requirement to notify the auditors. **15.51**

CA 2006, s 502 applies to auditors appointed on or after 6 April 2008. For auditors appointed before that date CA 1985, s 390 will continue to apply.[41] **15.52**

Conclusion

The changes that have been made by CA 2006, Part 13, Chapter 2 are to be welcomed and should result in written resolutions being useful to many more private companies than the regime that was in force prior to 1 October 2007. It is clear that the retreat from the need for unanimity required by the procedure under CA 1985 will result in more private companies, in particular those with more than the minimum number of members, using the procedure that is prescribed in CA 2006, Part 13, Chapter 2. The new written resolution procedure for private companies means that the procedure is put on the same basis as the required majorities that are required for resolutions passed at general meetings. It is likely that in the future a large proportion of private companies will choose to adopt the written resolution procedure to pass special resolutions, in particular those involving the amendment of their articles. **15.53**

[41] Schedule 4, para 12(3) and (4), Fifth Commencement Order.

16

MINUTES OF GENERAL MEETINGS AND DECISIONS OF MEMBERS

Introduction

An accurate and contemporaneous record of the decisions made by a duly constituted meeting is of fundamental importance for the good administration of any organization or institution. Minutes of meetings are a means by which all those who are concerned with the efficient management of an organization are kept informed of decisions that have been made at previous meetings. **16.01**

The Shorter Oxford English Dictionary[1] defines the word 'minutes' as '. . . a brief summary of the proceedings at a meeting'. At common law there is no duty on a company to keep minutes of its proceedings, but common sense and best practice dictate that a proper record of the proceedings of any decision-making body should be maintained. **16.02**

[1] Fifth edition, 2002, at p 1787.

Duty to Keep Minutes and Records under CA 1985

16.03 Every company registered and incorporated under CA 1985 had a duty pursuant to CA 1985, s 382(1) to keep minutes of all proceedings of general meetings. Such minutes had to be entered in a book kept for this express purpose. The duty imposed by CA 1985 was reflected in the content of regulation 100 of the 1985 Table A.[2] This provision, which is commonly incorporated into the articles of many companies, imposes a duty on directors to ensure that minutes are kept of the proceedings of a company and of any class of shareholders and of directors and any committee of directors. Minutes of meetings of directors are considered in Chapter 21. In addition, pursuant to CA 1985, s 382(A)(1), written resolutions passed pursuant to the provisions of s 381(A)[3] had to be recorded, together with the signatures of the members who gave their consent to the written resolution, in the same way that minutes of a general meeting are recorded.

Minutes of Members' Meetings under CA 2006

16.04 The new legislation largely reproduces the provisions contained in CA 1985 relating to minutes of members' meetings.[4] However, five important changes have been made to the law relating to minutes by CA 2006:

(1) The new legislation has abandoned the provisions in CA 1985, s 382(1) relating to meetings of managers.
(2) The law now requires that minutes and other pertinent records must be kept for a minimum period of 10 years.
(3) The new legislation extends the duty to keep minutes to class meetings.[5]
(4) Although records may be kept wherever a company decides, the minutes must be available for inspection at the registered office or at a place specified in the regulations.
(5) Unless the records have always been kept at the registered office, their location, and any change in their location, must be notified to the Registrar of Companies within 14 days. In addition CA 2006, Part 37 contains provisions which relate to the form in which company records, including minutes, must be kept as well as imposing a duty on companies to take proper and adequate precautions against falsification of records.

---

[2] See the commentary in Part 4 below.
[3] These provisions apply to private companies only.
[4] Under CA 2006 the requirement to maintain minutes of meetings of members is contained in Part 13, Chapter 6, whereas the requirement to maintain minutes of meetings of directors is found in Part 10.
[5] See further para 16.17 below.

By CA 2006, s 338(1) every company (public or private) must keep records comprising: 16.05

(a) copies of all resolutions passed otherwise than at general meetings;[6]
(b) minutes of all proceedings at general meetings; and
(c) details of the decisions taken by a sole member.

CA 2006, s 338 reflects the new statutory procedure for the passing of written resolutions by private companies contained in CA 2006, Part 13, Chapter 2, ss 288–300 (inclusive), which apply to decisions taken outside the context of a general meeting.[7] 16.06

Ten-year period of retention

Under CA 2006, s 355(2) company records must be retained by the company for a period of at least 10 years from the date of the relevant resolution, meeting or decision as the case may be. Although this prescribed period of retention is new, under the old law there was an indefinite period of retention. Accordingly, in practice the requirement to retain the records for a period of 10 years is unlikely to cause inconvenience or difficulty to companies that have adopted the practice of keeping minutes for relatively long periods of time. In relation to those companies whose record-keeping hitherto may not have been efficient, an improvement in their administrative procedures will be required in order to avoid a breach of the new legislation. The failure by a company to comply with these new provisions is an offence by every officer of the company who is in default.[8] 16.07

Single member companies

Special provision is made in CA 2006 for recording the decisions taken by single member companies. These are not new provisions. Under CA 1985, s 382B(1) required the member to provide the company with a written record of any decision taken by the member which might have been taken by the company in general meeting. Any default in complying with this requirement was expressly stated not to affect the validity of a decision that had been arrived at by such a single member. This last proposition followed from the provisions of CA 1985, s 382B(3). 16.08

---

[6] That is, written resolutions.

[7] See Ch 15. Under CA 1985, s 382A(1), written resolutions passed pursuant to CA 2006, s 381A had to be recorded as if they were the minutes of general meeting. That section also applied only to private companies.

[8] CA 2006, s 355(3) and (4).

CA 2006, s 357

16.09 CA 2006, s 357 which replaces CA 1985, s 382B now sets out the rules dealing with the need to maintain proper records of the decisions taken by a sole member where a company limited by shares or by guarantee has only one member. Where the member takes any decision that may be taken by the company in general meeting and has effect as if agreed by the company in general meeting, he is required to provide the company with details of his decision, unless the decision is taken by way of a written resolution. Once again, failure to comply with this requirement is an offence but that does not affect the validity of the decision made.[9]

Rights of inspection under CA 2006—s 358

16.10 It is important for minutes and other records to be drawn up and kept but such a provision will be of little efficacy in practice if the minutes and records cannot be inspected by members. Rights of inspection have therefore always formed an important part of the legislative scheme. The new statute is more rigorous in providing for rights of inspection of these company records than its predecessor.[10] A company must now 'at all times' keep available for inspection at its registered office the records referred to in s 355 relating to the previous 10 years and open those records to inspection by any member without charge.[11] In the alternative, the records may be kept available for inspection at such other place as specified in the regulations to be issued by the Secretary of State under CA 2006, s 1136. There is a duty on the part of the company to notify the Registrar of Companies of the place at which the records are kept available for inspection and of any change in that location, unless the records have at all times been kept at the registered office.[12]

16.11 By CA 2006, s 358(3) the company's records of this notice must be open to the inspection of any member without charge.

16.12 CA 2006, s 358(4) provides that any member is entitled on payment of a prescribed fee to be furnished with a copy of any of the company's records kept for this purpose. The time limit given for the company to comply with this obligation is 14 days. If an inspection is refused or a copy is not sent within 14 days an offence is committed by every officer of the company who is in default.[13]

16.13 The provisions of the Companies (Inspection and Copying of Registers, Indices and Documents) Regulations 1991[14] will continue to apply until 1 October 2009.

---

[9] See CA 2006, s 357(3), (4) and (5).
[10] CA 1985, s 383.
[11] CA 2006, s 358(1).
[12] See CA 2006, s 358(2).
[13] See CA 2006, s 358(5) and (6).
[14] SI 1991/1998.

The fees chargeable in respect of inspection and copying of records are set out in Sch 2 to these regulations. The levels of fees prescribed by Sch 2 have been amended by two recent statutory instruments: the Companies (Fees for Inspection and Copying of Company Records) Regulations 2007,[15] which came into force on 1 October 2007, and the Companies (Fees for Inspection and Copying of Company Records) (No. 2) Regulations 2007,[16] which came into force on 6 April 2008.

Court order for immediate inspection or copies under CA 2006, s 358(7)

It is open to a member to apply to the court for an order under CA 2006, s 358(7) compelling the immediate inspection of the records or directing that copies be sent to the person requesting them if an inspection has been refused or a document requested has not been supplied. This subsection does not refer to the 14-day period in the earlier part of the section. Accordingly, it is suggested that for the purposes of this provision, while the 14-day period (after which an offence is committed) will be a guide, it is likely that the court will be prepared to order an inspection or the supply of a copy document if these have not been provided within a reasonable time of the request having been made and refused. That period may, in certain circumstances, be less than 14 days. Refusal in this context must include a request that has been ignored. **16.14**

Only in rare cases should it be necessary for a member to have to resort to the time, trouble and expense of making such an application to the court. The reason for this is that well-advised directors understand the nature of their duties in relation to requests from members to inspect and take copies of the minutes and other records. However, it is likely that the greater use of written resolutions in private companies will lead to more frequent use of these provisions. **16.15**

Minutes as evidence—CA 2006, s 356

Section 356 of the new Act deals with the legal status of the company's records kept in accordance with s 355.[17] By s 356(4) the minutes of the proceedings of a general meeting, if purporting to be signed by the chairman of that meeting or of the next meeting are evidence (in Scotland, sufficient evidence) of the proceedings at that meeting. In addition, subs (5) raises a rebuttable statutory presumption that where there is a record of proceedings of a general meeting (a) the meeting is deemed duly held and convened, (b) all proceedings at the meeting are deemed **16.16**

---

15 SI 2007/2612.
16 SI 2007/3535.
17 This section replaces CA 1985, s 382(3).

to have duly taken place, and (c) all appointments at the meeting are deemed valid. It is open to a party to seek to rebut this presumption by contrary proof.

Class meetings

16.17 Shares in a company may of course be divided into different classes. Section 359 applies the provisions of CA 2006, Part 13, Chapter 6 to class meetings and resolutions passed by the holders of a particular class in the same way as they apply to general meetings and to resolutions of members generally. This is a new provision of CA 2006. The section applies the provisions of Chapter 6 with 'necessary qualifications'. The precise impact of this vague wording is unclear but it is to be assumed that every company at least must:

- (i) keep records of all class resolutions passed otherwise than at a class meeting;
- (ii) keep minutes of the proceedings of all class meetings;
- (iii) retain such records for at least 10 years from the date of the meeting or resolution;
- (iv) maintain those records available for inspection at the company's registered office or such other place as specified in the regulations issued by the Secretary of State under CA 2006, s 1136;
- (v) ensure that the records are open to inspection without charge by any member;
- (vi) supply copies to members on the payment of the requisite fee.

16.18 The prescribed enforcement and penalty provisions of ss 355 and 358 apply equally to the records of class meetings and class resolutions.

Transitional provisions

16.19 CA 2006, ss 355–359 are subject to transitional provisions which are found in Sch 3, para 40 to the Third Commencement Order. Paragraph 40 makes it clear that CA 2006, ss 355–359 apply to resolutions passed, meetings held or decisions taken on or after 1 October 2007. In respect of resolutions passed, meetings held or decisions taken prior to this date, CA 1985, ss 382, 382A, 382B and 383 continue to apply.

Form of company records

16.20 CA 2006, ss 1134 and 1135 govern the form in which company records must now be maintained.[18] The definition of the term 'company records' in s 1134 includes

[18] These provisions replace CA 1985, ss 382, 722 and 723.

amongst a wide range of documents any minutes or other document required by the Companies Acts[19] to be kept by a company.

CA 2006, s 1135 provides that such company records may be kept in hard copy or in electronic form. The arrangement of the contents may be kept in such manner as the directors think fit, provided that the information in question is adequately recorded for future reference.[20] Most importantly where the records are kept in electronic form they must be capable of being reproduced in a hard copy form.[21] The legislation thus sensibly enables the company to use electronic storage for its records, but insists that those are capable of being printed out and supplied in hard copy form to anyone who is entitled to such information and who prefers to receive the records in paper form. **16.21**

Any failure by a company to comply with the provisions of s 1135 constitutes an offence committed by every officer of the company who is in default.[22] A person who is guilty of such an offence is punishable by a fine. **16.22**

CA 2006, s 1138 imposes an additional obligation on a company where the records of the company (as defined in s 1134) are kept otherwise than in bound books. In such circumstances the company is required to take 'adequate precautions' in order to guard against falsification of the records and to facilitate the discovery of falsification. If a company fails to comply with this statutory requirement an offence is committed by every officer of the company who is in default and this offence is punishable by a fine. The impact of s 1138 in the context of minutes and records of resolutions is that the company must maintain a proper security system in order to safeguard its electronic records from any form of tampering. This may include an electronic firewall and the requirement for a password to access the relevant files. In addition, the security system must enable the company to detect where any attempt has been made to falsify the records. **16.23**

The content of minutes

How a company makes a record of its meetings will be a matter for each individual company to decide, but it is not unusual for the articles of association of a company to set out mandatory provisions relating to the form of minutes. It is clear that all minutes should strive to be concise, clearly drafted and devoid of ambiguity. It would be uncontroversial to suggest that minutes of a meeting should usually include the following information: **16.24**

- the date of the meeting;
- the venue of the meeting;

---

19 See CA 2006, s 2.
20 See CA 2006, s 1135(1).
21 See CA 2006, s 1135(2).
22 See CA 2006, s 1135(3) and 1135(4).

- the time of commencement of the meeting;
- the type of meeting;
- the persons present at the meeting as of right;
- the persons who are in attendance at the meeting, for example the company secretary or solicitor;
- apologies for absence;
- that a quorum was present;
- the identity of the chairman;
- matters arising from the last meeting;
- the precise text of every resolution put to the meeting for consideration and passed at the meeting;
- identification of documentation relevant to the meeting;
- appointments made at the meeting, including where relevant details of salaries, duties and powers;
- matters considered under the heading of 'Any other business';
- the date and time of the next meeting.

16.25 Minutes of a meeting are not a verbatim record or transcript of what has been said by everybody participating at a particular meeting. There is a clear distinction between a verbatim report and a minute. A verbatim report or a detailed report consists of what is said, whereas the minutes of a meeting consist of an accurate record of the business transacted or agreed upon. The minutes should be sufficiently intelligible to enable a member who was not present to understand what was decided at the meeting. Speeches, arguments and dissenting arguments that have been made at a general meeting may form the material of a report but the resolutions considered and passed and decisions taken are what is apposite for inclusion in the minutes. The minutes are only evidence of those matters properly entered in them.

16.26 It is not a statutory requirement but minutes are invariably read, or if previously circulated to members, taken as read at the next following meeting. This is the process by which the minutes of the former meeting are submitted for verification of their correctness. If the minutes are regarded as a correct summary of the proceedings of the preceding meeting by the members present at the next meeting, the minutes are signed by the chairman. If the minutes are considered to contain inaccuracies they may be modified and the modified version is signed by the chairman.

Amendment of minutes

16.27 Once the minutes have been approved and signed, they should not be altered or corrected. They are intended to form an agreed official record of the meeting. The same principle applies to the minutes of any meeting, including the meeting of members. In *Re Cawley & Co*[23] a meeting of directors was held at which it was resolved to make calls on shares. No dates were fixed for the calls, and after the minutes had been signed the secretary of the company, acting by his own initiative, inserted the dates of the calls. This unilateral alteration had the effect of giving the impression that the dates had been fixed at the original meeting. In the Court of Appeal Lord Esher MR observed:

> But they inserted no day or time or place when or where the calls were to become payable. Something happened with regard to that resolution which I cannot help thinking was most dangerously irregular; for the secretary, either in consequence of some supposed power vested in him, or of some idea of his own, some time afterwards inserted in the minutes of the meeting of the 18th certain dates as the dates of the calls. In my opinion that was the most dangerous thing that could well be done. Minutes of board-meetings are kept in order that the shareholders of the company may know exactly what their directors have been doing, why it was done, and when it was done; and any shareholder, looking at these minutes as they now stand, would suppose the dates were agreed upon at the meeting and were then filled in, whereas, in truth, no dates were agreed on by the directors at all. The dates formed no part of the resolution, and yet here is the entry made as if they formed part of the resolution then passed. I trust I shall never again see or hear of the secretary of a company, whether under superior directions or otherwise, altering minutes of meetings, either by striking out anything or adding anything. The proper mode of fixing the dates would have been by resolution, and then entering that resolution on the minutes.

Usually questions concerning the accuracy of the minutes are easily resolved. However, a member who considers that the contents of the draft minutes that have been supplied to him are not an accurate record of what took place at the meeting should, as a matter of best practice, inform the company secretary or the chairman as soon as possible. Ideally the member should explain that he believes that the minutes are inaccurate and provide a corrective draft of the relevant passage. Thereafter, at the next meeting at which the minutes of the previous meeting are considered, he should ask for the minutes to be amended as he has previously indicated and, if the meeting agrees, the document should be altered. If the draft minutes are so changed the chairman should ensure that the correct wording is inserted and initial the amendment or alteration for the purposes of future identification. **16.28**

In the event that there is opposition to the proposed amendment to the minutes the chairman must put this issue to the meeting and, if necessary, it must be put to a vote on a formal resolution to amend the minutes. For the purposes of such a resolution the proposed draft amendment to the minutes may be debated, but the chairman should endeavour to prevent a resumption of discussion concerning the business that was transacted at the previous meeting. **16.29**

[23] (1889) 42 Ch D 209 (CA).

16.30 There is no strict legal obligation on the chairman to sign the minutes but in the event that he does, CA 2006, s 356(4) will apply and the minutes will be treated as evidence of the proceedings at the relevant meeting.

Amendment of mistakes in signed minutes

16.31 In the event that signed minutes are found subsequently to be incorrect the apposite procedure to adopt is to add a further minute or a corrective note of the mistake, and for the chairman to sign that addition or note. If this procedure is adopted anyone who reads the minutes will know the correct position, whereas a minute that contains alterations and amendments has the effect of rendering the minute uncertain, as the reader thereof does not know whether the alterations were approved or indeed, if they were authorized to be made.

16.32 Minutes that have been signed are evidence of the proceedings to which they relate and the burden of proof of showing that the minutes are incorrect falls upon those who make that allegation.[24] This is a heavy burden of proof to discharge as evidence will have to be adduced to show what in fact was done at the meeting, even if that contradicts the minutes. The decision in *Re Fireproof Doors Ltd*[25] is authority for the proposition that evidence may be given of a resolution that has been passed at a meeting but not in fact recorded in the minutes.

16.33 Some articles of association may contain a provision to the effect that the minutes of a meeting if purporting to be signed by the authorized chairman shall be '. . . conclusive evidence without any further proof of the facts therein stated'. In *Kerr v John Mottram Ltd*[26] it was held that evidence cannot be given in such a case to contradict the minutes which have been signed, unless it can be shown as a preliminary matter that the minutes are not a bona fide record of what took place and that they have been written up falsely and fraudulently with a view to setting up a story which is not in accordance with the facts. This will not be possible if the minutes are substantially correct and are a bona fide record of what was transacted at the meeting. This decision has been much criticized and its correctness is doubted. It is thus imprudent to have an article framed in such a way.

Who should take the minutes?

16.34 Minutes must be taken by the person who is best placed to execute this important task. The person who undertakes this function must have a good understanding of the business that is to be transacted at the meeting. In the case of a large company, it is usual for the company secretary or someone in the company secretarial

---

[24] See *Re Indian Zoedone Co* (1884) 26 ChD 70 (CA) and CA 2006, s 356(5), discussed above.
[25] [1916] 2 Ch 142 (Astbury J).
[26] [1940] Ch 657 (Simonds J).

department to make notes at a general meeting and thereafter to write up the minutes of the meeting in the minute book. Plainly, the secretary should take care that what he records is both impartial and free from ambiguity. As stated above, the minutes should constitute a clear and precise account of what was actually agreed upon. What the person taking the minutes is striving to produce is a document that is sufficiently detailed and complete that an absent shareholder would be able to understand from the record what has been transacted at the meeting. Minutes that descend into unnecessary complexity, or lack clarity or are redolent with ambiguity and imprecise language are inappropriate, as clearly they will be difficult to comprehend.

Timing of the production of minutes

Minutes should be drafted and circulated in a timely fashion and without a long period of delay after the end of the relevant meeting. Although there is no mandatory time period for the production of minutes it is suggested that good corporate practice dictates that minutes should be produced and circulated in draft within approximately 48 hours of the meeting. In this way the draft will be produced while recollections of what was discussed and decided remain fresh, at least in the memories of the secretary and the chairman of the meeting. Delays in the production of minutes inevitably lead to disputes and confusion and such unnecessary delays should be avoided. **16.35**

A useful example of a case involving undue delay in the preparation of minutes is the decision of Scrutton J in *Toms v Cinema Trust Company Ltd.*[27] In that case no minutes were drawn up of a meeting for more than a year after it was held. The company's articles of association required that in the event of any conflict of interest a director would not be accountable to the company for any profit he obtained, provided that he disclosed his interest and that such disclosure and interest were entered in the minutes. Scrutton J held that as there was no time specified in the articles of association within which the entry had to be made it was required to be made within a reasonable time. A gap of over a year in the preparation of the minutes was not a reasonable time. Although this case turned on the construction of the terms of a particular article, the decision provides a useful warning as to the potential impact of undue procrastination in the preparation of minutes. **16.36**

[27] [1915] WN 29 (Scrutton J).

17

THE COMPANY COMMUNICATIONS PROVISIONS, INCLUDING ELECTRONIC COMMUNICATIONS

Introduction

17.01 Effective communication by a company with a wide range of persons including its members and debenture-holders is of fundamental importance to the efficient management of a company. Equally the ability of shareholders and others to be able to send communications to a company in an orderly manner is a matter of importance. Until modern times the companies legislation has always required documents, notices and other corporate literature such as reports and accounts to be sent by post or delivered to members in what in modern terminology is called 'hard copy form'. A company's articles of association, including the 1985 Table A, usually contain detailed provisions dealing with the service of such notices and documentation.[1] However, electronic communication is becoming the preferred method for shareholders to receive documents and communications from companies. In recent years, even before the enactment of CA 2006, a large number of public quoted companies with many thousands of members have taken active steps to encourage as many shareholders as

[1] See for example regs 111–116 of the 1985 Table A.

possible to elect to receive their documentation in this way rather than in paper format through the postal system substantially for reasons of cost-saving.

It is not surprising that the issue of electronic communications *by* a company and *to* a company is a subject that features in CA 2006. The aim of the new legislation relating to electronic communications is to encourage a greater use of this modern means of communication. Under the pre-existing law there had been a relatively modest adoption of electronic communications as the standard method of communication. In relation to the operation of the new provisions under CA 2006 the government has estimated that the introduction of the new electronic communications provisions will save UK companies in the region of £50m a year. It remains to be seen whether this estimate proves to be a realistic one in practice.[2] **17.02**

Advantages of Electronic Communication

There are obvious benefits of electronic communication both for companies and for shareholders. The advantages for shareholders are that they are able to view the information on the company's website as soon as it is available, view the documents online, choose which sections of documents they wish to print out and communicate with the company or its registrars quickly, relatively cheaply and effectively. Of course, it has to be recognized that there are still significant numbers of shareholders who will not have access to email and other methods of modern communication, and indeed some, who although having access to such methods of communication, do not want to use this method of communication. As a consequence, companies will have to continue to operate established and more conventional methods of communication with their members in tandem with the available modern methods of electronic communication. **17.03**

From the point of view of a company there are also significant advantages of communicating with its members by use of electronic means. These advantages include a reduction in printing costs and in postal charges, and a reduction in the use of natural and other resources. Accordingly, by persuading its shareholders to adopt the use of electronic communications companies will not only save considerable sums of money, but will also demonstrate that they are considering the impact of the company's operations on the environment.[3] Public companies will therefore make the following types of documents capable of being viewed electronically: **17.04**

- annual reports and accounts;
- interim reports;

[2] Standard Life plc has estimated that if all of its 1.5m shareholders opted for online communications the company could save the use of over 550 tonnes of paper a year.

[3] See the new statutory duty to promote the success of the company in CA 2006, s 172(1)(d).

- circulars to shareholders;
- notices of the annual general meeting and all other meetings of shareholders;
- forms of proxy;
- dividend re-investment plan documentation; and
- other documents relating to shareholder meetings.

Law Prior to 2000

17.05 Prior to 2000 the companies legislation did not make any specific provision for a company to communicate with its members by means of modern electronic methods, such as telephone, mobile telephone, text messaging, fax and email. At this time the most common and usual method by which a company sent notices of meetings to its members was by using first class pre-paid post. As alternatives to this method, which it has to be said, was not always known for its reliability, a company could effect personal service of documentation on a member or leave any documentation at the registered address of the member. However, as the use of modern forms of technology increased and other areas of the law made provisions for the service of documents by the use of fax, it would have been regrettable had it been found to be impossible to apply these modern technological advances to the legislation affecting companies.

The Companies Act (Electronic Communications) Order 2000[4]

17.06 In 2000, by means of secondary legislation in the form of the Companies Act (Electronic Communications) Order 2000 (the 2000 Order) made under the Electronic Communications Act 2000, ss 8 and 9, companies became empowered to use electronic communications in relation to certain aspects of communicating with their members.[5]

17.07 The effect of the 2000 Order was to amend certain specific provisions of CA 1985 and the 1985 Table A so as to permit electronic communication by a company with its members. However, under this legislative regime the default position (ie in the absence of agreement) applicable was that the member was always entitled

---

4 SI 3373/2000.

5 Electronic Communications Act 2000, s 15 defined 'electronic communication' as '. . . a communication transmitted (whether from one person to another, from one device to another or from one person to a device or vice versa)—

(a) by means of a telecommunication system (within the meaning of the Telecommunications Act 1948); or

(b) by other means while in electronic form'.

to documentation in hard copy form. However, a company was able to use electronic communications in relation to, amongst other things, the circulation of reports and accounts,[6] summary financial statements,[7] notices of general meeting[8] and the appointment of proxies[9] in the event that it had a member's express agreement. In the case of a private company notice of an elective resolution, for example to dispense with the laying of accounts and reports before a general meeting or to dispense with the holding of an annual general meeting, might be sent to a member using electronic communications to such address as notified by that person to the company for that purpose, or by means of a website where the company and that person had agreed that notices of meetings given to that person might instead be accessed by him on a website.[10] As a result, companies were permitted to use the electronic communications regime as promulgated by the 2000 Order so as to communicate with their members by email or via a website rather than via the postal system even before CA 2006 came into legal force.

As a result of this legislation companies, both public and private, were able to communicate with their members by a wide range of methods: **17.08**

- email;
- fax;
- telephone;
- mobile telephone;
- text message;
- website;
- supplying a CD-ROM;
- supplying a DVD;
- supplying a computer disk;
- supplying an audio tape.

Agreement required to communicate electronically

Under the 2000 Order there was no question that either members or indeed a company could be compelled to communicate by electronic means. Of critical importance to the effective operation of the 2000 Order was the requirement that a company obtain the express consent of the member to communication by electronic means. The company would have to issue a specific invitation to members offering the option to receive notices electronically and persuade them to provide an affirmative response. **17.09**

---

6 See CA 1985, ss 238 (4A)–(4E) and 239(2A) and (2B) which were inserted by Arts 12 and 13 of the 2000 Order.

7 See CA 1985, s 251(2A)–(2E), inserted by Art 14 of the 2000 Order.

8 See CA 1985, s 369(4A)–(4G), inserted by Art 18 of the 2000 Order.

9 See CA 1985, s 372(2A), (2B) and (6A), inserted by Art 19 of the 2000 Order.

10 See CA 1985, s 379A(2B)–(2F) and (5A), inserted by Art 21 of the 2000 Order.

What happened in practice was that it was difficult for companies to obtain such actual consent from their members, as many members simply failed to reply to companies' invitations for their consent to receive documentation in electronic form. This general inertia on the part of members to respond to such invitations has been recognized in the form of the new legislative regime set out in CA 2006.

17.10 Interestingly, the 2000 Order did not amend all the sections of CA 1985 that affected communication between a company and its members. For example, no express amendment was made to the important statutory provision which conferred power on members to requisition a meeting of members under CA 1985, s 368.[11] This section of CA 1985 contained wording that required the members' requisition notice to be 'deposited' by members at the registered office of the company. The time of the deposit of the requisition notice at a company's registered office was of central importance to the requisition procedure, because it was from that moment that all the timing provisions for the effective operation of the section started to operate.

17.11 In *PNC Telecom plc v Thomas*[12] the question arose as to whether a requisition notice sent by members by fax to the registered office of a company was valid. The claimant sought a declaration that the entitlement of the defendants to convene a meeting under CA 1985, s 368 had not arisen because the requisition notice was invalid as the use of a fax was not permitted service within the meaning of the word 'deposited' in s 368. The claimant argued that provision had been made in the 2000 Order for service by electronic means in respect of certain sections of the 1985 Act and of certain regulations contained in the 1985 Table A, but no mention had been made in these provisions of the procedure in relation to CA 1985, s 368 to requisition a meeting. The court acknowledged this fact but held that the requisition notice that had been sent by the requisitionists by fax and received by the company on its fax machine was valid. Accordingly, the requisitionists were entitled to convene a meeting.

17.12 The court noted that the 2000 Order had been made under the Electronic Communications Act 2000 and was primarily concerned with new electronic methods of communication such as email. However, it also applied to fax. Fax communication had been in use for a long time prior to the introduction of the 2000 Order and was not as new a method of communication. Further, a fax could transmit the contents of a form and a signature and the fax received was 'instructed' to duplicate its author's signature either by the author or on the author's authority. Service by fax was also more reliable, speedier and attracted no greater risk of forgery than service by post, the latter being an accepted form of service.

[11] Now called a request under CA 2006, s 303.

[12] [2004] 1 BCLC 88 (Morritt V-C). This case also demonstrates that the court will usually be very willing to uphold the right of members to require the directors to convene a meeting (such a right is now contained in CA 2006, ss 303–306), especially where the members wish to pass an ordinary resolution removing directors from office under CA 2006, s 168 (formerly CA 1985, s 303).

In the circumstances, a hard copy of the required notice with the relevant signatures had been validly served by fax and accordingly the defendants were entitled to requisition and convene a meeting under section 368 of the 1985 Act.

The Guidance of the Institute of Chartered Secretaries and Administrators

Schedule 1 to the 2000 Order inserted a number of amendments to the 1985 Table A. In particular reg 115 of the 1985 Table A[13] (as amended) made express reference to guidance issued by the Institute of Chartered Secretaries and Administrators (ICSA) in order to determine whether a notice had been given by a company.[14] The guidance to which reg 115 of the 1985 Table A referred was published by CSA in December 2000 in a booklet entitled 'Electronic Communications with Shareholders—a Guide to Recommended Best Practice'. By making express reference to this important publication of ICSA in reg 115 of the 1985 Table A, it was indirectly accredited with legal force, and as a consequence companies were well advised to pay due care and attention to the other recommendations contained therein. A revised edition of the ICSA guidance has been published to take account of the new legislative regime of CA 2006 regulating electronic communications.[15] **17.13**

As a consequence of the ICSA publication on best practice in this important area of the law a large number of listed companies amended their articles of association in order to permit them to communicate electronically with their members. Such provisions will continue to operate under the new statutory regime of CA 2006, but it is not clear whether the new deemed consent provisions will be capable of operation by relying on amendments to articles of association that were made to give effect to the 2000 Order. It is suggested that the better view is that in order for the deemed consent provisions of CA 2006 to apply with full effect, companies will be required to amend their articles of association again so as to reflect the new legislation. **17.14**

The Company Communication Provisions under CA 2006—Overview

The company communication provisions in CA 2006, ss 1143–1148 and Schs 4 and 5 came into force on 20 January 2007 by means of the Companies Act 2006 (Commencement No 1, Transitional Provisions and Savings) Order 2006.[16] These provisions take effect '. . . subject to any requirements that are imposed, or contrary **17.15**

---

[13] See the commentary in Part 4.

[14] The words inserted were: 'Proof that a notice contained in an electronic communication was sent in accordance with guidance issued by the Institute of Chartered Secretaries and Administrators shall be conclusive evidence that the notice was given.'—see Sch 1, para 8(2) of the 2000 Order.

[15] The document is called 'ICSA Guidance on Electronic Communications with Shareholders 2007'. It can be viewed on ICSA's website.

[16] SI 2006/3428.

provision made, by or under any enactment'.[17] These important sections and schedules are considered in detail below.

17.16 The provisions in CA 2006 relating to communications apply to both public and private companies, and are designed to allow any information or documents to be sent or supplied in either hard copy form or in electronic form, provided that the requirements of CA 2006 are fulfilled. Under the new statutory regime for electronic communications a company is permitted to apply the new electronic communication provisions to *any* provision of CA 2006 that authorizes or requires documents or information to be sent or supplied by or to members.[18] This is to be contrasted with the old regime under the 2000 Order which had amended certain specific legislative provisions of CA 1985 and regulations of the 1985 Table A by attaching wording that was applicable to electronic communication. This approach had engendered a degree of uncertainty as to whether other provisions of CA 1985 which required information to be communicated 'in writing' could be satisfied by the use of electronic communications.[19]

The need to opt out

17.17 Under the provisions of CA 2006 the legislation has made an effort to overcome the seeming inherent inertia of members to reply to companies' requests for consent to communicate with them electronically. As a result a 'deeming' provision in the new legislation applies to shareholders who have not replied and permits a company to communicate with them by means of website communications.[20]

17.18 Members will have to indicate their preference to receive documentation or information in hard copy format.[21] Many public companies have already sent letters to shareholders asking them to return a form if they wish to continue to receive paper copies of all shareholder communications. If no such express election is made by members the company will be permitted to use website communication as the default method of communicating with its members.[22] It is anticipated that requiring members to take positive action to receive documentation in hard copy format will produce advantageous cost savings for companies derived from using less paper and printing and minimizing distribution requirements.

---

[17] See CA 2006, s 1143(2).

[18] For example, a private company will be able to communicate written resolutions to members in electronic form or by means of a website, and members will be able to signify consent to written resolutions by electronic means—see CA 2006, ss 291(3)(a), 293(2)(a), 298 and 299.

[19] See *PNC Telecom plc v Thomas* [2004] 1 BCLC 88 (Morritt V-C).

[20] See further paras 17.63–17.68 below.

[21] Under CA 2006, s 1145.

[22] See Sch 5, Part 4, para 10 and the commentary below.

Distinction between communications *to* a company and *by* a company

In CA 2006, s 1144 a crucial distinction is drawn between communications that are made *to* a company and communications that are made *by* a company. Communications that are made *to* a company are regulated by s 1144(1) and the provisions of Sch 4. Communications that are made *by* a company are regulated by s 1144(2) and the provisions of Sch 5. These important schedules will be analysed in detail below. **17.19**

Two companies communicating with each other

Where a company is sending or supplying documents or information to another company, only the rules of Sch 5 relating to communications made *by* a company apply.[23] Accordingly, any shareholder which is itself a company is required to comply with the provisions of Sch 5 when communicating with the company in which it holds an investment. **17.20**

The Company Communication Provisions under CA 2006, ss 1143–1148 —Detailed Requirements

CA 2006, ss 1143–1148 set out a number of basic rules governing communications by or to a company and cross refer to Schs 4 and 5 for specific requirements. CA 2006, ss 1145, 1146 and 1148 contain provisions that are necessary for the proper understanding of Schs 4 and 5. In addition, reference must be made to s 1168 which defines what is meant by the phrases 'hard copy form', 'electronic form' and related expressions. In view of their importance these sections will be considered before examining the contents of Schs 4 and 5. **17.21**

Right of a member to demand a document in hard copy—CA 2006, s 1145

Companies that communicate with their members by electronic means are not permitted to abandon more conventional methods of communication because CA 2006, s 1145 enables a member who has received a document or information otherwise than in hard copy form to require the company to send a version of the document or information in hard copy form. A company that receives a request from a member under CA 2006, s 1145(1) is under a duty to send the document or information in hard copy form within 21 days of receiving the request and the company cannot make any charge for this service.[24] As a consequence of this **17.22**

23 See CA 2006, s 1144(3) and Sch 4, para 1(2).
24 See CA 2006, s 1145(2).

provision, it may well be that much of the perceived savings in costs will not materialize.

Consequences of breach of s 1145

17.23 Directors and officers, in addition to the company, who fail to comply with the requirements of CA 2006, s 1145 will commit an offence that is punishable by way of a fine.[25]

Definitions in CA 2006, s 1168

17.24 In order to understand the operation of the company communication provisions it is necessary to have regard to various definitions that are contained in CA 2006, s 1168. These definitions apply for all purposes of the Companies Acts.[26]

'Hard copy form'

17.25 CA 2006, s 1168(2) provides that a document or information is sent or supplied in hard copy form if it is sent or supplied in a paper copy or in a similar form that is capable of being read.[27]

'Electronic form'

17.26 Section 1168(3) provides that a document or information is sent or supplied in electronic form if it is sent or supplied by electronic means (eg by email or by fax) or by any other means while in electronic form (eg by sending a DVD, CD-ROM or disk by post). Where documents or information are sent or supplied in electronic form two requirements stipulated by s 1168(5) and (6) must be satisfied so far as the recipient is concerned. First, the recipient must be able to read the documents with the naked eye, or to the extent that the document consists of images such as photographs, pictures, maps, plans or drawings, see it with the naked eye. Secondly, the recipient must be able to retain a copy of the document or information. It would appear that the ability of the recipient to retain the document or information in electronic form only will be sufficient.

'Electronic means'

17.27 By CA 2006, s 1168(4) a document or information is sent or supplied by 'electronic means' if it is sent initially and received at its destination by means of electronic equipment for the processing[28] or storage of data and it is transmitted, conveyed and received by wire, radio, optical means or other electromagnetic means.

---

[25] See CA 2006, s 1145(4) and (5).

[26] See CA 2006, s 1168(1).

[27] As defined in CA 2006, s 1168(6).

[28] This includes digital compression—CA 2006, see s 1168(4)(a).

A document or information that is sent by electronic means must be sent in such a form that the sender reasonably considers will enable the recipient to read it and retain a copy of it.[29] This is no doubt to enable the document to be used for future reference. In this context the word 'read' means that the document or information can be read with the naked eye, or, if it consists of images or pictures, it can be seen with the naked eye.[30] **17.28**

Further definitions—CA 2006, s 1148

CA 2006, s 1148 contains further definitions for the purposes of the interpretation of the company communication provisions. Section 1148(1) provides that the word 'address' includes a number or address used for the purposes of sending documents or information by electronic means. Further, by means of the same provision the word 'document' is defined inexhaustively as *including* a summons, notice, order or other legal process and registers and the word 'company' includes any body corporate. **17.29**

Where references are made in the company communication provisions[31] to documents or information being sent or supplied by a company or to a company, such references include references to documents or information being sent or supplied by directors or to the directors of a company acting on behalf of a company.[32] This provision ensures that the legislation is construed in a practical and commonsense way, and that no artificial distinction is drawn between a company and the directors acting on its behalf for these purposes. **17.30**

Deemed delivery—CA 2006, s 1147

Provision is made in CA 2006, s 1147 for ascertaining the deemed time of delivery of documents and information sent or supplied by a company. In relation to members, this statutory provision is expressly subject to contrary provisions contained in the company's articles of association.[33] **17.31**

Deemed delivery by post

Where a company sends or supplies information by post (either in hard copy or electronic form) to an address in the United Kingdom and, provided that the company is able to show that the document or information was properly addressed, prepaid with the correct postage and posted, the document or information will be deemed to have been received by the recipient 48 hours after it was posted.[34] **17.32**

---

[29] See CA 2006, s 1168(5).
[30] See CA 2006, s 1168(6).
[31] CA 2006, ss 1144–1148.
[32] See CA 2006, s 1148(3).
[33] See CA 2006, s 1147(6)(a).
[34] CA 2006, s 1147(2).

This is an extremely important and helpful provision for a company. However, it is regrettable to note that even first class pre-paid post does not always meet the expectation of the legislation! Care must be taken by companies to ensure that in respect of any important communication there exists adequate evidence of the date and time of posting.

Deemed delivery by electronic means

17.33 Where a company sends documents or supplies information by electronic means, then provided that the company can show that what was sent or supplied was correctly addressed, the document or information will be deemed to have been received by the intended recipient 48 hours after it was sent.[35] This section rather strangely imposes the same timing on the deemed receipt of a document sent by virtually instantaneous communication as that sent by post.

Deemed delivery by website

17.34 Where a company sends or supplies documents or information by a website they are deemed to have been received by the intended recipient when the material was first available on the website or if later, when the recipient received, or is deemed to have received, notice of the fact that the material was available on the website.[36]

Calculation of the time period for deemed delivery

17.35 When calculating the time period for the purposes of CA 2006, s 1147, no account is to be taken of any part of a day that is not a working day.[37] A 'working day' is defined in s 1173(1) as meaning a day that is not a Saturday or a Sunday, Christmas Day, Good Friday or any day that is a bank holiday in the part of the United Kingdom where the company is registered. Accordingly, account must be taken only of normal working days, ignoring all weekends and bank holidays.

Schedule 4: Documents or Information Sent or Supplied *to* a Company

17.36 The provisions of CA 2006, Sch 4 regulate the sending or supply of documents or information to a company.[38] CA 2006, Sch 4 is divided into four parts:

Part 1—Introduction
Part 2—Communications in Hard Copy Form

[35] CA 2006, s 1147(3).
[36] See CA 2006, s 1147(4) and Sch 5, Part 4, para 13.
[37] See CA 2006, s 1147(5).
[38] Schedule 4, para 1(1).

Part 3—Communications in Electronic Form
Part 4—Other Agreed Forms of Communication

Schedule 4 does not apply where two companies are involved in the sending or supply of documents or information between each other. This situation is governed by the provisions of Sch 5. This is expressly stated in CA 2006, s 1144(3) and Sch 4, para 1(2). Accordingly, Sch 4 covers all communications with a company emanating from an individual, a partnership, a foreign corporation or a body corporate.[39] **17.37**

Sending or supplying documents or information in hard copy form to a company

It is possible to communicate with a company by sending or supplying documents or information in hard copy form by post to a specified address.[40] The relevant address may be either an address that has been supplied for a specific purpose, or the address of the company's registered office or an address to which any provision of the Companies Acts authorizes the document or information to be sent or supplied.[41] **17.38**

Under Sch 4, Part 2, para 3(2) a person will be held to have sent a document or information by post if he sends it in a pre-paid envelope containing the document or information. As the person who is communicating with a company will have the burden of proving that the document or information was sent by post it is prudent for the sender to obtain contemporaneous evidence of posting or use a guaranteed form of postal delivery, such as recorded delivery or special delivery. **17.39**

Communications to a company in electronic form—Sch 4, Part 3

Schedule 4, Part 3 deals with communications to a company in electronic form. If there is due and proper compliance with the provision of Sch 4, Part 3 the result is that a document or information will have been validly sent or supplied to the company.[42] Under Sch 4, Part 3, para 6 conditions are prescribed for effective communication to a company in electronic form. The recipient company must have agreed, either generally or specifically, that the document or information may be sent or supplied in electronic form and not revoked that agreement. Alternatively, a document or information may be sent or supplied in electronic form where the company is deemed to have agreed to be sent or supplied documents or information in electronic form by a specific provision in the Companies Acts. **17.40**

[39] See the definition of the word 'company' in CA 2006, s 1(1) and that of 'body corporate' in s 1173(1).
[40] CA 2006, Sch 4, Part 2, para 3(1).
[41] CA 2006, Sch 4, Part 2, para 4.
[42] CA 2006, Sch 4, Part 2, para 5.

Deemed agreement of a company under the Companies Acts

17.41 There are a number of provisions under CA 2006 where a company will be deemed to have agreed to accept communications at an electronic address. A company may include an electronic address[43] in a notice of a general meeting. If this is the case then the company will be deemed to have agreed that any document or information relating to proceedings at the meeting can be sent by electronic means to that address.[44] Another example where the company is deemed to have agreed that a document may be sent by electronic means also derives from CA 2006, s 333 and relates to the situation where a company has given an electronic address in an instrument of proxy or in an invitation to appoint a proxy issued by the company in relation to the meeting. This action on the part of the company means that the company is deemed to have agreed that any document or information relating to proxies for that meeting may be sent by electronic means to that address. The company is permitted to attach conditions or restrictions on the use of the address, but these must be stipulated in the notice.

17.42 Under CA 2006, s 298 a company may include in a document containing or accompanying a proposed written resolution an electronic address.[45] Where this situation pertains, a company will be deemed to have agreed that any document or information relating to that written resolution may be sent by electronic means to that address. Again, it is legitimate for the company to prescribe any conditions or limitations on the use of the electronic address in the document.

Address for electronic communication to a company

17.43 Schedule 4, Part 3, para 7 makes provision for the address to which communication in electronic form may be sent. The company must either specify an address for communications in electronic form or, if it is deemed to have specified such an address by a provision in the Companies Acts.

17.44 Documents or information may be sent or supplied in electronic form either by hand delivery or by postal delivery, for example, sending a CD-ROM through the post. In such a situation the document or information in electronic form must be sent or supplied to an address to which it could have been validly sent had the document or information been in hard copy form.[46]

---

[43] Defined in s 333(4) as 'any address or number used for the purpose of sending or receiving documents or information by electronic means'.

[44] See CA 2006, s 333(1).

[45] Section 298 defines 'electronic address' as '. . . any address or number used for the purpose of sending or receiving documents or information by electronic means'.

[46] CA 2006, Sch 4, Part 3, para 7(2).

CA 2006, Sch 4, Part 4

It is possible for documents or information to be sent or supplied to a company otherwise than in hard copy form or in electronic form if they are sent or supplied by some other form or manner which has been agreed by the company.[47] This provision appears to anticipate further developments in the technology of communications. **17.45**

Schedule 5: Communications *by* a Company

CA 2006, Sch 5

The provisions of CA 2006, Sch 5 govern communications that are made *by* a company. This includes the sending or supply of documents or information by a company to a company of which it is a shareholder. Schedule 5 is divided into six parts: **17.46**

Part 1—Introduction
Part 2—Communications in Hard Copy Form
Part 3—Communications in Electronic Form
Part 4—Communications by means of a Website
Part 5—Other Agreed Forms of Communication
Part 6—Supplementary Provisions

Schedule 5, Part 2—Communications in Hard Copy Form

If a company complies with the requirements of CA 2006, Sch 5, Part 2 the result will be that it will have sent or supplied a document or information in a lawful manner. **17.47**

In order to communicate by means of a document or information in hard copy form a company can:[48] **17.48**

(1) arrange for it to be handed to the recipient; or
(2) send or supply it by hand to a valid address; or
(3) send or supply it by post to a valid address.

Schedule 5, Part 2, para 4 determines what is an appropriate address for these purposes.

In order to send a document or information by post a company must place the document in a pre-paid envelope and consign that to the postal system.[49] **17.49**

---

[47] CA 2006, Sch 4, Part 4, para 8.
[48] Schedule 5, Part 2, para 3.
[49] Schedule 5, Part 2, para 2.

Addresses for communications in hard copy form

17.50 In order for a company to be able to communicate in an effective manner it must keep an up-to-date record of addresses. A valid address is an indispensable requirement to enable a company to comply with the provisions of Sch 5, Part 2.

17.51 Schedule 5, Part 2, para 4 enables a company to send or supply documents or information to five different addresses:

(1) an address that the intended recipient has specified;
(2) the registered office of a company;
(3) in respect of a member, the address of the member as shown in the register of members;[50]
(4) in respect of a director, the address of the director as shown in the register of directors;[51]
(5) an address authorized by a provision of the Companies Acts to which a document can be sent or supplied.

Last known address

17.52 In the absence of the company being able to send or supply a document or information to any of the addresses that are listed above, the company is permitted by Sch 5, Part 2, para 4 (2) to send or supply the document or information to the intended recipient's last address known to the company. Those responsible for the administration of a company's affairs are well advised to take all reasonable measures in order to keep addresses in the register of members as up to date as possible.

No valid address

17.53 A company is permitted by CA 2006, s 310(4) to make provision in its articles of association so that it will not be obliged to continue sending notice of general meetings to members who do not have a current address. A somewhat similar provision is to be found in s 423, dealing with the company's duty to circulate copies of its annual accounts and reports. Copies need not be sent to a person for whom the company does not have a current address as that term is defined in s 423(3). For this purpose a company has a current address for a person if an address has been notified to the company by the person as one at which documents may be sent to him, and the company has no reason to believe that documents sent to him at that address will not reach him.

---

[50] There is a statutory duty to maintain such a document.

[51] There is a statutory duty to maintain such a document.

Notice of general meeting

Under CA 2006, s 308 a notice of general meeting of a company may be given in hard copy form, or in electronic form or by means of a website or partly in one form and partly in another.[52] In order to notify a member of a general meeting in a regular and lawful manner by means of a notice in hard copy form[53] a company may (by virtue of Sch 5, Part 2, para 3): **17.54**

(i) hand to the member or other intended recipient a document which contains the notice of a general meeting; or
(ii) hand deliver to a member's registered address or an address specified by the intended recipient a notice of general meeting; or
(iii) place the notice of general meeting in a pre-paid envelope and send it by post to the member's registered address or the address specified by the intended recipient.

Of the various methods listed in sub-paras (i) to (iii) the most usual method of giving a notice of a general meeting is by using the postal system. Recourse to personal service on members as a means of giving notice of a general meeting must be very rare and as a practical matter may only operate as an adequate means of giving notice where the numbers of persons involved are very limited.

Schedule 5, Part 3—Communications in Electronic Form (other than by website)

Schedule 5, Part 3 deals with communications by a company in electronic form otherwise than by means of a website, which are governed by Part 4 (below). Although the term electronic form can encompass a number of forms of communication the most common will be the use of email. If a company complies with the prescribed requirements of CA 2006, Sch 5, Part 3 the result will be that it will have sent or supplied a document or information in a lawful manner.[54] Under s 308(b) a notice of a general meeting may be given in electronic form. **17.55**

Section 1168(3) provides that a document or information is sent or supplied in electronic form if it is sent or supplied by electronic means (eg by email or fax) or by any other means while in electronic form (for example by sending a DVD, CD-ROM or disk by post). By CA 2006, s 1168(4) a document or information is sent by 'electronic means' if it is sent initially and received at its destination by means of electronic equipment for the processing or storage of data and it is transmitted, conveyed and received by wire, radio, optical means or other electromagnetic means. **17.56**

---

[52] Regard will have to be had to ss 1143–1148 and Sch 5.

[53] CA 2006, s 308 of the CA 2006 also permits a notice of a general meeting to be given by electronic form or by means of a website publication in accordance with s 309.

[54] CA 2006, Sch 5, Part 3, para 5.

Agreement to receive information or documents in electronic form from a company

17.57 It is important to note that both the prior and continuing agreement of a person to receive documents or information in electronic form is a prerequisite of this method of communication by a company.[55] A person may agree to be sent or supplied with documents or information in this form either generally or specifically. Accordingly, in order for a company to be able to communicate with a member by email that person must give their specific permission in accordance with the requirements of Sch 5, Part 3, para 6(a).

17.58 In addition, by Sch 5, Part 3, para 6(b) in the case of a corporate recipient, agreement to receive documents or information in electronic form may not only arise as a result of its express agreement,[56] but may be deemed to have arisen by a provision in the Companies Acts.

Addresses for communications in electronic form

17.59 If a company has the agreement of a recipient to receive documents or information in electronic form it must ensure that the documents or information are sent or supplied by electronic means to an address that the intended recipient has specified for that purpose.[57] In relation to a corporate recipient, the address may be deemed to have been specified by a provision of the Companies Acts.[58]

Hand or postal delivery of documents or information in electronic form

17.60 It is possible for documents or information to be sent or supplied in electronic form either by hand delivery or by using the postal system—for example, a disk or CD-ROM may be hand delivered to a recipient or may be posted to a recipient. If such a method is employed the company must use the address of the recipient to which documents or information could be sent or supplied in hard copy form.[59]

Schedule 5, Part 4—Communications by a company by means of a website

17.61 Schedule 5, Part 4 deals with the publication of documents or the provision of information by a company by making it available on a website in accordance with the prescribed requirements of Sch 5, Part 4. These wide-ranging provisions govern agreements as to the use of a website, the availability of documents on the website, notification of their availability and the period during which they must

---

[55] CA 2006, Sch 5, Part 3, para 6(a).
[56] Either for a specific meeting or generally.
[57] Schedule 5, Part 3, paras 7(a), (b).
[58] Schedule 5, Part 3, para 7(b).
[59] Schedule 5, Part 3, para 7(2).

remain available. If a company complies with the requirements of CA 2006, Sch 5, Part 4 the result will be that it will have sent or supplied a document or information in a lawful manner by means of its availability on a website.

A company may give notice of a general meeting in a lawful manner if the notice for such a meeting appears on a website in compliance with the requirements of CA 2006, s 309. This does not mean that a company can make a unilateral decision to give notice of a general meeting in this manner. There must be due compliance with the requirements of Sch 5, Part 4. The express agreement or the deemed agreement of the members of the company concerned is of fundamental importance. **17.62**

Agreement to the use of communications by means of a website

The agreement of a recipient of documents or information to the use of communication by a company by means of a website can arise by two means. First, agreement can arise by the express consent (either generally or specifically) that the document or information may be sent or supplied to him in that manner. Secondly, agreement that a document or information may be sent or supplied by the company can arise through the deemed agreement of the recipient to the use of the website in accordance with Sch 5, paras 10 and 11. In both cases the agreement to the use of the website must not have been revoked. Each of these concepts is considered further below. **17.63**

Schedule 5, Part 4, para 9(1)(a)—Express Agreement

A company may communicate with a person by means of a website where that person has given his express agreement, either generally or on a specific occasion, that documents or information may be sent or supplied to him by that means. At the time that the company effects communication with a person by this method that person's express agreement must remain valid, that is, the agreement must not have been revoked. In this context it is suggested that revocation must require formal notice to the company. **17.64**

Schedule 5, Part 4, paras 9(1)(b) and 10—Deemed Agreement

As it has proved in practice rather difficult to obtain the express consent of recipients of documents or information, CA 2006 provides a mechanism for recipients to be taken to have given their consent to communications made by a company by means of a website. **17.65**

Who may be deemed to have agreed?[60]

17.66 Under Sch 5, Part 4, para 10(1)(a)–(c) there are three categories of person who may be deemed to have given their agreement to the use of a website. Those persons are:

(a) members of a company;
(b) another person who has been nominated by a member under provisions in a company's articles of association to enjoy or exercise all of any of the member's rights in relation to the company;
(c) a person nominated by a member under CA 2006, s 146 to enjoy information rights.[61]

Authority for the use of a website

17.67 Under Sch 5, Part 4, para 10(2) where the members of a company have resolved that the company may employ a website as a means of sending or supplying documents or information, or the company's articles of association contain a provision to that effect, a person will be taken to have agreed that documents or information may be sent or supplied to them in that manner provided that the two conditions stipulated by para 10(3) are satisfied. Accordingly, it is essential either that the members of the company have resolved that a company may use the website or that a company's articles of association contain a provision to that effect.

Conditions of Sch 5, Part 4, para 10(3)

17.68 In order for a company to be able to rely upon the deemed consent of the person, two conditions must be satisfied. The first condition is that the person has been asked individually by the company to agree that the company may send or supply documents or information generally, or particular documents or information, to him by means of a website. The second condition is that the company has not received a response to the invitation within a period of 28 days starting with the date upon which the request was made. It is suggested that this provision is likely to be strictly enforced and that the dates on which requests are made should be carefully recorded by the company.[62]

---

[60] Schedule 5, Part 4, para 11 also deals with the deemed agreement of debenture holders to the use of a website.

[61] See Ch 10.

[62] Since January 2007 when these provisions first came into force, it has become common for listed public companies in the UK to offer shareholders the opportunity to register to receive communications from the company either electronically or in printed form. Where members have not expressed a preference, and provided that the company has complied with the duty to warn the members of the consequences of failing to make such an election, the company is entitled thereafter to supply documentation via its website unless the member requests otherwise.

The failure of the company's request to warn of the consequences of silence

In order for the company to make a valid request for agreement that a person can be sent or supplied with documents by means of a website, the request must state in clear terms what the effect of a failure to respond will be,[63] that is, that no response from the person will enable the company to send or supply documents by means of a website because the invitee will be deemed to have consented to this method of communication. The use of language such as: 'You need to return this form by [a specified date] or you will be taken to have agreed to receive future communications by the website' will suffice. If the request made by the company does not comply with this important requirement, the person will not be deemed to have agreed to the company's request to send or supply documents by means of a website. **17.69**

Timing of company's request

The second condition with which the company must comply in order to be able to rely on a deemed consent from a person to be sent or supplied with documents or information by means of a website, is that it may only make a request at intervals of 12 months. If a member says he does not want to be sent or supplied with documentation via a website, the company must honour that decision and wait for a period of at least 12 months before it asks the member again for such consent. This restriction covers only requests made in relation to the specific documents for which consent was originally sought. Accordingly, it will be important for officers of a company to keep an accurate record of when requests have been sent to members and also how the member has reacted to such a request. **17.70**

The guidance issued by ICSA on the new electronic communications provisions states that communication during a year to encourage members to agree to the use of a website as a method of communication is permissible. What is prohibited, other than on an annual basis, is actively seeking to obtain the deemed agreement of members to the use of the website by repeated requests in the hope that the default provision will come into operation as a result of their failure to respond. This is an important check on the ability of the board of directors to impose change on the company. **17.71**

Resolutions under Sch 5, Part 4, para 10

Where a resolution is passed under Sch 5, Part 4, para 10 a copy of that resolution must be sent to the Registrar of Companies in accordance with the provisions of CA 2006, Part 3, Chapter 3. This is stipulated in Sch 5, Part 4, para 10(5). The cross reference is to CA 2006, ss 29 and 30. **17.72**

[63] CA 2006, Sch 5, Part 4, para 10(4).

Schedule 5, Part 4, para 12—availability of documents or information on a website

17.73 Having obtained the express or deemed consent of a person to communicate with them by means of a website the legislation makes express provisions for the format of the website. Companies will have to ensure that the website that is used complies with the requirements of para 12. Where documents or information can be sent or supplied by means of a website that documentation or information must be available in a form, and by a means, that the company reasonably believes will enable the recipient to both read it and to retain a copy of it. Accordingly, companies must take care that the technology that is employed on the website is not of such a sophisticated nature that it will preclude large numbers of persons, who are perhaps using less sophisticated technology, from gaining access to the documents or information that are posted on the website.

17.74 Paragraph 12(2) amplifies what is meant by the word 'read' in this context. A document or information can be read only if it can be read with the naked eye, and to the extent that the document or information is comprised of images (such as plans, pictures, photographs or diagrams) it can be seen with the naked eye. It is suggested that in order to comply with para 12 the size of the font used on a company's website should be sufficient to enable the information set out to be read from the computer screen.

Schedule 5, Part 4, para 13—notification of availability of information or documents on a website

17.75 Where the company has obtained the express consent, or can rely upon the deemed consent of the intended recipient to the use of a website as a means of communication, the company must in addition notify the intended recipient of four matters stipulated in Sch 5, Part 4, para 13 each time that a document or information appears on the website. Those four matters are:

(1) the presence of a document or information on the website;
(2) the address of the website;
(3) the place on the website where it may be accessed; and
(4) how to access the document or information.

17.76 As to timing, Sch 5, Part 4, para 13(2) provides that any document or information must be taken to have been sent by the company on the date on which the notification required by that paragraph is sent. Alternatively, if later, the document or information must taken to have been sent by the company on the date on which it first appears on the website after that notification is sent. This provision may have important repercussions in respect of notices of meetings where care must be taken to comply with the additional requirements of CA 2006, s 309.[64]

[64] See Ch 2.

These provide that the company must inform the members of the presence of the notice of meeting on the website and such notification must:

(a) state that it concerns a notice of a company meeting,
(b) specify the place, date and time of the meeting, and
(c) in the case of a public company, state whether the meeting will be an annual general meeting.

Method of complying with duty to notify under para 13

The statutory requirement that the intended recipient must also be notified each time that a document or information has been posted on the website may mean in practice that any cost savings arising from the use of a website will be illusory or less achievable. This will be the position in circumstances where members have consented to communication from the company by means of a website rather than by means of email. In such a situation, the company's notification in accordance with Sch 5, Part 4, para 13 that the document or information is available on the website will have to be sent by post, unless the member has expressed a wish to receive shareholder communications electronically in the future by registering with the company an email address, in which case he may be informed of the availability of documents on the website by email. If the document of which notification is being given amounts to a one-page notice of a general meeting, it is unlikely there will be much of a cost saving if a letter has to be sent to the members informing them that the documentation is available on the website. **17.77**

Schedule 5, Part 4, para 14(1)—period of availability of documents or information on a website

The company must make the document or information available on the website throughout the period specified by any applicable provision of the Companies Acts. If no time is specified by the legislation, the required period is one of 28 days beginning with the date on which the notification that the document or information is available on the website is sent to the person in question under para 13. A company will be well advised to keep an accurate record of relevant dates so that there will be no doubt as to when the relevant time period begins and ends and in order for there to be some documentary evidence which may be of assistance in case of difficulties. **17.78**

It would appear that if a company fails completely to comply with the requirements of Sch 5, Part 4, para 14(1) the result is that there has been no effective communication by means of a website. Partial default on the part of the company to comply with the requirements of para 14(1) is dealt with by the provisions contained in para 14(2). **17.79**

17.80 If the document or information has been on the website for only part of the period of time that is required by para 14(1) *and* the failure to make it available for the entire period is '. . . wholly attributable to circumstances that it would not be reasonable to have expected the company to prevent or avoid' the failure to comply with para 14(1) will be disregarded. This provision is no doubt designed to afford a modicum of protection to a company in the event of circumstances that may have an impact on the use of a website but which cannot be controlled by a company. A prolonged and perhaps widespread power failure could result in a large number of members of a company being unable to access the documents or information on a website. It is suggested that in such circumstances the non-availability of the document or information on the website for the prescribed period would be excused under Part 4, para 14(2).

17.81 Whether a failure is or is not wholly attributable to circumstances that are unreasonable to expect a company to have taken measures to avoid or prevent will be a question of degree and fact in each case. A company may well be expected to take reasonable steps to protect the integrity of a website in a similar way that responsible users of computer technology take steps to protect their operating systems from external but foreseeable risks such as computer viruses. However, widespread flooding of premises leading to a disruption in computer communication may be more easily excused.

Schedule 5, Part 5—Other Agreed Forms of Communication by a company

17.82 Under Sch 5, Part 5, para 15 the legislation provides that in addition to communication of documents or information in hard copy form or by electronic form or by means of a website it is permissible for communication by a company to take place in a manner that has been agreed to by the intended recipients. In view of the comprehensive nature of the legislation it is perhaps difficult to see what other forms of communication will apply. However, investment agreements and shareholders' agreements frequently contain specific provisions relating to the giving of notices by companies, for example by sending a notice to a party's solicitor at a prescribed address. Such agreed forms of communication are not prohibited under the new legislation.

Schedule 5, Part 6—Supplementary Provisions

17.83 Under these supplementary provisions (paras 16 and 17) two important issues are considered. First, provisions applicable to the joint holders of shares and secondly, provisions that are applicable in the event of death or bankruptcy of a member.

Schedule 5, Part 6, para 16—joint holders of shares

It is well established that shares may be registered in the names of more than one person.[65] In the absence of express provisions in a company's articles of association,[66] Sch 5, Part 6, para 16 contains default provisions applicable to the joint holders of shares or debentures. **17.84**

Under Sch 5, Part 6, para 16(2) where anything has to be agreed or specified by the holder of shares or debentures it must be agreed or specified by all of the holders of the shares or debentures.[67] **17.85**

Where anything is authorized or required to be sent or supplied to a holder of shares or debentures it may be sent or supplied to each of the joint holders[68] or to the holder whose name appears first in the register of members or debenture-holders. It is suggested that this latter requirement is more practical and express provision to this effect should be made in a company's articles of association. **17.86**

Schedule 5, Part 6, para 17—death or bankruptcy of members

Provision is made in Sch 5, Part 6, para 17 for communications by a company with those to whom shares devolve by operation of law such as executors, administrators and trustees in bankruptcy. All of para 17 is expressed to take effect subject to anything that is contained in a company's articles of association.[69] **17.87**

Under para 17(2) documents or information that are required or authorized to be sent or supplied to a member may be sent to the persons who can lawfully claim to be entitled to those shares as a consequence of a member's death or bankruptcy. The legal successors in title will have to supply to the company an address in the United Kingdom for this purpose, and until such an address has been so supplied, documentation or information may be sent or supplied in the same manner in which it might have been sent or supplied if the death or bankruptcy had not so occurred. **17.88**

---

65 Up to a maximum of four members.
66 See Sch 5, Part 6, para 16(4).
67 Subject to anything contained in a company's articles of association. The inherent practical difficulties with regard to obtaining the consent of all of the holders of shares may dictate that well-drafted articles of association will contain an express provision dealing with this situation.
68 See Sch 5, Part 6, para 16(3)(a).
69 See Sch 5, Part 6, para 17(4).

Part 2

MEETINGS OF DIRECTORS

18

INTRODUCTION TO DIRECTORS' MEETINGS AND DIRECTORS' DUTIES

In Part 2 of this book consideration is given to the legal issues concerning meetings of directors. Companies that are registered and incorporated under the Companies Acts vary in size and complexity and as a consequence the regulation of board meetings of such companies will inevitably involve different considerations and issues. What is required as a matter of practice in respect of the efficient management of large international companies, with many thousands of employees and multi-million pound turnovers, will be different from the needs of private unquoted companies with only a few employees and a smaller sphere of operation. **18.01**

Although there will be variations in the procedures regulating directors' meetings[1] that are dependant on the particular nature of a company, there are certain matters that apply generally and constitute fundamental requirements of proper corporate governance in relation to holding valid and lawful meetings of directors. For example, all directors must be given due notice[2] of a board meeting and receive the agenda and relevant papers in good time prior to the meeting. The chairman of the board of directors must ensure that the conduct of the board meeting is orderly so that the members of the board may discuss the issues on the agenda in a proper and regulated fashion. Accurate minutes of board meetings must be drawn up in a timely manner following the conclusion of the board meeting and circulated prior to the next board meeting. In the succeeding chapters various aspects concerning the meetings of directors will be discussed and analysed.

18.02 Companies that are registered and incorporated under the Companies Acts are creations of statute. A company is an artificial entity and as such has to operate through the agency of either the board of directors or the shareholders in general meeting. In a modern company the management of a company will be vested in the board of directors.[3] From time to time the board of directors will have to meet in order to consider, discuss and decide upon the many and varied issues that affect the affairs of a company. Just as with the meetings of any organization, the meetings of directors have to be the subject of due and proper regulation and board meetings have to be conducted with a degree of formality.

Statutory requirement for companies to have directors

18.03 CA 2006, s 154 requires that a private company must have at least one director and a public company must have at least two directors.[4] When CA 2006, s 155(1) comes into legal force[5] there will be a statutory requirement that a company must have at least one director who is a natural person.[6] Subject to this rule, a company can have one or more corporate directors. Under CA 2006, s 157(1) a person may not be appointed a director unless he has attained the age of 16 years.

Delegation of management powers to the board of directors

18.04 Companies that are registered and incorporated under the Companies Acts delegate the powers of management to the board of directors. This delegation reverses

---

[1] Regulation 88 of the 1985 Table A states that subject to the articles of association the directors may regulate their proceedings as they see fit.

[2] See *Portuguese Consolidated Mines Ltd* (1889) 42 ChD 160 (CA).

[3] See reg 70 of the 1985 Table A.

[4] These requirements derive from CA 1985, s 282.

[5] This is anticipated to be on 1 October 2008.

[6] This requirement is met if the office of director is held by a natural person as a corporation sole or otherwise by virtue of an office—see CA 2006, s 155(2).

the common law position that a company's powers must be exercised by the members in general meeting unless the memorandum and articles of association provide otherwise. The usual form of delegation to directors of managerial and administrative powers will be found in an article in the form of reg 70 of the 1985 Table A[7] which provides as follows:

> 70. Subject to the provisions of the Act, the memorandum and the articles and to any directions given by special resolution, the business of the company shall be managed by the directors who may exercise all the powers of the company. No alteration of the memorandum or articles and no such direction shall invalidate any prior act of the directors which would have been valid if that alteration had not been made or that direction had not been given. The powers given by this regulation shall not be limited by any special power given to the directors by the articles and a meeting of directors at which a quorum is present may exercise all powers exercisable by the directors.

The effect of a provision in the form that is cited above means that the management powers are vested lawfully in the board of directors. Directors will have to take decisions on a plethora of issues involving not only day-to-day decisions in relation to the internal management of the company but also planning for the future strategy of the company and regulating the company's dealings with third parties. **18.05**

In *Automatic Self-Cleansing Filter Syndicate Co v Cunningham* it was held by the Court of Appeal that where the articles of association vest the general powers of management in the directors, the shareholders in a general meeting cannot overrule the directors' proper and lawful exercise of their managerial powers.[8] The article in question in that case was in a very similar form to the wording of reg 70 of the 1985 Table A. At a general meeting of shareholders a resolution was passed instructing the directors to sell the undertaking of the company to a new company that had been incorporated for this purpose. The board of directors refused to comply with the resolution of the shareholders and thus declined to effect the sale. The Court of Appeal upheld the decision of Warrington J who had declined to grant the company a declaration that the directors were bound to put into effect the resolution of the shareholders concerning the proposed sale of the company's undertaking. This decision witnessed the start of the break with the nineteenth-century view[9] that regarded the shareholders in general meeting as constituting 'the company', with the directors being merely the agents of the shareholders. **18.06**

---

[7] See also the commentary in Part 4.

[8] [1906] 2 Ch 34 (CA); and see *Quinn & Axtens v Salmon* [1909] AC 442 (HL).

[9] This view was illustrated by the provisions of the Companies Clauses Consolidation Act 1845, s 90; see also the remarks of Cotton LJ in *Isle of White Rly v Tahourdin* (1883) 25 Ch D 320 on this piece of legislation.

18.07 In *Quin & Axtens Ltd v Salmon*[10] there were two managing directors who between them held the majority of the shares in the company. The articles of association of the company stipulated that the business of the company should be managed by the board of directors, who were empowered to exercise all the powers of the company 'subject to such regulations (not being inconsistent with the provisions of the articles) as may be prescribed by the shareholders in general meeting'. Another provision in the articles of association provided that no resolution of a meeting of the directors which had as its object the acquisition or letting of certain premises would be valid if either of the joint managing directors dissented. The directors resolved to acquire certain premises but one of the joint managing directors dissented. A meeting of shareholders was held at which a similar resolution was passed by a majority. The House of Lords held that the resolutions of the shareholders were inconsistent with the articles of association of the company, and thus the Court of Appeal had been right to grant an injunction restraining the company from acting on the shareholders' resolutions.

18.08 The principle that where the powers of general management are vested in the directors the shareholders have no power to give directions to the board or overrule their business decisions was summarized in *Shaw & Sons (Salford) Ltd v Shaw*[11] by Greer LJ who stated:

> A company is an entity distinct alike from its shareholders and its directors. Some of its powers may, according to its articles, be exercised by directors, certain other powers may be reserved for the shareholders in general meeting. If powers of management are vested in the directors, they and they alone can exercise these powers. The only way in which the general body of shareholders can control the exercise of powers by the articles in the directors is by altering the articles, or, if opportunity arises under the articles, by refusing to re-elect the directors of whose actions they disapprove. They cannot themselves usurp the powers which by the articles are vested in the directors any more than the directors can usurp the powers vested by the articles in the general body of shareholders.

18.09 It is to be noted that there is nothing in the law to prevent the inclusion of a provision in a company's articles of association which gives a supervisory power to the shareholders or permits them then to override the decisions of directors. Indeed, the text of reg 70 of the 1985 Table A has such a provision, but a special resolution is required for this purpose.

18.10 It is the board of directors of a company that is responsible for managing the affairs of the company and taking relevant and necessary management decisions. Lawfully appointed directors enter into transactions on behalf of the company for which they have stewardship and they occupy a fiduciary position in relation to the assets

---

10 [1909] AC 442 (HL).
11 [1935] 2 KB 113 (CA).

and property of the company. The powers of management that are vested in the directors of a company are fiduciary powers and as a result must be exercised by directors in accordance with their fiduciary duties. The obligations of directors are based on the well-established principles which have been codified in CA 2006, Part 10, Chapter 2.[12]

At first sight it may appear that the shareholders of a company have no powers at all in circumstances where they disagree with decisions that have been taken by the board of directors. Mere disagreement with a regular and lawful exercise of directors' powers and duties will not be capable of successful legal challenge. However, shareholders do have some effective sanctions at their disposal, and where they wish to challenge the authority of directors with regard to the management of a company's affairs it is possible for shareholders to: **18.11**

(a) remove directors from office by means of ordinary resolution;[13]
(b) pass a special resolution altering the company's articles of association; and
(c) in the most serious cases, apply to the court for relief from conduct of the affairs of the company by the directors that is both unfair and prejudicial to the interests of members.[14]

However, the sanctions that may be deployed by shareholders that are listed in para 18.11 above are not without their own problems. Although members have a right to remove a director from office before the expiration of his term of office by means of a duly passed ordinary resolution, such a removal from office does not operate so as to deprive the director concerned from his right to claim compensation from the company under the terms of his service contract. Further, it should be noted that the ability of members to effect a lawful change to a company's articles of association is predicated on the members concerned being able to command the requisite majority for the passing of a special resolution. Unless one member of a company controls 75% or more of the enfranchised shares, securing a lawful amendment to articles of association will require co-operation and agreement from other members. In the most serious of cases a member or members may have to have resort to their statutory remedy to challenge the conduct of the board of directors on the grounds that the affairs of the company are being or have been conducted in a manner that is unfairly prejudicial to their interests as members. The practicalities in terms of risk, time and expense of using the sanction of a petition presented to the court under CA 2006, s 994 must not be underestimated.[15] **18.12**

[12] See para 18.17 below and CA 2006, ss 170–181.

[13] Under the provisions of CA 2006, s 168, formerly CA 1985, s 303.

[14] Under the provisions of CA 2006, s 994, formerly CA 1985, s 459.

[15] The costs of, and incidental to, such a petition may be considerable and the length of time from presentation of a petition to its final determination usually takes more than 12 months.

Regulation of board meetings

18.13 The articles of association of a company, and in particular articles of association in standard form such as Table A, make provision for the regulation of the proceedings of directors. Regulation 88 of the 1985 Table A provides that subject to the provision of the articles the directors may regulate their affairs as they think fit. After giving this general regulatory power to the board of directors, reg 88 goes on to provide:

> . . . A director may, and the secretary at the request of the director shall, call a meeting of the directors. It shall not be necessary to give notice of a meeting to a director who is absent from the United Kingdom. Questions arising at a meeting shall be decided by a majority of votes. In the case of an equality of votes, the chairman shall have a second or casting vote. A director who is also an alternate director shall be entitled in the absence of the appointor to a second vote on behalf of his appointor in addition to his own vote.

18.14 Regulation 89 of the 1985 Table A stipulates the default provision for a quorum in order to constitute a valid meeting of directors; in the absence of any provision to the contrary the number of directors required for a valid meeting of directors is two. This matter will be considered in more detail in Chapter 19.

18.15 Where the approval of the board of directors is required for a particular matter or transaction there must either be a formal meeting of those directors or they must arrive at their decision by informal but unanimous agreement.[16] Indeed, that directors, provided they act unanimously, can act informally is clearly established by *Re Bonnelli's Telegraph Co, Collie's Claim*. In that case the articles of a company provided that three directors should be the quorum required at board meetings for the transaction of business. An agent was appointed to sell the business of the company. The letter of appointment was written at the company's office and signed by two directors. It was then forwarded to a third director, and confirmed and signed by himself and a fourth director. The letter was held to be binding upon the company even though it had been approved in this informal manner. Sir James Bacon V-C held that it was not necessary that the directors should all meet in one place, provided that it could be shown that all concurred, with full knowledge of what they were doing.[17]

Meetings of a sole director

18.16 Where there is only one director of a private company that individual alone can constitute a valid board meeting. As there are no other directors with whom the sole director can consult, and no directors who can provide an element of supervision

[16] See *Collie's Claim* (1871) 12 Eq 246 at 258; *In re Great Northern Salt and Chemical Works, Ex parte Kennedy* (1890) 44 Ch 472 at 481 (Stirling J).

[17] See also *Runciman v Walter Runciman plc* [1992] BCLC 1084 at 1092 and *Hunter v Senate Support Services* [2005] 1 BCLC 175 at [103].

of the sole director's conduct it is important in such a case that attention is paid to the form and content of the board minutes. A sole director who holds a board meeting must deliberate carefully and must scrupulously record his decisions in the board minutes.[18]

Introduction to the duties of directors

A detailed examination of the duties of directors is beyond the scope of this book but in considering the conduct of board meetings it is perhaps worthwhile to have regard to the framework of fiduciary and other obligations under which company directors must now operate. These will be reviewed in the remainder of this chapter. Subsequent chapters in Part 2 of this book will then deal with notices, agenda and quorum (Chapter 19), the role of the chairman (Chapter 20) and minutes and other records (Chapter 21). **18.17**

The general duties of directors are now set out in statutory form in CA 2006, ss 170–177. These provisions of CA 2006 introduce a new statutory code for directors. The intention of the new provisions is both to codify and to clarify the well-established common law duties of directors. CA 2006, ss 170–174 came into legal force on 1 October 2007.[19] It is anticipated that ss 175–177 will be brought into force with effect from 1 October 2008. **18.18**

Directors' duties are owed to the company

CA 2006, s 170(1) articulates a fundamental and well-established principle of English company law that the general duties of directors that are now set out in CA 2006, ss 171–177 are owed by a director to the company.[20] As a consequence, a director cannot be the subject of direct legal action from a company's members or creditors, and in any proceedings for breach of duty the proper claimant suing an allegedly errant director for breach of duty will be the company itself.[21] **18.19**

The new law is based on legal principles that date back to the nineteenth century. There is a significant corpus of jurisprudence which has refined and clarified the law **18.20**

[18] See *Neptune (Vehicle Washing Equipment) Ltd v Fitzgerald* [1995] BCLC 352 (Lightman J) and CA 2006, ss 186 and 231.

[19] The Companies Act 2006 (Commencement No 3) Order 2007, SI 2007/2194, art 2.

[20] *Percival v Wright* [1902] 2 Ch 421 (Swinfen Eady J). In some special circumstances, directors may owe duties to individual shareholders—see *Coleman v Myers* [1977] 2 NZLR 225, (NZ CA) 225 (especially 323–5, 328–30); the Court of Appeal of New South Wales in *Brunninghausen v Glavanics* (1999) 46 NSWLR 538 at 547–60; and *Peskin v Anderson* [2001] 1 BCLC 372 (CA).

[21] Of course it is possible for members to make a direct challenge to the conduct of directors on the ground that it is both unfair and prejudicial to the interests of members under the provisions of CA 2006, s 994 (formerly CA 1985, s 459). Such a challenge may be based on an allegation that a board of directors have acted in breach of their fiduciary duties—see *Re Saul D Harrison & Sons Plc* [1995] 1 BCLC 14 (CA).

relating to the duties of directors. The new legislation is mindful of that established case law. CA 2006, s 170(3) declares that the origins of the general duties set out in the sections are to be found in the common law rules and equitable principles in relation to directors, and that the statutory provisions replace the common law rules and equitable principles in relation to the duties that a director owes to his company.

18.21 The statement of the new statutory duties of directors has primacy over the established rules and principles, but the cadre of existing case law on the subject of directors' duties is likely to be of considerable importance in relation to the way in which the courts will interpret the new provisions.[22] CA 2006, s 170(4) provides some guidance as to how the general duties are to be interpreted. The new statutory general duties of directors must be interpreted and applied in the same way as the common law rules or equitable principles. Further, regard shall be had to the corresponding rules and principles when interpreting the statute and applying the general duties. By s 170(5) the general duties apply to shadow directors where, and to the extent that, the corresponding common law rules or equitable principles so apply.[23]

A continuing duty

18.22 Where a person ceases to be a director that individual continues to be subject to the duty to avoid conflicts of interest as regards the exploitation of any property, information or opportunity (of the company) of which he became aware at a time when he was a director.[24] It is no surprise that the new statutory code relating to the duties of directors contains such a provision, which has been an established part of the fabric of provisions designed to protect against self-dealing by fiduciaries. Directors must not place themselves in positions where there is a conflict between their personal interests and their duties. Such rules were established by the common law in the decision in *Keech v Sandford*[25] and have been upheld in important cases such as *Regal (Hastings) Limited v Gulliver*,[26] *Phipps v Boardman*[27] and *Industrial Development Consultants v Cooley*.[28]

18.23 Similarly s 170(2)(b) provides that the duty not to accept benefits from third parties, as set out in s 176, is also to continue after a director has ceased to hold office

[22] However, it is arguable that where the new provisions use new language, the value of precedents based on legislation that has been repealed will be negligible—see *Re M C Bacon Ltd (No 1)* [1990] BCLC 324 at 335 (Millett J).

[23] Clarification of the term 'shadow director' as defined in CA 1985, s 741(2) , now in CA 2006, s 251, is to be found in the judgment of Lewison J in *Ultaframe (UK) Ltd v Fielding and others* [2005] EWHC 1638 [2005] All ER (D) 397.

[24] CA 2006, s 170(2)(a) will be in legal force from 1 October 2008.

[25] (1726) 2 White and Tudor LC 693.

[26] [1942] 1 All ER 378, [1967] 2 AC 134n.

[27] [1967] 2 AC 46 (HL).

[28] [1972] 1 WLR 443 (Roskill J). See also *Canadian Aero Service Ltd v O'Malley* (1973) 40 DLR (3d) 371 Can SC; and *CMS Dolphin Ltd v Simonet* [2001] 2 BCLC 704 (Lawrence Collins J).

as regards things done or omitted by him before he ceased to be a director. A 'third party' for the purposes of this provision means someone other than the company or an associated body corporate or someone acting on their behalf. The aim of this provision is to prevent a person from resigning office as a director in order to escape from his duties and liabilities to the company.

Duty to act within powers

CA 2006, s 171 puts on a statutory basis the fundamental rule that a director must act in accordance with the company's constitution and only exercise powers for the purposes for which they are conferred. The general definition of the word 'constitution' in s 17 is extended for the purpose of Part 10 by CA 2006, s 257. **18.24**

The rule that is now given statutory force in s 171 is often referred to in the existing case law as the rule that directors' powers were not to be exercised for any improper or collateral purpose. A leading authority on this important aspect of the law is the decision of the Privy Council in *Howard Smith Limited v Ampol Petroleum Ltd*,[29] where a board of directors attempted to block a takeover bid by issuing new shares to their supporters. Lord Wilberforce stated that: **18.25**

> . . . it must be unconstitutional for directors to use their fiduciary powers over the shares in the company purely for the purpose of destroying an existing majority, or creating a new majority which did not previously exist.

Duty to promote the success of the company

Prior to the enactment of CA 2006, s 172 directors were required to exercise their powers in good faith in the interests of the company.[30] The phrase encapsulated an amalgam of different concepts such as that directors had duties of loyalty and good faith to their company. The common law rule contained a subjective element in that the directors were to act in what they, and not what a court, considered to be the interests of the company. The decision of the Court of Appeal in *Re Smith & Fawcett*[31] is the locus classicus of this principle. Lord Greene MR stated that directors: **18.26**

> . . . must exercise their discretion bona fide in what they consider – not what a court may consider – is in the interests of the company, and not for any collateral purpose. They must have regard to those considerations, and those considerations only, which the articles on their true construction permit them to take into consideration . . .

---

[29] [1974] AC 821 (PC) at 834, 837–8 (directors' use of fiduciary power to allot shares for a different purpose than that for which it was granted, and so as to dilute the voting power of the majority shareholding of issued shares).

[30] *Percival v Wright* [1902] 2 Ch 421 (Swinfen Eady J).

[31] [1942] Ch 304 (CA).

18.27 CA 2006, s 172 introduces a different concept, namely a duty to promote the success of the company. The section has not abandoned the former subjective element to this important duty by requiring the director to act '. . . in the way in which he considers, in good faith, would be most likely to promote the success of the company for the benefit of its members as a whole'.

18.28 Section 172(1) requires a director to have regard amongst other things to six specific matters:

(a) the likely consequences of any decision in the long term,
(b) the interests of the company's employees,
(c) the need to foster the company's business relationships with suppliers, customers and others,
(d) the impact of the company's operations on the community and the environment,
(e) the desirability of the company maintaining a reputation for high standards of business conduct, and
(f) the need to act fairly as between members of the company.

18.29 Many of the matters that are listed in CA 2006, s 172(1) which are set out above are ones which have been part of directors' duties under the law before 1 October 2007, such as taking into account the interests of the employees.[32] However, other matters are new, such as the need to foster the company's business relationships with suppliers, customers and others and the requirement to consider the impact of the company's operations on the environment. The list of matters in s 172(1) is by no means exhaustive. Further, there is no express statutory provision limiting the need of a director to have regard to the matters listed to the extent that they are reasonably relevant or practicable.

Duty to have regard to the interests of creditors

18.30 CA 2006, s 172(3) preserves the duty of directors to have regard in certain circumstances to the interests of creditors of the company. The subsection refers to any enactment or rule of law establishing that requirement. This duty is again well established in the existing case law and it arises where a company is insolvent or on the verge of becoming insolvent. In those circumstances, when considering their duties to the company the directors must have regard to and act in the interests of the company's creditors. The duty is not owed directly to the creditors but to the company and can later be enforced by a liquidator.[33] The separate reference in the subsection to 'any enactment' would incorporate the Insolvency Act 1986, s 214, dealing with the directors' liability for wrongful trading.

[32] See CA 1985, s 309.

[33] See *West Mercia Safetyware Ltd v Dodd* [1988] BCLC 250 (CA) where the reasoning in *Kinsela v Russell Kinsela Pty Ltd* (1986) 4 NSWLR 722 (NSW CA) was adopted.

Duty to exercise independent judgment

CA 2006, s 173 states that a director must exercise independent judgment. This is a basic principle, requiring the director to act in what he considers to be the interests of the company, and not someone else. A director must not fetter his discretion. A director is entitled to take advice from others, including the persons appointing him, but the final decision that is taken by a board of directors is the responsibility of the directors. Under s 173 it is the duty of a director to exercise his own discretion and not act merely as a cypher for others.[34] **18.31**

Exceptions from the duty in s 173

CA 2006, s 173(2) provides for two important exceptions to the rule. The duty is not infringed by the director acting in accordance with an agreement duly entered into by the company that restricts the future exercise of discretion by the directors. Further, the duty is not infringed by his acting in a way authorized by the company's constitution. **18.32**

Duty to exercise reasonable care, skill and diligence

The standard of reasonable skill care and diligence has been a controversial area of the law relating to the duties of directors. Section 174 puts on a statutory basis the modern judicial approach that has been adopted in relation to the standard of care expected from directors. In an age of professional directors the approach of Romer J in *Re City Equitable Fire Insurance Co Limited*[35] had become dated. In *Norman v Theodore Goddard (a firm) and others*,[36] Hoffmann J had been critical of the subjective approach towards directors' conduct in the old authorities,[37] and thought that the appropriate test was accurately laid down in the Insolvency Act 1986, s 214(4). This defines negligent conduct for the purposes of holding directors liable for 'wrongful trading' in terms of: **18.33**

> . . . the facts which a director of a company ought to know or ascertain, the conclusions which he ought to reach and the steps which he ought to take are those which would be known or ascertained, or reached or taken, by a reasonably diligent person having both—
>
> (a) the general knowledge, skill and experience that may reasonably be expected of a person carrying out the same functions as are carried out by that director in relation to the company, and
> (b) the general knowledge, skill and experience that that director has.[38]

---

[34] See *Colin Gwyer & Associates Ltd v London Wharf (Limehouse) Ltd* [2003] 2 BCLC 153.

[35] [1925] Ch 407 (Romer J).

[36] [1991] BCLC 1028 (Hoffmann J).

[37] Such as *Re City Equitable Fire Insurance Co Ltd* (op. cit.); and *Re Cardiff Savings Bank. The Marquis of Bute's case* [1892] 2 Ch 100 (Stirling J).

[38] See also *Re D'Jan of London Ltd* [1993] BCC 646 (Hoffmann J)—a case in which a director who signed an insurance proposal form without checking its contents was held to be liable in negligence.

18.34 The test in s 174 involves both subjective and objective elements in relation to the duty that is owed by a director to exercise reasonable care and skill. The test is a flexible one and it will require a director with specialist skills or responsibilities (such as a finance director)[39] to demonstrate the standard of skill, care and knowledge that a finance director in such a company would normally have in discharging his duties. It is right that the common law has given way to the statutory duty in s 174 that reflects the more demanding and rigorous standards required from modern company directors.

Duty to avoid conflicts of interest

18.35 At common law a person who is in a fiduciary position would be under a disability if they were in situation of conflict.[40] The duty was stated by Lord Herschell in *Bray v Ford*:[41]

> It is an inflexible rule of a court of equity that a person in a fiduciary position . . . is not, unless otherwise expressly provided, . . . allowed to put himself in a position where his interest and duty conflict. It does not appear to me that this rule is . . . founded upon principles of morality. I regard it rather as based on the consideration that, human nature being what it is, there is a danger, in such circumstances, of the person holding a fiduciary position being swayed by interest rather than by duty, and thus prejudicing those whom he was bound to protect.

CA 2006, s 175

18.36 CA 2006, s 175(1) imposes a positive duty on directors to avoid conflicts of interest. The new section is drafted in wide terms. It provides that a director of a company is under a duty to avoid a situation in which he has, or can have, a direct or indirect interest that conflicts, or possibly may conflict, with the interests of the company. CA 2006, s 175(2) gives an inexhaustive list of examples where a director must avoid conflicts of interest. The prohibition applies in particular to the exploitation of any property, information or opportunity and it is expressly provided that it is immaterial whether the company could take advantage of the property, information or opportunity in question. Section 175(2) is reflective of the position at common law that a director must not exploit a corporate opportunity even if the company did not have the resources to exploit it[42] or even where the company had decided not to pursue it.[43]

---

[39] See *Dorchester Finance Co Ltd v Stebbings* [1989] BCLC 498 (Foster J).

[40] See *Movitex v Bulfield* [1988] BCLC 104 (Vinelott J).

[41] [1896] AC 44 at 51–2 (HL).

[42] See *Regal Hastings Ltd v Gulliver* [1967] 2 AC 134n.

[43] See *Bhullar v Bhullar* [2003] 2 BCLC 241 (CA). See also *Industrial Development Consultants Ltd v Cooley* [1972] 2 All ER 162 (Roskill J); *CMS Dolphin Ltd v Simonet* [2001] 2 BCLC 704 (Lawrence Collins J).

Section 175(3) and (4) stipulate exceptions to the general rule. One exception is where the situation cannot reasonably be regarded as likely to give rise to a conflict of interest. In practice this may be a difficult test to apply. If the reasonable person looking at all of the relevant facts of a situation would think that there was a real possibility of conflict the requirements of s 175(4)(a) will not be satisfied.[44] The obvious cases of conflict may be easy to identify, but where there is any doubt in the matter great care should be exercised. If there is doubt or uncertainty as to whether or not a conflict of interest exists a director will be well advised to seek authorization from the board in accordance with the provisions of CA 2006, s 175(4)(b). If authorization is given, the duty imposed on directors by CA 2006, s 175 will not be infringed. However, the director will still be subject to the duty that is imposed by s 172 to promote the success of the company and to the duty of skill and care. **18.37**

Authorization of conflicts for directors of private companies

A director of a private company may be given authorization by the board of directors. This authorization from the board of directors is subject to the caveat that there is nothing in the constitution[45] of that private company which operates so as to invalidate such authorization. **18.38**

Authorization of conflicts for directors of public companies

Under s 175(5)(b) a director of a public company may also be given authorization by the board of directors. In relation to a public company there is a positive requirement that its constitution must contain a provision that empowers the directors to give such express authorization. **18.39**

Procedure for obtaining a valid authorization

Two important procedural requirements must be observed in order to achieve a valid authorization. First, the quorum for the board meeting must be arrived at without counting the director who is seeking the authorization or any other interested director. Secondly, the director who is seeking the authorization is disenfranchised or alternatively, it must be shown that the matter would have been agreed to if the director's votes had not been counted. The effect of these requirements is that the authorization is derived from an independent board of directors.[46] **18.40**

---

[44] See *Phipps v Boardman* [1967] 2 AC 46 (HL).

[45] As defined in CA 2006, ss 17 and 257.

[46] It should also be noted that s 180(4) preserves the common law position that permits members of the company to authorize conflicts that would otherwise contravene the no-conflict duty.

Duty not to accept benefits from third parties

18.41 CA 2006, s 176 codifies a well-established equitable rule that prohibits the exploitation of a fiduciary position for personal benefit or gain. The no-profit rule and the no conflict duty which are regulated by s 175 are core rules in ensuring that fiduciaries do not exploit their positions. In *Bray v Ford*[47] Lord Herschell took the view that there was only one rule, whilst in *Boardman v Phipps*[48] Lord Upjohn described the no-profit rule as being but a part of the wider no-conflict duty. In Australia in *Chan v Zacharia*[49] the court considered that the two rules were distinct although there was a certain amount of overlap. The statement of directors' duties in CA 2006, Part 10 divides the duty into two distinct duties. Accordingly, a transaction may be successfully impugned on the basis that it involved a director who had a real conflict of interest notwithstanding the fact that the director had not made a profit. This position is consistent with the important judgment of the House of Lords in *Regal (Hastings) Ltd v Gulliver*[50] where Lord Russell said:

> The rule of equity which insists on those, who by use of a fiduciary position make a profit, being liable to account for that profit, in no way depends on fraud, or absence of bona fides; or upon such questions or considerations as whether profit would or should otherwise have gone to the plaintiff, or whether the profiteer was under a duty to obtain the source of the profit for the plaintiff, or whether he took a risk or acted as he did for the benefit of the plaintiff, or whether the plaintiff has in fact been damaged or benefited by his action. The liability arises from the mere fact of a profit having, in the stated circumstances, been made.

18.42 Under s 176 a company director must not accept a benefit from a third party conferred by reason of his being a director, or his doing (or not doing) anything as director. It is clear from the debates in Parliament concerning this section that the word 'benefit' includes benefits of any description, including non-financial benefits. A 'third party' is defined in CA 2006, s 176(2) as 'a person other than the company, an associated body corporate or a person acting on behalf of the company or an associated body corporate'.

18.43 It is to be noted that there is no provision in s 176 for the directors to provide authorization to the director as there is in s 175(5) in respect of conflicts of interest. However, the company may be able to authorize the acceptance of benefits by virtue of s 180(4). As with s 175 it is expressly provided that the statutory duty is not infringed if the acceptance of the benefit cannot reasonably be regarded as likely to give rise to a conflict of interest.[51]

---

[47] [1896] AC 44.
[48] [1967] 2 AC 46, HL.
[49] (1984) 154 CLR 178.
[50] [1967] 2 AC 134n at 144.
[51] See s 176(4).

Duty to declare interest in proposed transaction or arrangement

CA 2006, s 177 replaces CA 1985, s 317(1). In addition to CA 1985, s 317 it was common for a company's articles of association[52] to permit directors to be interested in transactions or arrangements with the company provided they disclosed the nature and extent of any such interest to the board.[53] Section 317(1) was subject to criticism on the one hand for being too narrow in its scope because the extent of the directors' interest did not have to be disclosed, and on the other for being too wide in its ambit because *all* interests had to be disclosed. The need for a proper policy relating to disclosure of interests is, in the words of Lightman J in *Neptune (Vehicle Washing Equipment) Ltd v Fitzgerald* to achieve three objectives: **18.44**

> First, all the directors should know or be reminded of the interest; second, the making of the declaration should be the occasion for a statutory pause for thought about the existence of the conflict of interest and of the duty to prefer the interests of the company to their own; third, the disclosure . . . must be a distinct happening at the meeting. . . .[54]

Declaration of interest to other directors

Under CA 2006, s 177, if a director of a company is in any way, directly or indirectly, interested in a *proposed* transaction or arrangement with the company, he must declare both the nature and extent of that interest to the other directors of the company *before* the company enters into the transaction or arrangement. For a director to discharge his duty under s 177 it is not sufficient for a director to state that he has an interest. The director must go further and explain the extent of that interest. The legislation does not stipulate a minimum financial threshold. However, it may be that some comfort can be taken from s 177(6)(a) which provides that the interest in question must be such that it can reasonably be regarded as likely to give rise to a conflict of interest. **18.45**

The existing case law on disclosure contains some different approaches to the consequences of a failure of a director to disclose an interest. In *Lee Panavision Ltd v Lee Lighting Ltd*,[55] Dillon LJ took the view that a 'technical' failure to disclose an interest which in fact was well known to all the directors should not operate so as to invalidate the contract in question. This approach was followed in *Runciman v Walter Runciman plc*[56] and *MacPherson v European Strategic Bureau Ltd*.[57] A different approach was taken in *Neptune (Vehicle Washing Equipment) Ltd v Fitzgerald*,[58] **18.46**

[52] See for example reg 85 of the 1985 Table A.
[53] See *Guinness v Saunders* [1990] 2 AC 663 (HL).
[54] [1995] 1 BCLC 352 at 359.
[55] [1992] BCLC 22 (CA).
[56] [1992] BCLC 1084 (Simon Brown J).
[57] [1999] 2 BCLC 203 (Ferris J).
[58] [1996] Ch 274 (Lightman J).

where Lightman J held that due compliance with the statutory disclosure requirement was necessary even in the case of a company with a sole director and that a single director should make the declaration to himself and record the declaration in the board minutes. The provisions of s 177(6)(b) and (c) will settle differences of approach found in the case law prior to the enactment of the new law.

18.47 It is important to note that the statutory duty in CA 2006, s 177 is to declare an interest to the 'other directors'. No such disclosure is required where the company has only one director, consequently the conclusion of Lightman J in *Neptune (Vehicle Washing Equipment) Ltd v Fitzgerald* appears to have been overruled. This conclusion is based on s 177(6)(b) which makes it clear that there is no need to disclose matters that the other directors already know or ought reasonably to have known. If there are no other directors the section is complied with. Section 177(6)(c) relaxes the requirement of disclosure in relation to a director's interest in his service contract where it has been considered by a meeting of the directors or a committee appointed for such purpose, such as a remuneration committee.

Form of the declaration of interest

18.48 Section 177(2) provides the legislative regime as to how the director who is subject to the requirements of s 177(1) may make the necessary declaration. By s 177(2)(a) it may be made at a board meeting. As an alternative to this the director may make the declaration to the directors (under s 177(2)(b)(i)) by way of a notice in writing under s 184[59] or in accordance with a general notice under s 185 (under s 177(2)(b)(ii)). Section 184 deals with a notice relating to a specific issue, whereas s 185, which

---

[59] **184 Declaration made by notice in writing**
(1) This section applies to a declaration of interest made by notice in writing.
(2) The director must send the notice to the other directors.
(3) The notice may be sent in hard copy form or, if the recipient has agreed to receive it in electronic form, in an agreed electronic form.
(4) The notice may be sent—
  (a) by hand or by post, or
  (b) if the recipient has agreed to receive it by electronic means, by agreed electronic means.
(5) Where a director declares an interest by notice in writing in accordance with this section—
  (a) the making of the declaration is deemed to form part of the proceedings at the next meeting of the directors after the notice is given, and
  (b) the provisions of section 248 (minutes of meetings of directors) apply as if the declaration had been made at that meeting.

is based in large part on the provisions found in CA 1985, s 317, covers a notice of a general nature.[60]

The duty imposed on directors by CA 2006, s 177 is a continuing one in the sense that if the declaration becomes incomplete or inaccurate a further declaration must be made by the director concerned. 18.49

Exemptions from the duty in s 177

CA 2006, s 177(5) provides that the law does not require a declaration of an interest of which the director is not aware, or where the director is not aware of the transaction or arrangement in question. At first sight this appears to be a significant derogation from the statutory duty and a potential charter for errant directors. However, it is expressly stated that for the purposes of s 177(5) a director is treated as being aware of matters of which he ought reasonably to be aware. Accordingly, Nelsonian blindness or a disregard for the obvious will not come to the assistance of a director who has failed to declare an interest. 18.50

No disclosure in three instances

Under CA 2006, s 177(6) there are three prescribed instances where a director need not declare an interest. First, if it cannot reasonably be regarded as likely to give rise to a conflict of interest. In such a situation all of the relevant circumstances would have to be considered. Secondly, if, or to the extent that, the other directors are already aware of it (and for this purpose the other directors are treated as aware of anything of which they ought reasonably to be aware). In practice this may be very difficult to prove. Thirdly if, or to the extent that, it concerns terms of the director's service contract that have been or are to be considered either 18.51

---

[60] **185 General notice treated as sufficient declaration**

(1) General notice in accordance with this section is a sufficient declaration of interest in relation to the matters to which it relates.

(2) General notice is notice given to the directors of a company to the effect that the director—

(a) has an interest (as member, officer, employee or otherwise) in a specified body corporate or firm and is to be regarded as interested in any transaction or arrangement that may, after the date of the notice, be made with that body corporate or firm, or

(b) is connected with a specified person (other than a body corporate or firm) and is to be regarded as interested in any transaction or arrangement that may, after the date of the notice, be made with that person.

(3) The notice must state the nature and extent of the director's interest in the body corporate or firm or, as the case may be, the nature of his connection with the person.

(4) General notice is not effective unless—

(a) it is given at a meeting of the directors, or

(b) the director takes reasonable steps to secure that it is brought up and read at the next meeting of the directors after it is given.

by a meeting of the directors, or by a committee of the directors appointed for the purpose under the company's constitution.

Civil consequences of breach of directors' duties

18.52 CA 2006, s 178 provides for the civil consequences that will arise in the event of a breach (or threatened breach) of CA 2006, ss 171–177. An attempt was made to codify and state in the new legislation the remedies available for breach of directors' duties. However, this attempt was unsuccessful and in the final version of the legislation there is no codified statement of the remedies that are available.

18.53 CA 2006, s 178(1) provides that the consequences of a breach of the earlier sections are the same as would apply if the corresponding common law rule or equitable principle applied. The directors' duties contained in ss 171–177, but with the exception of s 174 (the duty to exercise reasonable care, skill and diligence) are, accordingly, enforceable in the same way as any other fiduciary duty owed to a company by its directors by virtue of s 178(2). Where there is a breach of a fiduciary duty owed to a company by its directors the consequences of such a breach may include liability as a constructive trustee, an account of any profits made by the director; damages or equitable compensation if the company has suffered loss; orders compelling the restoration of the corporate assets or property; and the rescission of a contract where the director failed to disclose an interest.

Ratification of acts of directors

18.54 At common law a breach of a director's fiduciary duty is capable of being 'cured' if the breach is ratified by the members of a company. What is ratification? Ratification is a procedure whereby those to whom duties are owed may release those who owe the duties from their legal obligations, and such a release may operate prospectively or retrospectively. At common law it was unclear when ratification would be effective and it would be impossible to reconcile all the decided cases. In addition jurisprudence in England has recognized a category of wrongs that were not capable of ratification, for example an act of illegality or where the matter was ultra vires. Many of these instances of non-ratification can be explained on the basis that the shareholders cannot ratify the wrong done to the company, either because the wrong is not done to the company but to the shareholders in their personal capacity (and the company is not, therefore, the proper plaintiff) or because the company itself is not 'legally competent' to deal with the question and therefore it is not possible for the company to ratify the act.

18.55 CA 2006, s 239 is a new provision that is reflective of the common law principle that a breach of duty that is committed by a director may be capable of ratification. At common law there have often been problems in deciding whether or not the ratification of a breach of duty has been effective and the new statutory procedure is to be welcomed. This provision is due to come into legal force on 1 October 2008.

Section 239 applies to the ratification by a company of conduct by a director which amounts to negligence, default, breach of duty or breach of trust in relation to the company. The ratification of such conduct will be effective only if the decision of the company to ratify it is made by resolution of the members of the company and without reliance on the votes of the director or any connected person with a personal interest in the ratification. The effect of this is to reverse the decision in *Northwest Transportation v Beatty*.[61] The legislation does not state whether the resolution should be an ordinary resolution or one requiring a higher majority. **18.56**

Ratification by written resolution

It is open to a private company to propose the resolution to ratify a breach of duty as a written resolution. If this procedure is adopted, s 239(3) stipulates that neither the director (if he is a member of the company) nor any member connected with him is an 'eligible member'. If the written resolution procedure is not employed the resolution may be proposed at a meeting of the members. In order for the resolution for ratification to be passed the necessary majority must be obtained by disregarding any votes cast by the director (if he is a member of the company) in favour of the resolution and by any member connected with him. **18.57**

Although the director is disenfranchised in the ratification procedure the legislation does not prevent the director whose conduct is the subject of a ratification resolution from attending the meeting, or from being counted towards the quorum or from taking part in the proceedings at any meeting at which the decision is considered. If the resolution is passed at a meeting in accordance with s 239(2) that concludes the matter. **18.58**

Ratification by unanimous consent of the members

The ability of members to ratify a breach of duty on the part of a director by their unanimous consent is preserved by CA 2006, s 239(6)(a). In practice this provision will only be useful in the context of a company with a small number of members. In addition, the board of directors is empowered under s 239(6)(b) to agree not to sue an errant director or to settle or release a claim made by them on behalf of the company. Section 239(7) makes it clear that the requirements imposed **18.59**

[61] (1887) 12 App Cas 587 (PC).

by s 239 are in addition to any other limitations or restrictions imposed by the law as to what may or may not be ratified.

Transitional provisions

18.60 It is to be noted that the new s 239 applies only to conduct by a director on or after 1 October 2007. Conduct by a director before that date is subject to the pre-existing law.[62]

[62] Companies Act 2006 (Commencement No 3, Consequential Amendments, Transitional Provisions and Savings) Order 2007 SI 2007/2194 Sch 3, para 17.

19

NOTICE, AGENDA AND QUORUM FOR MEETINGS OF DIRECTORS

Introduction

As has been discussed in Chapter 2 concerning the giving of notice of meetings to convene a valid meeting of members, the necessity to give due and proper notice of a meeting is a basic requirement for convening a meeting that can transact lawful business. In this chapter the requirements of notice of meetings are discussed with regard to meetings of the board of directors. The requirements of notice in relation to meetings of directors are less stringent than those relating to meetings of members, for in relation to the latter the applicable legislation prescribes requisite time periods for certain types of meeting and the passing of certain types of resolutions. There are no provisions in CA 2006 that regulate the giving of notice of directors' meetings. Provisions in relation to the giving of notice for board meetings are to be found in the articles of association of a company. **19.01**

19.02 In order for directors to discharge their duties to manage and administer the affairs of the company they need to be informed in advance of the issues which will be the subject matter of discussion at their meetings. To this end any well-organized institution will prepare and issue with the notice of the directors' board meeting an agenda which will give the members of the board an outline of the matters that will be debated at the forthcoming meeting. However, this is not a statutory requirement, nor is it required under the general law, but it is a standard procedure of good corporate practice and governance.

19.03 In relation to public listed companies regard has to be had to the provisions of the Combined Code on Corporate Governance (the Combined Code).[1] The first sentence of Main Principle A.5 provides that '[T]he board should be supplied in a timely manner with information in a form and of a quality appropriate to enable it to discharge its duties.' Public listed companies[2] are expected to comply with the provisions of the Combined Code although it is recognized in the preamble thereto that '. . . departure from the provisions of the Code may be justified in particular circumstances'.[3]

Notice

No statutory requirements for notice of directors' meetings

19.04 There are no statutory provisions in CA 2006 that stipulate a mandatory period of notice for meetings of a board of directors. This is a matter that is left to the internal constitution of a company. Provisions of a company's articles of association or any applicable shareholders' agreement may contain specific requirements regulating the timing of meetings of directors and any required period of notice for a meeting of the board. In the absence of any such provision all that is required is that reasonable notice of the meeting be given to the members of the board. What constitutes 'reasonable notice' will vary from company to company and according to circumstances.

The requirements of notice in articles of association

19.05 Well-drafted articles of association may make provision for giving notice of meetings of directors to all the members of the board of directors. Sometimes the articles of association of a company will stipulate that a certain number of days'

---

[1] June 2006 edition published by the Financial Reporting Council—<http://www.frc.org.uk>.

[2] The Combined Code recognizes in the Preamble that smaller listed public companies, in particular those that are new to listing, may judge that some of the provisions of the Combined Code are 'disproportionate or less relevant to their case'.

[3] Combined Code (2006) Preamble, para 3.

notice is required for a meeting of the board. A provision in a company's articles that fails to specify a specific number of days' notice for the convening of a board meeting will not be defective, but it may be harder to determine whether in any given situation adequate notice of a board meeting has been given. By way of illustration, reg 88 of the 1985 Table A provides:

> Subject to the provisions of the articles, the directors may regulate their proceedings as they think fit. A director may, and the secretary at the request of a director shall, call a meeting of directors. It shall not be necessary to give notice of a meeting to a director who is absent from the United Kingdom.[4]

Form and contents of the notice

A notice in writing for a board meeting may be very short, but its brevity will not necessarily invalidate its purpose and efficacy. The essential requirement of a valid notice for a board meeting is to communicate to the members of the board all of the pertinent information to enable them to attend the meeting. What is important for the members of the board to know is where and when the meeting will take place. Unless the articles of association of a company provide to the contrary, both the form and content of the notice of a board meeting will be left to the discretion of the board of directors and a verbal notification of a board meeting can constitute sufficient notice.[5] **19.06**

There is no requirement as a matter of law that notice need be given to a director of the business that is to be transacted at the board meeting. It has been held by the Court of Appeal in *La Compagnie de Mayville v Whitley*[6] that such a requirement would be 'extremely embarrassing',[7] 'most inconvenient' and 'one which would hamper in an unprecedented way the business of directors'.[8] In the same case AL Smith LJ held that a director is bound to go to a meeting of directors if he had notice when the meeting is to take place, whether he knows what business is to be transacted or not.[9] Under reg 88 of the 1985 Table A the board of directors has power to regulate such matters for themselves. Unless the articles of association make express provision for written notice a verbal notice for a meeting of directors will be sufficient. **19.07**

However, best practice requires that notice in general terms of the matters to be discussed should be given to the directors.[10] Care must be taken to ensure that if a notice is served on members of a board identifying the specific items of business **19.08**

4 Under CA 2006, s 270, a private company will no longer need to have a company secretary.
5 See *Browne v La Trinidad* (1888) 37 Ch D 1(CA).
6 See *La Compagnie de Mayville v Whitley* [1896] 1 Ch 788 (CA).
7 Op. cit. per Lindley LJ at 797.
8 Op. cit. per Kay LJ at 805–6.
9 Op. cit. at 810.
10 See paras 19.24–19.32 below concerning the agenda.

that are proposed to be discussed the notice is not in a misleading form. A notice that is designed to mislead, or has that effect, may result in the business transacted being held to be invalid.

Written notice is not compulsory

19.09 Although it is good practice, and it will be an invariable practice in the context of large companies, notice of a board meeting need not be given in writing unless there is a requirement for written notice prescribed in a company's articles of association[11] or in any relevant shareholders' agreement or joint venture agreement. Where such a requirement is stipulated either in the company's articles or in an applicable shareholders' or joint venture agreement written notice must be given to all of the directors.

Reasonable notice

19.10 It is to be noted that reg 88 of the 1985 Table A does not prescribe the actual period of time that is required in order for there to be a valid notice of a meeting of directors. If such a provision is applicable in the articles of association of a company then what is legally required in relation to the convening of a valid meeting of directors is a period of 'reasonable notice'. However, precisely what amounts to such reasonable notice cannot be stated in categorical terms and may vary in different circumstances. As a general rule it can be said that, in the absence of special circumstances, directors are entitled to receive sufficient notice of board meetings to enable them to attend. However, what is or is not sufficient notice will depend on the particular circumstances of each case.

19.11 Where circumstances dictate that a board meeting has to be convened and held in an emergency, for example in order to consider a hostile takeover bid, or some crisis or special situation that may have arisen unexpectedly, it must be accepted that the period of notice given to all of the directors may be much shorter than the period of notice that is given to directors in a normal, non-emergency situation. In these circumstances, the period of reasonable notice may of necessity have to be very short, but the shortness of the notice will not invalidate the notice of the board meeting if the situation so demands. It is suggested that special circumstances can dictate that even a few minutes' notice of a meeting to directors would constitute a valid notice of a board meeting if a director were able to attend and does not object.

[11] See *Browne v La Trinidad* (1888) 37 Ch D 1 (CA).

A question of fact

It is well established that what constitutes reasonable notice in a particular situation is in each case a question of fact and may also depend upon a course of previous conduct. It may be imprudent to depart from the period of notice that is normally given to directors unless there are objective circumstances that can justify such a decision. One faction of directors on a board must not use a shorter period of notice as a device or pretext to exclude other members of the board from the decision-making process.[12] **19.12**

Objection to the period of notice

If a director objects to the shortness of the period of notice that has been given for a board meeting then he must raise his objection at once. Any delay on the part of the director to object to the shortness of the period of notice will vitiate his objection to the shortness of the notice.[13] Accordingly, where a director is faced with short notice of a board meeting for which he which requires more time to prepare and where there is no obvious and pressing urgency, he should attempt to obtain the adjournment of the meeting. However, it must be remembered and noted that no director of a company with articles of association in the form of the 1985 Table A has the right to veto the convening of a meeting of the board simply because it turns out to be inconvenient for him to attend at the appointed time, provided that the period of notice given to him was reasonable.[14] **19.13**

Notice to all of the directors

It must be emphasized that notice of a board meeting must be given to all the members of the board who are entitled to receive such notice under the articles of association. If business is purportedly transacted at a board meeting of which some of the directors had no notice or insufficient notice, the business transacted will be invalid.[15] This proposition is true even if the directors who did not receive notice were in a minority. It is important to note that a director has no power to waive his right to receive notice of a board meeting.[16] On the other hand where a company adopts articles of association in the form of reg 88 of the 1985 Table A it is not necessary to give notice of a board meeting to a director who is absent from the United Kingdom.[17] **19.14**

---

[12] See *Re Homer District Consolidated Gold Mines Ltd, ex parte Smith* (1888) 39 ChD 546 (North J).

[13] See *Browne v La Trinidad* (1888) 37 Ch D 1 at 9–10 (CA).

[14] See *Colin Gwyer & Associates Ltd and another v London Wharf (Limehouse) Ltd and others; Eaton Bray Ltd and another v Palmer and others* [2003] 2 BCLC 153 at para [62].

[15] See *Colin Gwyer & Associates Ltd and another v London Wharf (Limehouse) Ltd and others; Eaton Bray Ltd and another v Palmer and others* [2003] 2 BCLC 153 at para [60].

[16] See *Re Portuguese Consolidated Copper Mines* (1888) 42 Ch D 160 (CA).

[17] See further para 19.19 below.

Directors who have no vote at board meetings

19.15 Sometimes, albeit rarely, the articles of association of a company will provide that a particular director has no entitlement to vote at board meetings, although he has the right to attend at such meetings. Is such a disenfranchised director entitled to receive notice of a board meeting? In *John Shaw & Sons (Salford) v Shaw*[18] the answer to this question was the subject of a conflict of judicial opinion. In this case, as part of a settlement of a dispute concerning sums of money owing to the plaintiff company by the three Shaw brothers, who were directors of and shareholders in the plaintiff company, the articles of association of the company were altered so that control of the company's financial affairs and management was transferred to three independent persons who were known collectively as 'permanent directors'. Two of the three Shaw brothers (Peter and John) did not adhere to the terms of the settlement, and at a board meeting the three permanent directors resolved to bring legal proceedings against them. Greer LJ held that under the company's articles the power to give instructions for the bringing of the actions was vested not in the directors generally but in the permanent directors, whose decision could not be overridden by the mere resolution of the shareholders, and therefore that the bringing of the actions was duly authorized. Greer LJ stated:[19]

> In my judgment on March 23, 1934, when the permanent directors decided to instruct the company's solicitors to bring these actions on behalf of the company, they had power under the articles to do so. The power was not in the board of directors but in the permanent directors. The ordinary directors were not entitled to any say on the question, which was the only one considered at the meeting. If they had been summoned and had come to the meeting they could have been directed by the permanent directors to retire and could not have refused.
>
> It seems to me in any case to be carrying technicality to an absurd length to say they ought to have been summoned to the meeting in order that they might be directed to retire. I do not, and am not entitled to differ from the decision of this Court in *Young v. Ladies' Imperial Club, Ld.* and *In re Portuguese Consolidated Copper Mines, Ld.* Those decisions mean that a meeting of directors having power to make a decision on a given matter is invalid if one of the directors entitled to take part has not been summoned. The decisions have no relation to the question we have to determine.

19.16 On the other hand in the same case, Slesser LJ held that the bringing of the actions was not authorized, as authority to do so could not be given at a meeting of directors to which the ordinary directors were not summoned. Slesser LJ stated:[20]

> I entertain no doubt that if it was necessary under the articles that a valid decision to bring an action must be arrived at at a meeting of the directors, that no such meeting

---

[18] [1935] 2 KB 113 (CA).
[19] [1935] 2 KB 113 at 133.
[20] [1935] 2 KB 113 at 138.

> was then held, by reason of the failure to summon the ordinary directors. The authority, if authority be needed for such a conclusion, is to be found in the case of *In re Homer District Consolidated Gold Mines*, where, on a failure to summon certain directors to a board meeting, North J. said: 'I come to the conclusion that what was done on that occasion was not the act of the board of directors, and did not bind the company.' *In re Portuguese Consolidated Copper Mines Ld.*,and on the same principle, in this Court, *Young v. Ladies' Imperial Club, Ld.*, are to the same effect. As was stated in *D'Arcy v. Tamar, &c., Ry. Co.*: 'it is quite clear that the directors are to act together, and in a meeting': per Martin B. But the argument in this case proceeds upon another footing, for it is said that the peculiar powers conferred upon the permanent directors by these articles and the exclusion of the ordinary directors from all the management of the affairs of the company, enabled the permanent directors to authorize the starting of proceedings as a part of their exclusive powers . . . .
>
> Article 87, so far as it is here material, provides that: 'the ordinary directors . . . shall have no right at directors' meetings to vote in respect of, nor shall they have any control over, the financial affairs of the company, and with regard to the management of the company's business they shall have only such rights of voting and such control over the management as may from time to time be conferred upon them by the permanent directors.' In fact the permanent directors did not at any time confer upon them any rights of voting or control over management. So that, in the result, the ordinary directors have no vote either on financial affairs or the management of the company's business. But it is to be noticed that it is at a directors' meeting, which for the reasons I have given they would be entitled to attend, and the article provides that they are debarred from the right to vote. Article 87 appears to contemplate their presence, but a limitation of their powers at such a meeting. So far as regards a directors' meeting, I cannot see why they are not entitled to attend and do all things at such meeting, except vote, in respect of the financial affairs of the company or the management. Thus article 118, as amended, for example, seems to assume their presence, if one permanent director is also present, under article 111, to authorize the affixing of the seal to an instrument.[21]

It is suggested that the more sound view is that of Slesser LJ and accordingly, if disenfranchised directors have the right to attend board meetings, such directors should receive due notice of every board meeting. Where a company has such directors its articles of association should make it clear that notice of the board meeting should be given to such directors. If notice is not given to all the directors the business transacted at that board meeting will be invalid. **19.17**

Board meetings that are held on a regular basis

Circumstances may arise where the board of directors of a company meets habitually on a regular weekly, fortnightly or monthly basis. It most articles, as the board may regulate the manner in which it conducts its affairs, it is open to the directors to resolve to hold their meetings at regular intervals. If this situation applies, then **19.18**

[21] It is interesting to note that the third judge in the Court of Appeal, Roche LJ, felt unable to support either of his brethren owing to lack of information—see [1935] 2 KB 113 at 148.

it is arguable that there is no need to give specific notice of each such meeting to the directors. If a board has resolved for the directors to meet on a fixed day and at a stipulated time on that day, for example, Thursday mornings at 9.15 am., or by reference to a formula, such as the first Monday of each month at 11.00 am, then it is suggested that there may be no need to issue a formal notice of the board meeting on each occasion. However, it is advisable, in order to avoid any subsequent legal dispute, that notice is given to every director of every such board meeting. Nowadays with the widespread use of electronic communications, including email, text message and fax, this should not impose an undue administrative burden on the company.

Directors who are abroad

19.19 For some companies it will be rare for the directors to be overseas on company business when a board meeting is convened. For other companies, particularly multinational institutions, it will be rare for all of the members of the board to be available in the United Kingdom when a board meeting takes place. Since the advent of the 1948 Table A, provision has been made to excuse the company secretary from giving notice to a director who is for the time being absent from the United Kingdom.[22] Naturally, this practice developed at a time when communications with, and travel to, foreign countries were both difficult and the exception rather than a commonplace occurrence.

19.20 Where there is a provision in the form of reg 88 of the 1985 Table A, it is not strictly necessary to give notice to a director who is overseas.[23] Where there is no such provision in the articles of association the decision in *The Halifax Sugar Refining Co Ltd v Franklyn*[24] is authority for the proposition that a valid meeting of directors can take place, even if no notice has been given to a director who is overseas, if he is out of reach of notices. However, this decision must be treated with caution. The case was decided in 1890 in an age when communication with persons overseas was far from easy. Technology relating to all forms of communication has progressed to an almost unimaginable degree both in terms of speed and availability. In these circumstances it is suggested that in an age of almost instantaneous communication and mobile technology great care should be taken with both the remit and efficacy of this decision.

19.21 Indeed, the true modern rule is that every director within reach of notice is entitled to receive notice of a board meeting. The mere absence of a director overseas does not dispense with the need to give him notice of a directors' meeting unless

[22] See reg 98 of the 1948 Table A.
[23] See *The Halifax Sugar Refining Co Ltd v Franklyn* (1890) 59 LJ 591; 42 LT 563n.
[24] Op. cit.

the articles of association so provide. In determining whether a director is within reach of notice, what has to be considered is whether his location and the ordinary means of communicating with him are such that if notice had to be given to him this would involve such delay as to seriously hamper the transaction of business of a company.[25]

Consequences of defective notice

Shorter notice than that which had been previously given was found to be invalid by North J in *Re Homer District Consolidated Gold Mines Ltd, ex parte Smith*.[26] In this case a duly constituted meeting of all five of the directors resolved not to allot preference shares until an application had been made for a certain number of shares. Shortly after this valid meeting of all of the directors, a meeting of only two of the directors was held and they resolved to cancel the previous resolution and to allot the shares that had been applied for. This second meeting was held on a few hours' notice to two of the other three directors. The evidence before the court disclosed that one director did not receive the notice until the day after the board meeting and the other director said that he could not attend at the stipulated time but that he could attend the meeting one hour later on the same day. In relation to the fifth director no notice was sent to him as he had travelled to America. The court held that the proceedings at the second meeting of the directors were invalid. **19.22**

This decision is an extreme example of what can happen where insufficient notice is given to members of a board. From the decided cases it appears that a director who does not receive adequate notice of a board meeting is entitled to a 'second' meeting if he did not in fact attend the board meeting convened at short notice. However, as stated above a director who contends that he has not received adequate notice must make known his objection to the chairman or other members of the board at once. If a director fails to make his objection within a reasonable time of the board meeting being convened, that omission may amount to a waiver of his right to insist on a meeting being called at his convenience. As a result the business that was transacted at that board meeting will not be capable of a successful challenge.[27] **19.23**

The Agenda

In the absence of express provision in the articles of association of a company or in any relevant shareholders' agreement or investment agreement there is no legal requirement to circulate an agenda for a board meeting. An agenda is a document **19.24**

---

25 *Mitropolus v The Greek Orthodox Church* (1993) 10 ACSR 134 at 137.

26 (1888) 39 ChD 546.

27 See *Browne v La Trinidad* (1888) 37 Ch D 1(CA); *Bentley-Stevens v Jones* [1974] 1 WLR 638.

that contains a list of items that will be the subject of debate and discussion at a forthcoming meeting. A list of items alone, without either explanatory briefing papers or some succinct notes relating to each item will be of little use to the persons who are to participate in the scheduled meeting. There is no doubt that guidance notes relating to each item on the agenda or a briefing paper on the important issues will make an agenda more useful to its recipients.

Purpose of an agenda

19.25 The purpose of an agenda is to give relevant information to the members of the board of directors relating to the business that is to be transacted at the forthcoming meeting. Sometimes the agenda for a board meeting will be included in the notice of the board meeting. It is also legitimate for the notice of a board meeting to have a full and detailed agenda sent with it. If the notice is accompanied by an agenda or if the latter is part of the notice the requirement to give members of the board details of the purpose of the meeting will have been satisfied.

Form and content of an agenda

19.26 It is unusual for the articles of association of a company[28] to set out in detail the precise requirements for the form and content of the agenda for a meeting of directors. As the directors generally have the power to regulate the conduct of their own proceedings, rules may be developed by the board of directors for the form and contents of an agenda for their meetings. If such rules have been developed, they should be observed. If a formal resolution has been submitted for discussion at a board meeting then it is prudent and good practice to set out the precise text thereof.

19.27 It is often the company secretary who will be responsible for the formulation and dissemination of the agenda for a meeting of a board of directors. The company secretary will act in consultation with the chairman of the board. Between them they will endeavour to ensure that no item for proper inclusion on the agenda for a board meeting has been overlooked or neglected.

19.28 In the event of a dispute between members of a board concerning an item for inclusion on the agenda for a board meeting it is suggested that the company secretary should in general err on the side of caution and include the disputed item on the agenda. This will avoid the risk of a successful legal challenge on the grounds that the rights of a director have been infringed and debate has been curtailed.

---

28 The 1985 Table A is silent on this issue.

As a matter of best practice important items or new issues arising for discussion at a board meeting should be set out conspicuously in an agenda and should be accompanied by pertinent explanatory notes and relevant documentation. **19.29**

'Any other business'

An item headed by the words 'Any other business' is invariably included on an agenda for a board meeting. Such a heading is not to be an indication that the board meeting is to degenerate into an open or unstructured debate on any particular matter that members of the board wish to discuss. The phrase 'Any other business' has become a convenient shorthand to indicate that other matters which can properly form the subject matter of debate and discussion at a board meeting are discussed. However, important and major issues should not be raised under the rubric of 'Any other business' unless there is good reason for so doing, for example, if some emergency or crisis has arisen. This is not a matter of law but a matter of good practice. On the other hand, if the articles of association of a company require a specific agenda and important items are omitted therefrom the legality of the meeting and the business transacted thereat may be open to challenge.[29] The law requires the form of the notice for a meeting of directors to be fair and reasonable and in deciding what meets that test the practice of the directors of the particular company is an important factor. **19.30**

Order of items on the agenda

There is no prescribed order of business for an agenda for a board meeting. No doubt, in most well-run organizations, an habitual order of business will have evolved that tends to be followed as a matter of routine. A logical order of business may be: **19.31**

(1) Welcome for new members
(2) Apologies for absence
(3) Minutes of the previous meeting
(4) Matters arising from the previous minutes
(5) Important items of business
(6) Reports
(7) Correspondence
(8) Any other business
(9) Date of next meeting

The precise sequence of the items for discussion at a board meeting need not follow the order in which items are listed on the agenda for the meeting. The chairman **19.32**

---

29 See *Toole v Flexihire Pty Ltd* (1991) 6 ACSR 455.

of a board meeting may wish to rearrange the order in which items on the agenda are discussed at the meeting. Of course, the chairman of the board should explain his reasons to the meeting for changing the order of business and the chairman must not exercise this power capriciously. Sometimes rearranging the order in which items on an agenda are discussed and debated at a board meeting can become controversial. Should this situation arise, the running order of items will itself become a topic for debate. Such debates on procedural matters inevitably detract from the main purpose of a board meeting, and in a well-run company the order of items on an agenda will be arrived at carefully in advance, and usually with the informal consent of the participants.

Quorum

19.33 The constitution of a company will regulate the quorum at board meetings. As in the case of a general meeting of shareholders, in order to transact lawful business at a meeting it must be quorate. A company's articles will state the minimum number of directors who must be present in order to constitute a quorum. It is the duty of the chairman of the meeting to ensure that a quorum is present before the meeting proceeds to transact business.

19.34 Where a company's articles incorporate reg 89 of the 1985 Table A the quorum for the transaction of business at a board meeting may be fixed by the directors, and in the absence of a decision fixing it at any other number, that quorum shall be two directors. Regulation 89 also states that a person who holds office only as an alternate director shall be counted in the quorum if his appointor is not present. Where a private company has only one director reg 89 must be excluded.

19.35 Attention should also be drawn to reg 90 of the 1985 Table A which provides that if the number of existing directors is fewer than the number fixed for the quorum the continuing directors or director may act, but only for the purpose of filling vacancies or calling a general meeting of shareholders.

19.36 It is also to be noted that articles which restrict a director from voting at a meeting of directors or of a committee of directors on a resolution concerning a matter in which he has or may have a conflict of interest or duty with the interests of the company frequently provide that the director shall not be counted in the quorum present at the meeting. For example, reference should be made to regs 94 and 95 of the 1985 Table A which are discussed in detail in Part 4 of this book.[30] Sometimes, the impact of such a provision makes it extremely difficult for a quorate board meeting to be held. In the event that this proves to be impossible, the proper procedure

[30] See also *Re Greymouth-Point Elizabeth Rly and Coal Co* [1904] 1 Ch 32 (Farwell J).

is for the directors to convene a general meeting of the shareholders to decide upon the matter in issue.

Committee meetings

Articles of association frequently permit the board to delegate their powers to committees appointed to deal with specific company business. When they contain such a provision the articles will invariably specify how the meetings of such committees should be regulated. If they take the form of reg 72 of the 1985 Table A, the proceedings of the committee are governed by the articles regulating the proceedings of meetings of the directors. Accordingly, committee meetings must be quorate and directors must comply with the requirements of the articles relating to the disclosure of conflicts of interest and any restrictions that exist on voting on resolutions in which they are interested. In addition, proper minutes should be kept of committee meetings.[31] Alternatively, the board may prescribe the mode of proceedings for committees by its own regulations. The committee must then conform to such regulations. **19.37**

[31] See Ch 21.

20

THE ROLE OF THE CHAIRMAN AT MEETINGS OF DIRECTORS

Introduction

It is usual for a valid board meeting to be chaired by one of the directors who will act as the chairman of the board. The person who occupies the position of chairman of the board of directors holds an important position in the hierarchy of a company. It is the responsibility of the chairman to manage the board meeting and, in consultation with the chief executive officer and the company secretary, to set the agenda for board meetings. In managing a board meeting a chairman must ensure that members of the board receive accurate and proper information in a timely manner so as to enable them to take informed management decisions. **20.01**

There is no statutory requirement for a board of directors to have a chairman equivalent to CA 2006, s 319 in relation to a general meeting of members.[1] However, articles of association contain provisions for the appointment of a **20.02**

[1] See also CA 2006, s 328, as to the rights of a proxy to be elected as chairman of a general meeting.

chairman of the board and good practice and corporate governance[2] dictate that it is usual for there to be a chairman of the board of directors. It is customary for the chairman of the board to preside as chairman at general meetings of the shareholders. The role of the chairman at general meetings is discussed in Chapter 7 above.

20.03 In a private company the position of chairman of the board will be of significance by reason of the powers that are given to him to control the agenda for board meetings and his role in conducting the meetings. In a public company, in particular a listed public company, the role of the chairman is even more significant in that he will frequently be the 'public face' of the company and the person with whom shareholders will be accustomed to communicate.

Appointment

20.04 The election of a chairman is a matter for the board of directors and not an issue for the shareholders in general meeting.[3] The manner in which a chairman of the board will be appointed will be a matter that is dealt with by a provision in a company's articles of association. By way of example, reg 91 of the 1985 Table A[4] provides as follows:

> 91. The board of directors may appoint one of their number to be the chairman of the board of directors and may from time to time remove him from office. Unless he is unwilling to do so, the director so appointed shall preside at every meeting of directors at which he is present. But if there is no director holding that office, or if the director holding it is unwilling to preside or is not present within five minutes after the time appointed for the meeting, the directors present may appoint one of their number to be chairman of the meeting.

A provision in very similar form and content to reg 91 of the 1985 Act Table A has been in existence since 1856.[5]

20.05 A director may be elected as chairman for a specific meeting of the board or for a specific period of time. Alternatively, the election of a director as chairman may be for meetings in general and for an indeterminate period of time. Whatever the terms applying to the appointment of the chairman, it is essential that a detailed record is kept in the minutes of the election of the chairman. The reason for this is to ensure that there is some contemporaneous documentary evidence which may prove to be helpful in the event of any later dispute.

---

[2] The phrase 'corporate governance' is a convenient shorthand for the concept of ensuring that decisions of a company are taken in a regular and proper manner by the relevant people who have given due and careful consideration to all of the salient facts.

[3] See *Clark v Workman* [1920] IR 107 (Ross J).

[4] See the commentary in Part 4 of this book.

[5] See Joint Stock Companies Act 1856, Table B.

Listed companies and the Combined Code

20.06 The Combined Code on Corporate Governance[6] (Combined Code) applying to UK listed companies refers to the position of the chairman of a public listed company. The Combined Code is not part of the Listing Rules, nor subject to enforcement by the Financial Services Authority (FSA). The Combined Code clearly contemplates that the board of directors of a listed company will have a chairman.[7] The Combined Code provides that for a listed company there should be a job description for the position of chairman, which should make clear the amount of time for which a person holding office will be expected to commit to the affairs of the company.

Independence criteria

20.07 At the time of appointment, the chairman of a public company should meet the independence criteria set out in the Combined Code.[8] The chairman of a public company must be someone of standing and integrity, who is capable of showing leadership within the company and representing it to the outside world.

Separation of the role of chairman and chief executive officer

20.08 Main Principle A.2 of the Combined Code is entitled 'Chairman and chief executive' and provides:

> There should be a clear division of responsibilities at the head of the company between the running of the board and the executive responsibility for the running of the company's business. No one individual should have unfettered powers of decision.

20.09 The Combined Code points out that the chairman is responsible for leadership of the board of directors, ensuring its effectiveness on all aspects of its role and setting its agenda.

20.10 The Combined Code takes the view that the roles of chairman and chief executive officer should not usually be held by the same person. Combined Code, Provision A.2.1 states that:

> The roles of chairman and chief executive should not be exercised by the same individual. The division of responsibilities between the chairman and chief executive should be clearly established, set out in writing and agreed by the board.

---

[6] 2006 version.

[7] See Main Principle A.2.

[8] See Combined Code, Provision A.2.2.

20.11 The separation of the roles of chief executive and chairman has been the subject of much debate in recent years. The Cadbury Report[9] took the view that, other things being equal, the roles of chairman and chief executive officer are best kept separate, whereas the Hampel Committee[10] recognized that in certain circumstances it may be appropriate to combine the roles during certain phases of a company's development.

20.12 This division of responsibilities between the chairman and chief executive officer is designed to ensure that there is a proper balance of power within the company and that no one individual has unlimited powers. The Combined Code does not prohibit[11] one person occupying the position of chairman and chief executive officer, but it provides that the chief executive should not go on to be the chairman of the company otherwise than in exceptional circumstances.[12] The Combined Code provides that if, exceptionally, a chief executive should become chairman, the board should consult major shareholders in advance and should set out its reasons to shareholders at the time of the appointment and in the next annual report.[13]

Duties and Responsibilities of the Chairman

20.13 The Supporting Principles of the Combined Code set out the responsibilities of the chairman. The chairman of the board is responsible for leadership of the board, and must take measures to ensure that it is effective in all aspects of its role and setting its agenda. The chairman is the person who is responsible for ensuring that the directors receive accurate and clear information in a timely fashion.

20.14 In respect of all companies, the chairman must start any meeting by ensuring that a quorum of the directors is present. In the absence of a quorum the board cannot proceed to business.[14] Thereafter it is his duty to keep order at the meeting and ensure that all items on the agenda are dealt with.

20.15 The chairman has responsibility for signing the minutes of the previous board meeting when they are approved by the board. This is an important function as,

---

[9] A report of a committee chaired by Adrian Cadbury which produced the first Code of Best Practice on corporate governance, in 1992. Its stated objective was 'to help raise the standards of corporate governance and the level of confidence in financial reporting and auditing by setting out clearly what it sees as the respective responsibilities of those involved and what it believes is expected of them'.

[10] Hampel Committee, Final Report (January 1998).

[11] The Higgs Report (2003) recommended a prohibition on a chief executive officer or managing director being appointed as chairman.

[12] The proposal in 2008 that one person should be both chairman and chief executive officer of Marks & Spencer plc has been controversial.

[13] See Combined Code, Provision A.2.2.

[14] See Ch 19 on the question of quorum at directors' meetings.

once they have been signed, the minutes constitute evidence of the proceedings at that meeting in accordance with CA 2006, s 249.[15]

In addition, the chairman's role is to ensure that there is effective communication with shareholders, and he must take steps to secure the effective contribution of non-executive directors. **20.16**

Only listed companies fall within the ambit of the Combined Code and the formal obligations that it imposes. However, even in the context of a private unquoted company the need to have good corporate governance must not be underestimated or overlooked. **20.17**

As the chairman will be one of the directors of a company he will be subject to the general duties set out in CA 2006, Part 10 that are applicable to persons who hold such office. These duties are considered in Chapter 18 above. In particular, due and proper regard must be had to the inexhaustive list of matters set out in CA 2006, s 172 when decisions are taken.[16] **20.18**

It is the chairman of the board who is primarily responsible for the organisation of board meetings. The chairman of the board will be the individual who will try to ensure that the board of directors is run efficiently and competently. Together with the secretary and in consultation with the chief executive officer, the chairman will set the agenda for board meetings. In setting the agenda the chairman must ensure that members of the board, both executive and non-executive, receive all proper and relevant information to enable them to take informed management decisions on behalf of the company. He should ensure that the non-executive directors are fully briefed in advance of board meetings. When the meeting takes place the chairman should take care to see that sufficient time is given for proper debate of the issues on the agenda.[17] On no account should discussion be stifled but, in practice, it may be necessary for the chairman, in the exercise of his judgment, to bring matters to a conclusion. **20.19**

Qualifications

No specific qualifications are required by the individual who will hold the position of chairman of the board of directors. For listed companies the Listing Rules[18] of the London Stock Exchange plc require that all directors have 'appropriate **20.20**

[15] See Ch 21.

[16] In this context see the discussion in Ch 21 relating to the content of minutes of board meetings.

[17] See the guidance for the chairman taken from the Higgs Report entitled 'Review of the role and effectiveness of non-executive directors' (January 2003) set out in the Related Guidance and Good Practice Suggestions of the Combined Code on Corporate Governance.

[18] See rule 3.8.

expertise and experience for the management of its business'. As the role of chairman is akin to that of an ambassador for the company it is essential that the person holding this important position has, and maintains, high standards of integrity and honesty and possesses real qualities of leadership. In addition, the role of chairman requires an individual who has good powers of communication with other members of the board, both executive and non-executive, with employees and shareholders of the company and with third parties who deal with the company.

Removal

20.21 It is usual to find a provision in a company's articles of association that empowers the board of directors to remove its chairman from office.[19] Regulation 91 of the 1985 Table A contains such a provision but it does not prescribe any procedure for such a removal. The removal of a chairman will be effected by way of a resolution of the board of directors passed by a simple majority of those directors present and voting. Such a resolution should be properly minuted. Frequently, a chairman is appointed for a specified period but may at any time be removed from office.

Resignation

20.22 It should be noted that the provisions of reg 91 of the 1985 Table A do not prescribe any specific procedure for the resignation of a chairman. Where a director resigns from the position as chairman it is prudent for an accurate written record to be made of this event and for that document to be kept in the minutes of the proceedings of directors. A written resignation is to be preferred to an oral one. As in the case of the resignation of a director, a person may resign from the office of chairman of the board at any time by notice to the company.[20]

Appointment in Breach of the Articles

20.23 In the event that an appointment of a director as chairman of the board is made in breach of a company's articles of association the appointment is void.[21] It is unlikely that a defective appointment of a chairman can be cured by acquiescence.[22] Accordingly, where a chairman has been appointed to hold that position in breach

[19] See reg 91, 1985 Table A.

[20] See *Glossop v Glossop* [1907] 2 Ch 370 at 374 (Neville J).

[21] See *Clark v Workman* [1920] IR 107 (Ross J).

[22] In *Clark v Workman* (op. cit.) the defective appointment of the chairman by means of a resolution of the shareholders in general meeting was not challenged for a period of 38 years.

of the articles of association it would appear that resolutions of the board of directors that have been carried by the casting vote of the chairman will be ineffective.[23]

The Chairman's Casting Vote at Board Meetings

Unless the articles of association or the provisions of any shareholders' agreement or investment agreement provide to the contrary,[24] decisions at board meetings will be taken by majority vote. However, in order to avoid deadlock the chairman of a board of directors will invariably be given a second or casting vote in the event of an equality of votes on a board resolution. Regulation 88 of the 1985 Table A confers a casting vote on the chairman of the board of directors. The chairman's casting vote is a fiduciary power which he must exercise in good faith and in what he perceives to be the best interests of the company. **20.24**

In many company disputes, especially those that arise in small private companies, there may be uncertainty as to who is entitled to take the chair at board meetings. This issue may be one of considerable significance where one faction of a board of directors is seeking to pass an important resolution in the context of opposition from another faction of directors. The existence and use of the chairman's casting vote on a board resolution may prove to be critical to the outcome. It is for this reason that the articles of many joint venture companies or shareholders' agreements provide that the chairman should not have a casting vote. **20.25**

[23] See *Clark v Workman* (op. cit.).

[24] For example, by requiring that a resolution receive the support of a specific majority of the directors or even the unanimous consent of the directors.

21

MINUTES OF MEETINGS OF DIRECTORS

Introduction

The keeping of proper records of meetings is a fundamental requirement for the efficient management of any institution. As has been discussed in Chapter 16, concerning minutes of shareholders' meetings, it is important to remember that minutes are not a verbatim transcript of the proceedings of a meeting but an accurate record in summary form of what has been decided. In general, minutes of directors' meetings will record what has been resolved upon, but there may be occasions when the minutes of a board meeting need to record the reasons for a particular decision or the main points from a discussion. Where directors of a public listed company have concerns about the way in which that company is being run or about a course of action being proposed by the board, directors should ensure that their concerns are recorded in the board minutes if they cannot be resolved.[1] **21.01**

Board minutes are a written record of a meeting and are designed to give an accurate overview of the proceedings of the meeting. There is no prescribed form that board minutes will take and there is room for latitude in terms of stylistic content and format. Board meeting minutes will usually be headed with the name of the company and the date, time and place of the meeting. It is also standard practice to start with a list of those attending the meeting in their capacity as directors and to list the names of other invited attendees, such as the company secretary and other participants. **21.02**

[1] See the Combined Code on Corporate Governance (2006) at A.1.4.

In some organisations the constitution will permit participation in board meetings by telephonic means or by audio-visual link. If persons attend by such means it is as well to record that they participated by means of the video-link or conference call.

21.03 The minutes must state the identity of the person who acts as chairman of the meeting. It is also common practice to record the names of those who are unable to attend and who have sent their apologies for their absence. Another standard feature is to record the fact that the board meeting is quorate. In established companies it is common for the minutes of a board meeting to start with the approval of the minutes of the previous board meeting and to deal with matters that arise from that previous meeting. If the members of a board agree that the written minutes reflect what happened at a previous meeting, then the minutes are approved, and the fact of their approval is recorded in the minutes of the current meeting. Where there are errors or omissions in the draft minutes, the minutes will have to be re-drafted and submitted again at a later date. Minor changes, such as typographical errors or small grammatical corrections may be made immediately, and the amended minutes may be approved 'as amended'. It is normally appropriate to give a draft copy of the minutes to all the members of the board of directors in advance of the board meeting.

21.04 Reference to the minutes of past meetings of directors can arise in a plethora of different situations. Frequently in litigation, reference will be made to board minutes and in that context, where the memory of the participants to a transaction might have faded, well-drafted minutes can serve as a very helpful aide memoire.

Statutory Requirements

21.05 CA 2006, Part 10, Chapter 9, ss 248 and 249 relate to minutes of board meetings. These sections are derived from CA 1985, s 382 but also introduce an important new requirement that all companies must keep records of board meetings for a period of 10 years. No doubt many public listed companies will have systems and procedures in place that make compliance with this new time period an easy task. However, as this new statutory requirement applies across the spectrum of all companies those entities that have less efficient methods of retaining board minutes will have to ensure that existing methods of keeping and accessing company records are adequate and, where necessary, are improved.

21.06 The legislation does not prescribe which officer of a company is to be responsible for drafting the minutes of a board meeting. This important role may be undertaken by the company secretary, or the chairman of the board or a member of the board. In the event that a company's articles of association identify a particular officer holder as the person required to take the minutes, then this task would have to be undertaken by that person. Such provisions are rare, as practical problems can arise if the particular officer is not available at a meeting.

CA 2006, s 248

CA 2006, s 248(1)[2] makes it a mandatory requirement for companies (both public and private) to maintain minutes of all proceedings at meetings of directors. This new statutory provision is derived from CA 1985, s 382(1), but the requirement under that section to record and maintain minutes of managers' meetings (where there are managers) has been abandoned. **21.07**

Ten-year period of retention

Under CA 2006, s 248(2) companies must retain such minutes for a period of 10 years from the date of the directors' meeting. As the prescribed 10-year time period is a new requirement imposed by CA 2006, companies must ensure that they have proper and workable procedures in place in order to comply with this mandatory time requirement. **21.08**

Consequences of a breach of s 248

A breach of CA 2006, s 248 by the company gives rise to an offence by every officer of the company who is in default. Under CA 1985, s 382(5) the company was made liable with the officers for the breach of the statutory requirement, but this liability on the company has been removed by CA 2006. **21.09**

Regulation 100 of the 1985 Table A

Companies that have adopted the 1985 Table A as part of their articles must also comply with Regulation 100. In addition to the statutory requirements of CA 2006, reg 100 of the 1985 Table A[3] imposes further obligations in respect of minutes of board meetings. This provision requires that the directors must ensure that minutes are made 'in books kept for the purpose' of the proceedings of meetings of the company, of any class of shareholders, of the directors and of committees of directors. Such minutes must include the names of the directors present at each such meeting. Regulation 100 also makes it mandatory for minutes to be kept of the appointment to the board of any officers. **21.10**

CA 2006, s 249—Minutes as evidence

Minutes of board meetings that are made in compliance with CA 2006, s 248, which purport to be authenticated by the chairman of that or the next directors' **21.11**

[2] This section came into force on 1 October 2007—see Third Commencement Order.
[3] See the commentary on this provision in Part 4.

meeting, are evidence of the proceedings at the directors' meeting.[4] There is a presumption (subject to proof to the contrary) that where minutes have been made pursuant to s 248, that the board meeting was duly held and convened, that all proceedings at the meeting are deemed to have taken place, and that all appointments at the meeting were validly made. As a consequence of CA 2006, s 249 a person who alleges that minutes of a board meeting are not accurate will have the evidential burden of proving the inaccuracy. The task of discharging this evidential burden is not to be underestimated.[5]

Transitional provisions

21.12 CA 2006, ss 248 and 249 came into force on 1 October 2007 and apply to meetings that are held on or after that date. CA 1985, s 382 continues to apply to meetings of directors held before that time.[6]

CA 2006, Part 37

21.13 It is to be noted that nothing is prescribed in CA 2006, ss 248 and 249 as to the form in which the minutes must be kept. The method of retaining minutes of board meetings is important because of the requirement that they are to be kept for a period of 10 years. In order to ascertain how a company should go about keeping its board minutes attention has to be paid to the provisions of CA 2006, Part 37.[7] Under CA 2006, Part 37 provision is made as to the form in which company records, including minutes of meetings, may be kept. In addition a statutory duty is imposed by s 1138 to take precautions against falsification. The precise measures that will be taken will vary from company to company. The more complex the operations of the company concerned, the more sophisticated the safety measures required to guard against falsification.

21.14 CA 2006, Part 37, entitled 'Companies: Supplementary Provisions' starts with a definition in s 1134 of the term company records.[8] Section 1134 provides that 'company records' in Part 37 means:

(a) any register, index, accounting records, agreement, memorandum, *minutes* or other document required by the Companies Acts to be kept by a company, and
(b) any register kept by a company of its debenture holders.

(emphasis added)

---

[4] See CA 2006, s 249(1).
[5] See *Re Fireproof Doors* [1916] 2 Ch 142 (Astbury J); *Re Pyle Works (No 2)* [1891] 1 Ch 173 at 184 (Stirling J).
[6] See Third Commencement Order, Sch 3, para 19.
[7] See in particular CA 2006, ss 1134–1138.
[8] This section is derived from CA 1985, s 722(1).

Minutes of board meetings fall within the definition that is set out above. CA 2006, s 1135 prescribes how company records including board minutes are to be kept. Under s 1135(1) company records may be kept in hard copy or electronic form, and may be arranged in such manner as the directors of the company think fit. The direct reference to company records in electronic form is to be welcomed. This is subject to the caveat that the information in question must be adequately recorded for future reference. This is an important consideration in view of the 10-year retention period stipulated by s 248. Section 1135(2) requires that where the records are kept in electronic form, they must be capable of being reproduced in hard copy form. Officers of a company who fail to comply with the requirements of s 1135 will commit an offence. **21.15**

Directors' entitlement to minutes of board meetings

By reason of his status a director of a company is entitled to see and have copies of the minutes of board meetings. This principle is derived from the common law rules entitling a director to have access to company records discussed by Slade J in *Conway v Petronius Clothing Co*[9] and the decision of the Court of Session in *McCusker v McRae*.[10] This right also extends to minutes of committees of directors, even if the director concerned is not a member of that committee. However, where a committee is formed because some members of a board would have a conflict, for example in relation to some transaction or in relation to litigation, it would not be appropriate for the conflicted directors to have unimpeded access to the minutes of that committee. **21.16**

Usually the company secretary will be permitted to have access to the board minutes. In addition under CA 1985, s 389A the auditors of a company had a statutory right to see the minutes of board meetings for the purposes of the audit. This section has been re-enacted as CA 2006, s 499.[11] **21.17**

No right for members to have access to board minutes

As a general rule shareholders of a company have no entitlement under the articles or under the provisions of CA 2006 to inspect and take copies of minutes of board meetings.[12] This position is to be contrasted with the provisions of CA 2006, s 358, from which is derived the members' rights to inspect and take copies of resolutions and minutes of shareholders' meetings. This principle was established **21.18**

---

[9] [1978] 1 WLR 72 (Slade J).

[10] (1966) SC 253.

[11] This section came into force on 6 April 2008.

[12] Shareholders may have the right to see minutes of board meetings under the terms of a shareholders' agreement or a subscription agreement.

as long ago as 1858. In *R v Mariquita and New Grenada Mining Company*[13] the application of a member of a joint stock company for an order permitting him to have access to the books containing the minutes of the company's board meetings was refused. In giving the judgment of the Court Lord Campbell CJ stated:[14]

> Both in common parlance, and in acts of parliament on this subject, the proceedings at meetings of the shareholders are considered as proceedings of the Company, and they are put in opposition to the proceedings of the directors, the select body to whom the general management of the business of the Company is entrusted. It is highly proper that an inspection of the books containing the proceedings of the directors should be obtained on special occasions and for special purposes: but the business of such Companies could hardly be conducted if any one, buying a share, might entitle himself at all times to gain a knowledge of every commercial transaction in which the directors engage, the moment that an entry is made in their books: and we cannot find that any such right of inspection is given.

21.19 However, the fact that shareholders are precluded from having access to the board minutes of a company under the general law does not mean that they may never see the contents of the minutes of directors' meetings. Such minutes are liable to be disclosed in the event of litigation, whether in a member's petition presented under the provisions of CA 2006, s 994 (unfairly prejudicial conduct) or in a derivative action brought under CA 2006, Part 11.[15] For this reason alone considerable care must always be taken with the accuracy, form and content of board minutes.

The impact of CA 2006, s 172

21.20 Chapter 18 discusses the general duties of directors which are now set out in statutory form in CA 2006, ss 172–177. Of those provisions the most important change has been the introduction of the new statutory duty to promote the success of the company that is contained in s 172.[16] Under that section a director is required to act in the way he considers, in good faith, would be likely to promote the success of the company for the benefit of its members as a whole, and in doing so must have regard (amongst other matters) to—

(a) the likely consequences of any decision in the long term;
(b) the interests of the company's employees;
(c) the need to foster the company's business relationships with suppliers, customers and others;
(d) the impact of the company's operations on the community and the environment;

[13] (1859) 1 El & El 289 (Campbell CJ).
[14] Op. cit. at 293–4.
[15] See *CAS Nominees Ltd v Nottingham Forest plc* [2001] 1 All ER 954 (Evans Lombe J).
[16] See Ch 18, paras 18.26–18.29.

(e) the desirability of the company maintaining a reputation for high standards of business conduct; and
(f) the need to act fairly as between members of the company.

One of the interesting questions that arises from the enactment of this provision is the extent to which directors must have regard to the matters listed in CA 2006, s 172(1) when reaching their decisions. Particular concern has arisen as to whether reference should be made in the minutes of board meetings to the fact that consideration has in fact been given by the board to these matters when reaching an important business decision. Moreover, it must be borne in mind that the list of matters in s 172(1) is not exhaustive, nor is there any reference in the section to questions of relevance or practicability. **21.21**

A number of ministerial statements made when the legislation was passing through Parliament have suggested that s 172 does not impose any requirement on directors to keep records in any circumstances in which they would not have had to do so previously. It has been stated that the words in s 172 '. . . have regard to . . .' mean '. . . give proper consideration to . . .'.[17] **21.22**

This view has been supported by GC 100[18] in a paper entitled 'Companies Act 2006—Director's Duties' published in February 2007. This paper points out that important board decisions will always be supported by a background paper prepared by the management team, possibly with the assistance of advisers. In practice, therefore, a thorough analysis of all the issues reflecting on the decision will already have been made by the management. It is the job of the directors to review the papers and any recommendations made in order to reach a decision. It is therefore suggested that it should be best practice for those members of the management team who are responsible for preparing the background paper on a topic to ensure that each of the relevant factors, including those that are referred to in CA 2006, s 172 is properly considered while the paper is being prepared. It is further suggested that responsibility for considering relevant factors can properly be delegated to the members of the management team preparing the paper in the usual way. Board minutes should not be used as the main medium for recording the extent to which each of the factors listed in CA 2006, s 172 was discussed. If this approach is adopted board minutes will continue to be simply a summary of the decisions taken by the board. It is to be noted that this view has been endorsed by the Institute of Chartered Secretaries and Administrators (ICSA) in its paper entitled 'Guidance on Directors' General Duties' (January 2008). **21.23**

[17] See Companies Act 2006, Duties of Company Directors Ministerial Statements, DTI, June 2007.
[18] This is an organization comprising senior legal officers of more than 70 FTSE 100 companies.

21.24 The view of the GC 100 must be respected in view of its members' extensive experience and involvement as the senior in-house legal advisers of some of the major listed companies in the United Kingdom. However, a note of caution regarding the approach recommended must be expressed. As yet, there has been no reported judicial consideration of s 172. Detailed board papers may be commonplace for listed public companies, but in practice that is not the case for unlisted companies, whether public or private. In such companies it would be prudent for board minutes to indicate in express terms the factors that have been taken into account when the directors were considering and taking important commercial decisions. Those factors will include, to the extent that they are in any way relevant, each of the items listed in sub-paras (a) to (f) of s 172(1). Such minutes will provide contemporaneous evidence of the facts and matters to which the directors have had regard when forming their business judgment.

21.25 The existence of board minutes in this form will serve to protect directors in the event that a decision that they have taken becomes the subject of a legal challenge, whether by shareholders or otherwise. If, as a result, the minutes of board meetings become longer and more detailed than hitherto, that is merely a consequence of the new legislation. The repeated assertions made by ministers that 'a paper trail' is not required in order to comply with s 172 will afford little comfort to a board of directors which is the subject of a claim for breach of fiduciary duty. When defending directors against an allegation of breach of duty there can be no substitute for well-drafted and accurate board minutes which reflect what occurred at the relevant board meeting. The preparation of such minutes is strongly recommended.

Part 3

COMMENTARY ON THE PROVISIONS OF THE COMPANIES ACT 2006, PART 13, SECTIONS 281 TO 361

22

COMMENTARY ON THE PROVISIONS OF THE COMPANIES ACT 2006, PART 13, SECTIONS 281 TO 361

General Note

22.01 The Companies Act 2006 (CA 2006), which contains 1,300 sections and 16 Schedules, received the Royal Assent on 8 November 2006. The preamble to CA 2006 states that it is 'An Act to reform company law and restate the greater part of the enactments relating to companies; to make other provision relating to companies and other forms of business organisation; to make provision about directors' disqualification, business names, auditors and actuaries; to amend Part 9 of the Enterprise Act 2002; and for connected purposes.' This new legislation is the result of a review and overhaul of the statutory provisions affecting registered companies and will, in time replace all the provisions of the Companies Act 1985 (CA 1985) and other associated statutes. The laudable aim of the new legislation is the simplification of corporate procedures and when it comes into full force it will have a widespread impact on those who are involved in the management of companies, whether as participant or as an adviser.

22.02 The provisions contained in CA 2006, Part 13 replace most of CA 1985, Part 11, Chapter 4 relating to meetings and resolutions. The changes that will be made to this important area of the law derive in the main from work carried out by the Company Law Review Steering Group, in particular, from the Company Law Review Steering Group's consultation paper entitled 'Modern Company Law for a Competitive Economy: Company General Meetings and Shareholder Communications'[1] and recommendations from Chapters 2, 6 and 7 of the Company Law Review Steering Group's 'Final Report'[2] plus two subsequent consultations: the 'Modernising Company Law' White Paper of July 2002[3] and the 'Company Law Reform' White Paper of March 2005.[4]

22.03 By CA 2006, s 1300(1) four parts of the new legislation came into force on the day that CA 2006 was passed. The four relevant parts are Part 43,[5] Part 44, ss 1274 and 1276, Part 46 and Part 47. CA 2006, s 1300(2) provides that the other provisions of the new legislation will come into force on such day as may be appointed by order of the Secretary of State or the Treasury.

22.04 In recent times there have been other pieces of complex and important legislation relating to commercial law that have received the Royal Assent and thereafter have been brought into force in a piecemeal fashion by means of an extended series of complex commencement orders. Whether this is an efficacious and practical method of producing new legislation is a moot point, but in relation to CA 2006 it is the system that has been adopted.[6] It had been envisaged when CA 2006 received the Royal Assent that all of the provisions of the new legislation would be brought into legal force by no later than 1 October 2008. This back stop date for the bringing into legal effect of all of the provisions in CA 2006 has now been put back to 1 October 2009.

22.05 By 6 April 2008 there have been a total of six commencement orders relating to various provisions of the CA 2006:

The Companies Act 2006 (Commencement No 1, Transitional Provisions and Savings) Order 2006 (SI 2006/3482);
The Companies Act 2006 (Commencement No 2, Consequential Amendments, Transitional Provisions and Savings) Order 2007 (S1 2007/1093);
The Companies Act 2006 (Commencement No 3, Transitional Provisions and Savings) Order 2007 (SI 2007/2194);

---

1 URN 99/1144 (London: DTI, 1999).
2 URN 01/942 and URN 01/943 (London: DTI, 2001).
3 Cm 5532, 2002, (London: DTI).
4 Cm 6456.
5 Save for the amendment in Sch 15, para 11(2) of the definition of 'regulated market' in the Financial Services and Markets Act 2000, Part 6.
6 Such a system may be correct where the commencement orders emerge in final form but as is set out below some of the commencement orders for CA 2006 have themselves been the subject of amendment and revision.

The Companies Act 2006 (Commencement No 4 and Commencement No 3 (Amendment)) Order 2007 (SI 2007/2607);
The Companies Act 2006 (Commencement No 5, Transitional Provisions and Savings) Order 2007 (SI 2007/3495);
The Companies Act 2006 (Commencement No 6, Saving and Commencement Nos 3 and 5 (Amendment)) Order 2008 (SI 2008/ 674).

Of these commencement orders the most significant in relation to the law on company meetings and resolutions has been the Companies Act 2006 (Commencement No 3, Transitional Provisions and Savings) Order 2007,[7] (the Third Commencement Order). **22.06**

The Third Commencement Order

This statutory instrument was published in draft on 29 June 2007 by the Office for Public Sector Information (OPSI) and was accompanied by explanatory notes. The Third Commencement Order was laid before Parliament in draft on 25 June 2007. In addition to bringing into legal force those provisions of CA 2006 that were scheduled to come into effect on 1 October 2007, the Third Commencement Order contained five schedules. Schedule 1 set out provisions dealing with transitional adaptations dealing with sections of CA 1985 that remain in force after 1 October 2007. Schedule 2 set out a list of the sections of CA 1985 that were repealed on 1 October 2007. Very importantly, Schedule 3 set out transitional provisions and savings. Schedule 4 set out consequential amendments relevant to the provisions of CA 2006 that came into force on 1 October 2007 and the repeals under CA 1985 that took effect on 1 October 2007, and Schedule 5 set out consequential repeals in other legislation. **22.07**

Amendment of the Third Commencement Order

On 13 July 2007, OPSI reissued the Third Commencement Order in the Companies Act 2006 (Commencement No 4 and Commencement No 3 (Amendment)) Order 2007.[8] The original draft order that had been published on 25 June 2007 was withdrawn on 5 July 2007 as a result of errors that had been found in the text of the order. **22.08**

---

[7] SI 2007/2194.
[8] SI 2007/2607.

The Fifth Commencement Order[9]

22.09 On 17 December 2007, the Fifth Commencement Order was made by Parliament. The Fifth Commencement Order refers to the sections of CA 2006 that are due to come into force on 6 April 2008, 29 June 2008 and 1 October 2008 respectively. The Fifth Commencement Order also repeals the sections of CA 1985 that will either be replaced by provisions of CA 2006 or that are redundant as a result of CA 2006. The Fifth Commencement Order makes transitional adaptations (in Sch 1) which, for the most part, involve applying provisions and concepts contained in CA 1985 to the provisions of CA 2006 that are coming into force, until the relevant provisions of the 2006 Act have come into effect. The transitional provisions and savings set out in Sch 4 in the Fifth Commencement Order deal with issues where there may be a straddling of the commencement dates of 6 April 2008, 29 June 2008 or 1 October 2008, as the case may be. Further it is to be noted that Sch 5 to the Fifth Commencement Order makes a number of amendments to earlier commencement orders.

Schedule 5, para 2(6) to the Fifth Commencement Order—annual general meeting of a private company

22.10 Schedule 5, para 2(6) to the Fifth Commencement Order deals with existing companies whose articles of association require them to hold an annual general meeting. The paragraph amends Sch 3, para 32 of the Third Commencement Order. Paragraph 32(4) now provides that a private company does not have to hold annual general meetings, even if its articles expressly state that annual general meetings must be held, if an elective resolution under CA 1985, s 366A (dispensing with the need to hold annual general meetings) was in force immediately prior to 1 October 2007. All elective resolutions (except those under CA 1985, s 80A) fell away on 1 October 2007 leading to uncertainty as to whether companies in this position needed to hold annual general meetings or amend their articles to remove the requirement to hold annual general meetings. Schedule 5, para 2(6) to the Fifth Commencement Order now clarifies the position with the effect that any relevant elective resolution remains operative.

New para 23A inserted into Sch 3 to the Third Commencement Order—the chairman's casting vote

22.11 It has been common for articles of association to contain a provision granting to the chairman of a general meeting a casting vote where there is an equality of votes on a resolution. Regulation 50 of the version of the 1985 Table A in the form that

[9] The Companies Act 2006 (Commencement No 5, Transitional Provisions and Savings) Order 2007 (SI 2007/3495).

was effective before 1 October 2007 is an example of such a provision. The article confers on the chairman power to pass or reject ordinary resolutions where there is a deadlock. CA 2006, ss 281 and 282, however, define an ordinary resolution as one that is passed by a simple majority. It appears that ss 281(3) and 282 have had the unintended consequence of overriding such an article. This matter is discussed further in the commentary under s 282 and in Chapter 11 above.

Schedule 5, para 2(5) to the Fifth Commencement Order inserts a new para 23A into Sch 3 to the Third Commencement Order in the following terms. **22.12**

> 23A—(1) This paragraph applies where, immediately before 1st October 2007, the articles of a company provided that in the event of equality of votes on an ordinary resolution, whether on a show of hands or on a poll, the chairman should have a casting vote in addition to any other vote that the chairman might have.
> (2) If that provision has not been removed by a subsequent alteration of the articles, it continues to have effect notwithstanding sections 281(3) and 282.
> (3) If that provision has been removed by a subsequent alteration of the articles, the company may at any time restore that provision, which shall have effect notwithstanding sections 281(3) and 282.

Paragraph 23A therefore provides that where, immediately before 1 October 2007, a company's articles provided for the chairman to have a casting vote in the case of an equality of votes, that article remains effective notwithstanding CA 2006, ss 281(3) and 282 and the chairman may retain his casting vote. Paragraph 23A also provides for the situation where a company has removed such an article since 1 October 2007. Such a company may validly reinstate the article and benefit from the saving provision. This amounts to an amendment to ss 281(3) and 282 for existing companies. Regrettably, it only serves to highlight the inadequacy of the original drafting of those sections and in particular the extraordinary failure to recognize the impact of the new legislation on the chairman's casting vote, which is a common feature of the articles of many companies. **22.13**

Extraordinary resolutions

Schedule 5, para 2(4) to the Fifth Commencement Order inserts a new sub-para 23(2) into Sch 3 of the Third Commencement Order. This provides that where extraordinary resolutions are still valid under the saving provision, such resolutions must continue to be filed with the registrar of companies under CA 2006, Part 3, Chapter 3. This is a reference to the requirements of CA 2006, ss 29 and 30. **22.14**

Commencement of CA 2006, Part 13

All of CA 2006, Part 13 (other than ss 308, 309 and 333 relating to electronic communications, which came into force on 20 January 2007) came into force on 1 October 2007 by reason of the provisions contained in the **22.15**

Third Commencement Order (as amended). The majority of the sections of Part 13[10] are the subject of transitional provisions.

22.16 Part 3 of this book deals with CA 2006, Part 13, ss 281– 381, which contains a comprehensive set of provisions governing the law relating to company resolutions and meetings of companies. The new provisions replicate much of the law previously found in CA 1985 and in related legislation, both primary and secondary, but introduce a number of new provisions. These include in Chapter 2 (ss 288–300 (inclusive)), a comprehensive code regulating written resolutions passed by the shareholders of private companies. There are important changes in nomenclature including the abolition of 'extraordinary resolutions', the introduction of a new power on the part of shareholders to request the calling of a general meeting (in place of the previous power to requisition an extraordinary general meeting), new and detailed procedures for the conduct of meetings and the appointment of proxies, and special provisions relating to public companies and quoted companies.

22.17 It is important to note that the provisions with regard to annual general meetings in Part 13, Chapter 4[11] relate to public companies only. Under the new legislation there is no longer any statutory requirement for a private company to hold an annual general meeting. Indeed, it is assumed by the draftsmen of the new legislation that private companies, however large, will not wish to hold an annual general meeting notwithstanding their previous history and practice. The statute removes entirely the provisions for elective resolutions for private companies which previously enabled their members to dispense with the holding of annual general meetings.[12] However, as pointed out in para 22.10 above, Sch 3, para 32(4) to the Third Commencement Order (as amended) preserves any elective resolution under CA 1985, s 366A which was in force immediately prior to 1 October 2007.

22.18 Part 13, Chapter 5[13] contains additional statutory provisions which apply only to quoted companies. By CA 2006, s 361 a quoted company for the purposes of Part 13 incorporates the definition in Part 15, s 385. A 'quoted company' means a company whose equity share capital has been included in the Official List[14] or is officially listed in an EEA state[15] or is admitted to dealing on either the New York Stock Exchange or on Nasdaq.

---

[10] CA 2006, ss 281, 288–290, 300, 303–306, 307, 310–331, 334–340, 342–354 and 355–359.
[11] See CA 2006, ss 336–340.
[12] See CA 1985, s 366A.
[13] CA 2006, ss 341–354.
[14] Within the meaning of the Financial Services and Markets Act 2000, s 103(1).
[15] See CA 2006, s 1170.

Part 13, Chapter 6[16] deals with the maintenance of records of resolutions and meetings and associated rights of inspection of such records. Supplementary provisions for Part 13 are contained in Chapter 7.[17] **22.19**

In addition, reference is made below to the new statutory provisions dealing with the sending or supplying of documents and information to or by a company in ss 1143–1148 and 1168 and Schs 4 and 5. These are defined in the statute as 'the company communications provisions'. The company communications provisions were brought into effect on 20 January 2007[18] and are discussed in Chapter 17. **22.20**

Provisions of CA 2006, Part 13

PART 13
RESOLUTIONS AND MEETINGS
CHAPTER 1
GENERAL PROVISIONS ABOUT RESOLUTIONS

281 Resolutions

(1) A resolution of the members (or of a class of members) of a private company must be passed—
    (a) as a written resolution in accordance with Chapter 2, or
    (b) at a meeting of the members (to which the provisions of Chapter 3 apply.
(2) A resolution of the members (or of a class of members) of a public company must be passed at a meeting of the members (to which the provisions of Chapter 3 and, where relevant, Chapter 4 apply).
(3) Where a provision of the Companies Acts—
    (a) requires a resolution of a company, or of the members (or a class of members) of a company, and
    (b) does not specify what kind of resolution is required, what is required is an ordinary resolution unless the company's articles require a higher majority (or unanimity).
(4) Nothing in this Part affects any enactment or rule of law as to—
    (a) things done otherwise than by passing a resolution,
    (b) circumstances in which a resolution is or is not treated as having been passed, or
    (c) cases in which a person is precluded from alleging that a resolution has not been duly passed.

---

[16] CA 2006, ss 355–359.
[17] CA 2006, ss 360 and 361.
[18] See the Companies Act 2006 (Commencement No 1, Transitional Provisions and Savings) Order 2006, SI 2006/3.

COMMENTARY: 281 Resolutions

Subsection (1):

22.21 Section 281(1) is a new provision which relates only to a private company. It prescribes that a resolution of the members or a class of the members must be passed either as a written resolution in accordance with Chapter 2 or at a meeting of the members, subject to Chapter 3. Notwithstanding its prescriptive wording this provision is subject to subs (4) and the developed jurisprudence recognizing the validity of corporate acts passed informally by the unanimous consent of the members.

Subsection (2):

22.22 Section 281(2) relates only to a public company. Resolutions of a public company may be passed only at duly convened meetings of its members. There is no provision for written resolutions in relation to a public company; this is not surprising as there would be very real practical difficulties. The provision is new and has the effect of nullifying reg 53 of the 1985 Table A, providing for written resolutions of the members. Previously reg 53 could be incorporated in the articles of association of a public company. It would appear that the draftsman of new statutory provisions in the new legislation has overlooked the fact that many public companies constitute part of a group of companies and may be wholly-owned subsidiaries. (The transitional provisions dealing with this important area have been introduced.) In respect of such companies informal resolutions under reg 53 of the 1985 Table A were commonplace. Under the new legislation a formal meeting of members will be required to pass any resolution. This provision may have a substantial impact on corporate reconstruction procedures.

Subsection (3):

22.23 This provision is inserted into the legislation for clarification. It provides that where the statute is silent as to the kind of resolution of a company or of the members or of a class of the members that is required, what is needed is an ordinary resolution unless the company's articles of association specify a higher majority or unanimity.

Subsection (4)(a):

22.24 This provision (which is based on CA 1985, s 381C) preserves the well-established rules of law concerning the validity of corporate matters determined by the unanimous, informal consent of the members. The principle is that if all of the shareholders have given their informal consent the fact that there has not been a formal meeting to pass a resolution does not vitiate the decision that has been made. Of course, this principle is subject to exceptions in that it does not apply in circumstances where the statute itself requires the passing of a resolution of the company in general meeting.[19]

Subsection (4)(b):

This provision widens the category of exceptions contemplated by subs (4)(a) and preserves the existing law. There may be a challenge to the efficacy of a resolution, for example on the ground that its passing has been procured by the means of a tricky or misleading circular to the members.[20] **22.25**

Subsection (4)(c):

This provision preserves the existing rules precluding a member, who has attended and voted at a meeting, from alleging that a resolution has not been passed when no such objection was raised at the general meeting. Such a rule is usually to be found in the company's articles. In this context reference may be made to reg 58 of the 1985 Table A. **22.26**

Transitional provisions

The transitional provisions relating to s 281 are to be found in the Third Commencement Order, Sch 3, para 22. These provisions are discussed in the commentary below s 287. **22.27**

282 Ordinary resolutions

(1) An ordinary resolution of the members (or of a class of members) of a company means a resolution that is passed by a simple majority.

(2) A written resolution is passed by a simple majority if it is passed by members representing a simple majority of the total voting rights of eligible members (see Chapter 2).

(3) A resolution passed at a meeting on a show of hands is passed by a simple majority if it is passed by a simple majority of—

(a) the members who, being entitled to do so, vote in person on the resolution, and

(b) the persons who vote on the resolution as duly appointed proxies of members entitled to vote on it.

(4) A resolution passed on a poll taken at a meeting is passed by a simple majority if it is passed by members representing a simple majority of the total voting

---

[19] See *Re New Cedos Engineering Co Ltd* [1994] 1 BCLC 797 at 814 (Oliver J); *R W Peak (Kings Lynn) Ltd* [1998] 1 BCLC 193 (Lindsay J) and *Wright v Atlas Wright (Europe) Ltd* [1999] 2 BCLC 301(CA).

[20] See *Carruth v Imperial Chemical Industries Ltd* [1937] AC 707 at 769 (HL) affirming sub-nom *Re Imperial Chemical Industries Ltd* [1936] Ch 587 (CA); *CAS (Nominees) Ltd v Nottingham Forest FC plc* [2002] 1 BCLC 613 at para [72] (Hart J); see further Ch 3.

rights of members who (being entitled to do so) vote in person or by proxy on the resolution.

(5) Anything that may be done by ordinary resolution may also be done by special resolution.

COMMENTARY: 282 Ordinary resolutions

Overview

22.28 Section 282 attempts to clarify a number of well-known principles concerning ordinary resolutions. The section provides a definition of an ordinary resolution, whether of the members generally or of a class of the members, and whether as a written resolution or as a resolution passed at a meeting. A simple majority of over 50% is required.

Subsection (1):

22.29 Section 282(1) refers to an ordinary resolution passed at a general meeting or at a class meeting and must be contrasted with a written resolution which is dealt with in subs (2). A simple majority is a bare numerical majority of those present in person or by proxy and voting.

Subsection (2):

22.30 Section 282(2) is entirely new. In the past the legislation did not permit a written resolution to be passed save with unanimous consent of the members who at the date of the written resolution would have been entitled to attend and vote at a meeting.[21] The effect of this provision is that a written resolution may now be passed by a simple majority of the total voting rights of eligible members, being the members who would have been entitled to vote on the resolution on the circulation date of the resolution.[22]

Subsection (3):

22.31 This provides a statutory definition of a resolution that is passed at a meeting on a show of hands where a simple majority is required. In effect the requirement is merely to count the people present who are entitled to vote.

Subsection (4):

22.32 This provides a statutory definition of a resolution that is passed at a meeting by means of a poll where a simple majority is required.

---

[21] See CA 1985, s 381A.

[22] See CA 2006, ss 289 and 290.

Subsection (5):

This new provision is for the avoidance of doubt and makes it clear that, in accordance with the principle that the greater includes the lesser, anything that may be done by an ordinary resolution may also be done by means of a special resolution. For example, if a company were to seek to remove a director by means of a special resolution rather than by an ordinary resolution under the provisions of CA 2006, s 168 that resolution, if passed, would be equally effective. **22.33**

A conundrum?

It is well known that the articles of association of many companies confer a casting vote on the chairman to be exercised in the event of an equality of votes, whether on a show of hands or on a poll. An example of such a provision is to be found in reg 50 of the 1985 Table A. Articles of association also frequently provide that the chairman, or some other director, should preside as chairman of a general meeting. On occasion the chairman of the meeting is himself not a member of the company; indeed reg 50 of the 1985 Table A assumes that this may be the case.[23] The statutory definition of an ordinary resolution in subss (3) and (4) appears not to take account of this situation. It seems to assume that the chairman exercising the casting vote on a show of hands or on a poll will always be a member. It is arguable that if the chairman is not a member of the company the resolution passed by the use of the casting vote will not constitute an ordinary resolution within the meaning of s 282. The resolution will however be effective under the articles of association of the company as a decision of the shareholders in general meeting. In the circumstances, consideration should be given to the provisions of the relevant articles of association of existing companies. Where those articles of association permit the chairman of a meeting to be a director or other person who is not a member to exercise a casting vote in the event of an equality of votes, they should be amended to remove this possibility. **22.34**

Resolution by means of the Fifth Commencement Order

The Fifth Commencement Order, Sch 5, para 2(5) attempts to resolve this conundrum (at least in part) by providing that where, immediately before 1 October 2007, a provision in a company's articles conferring on a chairman a casting vote in the event of an equality of votes on an ordinary resolution that provision will continue to have effect notwithstanding ss 281(3) and 282. Indeed, if that provision has been removed by a subsequent alteration of the articles the company is **22.35**

[23] Regulation 50 provides: ' In the case of an equality of votes, whether on a show of hands or on a poll, the chairman shall be entitled to a casting vote in addition to any other vote that he may have.' See Part 4 (below).

permitted at any time to restore it and it is deemed to have full effect notwithstanding ss 281(3) and 282.

Transitional provisions

22.36 The transitional provisions relating to s 282 are to be found in the Third Commencement Order, Sch 3, para 22. These provisions are discussed in the commentary below s 287.

283 Special resolutions

(1) A special resolution of the members (or of a class of members) of a company means a resolution passed by a majority of not less than 75%.

(2) A written resolution is passed by a majority of not less than 75% if it is passed by members representing not less than 75% of the total voting rights of eligible members (see Chapter 2).

(3) Where a resolution of a private company is passed as a written resolution—
  (a) the resolution is not a special resolution unless it stated that it was proposed as a special resolution, and
  (b) if the resolution so stated, it may only be passed as a special resolution.

(4) A resolution passed at a meeting on a show of hands is passed by a majority of not less than 75% if it is passed by not less than 75% of—
  (a) the members who, being entitled to do so, vote in person on the resolution, and
  (b) the persons who vote on the resolution as duly appointed proxies of members entitled to vote on it.

(5) A resolution passed on a poll taken at a meeting is passed by a majority of not less than 75% if it is passed by members representing not less than 75% of the total voting rights of the members who (being entitled to do so) vote in person or by proxy on the resolution.

(6) Where a resolution is passed at a meeting—
  (a) the resolution is not a special resolution unless the notice of the meeting included the text of the resolution and specified the intention to propose the resolution as a special resolution, and
  (b) if the notice of the meeting so specified, the resolution may only be passed as a special resolution.

COMMENTARY: 283 Special resolutions

Overview

22.37 Section 283 provides a definition of a special resolution, whether passed by the members as a whole or, where the share capital is divided into different classes, by a class of the members. The definition applies whether the special resolution is passed as a written resolution[24] or as a resolution passed at a general meeting.

---

[24] This applies only to a private company.

Much of the new section reflects the existing case law.[25] The main difference from the existing definition in CA 1985, s 378(2) is that there is no longer a requirement for 21 days' notice where a special resolution is to be passed at a meeting.

It is important to note that the concept of an 'extraordinary resolution' has now disappeared from the law,[26] at least so far as new companies are concerned.[27] A special resolution of the members or of a class of the members requires a majority of not less than 75% of those present and voting.

Subsection (3): Additional requirements

If a resolution is proposed as a special resolution, there is a requirement to say so, either in the text of the written resolution text or in the notice convening the relevant meeting. Where a resolution is proposed as a special resolution, it can only be passed as such. **22.38**

Subsections (4) and (5): The required majority

Subsection (4) provides that such a resolution may be passed on a show of hands if it is passed by not less than 75% of the members present who vote in person or by proxy. By subs (5) a special resolution will be passed on a poll taken at a meeting if it is passed by members representing not less than 75% of the members who vote in person or by proxy on the resolution. **22.39**

Subsection (6): Notice requirements

Note should be taken of the fact that a resolution will only take the form of a special resolution if (a) the notice of the meeting included the text of the proposed special resolution and (b) the notice specified the intention to propose the resolution as a special resolution. If the notice contains the requirements stipulated above the resolution may only be passed as a special resolution. Accordingly, it is not permissible to treat a failed special resolution, but one that attains more than a simple majority, as an effective ordinary resolution.[28] **22.40**

Private companies

With regard to private companies, a special resolution may now take a written form by virtue of the provisions of subs (2). Again, the special resolution is required to be passed by members representing not less than 75% of the total voting rights **22.41**

---

[25] See the important decision of Slade J in *Re Moorgate Mercantile Holdings Ltd* [1980] 1 WLR 227 [1980] 1 All ER 40.

[26] See CA 1985, s 378(1).

[27] See the note relating to the transitional provisions in respect of existing companies.

[28] For a fuller discussion of the different types of resolution and their amendment see Ch 11.

of eligible members.[29] In addition, for a written resolution of a private company to be effective as a special resolution certain formalities must be met: (1) it must be stated that the resolution is proposed as a special resolution and (2) if the resolution is so stated, it may only be passed as a special resolution. Once again there is no scope for a failed written special resolution that has been put forward as a special resolution taking effect as a written ordinary resolution if it fails to achieve the prescribed 75% majority, but more than a simple majority.

Transitional provisions

22.42 The transitional provisions relating to s 283 are to be found in the Third Commencement Order, Sch 3, para 22. These provisions are discussed in the commentary below s 287.

284 Votes: general rules

(1) On a vote on a written resolution—
  (a) in the case of a company having a share capital, every member has one vote in respect of each share or each £10 of stock held by him, and
  (b) in any other case, every member has one vote.
(2) On a vote on a resolution on a show of hands at a meeting—
  (a) every member present in person has one vote, and
  (b) every proxy present who has been duly appointed by a member entitled to vote on the resolution has one vote.
(3) On a vote on a resolution on a poll taken at a meeting—
  (a) in the case of a company having a share capital, every member has one vote in respect of each share or each £10 of stock held by him, and
  (b) in any other case, a member has one vote.
(4) The provisions of this section have effect subject to any provision of the company's articles.

COMMENTARY: 284 Votes: general rules

Overview

22.43 CA 2006, ss 284–287 contain a set of rules governing voting on resolutions considered at general meetings and in respect of written resolutions. These provisions have effect subject to any contrary provisions contained in a company's articles of association. General rules on votes of members taken by written resolution, on a show of hands at a meeting or on a poll taken at a meeting are set out in s 284. These provisions are based on CA 1985, s 370 and the relevant regulations in Table A. Section 284(4) allows these general rules to be varied by the articles of association of a company. It is to be anticipated that many draftsmen will wish to vary some of these provisions. For a detailed account of voting procedures see Chapter 9.

[29] See CA 2006, ss 289 and 290.

Subsection (1): Voting on a written resolution

In respect of a written resolution in a private company having a share capital, every member has one vote in respect of each share or each £10 of stock held by him. Stock is a very rare form of capital nowadays and it is surprising to find it retained in the provisions of CA 2006.[30] In every other case, such as a company limited by guarantee, every member has one vote. This provision takes effect subject to the company's articles of association which can provide otherwise. **22.44**

Subsection (2): Voting on a show of hands

A similar provision gives each member present in person and every duly appointed proxy for such member, one vote on a show of hands at a general meeting. Again this is subject to any contrary provisions in the articles of association of a company. The surprising effect of this provision is that where a member appoints more than one proxy in the exercise of his rights under s 324 each of those proxies have a vote on a show of hands. This may lead to considerable abuse in that a determined registered member may split his shares among several proxies, each of whom would be entitled to speak at the meeting[31] and vote on a show of hands thereby increasing what would otherwise have been the single vote of the member. Companies may consider that this is not an appropriate method of voting at general meetings and may wish to introduce an article ensuring that multiple proxies may only have one vote between them on a show of hands. However, the operation of such an article may cause difficulties for the chairman who might have to decide which of several proxies was the person entitled to vote. In any event it is suggested that whenever the outcome of voting on a show of hands may be determined by the votes of holders of multiple proxies or the outcome of the vote may be close the chairman should exercise his discretion and demand a poll. **22.45**

Where the same person has been appointed as a proxy by several members that proxy will have one vote on a show of hands by virtue of s 284(2)(b). Such a proxy is not entitled on a show of hands to one vote for every member for whom he acts.[32] The rule is that one human being is entitled to one vote on a show of hands. **22.46**

Subsection (3): Voting on a poll taken at a meeting

This provision deals with voting on a poll at a meeting. In the case of a company having a share capital the statute provides for one vote per share or for each £10 of stock. Every member similarly has one vote in every other case, including a company limited by guarantee. Again this is subject to the company's articles of association. **22.47**

---

[30] CA 2006 repeals the power to convert shares into stock. By s 620 stock may be reconverted into paid-up share capital of any nominal value if authority is given by ordinary resolution.

[31] See CA 2006, s 324(1).

[32] See Ch 9.

Subsection (4): The impact of the company's articles of association

22.48 This provision in s 284 allows these rules of general application to be varied by express provisions of a company's articles of association. Accordingly, articles of association will continue to contain tailor-made provisions designed to meet the special requirements of the particular company.

Transitional provisions

22.49 The transitional provisions relating to s 284 are to be found in the Third Commencement Order, Sch 3, para 22. These provisions are discussed in the commentary below s 287.

> **285 Votes: specific requirements**
>
> (1) Where a member entitled to vote on a resolution has appointed one proxy only, and the company's articles provide that the proxy has fewer votes in a vote on a resolution on a show of hands taken at a meeting than the member would have if he were present in person—
> (a) the provision about how many votes the proxy has on a show of hands is void, and
> (b) the proxy has the same number of votes on a show of hands as the member who appointed him would have if he were present at the meeting.
>
> (2) Where a member entitled to vote on a resolution has appointed more than one proxy, subsection (1) applies as if the references to the proxy were references to the proxies taken together.
>
> (3) In relation to a resolution required or authorised by an enactment, if a private company's articles provide that a member has a different number of votes in relation to a resolution when it is passed as a written resolution and when it is passed on a poll taken at a meeting—
> (a) the provision about how many votes a member has in relation to the resolution passed on a poll is void, and
> (b) a member has the same number of votes in relation to the resolution when it is passed on a poll as he has when it is passed as a written resolution.

COMMENTARY: 285 Votes: specific requirements

Overview

22.50 Section 285 sets out specific statutory requirements concerning the votes of members. These provisions may *not* be overridden by provisions in a company's articles of association. This section invalidates provisions in a company's articles of association which adversely discriminate against a proxy voting on a resolution on a show of hands at a meeting. The section also invalidates a member having a different number of votes on a written resolution when compared with a resolution passed on a poll.

Subsection (1): Proxies

Under subs (1) the proxy must always be afforded the same number of votes on a show of hands as the member who appointed him would have if he were present in person at the relevant general meeting of the company. This provision ensures that a company's articles of association do not disadvantage or otherwise discriminate against a member who is unable to attend in person and votes by appointing a proxy. **22.51**

Subsection (2): Multiple proxies

The same rules as are found in subs (1) apply where a member who is entitled to vote at a meeting has appointed more than one proxy in respect of his shareholding. The company's articles of association must not disadvantage that member. **22.52**

Subsection (3): Written resolutions of private companies

This provision only applies to a private company and makes new provision about voting rights on written resolutions. In this instance, in relation to a resolution required or authorized by a statute a member has the same number of votes when the resolution is passed on a poll as he has when it is passed as a written resolution. An example of the type of resolution covered by subs (3) is an ordinary resolution required to remove a director before the expiration of his period of office under CA 2006, s 168(1). **22.53**

Transitional provisions

The transitional provisions relating to s 285 are to be found in the Third Commencement Order, Sch 3, para 22. These provisions are discussed in the commentary below s 287. **22.54**

286 Votes of joint holders of shares

(1) In the case of joint holders of shares of a company, only the vote of the senior holder who votes (and any proxies duly authorised by him) may be counted by the company.
(2) For the purposes of this section, the senior holder of a share is determined by the order in which the names of the joint holders appear in the register of members.
(3) Subsections (1) and (2) have effect subject to any provision of the company's articles.

COMMENTARY: 286 Votes of joint holders of shares

Overview

Quite often shares will be registered in the names of more than one person as joint holders. Such a situation commonly arises where shares are held by executors or administrators. In such circumstances provision has to be made for deciding **22.55** which one of the joint holders of shares is entitled to exercise the votes attached to those shares at a meeting of the company. Plainly, although more than one person may have ownership rights to the shares that are registered in joint names, that tranche of shares cannot receive a greater enfranchisement than would occur if the shares happened to be registered in the name of a sole shareholder.

Subsections (1) and (2): The senior holder

22.56 Section 286 provides that where shares are registered in the name of more than one person only the vote of the senior holder, or a proxy appointed by him, as shown in the company's register of members may be counted by the company. The senior holder of the shares is determined by the order in which the names of the joint holders appear in a company's register of members. Section 286 enacts a provision that was commonly found in articles of association including reg 55 of the 1985 Table A[33] but was not found in CA 1985. The effect of this provision is that the company must accept only the proxy that has been duly authorized by the senior holder, to the exclusion of the votes of the other joint holders. It is to be noted that the subsection refers to the '... senior holder who votes ...'. This need not be the first named holder of shares in the register of members but could be the most senior who in fact votes or authorizes a proxy.

Subsection (3): The impact of the company's articles of association

22.57 Once again the provisions of s 286 take effect subject to anything to the contrary in a company's articles of association. It is desirable both for the efficient and effective conduct of a meeting that companies follow this sensible and practical provision.

Transitional provisions

22.58 The transitional provisions relating to s 286 are to be found in the Third Commencement Order, Sch 3, para 22. These provisions are discussed in the commentary below s 287.

> **287 Saving for provisions of articles as to determination of entitlement to vote**
> Nothing in this Chapter affects—
> (a) any provision of a company's articles—
> (i) requiring an objection to a person's entitlement to vote on a resolution to be made in accordance with the articles, and
> (ii) for the determination of any such objection to be final and conclusive, or

[33] See the commentary on reg 55 in Part 4 below.

(b) the grounds on which such a determination may be questioned in legal proceedings.

COMMENTARY: 287 Saving for provisions of articles as to determination of entitlement to vote

Section 287 contains a new statutory provision. This section preserves the effect of the provisions contained in a company's articles of association governing the requisite procedure that is to be followed for objecting to a person's right to vote on a resolution. It also preserves any provision in a company's articles of association stating that the determination of any such objection is final and conclusive. Regulation 58 of the 1985 Table A[34] provides that any objection to the qualification of any voter must be taken at the meeting or at any adjourned meeting at which the vote objected to is tendered, and every vote not disallowed at the meeting is valid. Regulation 58 also states, in standard form, that any objection should be referred to the chairman of the meeting whose decision in relation to this issue is final and conclusive.[35] **22.59**

Section 287(b) preserves the grounds on which such a determination (invariably made by the chairman of the meeting) may be questioned in legal proceedings. As may be seen from the cases cited at n 35 below these grounds are very limited and are usually restricted to cases involving fraud. The courts have held that questions of this nature should be determined in a summary manner and without the necessity of legal proceedings. The articles of association of a company should be, and are usually, framed in such a way as to ensure that this is the case. **22.60**

Transitional provisions on ss 281–287

The Third Commencement Order (as amended) contains the following transitional provisions in respect of CA 2006, ss 281–287. **22.61**

22. General provisions about resolutions (ss. 281 to 287)—

(1) Sections 281 to 287 of the Companies Act 2006 (general provisions about resolutions), apply—
  (a) to written resolutions to which sections 288 to 300 of that Act apply (see paragraph 24);
  (b) to resolutions (other than written resolutions)—
    (i) of which notice is given on or after 1st October 2007, or
    (ii) that are proposed at a meeting of which notice is given on or after 1st October 2007, other than a meeting convened in pursuance of a requisition made under section 368 or 376 of the 1985 Act or Article 376 or 384 of the 1986 Order made before that date.

[34] See the commentary on reg 58 in Part 4 below.

[35] See *Wall v London and Northern Assets Corporation* [1899] 1 Ch 550 (North J); *Colonial Gold Reef Ltd v Free State Rand Ltd* [1914] 1 Ch 382 (Sargant J); *Wall v Exchange Investment Corporation Ltd* [1926] Ch 13 (CA).

(2) The provisions of the 1985 Act or 1986 Order continue to apply to resolutions (other than written resolutions)—
   (a) of which notice is given before 1st October 2007, or
   (b) that are proposed at a meeting—
      (i) of which notice was given before 1st October 2007, or
      (ii) that is convened in pursuance of a requisition under section 368 or 376 of the 1985 Act or Article 376 or 384 of the 1986 Order made before that date.

(3) The provisions referred to in sub-paragraph (2) include—
section 370(6) of the 1985 Act or Article 378(6) of the 1986 Order (voting entitlement of members); and
section 378 of the 1985 Act or Article 386 of the 1986 Order (extraordinary and special resolutions).

(4) Where notice of a meeting is given over more than one day, it is treated for the purposes of this paragraph as given on the first of those days.

(5) Where copies of a requisition are deposited on more than one day, the references in this paragraph to the day on which the requisition is made shall be read as references to the first day on which the copies deposited are sufficient to require the company to act.

23. —[1] Any reference to an extraordinary resolution in a provision—
   (a) of a company's memorandum or articles, or
   (b) of a contract,

continues to have effect and shall continue to be construed in accordance with section 378 of the 1985 Act or Article 386 of the 1986 Order as if that section or Article had not been repealed.

[(2) Chapter 3 of Part 3 of the Companies Act 2006 (resolutions affecting a company's constitution) applies to any such resolution.][36]

[23A—(1) This paragraph applies where, immediately before 1st October 2007, the articles of a company provided that in the event of equality of votes on an ordinary resolution, whether on a show of hands or on a poll, the chairman should have a casting vote in addition to any other vote that the chairman might have.

(2) If that provision has not been removed by a subsequent alteration of the articles, it continues to have effect notwithstanding sections 281(3) and 282.

(3) If that provision has been removed by a subsequent alteration of the articles, the company may at any time restore that provision, which shall have effect notwithstanding sections 281(3) and 282.][37]

COMMENTARY: General provisions about resolutions (ss. 281–287)

22.62 The transitional provisions set out above make it clear that the new legislation applies only to resolutions of which notice was given on or after 1 October 2007 or are proposed at a meeting at which notice was given on or after that date. The only exception is a resolution proposed at a meeting convened in pursuance of a members' requisition under CA 1985, s 368 (members' requisition of an extraordinary

---

[36] Inserted by Fifth Commencement Order, Sch 5, para 2(4).
[37] Inserted by Fifth Commencement Order, Sch 5, para 2(5).

general meeting) or under CA 1985, s 376 (circulation of a members' resolution following a written requisition of members) made before 1 October 2007.

Sections 281–287 also apply to written resolutions for private companies circulated on or after 1 October 2007 pursuant to CA 2006, ss 288–300 (see below). **22.63**

The old law contained in CA 1985 continues to apply to resolutions (other than written resolutions) of which notice was given before 1 October 2007, or that were proposed at a meeting of which notice was given before that date or that was convened pursuant to a members' requisition under CA 1985, s 368 or 376. **22.64**

The transitional provisions in para 23 related to extraordinary resolutions. References to extraordinary resolutions may be found in an existing memorandum or articles or a contract, although no such concept is referred to in CA 2006. Paragraph 23 ensures that such provisions continue to have effect and are to be construed in accordance with CA 1985, s 378 as if that section had not been repealed. In addition, such resolutions must continue to be filed with the Registrar of Companies in accordance with CA 2006, ss 29 and 30. **22.65**

Paragraph 23A of the Third Commencement Order was introduced to deal with the problem relating to articles of existing companies that contained a provision that conferred a casting vote on the chairman of a general meeting for use in the event of an equality of votes on an ordinary resolution. Such provisions continue to have effect notwithstanding CA 2006, ss 281(3) and 282. If those provisions have been deleted from the articles they may now be restored at any time. **22.66**

CHAPTER 2
WRITTEN RESOLUTIONS
General provisions about written resolutions

288 Written resolutions of private companies

(1) In the Companies Acts a 'written resolution' means a resolution of a private company proposed and passed in accordance with this Chapter.

(2) The following may not be passed as a written resolution—

(a) a resolution under section 168 removing a director before the expiration of his period of office;

(b) [a resolution under section 391 of the Companies Act 1985 or Article 399 of the Companies (Northern Ireland) Order 1986][38] removing an auditor before the expiration of his term of office.

(c) [a resolution under section 80A of the Companies Act 1985 or Article 90A of the Companies (Northern Ireland) Order 1986 revoking, varying or renewing the authority of directors to allot securities].[39]

[38] Inserted by the Third Commencement Order, Sch 1, para 13(2)(a).

[39] Inserted by the Third Commencement Order, Sch 1, para 13(2)(b).

(3) A resolution may be proposed as a written resolution—
(a) by the directors of a private company (see section 291), or
(b) by the members of a private company (see sections 292 to 295).

(4) References in enactments passed or made before this Chapter comes into force to—
(a) a resolution of a company in general meeting, or
(b) a resolution of a meeting of a class of members of the company, have effect as if they included references to a written resolution of the members, or of a class of members, of a private company (as appropriate).

(5) A written resolution of a private company has effect as if passed (as the case may be)—
(a) by the company in general meeting, or
(b) by a meeting of a class of members of the company, and references in enactments passed or made before this section comes into force to a meeting at which a resolution is passed or to members voting in favour of a resolution shall be construed accordingly.

[(6) A written resolution under any of the provisions of the Companies Act 1985 or the Companies (Northern Ireland) Order 1986 mentioned in sections 300A and 300D is not effective unless the procedural requirements specified in those sections are complied with].[40]

COMMENTARY: 288 Written resolutions of private companies

Overview

22.67 CA 2006, Part 13, Chapter 2, which comprises ss 288–300 (inclusive) concerns written resolutions passed by members of private companies. The prescribed statutory procedure in Chapter 2 is *not* available to members of public companies, and it would seem that any article containing such a provision may no longer be relied upon as CA 2006 does not permit a written resolution in relation to a public company. The provisions of Part 13, Chapter 2 replace the present rules on written resolutions of private companies. Unlike the provisions relating to written resolutions contained in CA 1985 the new legislative requirements of CA 2006 (see ss 282 and 283) for effective written resolutions do not require unanimity and accordingly are more detailed than CA 1985, s 381A–381C.

Subsection (2): Exclusion of certain resolutions from the written resolution procedure

22.68 It is important to note that two important ordinary resolutions may not be passed by means of a written resolution. By virtue of s 288(2) a resolution under s 168 to remove a director from office before the expiration of his period of office[41] and a resolution under s 510 to remove an auditor before the expiration of his term of

[40] Inserted by the Third Commencement Order, Sch 1, para 13(3).
[41] This section is derived from CA 1985, s 303.

office are not capable of being passed by way of the written resolution procedure. In this respect the new legislation reproduces the two exceptions that were provided for in CA 1985, Sch 15A, Part 1. Apart from these two exemptions a private company may pass any other resolutions under the prescribed written resolution procedure.

Subsection (3): Who may propose a written resolution?

Two categories of person can propose that a resolution is passed as a written resolution. In the first instance the directors of a private company may make such a proposal under s 291. Secondly, the members of a private company may propose a resolution to be passed as a written resolution provided that they comply with the procedure that is prescribed in ss 292–295 (inclusive). **22.69**

Subsection (4):

Subsection (4) is somewhat curious in that within the main body of the new legislation provision has been made for transitional provisions relating to antecedent legislation. Subsection (4) provides that references in enactments passed or made before CA 2006, Part 13, Chapter 2 comes into force[42] to a resolution of the company in general meeting or a resolution of a class of members have effect as if they included references to a written resolution of members or of a class of members of a private company. **22.70**

Subsection (5):

Under subs (5) a written resolution of a private company has effect as if passed by the company in general meeting or by a meeting of a class of the members. The subsection goes on to refer to enactments passed or made before subs (5) comes into force and provides that references in those enactments to meetings at which a resolution is passed or to members voting in favour of a resolution have to be construed in accordance with the new provisions relating to written resolutions. **22.71**

Subsection (6):

This subsection was introduced into the legislataion by Sch 1, para 13(3) to the Third Commencement Order. It cross-refers to four additional sections that have been added to CA 2006 to deal with the transitional application of a number of important procedural requirements. Those sections (which are numbered 300A–300D) will be referred to below. **22.72**

---

[42] That is, on 1 October 2007.

Transitional provisions

22.73 The transitional provisions relating to s 288 are to be found in the Third Commencement Order, Sch 3, para 24. These provisions are discussed in the commentary below s 300D.

289 Eligible members

(1) In relation to a resolution proposed as a written resolution of a private company, the eligible members are the members who would have been entitled to vote on the resolution on the circulation date of the resolution (see section 290).

(2) If the persons entitled to vote on a written resolution change during the course of the day that is the circulation date of the resolution, the eligible members are the persons entitled to vote on the resolution at the time that the first copy of the resolution is sent or submitted to a member for his agreement.

COMMENTARY: 289 Eligible members

22.74 Provision is made under s 289 for the qualifying eligibility requirements of members of private companies who may participate in the written resolution procedure. Where a resolution is proposed as a written resolution of a private company the eligible members are the members who would have been entitled to vote on the resolution on the circulation date of that resolution. The circulation date is defined in s 290 (see below).

Subsection (2):

22.75 This provision is designed to ensure that the same shares cannot be voted more than once on the same written resolution. In the event that the persons entitled to vote on a written resolution change during the course of the day that is the circulation date of the resolution, the legislation provides in subs (2) that the eligible members are the persons entitled to vote on the resolution at the time the first copy of the resolution is sent or submitted to a member for his agreement. Although it is not free from doubt, this should be a single point in time.

Transitional provisions

22.76 The transitional provisions relating to s 289 are to be found in the Third Commencement Order, Sch 3, para 24. These provisions are discussed in the commentary below s 300D.

Circulation of written resolutions

290 Circulation date

References in this Part to the circulation date of a written resolution are to the date on which copies of it are sent or submitted to members in accordance with this Chapter (or if copies are sent or submitted to members on different days, to the first of those days).

COMMENTARY: 290 Circulation date

Section 290 defines the circulation date of a written resolution. The circulation date is the date on which copies of the written resolution are sent or submitted to members in accordance with the provisions of Part 13, Chapter 2. If copies are sent or submitted to members on different days, then the circulation date is the first of those days. As a consequence of s 290, those involved with the administration of a private company will have to take care to ensure that accurate records are kept of the time at which written resolutions and documentation associated therewith are circulated to the members of their companies. **22.77**

Transitional provisions

The transitional provisions relating to s 290 are to be found in the Third Commencement Order, Sch 3, para 24. These provisions are discussed in the commentary below s 300D. **22.78**

291 Circulation of written resolutions proposed by directors

(1) This section applies to a resolution proposed as a written resolution by the directors of the company.

(2) The company must send or submit a copy of the resolution to every eligible member.

(3) The company must do so—

  (a) by sending copies at the same time (so far as reasonably practicable) to all eligible members in hard copy form, in electronic form or by means of a website, or

  (b) if it is possible to do so without undue delay, by submitting the same copy to each eligible member in turn (or different copies to each of a number of eligible members in turn), or by sending copies to some members in accordance with paragraph (a) and submitting a copy or copies to other members in accordance with paragraph (b).

(4) The copy of the resolution must be accompanied by a statement informing the member—

  (a) how to signify agreement to the resolution (see section 296), and

  (b) as to the date by which the resolution must be passed if it is not to lapse (see section 297).

(5) In the event of default in complying with this section, an offence is committed by every officer of the company who is in default.

(6) A person guilty of an offence under this section is liable—

  (a) on conviction on indictment, to a fine;

  (b) on summary conviction, to a fine not exceeding the statutory maximum.

(7) The validity of the resolution, if passed, is not affected by a failure to comply with this section.

COMMENTARY: 291 Circulation of written resolutions proposed by directors

Overview

22.79 CA 2006, s 291 deals with the process of the circulation of written resolutions that are proposed by directors of private companies. The private company in question is under an obligation to send or submit a copy of the proposed written resolution to every eligible member. In order to comply with this requirement the private company will either send the proposed written resolution to all eligible members at the same time or, provided that it can be done without undue delay, submit the same copy of the resolution to each eligible member in turn or a combination of these methods. Consequently, a private company is permitted to circulate a document or email rather than sending out several copies of the proposed written resolution.

22.80 It is to be noted that the right to be sent a proposed written resolution under s 291 may be conferred by a company's articles on another person nominated by the member in accordance with s 145. This provision is examined in Chapter 10.

Subsection (3): Method of notification to members

22.81 How a company sends the proposed written resolution to its members is provided for in subs (3). The company must send copies at the same time so far as reasonably practicable to all eligible members in hard copy form or in electronic form or by means of a company website. As an alternative, if the company is able to do so, and is able to do so without undue delay, the company may submit the same copy of the written resolution to each eligible member in turn, or different copies to each of a number of eligible members in turn by sending copies to some members in accordance with para (a) and submitting a copy or copies to other members in accordance with para (b). This latter provision enables a company to pass around the same document or forward the same email to the members in turn.

Subsection (4): Guidance statement

22.82 Under subs (4) two important pieces of information must be imparted to the eligible members when they receive the copy of the proposed written resolution. First, the private company must inform the eligible members how to signify their agreement to the written resolution; this is dealt with in greater detail in s 296. In addition, the private company must inform the eligible members as to the date by which the resolution must be passed if it is not to fall into lapse under s 297.

Subsections (5) and (6): Offences

22.83 Subsection (5) creates a criminal offence which can be committed by the officers of a private company who fail to comply with the mandatory requirements of s 291(2), (3) and (4). The penalties applicable to officers who are found guilty of such an offence are set out in subs (6).

Subsection (7): Saving

However, notwithstanding any failure by any officer of a private company to comply with the mandatory provisions of s 291, the validity of the written resolution if it is passed is unaffected by any such failure to comply with the prescribed statutory process. **22.84**

Transitional provisions

The transitional provisions relating to s 291 are to be found in the Third Commencement Order, Sch 3, para 24. These provisions are discussed in the commentary below s 300D. **22.85**

292 Members' power to require circulation of written resolution

(1) The members of a private company may require the company to circulate a resolution that may properly be moved and is proposed to be moved as a written resolution.

(2) Any resolution may properly be moved as a written resolution unless—
- (a) it would, if passed, be ineffective (whether by reason of inconsistency with any enactment or the company's constitution or otherwise),
- (b) it is defamatory of any person, or
- (c) it is frivolous or vexatious.

(3) Where the members require a company to circulate a resolution they may require the company to circulate with it a statement of not more than 1,000 words on the subject matter of the resolution.

(4) A company is required to circulate the resolution and any accompanying statement once it has received requests that it do so from members representing not less than the requisite percentage of the total voting rights of all members entitled to vote on the resolution.

(5) The 'requisite percentage' is 5% or such lower percentage as is specified for this purpose in the company's articles.

(6) A request—
- (a) may be in hard copy form or in electronic form,
- (b) must identify the resolution and any accompanying statement, and
- (c) must be authenticated by the person or persons making it.

COMMENTARY: 292 Members' power to require circulation of written resolution

Overview

In addition to the ability of directors of a private company to propose a resolution in a written format, the members of a private company may require the company to circulate a resolution that is capable of being passed at a meeting and where they propose it to be moved as a written resolution. The act of circulation is to be carried out by the company itself. The duty arises when requests have been received **22.86** by the private company concerned from the requisite percentage of members defined in subss (4) and (5).

Subsection (2): Limits

22.87 This provision sets out the limits on the types of resolution that may be moved as a written resolution. They are restrictions which are intended to prevent the abuse of this statutory power. Any resolution can be proposed and moved as a resolution unless it would, if passed, be ineffective, whether because of inconsistency with any statutory provision or with the company's constitution[43] or otherwise or it is defamatory of any person or it is frivolous or vexatious.

Ineffective resolution

22.88 A resolution if passed would be ineffective if, for instance, it sought to achieve by an ordinary resolution something which required the passing of a special resolution. A common example of a resolution being ineffective is where such a resolution attempts to instruct the board of directors as to how they should exercise their powers of management of the company where there has been a lawful delegation to the board of directors of such management powers under the articles of association. Such an attempted instruction must take the form of a special resolution in order for it to have legal effect.[44] This legal distinction remains a trap for the unwary. Accordingly, great care should be taken in the formulation of any resolution when it is proposed by members of a company.

Subsection (2)(b) and (2)(c):

22.89 Deciding whether a written resolution falls within the ambit of s 292(2)(b) or (c) may give rise to difficult issues and great care should be taken by the company in reaching a conclusion on either of these issues. If a company is unsure whether a member's proposal to circulate a written resolution is defamatory of any person it will be well advised to take appropriate professional advice.[45] Another legitimate reason for not circulating a resolution that is proposed as a written resolution by members is if the proposed written resolution is 'frivolous or vexatious'. These two words are not defined in CA 2006 for the purposes of this section. The words 'frivolous and vexatious' have been used in other legal contexts and are familiar to lawyers, particularly to those involved with litigation in the context of applications

[43] The constitution of a company is defined in CA 2006, s 17 as follows:

'Unless the context otherwise requires, references in the Companies Acts to a company's constitution include—

(a) the company's articles, and

(b) any resolutions and agreements to which Chapter 3 applies (see Section 29).'

[44] See *Automatic Self-Cleansing Filter Syndicate Co Ltd v Cunninghame* [1906] 2 Ch 34 at 43 (CA); *Quinn & Axtens Ltd v Salmon* [1909] AC 442 (HL).

[45] See also the commentary in respect of s 295(1).

to strike out proceedings that constitute an abuse of process. Whether any assistance will be derived from cases where the meaning of the words 'frivolous and vexatious' has been discussed in a different legal context remains to be seen. It is suggested that a resolution may be deemed to be 'frivolous' if it is one that lacks sense or any serious purpose. The term 'vexatious' on the other hand may properly be applied to a resolution which has the characteristics of being troublesome, or burdensome or is proposed for no proper purpose connected with the company.

Subsection (3): Members' statement

Where the members of a private company exercise their statutory right under s 292 they are also entitled to have circulated with the proposed written resolution a statement of not more than 1,000 words on the subject matter of the resolution. If members try to persuade the company to circulate a document that contains a few more words than the stipulated 1,000 words it is suggested that it would be inopportune and perhaps unwise for a company to decline to circulate the statement. However, a line has to be drawn and a company would be well within its rights to refuse to circulate a statement that far exceeds the stipulated maximum number of words. Quite where the line is drawn will have to be decided after consideration of the particular facts of each case. It is important to note that by s 295 the company has power to apply to the court for an order that it is not required to circulate a members' statement where the court is satisfied that the rights conferred by ss 292 and 293 are being abused (see below). **22.90**

Subsections (4) and (5): The requisite percentage

A company is required to circulate a written resolution and an accompanying statement from its members provided it has had a request to do so from members who represent not less than 5% of the total voting rights of all members entitled to vote on the resolution or such lower percentage as is specified for this purpose in the company's articles of association. A sole member who controls 5% of the total voting rights of all members will be able to invoke this statutory provision without recourse to assistance from other shareholders. It is suggested that for practical reasons the 5% threshold that is provided for in the legislation should not be reduced to a lower figure by any provision in a company's articles of association. If the figure is reduced there is a real danger that the company may become inundated with large numbers of written resolutions from members which may be to the detriment of the efficient management of the affairs of the company. **22.91**

Subsection (6): Form of request

The format of the request that is received from members must comply with three provisions of subs (6). First, it may be in hard copy form or in electronic form, secondly it must identify the resolution and any accompanying statement and thirdly **22.92** it must be authenticated by the person or persons making the request. By virtue of CA 2006, s 1146 a document in hard copy form is sufficiently authenticated if it is signed by the person sending or supplying it. For a document in electronic form CA 2006, s 1146(3) requires the identity of the sender to be confirmed in the manner specified by the company or, in default, (where no such manner has been so specified) if the communication contains or is accompanied by the statement of the sender and the company has no reason to doubt the truth of that statement.

Transitional provisions

22.93 The transitional provisions relating to s 292 are to be found in the Third Commencement Order, Sch 3, para 24. These provisions are discussed in the commentary below s 300D.

293 Circulation of written resolution proposed by members

(1) A company that is required under section 292 to circulate a resolution must send or submit to every eligible member—
  (a) a copy of the resolution, and
  (b) a copy of any accompanying statement.

This is subject to section 294(2) (deposit or tender of sum in respect of expenses of circulation) and section 295 (application not to circulate members' statement).

(2) The company must do so—
  (a) by sending copies at the same time (so far as reasonably practicable) to all eligible members in hard copy form, in electronic form or by means of a website, or
  (b) if it is possible to do so without undue delay, by submitting the same copy to each eligible member in turn (or different copies to each of a number of eligible members in turn), or by sending copies to some members in accordance with paragraph (a) and submitting a copy or copies to other members in accordance with paragraph (b).

(3) The company must send or submit the copies (or, if copies are sent or submitted to members on different days, the first of those copies) not more than 21 days after it becomes subject to the requirement under section 292 to circulate the resolution.

(4) The copy of the resolution must be accompanied by guidance as to—
  (a) how to signify agreement to the resolution (see section 296), and
  (b) the date by which the resolution must be passed if it is not to lapse (see section 297).

(5) In the event of default in complying with this section, an offence is committed by every officer of the company who is in default.

(6) A person guilty of an offence under this section is liable—
  (a) on conviction on indictment, to a fine;
  (b) on summary conviction, to a fine not exceeding the statutory maximum.

(7) The validity of the resolution, if passed, is not affected by a failure to comply with this section.

COMMENTARY: 293 Circulation of written resolution proposed by members

Overview

Section 293 prescribes the procedure to be followed by a private company when it is required under s 292 to circulate a members' resolution and accompanying statement. This section covers the same ground (with appropriate modifications) as s 291, which applies only to the circulation of written resolutions that have been proposed by the directors. **22.94**

It is to be noted that the right to receive a written resolution proposed by members under s 293 may be conferred by a company's articles on another person nominated by the member in accordance with s 145. This provision is examined in Chapter 10. **22.95**

Subsections (1) and (2):

The private company must circulate the resolution and any accompanying statement by sending them to all eligible members at the same time or, if it can be done without undue delay, by submitting the same copy of the resolution and statement to each eligible member in turn or a combination of these methods. The copy may be sent in hard copy form, or in electronic form or by means of a website. **22.96**

Subsection (3): Timing

In general, the private company is required to circulate the members' written resolution within 21 days of the company being requested to do so by those members. This general rule is subject to the exception that if the written resolution is circulated to members on different days, then the first copy should be dispatched not more than 21 days after the request to circulate the resolution. **22.97**

Subsection (4): Guidance statement

The copy of the resolution must be accompanied by what is described as 'guidance' as to how the member can signify his agreement to the resolution and the date by which the resolution must be passed if it is not to lapse. This guidance will properly take the form of a letter or circular from the board explaining to the members what they have to do. **22.98**

Subsections (5) and (6): Offences

Officers of private companies who fail to comply with this statutory procedure will commit an offence, and if found guilty of this offence they will be liable to a fine. **22.99**

Subsection (7): Saving

22.100 Notwithstanding any failure to comply with the requisite procedure the efficacy of a resolution that has been passed is unaffected.

Transitional provisions

22.101 The transitional provisions relating to s 293 are to be found in the Third Commencement Order, Sch 3, para 24. These provisions are discussed in the commentary below s 300D.

294 Expenses of circulation

(1) The expenses of the company in complying with section 293 must be paid by the members who requested the circulation of the resolution unless the company resolves otherwise.

(2) Unless the company has previously so resolved, it is not bound to comply with that section unless there is deposited with or tendered to it a sum reasonably sufficient to meet its expenses in doing so.

COMMENTARY: 294 Expenses of circulation

22.102 It is plain that there is some concomitant cost of, and incidental to, the circulation by the company of members' resolutions and statements under CA 2006, s 293. Section 294 provides that the expenses of the company in complying with the duty under s 293 must be paid by the members who have requested the circulation of the resolution unless the company resolves otherwise. CA 2006 does not say whether it is the resolution of the company in general meeting or the resolution of the board that can absolve the member or members from providing the expenses. It is suggested that in the absence of a clear statement of statutory intention, the resolution may be passed by either body. It is also unclear as to whether a provision for the payment of the expenses incurred in the circulation of a members' resolution and statement may be included in the company's articles of association. It is suggested that this must be the case and that the presence of such a provision could be relied upon by members exercising their rights under s 293. In every other case the company is not bound to comply with s 293 unless there is deposited with or tendered to it a sum that is reasonably sufficient to meet the company's expenses of effecting the circulation. This is always subject to any decision that the company may have made previously to waive such a requirement.

Transitional provisions

22.103 The transitional provisions relating to s 294 are to be found in the Third Commencement Order, Sch 3, para 24. These provisions are discussed in the commentary below s 300D.

295 Application not to circulate members' statement

(1) A company is not required to circulate a members' statement under section 293 if, on an application by the company or another person who claims to be aggrieved, the court is satisfied that the rights conferred by section 292 and that section are being abused.

(2) The court may order the members who requested the circulation of the statement to pay the whole or part of the company's costs (in Scotland, expenses) on such an application, even if they are not parties to the application.

COMMENTARY: 295 Application not to circulate members' statement

Overview

Circulation of resolutions by members and accompanying statements can become a platform for minority, special-interest groups who happen to hold shares in a company. Accordingly, provision has been made for an application to the court for an order to exempt the private company from the requirement to circulate a member's statement under CA 2006, s 293 in cases of abuse. This provision is in similar terms to CA 2006, s 317 which confers a like jurisdiction on the court in relation to the circulation of a members' statement prepared for the purposes of a general meeting of a company. Where the court makes an order under this section the company is relieved of the duty to circulate the members' statement. **22.104**

Subsection (1):

The application to the court may be made by the company or indeed by any other person who claims to be aggrieved. A person who claims to be aggrieved is not defined within the legislation, but it is suggested that such a person will have to show sufficient nexus with the content and subject matter of the proposed resolution and statement in order to satisfy the requirement of being an aggrieved person. It may also be possible for the company to use this procedure to obtain clarification as to whether the written resolution offends the limits of s 292(2), although this is not clear from the wording of the statute. **22.105**

Subsection (2): Costs of application

If the court is satisfied that the rights conferred by s 292 are being abused it may make an order that exempts the private company from the duty to circulate the members' statement under s 293. The court is expressly empowered to make an order against the members who requested the circulation of the statement to pay all or part of the private company's costs on such an application, even if those persons do not attend the application or are not parties to the application. **22.106**

Transitional provisions

22.107 The transitional provisions relating to s 295 are to be found in the Third Commencement Order, Sch 3, para 24. These provisions are discussed in the commentary below s 300D.

Agreeing to written resolutions

296 Procedure for signifying agreement to written resolution

(1) A member signifies his agreement to a proposed written resolution when the company receives from him (or from someone acting on his behalf) an authenticated document—
  (a) identifying the resolution to which it relates, and
  (b) indicating his agreement to the resolution.
(2) The document must be sent to the company in hard copy form or in electronic form.
(3) A member's agreement to a written resolution, once signified, may not be revoked.
(4) A written resolution is passed when the required majority of eligible members have signified their agreement to it.

COMMENTARY: 296 Procedure for signifying agreement to written resolution

Overview

22.108 The purpose of s 296 is to set out the procedure for members of a private company to signify their agreement to a written resolution. It is designed to provide the company with a degree of clarity as to when the required majority of eligible members has been attained. The section applies to all written resolutions, whether proposed by the directors or by members.

Subsection (2):

22.109 By s 296(2), a member of a private company may signify his agreement to a written resolution in hard copy or electronic form. CA 2006, s 298 and Schs 4 and 5 provide for the sending of documents in hard copy form (Sch 4, Part 2 and Sch 5, Part 2) or in electronic form (Sch 4, Part 3 and Sch 5, Part 3). The provisions of Schs 4 and 5 are examined in Chapter 17.[46] By Schs 4 and 5, Part 3, para 6, a document may only be sent to a company in electronic form if the company has agreed, either generally or specifically, that the document may be sent in that form (and the agreement has not been revoked) or the company is deemed to have so agreed by a provision in the statutes. In fact, by reason of CA 2006, s 298 (see below) where a company has given an electronic address in any document containing or accompanying a proposed

[46] It is to be noted that Sch 4 deals with documents and information sent or supplied *to* a company; Sch 5 deals with communications *by* a company and *between* companies, including corporate shareholders of a company.

written resolution it is deemed to have agreed that any document may be sent to that stated address by electronic means.

Subsection (3): Inability to revoke consent

Once a member of a private company has signified agreement to a written resolution, he is not permitted to withdraw his agreement. This is a vital provision which is designed to ensure clarity of outcome. However, as a result of this provision members need to take great care before signifying their consent. **22.110**

Subsection (4): When the resolution is passed

The written resolution is passed at the time when the required majority of members has been achieved by notification to the company. The effect of this provision is that a written resolution may come into force as soon as the requisite majority in favour of the resolution has been achieved. In the case of an ordinary resolution this means that it will take effect as soon as a simple majority has been obtained, that is, a simple majority of the total voting rights of eligible members—see CA 2006, s 282(2). In the case of a special resolution such a resolution will be passed when it is approved by members representing not less than 75% of the total voting rights of eligible members—see CA 2006, s 283(2). The time limit on members for giving their consent is governed by CA 2006, s 297. **22.111**

Transitional provisions

The transitional provisions relating to s 296 are to be found in the Third Commencement Order, Sch 3, para 24. These provisions are discussed in the commentary below s 300D. **22.112**

297 Period for agreeing to written resolution

(1) A proposed written resolution lapses if it is not passed before the end of—
  (a) the period specified for this purpose in the company's articles, or
  (b) if none is specified, the period of 28 days beginning with the circulation date.
(2) The agreement of a member to a written resolution is ineffective if signified after the expiry of that period.

COMMENTARY: 297 Period for agreeing to written resolution

Section 297 applies to all written resolutions, whether proposed by the directors or by the members. The section imposes a time limit of 28 days for passing a written resolution, unless the articles of association of the private company specify a different period. This means that there will be a definite time when the private company can say that a written resolution has received inadequate support and has consequently not been passed. It is suggested that the period of 28 days **22.113** provides an adequate and reasonable period of time and that generally the articles of association of a private company need not stipulate a different time period.

22.114 The period stipulated for agreeing to a written resolution applies to resolutions that are proposed by either the directors or by the members. The proposed written resolution will lapse if it is not passed before the end of the relevant period. By subs (2), if a member of a private company gives his agreement to a written resolution after the expiry of the relevant period that agreement is of no effect. A resolution therefore cannot be revived by the late delivery of written assents.

Transitional provisions

22.115 The transitional provisions relating to s 297 are to be found in the Third Commencement Order, Sch 3, para 24. These provisions are discussed in the commentary below s 300D.

Supplementary

298 Sending documents relating to written resolutions by electronic means

(1) Where a company has given an electronic address in any document containing or accompanying a proposed written resolution, it is deemed to have agreed that any document or information relating to that resolution may be sent by electronic means to that address (subject to any conditions or limitations specified in the document).

(2) In this section 'electronic address' means any address or number used for the purposes of sending or receiving documents or information by electronic means.

COMMENTARY: 298 Sending documents relating to written resolutions by electronic means

22.116 The next three sections of Part 13, Chapter 2, ss 298–300, are supplementary provisions relating to the written resolution procedure. Section 298 must be read together with the provisions concerning electronic communications to companies in Part 3 (communications in electronic form) of Schs 4 and 5. Taken together, these provisions allow a member to communicate with the company by electronic means where the company has given an electronic address in a document containing or accompanying a proposed written resolution.

22.117 Under s 298 where a company has given an electronic address in a document containing or accompanying a proposed written resolution the company is deemed to have agreed that any document or information relating to that written resolution can be sent by electronic means to the company's stated address. This is subject to the caveat that if there is any conditionality or limitation specified in the company's document stipulating its electronic address then those conditions and limitations will apply. An electronic address for this purpose means any address or number used for the purposes of sending or receiving documents or information by electronic means. The phrase 'electronic means' is defined in CA 2006, s 1168(4) as follows:[47]

> A document or information is sent or supplied by electronic means if it is—
> (a) sent initially and received at its destination by means of electronic equipment for the processing which expression includes (digital compression) or storage of data, and
> (b) entirely transmitted, conveyed and received by wire, by radio, by optical means or by other electro-magnetic means.
>
> References to electronic means have a corresponding meaning.

Transitional provisions

The transitional provisions relating to s 298 are to be found in the Third Commencement Order, Sch 3, para 24. These provisions are discussed in the commentary below s 300D. **22.118**

> **299 Publication of written resolution on website**
>
> (1) This section applies where a company sends—
> (a) a written resolution, or
> (b) a statement relating to a written resolution,
> to a person by means of a website.
>
> (2) The resolution or statement is not validly sent for the purposes of this Chapter unless the resolution is available on the website throughout the period beginning with the circulation date and ending on the date on which the resolution lapses under section 297.

COMMENTARY: 299 Publication of written resolution on website

Where a private company uses a website as a means of sending a written resolution and/or a statement relating to such a resolution to members it must comply with the requirements of subs (2). In order to so comply, the written resolution must be available on the website for the period starting with the circulation date, as defined in s 290, and finishing with the date on which the proposed written resolution will lapse under s 297. Detailed provisions dealing with communications by a company by means of a website are prescribed in CA 2006, Sch 5, Part 4.[48] **22.119**

The legislation is cast in absolute terms and the natural meaning of the language used by the section suggests that if the resolution is not available on the website for the whole of the period it will not be validly sent. The legislation does not say what is to happen if, for reasons beyond the reasonable control of the company, the **22.120**

[47] Reference should also be made to CA 2006, s 1168(3) which states when documents are sent or supplied in electronic form.

[48] The provisions are discussed in Ch 17.

website is unavailable for part of the prescribed period of time.[49] It is to be presumed that non-compliance with this section will render the resolution ineffective.

Transitional provisions

22.121 The transitional provisions relating to s 299 are to be found in the Third Commencement Order, Sch 3, para 24. These provisions are discussed in the commentary below s 300D.

300 Relationship between this Chapter and provisions of company's articles

A provision of the articles of a private company is void in so far as it would have the effect that a resolution that is required by or otherwise provided for in an enactment could not be proposed and passed as a written resolution.

COMMENTARY: 300 Realtionship between this Chaptet and provisions of company's articles

22.122 CA 2006, s 300 governs the relationship between the provisions of Part 13, Chapter 2 and a company's articles of association. CA 2006, s 300 declares void any provision that is contained in the articles of association of a private company which has the effect of making it impossible to pass a resolution as a written resolution. The section refers to any statutory provision. The word 'enactment' is defined in CA 2006, s 1293 in the following broad terms:

In this Act, unless the context otherwise requires, 'enactment' includes—

(a) an enactment contained in subordinate legislation within the meaning of the Interpretation Act 1978 (c.30),

(b) an enactment contained in, or in an instrument made under, an Act of the Scottish Parliament, and

(c) an enactment contained in, or in an instrument made under, Northern Ireland legislation within the meaning of the Interpretation Act 1978.

22.123 The effect of s 300 is to preserve the right of any private company to pass any resolution required by statute in the form of a written resolution under Part 13, Chapter 2. The articles of association of a private company therefore cannot dilute these important statutory rights.

Transitional application of procedural requirements

Disapplication of pre-emption rights

300A.—(1) This section applies to a written resolution—

(a) under section 95(2) of the Companies Act 1985 or Article 105(2) of the Companies (Northern Ireland) Order 1986 (disapplication of pre-emption rights), or

(b) renewing a resolution under that provision.

---

[49] There is no equivalent to s 353(5).

(2) The statement required by section 95(5) of that Act or Article 105(5) of that Order (statement by directors to be circulated with notice of meeting) must be sent or submitted to every eligible member at or before the time at which the resolution is sent or submitted to him.

(3) Section 95(6) of that Act or Article 105(6) of that Order (offences) applies in relation to the inclusion in any such statement of matter that is misleading, false or deceptive in a material particular.

COMMENTARY: 300A.—(1) This section applies to a written resolution

Section 300A enables the written resolution procedure for private companies in CA 2006 to be used for the passing of a special resolution disapplying the statutory pre-emption rights in respect of new issues of capital contained in CA 1985, s 89(1). Under CA 1985, s 95(5) a special resolution to disapply those rights must be recommended by the directors and accompanied by a written statement of the directors setting out their reasons for making the recommendation, the amount to be paid to the company in respect of the equity securities to be allotted and the directors' justification of that amount. Section 300A(2) provides that that statement must be sent or submitted to every eligible member along with or before the time at which the resolution is sent or submitted to that member. **22.124**

Section 300A (3) applies CA 1985, s 95(6) which creates an offence punishable by a fine or imprisonment or both for any person who knowingly or recklessly permits the inclusion in any such statement of matter that is misleading, false or deceptive in a material particular. **22.125**

300B.— Financial assistance for purchase of company's own shares or those of holding company

(1) This section applies to a written resolution under section 155(4) or (5) of the Companies Act 1985 or Article 165(4) or (5) of the Companies (Northern Ireland) Order 1986 (financial assistance for purchase of company's own shares or those of holding company).

(2) The documents referred to in section 157(4)(a) of that Act or Article 167(4)(a) of that Order (documents to be available at meeting) must be sent or submitted to every eligible member at or before the time at which the resolution is sent or submitted to him.

COMMENTARY: 300B.— Financial assistance for purchase of company's own shares or those of holding company

Section 300B enables the written resolution procedure for private companies in CA 2006 to be used for the passing of a special resolution by a private company proposing to give financial assistance in respect of the acquisition of its own shares or those of its holding company. **22.126**

Section 300B(2) provides that the statutory declaration of the directors under CA 1985, s 155(6) together with the auditors' report annexed to it must be sent **22.127** or submitted to every eligible member at the same time as or before the written resolution is sent or submitted to him.

300C.— Authority for off-market purchase or contingent purchase contract of company's own shares

(1) This section applies to a written resolution—
  (a) conferring authority to make an off-market purchase of the company's own shares under section 164(2) of the Companies Act 1985 or Article 174(2) of the Companies (Northern Ireland) Order 1986,
  (b) conferring authority to vary a contract for an off-market purchase of the company's own shares under section 164(7) of that Act or Article 174(7) of that Order, or
  (c) varying, revoking or renewing any such authority under section 164(3) of that Act or Article 174(3) of that Order.

(2) Section 164(5) of that Act or Article 174(5) of that Order (resolution ineffective if passed by exercise of voting rights by member holding shares to which the resolution relates) does not apply.

But for the purposes of section 289 of this Act (eligible members) a member holding shares to which the resolution relates shall not be regarded as a member who would be entitled to vote on the resolution.

(3) The documents referred to in section 164(6) of that Act or Article 174(6) of that Order (documents to be available at company's registered office and at meeting), and, where that provision applies by virtue of section 164(7) of that Act or Article 174(7) of that Order, the further documents referred to in that provision, must be sent or submitted to every eligible member at or before the time at which the resolution is sent or submitted to him.

(4) Subsections (2) and (3) above also have effect in relation to a written resolution in relation to which the provisions of section 164(3) to (7) of the Companies Act 1985 or Article 174(3) to (7) of the Companies (Northern Ireland) Order 1986 apply by virtue of—
  (a) section 165(2) of that Act or Article 175(2) of that Order (authority for contingent purchase contract), or
  (b) section 167(2) of that Act or Article 177(2) of that Order (approval for release of rights under contracts approved under section 164 or 165 or Article 174 or 175).

COMMENTARY: 300C.— Authority for off-market purchase or contingent purchase contract of company's own shares

22.128 Section 300C enables the written resolution procedure for private companies in CA 2006 to be used in transactions in respect of an off-market purchase of a company's own shares. It is to be noted that s 300C(2) provides that for the purposes of s 289(6) and its definition of the term 'eligible member', a member holding shares to which the resolution relates must not be regarded as a member who would be entitled to vote on the resolution. Such members are disenfranchised.

22.129 By s 300C(3) copies of the relevant contract or the written memorandum of its terms must be sent or submitted to every eligible member at or before the time at which the written resolution is sent to him. Section 300C(4) applies these provisions to a written resolution for authority to enter into a contingent purchase contract as defined in CA 1985, s 165(1) or a special resolution for the release of a company's rights under a contract approved under CA 1985, s 164 or 165.

300D.— Approval for payment out of capital

(1) This section applies to a written resolution giving approval under section 173(2) of the Companies Act 1985 or Article 183(2) of the Companies (Northern Ireland) Order 1986 (redemption or purchase of company's own shares out of capital).

(2) Section 174(2) of that Act or Article 184(2) of that Order (resolution ineffective if passed by exercise of voting rights by member holding shares to which the resolution relates) does not apply.

But for the purposes of section 289 of this Act (eligible members) a member holding shares to which the resolution relates shall not be regarded as a member who would be entitled to vote on the resolution.

(3) The documents referred to in section 174(4) of that Act or Article 184(4) of that Order (documents to be available at meeting) must be sent or submitted to every eligible member at or before the time at which the resolution is sent or submitted to him..

COMMENTARY: 300D.— Approval for payment of capital

Section 300D enables the written resolution procedure for private companies in CA 2006 to be used for the passing of a special resolution in respect of a redemption or purchase by a private company of its own shares out of capital. Section 300D(2) provides that for the purposes of s 289(6) and its definition of the term 'eligible member', a member holding shares to which the resolution relates must not be regarded as a member who would be entitled to vote on the resolution. **22.130**

By s 300D(3) the statutory declaration of the directors and the auditors' report required by CA 1985, s 173 must be sent or submitted to every eligible member at the same time as or before the written resolution is sent or submitted to that member. **22.131**

Transitional provisions

Written resolutions (ss. 288 to 300)

24.—(1) Sections 288 to 300 of the Companies Act 2006 (written resolutions) apply to resolutions for which the circulation date (see section 290) is on or after 1st October 2007.

(2) Section 381A to 381C of, and Schedule 15A to, the 1985 Act or Article 389A to 389C of, and Schedule 15A to, the 1986 Order continue to apply to resolutions sent or circulated to any relevant member before that date.

A 'relevant member' means one whose signature is required by section 381A(1) or Article 389A(1).

COMMENTARY: Written resolutions (ss. 288 to 300)

22.132 The new legislation applies only to written resolutions where the circulation date as defined in s 290 is on or after 1 October 2007. The provisions of CA 1985 dealing with written resolutions in ss 381A–381C and Sch A continue to apply to resolutions sent or circulated to members before that date.

CHAPTER 3
RESOLUTIONS AT MEETINGS
General provisions about resolutions at meetings

301 Resolutions at general meetings

A resolution of the members of a company is validly passed at a general meeting if—

(a) notice of the meeting and of the resolution is given, and

(b) the meeting is held and conducted,

in accordance with the provisions of this Chapter (and, where relevant, Chapter 4) and the company's articles.

COMMENTARY: 301 Resolutions at general meetings

Overview of Chapter 3

22.133 The provisions contained in Part 13, Chapter 3 (ss 301–335), are based on CA 1985, ss 368–377, 379 and 381 and make provision concerning resolutions passed at a duly convened general meeting. The provisions of Chapter 3 apply to both private companies and public companies. It is important to note that a private company will no longer be obliged to hold a meeting that is designated as its annual general meeting. The statutory provisions about circulation of statements in CA 1985, ss 376 and 377 have been separated from the provisions dealing with the circulation of resolutions prior to an annual general meeting. These are now to be found in Part 13, Chapter 4, entitled 'Public Companies: Additional Requirements for AGMs'. CA 1985, s 367 which gave the Secretary of State jurisdiction to convene a meeting in circumstances where there had been no annual general meeting, is repealed and is not replaced.

Section 301

22.134 Section 301 prescribes how a resolution of the members of a company will be passed validly. In the first instance the company must give due notice of the meeting and of the resolution that is to be passed. Secondly, the meeting must be held and conducted in accordance with the prescribed legislation and any other pertinent provisions contained in the company's articles of association.

22.135 All members of a company are entitled to expect that meetings of the company will be held and conducted in accordance with the relevant provisions of the articles of association and/or any pertinent shareholders' agreement. The effect of s 301, with its general statement about the circumstances in which resolutions at meetings are validly passed, is to extend to all resolutions the principle found in CA 1985, s 378(6) which related to extraordinary and special resolutions. That principle is that passing a resolution in a meeting is not just a question of obtaining the requisite majority, but of using the correct and relevant corporate procedures. Under s 301 a resolution must be passed in accordance with the relevant provisions of CA 2006 and any additional requirements imposed by the company's articles. Mandatory provisions in CA 2006 cannot be avoided by making alternative provision in the articles of association.

Calling meetings

302 Directors' power to call general meetings

The directors of a company may call a general meeting of the company.

COMMENTARY: 302 Directors' power to call general meetings

Section 302 reflects part of reg 37 of the 1985 Table A, which allows the directors to call a general meeting at the time of their choosing. **22.136**

Section 302 makes it clear that the board of directors of a company are empowered to convene a meeting of the members of the company. Plainly, the power must be used for the proper purposes of the company and must not be abused for private or collateral purposes of the directors. The date, time and venue for a meeting of members ought to be chosen with due and proper consideration so that, so far as is possible, as many members as possible may be able to attend and participate. **22.137**

303 Members' power to require directors to call general meeting

(1) The members of a company may require the directors to call a general meeting of the company.

(2) The directors are required to call a general meeting once the company has received requests to do so from—

(a) members representing at least the required percentage of such of the paid-up capital of the company as carries the right of voting at general meetings of the company (excluding any paid-up capital held as treasury shares); or

(b) in the case of a company not having a share capital, members who represent at least the required percentage of the total voting rights of all the members having a right to vote at general meetings.

(3) The required percentage is 10% unless, in the case of a private company, more than twelve months has elapsed since the end of the last general meeting—

(a) called in pursuance of a requirement under this section, or

(b) in relation to which any members of the company, had (by virtue of an enactment, the company's articles or otherwise) rights with respect to the circulation of a resolution no less extensive than they would have had if the meeting had been so called at their request, in which case the required percentage is 5%.

(4) A request—

(a) must state the general nature of the business to be dealt with at the meeting, and

(b) may include the text of a resolution that may properly be moved and is intended to be moved at the meeting.

(5) A resolution may properly be moved at a meeting unless—
  (a) it would, if passed, be ineffective (whether by reason of inconsistency with any enactment or the company's constitution or otherwise),
  (b) it is defamatory of any person, or
  (c) it is frivolous or vexatious.

(6) A request—
  (a) may be in hard copy form or in electronic form, and
  (b) must be authenticated by the person or persons making it.

COMMENTARY: 303 Members' power to require directors to call general meeting

Overview

22.138 This section, together with CA 2006, ss 304 and 305, is based upon the provisions previously contained in CA 1985, s 368. CA 1985, s 368 enabled the members of a company to compel the board of directors to convene a meeting of members. Such a power is particularly useful when members of a public or a private company wish to remove directors from office before the expiration of their term of office. The right of members is not unfettered and is subject to the precise statutory requirements. The member requiring a meeting to be convened must comply with the stipulated procedure. Sometimes members fail to follow the prescribed procedure and as a result are frustrated in their efforts to obtain a valid meeting. It is suggested that in practice often a company's best interests may not be well served by taking issue with what may be fairly described as minor procedural points.

Alterations to the existing law

22.139 There are a number of important changes in this area of the law, which are considered in detail in Chapter 5. There is a change in the threshold required in order to make a valid request for a meeting. For public companies the threshold remains members with voting rights holding at least 10% of the paid-up share capital. In relation to private companies, the threshold is 5% or 10% of the paid-up capital (or, in a company with no share capital, 5% or 10% of the total voting rights) depending on when there was last a meeting in advance of which members had a right equivalent to the right under this section to circulate resolutions. This is unfortunately obscure drafting. It seems that the threshold is lower only if there has been no such meeting in the last twelve months. Second, subs (4)(b) extends the provisions of CA 1985 by enabling members to include the text of a resolution to be moved at the requested meeting. Subsection (5) defines the type of resolution that can be ignored. Requests in electronic form are expressly permitted.

22.140 It is to be noted that the right to require the directors to call a general meeting under s 303 may be conferred by a company's articles on another person nominated by the member in accordance with s 145. This provision is examined in Chapter 10.

Subsection (2): A valid request

The board of directors must receive a valid request in order to trigger the statutory duty to convene a meeting. In the case of a company limited by shares a request will be valid if it is received from members representing at least the required percentage of such of the paid-up capital of the company as carries the right of voting at general meetings of the company. For this purpose any paid-up capital held as treasury shares is excluded from the calculation. **22.141**

Where a company does not have a share capital, the request for a meeting has to be received from members who represent at least the required percentage of the total voting rights of all the members having a right to vote at general meetings. **22.142**

Subsection (3): Required percentage

As a general rule the required percentage is 10%. However, in relation to a private company this figure is reduced to 5% in two particular instances. First, where more than 12 months have elapsed since the end of the last general meeting called in pursuance of a request under s 303. Secondly, where more than 12 months have elapsed since the end of the last general meeting in relation to which any members of the company had (by virtue of an enactment, the company's articles or otherwise) rights with respect to the circulation of a resolution no less extensive than they would have had if the meeting had been so called at their request. It is unclear why the draftsman has chosen to use the phrase '... the end of the last general meeting ...' when the subsection could have referred simply to the date of the last general meeting. The time at which a meeting ends is of no significance. It would appear that the concern to permit private companies to avoid holding meetings has influenced the drafting of this subsection. The lower threshold of 5% applies where there has been no meeting for 12 months. **22.143**

Qualifying shares held by one member

If a single member holds the qualifying percentage of shares or voting rights, that person alone has the requisite standing to make a valid request. Such a member is not obliged to find support for his action from other members. **22.144**

Subsection (4): Content of the request

The request from members must state the general nature of the business to be dealt with at the proposed meeting. It is not a mandatory requirement for the request to contain the precise text of the resolution. It is permissible and, some may say, desirable and good practice for the request to include the text of the resolution that is intended to be moved at the meeting. A board of directors would be ill advised to reject a request for a meeting on the grounds that the text of the resolution was not drafted clearly, if the general words of the request make it apparent what the requesting members wanted to have passed as a resolution at the forthcoming meeting. **22.145**

However, from the point of view of the requesting members, care should be taken where possible to draft the precise text of the proposed resolution.

Subsection (5): Power to reject a request

22.146 It is not the case that a board of directors must accede to all requests from members. A board of directors is entitled to reject a request in accordance with s 303(5) if a proposed resolution would, if passed, be ineffective or would be defamatory of any person or would be frivolous or vexatious or a combination of these grounds. The legislation does not define the words 'frivolous or vexatious'. No doubt in practice it may be relatively easy to identify resolutions that fall well within the ambit of these words. As with many matters, harder questions will arise when the decision on the phrase 'frivolous or vexatious' is more borderline. It is suggested that directors and those who advise them should take care not to resort to too wide a construction of the term 'frivolous or vexatious' as this may lead to a legal challenge from members. These important restrictions are further considered in relation to s 292(2) above, which contains identical wording.

Subsection (6): Form of the request

22.147 A valid request may be made in hard copy or in electronic form and must be authenticated by the person or persons making it. By virtue of CA 2006, s 1146 a document in hard copy form is sufficiently authenticated if it signed by the person sending or supplying it. For a document in electronic form CA 2006, s 1146(3) requires the identity of the sender to be confirmed in the manner specified by the company or, in default (where no such manner has been so specified) if the communication contains or is accompanied by the statement of the sender and the company has no reason to doubt the truth of that statement.

Transitional provisions

22.148 The transitional provisions relating to s 303 are to be found in the Third Commencement Order, Sch 3, para 25. These provisions are discussed in the commentary below s 305.

304 Directors' duty to call meetings required by members

(1) Directors required under section 303 to call a general meeting of the company must call a meeting—
  (a) within 21 days from the date on which they become subject to the requirement, and
  (b) to be held on a date not more than 28 days after the date of the notice convening the meeting.

(2) If the requests received by the company identify a resolution intended to be moved at the meeting, the notice of the meeting must include notice of the resolution.

(3) The business that may be dealt with at the meeting includes a resolution of which notice is given in accordance with this section.
(4) If the resolution is to be proposed as a special resolution, the directors are treated as not having duly called the meeting if they do not give the required notice of the resolution in accordance with section 283.

COMMENTARY: 304 Directors' duty to call meetings required by members

Section 304 is cast in mandatory terms and upon receipt of a valid request from the prescribed member or members s 303 imposes a strict statutory duty on the directors to convene the requested meeting. The directors are required to convene the meeting within 21 days from the date when they become subject to the requirement to do so. This important timing provision is not defined in the legislation. This contrasts unfavourably with the old law, where timings imposed on the directors to comply with their statutory duty were measured from the date of the deposit of the requisition notice. In future, directors will be well advised to make an accurate record of the date and time when they receive a valid request from members so as to minimize the risk of disputes arising with the requesting members as to when the statutory duty of the directors to convene the meeting expires. **22.149**

Although the directors have a period of three weeks in which to respond to the members, the meeting that has to be called will be valid if it is convened for a date not more than 28 days after the notice of the meeting is issued. Shareholders who use s 303 should realize that the process is not instantaneous and there is a potential gap of some seven weeks if directors use, as they are entitled to do, the full extent of the prescribed statutory time limits. **22.150**

Subsection (2): Contents of the notice of the meeting

A notice issued under s 304 must give all of the relevant information that is required to evidence a valid meeting: date, time and venue. In addition, subs (2) provides that where the requesting members have gone to the effort of drafting a resolution for the meeting, the notice should include the text of that resolution. **22.151**

Subsection (3):

The business of the meeting will include any resolution of which notice has been given under subs (2). This provision is a statement of the obvious. **22.152**

Subsection (4): Notice of a special resolution

Where the members make a lawful request and such request concerns a special resolution, the notice convening the meeting to be sent out by the directors must give notice of the special resolution in compliance with CA 2006, s 283. CA 2006, s 283(6) requires the notice to include the text of the proposed special resolution **22.153** and a statement that it will be proposed as a special resolution.[50] If directors omit to comply with s 283 the result is that the meeting requested by the members will not have been duly convened. The result will be that the members will be entitled to convene a meeting themselves under the provisions of s 305.

Transitional provisions

22.154 The transitional provisions relating to s 304 are to be found in the Third Commencement Order, Sch 3, para 25. These provisions are discussed in the commentary below s 305.

305 Power of members to call meeting at company's expense

(1) If the directors—
 (a) are required under section 303 to call a meeting, and
 (b) do not do so in accordance with section 304,
 the members who requested the meeting, or any of them representing more than one half of the total voting rights of all of them, may themselves call a general meeting.
(2) Where the requests received by the company included the text of a resolution intended to be moved at the meeting, the notice of the meeting must include notice of the resolution.
(3) The meeting must be called for a date not more than three months after the date on which the directors become subject to the requirement to call a meeting.
(4) The meeting must be called in the same manner, as nearly as possible, as that in which meetings are required to be called by directors of the company.
(5) The business which may be dealt with at the meeting includes a resolution of which notice is given in accordance with this section.
(6) Any reasonable expenses incurred by the members requesting the meeting by reason of the failure of the directors duly to call a meeting must be reimbursed by the company.
(7) Any sum so reimbursed shall be retained by the company out of any sums due or to become due from the company by way of fees or other remuneration in respect of the services of such of the directors as were in default.

COMMENTARY: 305 Power of members to call meeting at company's expense

22.155 Section 305, which is derived from the provisions of CA 1985, s 368(4), empowers the members of a company to call a meeting at the company's expense in circumstances where the directors fail to call a meeting in response to a valid and legitimate request from the members. The power may be exercised by either all the members who made the valid request for a meeting, or by any number of those requesting members provided that they represent more than one half of the total voting rights of the entire group. It is to be hoped, and indeed, expected that responsible directors of a company, acting in accordance with their fiduciary duties, who receive a

[50] See the commentary on s 283 (above).

lawful request from members will comply in a timely manner with their statutory duty. In those rare cases where the directors do not comply with their duty in this regard, express provision is made for the members themselves to convene the meeting. Accordingly, there is no need for members who find themselves in such a situation to make an application to the court under the provisions of s 306.

Subsection (2):

This subsection requires that if the members' request for a meeting has set out the text of a resolution the notice convening that meeting must replicate the text of the resolution. **22.156**

Subsection (3): Timing

The power that is conferred upon members to convene a meeting under s 305 accrues only where the board of directors is in default of its statutory duty under s 304. The accrued power does not endure for an indefinite period and as a consequence must be used in a timely manner. Under subs (3) the members must call the meeting for a date that is within the period of three months after the date on which the directors became subject to the requirement to call the meeting. That date is determined by reference to s 303(2), and is the date on which the company has received requests to call the meeting from members with the required percentage of total voting rights (as defined in s 303(3)). **22.157**

Subsection (4): Formalities

The members must observe the requirements of the company's articles of association and call the meeting in the same way as nearly as possible that meetings of the company are usually called by the board of directors. Total replication is not required but substantial compliance is both necessary and desirable. The members must send out the notice of the meeting in the same way and to the same persons as if the meeting had been convened by the board. **22.158**

Subsection (5):

The business which may be dealt with at a meeting convened by members includes but is not confined to the resolution of which notice has been given in accordance with s 305. The subsection therefore appears to extend the scope of the business that may be dealt with at such a meeting and enlarges the right of the requesting members to fix the agenda. **22.159**

Subsection (6): Recovery of reasonable expenses

The reasonable expenses of members who are put to the time, trouble and inconvenience of convening a meeting for themselves where the directors have failed to **22.160** comply with their statutory duty can be reimbursed pursuant to the provisions of subs (6). The company has the primary responsibility to reimburse the expenses to the members. Care should be taken to ascertain what falls within the ambit of the phrase 'reasonable expenses'. Accordingly, members convening a meeting for themselves under s 305(1) will be well advised to keep a contemporaneous and accurate record of the proper expenses which they incur in connection with convening and holding the meeting. Such expenses may include printing and postage costs. Whether the expenses incurred by the members will fall to be characterized as reasonable will be a question of fact in each case.

Subsection (7): Directors to be responsible for the expenses

22.161 Reimbursement of the reasonable expenses incurred by members of the company under the provisions of subs (6) might give little comfort to members if errant directors suffer no personal financial penalty as a result of their default. Accordingly, subs (7) provides that the directors are to be penalized directly by the reimbursement of the reasonable expenses being taken out of the fees or other remuneration that is due to them. There are sound policy reasons for this provision and it may act as some encouragement to directors to comply with their statutory duty under s 304.

Transitional provisions

22.162 Schedule 3, para 25 to the Third Commencement Order provides as follows:

> Members' power to require directors to call meeting (ss. 303 to 305)
> 25.—(1) Sections 303 to 305 of the Companies Act 2006 (meetings required by members) apply to requests made on or after 1st October 2007.
> (2) Section 368 of the 1985 Act or Article 376 of the 1986 Order continues to apply to requisitions made before that date.
> (3) Where requests are made or copies of a requisition are deposited on more than one day, the references in this paragraph to the day on which the request or requisition is made shall be read as references to the first day on which the requests made or copies deposited are sufficient to require the company to act.

22.163 It is apparent that the new legislation applies only to requests that are made on or after 1 October 2007.

> **306 Power of court to order meeting**
> (1) This section applies if for any reason it is impracticable—
> (a) to call a meeting of a company in any manner in which meetings of that company may be called, or
> (b) to conduct the meeting in the manner prescribed by the company's articles [this Act, the Companies Act 1985 or the Companies (Northern Ireland) Order 1986].[51]

[51] Words in square brackets inserted by Third Commencement Order, Sch 1, para 14.

(2) The court may, either of its own motion or on the application—
(a) of a director of the company, or
(b) of a member of the company who would be entitled to vote at the meeting,
order a meeting to be called, held and conducted in any manner the court thinks fit.
(3) Where such an order is made, the court may give such ancillary or consequential directions as it thinks expedient.
(4) Such directions may include a direction that one member of the company present at the meeting be deemed to constitute a quorum.
(5) A meeting called, held and conducted in accordance with an order under this section is deemed for all purposes to be a meeting of the company duly called, held and conducted.

COMMENTARY: 306 Power of court to order meeting

This section derives from, and is in substantially the same form as, CA 1985, s 371. Where, for any reason, it is impracticable to hold a meeting of a company application can be made to the court by the company or a member for an order convening a meeting of the company. In addition, the court has jurisdiction to use the power in this section in circumstances where there is no application made by a member or by the company itself; this power may prove useful to a court where it is trying to resolve a corporate dispute between different factions of shareholders. **22.164**

It is to be noted that this section applies only to general meetings of members of public and private companies and it has no application to meetings of directors. Further, by s 334(2)(b) the provisions of s 306 do not apply to class meetings of members. It is most regrettable that the legislation does not specify this restriction in s 306 itself. **22.165**

'Impracticability'

Unless the court decides that the evidence discloses that there is real impracticability the court has no jurisdiction to use the statutory power. Impracticability may take many and diverse forms and it could be said that the categories of impracticability are not closed. One very common application of the jurisdiction under CA 1985, s 371 was where a meeting could not proceed to transact business because it was inquorate. Reference should be made to Chapter 6 above for a more detailed discussion of this issue. **22.166**

Subsections (3) and (4): Directions from the court

Where an order is made under subs (2) the court is empowered by subs (3) to give ancillary and consequential directions in relation to the meeting. Although such directions take some cognizance of provisions in a company's articles of association and of the terms of any applicable shareholders' agreement, the court can give such directions as it thinks fit so as to ensure that an effective meeting can take place—after all, the application to the court will have been precipitated by the fact **22.167** that it has not been possible to hold a meeting as envisaged by the terms of the constitution of the company. The direction that is most commonly given to overcome the apparent misuse of the quorum provisions is one that the meeting may proceed to transact lawful business with a quorum of only one member present. This is dealt with in subs (4).

Subsection (5):

22.168 The effect of this subsection is to put the status of the court-ordered meeting beyond any doubt. It is deemed for all purposes to be a meeting of the company duly convened and held.

Notice of meetings

307 Notice required of general meeting

(1) A general meeting of a private company (other than an adjourned meeting) must be called by notice of at least 14 days.

(2) A general meeting of a public company (other than an adjourned meeting) must be called by notice of—

(a) in the case of an annual general meeting, at least 21 days, and

(b) in any other case, at least 14 days.

(3) The company's articles may require a longer period of notice than that specified in subsection (1) or (2).

(4) A general meeting may be called by shorter notice than that otherwise required if shorter notice is agreed by the members.

(5) The shorter notice must be agreed to by a majority in number of the members having a right to attend and vote at the meeting, being a majority who—

(a) together hold not less than the requisite percentage in nominal value of the shares giving a right to attend and vote at the meeting (excluding any shares in the company held as treasury shares), or

(b) in the case of a company not having a share capital, together represent not less than the requisite percentage of the total voting rights at that meeting of all the members.

(6)[52] The requisite percentage is—

(a) in the case of a private company, 90% or such higher percentage (not exceeding 95%) as may be specified in the company's articles;

(b) in the case of a public company, 95%.

(7) Subsections (5) and (6) do not apply to an annual general meeting of a public company (see instead section 337(2)).

COMMENTARY: 307 Notice required of general meeting

22.169 Section 307 is based on part of CA 1985, s 369 but also contains a number of important changes.

[52] Note: there are important transitional provisions in s 307(6)—see further the commentary below s 311.

Subsections (1) and (2): Length of notice

The minimum notice period requirement of 21 days for the annual general meetings of a public company is maintained. However, a period of 14 days' notice is required for all other general meetings, whether they be general meetings of public or private companies and whatever the nature of the business that is to be transacted. Thus, the previous requirement of at least 21 days' notice for a meeting at which a special resolution is to be proposed is abolished. **22.170**

Subsection (3):

This provision permits the articles of association of companies to contain provisions requiring longer periods of notice for meetings than is required by subss (1) and (2). **22.171**

Subsections (4) to (6): Members' agreement to a shorter period of notice

A general meeting may be called on shorter notice if the requisite majority of members give their informed agreement to such a proposal. A further important substantive change from the position under CA 1985 is that by subss (5) and (6) the requisite majority required to agree to a short notice period has been reduced for private companies from 95% to 90% of the voting rights, although the articles may specify up to 95% if the company wishes. For public companies, the majority required to agree to a short notice period remains at 95% of the voting rights. The provisions of s 360 (computation of periods of notice etc: clear day rule) apply for the purposes of calculating the requisite period of notice under s 307(1) and (2).[53] **22.172**

Subsection (7): Private companies only

It is important to note that by reason of subs (7) the provisions contained in subss (5) and (6) do not apply to the annual general meeting of a public company. The provisions of CA 2006, s 337(2) have to be observed in relation to the notice period for an annual general meeting of a public company. That section imposes a requirement of unanimous consent from members to a shorter period of notice.[54] **22.173**

Transitional provisions

The transitional provisions relating to s 307 generally are to be found in the Third Commencement Order, Sch 3, para 26. These provisions are discussed in the commentary below s 311. However, the Sixth Commencement Order introduces a further transitional provision applicable only to s 307(6). This transitional provision is found in Sch 3, para 2(2) of the Sixth Commencement Order and came **22.174**

[53] See the commentary to s 360 (below).
[54] See the commentary to s 337 (below).

into force on 6 April 2008. It inserts a new para 26A into Sch 3 to the Third Commencement Order dealing with notice of meetings. This provision and commentary appear below s 311.

308 Manner in which notice to be given

Notice of a general meeting of a company must be given—
(a) in hard copy form,
(b) in electronic form, or
(c) by means of a website (see section 309),
or partly by one such means and partly by another.

COMMENTARY: 308 Manner in which notice to be given

22.175 CA 2006, s 308, which came into force on 20 January 2007[55] stipulates three methods by which a company may give due notice of a general meeting. The three stipulated methods are in a hard copy format, or in electronic format or by means of a website. In relation to the last mentioned method further important detail is set out in s 309.[56] The three stipulated methods are not mutually exclusive and accordingly a company is permitted to use an amalgam of the stipulated methods in order to give valid notice of a meeting. It would seem that the wording '… or partly by one such means and partly by another …' means that only two methods can be used. It may be anticipated that many companies will in future decide to give notice of their general meetings to members by both direct communication with their members and via a website. Such a development is to be encouraged as it will increase the likelihood of shareholder participation at meetings. In this context reference should also be made to the 'company communication provisions' in CA 2006, ss 1144–1148 and Sch 5. These provisions are discussed in Chapter 17.

309 Publication of notice of meeting on website

(1) Notice of a meeting is not validly given by a company by means of a website unless it is given in accordance with this section.
(2) When the company notifies a member of the presence of the notice on the website the notification must—
(a) state that it concerns a notice of a company meeting,
(b) specify the place, date and time of the meeting, and
(c) in the case of a public company, state whether the meeting will be an annual general meeting.
(3) The notice must be available on the website throughout the period beginning with the date of that notification and ending with the conclusion of the meeting.

---

[55] See the Companies Act 2006 (Commencement No 1, Transitional Provisions and Savings) Order 2006, SI 2006/3482, para 3.

[56] See the commentary on this section below.

COMMENTARY: 309 Publication of notice of meeting on website

Overview

Section 309, which came into force on 20 January 2007,[57] should be read in conjunction with the 'company communications provisions' which contain the general requirements for companies in sending and supplying information to members as set out in ss 1144–1148[58] and Sch 5. The requirement to give due and proper notice of a meeting is a fundamental requirement of a company's administration. The new legislation, which reflects the provisions of subss (4A)–(4G) introduced into CA 1985, s 369 by the Companies Act 1985 (Electronic Communications) Order 2000,[59] recognizes the extensive technological developments that have been made in modern communications, and makes provision for notice of meetings to be given to members by means of a website. **22.176**

Subsection (1):

For such notification to be valid there must be due compliance with the requirements that are stipulated in s 309. **22.177**

Subsection (2): Basic requirements

Notification to members of a meeting by means of a website must comply with the requirements of subs (2). Thus, the notification must state that it concerns a meeting of the company and specify the date, the time and place of the meeting. An additional requirement, applicable only to public companies, is imposed by subs (2)(c); a public company must state whether the proposed meeting is the company's annual general meeting. **22.178**

Subsection (3): Duration of the notification

The notification of a meeting to members by use of a website must appear on the website for the entire period beginning with the date of the notification and ending with the conclusion of the meeting. It seems that where default is made with the provisions of subs (3) the notice of meeting will not be valid. This section takes no account of possible technical problems with the website. It therefore imposes on the company an obligation to ensure that its website is properly maintained and is functioning at all times. **22.179**

310 Persons entitled to receive notice of meetings

(1) Notice of a general meeting of a company must be sent to—

---

[57] See the Companies Act 2006 (Commencement No 1, Transitional Provisions and Savings) Order 2006, SI 2006/3482, para 3.

[58] In CA 2006, Part 37.

[59] SI 2000/373, art 18.

(a) every member of the company, and
(b) every director.

(2) In subsection (1), the reference to members includes any person who is entitled to a share in consequence of the death or bankruptcy of a member, if the company has been notified of their entitlement.

(3) In subsection (2), the reference to the bankruptcy of a member includes—
(a) the sequestration of the estate of a member;
(b) a member's estate being the subject of a protected trust deed (within the meaning of the Bankruptcy (Scotland) Act 1985 (c. 66)).

(4) This section has effect subject to—
(a) any enactment, and
(b) any provision of the company's articles.

COMMENTARY: 310 Persons entitled to receive notice of meetings

22.180 Section 310 incorporates part of the familiar provisions of reg 38 of the 1985 Table A.[60] Section 310 identifies the recipients entitled to due notice in order to convene a valid meeting of a company. They include every member of the company and, for the first time in statute, every director. The section is subject to any provision in a company's articles and any enactment. Although the section is silent on the subject of the auditors, in fact by s 502(2)(a) a company's auditor is entitled to receive all notices of and other communications concerning any general meeting which a member is entitled to receive.

22.181 It is to be noted that the right to receive notice of general meetings under s 310 may be conferred by a company's articles on another person nominated by a member in accordance with s 145. This provision is examined in Chapter 10.

Subsection (2): Who is a member?

22.182 The scope of what is contemplated by the word 'member'[61] is extended by subs (2). This provision means that members include persons who are entitled to the

[60] Regulation 38 of 1985 Table A provides: 'An annual general meeting and an extraordinary general meeting called for the passing of a special resolution or a resolution appointing a person as a director shall be called by at least twenty one clear days' notice. All other extraordinary general meetings shall be called by at least fourteen clear days' notice but a general meeting may be called by shorter notice if it is so agreed–

in the case of an annual general meeting, by all the members entitled to attend and vote thereat; and

in the case of any other meeting by a majority in number of the members having a right to attend and vote being a majority together holding not less than ninety-five per cent in nominal value of the shares giving that right.

The notice shall specify the time and place of the meeting and the general nature of the business to be transacted and, in the case of an annual general meeting, shall specify the meeting as such.

Subject to the provisions of the articles and to any restrictions imposed on any shares, the notice shall be given to all the members, to all persons entitled to a share in consequence of the death or bankruptcy of a member and to the directors and auditors.'

[61] 'Member' is defined in CA 2006, s 112.

shares of a registered member as a result of the death or bankruptcy of such a member. However, in order to fall within the ambit of subs (2) the company must have been notified of the entitlement of the person claiming title to the shares as a result of the death or bankruptcy of a registered member.

Subsection (3): Bankruptcy

Subsection (3) gives further clarification in relation to the bankruptcy of a member which includes sequestration of the estate of a member, and in Scotland, the subjecting of a member's estate to a protected trust deed. **22.183**

Subsection (4): The impact of statute and a company's articles of association

This provision stipulates that the entire section has effect subject to any enactment and to any provision in a company's articles of association. As a consequence a company may expressly provide in its articles of association that it is not obliged to send notice of a meeting to a particular type of member. Examples are members for whom the company has ceased to have a valid address or to members whose registered address is overseas. This is a standard provision in the articles of association of many private companies and forms part of reg 112 of the 1985 Table A. Importantly, the new legislation does not invalidate these provisions in a company's articles of association. **22.184**

Definition of enactment

The word 'enactment' is defined in CA 2006, s 1293. Unless the context requires otherwise there are three inexhaustive definitions of the word 'enactment'. They include an enactment contained in subordinate legislation within the meaning of the Interpretation Act 1978 or one contained in or in an instrument made under an Act of the Scottish Parliament or under Northern Ireland legislation. **22.185**

Transitional provisions

The transitional provisions relating to s 310 are to be found in the Third Commencement Order, Sch 3, para 26. These provisions are discussed in the commentary below s 311. **22.186**

311 Contents of notices of meetings

(1) Notice of a general meeting of a company must state—
   (a) the time and date of the meeting, and
   (b) the place of the meeting.
(2) Notice of a general meeting of a company must state the general nature of the business to be dealt with at the meeting.

This subsection has effect subject to any provision of the company's articles.

COMMENTARY: 311 Contents of notices of meetings

22.187 Having identified in s 310 the persons who are to be the recipients of a valid notice, the legislation proceeds to make provision for the content of a valid notice.

Subsection (1): Time, date and location

22.188 This provision requires that the notice of a general meeting must state the time, date and location of the meeting. It is axiomatic that any well-drafted notice for any meeting would contain such fundamentally important information. It is suggested that the time for the start of the meeting which must be specified is not confined to a fixed time but may include a reference to the conclusion of a previous meeting. For example, it is permissible to stipulate the time as '… at 10.15 a.m. or as soon thereafter as the meeting of the [x shareholders] preceding it shall have concluded or been adjourned'. Equally, it is suggested that it is not valid to convene a meeting to be held '… immediately after the meeting of the [x shareholders]'. The obvious reason for this is that the statute requires the notice of the meeting to state the time of the meeting, thereby providing for a degree of certainty as to when the meeting will take place. Equally, it is essential that the date of the meeting is clearly given. It is vital to avoid stating the wrong day of the week! If the wrong day of the week is included in the notice this may cause considerable confusion for shareholders and the notice may be invalid. In such circumstances the meeting may have to be abandoned and reconvened for another day with a new, correctly drafted notice.

Subsection (2): Notice of the general business

22.189 As to the business of the meeting, subs (2) provides that the notice must state the general nature of the business to be transacted at the meeting. It is customary for a well-drafted notice of a meeting to set out the precise text of resolutions that are to be proposed and it is suggested that the new legislation should not encourage a departure from this practice. All of this commonsense information is subject to any provision of a company's articles of association. It is highly unlikely that a company would wish to derogate in any substantial way from the requirements of the statutory provision.

Transitional provisions

22.190 Schedule 3, paras 26 and 26A of the Third Commencement Order provide as follows:

> **Notice of meetings (ss. 307, 310 and 311)**
>
> 26.—(1) Sections 307, 310 and 311 of the Companies Act 2006 (notice of meetings) apply in relation to meetings of which notice is given on or after 1st October 2007.

(2) The provisions of the 1985 Act or the 1986 Order continue to apply in relation to a meeting of which notice was given before that date.
(3) The provisions referred to in sub-paragraph (2) include sections 369 and 370(2) of the 1985 Act or Articles 377 and 378(2) of the 1986 Order.
(4) Where notice of a meeting is given over more than one day, it is treated for the purposes of this paragraph as given on the first of those days.

26A.—(1) The following provisions have effect for the purposes of section 307(6)
(a) of the Companies Act 2006(private companies: requisite percentage for calling general meeting a short notice).
(2) If immediately before 1st October 2007 there was in force in relation to a company a resolution under section 369(4) of the 1985 Act or Article 377 (4) of the 1986 Order—
(a) specifying 90%, or
(b) under which the company in general meeting had determined that the percentage should be 90%,
any provision of the company's articles specifying a higher percentage shall be disregarded.
(3) If immediately before 1st October 2007 there was in force in relation to a company a resolution under section 369(4) of the 1985 Act or Article 377 (4) of the 1986 Order—
(a) specifying a percentage greater than 90% but less than 95%, or
(b) under which the company in general meeting had determined a percentage greater than 90% but less than 95%,
any provision of the company's articles specifying a different percentage shall be disregarded.
(4) Sub-paragraph (2) and (3) does not apply in relation to provisions of the company's articles adopted on or after 1st October 2007.[62]

COMMENTARY: Notice of meetings (ss. 307, 310 and 311)

Paragraph 26

22.191 Accordingly, ss 307, 310 and 311 dealing with notices of general meetings apply in relation to any meeting of which notice has been given on or after 1 October 2007. The previous legislation continues to apply in relation to a meeting when notice was given before that date.

Paragraph 26A

22.192 The effect of para 26A is that where a private company has passed an elective resolution in accordance with CA 1985, s 379A reducing the majority that is required to authorize short notice of a meeting, any provision in a company's articles specifying a higher percentage must be disregarded. This applies notwithstanding the wording

[62] This is inserted as an amendment to the Third Commencement Order by Sch 3, para 2(2) of the Sixth Commencement Order.

of CA 2006, s 307(6)(a) which renders paramount the percentage specified in the company's articles. In addition, if there was such an elective resolution specifying a percentage greater than 90% but less than 95%, any provision of the company's articles specifying a different percentage is again to be disregarded.

22.193 This modification to s 307(6)(a) applies only to existing articles of a company and does not apply in relation to any articles adopted on or after 1 October 2007. Accordingly, in the case of new articles, s 307 (6)(a) will apply without any modification and the requisite percentage for a private company will be 90% or such higher percentage (not exceeding 95%) as may be specified in the company's articles.

312 Resolution requiring special notice

(1) Where by any provision of the Companies Acts special notice is required of a resolution, the resolution is not effective unless notice of the intention to move it has been given to the company at least 28 days before the meeting at which it is moved.

(2) The company must, where practicable, give its members notice of any such resolution in the same manner and at the same time as it gives notice of the meeting.

(3) Where that is not practicable, the company must give its members notice at least 14 days before the meeting—
   (a) by advertisement in a newspaper having an appropriate circulation, or
   (b) in any other manner allowed by the company's articles.

(4) If, after notice of the intention to move such a resolution has been given to the company, a meeting is called for a date 28 days or less after the notice has been given, the notice is deemed to have been properly given, though not given within the time required.

COMMENTARY: 312 Resolution requiring special notice

Overview

22.194 Section 312 is based upon the provisions of CA 1985, s 379. That section and its statutory predecessors made provision for special notice to be given of certain resolutions, for example, an ordinary resolution to remove a director from office before the expiration of his period of office under CA 1985, s 303. It is to be noted that CA 2006, s 312 contemplates only resolutions that are passed at meetings of a company. The reason for this is that the resolutions for which special notice is required are either resolutions which cannot as a matter of law be passed as a valid written resolution,[63] or are written resolutions which have their own specifically prescribed procedure.[64] It is a matter for regret that the additional procedural hurdle of requiring special notice to the company in certain limited circumstances has been retained in the new legislation.

[63] For example, resolutions under CA 2006, ss 168 and 510.

[64] For example, under CA 2006, ss 514 and 515.

Subsection (1):

Certain resolutions, such as a resolution to remove a director before the expiration of his term of office, require special notice under the Companies Acts; such a provision existed in CA 1985. Where such special notice is required under CA 2006 the resolution will not be effective unless notice of the intention to move the resolution has been given to the company at least 28 days before the meeting at which the resolution is to be moved. **22.195**

Subsection (2):

By subs (2) the company to whom notice has been given must, if it is practicable, give notice to its members of the resolution that requires special notice. In order to give notice of a resolution requiring special notice the company can give notice of this in the same way that it gives notice of a meeting. Accordingly, the duty on the company to give notice is qualified and not absolute. It would appear that it is the company itself that has to make the judgment as to whether or not it is practicable to give notice under subs (2). It is suggested that the company's assessment of whether or not it is practicable to give notice must be based on cogent objective criteria. In the event that it is not practicable for the company to give notice of a resolution requiring special notice then the provisions of subs (3) apply. **22.196**

Subsection (3):

The contents of this subsection may encourage companies to conclude that it is practical to give notice under subs (2). Under subs (3) notice has to be given to members at least 14 days before the meeting by either an advertisement in a newspaper with an appropriate circulation or in any other way permitted by the company's articles of association. It would be prudent for a company's articles of association to make express provision to deal with the situation contemplated by subs (3). **22.197**

The provisions of s 360 apply for the purposes of calculating the requisite period of notice under s 312(1) and (3).[65] **22.198**

Subsection (4):

Where a company has received notice of an intention to move a resolution requiring special notice and a meeting is called for a date 28 days or less after the notice has been given, the notice is deemed to have been properly given, though it has not been given within the required time. This provision is designed to validate the **22.199**

[65] See the commentary on s 360 (below).

passing of a resolution which requires special notice even though the strict 28 day time limit has not been complied with.

Transitional provisions

22.200 Schedule 3, para 27 of the Third Commencement order provides as follows:

> Special notice (s. 312)
>
> 27. (1) Section 312 of the Companies Act 2006 (special notice) applies in relation to resolutions for which special notice is required where notice of the intention to move the resolution is given to the company on or after 1st October 2007.
>
> (2) Section 379 of the 1985 Act or Article 387 of the 1986 Order continues to apply to resolutions for which special notice is required where notice of the intention to move the resolution is given to the company before that date.

22.201 This provision is self-explanatory. The new section applies only to resolutions for which special notice is required where notice has been given to the company on or after 1 October 2007. Prior to that date the previous statute will apply.

> **313 Accidental failure to give notice of resolution or meeting**
>
> (1) Where a company gives notice of—
>
> (a) a general meeting, or
>
> (b) a resolution intended to be moved at a general meeting,
>
> any accidental failure to give notice to one or more persons shall be disregarded for the purpose of determining whether notice of the meeting or resolution (as the case may be) is duly given.
>
> (2) Except in relation to notice given under—
>
> (a) section 304 (notice of meetings required by members),
>
> (b) section 305 (notice of meetings called by members), or
>
> (c) section 339 (notice of resolutions at AGMs proposed by members),
>
> subsection (1) has effect subject to any provision of the company's articles.

COMMENTARY: 313 Accidental failure to give notice of resolution or meeting

Overview

22.202 In general at common law, an omission to give due notice to any person entitled to receive it will invalidate a meeting.[66] This rule is invariably relaxed by provisions in a company's articles of association. Section 313 reflects in part the existing provisions of reg 39 of the 1985 Table A.[67] This standard form provision contains a general rule of practical importance to the effect that the accidental failure to give notice of a resolution or of a general meeting will normally be disregarded.

---

[66] See *Smyth v Darley* (1849) 2 HLC 789.

[67] Regulation 39 of the 1985 Table A provides: 'The accidental omission to give notice of a meeting to, or the non-receipt of notice of a meeting by, any person entitled to receive notice shall not invalidate the proceedings at that meeting.'

Section 313 provides that where a company has given notice of a meeting (ie under s 310) or notice of a resolution intended to be moved at a general meeting (eg, under s 312(2)), the accidental omission to give notice to one or more persons will be disregarded for the purpose of deciding whether or not notice of the meeting or resolution has been duly given. **22.203**

'Accidental omission'

The legislation does not define the phrase 'accidental omission'. Accordingly, it would appear that the established law on the meaning of this phrase will continue to be relevant. The courts have construed the word 'accidental' narrowly. The provision will not assist in cases where the omission to give notice has been deliberate in the sense that it reflected a mistaken belief that a member was not entitled to receive notice[68] or an erroneous miscalculation of the number of days' notice required for the meeting. The onus of proof is placed by the courts on the persons claiming that the omission to give due notice was accidental.[69] The mistaken belief may be based on a mistake of fact or on a mistake of law. **22.204**

Subsection (2):

Articles of association may deal with the consequences of accidental omission to give notice. This has always been permitted and no doubt will continue to be good corporate practice. However, it is important to note that subs (1) has effect subject to any provision in a company's articles of association relating to accidental omission to give notice except in relation to notices given under s 304 (notice of meetings required by members), s 305 (notice of meetings called by members) and s 339 (notice of resolutions at the annual general meeting of public companies proposed by members). This subsection provides additional protection for members when exercising their statutory rights under ss 304, 305 and 339. **22.205**

Transitional provisions

Schedule 3, para 28 of the Third Commencement Order provides as follows: **22.206**

> 28. (1) Section 313 of the Companies Act 2006 (accidental failure to give notice of resolution or meeting) applies to resolutions or meetings of which notice is given on or after 1st October 2007.

---

68 See *Musselwhite v C H Musselwhite & Sons Ltd* [1962] Ch 964 at 978 (Russell J) and *Re Compaction Systems Pty Ltd* (1976) 2 ACLR 135 (Supreme Court of New South Wales). Contrast *Re West Canadian Collieries Ltd* [1962] Ch 370 (Plowman J)—a case where in error notice of a meeting was not served on nine members.

69 See *POW Services Ltd v Clare* [1995] 2 BCLC 435 at 450h (Jacob J).

(2) The reference in sub-paragraph (1) to cases in which notice is given on or after 1st October 2007 includes cases in which notice would be regarded as so given if section 313 applied.

COMMENTARY

22.207 The start date for s 313 is again 1 October 2007. The meaning of the second sub-paragraph is obscure. It is perhaps intended to widen the scope of s 313 to include cases where notice was by accident not given, but should be regarded as having been given by reason of the section.

Members' statements

314 Members' power to require circulation of statements

(1) The members of a company may require the company to circulate, to members of the company entitled to receive notice of a general meeting, a statement of not more than 1,000 words with respect to—
   (a) a matter refered to in a proposed resolution to be dealt with at that meeting, or
   (b) other business to be dealt with at that meeting.

(2) A company is required to circulate a statement once it has received requests to do so from—
   (a) members representing at least 5% of the total voting rights of all the members who have a relevant right to vote (excluding any voting rights attached to any shares in the company held as treasury shares), or
   (b) at least 100 members who have a relevant right to vote and hold shares in the company on which there has been paid up an average sum, per member, of at least £100.

See also section 153 (exercise of rights where shares held on behalf of others).

(3) In subsection (2), a 'relevant right to vote' means—
   (a) in relation to a statement with respect to a matter referred to in a proposed resolution, a right to vote on that resolution at the meeting to which the requests relate, and
   (b) in relation to any other statement, a right to vote at the meeting to which the requests relate.

(4) A request—
   (a) may be in hard copy form or in electronic form,
   (b) must identify the statement to be circulated,
   (c) must be authenticated by the person or persons making it, and
   (d) must be received by the company at least one week before the meeting to which it relates.

COMMENTARY: 314 Members' power to require circulation of statements

Overview

22.208 Sections 314 and 315 are based upon the provisions found in CA 1985, ss 376 and 377. The sections confer upon members of both public and private companies the right to have a statement of up to one thousand words circulated by the company to all the other members. In the context of a company with a large number of shareholders the exercise of this right can prove to be expensive.[70]

Changes to the existing law

The new provisions will introduce three significant changes. The first difference from the existing provisions under CA 1985 is that where the statement relates to a resolution or other matter which will be dealt with at an annual general meeting of a public company and the statement is received before the end of the public company's financial year, the shareholders who require the statement to be circulated are not required to cover the company's costs of the circulation process. The second change is that the shares of members that are relied upon in order to trigger the right to have a statement circulated must have voting rights relating to the relevant resolution, rather than have rights to vote at a meeting in general. The third change is that the members may make their requests in electronic form. **22.209**

Subsection (1): The members' statement

The members have the right to require the company to circulate a statement with respect to a matter referred to in a proposed resolution to be dealt with at the meeting or some other business that is to come before the meeting. The wording in the legislation permits members to circulate a statement through the company in respect of resolutions or general business that is to come before a meeting of whatever kind. A company does not have to circulate whatever the members produce as the length of the statement is subject to a limitation of 1,000 words. The right of the company to reject a statement longer than 1,000 words should be exercised with circumspection in order to avoid unnecessary criticism or controversy. **22.210**

Subsections (2) and (3):

This provision sets the limit on the number of members required for the regular exercise of this statutory right. The required limit in sub-para (b) may be difficult to achieve in circumstances where the share capital of the company is divided into shares of a small nominal value; at least £10,000 in the aggregate of paid-up share capital is required. The subsection cross-refers to CA 2006, s 153 which governs the exercise of rights where shares are held on behalf of others.[71] **22.211**

Subsection (4): Form of the request and timing

The form of the request may be in hard copy or electronic form. It would appear that sub-para (b) requires the statement that is to be circulated to be included with **22.212**

---

[70] This subject is considered further in Ch 3.

[71] See Ch 10.

the request. The document must be authenticated within the meaning of CA 2006, s 1146. To be effective the members' request must be received at least one week before the meeting to which the request relates. This prescribed time period of one week is very short and may give rise to serious practical difficulties. For example, there may be insufficient time for the company to circulate the statement to members and to receive back from the members a valid proxy. Members will be well advised to serve on the company their statement well in advance of the meeting and not to rely on the prescribed period of one week.

Transitional provisions

22.213 The transitional provisions relating to s 314 are to be found in the Third Commencement Order, Sch 3, para 29. These provisions are discussed in the commentary below s 317.

315 Company's duty to circulate members' statement

(1) A company that is required under section 314, to circulate a statement must send a copy of it to each member of the company entitled to receive notice of the meeting—
  (a) in the same manner as the notice of the meeting, and
  (b) at the same time as, or as soon as reasonably practicable after, it gives notice of the meeting.

(2) Subsection (1) has effect subject to section 316(2) (deposit or tender of sum in respect of expenses of circulation) and section 317 (application not to circulate members' statement).

(3) In the event of default in complying with this section, an offence is committed by every officer of the company who is in default.

(4) A person guilty of an offence under this section is liable —
  (a) on conviction on indictment, to a fine;
  (b) on summary conviction, to a fine not exceeding the statutory maximum.

COMMENTARY: 315 Company's duty to circulate members' statement

22.214 Section 315 is based on the remainder of CA 1985, ss 376 and 377. The purpose of s 315 is to make provision for the action to be taken by a company in circumstances where it is required to circulate a members' statement made in accordance with s 314.

Subsection (1): Obligation to circulate statement

22.215 Where a company has received a valid request to circulate a statement made under s 314, it becomes under a duty to send a copy of the statement to all the other members of the company who are entitled to receive due and proper notice of the meeting. The obligation on the company is to circulate the statement in the same way as circulating the notice of a meeting and at the same time as, or as soon as reasonably practicable after, the company has given notice of the meeting.

Subsection (2): Qualifications to the duty to circulate

The duty of the company is not absolute because subs (2) stipulates that the company's duty to circulate a statement is qualified by the provisions of s 316(2) concerning the deposit or tender of the requisite funds to meet the expense of consultation. The problems and practical difficulties that may be associated with complying with s 316(2) are considered in detail below. The duty is also qualified by the ability of the company to make an application to court under s 317. This last-mentioned provision empowers the court to grant a company relief from the statutory duty if circumstances disclose that the members' right to require the circulation of a statement is being abused. **22.216**

Subsections (3) and (4): Offence

If a company fails to comply with the requirements of s 315 every officer who is in default will have committed a criminal offence created by subs (3). The penalties are stipulated in subs (4). **22.217**

Transitional provisions

The transitional provisions relating to s 315 are to be found in the Third Commencement Order, Sch 3, para 29. These provisions are discussed in the commentary below s 317. **22.218**

316 Expenses of circulating members' statement

(1) The expenses of the company in complying with section 315 need not be paid by the members who requested the circulation of the statement if—
   (a) the meeting to which the requests relate is an annual general meeting of a public company, and
   (b) requests sufficient to require the company to circulate the statement are received before the end of the financial year preceding the meeting.

(2) Otherwise—
   (a) the expenses of the company in complying with that section must be paid by the members who requested the circulation of the statement unless the company resolves otherwise, and
   (b) unless the company has previously so resolved, it is not bound to comply with that section unless there is deposited with or tendered to it, not later than one week before the meeting, a sum reasonably sufficient to meet its expenses in doing so.

COMMENTARY: 316 Expenses of circulating members' statement

Section 316 deals with the expenses of the circulation of a members' statement. These may be considerable in respect of a public company with a large share register. **22.219**

Subsection (1):

22.220 This provides that the members need not pay the expenses of circulating a statement if the meeting to which the valid request relates is the annual general meeting of a public company and sufficient numbers of valid requests are received before the financial year-end of the public company in question.

Subsection (2):

22.221 If the requirements of subs (1) do not apply the expenses of the company will have to be paid by the members who have requested the circulation of the statement. This means that the members requesting the circulation of the statement must deposit with, or tender to the company a sum of money reasonably sufficient to meet the costs of circulating the statement. This sum of money must be deposited or tendered to the company not later than one week before the relevant meeting. This rule will apply unless the company resolves otherwise. The legislation does not state whether it is the resolution of the company in general meeting or the resolution of the board of directors that can absolve the member or members from the obligation to provide the expenses. It is suggested that in the absence of a clear statement of statutory intention the necessary resolution may be passed by the shareholders in general meeting. It is also arguable that an appropriate provision may be inserted in a company's articles of association. The adoption of such a provision by special resolution will constitute a resolution of a company within the meaning of s 316(2)(b).

Timing and compliance

22.222 In this context s 315(2) is of importance in that it makes the company's compliance with the request to circulate a members' statement under s 314 dependent upon compliance by the relevant members with s 316(2)(b). In effect the company is not bound to comply with ss 314 and 315 unless it has received by way of deposit, or has had tendered to it, not later than one week before the meeting, a sum that is reasonably sufficient to meet its expenses of compliance.

22.223 Unfortunately, the wording of the statute is likely to result in a great deal of uncertainty on the part of those concerned with the management of the company's affairs. This results from the fact that the members making the request need not make it earlier than a week before the meeting, and are not required to deposit the expenses at the same time unless they leave it to the very end of the stipulated period to make their request. There may therefore be a gap between the lodging of a request under s 314(4) and the provision of the costs in accordance with s 316(2). Where such a gap exists the company will not know whether it will in fact be obliged to send a copy of the members' statement to each member in advance of the meeting, as there will not yet have been compliance with s 316(2).

It is also likely that disputes may arise as to the amount that is reasonably sufficient to meet the company's expenses in complying with s 315. **22.224**

It is suggested that in order to avoid such problems an officer of the company should write to the relevant members upon receipt of their request made under s 314, explaining to them the probable amount of the company's expenses and how this sum has been calculated. At the same time a request should be made of the members for the deposit or tender of the estimate sum within the statutory timetable. It is hoped that if such a procedure is adopted the scope for uncertainty will be diminished. **22.225**

Transitional provisions

The transitional provisions relating to s 316 are to be found in the Third Commencement Order, Sch 3, para 29. These provisions are discussed in the commentary below s 317. **22.226**

> **317 Application not to circulate members' statement**
>
> (1) A company is not required to circulate a members' statement under section 315 if, on an application by the company or another person who claims to be aggrieved, the court is satisfied that the rights conferred by section 314 and that section are being abused.
>
> (2) The court may order the members who requested the circulation of the statement to pay the whole or part of the company's costs (in Scotland, expenses) on such an application, even if they are not parties to the application.

COMMENTARY: 317 Application not to circulate members' statement

Section 317 is based on CA 1985, s 377(3). The court is given jurisdiction to grant relief to a company from the statutory duty to circulate a members' statement if the court reaches the view that the members' right to require circulation of a statement is being abused. The application may be made by the company or by another person (being a legal person) who claims to be aggrieved. The right of a company to apply to the court for relief from the obligation to circulate members' statements if the statutory procedure is being abused is most valuable. Obviously, the court hearing any such application has to strike a fair balance between the interests of the members on the one hand and the interests of the company on the other. It is likely that applications under this section will be infrequent. In order to bring an application in the capacity of a person who claims to be aggrieved such an applicant must show a sufficient connection with the proposed statement. For example, a person who is named in the proposed statement might apply to the court in order to prevent the circulation of defamatory matter, or where the statement contains material that is misleading or inaccurate. However, in practical terms this right will be of little value as it can only be utilized by someone who knows the contents of the proposed statement. **22.227**

Subsection (2):

22.228 In the event that a successful application is made, the court has jurisdiction to make an adverse order for costs against the members concerned, even if they do not appear before the court on the hearing of the company's application or even if they are not parties to the application.

Transitional provisions

22.229 Schedule 3, para 29 of the Third Commencement Order provides as follows:

> **Circulation of members' statements (ss. 314 to 317)**
>
> 29.—(1) Sections 314 to 317 of the Companies Act 2006 (circulation of members' statements) apply to requests made on or after 1st October 2007.
>
> (2) Sections 376 and 377 of the 1985 Act or Articles 384 and 385 of the 1986 Order continue to apply in relation to requisitions made before that date.
>
> (3) So long as such a requisition made to a private company under section 376(1)(b) or Article 384(1)(b) is not complied with, section 366 of the 1985 Act or Article 374 of the 1986 Order (duty to hold annual general meeting) continues to apply in relation to the company.
> This does not apply if the company is not required to comply with the requisition (see section 377 of the 1985 Act or Article 385 of the 1986 Order).
>
> (4) Where requests are made or copies of a requisition are deposited on more than one day, the references in this paragraph to the day on which the request or requisition is made shall be read as references to the first day on which the requests made or copies deposited are sufficient to require the company to act.

COMMENTARY: Circulation of members' statements (ss. 314 to 317)

22.230 Sections 314 to 317 once again apply to requests for the circulation of members' statements that are made on or after 1 October 2007. The old law found in CA 1985, ss 376 and 377 continues to apply to requisitions in writing made by members before that date. Such requisitions could only be made in respect of the next annual general meeting. Indeed, sub-para 29(3) is designed to ensure that CA 1985, s 366 requiring every company to hold an annual general meeting will continue to apply to a private company if that company has not yet complied with a requisition made under CA 1985, s 376(1)(b). By this means a private company with an outstanding requisition to circulate a members' statement under CA 1985 must hold an annual general meeting for this purpose. This is likely to be extremely rare.

Procedure at meetings

> **318 Quorum at meetings**
>
> (1) In the case of a company limited by shares or guarantee and having only one member, one qualifying person present at a meeting is a quorum.
>
> (2) In any other case, subject to the provisions of the company's articles, two qualifying persons present at a meeting are a quorum, unless—

(a) each is a qualifying person only because he is authorised under section 323 to act as the representative of a corporation in relation to the meeting, and they are representatives of the same corporation; or
(b) each is a qualifying person only because he is appointed as proxy of a member in relation to the meeting, and they are proxies of the same member.

(3) For the purposes of this section a 'qualifying person' means—
(a) an individual who is a member of the company,
(b) a person authorised under section 323 (representation of corporations at meetings) to act as the representative of a corporation in relation to the meeting, or
(c) a person appointed as proxy of a member in relation to the meeting.

COMMENTARY: 318 Quorum at meetings

Overview

Sections 318 to 323 are grouped under the heading 'Procedure at Meetings'. These important sections deal with procedural and administrative matters that are fundamental to the proper conduct of company meetings. They set out a basic procedural framework governing the quorum, the appointment of a chairman, methods of voting and the representation of corporate members at meetings. **22.231**

Quorum

CA 2006, s 318 is based on CA 1985, s 370(4) and 370A. A meeting cannot proceed to transact lawful business unless it is quorate, that is to say, it is attended by at least the minimum number of persons that are required in order to confer capacity on the meeting. The essential importance of achieving a quorum at the start of a meeting is discussed in detail in Chapter 1. The concept of a 'qualifying person' is new and is defined in subs (3). **22.232**

Subsection (1):

The quorum for companies limited by shares or by guarantee and having only a single member is one qualifying member. **22.233**

Subsection (2):

This provision applies to all companies except single member companies. If the articles of association make provision for the quorum required for an effective meeting of members then that stated requirement is the governing provision. However, if the articles of association of a company are silent on the matter, subs (2) provides that the quorum is two qualifying persons present at the meeting. However, this statutory provision is subject to two important caveats. First, the presence of two qualifying persons will not constitute a quorum if each such person is only a qualifying person because he is authorized to act as a corporate **22.234** representative under s 323 and the two persons are representatives of the same corporation. The second caveat is that each person is a qualifying person only because he is appointed as a proxy of a member and they are proxies of the same person.

Subsection (3):

22.235 The new term 'qualifying person' means an individual who is a member of a company, an authorized corporate representative appointed under s 323, or a person who is appointed as a proxy for a member. This is an exhaustive definition.

General

22.236 The combined effect of subss (2) and (3) is that a member, or a duly appointed corporate representative or a duly appointed proxy present at a meeting may all be counted as 'qualifying members'. However, two or more duly appointed corporate representatives or proxies of the same member are not 'qualifying members' for the purpose of quorum. In short, two human beings representing more than one member are required to constitute a quorum.

Transitional provisions

22.237 The transitional provisions relating to s 318 are to be found in the Third Commencement Order, Sch 3, para 30. These provisions are discussed in the commentary below s 331.

319 Chairman of meeting

(1) A member may be elected to be the chairman of a general meeting by a resolution of the company passed at the meeting.
(2) Subsection (1) is subject to any provision of the company's articles that states who may or may not be chairman.

COMMENTARY: 319 Chairman of meeting

22.238 This section makes provision for the appointment of a person to act as the chairman of a meeting of members of a company. It is customary in very many companies for the chairman of the board of directors to take the role of chairman at a duly convened meeting of members. Under CA 2006, s 319 it is possible for a member to be elected as chairman of a general meeting. Such an appointment will be made at the relevant meeting. The ability of members to elect one of their number to be the chairman of a meeting is made subject to any provisions contained in a company's articles of association which regulate who may or may not act as chairman.

The role and duties of the chairman[72] are very important and those concerned with the administration of company meetings should give careful consideration as to whether or not it is desirable and practical that a member who is not a director should have the capacity to act as the chairman of a meeting. It is suggested that leaving the identity of the chairman to the decision of the members as a whole may produce infelicitous results, and that a company's articles of association should make express provision regarding who may and who may not occupy the position of chairman. **22.239**

The chairman of the board of directors may himself not be a member of the company but may have the casting vote at a meeting of members under reg 50 of the 1985 Table A. This provision may conflict with ss 281(3) and 282. This point is discussed in the commentary in relation to s 282 above and in relation to reg 50 of the 1985 Table A in Part 4 below. **22.240**

In addition, it is to be noted that by s 328 a proxy may be elected to act as the chairman.[73] **22.241**

Transitional provisions

The transitional provisions relating to s 319 are to be found in the Third Commencement Order, Sch 3, para 30. These provisions are discussed in the commentary below s 331. **22.242**

> **320 Declaration by chairman on a show of hands**
>
> (1) On a vote on a resolution at a meeting on a show of hands, a declaration by the chairman that the resolution—
> (a) has or has not been passed, or
> (b) passed with a particular majority,
> is conclusive evidence of that fact without proof of the number or proportion of the votes recorded in favour of or against the resolution.
>
> (2) An entry in respect of such a declaration in minutes of the meeting recorded in accordance with section 355 is also conclusive evidence of that fact without such proof.
>
> (3) This section does not have effect if a poll is demanded in respect of the resolution (and the demand is not subsequently withdrawn).

COMMENTARY: 320 Declaration by chairman on a show of hands

Overview

Section 320 is a restatement of CA 1985, s 378(4) and part of reg 47 of the 1985 Table A.[74] The purpose of the section is to provide certainty in relation to **22.243**

---

72 See Ch 7.

73 See commentary on s 328 below.

74 Regulation 47 of 1985 Table A provides: 'Unless a poll is demanded a declaration by the Chairman that a resolution has been carried or carried unanimously, or by a particular majority, or

corporate decision making taken at a duly convened meeting. In order to promote certainty members of a company are precluded from impugning a declaration by the chairman of the meeting as to the votes cast on a particular resolution. The only lawful method by which a member can challenge the declaration by the chairman of the meeting as to the votes cast on a resolution is by demanding a poll. This important right is governed by CA 2006, s 321.

Voting on a show of hands

22.244 Decision making at meetings can be effected in a number of ways. Voting on a show of hands is a well-established method. On such a vote each member who is present in person will have one vote irrespective of the number of shares he holds in the issued share capital of the company. Provision has to be made for the counting of such votes. No doubt, the chairman will be assisted by other members of the board, or the company secretary or indeed by independent persons especially appointed to carry out such a task. Whatever assistance is afforded to the chairman by other attendees at the meeting, it is the chairman who has to declare the result of a vote that is taken on a show of hands to the members assembled at the meeting. The chairman will declare that the resolution on a show of hands has been passed or not passed, or passed with a particular majority.

22.245 The chairman's declaration is conclusive evidence of the result. An accurate record of the declaration made by the chairman as to the result must be made in the minutes of the meeting. Such an entry has to be made in accordance with the provisions of s 355.[75] Where there is cogent evidence of a manifest error on the part of the chairman, for example where the chairman acts in a completely perverse manner and overtly disregards the true result of the members' voting, this provision may produce injustice. The remedy of the members is to demand a vote on a poll, while at the same time reminding the chairman of his duties to the meeting.

Subsection (3):

22.246 It is important to note that the provisions of s 320 do not apply if there has been a request for a vote to be taken on a poll, and that demand has not been withdrawn.

Transitional provisions

22.247 The transitional provisions relating to s 320 are to be found in the Third Commencement Order, Sch 3, para 30. These provisions are discussed in the commentary below s 331.

---

lost, or not carried by a particular majority and an entry to that effect in the minutes of the meeting shall be conclusive evidence of that fact without proof of the number or proportion of the votes recorded in favour of or against the resolution.'

[75] See the commentary on s 355 below.

321 Right to demand a poll

(1) A provision of a company's articles is void in so far as it would have the effect of excluding the right to demand a poll at a general meeting on any question other than—
 (a) the election of the chairman of the meeting, or
 (b) the adjournment of the meeting.

(2) A provision of a company's articles is void in so far as it would have the effect of making ineffective a demand for a poll on any such question which is made—
 (a) by not less than 5 members having the right to vote on the resolution; or
 (b) by a member or members representing not less than 10% of the total voting rights of all the members having the right to vote on the resolution (excluding any voting rights attached to any shares in the company held as treasury shares); or
 (c) by a member or members holding shares in the company conferring a right to vote on the resolution, being shares on which an aggregate sum has been paid up equal to not less than 10% of the total sum paid up on all the shares conferring that right (excluding shares in the company conferring a right to vote on the resolution which are held as treasury shares).

COMMENTARY: 321 Right to demand a poll

Overview

22.248

The right of a shareholder to call for a vote to be taken on a poll is well established and is preserved in the new statute. A company cannot exclude this right by means of a provision in its articles of association. CA 2006, s 321 is based on CA 1985, s 373. The objective of this provision is to restrict the capacity of a company by means of provisions in its articles of association, to exclude the right of members to call for a vote to be taken on a poll.

Subsection (1):

22.249

Contrary to the general rule that provisions in a company's articles of association are void in so far as they exclude the rights of members to demand a poll, the legislation allows the articles of association of a company to exclude the right to a vote on a poll in relation to two matters: first, in relation to the election of the chairman of the meeting and secondly, on the question of the lawful adjournment of the meeting.

Subsection (2):

22.250

Section 321(2) permits three methods of making an effective demand for a vote on a poll. First, a demand can be made by at least five members who have the right to vote on the resolution. Secondly, a demand can be made by a single member or a number of members who represent not less than 10% of the total voting rights of all the members who are enfranchised in relation to the particular resolution. Shares held by the company as treasury shares are excluded from the calculation of the requisite percentage. Finally a lawful demand for a poll can be made by a member or members holding shares in the company that are capable of being lawfully voted on the particular resolution, being shares on which there has been paid up an aggregate sum equal to or not less than 10% of the total paid up or all of the shares that are enfranchised on the particular resolution. Again, there are excluded from the calculation shares held as treasury shares.

22.251 Section 321(2) must be read in conjunction with the rights of a proxy to join in the demand for a poll as set out in s 329(2).[76] Each proxy who joins in a demand counts as one of the five members who demands a poll under s 321(2)(a). Similarly, a demand by a proxy is to be treated as a demand by a member representing the voting rights that the proxy is authorized to exercise for the purposes of s 321(2)(b). A proxy's demand for a poll will similarly be treated as backed by a member holding the shares to which the rights are attached for the purposes of s 321(2)(c).

Transitional provisions

22.252 The transitional provisions relating to s 321 are to be found in the Third Commencement Order, Sch 3, para 30. These provisions are discussed in the commentary below s 331.

322 Voting on a poll

On a poll taken at a general meeting of a company, a member entitled to more than one vote need not, if he votes, use all his votes or cast all the votes he uses in the same way.

COMMENTARY: 322 Voting on a poll

22.253 Section 322 is based upon CA 1985, s 374. CA 1985, s 374 also deals with class meetings and in CA 2006 this aspect of the law is dealt with by s 334.[77] What s 322 recognizes is that a registered member may hold shares for and on behalf of a third party. The provisions of s 322 permit such a registered member to cast votes in different ways. Such a person may have to cast votes relating to tranches of shares in different ways because he is in receipt of different instructions from different clients. This provision is of no assistance and has no application where a vote is taken on a show of hands. Accordingly, whenever a registered member is required to cast votes in different ways he must seek a vote on a poll in order to do so.

Transitional provisions

22.254 The transitional provisions relating to s 322 are to be found in the Third Commencement Order, Sch 3, para 30. These provisions are discussed in the commentary below s 331.

---

[76] See s 329 (below).

[77] See the commentary on s 334 below.

323 Representation of corporations at meetings

(1) If a corporation (whether or not a company within the meaning of this Act) is a member of a company, it may by resolution of its directors or other governing body authorise a person or persons to act as its representative or representatives at any meeting of the company.

(2) Where the corporation authorises only one person, he is entitled to exercise the same powers on behalf of the corporation as the corporation could exercise if it were an individual member of the company.

(3) Where the corporation authorises more than one person, any one of them is entitled to exercise the same powers on behalf of the corporation as the corporation could exercise if it were an individual member of the company.

(4) Where the corporation authorises more than one person and more than one of them purport to exercise a power under subsection (3)—

(a) if they purport to exercise the power in the same way, the power is treated as exercised in that way,

(b) if they do not purport to exercise the power in the same way, the power is treated as not exercised.

COMMENTARY: 323 Representation of corporations at meetings

Section 323 deals with the appointment of corporate representatives to represent corporate shareholders at general meetings. It is common for financial institutions and other substantial investors to have their shareholdings registered in the name of nominee companies. Such nominee companies will invariably attend general meetings by corporate representatives rather than by proxies as the appointment of such a representative may be more flexible and may allow further time for deliberation before the meeting. This arises because there is no requirement to notify the company in advance of their appointment as in the case of proxies, which are required to be delivered to the company not later than 48 hours before the meeting. **22.255**

CA 2006, s 323 is not subject to the company's articles of association and there is nothing in the statute permitting the company to grant greater rights than those that are set out in the section. **22.256**

Multiple corporate representatives

Under CA 1985, s 375 the consequence of appointing a number of representatives was uncertain as the statute only contemplated the appointment of a single representative. CA 2006, s 323 now makes express provision for the appointment of multiple corporate representatives. Under the new legislation any one of multiple corporate representatives will be entitled to vote and exercise other membership rights on behalf of the registered member at a meeting. Those other rights include the right to speak at the meeting and the right to demand a poll. **22.257**

Section 323(4)(b)

22.258 However, CA 2006, s 323(4)(b) provides that where the votes or other exercise of powers conflict, the appointing corporation will be deemed to have abstained from voting or exercising any other power as a member. There has been a considerable difference of opinion as to the correct interpretation of this provision. As stated above it is common practice for corporate representatives to be appointed by financial institutions who may hold a number of different designated accounts on behalf of separate beneficial owners. Whereas the new section would permit each of such accounts to have a separate corporate representative, thereby treating each beneficial owner as if he were a separate shareholder, taken literally s 323(4)(b) no longer permits this in the event that some corporate representatives were to vote one way and some to vote the other way. The explanatory note[78] to s 323 states: 'If a corporation wishes to appoint people with different voting intentions or with authority to vote different blocks of shares, they should appoint proxies'. This view is to be endorsed. It is suggested that where a corporation wishes to appoint more than one corporate representative with different voting instructions or voting in respect of different tranches of shares, the corporation should ideally properly appoint valid proxies with such instructions so as to avoid any resulting confusion at the general meeting. The rights of proxies have been extended under CA 2006 and under s 324 a duly appointed proxy may always speak and vote at the general meeting and may be elected as chairman. However, it must be recognized that the appointment of proxies under s 324 may not always be possible because of the time constraints that are involved.

Single corporate representative

22.259 The next alternative would be to employ only a single corporate representative as happened in the past. In that event s 323(4) would have no application. Under s 323(2) the corporate representative would be entitled to be treated as if he were an individual member of the company and s 322 provides that on a poll a member need not cast all of his votes in the same way.

Interaction with CA 2006, s 152

22.260 It has been suggested that s 323(4) may be subject to an implied exception where shares are held on behalf of others within the meaning of s 152. That section provides that where a member holds shares in a company on behalf of more than one person the rights attached to the shares, if exercised, need not all be exercised in the same way. However, neither s 152 nor s 323 makes any reference to the other section. Accordingly, the status of this interpretation is unclear.

---

[78] CA 2006 Explanatory Notes, para 569 .

'Designated corporate representative'

An alternative but more complex procedure that has been recommended is for the appointment of one of the multiple corporate representatives as the 'designated corporate representative' who will be the only one to vote on a poll. Such a designated corporate representative will be treated for voting purposes as a single corporate representative. It has been suggested that the ideal person to be appointed would be the chairman of the meeting who before voting will receive directions from each of the corporate representatives present. It has even been suggested that in order to facilitate this process a document entitled a 'directions card' can be supplied to the chairman indicating how the votes of each corporate representative/beneficial owner should be voted. If the method of appointing a designated corporate representative is adopted it would be best practice for the company to include a statement to this effect in the notice of the meeting.[79] **22.261**

Vote on a show of hands

A corporate representative is entitled to vote on a show of hands. Where there are multiple corporate representatives it follows from s 323(3) that any one of those corporate representatives is entitled to exercise the voting power 'as if it were an individual member of the company'. Accordingly, the corporate representatives collectively have only one vote on a show of hands. It is suggested that this will be unsatisfactory in many cases where the corporate representatives represent different shareholder accounts and have different accounts. In those circumstances voting should be clarified by the demand for a poll. **22.262**

The right to appoint a proxy

By virtue of CA 2006, s 323(2) where a corporation authorizes only one person to be its representative that single corporate representative is entitled to exercise the same rights on behalf of the corporation as if it were an individual member. Section 324 declares the right of an individual member to appoint another person as his proxy. That right would appear to extend to a single corporate representative. Such a right may also be exercised by one only of multiple corporate representatives under s 323(3). In practice it is likely that this power will be used only on rare occasions as the purpose of appointing a corporate representative is that that person should attend the general meeting on behalf of the corporate shareholder. **22.263**

---

79 See ICSA Guidance on Proxies and Corporate Representatives at General Meetings (January 2008) at <http://www.icsa.org.uk>.

Transitional provisions

22.264 The transitional provisions relating to s 323 are to be found in the Third Commencement Order, Sch 3, para 30. These provisions are discussed in the commentary below s 331.

Proxies

324 Rights to appoint proxies

(1) A member of a company is entitled to appoint another person as his proxy to exercise all or any of his rights to attend and to speak and vote at a meeting of the company.

(2) In the case of a company having a share capital, a member may appoint more than one proxy in relation to a meeting, provided that each proxy is appointed to exercise the rights attached to a different share or shares held by him, or (as the case may be) to a different £10, or multiple of £10, of stock held by him.

COMMENTARY: 324 Rights to appoint proxies

Overview

22.265 CA 2006, ss 324–331 contain important provisions relating to proxies, some of which reflect CA 1985, s 372 and others which are entirely new. It is well established in articles of association that a member of a company who is unable to attend a meeting of members may appoint another person to attend a meeting in his place. The person appointed by the member to stand in for him at a meeting is called a proxy. Under the new legislation a duly appointed proxy of a member is entitled to exercise all or any of the rights of the member who appointed him, including the right of the member to speak and vote at meetings.[80] The statutory rights concerning the appointment of proxies are basic requirements and the legislation lays down minimum criteria. A company does not have the capacity to abrogate or negate the statutory proxy rights of its members by means of provisions in its articles of association. However, a company may confer on members greater rights in relation to proxies than those set out in the statute. Consideration may have to be given to the existing provisions of the articles of association of many private companies which may not reflect these provisions of the new legislation.

22.266 These eight sections apply to both public and private companies. Section 324 contains new statutory provisions regulating the appointment of proxies. The aim of the new statutory provision is to give statutory force to certain existing rights which under CA 1985 are subject to provisions contained in a company's articles of association. Reference should also be made to the important provisions regarding electronic communications that are dealt with in CA 2006, s 333 as these set

80 As to the rights of a proxy on voting see CA 2006, ss 284(2)(b) and 285(1).

out the method by which an instrument of proxy may be returned to the company by electronic means.

Subsection (1):

A member of a company has a statutory right to appoint any other person to act as his proxy. The person appointed need not be a member of the company although this is not expressly stated in the statute.[81] The proxy may exercise all or any of the rights of the member to attend, to speak and to vote at a meeting of the company. It is apparent that this rule applies to both public companies and to private companies. **22.267**

Subsection (2):

In the case of a company that has a share capital a registered member may appoint more that one person to act as his proxy for a particular meeting. This is subject to the proviso that where a member appoints more than one person to act as his proxy for a meeting the persons so appointed do so in respect of different shares held by the member. **22.268**

Voting by proxies

The right of a proxy to vote at a meeting under s 324 is to be read in conjunction with CA 2006, ss 284 and 285. Subject to the articles of association of the company, on a vote on a resolution on a show of hands at a meeting every duly appointed proxy present has one vote.[82] By s 285(1) a proxy must have the same number of votes on a show of hands as the member who appointed him would have had if he were present at the meeting. The effect of this provision is that if there is more than one duly appointed proxy for a member they must be afforded at least one vote between them on a vote on a show of hands.[83] **22.269**

Transitional provisions

The transitional provisions relating to s 324 are to be found in the Third Commencement Order, Sch 3, para 30. These provisions are discussed in the commentary below s 331. **22.270**

> **325 Notice of meeting to contain statement of rights**
>
> (1) In every notice calling a meeting of a company there must appear, with reasonable prominence, a statement informing the member of—
>
> (a) his rights under section 324, and

---

[81] In contrast to CA 1985, s 372(1), which used the phrase '…whether a member or not…'.

[82] See CA 2006, s 284(2)(b).

[83] See the commentary on CA 2006, ss 284 and 285.

(b) any more extensive rights conferred by the company's articles to appoint more than one proxy.

(2) Failure to comply with this section does not affect the validity of the meeting or of anything done at the meeting.

(3) If this section is not complied with as respects any meeting, an offence is committed by every officer of the company who is in default.

(4) A person guilty of an offence under this section is liable on summary conviction to a fine not exceeding level 3 on the standard scale.

COMMENTARY: 325 Notice of meeting to contain statement of rights

Overview

22.271 Section 325 replaces CA 1985, s 372(3) and (4). Certain aspects of s 325 are new in order to take account of the enhanced right of a member to appoint proxies under s 324.

Subsection (1):

22.272 When a company issues a notice of a meeting of members the notice must contain a statement informing the member of his rights under section 324 to appoint another person as his proxy, and any other more extensive rights that may be contained in the articles of association of the company. A standard form of such a notice could be along the following lines, subject to the provisions of the company's articles:

> **Nominating a proxy**
> A member entitled to attend, speak and vote at the Meeting is entitled to appoint another person as his or her proxy to exercise all or any of his or her rights to attend, speak and vote instead of the member. A member may appoint more that one proxy in relation to the Meeting, provided that each proxy is appointed to exercise the rights attached to a different share or shares held by the member. A proxy need not be a member of the company. Completion and submission of an instrument appointing a proxy will not preclude a member from attending and voting in person at the Meeting. If a member wishes to appoint more than one proxy and so requires additional proxy forms the original proxy form may be photocopied or additional forms can be obtained from [Registrar's or company's address]. It will also be necessary to state the number of shares in relation to which each such person is authorised to act as a proxy.

Subsection (2): Validity of meeting and business transacted

22.273 The failure of a company to furnish the information that is required by s 325(1) to its members does not invalidate the meeting or any business that is transacted at the meeting. Subsection (2) is designed to meet the situation where the failure of the company to inform the member of his rights was an accidental or inadvertent one. Notwithstanding the provisions of subs (2), if there was cogent and compelling evidence that members had not been informed of their rights to appoint proxies so that the incumbent board of directors had engineered the result of the general meeting to their own ends, it is suggested that such conduct could amount to unfairly prejudicial conduct and give rise to a remedy under CA 2006, s 994.[84]

Subsections (3) and (4): Offence

Officers of companies who fail to comply with the requirements of subs (1) commit an offence. Subsection (4) stipulates the penalty if officers are found guilty of the prescribed offence. **22.274**

Transitional provisions

The transitional provisions relating to s 325 are to be found in the Third Commencement Order, Sch 3, para 30. These provisions are discussed in the commentary below s 331. **22.275**

326 Company-sponsored invitations to appoint proxies

(1) If for the purposes of a meeting there are issued at the company's expense invitations to members to appoint as proxy a specified person or a number of specified persons, the invitations must be issued to all members entitled to vote at the meeting.
(2) Subsection (1) is not contravened if—
  (a) there is issued to a member at his request a form of appointment naming the proxy or a list of persons willing to act as proxy, and
  (b) the form or list is available on request to all members entitled to vote at the meeting.
(3) If subsection (1) is contravened as respects a meeting, an offence is committed by every officer of the company who is in default.
(4) A person guilty of an offence under this section is liable on summary conviction to a fine not exceeding level 3 on the standard scale.

COMMENTARY: 326 Company-sponsored invitations to appoint proxies

Section 326 replaces CA 1985, s 372(6). Very often a company will want the chairman of the meeting or some other approved persons to be nominated by members to act as proxies for absent members. For that reason a listed company will send to its members a voting form appointing the chairman of the general meeting as proxy. However, the notice must make it clear that while most members choose the chairman of the meeting to vote on their behalf, a member is entitled if he so wishes to appoint someone else to attend the meeting and to vote on his behalf. Such a person is often referred to as a nominated proxy. **22.276**

---

[84] Formerly CA 1985, s 459.

Subsection (1):

22.277 If a company wishes to invite members to appoint a specified person or persons as a proxy (for example, the chairman), the company must ensure that the invitation is issued to all persons who are entitled to vote at the relevant meeting.

Subsection (2):

22.278 Subsection (2) makes it clear that subs (1) will not be contravened if a member receives at his request a form of appointment naming a specified proxy or a list of persons who are willing to act as proxy, and the form or list is available on request to all members who are entitled to vote at the meeting.

Subsections (3) and (4): Offence

22.279 Officers of companies who fail to comply with the requirements of subs (1) commit an offence. Subs (4) stipulates the penalty if officers are found guilty of the offence.

Transitional provisions

22.280 The transitional provisions relating to s 326 are to be found in the Third Commencement Order, Sch 3, para 30. These provisions are discussed in the commentary below s 331.

327 **Notice required of appointment of proxy etc**

(1) This section applies to—
  (a) the appointment of a proxy, and
  (b) any document necessary to show the validity of, or otherwise relating to, the appointment of a proxy.
(2) Any provision of the company's articles is void in so far as it would have the effect of requiring any such appointment or document to be received by the company or another person earlier than the following time—
  (a) in the case of a meeting or adjourned meeting, 48 hours before the time for holding the meeting or adjourned meeting;
  (b) in the case of a poll taken more than 48 hours after it was demanded, 24 hours before the time appointed for the taking of the poll;
  (c) in the case of a poll taken not more than 48 hours after it was demanded, the time at which it was demanded.[85]
(3) In calculating the periods mentioned in subsection (2) no account shall be taken of any part of a day that is not a working day.

[85] CA 2006, s 327(2)(c) can be ignored as it is not being commenced; see further Ch 8.

COMMENTARY: 327 Notice required of appointment of proxy etc

Overview

CA 2006, s 327 replaces CA 1985, s 372(5). It is to be noted that the timing requirements under the new legislation are different from those under CA 1985. Compliance with these requirements is of essential importance both for members and the company. Although the company has a duty to inform members of their rights to appoint a proxy, responsibility for the efficacy of the exercise of these important rights remains with the members themselves. The prescribed rules are not that onerous in their terms, but if they are not complied with a company is entitled to reject a member's appointment of a proxy. A company should adopt a consistent and clear approach to dealing with disputes that may arise as to the validity of a proxy. **22.281**

Section 327 makes provisions for regulating the effective appointment of a proxy and for the requisite documentation to show the validity of the appointment of the proxy. An important requirement concerns members informing the company of the appointment of proxies for a particular meeting. Adequate time must be given to members to make the appointment. Equally a company must have adequate time to receive the notification of the appointment of a proxy or proxies prior to a meeting. **22.282**

Subsection (2):

This provision invalidates any part of a company's articles which would require the appointment of a proxy or any document required to show the validity of such appointment to be received by the company or its registrars (described as 'another person') earlier than the prescribed times in sub-paras (a) and (b).[86] Accordingly, it is not lawful for a company to include provisions in its articles of association requiring documentation relating to the appointment of proxies to be received by it earlier than any of the times prescribed by subs (2). **22.283**

Subsection (2)(a): 48 hours minimum

The effect of s 327(2)(a) is to require that documentation relating to a proxy appointment for a meeting or an adjourned meeting must be received by the company 48 hours before the time for holding the meeting or the adjourned meeting. Any provision in a company's articles of association requiring service at an earlier time will be void. **22.284**

---

[86] CA 2006, s 327(2)(c) has not been brought into force and is unlikely to be brought into force.

Subsection (2)(b): 24 hours minimum

22.285 The effect of s 327(2)(b) is to require that documentation relating to a proxy appointment for a poll taken more than 48 hours after it is demanded, must be received by the company 24 hours before the time appointed for the taking of the poll. Any provision in a company's articles of association requiring service at an earlier time will be void.

Subsection (2)(c):

22.286 The effect of s 327(2)(c) is to require that documentation relating to a proxy appointment for a poll taken not more than 48 hours after it was demanded must received by the company at the time when the poll is demanded. Any provision in a company's articles of association requiring service at an earlier time will be void. This subsection was thought to validate the late delivery and receipt of proxies that were brought to a meeting by a member. The decision has been taken by the Secretary of State not to bring this paragraph into legal force and it has been deliberately excluded from art 2(1)(f) of the Third Commencement Order.[87]

Subsection (3): Calculation of time limits

22.287 Subsection (3) makes provision for the calculation of the time periods specified in subs (2). When calculating the relevant period of time no account must be taken of any part of a day that is not a working day. This represents a significant change in the law. CA 2006, s 1173(1) defines the term 'working day' as follows:

> 'working day' in relation to a company means a day that is not a Saturday or Sunday, Christmas Day or Good Friday or any day that is a bank holiday under the Banking and Financial Dealings Act 1971 (c.80) in the part of the United Kingdom where the company is registered.

Selecting the day for a meeting

22.288 In the light of these provisions great care should be taken in selecting a particular day of the week for a meeting. It would appear that the statutory requirements of subs (2), combined with the vagaries of the postal system and the opening hours of company registrars' offices may make it singularly inopportune to convene a meeting of a company for a Monday or on occasion a Tuesday. For example, if a meeting is convened to start at 3.00 pm on a Tuesday proxies will need to have been deposited with the company by 3.00 pm on the preceding Friday in order to be valid. Where there is an intervening bank holiday Monday proxies will need to have been deposited with the company by 3.00 pm the preceding Thursday in

---

87 See Ch 8.

order to be valid. In all the circumstances it is suggested that the safest course in the future may be to convene meetings for a Wednesday or a Thursday.

Standard form of notice

It is customary for a notice of general meeting to contain a note reminding members of the period of time within which a proxy must be lodged or received by the company in order for it to be valid. Such note may take the following form with appropriate modifications: **22.289**

> In order to be valid, the instrument appointing a proxy and the power of attorney or other authority (if any) under which it is signed, or a copy of such authority certified notarially or in some other way approved by the Board, must be deposited not less than 48 hours before the time of the holding of the meeting (or any adjourned meeting) at: [address]. In the case of an appointment of a proxy submitted in electronic form, such appointment must be received not less than 48 hours before the time of the holding of the Meeting (or any adjourned meeting). It should be noted, however, that any power of attorney or other authority relating to an appointment of a proxy cannot be submitted electronically and must be deposited as referred to above for the appointment to be valid.

Transitional provisions

The transitional provisions relating to s 327 are to be found in the Third Commencement Order, Sch 3, para 30. These provisions are discussed in the commentary below s 331. **22.290**

> **328 Chairing meetings**
>
> (1) A proxy may be elected to be the chairman of a general meeting by a resolution of the company passed at the meeting.
>
> (2) Subsection (1) is subject to any provision of the company's articles that states who may or who may not be chairman.

COMMENTARY: 328 Chairing meetings

Section 328 makes it clear that a proxy who has been validly appointed may be elected as the chairman of the meeting. The appointment of a proxy as chairman may well be by means of a resolution of the members passed at the meeting. This is not an absolute right, in that it is legitimate for a company's articles of association to make express provision relating to the identity of persons who are and are not entitled to act as chairman of a meeting of members. For example, reg 42 of the 1985 Table A[88] provides that the chairman of the board or in his absence a director nominated by the other directors shall preside as chairman. **22.291**

---

[88] See the commentary in Part 4 (below).

Transitional provisions

22.292 The transitional provisions relating to s 328 are to be found in the Third Commencement Order, Sch 3, para 30. These provisions are discussed in the commentary below s 331.

329 Right of proxy to demand a poll

(1) The appointment of a proxy to vote on a matter at a meeting of a company authorises the proxy to demand, or join in demanding, a poll on that matter.
(2) In applying the provisions of section 321(2) (requirements for effective demand), a demand by a proxy counts—
  (a) for the purposes of paragraph (a), as a demand by the member;
  (b) for the purposes of paragraph (b), as a demand by a member representing the voting rights that the proxy is authorised to exercise;
  (c) for the purposes of paragraph (c), as a demand by a member holding the shares to which those rights are attached.

COMMENTARY: 329 Right of proxy to demand a poll

22.293 CA 2006, s 329 prescribes how a duly appointed proxy may participate in the demand for a vote on a poll. As a proxy stands in place of the member who has appointed him he is entitled to demand, or to join in a demand, that a vote on any matter at a meeting of the company is taken on a poll.

Subsection (2):

22.294 Section 321(2) states how an effective demand for a poll is made. Subsection 329(2)(a) provides that a demand made by a duly appointed proxy counts as a demand by a member under s 321(2) (a). Subsection 329(2)(b) similarly provides that the voting rights that the proxy may exercise are to be taken into account in calculating whether persons representing not less than 10% of the total voting rights have made an effective demand for a poll under s 321(2)(b). Equally, s 329(2)(c) provides that a demand by a proxy for a vote on a poll counts as a demand by a member holding the shares to which those voting rights are attached for the purposes of s 321(2)(c).

Transitional provisions

22.295 The transitional provisions relating to s 329 are to be found in the Third Commencement Order, Sch 3, para 30. These provisions are discussed in the commentary below s 331.

330 Notice required of termination of proxy's authority

(1) This section applies to notice that the authority of a person to act as proxy is terminated ('notice of termination').
(2) The termination of the authority of a person to act as proxy does not affect—
  (a) whether he counts in deciding whether there is a quorum at a meeting,

(b) the validity of anything he does as chairman of a meeting, or
(c) the validity of a poll demanded by him at a meeting, unless the company receives notice of the termination before the commencement of the meeting.

(3) The termination of the authority of a person to act as proxy does not affect the validity of a vote given by that person unless the company receives notice of the termination—
(a) before the commencement of the meeting or adjourned meeting at which the vote is given, or
(b) in the case of a poll taken more than 48 hours after it is demanded, before the time appointed for taking the poll.

(4) If the company's articles require or permit members to give notice of termination to a person other than the company, the references above to the company receiving notice have effect as if they were or (as the case may be) included a reference to that person.

(5) Subsections (2) and (3) have effect subject to any provision of the company's articles which has the effect of requiring notice of termination to be received by the company or another person at a time earlier than that specified in those subsections.
This is subject to subsection (6).

(6) Any provision of the company's articles is void in so far as it would have the effect of requiring notice of termination to be received by the company or another person earlier than the following time—
(a) in the case of a meeting or adjourned meeting, 48 hours before the time for holding the meeting or adjourned meeting;
(b) in the case of a poll taken more than 48 hours after it was demanded, 24 hours before the time appointed for the taking of the poll;
(c) in the case of a poll taken not more than 48 hours after it was demanded, the time at which it was demanded.[89]

(7) In calculating the periods mentioned in subsections (3)(b) and (6) no account shall be taken of any part of a day that is not a working day.

COMMENTARY: 330 Notice required of termination of proxy's authority

Provision is made in s 330 for the manner in which a member may terminate the appointment of a proxy. The new section covers the same ground as reg 63 of the 1985 Table A. **22.296**

Subsection (2): Continuing validity

In order to operate as an effective termination of the authority of a duly appointed proxy the notice of termination must be received by the company before the start of the relevant meeting. If the notice of termination is not so received, subs (2) declares that the non-receipt of the termination does not affect the determination of the quorum of the meeting, the validity of any act done by a proxy who has **22.297**

[89] Section 330(6)(c), CA 2006 is not being commenced.

been elected as chairman of the meeting or the validity of any poll demanded by the proxy at the meeting.

Subsection (3):

22.298 This provision deals only with the effect on voting of the termination of a proxy's authority. By virtue of subs (3) the termination of the authority of a person to act as proxy does not affect the validity of a vote given by the proxy unless the company has received notice of the termination of the proxy before the start of the meeting, or the adjourned meeting, or in relation to a poll taken more than 48 hours after it is demanded, before the time appointed for the taking of the poll.

Subsection (4):

22.299 It is permissible for a company's articles of association to stipulate or allow that an entity other than the company, for example the registrars of the company, must be given notice of the termination of the authority of a person to act as proxy. If there is such a stipulation or permission then the provisions of subs (3) apply to the identified entity.

Subsections (5) and (6): Timing under the articles of association

22.300 The provisions of subss (2) and (3) are stated to be subject to any provision in a company's articles of association requiring notices of termination of a proxy's authority to be received at an earlier time However, subs (6) invalidates any provision in a company's articles of association which would reduce the time periods below the stated statutory minimum. These are (a) earlier than 48 hours before the time of the meeting or of the adjourned meeting; (b) earlier than 24 hours before the taking of a poll of the type which is taken more than 48 hours after the time when it was demanded; or (c) earlier than the time at which the poll was demanded when it is taken within that 48-hour period.

22.301 The decision has been taken by the Secretary of State not to bring s 330(6)(c) into force for the same practical reasons mentioned above in relation to s 327(2)(c). It has been deliberately excluded from art 2(1)(f) of the Third Commencement Order.[90]

Subsection (7):

22.302 For the purpose of subss 330(3)(b) and 330(6) (ie in calculating the periods of 24 hours and 48 hours respectively) no account must be taken of any part of a day that is not a working day as defined in s 1173(1).[91]

---

[90] See Ch 8.

[91] This definition is set out in para 22.287 above.

Transitional provisions

The transitional provisions relating to s 330 are to be found in the Third Commencement Order, Sch 3, para 30. These provisions are discussed in the commentary below s 331. **22.303**

> **331 Saving for more extensive rights conferred by articles**
>
> Nothing in sections 324 to 330 (proxies) prevents a company's articles from conferring more extensive rights on members or proxies than are conferred by those sections.

COMMENTARY: 331 Saving for more extensive rights conferred by articles

Section 331 makes is clear that a company may confer more extensive rights on its members in relation to the appointment of proxies. The statutory provisions relating to proxy rights set out the minimum rights in relation to proxies to which a member or his duly appointed proxy are entitled. Accordingly, there is scope for a company's articles of association to afford more generous rights to members and to proxies. In practice it is considered to be unlikely that many companies in particular private companies, will wish to adopt provisions concerning proxies that go beyond the basic legislative requirements. **22.304**

Transitional provisions

Schedule 30, para 30 of the Third Commencement Order provides as follows: **22.305**

> **Procedure at meetings and proxies (ss. 318 to 331)**
>
> 30.—(1) Sections 318 to 323 of the Companies Act 2006 (procedure at meetings) and sections 324 to 331 (proxies) apply to meetings of which notice is given on or after 1st October 2007.
>
> (2) The provisions of the 1985 Act or the 1986 Order continue to apply to meetings of which notice was given before that date.
>
> (3) The provisions referred to in sub-paragraph (2) include sections 370, 370A, 372 to 375 and 378(4) of the 1985 Act or Articles 378, 378A, 380 to 383 and 386(4) of the 1986 Order.
>
> (4) Where notice of a meeting is given over more than one day, it is treated for the purposes of this paragraph as given on the first of those days.

COMMENTARY: Procedure at meetings and proxies (ss. 318 to 331)

Sections 318 to 323 dealing with the procedure at meetings and the appointment of proxies apply only to meetings of which notice was given on or after 1 October 2007. The earlier provisions of CA 1985 continue to apply to meetings where notice was given before that date. **22.306**

Adjourned meetings

332 Resolution passed at adjourned meeting

Where a resolution is passed at an adjourned meeting of a company, the resolution is for all purposes to be treated as having been passed on the date on which it was in fact passed, and is not to be deemed passed on any earlier date.

COMMENTARY: 332 Resolution passed at adjourned meeting

22.307 Section 332 is based on the part of CA 1985, s 381 that applied to meetings of members. It is well established that an adjourned meeting is to be regarded as a continuation of the original meeting.[92] Section 332 stipulates that in the event that a resolution is passed at an adjourned meeting of members the resolution is treated as having been passed on that day, and the resolution is not deemed to have been passed on the earlier date of the antecedent meeting. CA 1985, s 381 applied the same rule to class meetings of members and to meetings of directors, neither of which are mentioned in s 332. CA 2006, s 334 now regulates the position so far as class meetings are concerned.

Electronic communications

333 Sending documents relating to meetings etc in electronic form

(1) Where a company has given an electronic address in a notice calling a meeting, it is deemed to have agreed that any document or information relating to proceedings at the meeting may be sent by electronic means to that address (subject to any conditions or limitations specified in the notice).

(2) Where a company has given an electronic address—
   (a) in an instrument of proxy sent out by the company in relation to the meeting, or
   (b) in an invitation to appoint a proxy issued by the company in relation to the meeting,

   it is deemed to have agreed that any document or information relating to proxies for that meeting may be sent by electronic means to that address (subject to any conditions or limitations specified in the notice).

(3) In subsection (2), documents relating to proxies include—
   (a) the appointment of a proxy in relation to a meeting,
   (b) any document necessary to show the validity of, or otherwise relating to, the appointment of a proxy, and
   (c) notice of the termination of the authority of a proxy.

(4) In this section 'electronic address' means any address or number used for the purposes of sending or receiving documents or information by electronic means.

---

[92] See *McLaren v Thomson* [1917] 2 Ch 261 (CA).

COMMENTARY: 333 Sending documents relating to meetings etc in electronic form

Overview

Section 333 deals with the very important issue of the company communicating with its members about meetings by means of electronic communications. CA 2006, ss 333 and 1143–1148, together with Schs 4 and 5 came into force on 20 January 2007 by virtue of para 3 (1) of the Companies Act 2006 (Commencement No 1, Transitional Provisions and Savings) Order 2006.[93] Schedule 4 contains provisions regulating how documents and information may be sent or supplied *to* a company by an individual member, that is to say by a member who is not a company within the meaning of a statute.[94] This must be contrasted with Sch 5 which governs communications *by* and between a company. **22.308**

Part 3, para 6 of both Schs 4 and 5 provides that a document may only be sent to a company in electronic form if the company has agreed to this method or it is deemed to have so agreed by reason of a provision of the Companies Act. Section 333(1) and 333(2) constitutes deeming provisions within the meaning of those paragraphs. Accordingly, the effect of s 333 (coupled with the provisions of Schs 4 and 5, Part 3) is to permit a member of a company to communicate with the company by electronic means in circumstances where the company has given an electronic address in a notice convening a meeting or in an instrument of proxy or proxy invitation. **22.309**

Subsections (1) and (2):

Both of these provisions are subject to any conditions or limitations on the use of the electronic address that may be specified in the notice of meeting. **22.310**

Subsection (3):

The documents that may be sent to the company relating to proxies under this section include the notice of appointment of a proxy, any document that evidences the validity of or relates to the appointment and a notice of termination of the authority of a proxy. It is likely that the ability to give notice of termination of a proxy's authority by email under this section will be of considerable value. Indeed, if the section applies, notice of termination of a proxy's authority may be given by email even where the appointment of the proxy itself was made in hard copy form. **22.311**

Subsection (4): 'Electronic address'

'Electronic address' is defined for the purposes of s 333 as any address or number used for the purposes of sending or receiving documents or information by **22.312**

---

93 SI 2006/3428.

94 Communications by a company are regulated by Sch 5—see s 1144(2).

electronic means. CA 2006, s 1168(3) gives as examples of electronic means email and fax. A document or information is sent or supplied by electronic means if it is sent initially and received at its destination by means of electronic equipment for the processing or storage of data and is entirely transmitted, conveyed and received by wire, by radio, by optical means or by any other electromagnetic means.[95] For further discussion of these issues see Chapter 17.

Online voting

22.313 Listed public companies have been making increasing use of this provision. Shareholders are regularly encouraged to vote online using the company's website. Many companies are sending voting forms to members recommending them to nominate a proxy or in the alternative to vote using their 'unique shareholder reference number'. Where such an approach is adopted it is essential that shareholders are told that if they send in both their hard copy voting form and vote online the last instruction that the company receives will be the one that counts. However, members are of course still entitled to attend the company's general meeting and vote in person and they must told that where they do so the vote which counts will be that given by them at the meeting.

Application to class meetings

334 Application to class meetings

(1) The provisions of this Chapter apply (with necessary modifications) in relation to a meeting of holders of a class of shares as they apply in relation to a general meeting.This is subject to subsections (2) and (3).

(2) The following provisions of this Chapter do not apply in relation to a meeting of holders of a class of shares—

  (a) sections 303 to 305 (members' power to require directors to call general meeting), and

  (b) section 306 (power of court to order meeting).

(3) The following provisions (in addition to those mentioned in subsection (2)) do not apply in relation to a meeting in connection with the variation of rights attached to a class of shares (a 'variation of class rights meeting')—

  (a) section 318 (quorum), and

  (b) section 321 (right to demand a poll).

(4) The quorum for a variation of class rights meeting is—

  (a) for a meeting other than an adjourned meeting, two persons present holding at least one-third in nominal value of the issued shares of the class in question (excluding any shares of that class held as treasury shares);

  (b) for an adjourned meeting, one person present holding shares of the class in question.

[95] See CA 2006, s 1168(4).

(5) For the purposes of subsection (4), where a person is present by proxy or proxies, he is treated as holding only the shares in respect of which those proxies are authorised to exercise voting rights.

(6) At a variation of class rights meeting, any holder of shares of the class in question present may demand a poll.

(7) For the purposes of this section—

(a) any amendment of a provision contained in a company's articles for the variation of the rights attached to a class of shares, or the insertion of any such provision into the articles, is itself to be treated as a variation of those rights, and

(b) references to the variation of rights attached to a class of shares include references to their abrogation.

COMMENTARY: 334 Application to class meetings

Overview

Where the share capital of a company is divided into different classes separate meetings of the members of those classes are often required. Just as with a general meeting it is important that class meetings are duly convened and conducted strictly in accordance with the applicable legislation, the relevant articles of association and the provisions of any applicable shareholders' agreement. CA 2006, s 334 sets out the minimum requirements for valid class meetings and deals in particular with meetings that are held to vary class rights. **22.314**

Subsections (1) and (2):

By s 334(1) the provisions of Part 13, Chapter 3 are declared to apply, with necessary modifications, to meetings of the holders of shares of different classes as they apply to general meetings. Among the important provisions that apply to class meetings is s 324 entitling any member of a company to appoint another person as his proxy to attend, speak and vote. **22.315**

However, this is subject to subs (2) which provides that ss 303 (the members' power to require directors to call general meeting); 304 (the directors' duty to call meeting required by members); 305 (the power of members to call a meeting at the company's expense); and 306 (the power of court to order a meeting) do not apply to class meetings. Accordingly, there is no statutory power enabling a member to require the calling of a class meeting by the directors and it is not possible to apply to the court for a class meeting to be convened by order of the court. **22.316**

Subsection (3):

This provision contains a further caveat in relation to the applicability of Part 13, Chapter 3 to class meetings. Where a meeting of a class of members is convened in connection with the variation of the class rights attached to those shares the provisions of s 318 (quorum) and s 321 (the right to demand a poll) do not apply. In place of s 318 the provisions of subss (4) and (5) apply. In place of s 321 the provisions of subs (6) apply. **22.317**

Subsections (4) and (5):

22.318 Subsection (4) provides that the required quorum for a lawful meeting to vary the class rights of that class is two persons present holding at least one-third in nominal value of the issued shares of that class. This requirement excludes any shares that are held as treasury shares as defined by CA 2006, s 724. For an adjourned meeting dealing with a proposed variation of rights the required quorum is one member present who is a holder of the class of shares in question. A member may be present at a class meeting by means of a duly appointed proxy. This is the inevitable impact of the wording of s 334(1) and is a necessary implication of subs (5). Where a member is present by one or more proxies he is treated for the purpose of the quorum requirements in subs (4) as holding only the shares in respect of which those proxies are authorized to exercise voting rights.

Subsection (6):

22.319 In relation to a meeting for the variation of class rights under s 334(6) any holder of shares of that class who is present at the meeting may make a demand for a poll. Section 329(1) extends the right to demand a poll or to join in the demand for a poll to a duly appointed proxy. By virtue of subs (5) the proxy is to be treated as the holder of the shares of the class in question.

Subsection (7):

22.320 Subsection (7) clarifies the scope of the phrase 'variation of class rights' for the purposes of s 334. A variation of class rights includes any amendment to a provision in a company's articles of association for the variation of class rights and the insertion of any such provision into the articles of association. Further, the phrase '… the variation of rights attached to a class of shares …' includes, but is not limited to, references to the abrogation of such rights.

Transitional provisions

22.321 The transitional provisions relating to s 334 are to be found in the Third Commencement Order, Sch 3, para 31. These provisions are discussed in the commentary below s 335.

> **335 Application to class meetings: companies without a share capital**
>
> (1) The provisions of this Chapter apply (with necessary modifications) in relation to a meeting of a class of members of a company without a share capital as they apply in relation to a general meeting.
> This is subject to subsections (2) and (3).
>
> (2) The following provisions of this Chapter do not apply in relation to a meeting of a class of members—
>
> (a) sections 303 to 305 (members' power to require directors to call general meeting), and

(b) section (306) (power of the court to order a meeting).

(3) The following provisions (in addition to those mentioned in subsection (2)) do not apply in relation to a meeting in connection with the variation of the rights of a class of members (a 'variation of class rights meeting')—
  (a) section 318 (quorum), and
  (b) section 321 (right to demand a poll).

(4) The quorum for a variation of class rights meeting is—
  (a) for a meeting other than an adjourned meeting, two members of the class present (in person or by proxy) who together represent at least one-third of the voting rights of the class;
  (b) for an adjourned meeting, one member of the class present (in person or by proxy).

(5) At a variation of class rights meeting, any member present (in person or by proxy) may demand a poll.

(6) For the purposes of this section—
  (a) any amendment of a provision contained in a company's articles for the variation of the rights of a class of members, or the insertion of any such provision into the articles, is itself to be treated as a variation of those rights; and
  (b) references to the variation of rights of a class of members include references to their abrogation.

COMMENTARY: 335 Application to class meetings: companies without a share capital

Section 335 provides for the application of the provisions of Part 13, Chapter 3 with certain modifications to class meetings of companies that do not have a share capital. This section will in the main apply to companies that are limited by guarantee. In such companies members may enjoy different rights of participation and entitlement. The section is the mirror image of s 334, save that there is no reference to share holdings or to share capital. Subsection (5) mirrors the wording of s 334(6) and states clearly that at a variation of class rights meeting (ie a meeting in connection with the variation of the rights of a class of members) any member present in person or by proxy may demand a vote to be taken on a poll. **22.322**

Transitional provisions

Schedule 3, para 31 of the Third Commencement Order provides as follows: **22.323**

Application of provisions to class meetings (ss. 334 and 335)

31.—(1) Sections 334 and 335 of the Companies Act 2006 (application of provisions of Chapter 3 to class meetings) apply to requests and meetings in relation to which the provisions applied by those sections have effect.

(2) Section 125(6) of the 1985 Act or Article 135(6) of the 1986 Order continues to apply to meetings of which notice is given before 1st October 2007.

(3) Where notice of a meeting is given over more than one day, it is treated for the purposes of sub-paragraph (2) as given on the first of those days.

COMMENTARY: Application of provisions to class meetings (ss. 334 and 335)

22.324 These transitional provisions preserve the existing statutory requirements for class meetings contained in CA 1985, s 125(6) where notice of the class meeting was given before 1 October 2007. It would seem that the new legislation applies to class meetings where notice is given on or after that date. It is difficult to conceive why it was thought necessary to use the cryptic wording in para 31(1).

CHAPTER 4
PUBLIC COMPANIES: ADDITIONAL REQUIREMENTS FOR AGMs

336 Public companies: annual general meeting

(1) Every public company must hold a general meeting as its annual general meeting in each period of 6 months beginning with the day following its accounting reference date (in addition to any other meetings held during that period).

(2) A company that fails to comply with subsection (1) as a result of giving notice under section 392 (alteration of accounting reference date)—

(a) specifying a new accounting reference date, and

(b) stating that the current accounting reference period or the previous accounting reference period is to be shortened,

shall be treated as if it had complied with subsection (1) if it holds a general meeting as its annual general meeting within 3 months of giving that notice.

(3) If a company fails to comply with subsection (1), an offence is committed by every officer of the company who is in default.

(4) A person guilty of an offence under this section is liable—

(a) on conviction on indictment, to a fine;

(b) on summary conviction, to a fine not exceeding the statutory maximum.

COMMENTARY: 336 Public companies: annual general meeting

Overview

22.325 Part 13, Chapter 4 (ss 336–340) deals with the important matter of annual general meetings of public companies. The provisions in Chapter 4 apply to public companies only and are additional requirements applicable to their annual general meetings. Unlike private companies, a public company remains under a statutory duty imposed by CA 2006 every year to hold a meeting designated as its annual general meeting. As has been discussed in Chapter 4 of this book, many existing private companies may well continue to hold an annual general meeting. If the articles of association of a private company require an annual general meeting and the company no longer desires to hold such a meeting, the relevant provisions of the articles will require amendment. There are extensive transitional provisions dealing with the implementation of ss 336–340. These are considered below.[96] These sections came into force on 1 October 2007 pursuant to art 2 of the Third Commencement Order.

[96] The transitional provisions appear in Sch 3, paras 32–38 to the Third Commencement Order (see below).

Subsection (1):

Section 336(1) sets out the statutory duty on a public company to hold a general meeting which is designated as the annual general meeting of that public company. An annual general meeting of a public company must be held once a year, in the period of six months that begins with the day following the accounting reference date of the company. In effect this means that a company must hold its annual general meeting within 26 weeks of the end of its financial year. The statutory requirement to designate a meeting as an annual general meeting does not preclude the public company from holding other meetings of its members that may be required from time to time. Of course, for large public companies having extensive numbers of shareholders the costs of and incidental to convening and holding a meeting of its shareholders may be considerable. In such circumstances it may be in the best interests of the company to avoid the need for a multiplicity of meetings of its members during a year. **22.326**

Subsection (2):

Subsection (2) provides in effect that a public company shall be treated as having complied with the requirement in subs (1) to hold an annual general meeting in each period of six months beginning with the day following its accounting reference date, if it has given notice of the alteration of its accounting reference date under s 392 and holds its annual general meeting within three months of giving that notice. A notice under s 392 must specify the new accounting reference date and state that the existing accounting reference period or previous accounting reference period is to be shortened. **22.327**

Subsections (3) and (4): Offence

By subs (3) all of the officers of a public company will commit an offence if their company fails to comply with the statutory obligation to hold an annual general meeting. If such persons are found guilty of the statutory offence subs (4) prescribes the criminal sanctions. **22.328**

Transitional provisions

The transitional provisions relating to s 336 are to be found in the Third Commencement Order, Sch 3, paras 32–38. These provisions are discussed in the commentary below s 340. **22.329**

> **337 Public companies: notice of AGM**
>
> (1) A notice calling an annual general meeting of a public company must state that the meeting is an annual general meeting.
>
> (2) An annual general meeting may be called by shorter notice than that required by section 307(2) or by the company's articles (as the case may be), if all the members entitled to attend and vote at the meeting agree to the shorter notice.

COMMENTARY: 337 Public companies: notice of AGM

22.330 This section replaces CA 1985, s 369. Section 337 prescribes requirements for a valid notice to convene an annual general meeting of a public company. By subs (1) the requisite notice must state that the meeting of the company is to be the annual general meeting. This requirement is clearly designed to ensure that the members are aware of the importance of the meeting.

Subsection (2):

22.331 As to the required period of notice for the convening of an annual general meeting of a public company, subs (2) refers back to s 307(2) which stipulates a notice period of 21 days. It is permissible for a public company to hold an annual general meeting by a period of notice of less than 21 days provided that there is unanimous agreement to a shorter period of notice from the members who are entitled to attend and vote at the meeting. The new provision therefore reflects in its wording the previous legislation.[97]

Difficulties of obtaining unanimous consent

22.332 It is doubtful whether a listed public company with a vast number of members entitled to attend and vote at an annual general meeting would ever be able, as a matter of practicality, to obtain such unanimous agreement. However, in the context of an unlisted public company with more modest numbers of registered members such unanimous consent might be achieved. The legislation does not indicate how the public company should go about the not insignificant task of obtaining the consent of all of its members who are entitled to attend and vote at the annual general meeting; the logistics of such an exercise may prove to be difficult to achieve in practice. It would be essential for any public company seeking to rely upon s 337(2) to have an adequate evidential record of the unanimous consent of the members entitled to attend and vote at the annual general meeting so that it is in a position to meet any objection with credible evidence.

22.333 Abrogating the right of a member to receive the requisite period of notice for a meeting is a serious matter and one that will be permitted only if the strict requirements of the section are met. Section 337(2) requires the agreement of all the members entitled to attend and vote and the statutory requirement is not subject to any de minimis exception.

[97] See CA 1985, s 369.

Transitional provisions

The transitional provisions relating to s 337 are to be found in the Third Commencement Order, Sch 3, paras 32–38. These provisions are discussed in the commentary below s 340. **22.334**

338 Public companies: members' power to require circulation of resolutions for AGMs

(1) The members of a public company may require the company to give, to members of the company entitled to receive notice of the next annual general meeting, notice of a resolution which may properly be moved and is intended to be moved at that meeting.

(2) A resolution may properly be moved at an annual general meeting unless—

(a) it would, if passed, be ineffective (whether by reason of inconsistency with any enactment or the company's constitution or otherwise),

(b) it is defamatory of any person, or

(c) it is frivolous or vexatious.

(3) A company is required to give notice of a resolution once it has received requests that it do so from—

(a) members representing at least 5% of the total voting rights of all the members who have a right to vote on the resolution at the annual general meeting to which the requests relate (excluding any voting rights attached to any shares in the company held as treasury shares), or

(b) at least 100 members who have a right to vote on the resolution at the annual general meeting to which the requests relate and hold shares in the company on which there has been paid up an average sum, per member, of at least £100.

See also section 153 (exercise of rights where shares held on behalf of others).

(4) A request—

(a) may be in hard copy form or in electronic form,

(b) must identify the resolution of which notice is to be given,

(c) must be authenticated by the person or persons making it, and

(d) must be received by the company not later than—

(i) 6 weeks before the annual general meeting to which the requests relate, or

(ii) if later, the time at which notice is given of that meeting.

COMMENTARY: 338 Public companies: members' power to require circulation of resolutions for AGMs

Overview

22.335

Section 338 and 339 together replace CA 1985, ss 376 and 377. Section 338 deals with the rights of members of public companies to require the company to circulate resolutions which they intend to move at the next annual general meeting of the company. There are limits as to the sort of resolution that can be proposed and the shareholders who wish to use this statutory power must have the requisite standing to do so. It is to be noted that this section is a useful right for shareholders in public companies who want to raise an issue at the annual general meeting. However, it is a right that has bounds and limitations and it is not an unfettered tool of shareholder activism.

Subsections (1) and (2):

22.336 Section 338(1) refers to resolutions that may properly be moved at an annual general meeting. This phrase is explained further in s 338(2). Any resolution may be moved at an annual general meeting unless it would, if passed, be ineffective or it is defamatory of any person or it is frivolous or vexatious. These three grounds are alternative rather than cumulative requirements, entitling a company to decline to circulate a resolution from its members. Probably it will be relatively straightforward to identify resolutions which would, if passed, be ineffective or are defamatory of any person. If a public company is in any doubt as to whether or not a resolution is defamatory it should seek appropriate professional advice. However, precisely what resolutions will be properly characterised as being frivolous or vexatious may be harder to determine. CA 2006 does not give a definition of what constitutes a resolution that is frivolous or vexatious.

Subsection (3): Numbers required for a valid request

22.337 The right of members of a public company to require the circulation of a resolution is subject to a standing requirement set out in s 338(3). Two categories of members of public companies may make use of the power under s 338(1). First, members of a public company who wish to use the power must have at least 5% of the total voting rights of all the members who have a right to vote on the resolution. In the alternative, at least 100 members of a public company who have the right to vote on the resolution and hold shares in the company on which there has been paid up an average sum per member of at least £100. Although this appears to be a modest figure, in fact in the case of many public companies it may be very difficult to comply with this test. A substantial number of public companies have shares of a low nominal value, often just a few pence or fractions thereof. The statutory provision takes no account of the traded market value of such shares.

22.338 In general it will be a group of members of a public company who will have the ability to make use of the statutory power but a single member with a shareholding of at least 5% of the total voting rights of all the members who have a right to vote on the resolution would fall within the ambit of s 338(3) (a). This is to be contrasted with s 338(3)(b) where the legislation requires a minimum of 100 members.

The impact of CA 2006, s 153

The final sentence of s 338(3) refers to s 153[98] which governs the exercise of rights where shares are held on behalf of others. Section 153 applies for the purposes of s 314 (power to require circulation of statement), s 342 (power to require an independent report on a poll) and s 527 (power to require website publication of audit concerns), as well as s 338. Section 153(2) provides a third category of persons[99] who may request the company to give notice of a resolution. This provision provides as follows: **22.339**

> (1) A company is required to act under any of those sections if it receives a request in relation to which the following conditions are met—
> (a) section 314 (power to require circulation of statement),
> (b) section 338 (public companies: power to require circulation of resolution for AGM),
> (c) section 342 (power to require independent report on poll), and
> (d) section 527 (power to require website publication of audit concerns).
>
> (2) A company is required to act under any of those sections if it receives a request in relation to which the following conditions are met—
> (a) it is made by at least 100 persons;
> (b) it is authenticated by all the persons making it;
> (c) in the case of any of those persons who is not a member of the company, it is accompanied by a statement—
> (i) of the full name and address of a person ('the member') who is a member of the company and holds shares on behalf of that person,
> (ii) that the member is holding those shares on behalf of that person in the course of a business,
> (iii) of the number of shares in the company that the member holds on behalf of that person,
> (iv) of the total amount paid up on those shares,
> (v) that those shares are not held on behalf of anyone else or, if they are, that the other person or persons are not among the other persons making the request,
> (vi) that some or all of those shares confer voting rights that are relevant for the purposes of making a request under the section in question, and
> (vii) that the person has the right to instruct the member how to exercise those rights;
> (d) in the case of any of those persons who is a member of the company, it is accompanied by a statement—
> (i) that he holds shares otherwise than on behalf of another person, or
> (ii) that he holds shares on behalf of one or more other persons but those persons are not among the other persons making the request;
> (e) it is accompanied by such evidence as the company may reasonably require of the matters mentioned in paragraph (c) and (d);
> (f) the total amount of the sums paid up on—

[98] A detailed analysis of section 153 is found in Chapter 10.
[99] ie in addition to those in subparagraphs (a) and (b) of section 338(3), CA 2006.

(i) shares held as mentioned in paragraph (c), and
(ii) shares held as mentioned in paragraph (d),

divided by the number of persons making the request, is not less than £100;

(g) the request complies with any other requirements of the section in question as to contents, timing and otherwise.

22.340 It can be seen from the above that such a request must be made by at least 100 persons and, in the case of any of those who are not members of the company, it must be accompanied by a detailed statement particularizing the matters listed in (i) to (vii). In all cases the total amount of the sums paid up on the relevant shares must be an average of not less than £100 per person. The same considerations apply as to the difficulties in practice of meeting this test, which is in no way referable to the true value of the shares but only to their nominal value.

Subsection (4): Form and timing of the request

22.341 Section 338(4) contains information relating to the form and contents of a request. There are compulsory and optional requirements. The compulsory requirements are that the request must:

(i) identify the resolution; and
(ii) be authenticated by the person or persons making the request; and
(iii) be received by the company not later than six weeks before the annual general meeting to which it relates or if later (ie than the six weeks) not later than the time at which notice is given of the annual general meeting.

22.342 These timing requirements are of essential importance in that the members' power to require the circulation of a resolution will be lost if the request is not received by the company within the requisite period of time. The last possible date for an effective request from members is the time at which notice is given of the meeting by the company. Practitioners should note that if a valid request is to be made, care should be taken to ensure that it is received by the company in good time. Secretaries of public companies will no doubt be alert to ensure that requests from members that are made out of time are disregarded.

22.343 Section 338(4)(a) also provides that at the option of the requesting members the request may be in hard copy form or in electronic form. For the meaning of 'electronic form' see CA 2006, s 1168(3)–(6).[100] The form in which a request is provided may depend to some extent on the members' ability to comply with the important timing requirements.

---

[100] See further Ch 17.

Transitional provisions

The transitional provisions relating to s 338 are to be found in the Third Commencement Order, Sch 3, paras 32–38. These provisions are discussed in the commentary below s 340. **22.344**

339 Public companies: company's duty to circulate members' resolutions for AGMs

(1) A company that is required under section 338 to give notice of a resolution must send a copy of it to each member of the company entitled to receive notice of the annual general meeting—
  (a) in the same manner as notice of the meeting, and
  (b) at the same time as, or as soon as reasonably practicable after, it gives notice of the meeting.
(2) Subsection (1) has effect subject to section 340(2) (deposit or tender of sum in respect of expenses of circulation).
(3) The business which may be dealt with at an annual general meeting includes a resolution of which notice is given in accordance with this section.
(4) In the event of default in complying with this section, an offence is committed by every officer of the company who is in default.
(5) A person guilty of an offence under this section is liable—
  (a) on conviction on indictment, to a fine;
  (b) on summary conviction, to a fine not exceeding the statutory maximum.

COMMENTARY: 339 Public companies: company's duty to circulate members' resolutions for AGMs

Where a public company is required to give notice of resolutions under s 338 it is under a statutory duty to give such notice in the same manner in which it gives notice of the annual general meeting and at the same time as it gives notice of the annual general meeting, or as soon as reasonably practicable after. This statutory duty is stated to be subject to s 340(2) which deals with the important issue of the payment of expenses. As will be seen below, the company is only under an obligation to comply with a request to circulate a resolution if its expenses in connection with due compliance with the section have been paid.[101] The persons who must receive notice of the resolutions under s 338 are each member of the company entitled to receive notice of the annual general meeting. **22.345**

Subsection (3):

This provision states that the business of the annual general meeting which may be dealt with includes a resolution of which notice is given in accordance with the section. This permissive language ignores the fact that if the members' rights under ss 338 and 339 are exercised, the business of the annual general meeting must include the members' resolution. **22.346**

101 See s 340 (below).

Subsections (4) and (5): Offence

22.347 If the officers of a public company fail to comply with the requirements of s 339 they all commit an offence under s 339(4), and those officers who are proved to be guilty of this offence are subject to the penalties stated in s 339(5).

Transitional provisions

22.348 The transitional provisions relating to s 339 are to be found in the Third Commencement Order, Sch 3 at paras 32–38. These provisions are discussed in the commentary below s 340.

> **340 Public companies: expenses of circulating members' resolutions for AGM**
>
> (1) The expenses of the company in complying with section 339 need not be paid by the members who requested the circulation of the resolution if requests sufficient to require the company to circulate it are received before the end of the financial year preceding the meeting.
>
> (2) Otherwise—
>
> (a) the expenses of the company in complying with that section must be paid by the members who requested the circulation of the resolution unless the company resolves otherwise, and
>
> (b) unless the company has previously so resolved, it is not bound to comply with that section unless there is deposited with or tendered to it, not later than—
>
> (i) six weeks before the annual general meeting to which the requests relate, or
>
> (ii) if later, the time at which notice is given of that meeting,
>
> a sum reasonably sufficient to meet its expenses in complying with that section.

COMMENTARY: 340 Public companies: expenses of circulating members' resolutions for AGM

22.349 Section 340 applies to public companies only. The costs and expenses associated with the circulation of resolutions under ss 338 and 339 may be considerable where a public company has an extensive number of shareholders. In practice the costs of and incidental to this process may act as an effective deterrent to prevent shareholders using the rights under s 338.

22.350 However, there are two circumstances in which the expenses of the circulation of a resolution may not fall to be paid by the shareholders themselves. First, where they apply before the end of the company's financial year and secondly, where the company has resolved that the expenses need not be paid by the members.

Subsection (1):

22.351 By s 340(1) the shareholders are absolved from the requirement to pay the expenses of the circulation if the request has been received by the public company before the end of the financial year that preceded the annual general meeting. For example, if a public company's accounting reference date was 30 April its annual general meeting would have to be held by 31 October in any year. If members were to send in a valid request to the public company to require circulation of a resolution for the annual general meeting at any time before 30 April there will be no costs chargeable to those members. This is an important statutory concession which may encourage members to lodge their requests with the company earlier than they otherwise would. However, the benefits of the statutory concession on payment of expenses will not assist a member in relation to a proposed resolution regarding a matter that has only recently arisen.

Subsection (2):

Section 340(2) provides that in every other case the general rule is that the company's expenses in complying with the section and circulating the members' resolution must be paid by those members who make the request. There is an exception to this general rule where the company has resolved otherwise. The legislation is silent as to whether 'the company' in this context refers to the board of directors or to the shareholders in general meeting. It is suggested that in this context 'the company' refers to the company in general meeting who may resolve to exempt the members from payment of these expenses. An appropriate provision may also be inserted in the articles of association of a public company authorizing the board of directors to grant such exemption to members. **22.352**

Timing and compliance

Section 340(2)(b) is of vital significance in that it makes the public company's compliance with the request dependant upon the members' willingness to meet the associated costs. It applies in all cases unless the public company in question has resolved previously to grant an exemption as to the payment of expenses by the members who make the request. The public company is not bound to comply with s 339 and circulate the members' resolution unless it has received by way of deposit or has had tendered to it a sum reasonably sufficient to meet its compliance expenses. The timing of this deposit or tender of funds is also important. Again it has to be provided not later than six weeks before the annual general meeting or, if later, at the time at which notice is given of that meeting. **22.353**

The wording of this provision is almost guaranteed to lead to legal disputes as it is likely that companies will be faced with a period of uncertainly after the lodging of a request from members as to whether the expenses of circulation will in fact be met. As the members making the request are entitled to deposit the funds as late as just before the time when notice is given of the meeting, those involved with the administration of the meeting will be required in practice to take preliminary steps to comply with the request. The weakness in the drafting of the legislation has arisen from the failure of the statute to require that the request is accompanied by **22.354** the deposit or tender of the sum of money that is reasonably sufficient to meet the company's expenses. Under CA 1985, s 377(1)(b) this was an express requirement which had practical effect. Regrettably, this provision in the new legislation creates uncertainty and may leave public companies in the infelicitous situation that they will not know whether they are obliged to give notice of a members' resolution until relatively late in the period prior to the date fixed for the annual general meeting.

22.355 Disputes may also arise as to the size of the sum that is considered to be reasonably sufficient to meet the company's expenses in complying with the requirements of s 399. In order to try to avoid such problems it is recommended that upon receipt of a request made under s 338 the company secretary or other officer should write to the relevant members explaining the likely amount of the company's expenses and their composition. At the same time a request should be made of the members for the deposit or tender of this amount within the time period that is permitted by the statutory timetable. It is to be hoped that such a response by a public company will minimize the risk of a legal dispute on this subject.

Transitional provisions

22.356 Schedule 3, paras 32–38 of the Third Commencement Order (as amended by the Sixth Commencement Order) provides as follows:

> **Annual general meetings (ss. 336 to 340)**
>
> 32.—(1) The repeal of section 366 of the 1985 Act or Article 374 of the 1986 Order (duty to hold annual general meeting) does not affect any provision of a private company's memorandum or articles that expressly requires the company to hold an annual general meeting.
>
> (2) Any such provision continues to have such effect as it had immediately before 1st October 2007.
>
> (3) Provision specifying that one or more directors are to retire at an annual general meeting of the company is not provision expressly requiring the company to hold an annual general meeting.
>
> [(4) A company is not to be treated as one whose articles expressly require it to hold an annual general meeting if immediately before 1st October 2007 there was in force a resolution under section 366A of the 1985 Act or Article 374A of the 1986 Order (election to dispense with annual general meetings).][102]
>
> 33. The repeal of section 367 of the 1985 Act (default power of Secretary of State to call AGM) has effect in relation to a private company as from 1st October 2007, even if an application under that section has been made, or the Secretary of State has called or directed the calling of a meeting under that section, before that date.

---

[102] Text in square brackets added to Sch 3, para 32 of the Third Commencement Order by Sch 5, para 2(6) of the Fifth Commencement Order, SI 2007/3495.

34.—(1) The repeal of sections 376 and 377 of the 1985 Act or Articles 384 and 385 of the 1986 Order does not affect their application in relation to a requisition under section 376(1)(a) or Article 384(1)(a) made to a private company before 1st October 2007.

(2) So long as such a requisition has not been complied with, section 366 of the 1985 Act or Article 374 of the 1986 Order (duty to hold annual general meeting) continues to apply in relation to the company.

This does not apply if the company is not required to comply with the requisition (see section 377 of the 1985 Act or Article 385 of the 1986 Order).

(3) Where copies of the requisition are deposited on more than one day, the reference in sub-paragraph (1) to the day on which the request or requisition is made shall be read as a reference to the first day on which the copies deposited are sufficient to require the company to act.

35.—(1) In the case of an existing public company—

(a) section 366 of the 1985 Act or section 374 of the 1986 Order (duty to hold annual general meeting) continues to apply to determine the date by which the company must hold its first annual general meeting after 30th September 2007, and

(b) section 336 of the Companies Act 2006 (public companies: annual general meeting) applies in relation to subsequent annual general meetings.

(2) An 'existing public company' means a company formed and registered before 1st October 2007 that is a public company immediately before that date.

36. The repeal of section 367 of the 1985 Act (default power of Secretary of State to call AGM) does not affect the operation of that section in relation to a public company where an application under that section was made before 1st October 2007.

37.—(1) Section 337 of the Companies Act 2006 (public companies: notice of AGM) applies to meetings of which notice is given on or after 1st October 2007.

(2) Section 369 of the 1985 Act or Article 377 of the 1986 Order continues to apply in relation to meetings of which notice is given before that date.

(3) Where notice of a meeting is given over more than one day, it is treated for the purposes of this paragraph as given on the first of those days.

38.—(1) Sections 338 to 340 of the Companies Act 2006 (public companies: members' power to require circulation of resolutions for AGMs) apply to requests made on or after 1st October 2007.

(2) Sections 376 and 377 of the 1985 Act or Articles 384 and 385 of the 1986 Order continue to apply to requisitions made to a public company before that date.

(3) Where requests are made or copies of a requisition are deposited on more than one day, the references in this paragraph to the day on which the request or requisition is made shall be read as references to the first day on which the requests made or copies deposited are sufficient to require the company to act.

COMMENTARY: Annual general meetings (ss. 336 to 340)

22.357

These extensive transitional provisions have arisen as a consequence of the decision taken in CA 2006 to abolish the previous statutory requirement for annual general meetings of private companies. The decision has left many tens of thousands of existing private companies with articles of association which reflect the previous law. Paragraph 32 makes it clear beyond doubt that such articles will continue to apply and to govern the affairs of those companies. However, sub-para (3) provides that where the provision in the articles simply requires the retirement of directors by rotation at an annual general meeting, that provision is not to be interpreted as expressly requiring the company to hold an annual general meeting. Regulation 73 of the 1985 Table A is in this form, dealing only with retirements by rotation.[103] It is to be contrasted with reg 89 of the 1948 Table A which, when read with reg 47, unquestionably requires the company to hold a general meeting as its annual general meeting in each year.

22.358 Paragraph 32(6) preserves the right of companies which adopted an elective resolution under CA 1985, s 366A to dispense with annual general meetings, to continue to do so notwithstanding the express provisions of their articles.

22.359 Paragraph 36 concerns the power, now removed, to apply to the Secretary of State to call an annual general meeting. Applications made in relation to a public company before 1 October 2007 are unaffected by the repeal. There is no such saving for applications in respect of private companies.

22.360 Paragraph 37 provides that s 337, dealing with the notice requirements for an annual general meeting of a public company, will apply to meetings of which notice is given on or after 1 October 2007. Similarly, by para 38, ss 338–340 dealing with the members' power to require the circulation of resolutions for an annual general meeting, will apply to requests made on or after 1 October 2007.

CHAPTER 5
ADDITIONAL REQUIREMENTS FOR QUOTED COMPANIES

Website publication of poll results

341 Results of poll to be made available on website

(1) Where a poll is taken at a general meeting of a quoted company, the company must ensure that the following information is made available on a website—
   (a) the date of the meeting,
   (b) the text of the resolution or, as the case may be, a description of the subject matter of the poll,
   (c) the number of votes cast in favour, and
   (d) the number of votes cast against.

(2) The provisions of section 353 (requirements as to website availability) apply.

(3) In the event of default in complying with this section (or with the requirements of section 353 as it applies for the purposes of this section), an offence is committed by every officer of the company who is in default.

(4) A person guilty of an offence under subsection (3) is liable on summary conviction to a fine not exceeding level 3 on the standard scale.

---

[103] See the commentary on reg 73 of the 1985 Table A in Part 4 of this book.

(5) Failure to comply with this section (or the requirements of section 353) does not affect the validity of
   (a) the poll, or
   (b) the resolution or other business (if passed or agreed to) to which the poll relates.
(6) This section only applies to polls taken after this section comes into force.

COMMENTARY: 341 Results of poll to be made avaliable on website

Overview

Chapter 5, comprising CA 2006, ss 341–354, stipulates additional requirements for quoted companies in respect of the publication of the results of voting on a poll and procedures regulating the obtaining of an independent report. **22.361**

Definition of quoted company

A quoted company for the purposes of CA 2006, Part 13 is defined in s 361 which states that it has the same meaning as in CA 2006, Part 15. That is in fact a reference to the definition found in s 385(2): a quoted company means a company whose equity share capital (a) has been included in the official list[104] in accordance with the provisions of the Financial Services and Markets Act 2000, Part 6, or (b) is officially listed in an EEA State, or (c) is admitted to dealing on either the New York Stock Exchange or Nasdaq. **22.362**

Subsections (1) and (2):

In relation to a public company where a poll is taken on a vote at a general meeting the quoted company has to ensure that certain information is made available on a website concerning the result of the poll. The information that has to be provided on a website is the date of the meeting, the text of the resolution or a description of the subject matter of the poll, the number of votes cast in favour of the resolution or the subject matter of the poll and finally the number of votes cast against the resolution or the subject matter of the poll. The provisions of s 353 concerning the availability of the website apply for the purposes of s 341. Logging the data on the relevant website is an important matter and will frequently be the responsibility of the company secretary and his staff. **22.363**

Subsection (3) and (4): Offence

The legislation goes on to provide in subs (3) that an offence is committed by every officer of the company if the requirements of s 341 and s 353 are not complied with. Officers who commit the offence prescribed by subs (3) are liable on summary conviction to a fine under subs (4). It is to be noted that the company itself does not commit an offence. **22.364**

---

104 The 'official list' is defined in the Financial Services and Markets Act 2000, s 103(1).

Subsections (5): Validity of business

22.365 Importantly, the legislation provides in subs (5) that the failure to comply with the provisions of ss 341 or 353 does not affect the validity of the poll or the resolution or other business passed or agreed to which the poll relates. This section only applies to polls that will be taken after s 341 comes into force. As at the date of writing s 341 has not yet come into force.

Subsection (6):

22.366 Section 341(6) makes it clear that the new legislation does not have retrospective effect. Accordingly, there are no transitional provisions in respect of this section.

Class meetings

22.367 It is to be noted that s 341 applies in relation to a class meeting of a quoted company in connection with a meeting held to vary the rights attached to shares of that class. This is the effect of CA 2006, s 352(1) which is considered below.

Timing

22.368 The information that is to be published on the company's website must be made available as soon as reasonably practicable and be kept available for a period of two years in accordance with CA 2006, s 353(4). For further details concerning the requirements as to website availability see s 353 below.

Independent report on poll

342 Members' power to require independent report on poll

(1) The members of a quoted company may require the directors to obtain an independent report on any poll taken, or to be taken, at a general meeting of the company.

(2) The directors are required to obtain an independent report if they receive requests to do so from—

(a) members representing not less than 5% of the total voting rights of all the members who have a right to vote on the matter to which the poll relates (excluding any voting rights attached to any shares in the company held as treasury shares), or

(b) not less than 100 members who have a right to vote on the matter to which the poll relates and hold shares in the company on which there has been paid up an average sum, per member, of not less than £100.

See also section 153 (exercise of rights where shares held on behalf of others).

(3) Where the requests relate to more than one poll, subsection (2) must be satisfied in relation to each of them.

(4) A request—

(a) may be in hard copy form or in electronic form,

(b) must identify the poll or polls to which it relates,

(c) must be authenticated by the person or persons making it, and
(d) must be received by the company not later than one week after the date on which the poll is taken.

COMMENTARY: 342 Members' power to require independent report on poll

Overview

CA 2006, ss 342–351 set a new statutory procedure under which members may obtain an independent report on a poll which is taken, or is to be taken, at a general meeting of a quoted company. By virtue of s 352 these sections also apply to polls taken at a class meeting of the holders of a class of shares of a quoted company where the meeting is held in connection with a variation of the rights attached to that class. The sections provide a comprehensive procedure for the obtaining of the independent report, the appointment of an independent assessor and the publication of the resulting report. **22.369**

Section 342(1)

Section 342 confers on members of a quoted company a new right to require the directors to obtain an independent report on any poll that has been taken, or is to be taken at a general meeting of that company. This is an important new statutory provision which may come to be used frequently by members. The section is designed to ensure that voting on a poll is properly conducted and that the outcome is capable of independent verification. This new statutory right is arguably an adjunct to the existing ability of the board of directors, in the proper exercise of their powers of management under the articles of association or pursuant to a specific provision, to authorize the appointment of independent scrutineers for the purposes of conducting a poll. **22.370**

Subsection (2):

There is a minimum threshold requirement in order to trigger the procedure, which is set out in s 342(2). That threshold requirement stipulates that the directors are under an obligation to obtain an independent report if they receive requests from either members representing not less than 5% of the total voting rights of all the members who have a right to vote on the matter to which the poll relates, or a request is received from not less than 100 members who have a right to vote on the matter to which the poll relates and hold shares in the company on which there has been paid up an average sum per member of not less than £100. The concluding sentence of s 342(2) indicates that CA 2006, s 153 (which concerns the exercise of rights where shares are held on behalf of others) applies to s 342. Frequently members will wish to ensure that they meet this minimum **22.371** threshold requirement in advance of the meeting so as to procure the attendance at the relevant meeting of the duly appointed assessor.[105]

Subsection (3):

22.372 Where a request relates to more than one vote that has been taken on a poll the threshold requirements relating to the requests must be satisfied in relation to each poll. Accordingly, in the event that a quoted company receives a valid request in relation to one poll satisfying the requirements of s 342(2)(a) it would be under an obligation to obtain a report on a poll, but if the threshold requirements are not satisfied in relation to a different vote there would be no requirement to obtain a report on that specific poll.

Subsection (4): Form and timing of the request

22.373 Members requesting the directors of a quoted company to obtain an independent report on a poll may make their request in hard copy form or in electronic form. They must also identify the poll or polls to which their request relates and the request must be authenticated by the person or persons making the request. As to the time at which the request must be received, it is stipulated by s 342(4)(d) that it must be received by the company not later than one week after the date on which the poll is taken. This is an important time constraint and one which must be adhered to strictly.

Class meetings

22.374 By virtue of s 352, this section and ss 343–351 also apply in respect of a class meeting of a quoted company that is held to consider the variation of the rights attached to any class of shares.

Transitional provisions

22.375 The transitional provisions relating to s 342 are to be found in the Third Commencement Order, Sch 3, para 39. These provisions are discussed in the commentary below s 354.

> **343 Appointment of independent assessor**
>
> (1) Directors who are required under section 342 to obtain an independent report on a poll or polls must appoint a person they consider to be appropriate (an 'independent assessor') to prepare a report for the company on it or them.
>
> (2) The appointment must be made within one week after the company being required to obtain the report.
>
> (3) The directors must not appoint a person who—

[105] See CA 2006, s 348(1) (below).

(a) does not meet the independence requirement of section 344, or
(b) has another roll in relation to any poll on which he is to report (including, in particular, a role in connection with collecting or counting votes or with the appointment of proxies).

(4) In the event of default in complying with this section, an offence is committed by every officer of the company who is in default.

(5) A person guilty of an offence under this section is liable on summary conviction to a fine not exceeding level 5 on the standard scale.

(6) If at the meeting no poll on which a report is required is taken—
(a) the directors are not required to obtain a report from the independent assessor, and
(b) his appointment ceases (but without prejudice to any right to be paid for work done before the appointment ceased).

COMMENTARY: 343 Appointment of independent assessor

Where directors of a quoted company receive a valid request under s 342 to obtain an independent report on a poll or polls they must thereafter appoint a person whom they consider to be an appropriate person to fulfil the role as an independent assessor. It is important to note that the appointment of the independent assessor can be made only by the board of directors in the exercise of their discretion on this matter. The duly appointed independent assessor is then required to prepare a report for the company on the poll or polls. **22.376**

Subsection (2):

The directors must not delay in making the appointment because s 343(2) provides that the appointment must be made within one week after the company has been requested to obtain the independent report. **22.377**

Subsection (3):

The person who is appointed must satisfy the independence requirements stipulated in s 344, which is considered further below. The directors must not appoint a person who does not meet the independence criteria of s 344 and must not appoint a person who has another role in relation to any poll on which he is to report, including a role in connection with collecting or counting votes or with the appointment of proxies. **22.378**

Subsections (4) and (5): Offence

A criminal offence is committed if the company does not comply with the requirements of s 343 and officers who are found guilty of such an offence are liable on summary conviction to a fine. **22.379**

Subsection (6):

22.380 By subs (6) if at the meeting no poll is taken in respect of a resolution on which a report has been requested, the directors are not required to obtain a report from the independent assessor and the appointment of that independent assessor ceases. The cessation of the independent assessor's role is stated to be without prejudice to any right he may have to be paid for work done before his appointment ceased.

Transitional provisions

22.381 The transitional provisions relating to s 343 are to be found in the Third Commencement Order, Sch 3, para 39. These provisions are discussed in the commentary below s 354.

344 Independence requirement

(1) A person may not be appointed as an independent assessor—
  (a) if he is—
    (i) an officer or employee of the company, or
    (ii) a partner or employee of such a person, or a partnership of which such a person is a partner;
  (b) if he is—
    (i) an officer or employee of an associated undertaking of the company, or
    (ii) a partner or employee of such a person, or a partnership of which such a person is a partner;
  (c) if there exists between—
    (i) the person or an associate of his, and
    (ii) the company or an associated undertaking of the company,

a connection of any such description as may be specified by regulations made by the Secretary of State.

(2) An auditor of the company is not regarded as an officer or employee of the company for this purpose.

(3) In this section—

'associated undertaking' means—
  (a) a parent undertaking or subsidiary undertaking of the company, or
  (b) a subsidiary undertaking of a parent undertaking of the company;

and 'associate' has the meaning given by section 345.

(4) Regulations under this section are subject to negative resolution procedure.

COMMENTARY: 344 Independence requirement

Overview

22.382 The independence requirements prescribed for an independent assessor are set out in s 344, which is expressed to be subject to further regulations that may be made in the future by the Secretary of State. At the time of writing no such regulations had been made or suggested. The requirements of the section are not unduly onerous. However, to ensure that an appropriate person is appointed as an independent assessor it may in practice be necessary for that person to be interviewed by a senior officer of the company. Such a task may be one for the company secretary.

Subsection (1):

A person may not be appointed to hold office as an independent assessor if he is either an officer or employee of the company, or a partner or employee of such a person or a partnership of which such a person is a partner. In addition, officers and employees of associated undertakings of the company are not eligible to be appointed, nor are partners or employees of such a person or a partnership of which such a person is a partner. Additionally, if there exists between the person or an associate of his or the company and the company or an associated undertaking of the company a connection of any description which may be specified in regulations to be made by the Secretary of State, then that will debar such persons from taking on the role of an independent assessor. **22.383**

Subsection (2):

It might be thought that an auditor of a quoted company is an inapposite person to carry out the independent report. However by s 344(2) an auditor of the company is not regarded as an officer or employee of the company for this purpose and may therefore qualify for appointment. The meaning of the phrase 'associated undertaking' is given further clarification by s 344(3). This is a reference to a parent or subsidiary undertaking of the company or a subsidiary undertaking of a parent undertaking of the company. 'Associate' has the meaning given by s 345. **22.384**

Subsection (3):

The meaning of the phrase 'associated undertaking' for the purposes of s 344(1)(b)(i) and 344(1)(c)(ii) is defined in subs (3). The meaning of the word 'associate' is defined in s 345 (see below). **22.385**

Transitional provisions

The transitional provisions relating to s 344 are to be found in the Third Commencement Order, Sch 3, para 39. These provisions are discussed in the commentary below s 354. **22.386**

345 Meaning of 'associate'

(1) This section defines 'associate' for the purposes of section 344 (independence requirement).

(2) In relation to an individual, 'associate' means—
   (a) that individual's spouse or civil partner or minor child or step-child,
   (b) any body corporate of which that individual is a director, and
   (c) any employee or partner of that individual.

(3) In relation to a body corporate, 'associate' means—
 (a) any body corporate of which that body is a director,
 (b) any body corporate in the same group as that body, and
 (c) any employee or partner of that body or of any body corporate in the same group.

(4) In relation to a partnership that is a legal person under the law by which it is governed, 'associate' means—
 (a) any body corporate of which that partnership is a director,
 (b) any employee of or partner in that partnership, and
 (c) any person who is an associate of a partner in that partnership.

(5) In relation to a partnership that is not a legal person under the law by which it is governed, 'associate' means any person who is an associate of any of the partners.

(6) In this section, in relation to a limited liability partnership, for 'director' read 'member'.

COMMENTARY: 345 Meaning of 'associate'

22.387 The word 'associate' is defined for the purposes of s 344 in s 345. In relation to an individual, 'associate' means that individual's spouse or civil partner or minor child or stepchild or any body corporate of which that individual is a director and any employee or partner of that individual. In relation to a body corporate, the term 'associate' is defined to mean any body corporate of which that body is a director, any body corporate in the same group as that body, and any employee or partner of that body or of any body corporate in the same group. In relation to a partnership that is a legal person under the law by which it is governed the word 'associate' means any body corporate of which that partnership is a director, or any employee of or partner in that partnership, and any person who is an associate of a partner in that partnership.

22.388 In relation to a partnership that is not a legal person under the law by which it is governed, the phrase 'associate' means any person who is an associate of any of the partners. Limited liability partnerships fall within the ambit of the section because by subs (6) the word 'director' is to be construed as a member in relation to a limited liability partnership.

Transitional provisions

22.389 The transitional provisions relating to s 345 are to be found in the Third Commencement Order, Sch 3, para 39. These provisions are discussed in the commentary below s 354.

346 Effect of appointment of a partnership

(1) This section applies where a partnership that is not a legal person under the law by which it is governed is appointed as an independent assessor.

(2) Unless a contrary intention appears, the appointment is of the partnership as such and not of the partners.

(3) Where the partnership ceases, the appointment is to be treated as extending to—
   (a) any partnership that succeeds to the practice of that partnership, or
   (b) any other person who succeeds to that practice having previously carried it on in partnership.

(4) For the purposes of subsection (3)—
   (a) a partnership is regarded as succeeding to the practice of another partnership only if the members of the successor partnership are substantially the same as those of the former partnership, and
   (b) a partnership or other person is regarded as succeeding to the practice of a partnership only if it or he succeeds to the whole or substantially the whole of the business of the former partnership.

(5) Where the partnership ceases and the appointment is not treated under subsection (3) as extending to any partnership or other person, the appointment may with the consent of the company be treated as extending to a partnership, or other person, who succeeds to—
   (a) the business of the former partnership, or
   (b) such part of it as is agreed by the company is to be treated as comprising the appointment.

COMMENTARY: 346 Effect of appointment of a partnership

Under s 346 the legislation deals with the appointment of a partnership that is not a legal person under the law by which the partnership is governed. Where a partnership that is not a legal person under the law by which it is governed is appointed as an independent assessor the appointment is of the partnership as such and not of the individual partners. This is expressed to be subject to any contrary intention. In the event that such a partnership ceases, the appointment is treated as extending to any partnership that succeeds to the practice of the first practice or any other person who succeeds to that practice having previously carried it on in partnership. **22.390**

Transitional provisions

22.391 The transitional provisions relating to s 346 are to be found in the Third Commencement Order, Sch 3, para 39. These provisions are discussed in the commentary below s 354.

347 The independent assessor's report

(1) The report of the independent assessor must state his opinion whether—
   (a) the procedures adopted in connection with the poll or polls were adequate;
   (b) the votes cast (including proxy votes) were fairly and accurately recorded and counted;
   (c) the validity of members' appointments of proxies was fairly assessed;
   (d) the notice of the meeting complied with section 325 (notice of meeting to contain statement of rights to appoint proxy);
   (e) section 326 (company-sponsored invitations to appoint proxies) was complied with in relation to the meeting.

(2) The report must give his reasons for the opinions stated.

(3) If he is unable to form an opinion on any of those matters, the report must record that fact and state the reasons for it.

(4) The report must state the name of the independent assessor.

COMMENTARY: 347 The independent assessor's report

22.392 Section 347 deals with the independent assessor's report. The report of the independent assessor must state his opinion as to whether the procedures adopted in connection with the poll or polls were adequate, whether the votes cast including proxy votes were fairly and accurately recorded and counted, whether the validity of member's appointments of proxies was fairly assessed, whether the notice of meeting complied with s 325 (in that it contained a statement of the members' rights to appoint a proxy) and whether s 326 (dealing with company-sponsored invitations to appoint proxies) was complied with in relation to the particular meeting.

Subsections (2) to (4):

22.393 The independent assessor is required to give reasons for the opinions that are stated in his report. It would therefore be imprudent for an independent assessor just to state his finding without an adequate and considered assessment of his reasons. In the event that an independent assessor is unable to form an opinion on any of the prescribed matters in s 347(1) the report must record that fact and state the reasons for it. In addition, and obviously, the report must state the name of the independent assessor.

Timing

22.394 Surprisingly, the section does not prescribe any timetable for the production of the independent assessor's report. This is the case notwithstanding the extensive powers given to the independent assessor by s 349 to require the provision of information or explanations and the creation of a new criminal offence of failing to comply with that requirement without delay in s 350(1).

Transitional provisions

22.395 The transitional provisions relating to s 347 are to be found in the Third Commencement Order, Sch 3, para 39. These provisions are discussed in the commentary below s 354.

348 Rights of independent assessor: right to attend meeting etc

(1) Where an independent assessor has been appointed to report on a poll, he is entitled to attend—

(a) the meeting at which the poll may be taken, and

(b) any subsequent proceedings in connection with the poll.

(2) He is also entitled to be provided by the company with a copy of—
   (a) the notice of the meeting, and
   (b) any other communication provided by the company in connection with the meeting to persons who have a right to vote on the matter to which the poll relates.

(3) The rights conferred by this section are only to be exercised to the extent that the independent assessor considers necessary for the preparation of his report.

(4) If the independent assessor is a firm, the right under subsection (1) to attend the meeting and any subsequent proceedings in connection with the poll is exercisable by an individual authorised by the firm in writing to act as its representative for that purpose.

COMMENTARY: 348 Rights of independent assessor: right to attend meeting etc

Overview

Being appointed as an independent assessor is obviously an important role and certain statutory rights are extended to the independent assessor in order to enable him to carry out his functions. Section 348 presupposes that the independent assessor has been chosen by the company in advance of the meeting. This will be the case where the board of directors has received a request from the requisite number of members in advance of the meeting in accordance with s 342(2). Where such a person has been appointed to report on a poll he is entitled to attend the meeting at which the poll may be taken and any subsequent proceedings in connection with the poll. There is no guidance in the legislation as to the meaning of the phrase '... subsequent proceedings in connection with the poll'. It is to be presumed that this would include the right to be present during the count of the votes. **22.396**

In addition, the independent assessor is entitled to be provided by the company with a copy of the notice of the meeting and any other communication provided by the company in connection with the meeting to persons who have a right to vote on the matter to which the poll relates. It is to be noted that the phrase '... any other communication provided by the company in connection with the meeting ...' is one of extremely wide ambit and care must be taken that all relevant documentation is provided to the independent assessor. This is not to say that the independent assessor has an unfettered ability to call for corporate documentation because it is expressly provided by subs (3) that the rights conferred by s 348 are only to be exercised to the extent that the independent assessor considers them necessary for the preparation of his report. **22.397**

Subsection (4):

Where the independent assessor is a firm, the right to attend a meeting and any subsequent proceedings in connection with a poll are exercisable by an individual authorized by the firm in writing to act as its representative for that purpose. **22.398**

General

22.399 It is to be noted that the independent assessor has the right to apply for an injunction to enforce his rights under this section. This is apparent from the wording of s 350(5).

Transitional provisions

22.400 The transitional provisions relating to s 348 are to be found in the Third Commencement Order, Sch 3, para 39. These provisions are discussed in the commentary below s 354.

> **349 Rights of independent assessor: right to information**
>
> (1) The independent assessor is entitled to access to the company's records relating to—
> (a) any poll on which he is to report;
> (b) the meeting at which the poll or polls may be, or were, taken.
>
> (2) The independent assessor may require anyone who at any material time was—
> (a) a director or secretary of the company,
> (b) an employee of the company,
> (c) a person holding or accountable for any of the company's records,
> (d) a member of the company, or
> (e) an agent of the company,
>
> to provide him with information or explanations for the purpose of preparing his report.
>
> (3) For this purpose 'agent' includes the company's bankers, solicitors and auditor.
>
> (4) A statement made by a person in response to a requirement under this section may not be used in evidence against him in criminal proceedings except proceedings for an offence under section 350 (offences relating to provision of information).
>
> (5) A person is not required by this section to disclose information in respect of which a claim to legal professional privilege (in Scotland, to confidentiality of communications) could be maintained in legal proceedings.

COMMENTARY: 349 Rights of independent assessor: right to information

22.401 In addition to the rights of access to meetings and subsequent proceedings in connection with a poll, an independent assessor has a right to information. In particular, he has the right to access the company's records relating to any poll on which he is to report and in relation to the meeting at which the poll or polls may be or were taken.

Subsection (2):

22.402 The independent assessor may require anyone who at any material time was a director or secretary of the company, an employee of the company, a person holding or accountable for any of the company's records, or a member of the company, or an agent of the company to provide him with information or explanations for the purposes of preparing the report. The legislation does not stipulate how the independent assessor may require such persons to provide him with information or explanations.

Subsection (3):

By s 349(3) an agent is stated to include the company's bankers, its solicitors and its auditors. The list is inexhaustive and may include other agents. **22.403**

Subsections (4) and (5): Privilege against self-incrimination

Where a person is required by the independent assessor to make a statement under s 349 the statement made may not be used in evidence against the maker of it in criminal proceedings, except proceedings for an offence relating to the omission to provide information under s 350. There is therefore privilege against self-incrimination in this context. In addition, a person is not required by s 349 to disclose information in respect of which there is a claim to legal professional privilege. It is to be noted that the independent assessor has the right to apply for an injunction to enforce his rights under this section. This is apparent from s 350(5). **22.404**

Transitional provisions

The transitional provisions relating to s 349 are to be found in the Third Commencement Order, Sch 3, para 39. These provisions are discussed in the commentary below s 354. **22.405**

350 Offences relating to provision of information

(1) A person who fails to comply with a requirement under section 349 without delay commits an offence unless it was not reasonably practicable for him to provide the required information or explanation.

(2) A person guilty of an offence under subsection (1) is liable on summary conviction to a fine not exceeding level 3 on the standard scale.

(3) A person commits an offence who knowingly or recklessly makes to an independent assessor a statement (oral or written) that—
   (a) conveys or purports to convey any information or explanations which the independent assessor requires, or is entitled to require, under section 349, and
   (b) is misleading, false or deceptive in a material particular.

(4) A person guilty of an offence under subsection (3) is liable—
   (a) on conviction on indictment, to imprisonment for a term not exceeding two years or a fine (or both);
   (b) on summary conviction—
      (i) in England and Wales, to imprisonment for a term not exceeding twelve months or to a fine not exceeding the statutory maximum (or both);
      (ii) in Scotland or Northern Ireland, to imprisonment for a term not exceeding six months, or to a fine not exceeding the statutory maximum (or both).

(5) Nothing in this section affects any right of an independent assessor to apply for an injunction (in Scotland, an interdict or an order for specific performance) to enforce any of his rights under section 348 or 349.

COMMENTARY: 350 Offences relating to provision of information

22.406 Section 350 creates a number of new statutory offences in connection with the provision of information to the independent assessor. The legislation makes it clear that timely compliance with the request to provide information or an explanation is necessary. An offence is committed if a person fails to provide the required information or explanation to the independent assessor stipulated in s 349 without delay, unless it was not reasonably practicable for him to provide that required information or explanation. The section provides no assistance as to the meaning of the word 'delay' in this context. A person found guilty of such an offence is liable on summary conviction to a fine.

Subsections (3) and (4):

22.407 A more serious offence is committed by a person who knowingly or recklessly makes a statement, whether oral or written, to an independent assessor that is misleading, false or deceptive in a material particular. Such a person if found guilty of such an offence is liable on conviction on indictment to imprisonment for a term not exceeding two years or a fine or both.

Subsection (5):

22.408 Notwithstanding the criminal offences that may be committed by failing to cooperate with the independent assessor, s 350(5) makes it clear that nothing in this section affects the right of the independent assessor to apply for an injunction to enforce his rights under either s 348 or s 349. It is anticipated that such applications will be extremely rare.

Transitional provisions

22.409 The transitional provisions relating to s 350 are to be found in the Third Commencement Order, Sch 3, para 39. These provisions are discussed in the commentary below s 354.

351 Information to be made available on website

(1) Where an independent assessor has been appointed to report on a poll, the company must ensure that the following information is made available on a website—
- (a) the fact of his appointment,
- (b) his identity,
- (c) the text of the resolution or, as the case may be, a description of the subject matter of the poll to which his appointment relates, and
- (d) a copy of a report by him which complies with section 347.

(2) The provisions of section 353 (requirements as to website availability) apply.
(3) In the event of default in complying with this section (or with the requirements of section 353 as it applies for the purposes of this section), an offence is committed by every officer of the company who is in default.
(4) A person guilty of an offence under subsection (3) is liable on summary conviction to a fine not exceeding level 3 on the standard scale.
(5) Failure to comply with this section (or the requirements of section 353) does not affect the validity of—
  (a) the poll, or
  (b) the resolution or other business (if passed or agreed to) to which the poll relates.

COMMENTARY: 351 Information to be made avaliable on website

Section 351 deals with the publication on the company's website of the independent assessor's report. Following the completion of the report that is made by the independent assessor sufficient publicity must be given to the information contained in that report. Accordingly the quoted company must ensure that the fact of the appointment of the assessor, his identity, the text of the resolution or a description of the subject matter at the poll, and a copy of his report is made available on the company's website. Once again the general requirements as to website availability under s 353 apply to s 351. Officers of a company who fail to make available the information required by s 351 or comply with the requirements of s 353 commit an offence and an offence is committed by every officer of the company who is in default. Summary conviction for this offence will result in a fine. **22.410**

Subsection (5): Validity

Section 351(5) provides that the failure to comply with the requirement to publicize the information required does not affect the validity of the poll or of the resolution or other business to which the poll relates. **22.411**

Transitional provisions

The transitional provisions relating to s 351 are to be found in the Third Commencement Order, Sch 3, para 39. These provisions are discussed in the commentary below s 354. **22.412**

Supplementary

352 Application of provisions to class meetings

(1) The provisions of—
  section 341 (results of poll to be made available on website), and
  sections 342 to 351(independent report on poll),

apply (with any necessary modifications) in relation to a meeting of holders of a class of shares of a quoted company in connection with the variation of rights attached to such shares as they apply in relation to a general meeting of the company.

(2) For the purposes of this section—
   (a) any amendment of a provision contained in a company's articles for the variation of the rights attached to a class of shares, or the insertion of any such provision into the articles, is itself to be treated as a variation of those rights, and
   (b) references to the variation of rights attached to a class of shares include references to their abrogation.

COMMENTARY: 352 Application of provisions to class meetings

22.413 Section 352 applies the provisions of ss 341–351 to class meetings of quoted companies dealing with the variation of class rights in the same way as they apply to general meetings of companies. This is an important extension of the application of these provisions and indicates the importance attached by the legislature to the class rights that may be attached to shares of quoted companies.

22.414 The result of any poll conducted at a class meeting must be made available on the company's website under s 341 along with information as to the date of the meeting, the text of the resolution. Default in complying with the requirements of s 341 constitutes an offence under that section.

22.415 By reason of s 352 a member of a class has the statutory right to require an independent report on a poll in accordance with the detailed procedures set out in ss 342–351 inclusive.

Transitional provisions

22.416 The transitional provisions relating to s 352 are to be found in the Third Commencement Order, Sch 3, para 39. These provisions are discussed in the commentary below s 354.

353 Requirements as to website availability

(1) The following provisions apply for the purposes of—
   section 341 (results of poll to be made available on website), and
   section 351 (report of independent observer to be made available on website).
(2) The information must be made available on a website that—
   (a) is maintained by or on behalf of the company, and
   (b) identifies the company in question.
(3) Access to the information on the website, and the ability to obtain a hard copy of the information from the website, must not be conditional on the payment of a fee or otherwise restricted.
(4) The information—
   (a) must be made available as soon as reasonably practicable, and
   (b) must be kept available throughout the period of two years beginning with the date on which it is first made available on a website in accordance with this section.

(5) A failure to make information available on a website throughout the period specified in subsection (4)(b) is disregarded if—
   (a) the information is made available on the website for part of that period, and
   (b) the failure is wholly attributable to circumstances that it would not be reasonable to have expected the company to prevent or avoid.

COMMENTARY: 353 Requirements as to website availability

Section 353 sets out the statutory requirements that are applicable to the information which must be published on the website of a quoted company for the purposes of ss 341 and 351. Section 341 deals with the result of a poll at a general meeting of a quoted company. Section 351 deals with the report of the independent assessor who has been duly appointed in accordance with ss 342 and 343 to provide an independent report on a poll. **22.417**

Subsections (2) and (3): Requirements for the website

These provisions regulate the website and require that the information is made available on a website that is maintained by or on behalf of the company and which identifies the company. The wording of the subsection is believed to provide flexibility as to whether the website is one that is maintained by the company itself or is operated by a website service provider on behalf of the company. The essential condition is contained in subs (3), which requires that the information on the website and the ability to obtain a hard copy of it from the website is free of charge and unrestricted. It would appear that access to the information must be available on this basis to all members of the public, whether or not they are members of the quoted company. **22.418**

Subsections (4) and (5):

The information required under ss 341 and 351 must be made available as soon as reasonably practicable and kept available for a minimum period of two years from the date of its first publication on the website. If there is a failure to comply with s 353(4)(b) for the whole of the two-year period no offence will be committed under s 341(3) or 351(3) if the information was available for some of the time, and the failure was wholly attributable to circumstances that were beyond the company's reasonable control. **22.419**

Transitional provisions

The transitional provisions relating to s 353 are to be found in the Third Commencement Order, Sch 3, para 39. These provisions are discussed in the commentary below s 354. **22.420**

354 Power to limit or extend the types of company to which provisions of this Chapter apply

(1) The Secretary of State may by regulations—
  (a) limit the types of company to which some or all of the provisions of this Chapter apply, or
  (b) extend some or all of the provisions of this Chapter to additional types of company.

(2) Regulations under this section extending the application of any provision of this Chapter are subject to affirmative resolution procedure.

(3) Any other regulations under this section are subject to negative resolution procedure.

(4) Regulations under this section may—
  (a) amend the provisions of this Chapter (apart from this section);
  (b) repeal and re-enact provisions of this Chapter with modifications of form or arrangement, whether or not they are modified in substance;
  (c) contain such consequential, incidental and supplementary provisions (including provisions amending, repealing or revoking enactments) as the Secretary of State thinks fit.

COMMENTARY: 354 Power to limit or extend the types of company to which provisions of this Chapter apply

22.421 Section 354 confers a broad power on the Secretary of State to limit or to extend both the types of company to which the provision of Part 13, Chapter 5 may apply or to extend the provisions to additional types of company. In addition, the regulations may amend, repeal or modify the provisions of Chapter 5. As can be seen above some of the new provisions in Chapter 5 are very wide-ranging in scope and may in practice give rise to difficulties for quoted public companies. In the circumstances the reservation to the Secretary of State of this wide power to amend or adapt the legislation is to be welcomed.

Transitional provisions

22.422 Schedule 3, para 39 of the Third Commencement Order provides as follows:

Additional requirements for quoted companies (ss. 342 to 354)

39.—(1) Sections 342 to 354 of the Companies Act 2006 apply to polls taken at meetings of which notice was given on or after 1st October 2007.

(2) Where notice of a meeting is given over more than one day, it is treated for the purposes of this paragraph as given on the first of those days.

COMMENTARY: Additional requirements for quoted companies (ss. 342 to 354)

22.423 The transitional provisions make it clear that ss 342–354 apply in respect of any general meeting or class meeting where notice was given on or after 1 October 2007. The use of the phrase in para 39 '... polls taken at meetings ...' is somewhat vague and unfortunate as this wording does not take account of the power contained in many articles of association to direct the taking of a poll after the conclusion of a meeting as is reflected in s 330(3) and (6).

CHAPTER 6
RECORDS OF RESOLUTIONS AND MEETINGS

355 Records of resolutions and meetings etc

(1) Every company must keep records comprising—
  (a) copies of all resolutions of members passed otherwise than at general meetings,
  (b) minutes of all proceedings of general meetings, and
  (c) details provided to the company in accordance with section 357 (decisions of sole member).

(2) The records must be kept for at least ten years from the date of the resolution, meeting or decision (as appropriate).

(3) If a company fails to comply with this section, an offence is committed by every officer of the company who is in default.

(4) A person guilty of an offence under this section is liable on summary conviction to a fine not exceeding level 3 on the standard scale and, for continued contravention, a daily default fine not exceeding one-tenth of level 3 on the standard scale.

COMMENTARY: 355 Records of resolutions and meetings etc

Overview

Part 13, Chapter 6 (ss 355–359) deals with the important obligation of a company to maintain proper records of both resolutions and meetings. This Chapter replaces CA 1985, ss 382–383. The most important change that has been made to the existing law is the introduction of a 10-year minimum period for the keeping of company records. No such time limit existed under the previous legislation. In addition, it should be noted that s 355 makes no reference to the minutes of meetings of directors. The requirement to keep minutes of directors' meetings is contained in s 248 and their evidential significance is dealt with by s 249. These two sections are considered in Chapter 16 of this book. **22.424**

Subsection (1):

This provision requires all companies to maintain proper records of proceedings, which will comprise copies of all resolutions passed otherwise than at a general meeting of the company, minutes of all proceedings of general meetings and the proper details of decisions taken by a sole member under s 357. The phrase '... otherwise than at general meetings ...' in s 355(1)(a) refers to written resolutions of private companies and to resolutions of class meetings. **22.425**

Subsection (2):

Subsection (2) provides that the records prescribed by subs (1) must be kept for at least 10 years from the date of the resolution, meeting or decision as appropriate. **22.426**

These provisions for the lengthy retention of company records of proceedings emphasize their significance as important documents that have to be created and maintained in accordance with the statute.

Subsections (3) and (4): Offence

22.427 In the event that a company fails to comply with these important statutory requirements an offence is committed by every officer of the company who is in default. Subsection (4) goes on to provide that where an officer is found guilty of an offence under s 355 he is liable on summary conviction to a fine. In cases of continued contravention, provision is made for a daily default fine.

Transitional provisions

22.428 The transitional provisions relating to s 355 are to be found in the Third Commencement Order, Sch 3, para 40. These provisions are discussed in the commentary below s 359.

356 Records as evidence of resolutions

(1) This section applies to the records kept in accordance with section 355.
(2) The record of a resolution passed otherwise than at a general meeting, if purporting to be signed by a director of the company or by the company secretary, is evidence (in Scotland, sufficient evidence) of the passing of the resolution.
(3) Where there is a record of a written resolution of a private company, the requirements of this Act with respect to the passing of the resolution are deemed to be complied with unless the contrary is proved.
(4) The minutes of proceedings of a general meeting, if purporting to be signed by the chairman of that meeting or by the chairman of the next general meeting, are evidence (in Scotland, sufficient evidence) of the proceedings at the meeting.
(5) Where there is a record of proceedings of a general meeting of a company, then, until the contrary is proved—
  (a) the meeting is deemed duly held and convened,
  (b) all proceedings at the meeting are deemed to have duly taken place, and
  (c) all appointments at the meeting are deemed valid.

COMMENTARY: 356 Records as evidence of resolutions

22.429 CA 2006, s 356 is linked to s 355. It ensures that records of all resolutions (including written resolutions of private companies and of class meetings) and the minutes of meetings are signed off by a director or by the company secretary, or by the chairman in the case of a general meeting. Where records are so signed off they will be evidence as to the passing of a resolution or as to the proceedings transacted at a meeting.

Subsection (5): Records as evidence

22.430 Unless the contrary is proved, where there is a record of a general meeting of the company the legislation stipulates under s 356(5) that the meeting is deemed to have been duly held and convened, that all the proceedings are deemed to have duly taken place and that all the appointments made at the meeting are deemed to be valid. In strict legal terms this subsection creates a rebuttable presumption, placing the onus of proof to the contrary on the persons who challenge the record of the meeting. This provision replaces CA 1985, ss 382(4) and 382A(2).

Transitional provisions

The transitional provisions relating to s 356 are to be found in the Third Commencement Order, Sch 3, para 40. These provisions are discussed in the commentary below s 359. **22.431**

357 Records of decisions by sole member

(1) This section applies to a company limited by shares or by guarantee that has only one member.

(2) Where the member takes any decision that—

  (a) may be taken by the company in general meeting, and

  (b) has effect as if agreed by the company in general meeting, he must (unless that decision is taken by way of a written resolution) provide the company with details of that decision.

(3) If a person fails to comply with this section he commits an offence.

(4) A person guilty of an offence under this section is liable on summary conviction to a fine not exceeding level 2 on the standard scale.

(5) Failure to comply with this section does not affect the validity of any decision referred to in subsection (2).

COMMENTARY: 357 Records of decisions by sole member

CA 2006, s 357 applies to a company limited by shares or by guarantee that has only one member. In such a company decisions still have to be taken and an adequate record of those decisions must be kept. Subsection (2) provides that where a single member takes any decision that may otherwise be taken by a company in general meeting and that has effect as if agreed by the company in general meeting, the single member must provide the company with details of that decision. The single member is excused from this requirement if the decision has been taken by way of a written resolution. In the event that the single member fails to comply with s 357 he commits an offence and if found guilty of that offence, he is liable on summary conviction to a fine. However, subs (5) stipulates that any failure to comply with the provisions of s 357 does not affect the validity of any decision to which the provisions of subs (2) apply. **22.432**

Transitional provisions

The transitional provisions relating to s 357 are to be found in the Third Commencement Order, Sch 3, para 40. These provisions are discussed in the commentary below s 359. **22.433**

358 Inspection of records of resolutions and meetings

(1) The records referred to in section 355 (records of resolutions etc) relating to the previous ten years must be kept available for inspection—
   (a) at the company's registered office, or
   (b) at a place specified in regulations under section 1136.

(2) The company must give notice to the registrar—
   (a) of the place at which the records are kept available for inspection, and
   (b) of any change in that place,

unless they have at all times been kept at the company's registered office.

(3) The records must be open to inspection of any members of the company without charge.

(4) Any member may require a copy of any of the records on payment of such fee as may be prescribed.

(5) If default is made for 14 days in complying with subsection (2) or an inspection required under subsection (3) is refused, or a copy requested under subsection (4) is not sent, an offence is committed by every officer of the company who is in default.

(6) A person guilty of an offence under this section is liable on summary conviction to a fine not exceeding level 3 on the standard scale and, for continued contravention, a daily default fine not exceeding one-tenth of level 3 on the standard scale.

(7) In a case in which an inspection required under subsection (3) is refused or a copy requested under subsection (4) is not sent, the court may by order compel an immediate inspection of the records or direct that the copies required be sent to the persons who requested them.

COMMENTARY: 358 Insepection of records of resolutions and meetings

22.434 Section 358 replaces CA 1985, s 383 and contains important requirements relating to the inspection of a company's records by members.

Subsections (1) and (2):

22.435 This provides that the records of a company maintained in accordance with the provisions of s 355 must be kept available for inspection at the company's registered office or at some other location in accordance with regulations that will be made by the Secretary of State under CA 2006, s 1136. That section empowers the Secretary of State to make provision by regulations as to where certain company records must be kept available for inspection where the records are kept other than at the registered office.

22.436 A company is obliged by subs (2) to give notice to the Registrar of the place at which records are kept available for inspection and of any change in that location, unless the records have always been kept at the registered office of the company. This provision may be a trap for the unwary in that notification to the Registrar will be required if at any time these records have not been kept available for inspection at the registered office.

Subsection (3): Inspection by members

The members of a company continue to enjoy the right to inspect the records without incurring any charge. This obligation to keep the company's minute book available for inspection by any member without charge has operated since 1929. It is an important right of all shareholders and is of particular value to minority shareholders who may be engaged in a dispute with the company of which they are members. However, as noted above, s 355 is limited in scope and does not include the minutes of meetings of directors. There is no statutory right for a member to inspect board minutes. **22.437**

Subsection (4):

Where a member requires any copy of any of the records he may be required to pay a prescribed fee. A prescribed fee means one that is prescribed by order or by regulations made by the Secretary of State. The power to make such regulations is contained in s 1137. Under CA 1985, regulations were made for this purpose and the fee prescribed for copies of minutes was '10 pence per 100 words, or part thereof, copied'.[106] The new regulations under CA 2006 state that the fee now prescribed is: **22.438**

(i) 10 pence per 500 words or part thereof copied; and
(ii) the reasonable costs incurred by the company in delivering the copy of the company record to the person entitled to be provided with that copy.[107]

Subsections (5) and (6): Offences

Officers of a company who fail to comply with the notification requirements in subs (2), or with the members' right to require inspection under subs (3), or fail to send a copy a requested under subs (4) commit an office which is punishable by a fine. In cases of continued contravention provision is made for a daily default fine. **22.439**

Subsection (7):

The court has jurisdiction to make an order compelling the immediate inspection of the records kept under s 355, or to direct that copies required under subs (4) but not sent are provided to the persons who requested them. Such an order takes the form of a mandatory injunction. **22.440**

---

[106] Companies (Inspection and Copying of Registers, Indices and Documents) Regulations 1991 (SI 1991/1998).

[107] Companies (Fees for Inspection and Copying of Company Records) Regulations 2007 (SI 2007/2612).

Transitional provisions

22.441 The transitional provisions relating to s 358 are to be found in the Third Commencement Order, Sch 3, para 40. These provisions are discussed in the commentary below s 359.

> **359 Records of resolutions and meetings of class of members**
>
> The provisions of this Chapter apply (with necessary modifications) in relation to resolutions and meetings of—
>
> (a) holders of a class of shares, and
>
> (b) in the case of a company without a share capital, a class of members,
>
> as they apply in relation to resolutions of members generally and to general meetings.

COMMENTARY: 359 Records of resolutions and meetings of class of members

22.442 Section 359 is a new provision relating to class meetings. This section makes it clear that the provisions in Chapter 6 apply not only to general meetings and to resolutions but also to the resolutions and meetings of a class of members. Accordingly, there are similar rights of inspection and similar rights to require copies in relation to class meetings and class resolutions. Such records must also be kept by the company for a period of at least 10 years.

Transitional provisions

22.443 Schedule 3, para 40 of the Third Commencement Order provides as follows:

> **Records of resolutions and meetings (ss. 355 to 359)**
>
> 40.—(1) Sections 355 to 359 of the Companies Act 2006 (records of resolutions and meetings) apply to resolutions passed, meetings held or decisions taken on or after 1st October 2007.
>
> (2) Sections 382, 382A, 382B and 383 of the 1985 Act or Articles 390, 390A, 390B and 391 of the 1986 Order continue to apply to resolutions passed, meetings held or decisions taken before that date.

COMMENTARY: Records of resolutions and meetings (ss. 355 to 359)

22.444 These transitional provisions are self-explanatory. The new sections apply only to matters decided, resolutions passed or meetings held on or after 1 October 2007. The provisions of CA 1985 apply before that date.

CHAPTER 7
SUPPLEMENTARY PROVISIONS

> **360 Computation of periods of notice etc: clear day rule**
>
> (1) This section applies for the purposes of the following provisions of this Part—
>
> section 307(1) and (2) (notice required of general meeting),

section 312(1) and (3) (resolution requiring special notice),
section 314(4)(d) (request to circulate members' statement),
section 316(2)(b) (expenses of circulating statement to be deposited or tendered before meeting),
section 338(4)(d)(i) (request to circulate member's resolution at AGM of public company), and
section 340(2)(b)(i) (expenses of circulating statement to be deposited or tendered before meeting).

(2) Any reference in those provisions to a period of notice, or to a period before a meeting by which a request must be received or sum deposited or tendered, is to a period of the specified length excluding—
  (a) the day of the meeting, and
  (b) the day on which the notice is given, the request received or the sum deposited or tendered.

COMMENTARY: 360 Computation of periods of notice etc: clear day rule

This provision contains essential rules for the calculation of the requisite time periods under Part 13. The provisions set out what is known as the 'clear day rule'. **22.445**

Subsection (1) lists the six sections to which it applies. By subs (2) the general rule is that any reference in those provisions to a period of notice is to be calculated by excluding (a) the date of the meeting and (b) the day on which the notice is given. **22.446**

The same rule applies to the calculation of the period before a meeting by which a request (such as a request to circulate a members' statement or a members' resolution at an annual general meeting of a public company) must be received. Equally, the rules also apply to the calculation of the period before a meeting by which time a sum to cover the company's expenses must be deposited or tendered. **22.447**

There are no transitional provisions relating to this section. **22.448**

361 Meaning of 'quoted company'

In this Part 'quoted company' has the same meaning as in Part 15 of this Act.

COMMENTARY: 361 Meaning of 'quoted company'

For the purposes of CA 2006, Part 13 dealing with resolutions and meetings, the term 'quoted company' has the meaning ascribed to it by CA 2006, Part 15. CA 2006, s 385(2) defines a 'quoted company' as follows: **22.449**

A 'quoted company' means a company whose equity share capital—
  (a) has been included in the official list in accordance with the provisions of Part 6 of the Financial Services and Markets Act 2000 (c.8), or
  (b) is officially listed in an EEA State, or
  (c) is admitted to dealing on either the New York Stock Exchange or the exchange known as the Nasdaq.

In paragraph (a) 'the official list' has the meaning given to it by section 103(1) of the Financial Services and Markets Act 2000.

22.450 The ambit of s 385(1) and (2) may be extended or limited by the Secretary of State for Trade and Industry so as to expand or restrict the categories of companies that are quoted companies.[108]

108 See CA 2006, s 385(5).

PART 4

ANNOTATION OF 1985 TABLE A REGULATIONS RELATING TO MEETINGS OF MEMBERS AND PROCEEDINGS OF DIRECTORS

23

ANNOTATION OF 1985 TABLE A REGULATIONS RELATING TO MEETINGS OF MEMBERS AND PROCEEDINGS OF DIRECTORS

Introduction

23.01 In addition to the statutory provisions regulating the proceedings of meetings of members and of directors, a company's articles of association will contain rules and regulations governing these types of meeting. Plainly, where the legislation prescribes minimum requirements a company is not entitled to have provisions in its articles of association that depart or derogate from these basic rules. For a long time as an adjunct to the statutory provisions relating to meetings there have been articles of association in what may be called a 'standard form'. Companies may choose to adopt these standard form provisions in their entirety, or with certain amendments, modifications and exclusions. In this part of the book the familiar provisions relating to meetings of members and of directors that are contained in the Companies (Tables A to F) Regulations 1985 (SI 1985/805)[1] (1985 Table A) are considered and analysed.

23.02 The history of standard-form provisions in Table A as a supplement to the legislation regulating the conduct of registered companies dates back to the nineteenth

---

1 The 1985 Table A came in to force on 1 July 1985.

century and as a consequence there is a well-established jurisprudence.[2] In addition, over the years amendments have been made to Table A reflecting both legislative changes and changes in practice and procedure. The version which applies to a company in the absence of any special resolution adopting different articles of association is that contained in, or made under the Companies Act under which the company was originally registered. CA 1985, s 8(3) provided that any amendment to the 1985 Table A made by new regulation would not affect a company registered before the alteration or repeal took effect. That section has been repealed by CA 2006, s 1295 and Sch 16 and has not been replaced so far as Table A is concerned. CA 2006, ss 18–20 provide for model articles of association to be prescribed by the Secretary of State for different types of company. By CA 2006, s 19(3) a company may adopt all or any of the provisions of the model articles of association.

23.03 Section 19(4) mirrors CA 1985 by providing that an amendment of model articles by regulations under that section does not affect a company registered before the amendment takes effect. As at the date of publication no model articles in final form have been published. The provisions dealing with meetings of directors and members in the latest version of the draft model articles are reproduced in Part 5 together with a commentary.

The 2007 Regulations

23.04 As part of the process of implementing CA 2006, amendments have been made to the 1985 Table A by the Companies (Tables A to F) (Amendment) Regulations 2007[3] (the 2007 Regulations). This new amended version of the 1985 Table A applies only to companies that are incorporated on or after 1 October 2007 which adopt Table A as their articles of association. It therefore does not automatically apply to existing companies, but may be adopted by such companies by the passing of a special resolution. Part 1 of the 2007 Regulations provides for citation, commencement and interpretation. Part 2 of the 2007 Regulations makes amendments which apply to all companies. Part 3 of the 2007 Regulations applies to private companies limited by shares only. Part 4 of the 2007 Regulations applies to public companies limited by shares only. Part 5 of the 2007 Regulations makes amendments to Table C, applicable to companies limited by guarantee.

23.05 As will be seen below, the 2007 Regulations introduce two versions of Table A—one for private companies and one for public companies. The definition of 'the

---

[2] There have been six earlier versions of Table A namely, 1856, 1862, 1906, 1908, 1929 and 1948.

[3] SI 2007/2541. These Regulations were made on 3 September 2007 and came into force on 1 October 2007.

Act' used in reg 1 of the 1985 Table A has been extended to include both CA 1985 and any provisions of CA 2006 that are for the time being in force.[4]

In the commentary that follows attention will be drawn to the specific amendments that have been made by the 2007 Regulations. **23.06**

On 27 September 2007 it was announced that the Government had made regulations making two further amendments to the Table A regulations which came into force on 1 October 2007. The purpose of the latest amendments was to correct inconsistencies between Table A and corresponding provisions of the Companies Act 2006. These further amendments are in addition to amendments made on 3 September 2007 by the 2007 Regulations. **23.07**

The 2007 Amendment Regulations

The Regulations that were made on 27 September 2007 are called the Companies (Tables A to F) (Amendment) (No 2) Regulations 2007) (SI 2007/2826). In this Part those Regulations are referred to as the 2007 Amendment Regulations. These amend regs 50 and 54 of the 1985 Table A and apply to a company registered on or after 1 October 2007 which adopts Table A as its articles of association. According to a departmental release, dated 28 September 2007, reg 50 of the 1985 Table A has been deleted because the content of that provision conflicts with CA 2006, ss 281 and 282. It is suggested that the combined effect of these sections of CA 2006, which came into force on 1 October 2007, is that a resolution cannot be passed by use of a casting vote by a chairman. That proposition is of questionable validity.[5] In addition, reg 54 of the 1985 Table A is amended to reflect the new rights for proxies to vote on a show of hands provided by CA 2006, ss 284(2)(b) and 324(1). The text of the 2007 Amendment Regulations are set out in the commentary below. **23.08**

The standard form provisions of the 1985 Table A apply to very many companies, both public and private. Companies that are incorporated and registered under the Companies Acts will vary in size and proper attention must be paid to their specific administrative requirements. It is pointless in the context of a small family company to impose complex and elaborate procedural requirements for board meetings when there may be a sole director or only two directors. Similarly, although undue complexity should be avoided, a large multinational organization may well require more highly regulated procedures in order to engender the efficient conduct of its management. **23.09**

---

4 SI 2007/2541 Part 2, para 3.

5 See the Commentary on CA 2006, s 282 at Part 3 (above).

Regulations of the 1985 Table A Relating to Meetings of Members

23.10 Regulations 36 to 63 (inclusive) of the 1985 Table A set out rules for the conduct of meetings of members. Each one of these regulations is set out below and is commented upon in turn. Where the regulations have been amended by the 2007 Regulations this will be made clear. For further detailed discussion of the practice and procedures arising out of the commentary on regs 36–63 of the 1985 Table A, reference should be made to the earlier chapters of this book.

> REGULATION 36
>
> All general meetings other than annual general meetings shall be called extraordinary general meetings.

COMMENTARY: REGULATION 36

23.11 Regulation 36 reflected the legal requirements of CA 1985, s 366 that all companies were to hold a meeting designated as an annual general meeting at least once in every calendar year. Under CA 1985, s 366A a procedure existed where by means of an 'elective resolution' the members of a private company might dispense with the requirement to hold an annual general meeting. However, prior to the enactment of CA 2006 it was questionable whether it was good practice to dispense with the need to hold an annual general meeting even in the context of a private unquoted company with a small number of members. The need for directors of a company to be accountable on an annual basis to their members at an annual general meeting is likely to promote greater efficiency and better communication, and may prevent small problems developing into more serious disputes.

23.12 Under CA 1985, s 367 the Secretary of State had power to call a meeting where a company had not complied with the provisions of CA 1985, s 366. Recourse to and use of this power was very rare and it has now been repealed.

23.13 Under CA 2006 a private company is no longer under a statutory obligation to hold an annual general meeting. In view of this legislative change it is likely that many existing companies will dispense with the holding of an annual general meeting. Accordingly, an article in the form of reg 36 for private companies will need amendment. The duty of public companies to hold an annual general meeting is preserved by CA 2006, s 336. Reference should also be made to CA 2006, ss 337–340 for the additional requirements applicable to annual general meetings of public companies.

2007 Regulations

23.14 Paragraph 4 of the 2007 Regulations provides as follows:

> 4. Regulation 36 of Table A ceases to have effect.

The 2007 Regulations have deleted reg 36 of the 1985 Table A for all new companies that are limited by shares.[6]

REGULATION 37

The directors may call general meetings and, on the requisition of members pursuant to the provisions of the Act, shall forthwith proceed to convene an extraordinary general meeting for a date not later than eight weeks after receipt of the requisition. If there are not within the United Kingdom sufficient directors to call a general meeting, any director or any member of the company may call a general meeting.

COMMENTARY: REGULATION 37

A duly constituted board of directors has the authority to convene a meeting of the members. The board of directors is the organ of the company that is entrusted with the duty to manage the affairs of the company. It is axiomatic that the board of directors have the power to convene a meeting of the members. Indeed, there will be some instances where the board of directors will be compelled by statute to convene a meeting of members; for example, in order to pass a special resolution for the amendment of the articles of association. However, the power of directors to convene a meeting of members is a fiduciary power and must be exercised for proper corporate purposes and not for ulterior and collateral purposes of the directors themselves. It must also be remembered that where companies have large numbers of shareholders the costs of convening and holding a meeting can constitute a considerable expense to the company, and thus care should be taken not to call excessive numbers of meetings or meetings that are in fact unnecessary. **23.15**

The directors may choose the date, time and venue of the meeting.[7] Again, this ability to control the time and place of the meeting must not be abused and care should be taken that the selected date, time and, in particular the venue are such that they are convenient to the members as a whole. It is suggested that the convenience of the directors, in the sense of their ability to attend and participate in a meeting of members, may be a factor in deciding where a meeting of members should be held, but it should not be an overriding or dominant factor. **23.16**

CA 2006, s 303, which is derived from CA 1985, s 368, confers upon members the right to require the directors to call a meeting and this right is recognized in reg 37. Directors of a company who receive a valid request from members are under a statutory duty under CA 2006, s 304 to proceed to convene a meeting. Directors are given a period of 21 days in which to respond in a positive manner to a valid request from the members of the company. If the directors fail to comply with their statutory duty to respond to the members' requisition notice the members **23.17**

---

6 SI 2007/2541, Part 2, para 4.

7 See CA 2006, s 311. See Ch 2.

themselves are empowered by CA 2006, s 305 to convene a meeting of members themselves. In convening a meeting themselves under s 305 the members should try, so far as is possible, to follow the usual procedures of the company.

23.18 In addition to the power of directors and members to convene meetings there is a residual discretionary jurisdiction vested in the court under CA 2006, s 306 to call, or direct the calling of a general meeting in circumstances where it is for any reason impracticable to hold a meeting. This power is a well-established jurisdiction of the court that was previously to be found in CA 1985, s 371.[8]

2007 Regulations

23.19 Paragraph 5 of the 2007 Regulations provides as follows:

> 5.—(1) Regulation 37 of Table A is amended as follows.
> (2) After the words 'proceed to convene' omit the words the word 'an extraordinary' and insert the word 'a'.
> (3) After the first reference to 'general meeting' omit the words 'for a date not later than eight weeks after receipt of the requisition' and insert the words 'in accordance with the provisions of the Act'.
>
> The effect of the amendment: the 2007 form of Regulation 37:
> '37. The directors may call general meetings and, on the requisition of members pursuant to the provisions of the Act, shall forthwith proceed to convene a general meeting in accordance with the Act. If there are not within the United Kingdom sufficient directors to call a general meeting, any director or any member of the company may call a general meeting.'

23.20 This amendment is applicable to both public and private companies limited by shares. It reflects the combined requirements of s 304(1)(a): that the directors must call the general meeting within 21 days from the date on which they become subject to that requirement under s 303, and s 304(1)(b): that a general meeting called by the directors in response to a members' request must be held on a date not more than 28 days after the date of the notice convening the meeting. The potential gap in time from the date of the request is now some seven weeks only. The older version of the 1985 Table A is therefore positively misleading and should be amended in the form of this revised regulation as it implies a time period of eight weeks rather than the seven allowed by the statute. This has in fact been an unfortunate feature of the 1985 Table A since the insertion of subs (8) of CA 1985, s 368(8) in March 1990 under CA 1989.

23.21 The second sentence of Regulation 37, which is largely unchanged in the 2007 version, gives a wide power to a single director or a member to call a general meeting when directors are absent from the UK. Proof of the absence of sufficient directors

[8] See Ch 6.

from the UK will be an essential aspect for proving the validity of any notice of meeting sent out in these circumstances. Recourse to this power is rare in practice.

REGULATION 38

An annual general meeting and an extraordinary general meeting called for the passing of a special resolution or a resolution appointing a person as a director shall be called by at least twenty one clear days' notice. All other extraordinary general meetings shall be called by at least fourteen clear days' notice but a general meeting may be called by shorter notice if it is so agreed—

(a) in the case of an annual general meeting, by all the members entitled to attend and vote thereat; and

(b) in the case of any other meeting by a majority in number of the members having a right to attend and vote being a majority together holding not less than ninety-five per cent in nominal value of the shares giving that right.

The notice shall specify the time and place of the meeting and the general nature of the business to be transacted in the case of any other meeting

Subject to the provisions of the articles and to any restrictions imposed on any shares, the notice shall be given to all the members, to all persons entitled to a share in consequence of the death or bankruptcy of a member and to the directors and auditors.

COMMENTARY: REGULATION 38

CA 1985, s 369 set out the minimum requirements for the giving of notice of **23.22**
meetings of members under CA 1985. Those statutory requirements are reflected in the contents of reg 38 in its original form set out above. Under this regulation annual general meetings and meetings that are convened for the passing of a special resolution require at least 21 clear days' notice. All other meetings require at least 14 clear days' notice.

Accordingly, a company which retains the 1985 Table A in this original form can- **23.23**
not make use of the provision for shorter periods of notice contained in CA 2006, s 307(1). That section provides that for a private company a general meeting (other than an adjourned meeting) requires only at least 14 days' notice, although 21 days' notice is still required for an annual general meeting of a public company. Section 307(3) expressly recognizes that the articles of a company may requirea longer period of notice than that specified in s 307(1) and (2). Moreover, CA 2006 makes no requirement for a longer period of notice when a meeting is to consider a special resolution. This is apparent from the absence of any prescribed notice period in s 283, which defines a special resolution.

CA 2006 no longer requires a private company to hold an annual general meeting. **23.24**
Sections 336 to 340 concern only public companies in respect of which there remains a statutory duty to convene an annual general meeting.

It is to be noted that although reg 38 was introduced when the requirement for an **23.25**
annual general meeting was applicable to both public and private companies, it

does not strictly require an annual general meeting for a private company. In this respect, reg 38 differs from the express requirements of reg 47 in the 1948 Table A which states: 'The company shall in each year hold a general meeting as its annual general meeting in addition to any other meetings in that year....'

23.26 It is therefore open to a private company incorporated with the 1985 Table A articles not to hold an annual general meeting from 1 October 2007. However, if a private company chooses to continue to do so it may hold such an annual meeting and must then comply with the notice requirements of reg 38 incorporated into its articles. The paragraphs which follow examine the requirements of reg 38 in that context.

23.27 As stated in sub-para (a) of reg 38, it possible that an annual general meeting can be held on a shorter period of notice than 21 clear days if all the members who are entitled to attend and vote at such a meeting agree to such a course. Save in the context of a company with very few shareholders or where a company is a wholly owned subsidiary of another company, in practice it may be very difficult to obtain the required unanimous consent. In relation to other meetings, the members may agree to a shorter period of notice than that prescribed by the legislation. In this case, under reg 38 in its original form, the consent does not have to be unanimous but has to be given by members who have the right to attend and vote at the meeting holding not less than 95% in nominal value of the voting shares.[9] There is no concept of de minimis compliance with the numbers required to consent to a period of shorter notice. Great care should be taken with the calculation of the requisite number of members.

23.28 Regulation 38 requires that the notice of the meeting must state the time (meaning the date and precise time of day) of the meeting, the venue of the meeting and the general nature of the business that it is proposed to be transacted. This provision reflects the requirements of CA 2006, s 311. In relation to an annual general meeting the notice shall make it clear that the meeting is to be an annual general meeting.[10]

23.29 Notice of meetings must be given to all the members and to any person who is entitled to a share in consequence of the death or bankruptcy of a member. This obvious requirement, which is reflected in CA 2006, s 310(1)(a) and (2), is subject to any provision in the company's articles of association. For example, where share capital is divided into shares of different classes the rights attached to the various classes of shares may contain restrictions and reservations upon the right to receive notice of general meetings and to attend and vote at meetings.

---

[9] Different percentages are required under the 2007 amended form of reg 38—see below.

[10] See CA 2006, s 337(1) for public companies.

Certain non-members are also entitled to receive due notice of meetings. Regulation 38 requires notice of meetings to be given to the directors. This reflects the requirement of CA 2006, s 310(1)(b). The auditors of a company are also entitled to receive due notice of a meeting of the members of a company. This is an express requirement of reg 38 and CA 2006, s 502(2). The final sentence of reg 38 is itself subject to the provisions of the articles and any restrictions imposed on the shares. If a company's articles of association stipulate that notice of a general meeting is not to be given to shareholders who do not have the right to attend and vote, care should be taken to comply with this requirement because members are entitled to have the affairs of the company conducted in accordance with the requirements of the articles. In the event that notice is given to members who have no right to receive such notice, consideration has to be given to the effect of the attendance of such members on the meeting. In the event that the business of a meeting came to be dominated by the presence of members who were not entitled to have notice other members may be able to challenge the efficacy of any resolution that was passed—see *Re Smiths of Smithfield Ltd* [2003] BCC 769. However, if persons are present at a meeting who in fact have no entitlement to attend but such attendees do not play any role in, or take part in the meeting their presence will not operate so as to render the meeting or any business transacted thereat invalid—see *Re Quinn and National Catholic Benefit and Thrift Society's Arbitration* [1921] 2 Ch 318 (Eve J). **23.30**

2007 Regulations

Paragraph 9 of the 2007 Regulations provides as follows:

> Notice of general meetings
>
> 9. (1) Regulation 38 of Table A is amended as follows.
>
> (2) Omit the words 'An annual general meeting and an extraordinary general meeting called for the passing of a special resolution or a resolution appointing a person as a director shall be called by at least twenty-one clear days' notice. All other extraordinary '.
>
> (3) Omit paragraph (a).
>
> (4) In paragraph (b), omit the words 'in the case of any other meeting' and '-five'.
>
> (5) Omit the words 'and, in the case of an annual general meeting shall specify the meeting as such'.

The effect of the amendment: the 2007 form (for private companies only):

> 38. General meetings shall be called by at least fourteen clear days' notice but a general meeting may be called by shorter notice if it is so agreed by a majority in number of the members having a right to attend and vote being a majority together holding not less than ninety per cent in nominal value of the shares giving that right.
>
> The notice shall specify the time and place of the meeting and the general nature of the business to be transacted.

> Subject to the provisions of the articles and to any restrictions imposed on any shares, the notice shall be given to all the members, to all persons entitled to a share in consequence of the death or bankruptcy of a member and to the directors and auditors.

COMMENTARY: Regulation 38 amendment (for private companies)

23.31 The amendment set out above applies only to a private company limited by shares. The amended version reflects the new statutory requirement of at least 14 clear days' notice for all general meetings. It also mirrors CA 2006, s 307(5) and (6) in that it permits shorter notice to be agreed by a majority of members having the right to attend and vote who together hold not less than 90% in nominal value of the voting shares, rather than the previous higher proportion of 95% under CA 1985, s 369(4).

Public companies only

Paragraph 20 of the 2007 Regulations provides as follows:

> Notice of general meetings
>
> 20. (1) Regulation 38 of Table A is amended as follows.
>
> (2) After the words 'annual general meeting' omit the words 'and an extraordinary general meeting called for the passing of a special resolution or a resolution appointing a person as a director'.
>
> (3) After the words 'All other' omit the word 'extraordinary'.

The effect of the amendment: the 2007 form (for public companies only):

> 38. An annual general meeting shall be called by at least twenty-one clear days' notice. All other general meetings shall be called by at least fourteen clear days' notice but a general meeting may be called by shorter notice if it is so agreed—
>
> (a) in the case of an annual general meeting, by all the members entitled to attend and vote thereat; and
>
> (b) in the case of any other meeting by a majority in number of the members having a right to attend and vote being a majority together holding not less than ninety-five per cent in nominal value of the shares giving that right.
>
> The notice shall specify the time and place of the meeting and the general nature of the business to be transacted and in the case of an annual general meeting, shall specify the meeting as such.
>
> Subject to the provisions of the articles and to any restrictions imposed on any shares, the notice shall be given to all the members, to all persons entitled to a share in consequence of the death or bankruptcy of a member and to the directors and auditors.

COMMENTARY: Regulation 38 amendment (for public companies)

23.32 The amendment set out above applies only to a public company limited by shares. The amended version continues to refer to the public company holding an annual general meeting in accordance with CA 2006, s 336. Subparagraph (a) reflects the terms of s 337(2) which permits an annual general meeting of a public company to be called by shorter notice than that required by s 337(2) or by the company's articles if all the members entitled to attend and vote agree. In the case of any other meeting, under subpara (b) shorter notice requires the agreement of members holding 95% in nominal value of the shares giving a right to attend and vote at the meeting in accordance with CA 2006, s 307(5) and (6)(a).

> **REGULATION 39**
>
> The accidental omission to give notice of a meeting to, or the non-receipt of notice of a meeting by, any person entitled to receive notice shall not invalidate the proceedings at that meeting.

COMMENTARY: REGULATION 39

Where by reason of an accidental omission, as opposed to an omission which is deliberate, a person who is entitled to notice does not receive due notice of a meeting, that accidental omission will not render invalid the proceedings of the meeting. Something that arises because of carelessness or through unexpected or unforeseen circumstances may be construed as 'accidental' within the meaning of the regulation. However, an article in the form of reg 39 will not assist in circumstances where the omission to give due notice of a meeting was deliberate and the result of a reasoned determination. See generally: *Re West Canadian Collieries Ltd* [1962] Ch 370 (Plowman J); *Musselwhite v CH Musselwhite & Son Ltd* [1962] Ch 964 (Russell J); *Re Peninsular and Oriental Steam Navigation Co* [2006] EWHC 389 (Ch), [2006] All ER (D) 36 (Mar) at [104] (Warren J). **23.33**

The content of reg 39 is now reflected in CA 2006, s 313(1) which covers not only an accidental failure to give notice of a general meeting but also to give notice of a resolution that is intended to be moved at a general meeting. A company remains at liberty to include in its articles a provision dealing with the consequences of an accidental failure of this type which differs in its wording and effect from s 313(1). However, three types of notice may only be subject to the statutory code, namely those given under ss 304 (notice of meetings required by members), 305 (notice of meetings called by members) and 339 (notice of resolutions proposed by members at the annual general meetings of public companies). **23.34**

> **REGULATION 40**
>
> No business shall be transacted at any meeting unless a quorum is present. Two persons entitled to vote upon the business to be transacted, each being a member or a proxy for a member or a duly authorised representative of a corporation, shall be a quorum.

COMMENTARY: REGULATION 40

It is an indispensable prerequisite of a valid meeting that it must be quorate. In order for there to be a valid meeting of members capable of proceeding to transact **23.35** lawful business there must be two persons entitled to vote, each being a member or a proxy for a member or a duly authorized representative of a corporation. In the light of the provisions of reg 41 (see below) it is clear that there must be a valid quorum present throughout the entire meeting.

23.36 It should be noted by way of contrast that under reg 53 of the 1948 Table A the quorum was required to be present only when the meeting proceeded to business. As a result, in the event that a member left after the meeting had started the rest of the meeting was not invalid provided that at least two persons remained—see *Re Hartley Baird Ltd* [1955] Ch 143 (Wynn-Parry J) and *Re London Flats Ltd* [1969] 1 WLR 711 (Plowman J).

23.37 CA 1985, s 1(3A) as amended by the Companies (Single Member Private Limited Companies) Regulations 1992, SI 19992/1699 introduced the concept of single member private companies. [11] The articles of association of a private company with a sole member will provide that one member present in person or by proxy will be a quorum. Now, by virtue of CA 2006, s 7(1) a single person may form any type of company, not just a private company.

2007 Regulations

Paragraph 10 of the 2007 Regulations provides as follows:

> 10. (1) Regulation 40 of Table A is amended as follows
> (2) At the beginning of the second sentence insert the words 'Save in the case of a company with a single member'.

The effect of the amendment: the 2007 form (for private companies only):

> 40. No business shall be transacted at any meeting unless a quorum is present. Save in the case of a company with a single member two persons entitled to vote upon the business to be transacted, each being a member or a proxy for a member or a duly authorised representative of a corporation, shall be a quorum.

COMMENTARY: Regulation 40 amendment (for private companies)

23.38 This amendment applies only to private companies limited by shares. The amended version makes express reference to the possibility of a company having a single member, in which event one qualifying person who is present will constitute the quorum for a meeting. This reflects CA 2006, s 318(1). In all other cases under reg 40, two persons physically present, who are entitled to vote on the business before the meeting, are required for there to be a valid meeting.

---

[11] This provision came into force on 15 July 1992.

REGULATION 41

If such a quorum is not present within half an hour from the time appointed for the meeting, or if during a meeting such a quorum ceases to be present, the meeting shall stand adjourned to the same day in the next week at the same time and place or to such time and place as the directors may determine.

COMMENTARY: REGULATION 41

Starting a meeting of members on time is good practice but sometimes circumstances dictate that this may not be possible. Regulation 41 deals with the situation where a quorum is not present, either when the meeting proceeds to business or at any time during the meeting itself. In such circumstances, the meeting will automatically be adjourned to the same day in the following week at the same time and venue, unless the directors determine that the time and place shall change. This regulation also makes it clear that an effective quorum must be present throughout the duration of the general meeting. **23.39**

REGULATION 42

The chairman, if any, of the board of directors or in his absence some other director nominated by the directors shall preside as chairman of the meeting, but if neither the chairman nor such other director (if any) be present within fifteen minutes after the time appointed for holding the meeting and willing to act, the directors present shall elect one of their number to be chairman and, if there is only one director present and willing to act, he shall be chairman.

COMMENTARY: REGULATION 42

If a person has been appointed to hold office as the chairman of the board of directors that person has capacity to act as the chairman of a meeting of members. Such an appointment arises by reason of holding office as chairman of the board of directors. Alternatively, the members of the board can nominate another director to be the chairman of a forthcoming meeting of members. Accordingly, it can be seen that reg 42 confers authority on a board of directors to decide in advance of a general meeting who is to take on the important role of chairman of such a meeting. Deciding in advance who is to act as the chairman is a sensible and prudent course of action, as it is sometimes unwise to leave to chance the identity of the chairman of a general meeting of members.[12] **23.40**

In the event that the chairman of the board cannot attend a meeting of members, and a director who has been nominated in advance to chair the meeting is also not present, the role of chairman is to be filled by one of the other directors **23.41**

[12] See Ch 7.

present. If circumstances dictate that only one director is present and that director is willing to act as the chairman, then he is to be the chairman.

23.42 CA 2006, s 319 permits a member to be elected as the chairman of a general meeting by a resolution of the company passed at the meeting. However, this entitlement is subject to any provision of the company's articles which regulates who may or may not be the chairman. Regulation 42 constitutes such a restrictive provision. It would not allow a member to be imposed on the meeting as chairman in the absence of a director. However, reg 43 applies in this situation, where no directors are present or willing to act as chairman.

REGULATION 43

If no director is willing to act as chairman, or if no director is present within fifteen minutes after the time appointed for holding the meeting, the members present and entitled to vote shall choose one of their number to be chairman.

COMMENTARY: REGULATION 43

23.43 The effect of this regulation is to ensure that a general meeting of members will not fail by reason of the absence of a chairman. In the absence of any director who is willing to act as chairman, the members of the company who are present and have the right to vote have the authority to elect a member to act as chairman of that meeting—see *Re Bradford Investments plc* [1991] BCLC 224 (Hoffmann J).

23.44 A member will be present for the purposes of reg 43 if he is present at the meeting by means of a lawful proxy. CA 2006, s 324(1) provides that a member is entitled to appoint another person as his proxy to exercise all or any of his rights to attend and to speak and vote at a meeting of the company. Under CA 2006, s 328(1) the proxy himself may be elected as chairman of the meeting by a resolution of the company passed at the meeting. Again, this latter entitlement is subject to any contrary provision of the company's articles. There is nothing in reg 43 to detract from this provision.

REGULATION 44

A director shall, notwithstanding that he is not a member, be entitled to attend and speak at any general meeting and at any separate meeting of the holders of any class of shares in the company.

COMMENTARY: REGULATION 44

23.45 Regulation 44 applies to general meetings and, where a company's issued share capital is divided into different classes of shares, to class meetings of members. The regulation ties in with the right of a director to receive notice of general meetings under reg 38 and CA 2006, s 310(1)(b). Regulation 44 was a new provision in the 1985 Table A. It is suggested the omission of such a regulation in earlier versions of Table A was because it was thought that a director of a company had an inherent right to attend and speak at a meeting of members, even though he might not be a shareholder in the company. The decision of the Court of Appeal in *Peel v London and North Western Railway Co* [1907] 1 Ch 5 at 16–17 suggests that this was the case (although not directly on point). Regulation 44 puts the matter beyond dispute. A director is entitled to address any general meeting of a company or, where apposite, any class meeting of members.

REGULATION 45

The chairman may, with the consent of a meeting at which a quorum is present (and shall if so directed by the meeting), adjourn the meeting from time to time and from place to place, but no business shall be transacted at an adjourned meeting other than business which might properly have been transacted at the meeting had the adjournment not taken place. When a meeting is adjourned for fourteen days or more, at least seven clear days' notice shall be given specifying the time and place of the adjourned meeting and the general nature of the business to be transacted. Otherwise it shall not be necessary to give any such notice.

COMMENTARY: REGULATION 45

Questions often arise concerning adjournments of general meetings. It is most **23.46** important to note that a chairman of a meeting has no authority by reason of his position as chairman to stop or to adjourn a meeting—see *Salisbury Gold Mining Co v Hathorn* [1897] AC 268 (PC). If a chairman of a meeting walked out of the meeting or absented himself in any other manner, the remaining members would be entitled to continue with the business on the designated agenda for the meeting and would be able to appoint a new chairman—see *National Dwellings Society v Sykes* [1894] 3 Ch 159 (Chitty J); *Catesby v Burnett* [1916] 2 Ch 325 (Eve J).

Under the provisions of reg 45 a chairman is bound to adjourn a meeting if a **23.47** majority of the persons present eligible to vote want the meeting to be adjourned. It would be a serious abuse of the role of the chairman if he declined to adjourn the meeting in response to a direction to this effect from the majority of the members.

A chairman will be able to adjourn a meeting in circumstances where it is neces- **23.48** sary to afford all the members the opportunity of casting their votes, but this power is limited in its scope as it appears to arise only in exceptional or unusual circumstances where it is not possible to ascertain the wishes of the members—see *Byng v London Life Association* [1989] BCLC 400 (CA).

Under reg 45, where a general meeting is correctly adjourned by the chairman **23.49** with the consent of the members it is not permissible for the chairman simply to declare that the meeting stands adjourned. The chairman is required to state the time and the place of the adjourned meeting and the wording of the regulation requires the chairman to do this when he announces the adjournment.

23.50 At the adjourned meeting it is impermissible for the members to transact business that was not properly before the original meeting. CA 2006, s 332 provides that where a resolution is passed at an adjourned meeting of a company, the resolution is for all purposes treated as having been passed on the date on which it was in fact passed, and it is not deemed to have been passed on any earlier date.

23.51 Generally notice to the members and other persons who are entitled to receive due notice of an adjourned meeting is not required. The minimum notice requirements contained in CA 2006, s 307 do not apply to adjourned meetings. However, under reg 45, where the adjournment of a meeting is for a period of 14 days or more, the mandatory wording requires that a minimum period of seven clear days' notice shall be given, specifying the time and place of the adjourned meeting and the general nature of the business to be transacted—see *Robert Batcheller & Sons v Batcheller* [1945] Ch 169 (Romer J).

REGULATION 46

A resolution put to the vote of a meeting shall be decided on a show of hands unless before, or on the declaration of the result of, the show of hands a poll is duly demanded. Subject to the provisions of the Act, a poll may be demanded—

(a) by the chairman; or
(b) by at least two members having the right to vote at the meeting; or
(c) by a member or members representing not less than one-tenth of the total voting rights of all the members having the right to vote at the meeting; or
(d) by a member or members holding shares conferring a right to vote at the meeting being shares on which an aggregate sum has been paid up equal to not less than one-tenth of the total sum paid up on all the shares conferring that right;

and a demand by a person as proxy for a member shall be the same as a demand by the member.

COMMENTARY: REGULATION 46

23.52 The conventional method of decision making at a meeting of members is for a vote to be taken on a show of hands. Where a vote is taken on a show of hands each member has one vote, irrespective of the actual number of shares held by him as recorded in the company's register of members. However, the impact of a combination of CA 2006, s 324 (the right of a member to appoint more than one proxy for a meeting) and s 284(2) (every duly appointed proxy present being entitled to vote on a show of hands) means that where more than one proxy is appointed a member may obtain multiple representation on a show of hands. For further discussion of this issue reference should be made to Chapter 9.

23.53 The orthodox method of voting will be displaced if at the meeting a lawful demand for a vote to be taken on a poll is made. In addition, a company's articles of association or the terms of a shareholders' agreement may stipulate that on certain matters or resolutions voting must take place by means of a poll. Large public companies invariably put all resolutions to a vote taken on a poll.

Regulation 46 was reflective of the provisions contained in CA 1985, s 373, which have been replaced by CA 2006, ss 321 and 329. If a company's articles of association contain provisions that are inconsistent with the legislative regime prescribed by s 321 such provisions will be void and of no effect. Regulation 46 does not contravene those statutory requirements. **23.54**

Regulation 46 empowers four categories of person to make a lawful demand for a vote on a resolution to be taken on a poll. As to the ability of the chairman of the meeting to make a demand for a poll, this power is not a personal right that is vested in the chairman himself. The power is a fiduciary power and must be exercised for proper purposes and in the interests of ascertaining the true wishes of the general meeting. The power must not be exercised in a manner that is self-serving, capricious or partial. Where the chairman is not certain about the sense of the meeting he will be well advised to demand a poll—see *Byng v London Life Association* [1989] BCLC 400 (CA). **23.55**

Where a member appoints a proxy to attend a meeting on his behalf that appointment carries with it the ability for the duly appointed proxy to demand, or join in demanding, a poll. This right is enshrined in CA 2006, s 329. **23.56**

A single member holding the qualifying number of shares that is stipulated by sub-para (c) of reg 46 will be able to demand a poll just as if the number of qualifying shares were held by a number of members. **23.57**

REGULATION 47

Unless a poll is duly demanded a declaration by the chairman that a resolution has been carried or carried unanimously, or by a particular majority, or lost, or not carried by a particular majority and an entry to that effect in the minutes of the meeting shall be conclusive evidence of the fact without proof of the number or proportion of the votes recorded in favour of or against the resolution.

COMMENTARY: REGULATION 47

Subject to one caveat, reg 47 stipulates that the declaration by the chairman of the result of a vote taken on a show of hands is 'conclusive evidence' of the result and there is no need for the chairman to record either the number or the proportion of the votes cast in favour or against a resolution. Although there is no requirement in reg 47 to record the numbers of votes cast in favour or against a particular resolution there is no doubt that it is good practice so to do in case there is any subsequent dispute about the matter. The one caveat to the rule contained in reg 47 is that where a poll (ie a vote that takes account of the actual numbers of shares held by individual members) is demanded, the declaration of the result of the vote by the chairman is not conclusive evidence of the outcome. **23.58**

The terms of reg 47 are now reflected in CA 2006, s 320. That section provides that on a vote on a resolution on a show of hands a declaration by the chairman **23.59** that the resolution has been passed or not passed is conclusive evidence of that fact, without proof of the number or proportion of the votes recorded in favour or against the resolution. If the minutes record such a declaration they constitute conclusive evidence of that fact without further proof. However, the section does not have effect if a poll is demanded in respect of the resolution and the demand is not later withdrawn.

REGULATION 48

The demand for a poll may, before the poll is taken, be withdrawn but only with the consent of the chairman and a demand so withdrawn shall not be taken to have invalidated the result of a show of hands declared before the demand was made.

COMMENTARY: REGULATION 48

23.60 Once a lawful demand has been made for a vote to be taken on a poll the maker of that demand does not have an unqualified right to withdraw the demand. The request to withdraw the demand for the poll may only be made by the person who demanded the poll before the vote on the poll is taken, but this request will only become effective if the consent of the chairman is forthcoming. If the circumstances are such that prior to the lawful demand for a vote on a poll being made there has been a vote on a show of hands, the later withdrawal of the demand for a poll does not operate so as to invalidate the earlier vote taken on a show of hands.

REGULATION 49

A poll shall be taken as the chairman directs and he may appoint scrutineers (who need not be members) and fix a time and place for declaring the result of the poll. The result of the poll shall be deemed to be the resolution of the meeting at which the poll was demanded.

COMMENTARY: REGULATION 49

23.61 If a vote on a poll is lawfully demanded then, unless the articles of association provided to the contrary, the chairman has an unfettered discretion under the terms of reg 49 to direct how and when the poll is to be taken and he has the jurisdiction to direct that the poll is taken at once—see *Re Chillington Iron Co* (1885) 29 Ch D 159 (Kay J). In accordance with the provisions of reg 51 a poll on the election of a chairman or on a question of an adjournment of the meeting must be forthwith and all other polls must take place within 30 days of being demanded.

23.62 Very sensibly reg 49 confers express authority on the chairman of the meeting to appoint scrutineers to assist in the counting of the votes cast on a poll. In view of this express power to appoint scrutineers there can be no doubt that the costs of, and incidental to, their appointment fall to be paid by the company. Regulation 49 applies to both public and private companies. CA 2006, Part 13, Chapter 5 (ss 341–354) introduces additional requirements for quoted companies, including the right of members to require the directors to obtain an independent report on any poll that is taken or to be taken at a general or class meeting of the company. They also provide in CA 2006, s 341 for the results of the poll to be published on the company's website. These detailed provisions are examined in Chapter 9 and in the commentary in Part 3.

For companies other than a quoted company, in the absence of an express authorization in the articles to appoint scrutineers to assist with the conduct of a poll, it is suggested that the chairman should exercise a degree of caution in relation to the appointment of scrutineers. In most circumstances he should obtain the consent of the meeting to that proposal before its implementation. **23.63**

REGULATION 50

In the case of an equality of votes, whether on a show of hands or on a poll, the chairman shall be entitled to a casting vote in addition to any other vote he may have.

COMMENTARY: REGULATION 50

In order to avoid impasse and uncertainty reg 50 confers on the chairman of the meeting a casting vote if an equal number of votes is exercised either on a show of hands or on a vote that is taken on a poll. Without a provision conferring a casting vote on the chairman there is no inherent right at common law to have such a vote—see *Nell v Longbottom* [1894] 1 QB 767 (Divisional Court). **23.64**

Table A has contained a provision for the chairman of a meeting to have a second or casting vote since 1862. In its original form the casting vote was given for use where there was an equality of votes on a poll.[13] In the 1906 Table A the wording was extended to confer a casting vote on the chairman in the event of an equality of votes whether on a show of hands or a poll.[14] This was repeated in the 1908 Table A.[15] Identical wording is to be found in reg 52 of the 1929 Table A and in reg 60 of the 1948 Table A. **23.65**

The concluding phrase of reg 50 makes it clear that if the chairman of the meeting has cast votes at the meeting in any other capacity, for example, in his capacity as a member of the company or as a proxy-holder for a member, his casting vote is in addition to those other votes. **23.66**

2007 Amendment Regulations

Regulation 50 has now been deleted for both private and public companies registered on or after 1 October 2007 under the 2007 Amendment Regulations. **23.67**

---

[13] Regulation 43 of the 1862 Table A.
[14] Regulation 58 of the 1906 Table A.
[15] Regulation 58 of the 1908 Table A.

The stated reason for this change is the perceived conflict between reg 50 and CA 2006, ss 281 and 282. It has been suggested that the effect of those sections is that a resolution can no longer be passed by the use of the chairman's casting vote. This interpretation of these new sections requires closer examination.

23.68 Both sections do not expressly deal with the question of the chairman's casting vote and, in particular, do not in terms prohibit the passing of a resolution on the exercise of a casting vote. Section 281 prescribes how a resolution of the members may be passed. Under CA 2006, s 281(1) a resolution of members of a private company can be passed by use of the written resolution procedure or at a meeting of members. A resolution of a public company can only be passed at a general meeting of the members. This section is not capable of being modified by a company's articles.

23.69 CA 2006, s 282, which is also incapable of modification by provisions in a company's articles, defines an ordinary resolution of the members or a class of members as a resolution that is passed by a simple majority. Section 282(3) provides that a resolution is passed at a meeting on a show of hands by a simple majority if it is passed by a simple majority of (a) members who, being entitled to vote, vote in person and (b) the persons who are duly appointed proxies of members entitled to vote on it. In the event that a resolution is put to a vote on a poll, by s 282(4) the resolution is passed by a simple majority if it is passed by members representing a simple majority of the total voting rights of members who vote in person or by proxy on the resolution.

23.70 There is no mention in s 282 of a vote exercised by a chairman as a casting vote, whether on a show of hands or a poll. However, the section does appear to exclude from the definition of an ordinary resolution any resolution passed by votes other than those exercised by a member or his duly appointed proxy. The ramifications of this wording may be very far reaching, albeit unintentional. It is to be noted that there is no reference to what would be a major change in the law in the Explanatory Notes to CA 2006.

23.71 The 2007 Amendment Regulations only amend Table A in respect of new companies (or those which adopt Table A in its new amended form). This will leave many existing companies, both public and private, with reg 50 as part of their articles. This is likely to cause much confusion and uncertainty. The articles, which form part of the company's constitution, constitute a contract between the company and its members.[16] In the case of many private companies, including joint ventures, a chairman may often not be a member of the company. Indeed, he may have been appointed expressly for the purpose of acting independently of two rival factions of shareholders and, where necessary, resolving disputes by the exercise of his or her casting vote. The loss of a casting vote in these circumstances may have a substantial impact on the company.

---

[16] CA 2006, s 33.

Section 281(4)(b) states that nothing in CA 2006, Part 13 affects any enactment or rule of law as to the circumstances in which a resolution is or is not treated as having been passed. However, this wording may be insufficient to validate a resolution carried by the chairman's casting vote. Section 281(4)(c) on the other hand provides that nothing in this Part of CA 2006 affects any enactment or rule of law as to cases in which a person is precluded from alleging that a resolution has not been duly passed. It is suggested that this subsection may enable the argument to be put that a member of a company, whose articles contain reg 50, will be estopped from contending that a resolution passed by the use of the chairman's casting vote is invalid. **23.72**

One possible solution may be found by restricting the role of chairman to that of a member of the company or his proxy and ensuring that the vote on ordinary resolutions is carried out by means of a poll. In that event, any resolution passed on a poll will be passed by members 'representing a simple majority of the total voting rights of members who (being entitled to do so) vote in person or by proxy on the resolution' within the meaning of s 282(4). This wording may be of greater assistance than that of s 282(3) which refers to voting on a show of hands. **23.73**

Perhaps it would have been more sensible to have amended reg 50 to exclude the use of a casting vote on a resolution on a show of hands or by any chairman who was not a member of the company, alternatively to have provided that to preside as chairman at a general meeting the person must be a member or his proxy.[17] The deletion of reg 50 for all new companies deprives such companies of the ability to make provision in its articles for a mechanism to avoid deadlock at meetings. It is most unfortunate that such a fundamental change in corporate procedure should have been introduced in such an indirect and haphazard manner. **23.74**

REGULATION 51

A poll demanded on the election of a chairman or on a question of adjournment shall be taken forthwith. A poll demanded on any other question shall be taken either forthwith or at such time and place as the chairman directs not being more than thirty days after the poll is demanded. The demand for a poll shall not prevent the continuance of a meeting for the transaction of any business other than the question on which the poll was demanded. If a poll is demanded before the declaration of the result of a show of hands and the demand is duly withdrawn, the meeting shall continue as if the demand had not been made.

COMMENTARY: REGULATION 51

Regulation 51 stipulates in mandatory terms that a poll demanded on the election of a chairman or on the question of an adjournment of the meeting shall be taken forthwith. Other polls may be taken forthwith but, if they are not taken immediately, there is a period of 30 days from the time that the poll was demanded **23.75**

[17] See CA 2006, s 328(1).

within which the poll must take place. A valid demand for a poll in relation to a particular resolution does not operate as any form of impediment to the continuation of the general meeting in relation to other business and resolutions.

REGULATION 52

No notice need be given of a poll not taken forthwith if the time and place at which it is to be taken are announced at the meeting at which it is demanded. In any other case at least seven clear days' notice shall be given specifying the time and place at which the poll is to be taken.

COMMENTARY: REGULATION 52

23.76 When a poll is not taken at once it is important to ensure that the members know precisely when the poll is going to be conducted. Accordingly, it is usual for the chairman to announce at the general meeting the precise time and venue for the poll. If such an announcement concerning a subsequent poll is made at the meeting then there is no need for the company to give any further form of notice to the members. If an announcement concerning the time and place of a poll is not made at the meeting, it is incumbent on the company to give at least seven clear days' notice of the time and place of the poll.

REGULATION 53

A resolution in writing executed by or on behalf of each member who would have been entitled to vote upon it if it had been proposed at a general meeting at which he was present shall be as effectual as if it had been passed at a general meeting duly convened and held and may consist of several instruments in the like form each executed by or on behalf of one or more members.

COMMENTARY: REGULATION 53

23.77 CA 1989, ss 113 and 114 introduced ss 381A, 381B, 381C, 382A and Sch 15A to CA 1985. These legislative amendments introduced a new statutory procedure for written resolutions. Such written resolutions had to be signed by all the members entitled to vote and once the unanimous written approval has been obtained the written resolution took effect as if passed by the company in general meeting. The difficulties of obtaining the unanimous consent of the members were formidable save in the case of a company with only a small number of members. These difficulties reduced the utility and efficacy of the procedure under CA 1985, Sch 15A.

23.78 CA 2006, Part 13, Chapter 2 (ss 288–300) introduces a new code for written resolutions which is applicable to private companies only.[18] This provides a

[18] See CA 2006, ss 281(1)(a) and 288(1).

comprehensive procedure dealing with the persons eligible to sign such resolutions (known as 'eligible members'), the procedure for the circulation of resolutions, expenses, the procedure for signifying agreement, the timetable, modes of sending and publication. This procedure in effect replaces that in reg 53 which has become redundant because it is clearly much more restrictive than the statutory procedure, which is of general application to private companies.[19]

23.79 The statutory written resolution procedure provided for in CA 2006 does not change the common law position concerning the unanimous consent of members. If all the members of a company who have the right to attend and vote at a general meeting give their approval to a matter which could form the subject matter of a valid resolution at a general meeting that informal consent is as effective as a resolution passed at a valid meeting—see *Re Express Engineering Works* [1920] 1 Ch 466 (CA); *Re Duomatic Ltd* [1969] 2 Ch 365 (Buckley J); *Atlas Wright (Europe) Ltd v Wright* [1999] 2 BCLC 301 (CA); *Euro Brokers Holdings Ltd v Monecor (London) Ltd* [2003] 1BCLC 506 (CA).

2007 Regulations

Paragraph 6 of the 2007 Regulations provides as follows:

> 6. Regulation 53 of Table A ceases to have effect.

COMMENTARY: 2007 Regulations

23.80 This amendment is applicable to both public and private companies limited by shares incorporated on or after 1 October 2007 or which adopt the new version of Table A. Accordingly, there remain many thousands of companies where the articles continue to incorporate reg 53.

23.81 It is important to note that the new statutory procedure cannot apply to a public company (see above). CA 2006, s 281(2) provides that a resolution of the members of a public company must be passed at a meeting of the members. This means that it is no longer possible for a public company to rely upon reg 53 for the purposes of a written resolution, even if that regulation has not been deleted from its articles. However, a public company that is small enough to garner unanimous consent may be able to rely upon the common law position as illustrated by the decision in *Re Duomatic Ltd* [1969] 2 Ch 365 (Buckley J) which is preserved by CA 2006, s 281(4)(a).

> **REGULATION 54**
>
> Subject to any rights or restrictions attached to any shares, on a show of hands every member who (being an individual) is present in person or (being a corporation)

---

[19] See also CA 2006, s 300.

is present by a duly authorised representative, not being himself a member entitled to vote, shall have one vote and on a poll every member shall have one vote for every share of which he is the holder.

COMMENTARY: REGULATION 54

23.82 Regulation 54 prescribes the manner of voting and the number of votes that can be cast at a general meeting of members. The conventional method of voting is by way of a vote taken on a show of hands. When voting is conducted on a show of hands, no reference is made to the actual number of shares that are registered in the company's register of members against the name of each member. On a show of hands each member will have just one vote.

23.83 The existing wording of reg 54 makes no mention of the right of a proxy to vote on a show of hands, now to be found in CA 2006, s 284(2)(b). Although the provisions of that section may be modified by a company's articles,[20] s 285(1) imposes certain minimum requirements for all companies which cannot be disapplied by the articles. A proxy cannot have fewer votes in a vote on a resolution on a show of hands than the member himself if he were present in person and he must be afforded the same voting rights as the member. Although the wording of this provision is convoluted, this would seem to be its meaning. The existing reg 54 is therefore somewhat misleading and companies are well advised to adopt the modified version introduced in the 2007 Amendment Regulations referred to below.

23.84 The articles of association of a company constitute a statutory contract between the company and its members, and as between each of the members themselves. In these circumstances, it is permissible for articles of association to contain provisions which confer different voting rights on members holding different classes of shares. Sometimes a class of shares, for example preference shares, will have no voting rights at all, or, alternatively, restricted voting rights that only arise in prescribed circumstances, where, for example, a preferential dividend is in arrears.

23.85 As a matter of law, shares constitute personal property as opposed to realty, and the rights that are attached to shares, such as a right to cast a vote at a general meeting, are personal property rights—see *Borland's Trustee v Steel Bros & Co Ltd* [1901] Ch 279 (Farwell J); *Government of Mauritius v Union Flacq Sugar Estates Co. Ltd* [1992] 1 WLR 903 (PC). As a consequence, a member of a company may cast his vote as he sees fit and in his own personal interests even though to vote in such a manner may be inimical to the interests of the company as a whole—see *North-West Transportation Co v Beatty* (1887) 12 App Cas 589 (PC).

[20] See CA 2006, s 284(4).

Where a shareholder is also a director of the company, that individual is still able to cast the votes in respect of his personal shareholding as he sees fit—see *Northern Counties Securities Ltd v Jackson and Steeple Ltd* [1974] 1 WLR 1133 (Walton J). **23.86**

2007 Amendment Regulations

> 4.—(1) Regulation 54 of Table A is amended as follows.
> (2) After the words 'is present in person' insert the words 'or by proxy'.
> (3) After the words 'is present by a duly authorised representative' insert the words 'or by proxy'.
> (4) Omit the words 'not being' and insert the words 'unless the proxy (in either case) or the representative is'.

The effect of the amendment: the 2007 form:

> 54. Subject to any rights or restrictions attached to any shares, on a show of hands every member who (being an individual) is present in person or by proxy or (being a corporation) is present by a duly authorised representative or by proxy, unless the proxy (in either case) or the representative is himself a member entitled to vote, shall have one vote and on a poll every member shall have one vote for every share of which he is the holder.

The amendment of reg 54 has been introduced to reflect the fact that under CA 2006, ss 284(2)(b) and 324(1) a proxy must be permitted to vote both on a show of hands and on a poll. A proxy is entitled to exercise all or any of the rights of the member to attend and to speak and vote. **23.87**

> **REGULATION 55**
>
> In the case of joint holders the vote of the senior who tenders a vote, whether in person or by proxy, shall be accepted to the exclusion of the votes of the other joint holders; and seniority shall be determined by the order in which the names of the holders stand in the register of members.

COMMENTARY: REGULATION 55

Shares are capable of being owned by more than one person. The names of joint holders of shares should be entered in the company's register of members. Although shares can be owned jointly it does not follow that each joint shareholder is entitled to vote at a general meeting. Regulation 55 stipulates that where shares are held jointly it is only the vote of the 'senior' that will be accepted. Seniority will be determined on the basis of the order in which the names of the members are entered in the company's register of members. This regulation reflects the wording of CA 2006, s 286 which also states that only the votes of the proxies duly appointed by the senior holder may be counted by the company. **23.88**

It is permissible for two joint holders to have their holding split so that different tranches of shares are registered with their names in a different order so as to increase **23.89** their voting power and enable both of them to attend and vote at a general meeting—see *Burns v Siemens Brothers Dynamo Works* [1919] 1 Ch 225 (Astbury J).

REGULATION 56

A member in respect of whom an order has been made by any court having jurisdiction (whether in the United Kingdom or elsewhere) in matters concerning mental disorder may vote, whether on a show of hands or on a poll, by his receiver, curator bonis or other person authorised in that behalf appointed by that court, and any such receiver, curator bonis or other person may, on a poll, vote by proxy. Evidence to the satisfaction of the directors of the authority of the person claiming to exercise the right to vote shall be deposited at the office, or at such other place as is specified in accordance with the articles for the deposit of instruments of proxy, not less than 48 hours before the time appointed for holding the meeting or adjourned meeting at which the right to vote is to be exercised and in default the right to vote shall not be exercisable.

COMMENTARY: REGULATION 56

23.90 In the event that a registered member becomes subject to mental incapacity and has his affairs regulated by a court order, he remains entitled to vote at a general meeting via the person who is appointed to have jurisdiction over his affairs. The court order contemplated by reg 56 may be made by any court in the United Kingdom or a court that situated elsewhere. As a safeguard designed to ensure that the voting rights of an incapacitated member may not be abused, a company is entitled to have produced to it proper evidence relating to the entitlement of the person who claims to be entitled to vote on behalf of the incapacitated member. Such evidence must be deposited with the company not less than 48 hours before the time designated for the start of the general meeting. A copy of the order of the court which confers on the person who is the substitute for the member the authority to act is the most apposite form of evidence in this regard. If the evidence is not deposited at the registered office within the prescribed time limit, or if the evidence is not satisfactory in the considered opinion of the board of directors, the votes in respect of the shares in question will not be capable of being exercised at the relevant general meeting.

REGULATION 57

No member shall vote at any general meeting or at any separate meeting of the holders of any class of shares in the company, either in person or by proxy, in respect of any share held by him unless all moneys presently payable by him in respect of that share have been paid.

COMMENTARY: REGULATION 57

23.91 A shareholder has important rights as a member of a company but he also has responsibilities to that company. Although the well-established twin concepts of corporate personality and limited liability confer a degree of protection to those who wish to invest in registered companies, a shareholder does have an obligation to pay for the shares which he holds and to pay any lawful calls that are made on shareholders as a whole. Accordingly, it is common for articles of association to contain a provision that prohibits members from exercising the voting rights attached to their shares if a call or any other sum of money is due and owing in respect of those shares. If a member holds 100 shares and a call is outstanding on 40 of those shares, reg 57 permits the member to vote in respect of 60 shares on which no money is owed, but operates so as to disenfranchise the member in respect of the remaining 40 shares.

Sometimes articles of association will empower the company to take remedial action against a member who has not paid a call. Ultimately, such action may lead to the forfeiture of the shares—see, for example, regs 19 and 20 of the 1985 Table A and the decision in *Hunter v Senate Support Services* [2005] 1 BCLC 175. Where a company has implemented the forfeiture provisions correctly the forfeited shares may be re-allotted to another person. However, the new member who becomes the holder of the forfeited shares will not inherit with those shares the previous impediment to voting. In *Randt Gold Mining Co Ltd v Wainwright* [1901] 1 Ch 184 (Kekewich J), the original shareholder had outstanding calls on his shares and as a consequence his shares were forfeited. Thereafter the forfeited shares were allotted to a new member. As there remained an outstanding sum due from the original holder of the shares, it was held that the new member was not entitled to cast votes in respect of these shares. However, had the Randt Gold Mining Co Ltd had a provision in its articles of association in the form of reg 57, the new member would have been able to vote as the restriction is a personal one under this regulation. **23.92**

REGULATION 58

No objection shall be raised to the qualification of any voter except at the meeting or adjourned meeting at which the vote objected to is tendered, and every vote not disallowed at the meeting shall be valid. Any objection made in due time shall be referred to the chairman whose decision shall be final and conclusive.

COMMENTARY: REGULATION 58

In order to promote certainty and in an effort to avoid disputes, reg 58 stipulates that an objection to the qualification of a member to vote must be taken at the general meeting where the vote is tendered. If no objection is tendered the vote will be allowed. Where an objection is taken it must be made to the chairman of the meeting, and his decision on the matter is declared to be final and binding. Accordingly, where an objection is made in time and the chairman makes his ruling on the matter the issue is at an end and cannot be impugned. The decisions in *Wall v London and Northern Assets Corpn* [1899] 1 Ch 550 (North J); *Wall v Exchange Investment Corpn* [1926] Ch 143 (CA); and *In re Hadeligh Castle Gold Mines* [1900] 2 Ch 419 (Cozens-Hardy J) indicate the importance of the finality of the chairman's decision, but do admit to the possibility of an effective **23.93** subsequent legal challenge where there is cogent evidence of fraud or bad faith; in practice such cases are likely to be extremely rare.

23.94 CA 2006, s 287 provides that nothing in CA 2006, Part 13, Chapter 1 (ss 281–287) affects a provision of a company's articles of this nature or the grounds on which such a determination of any objection may be questioned in legal proceedings.

> **REGULATION 59**
>
> On a poll votes may be given either personally or by proxy. A member may appoint more than one proxy to attend on the same occasion.

COMMENTARY: REGULATION 59

23.95 Regulation 59 makes it clear that where a vote is taken on a poll those votes can be cast by the member in person or by means of a duly appointed proxy. Members of both public and private companies are now entitled to appoint more than one proxy. CA 2006, s 324(2) expressly states that a member may appoint more than one proxy in relation to a meeting, provided that each proxy is appointed to exercise the rights attached to a different share or shares. This statutory provision enables duplication of representation, albeit not in respect of the same shares.

> **REGULATION 60**
>
> The appointment of a proxy shall be ...[21] executed by or on behalf of the appointor and shall be in the following form (or in a form as near thereto as circumstances allow or in any other form which is usual or which the directors may approve)
>
> ' PLC/Limited
>
> I/We, ____________, of ____________, being a member/members of the above-named company, hereby appoint ____________ of ____________, or failing him, ____________ of ____________, as my/our proxy to vote in my/our name[s] and on my/our behalf at the annual/extraordinary general meeting of the company to be held on 19____________, and at any adjournment thereof.
>
> Signed on ____________ 19 ____________.'

COMMENTARY: REGULATION 60

23.96 Regulation 60 contains a standard form precedent for use by members to appoint a proxy. The directors of a company have a discretion to permit a proxy in another format.

23.97 The Companies Act (Electronic Communications) Order 2000, SI 2000/3373, Sch 1, para 2 amended reg 60 with effect from 22 December 2000 so as to permit

[21] The omission of the words '...in writing...' was as a result of the amendment to reg 60 that was effected by the Companies Act (Electronic Communications) Order 2000, SI 2000/3373 with effect from 22 December 2000.

members to appoint proxies by electronic means. These powers are now contained in CA 2006, s 333.[22]

2007 Regulations—Private companies

Paragraph 11 of the 2007 Regulations provides as follows:

> Votes of members
> 11. (1) Regulation 60 of Table A is amended as follows.
> (2) After the words 'our behalf at the' omit the words 'annual/extraordinary'.

This amendment applies only to a *private* company limited by shares, which is no longer required by statute to hold an annual general meeting.[23] The amendment to reg 60 reflects this change in the law. 23.98

The effect of the amendment: the 2007 form (for private companies only):

> **REGULATION 60**
>
> The appointment of a proxy shall be ...[24] executed by or on behalf of the appointor and shall be in the following form (or in a form as near thereto as circumstances allow or in any other form which is usual or which the directors may approve)
>
> ' PLC/Limited
>
> I/We, _____________, of _____________, being a member/members of the above-named company, hereby appoint _____________ of _____________, or failing him, _____________ of _____________, as my/our proxy to vote in my/our name[s] and on my/our behalf at the general meeting of the company to be held on 19 _____________, and at any adjournment thereof.
>
> Signed on _____________ 19 _____________.'

2007 Regulations—Public companies

Paragraph 21 of the 2007 Regulations provides as follows:

> 21. (1) Regulation 60 of Table A is amended as follows.
> (2) After the words 'our behalf at the annual' omit the word 'extraordinary' and insert the words 'any other'.

This amendment applies only to a *public* company limited by shares and simply removes reference to extraordinary general meetings which no longer exist. The amendment preserves the form for use at both the annual general meeting of a public company and at any other general meeting. 23.99

---

[22] See also CA 2006, s 1144 and Schs 4 and 5.

[23] See CA 2006, s 336(1) which requires only a public company to hold an annual general meeting.

[24] The omission of the words '... in writing ...' was as a result of the amendment to reg 60 that was effected by the Companies Act (Electronic Communications) Order 2000, SI 2000/3373 with effect from 22 December 2000.

The effect of the amendment: the 2007 form (for public companies only):

REGULATION 60

The appointment of a proxy shall be ...[25] executed by or on behalf of the appointor and shall be in the following form (or in a form as near thereto as circumstances allow or in any other form which is usual or which the directors may approve)

'

PLC/Limited

I/We, ____________, of ____________, being a member/members of the above-named company, hereby appoint ____________ of ____________, or failing him, ____________ of ____________, as my/our proxy to vote in my/our name[s] and on my/our behalf at the general meeting of the company to be held on 19 ____________, and at any adjournment thereof.

Signed on ____________ 19 ____________.'

REGULATION 61

Where it is desired to afford members an opportunity of instructing the proxy how he shall act the appointment of a proxy shall be in the following form (or in a form as near thereto as circumstances allow or in any other form which is usual or which the directors may approve)—

'

PLC/Limited

I/We, ____________, of ____________ being a member/members of the above-named company, hereby appoint ____________ of ____________, or failing him, ____________ of ____________, as my/our proxy to vote in my/our name[s] and on my/our behalf at the annual/extraordinary general meeting of the company to be held on 19 ____________, and at any adjournment thereof.
This form is to be used in respect of the resolutions mentioned below as follows:
Resolution No 1 *for *against
Resolution No 2 *for *against.
*Strike out whichever is not desired.
Unless otherwise instructed, the proxy may vote as he thinks fit or abstain from voting. Signed this ____________ day of ____________ 19____________.'

COMMENTARY: REGULATION 61

23.100 An article in this form enables a member to indicate specific instructions to his duly appointed proxy. The final sentence of reg 61 provides that if no instructions are indicated to the proxy then the latter will vote as he sees fit, and he may abstain from voting altogether. Where the original text of a resolution is subject to a legitimate amendment at a meeting difficulties may occur for a proxy if the amendment comes to be voted upon. In *Re Waxed Papers Ltd* [1937] 2 All ER 481 (CA) shareholders appointed proxies to act for them at a general meeting convened by the court for the purpose of considering and, if thought fit, approving, with or without

[25] The omission of the words '... in writing ...' was as a result of the amendment to reg 60 that was effected by the Companies Act (Electronic Communications) Order 2000, SI 2000/3373 with effect from 22 December 2000.

modification, a scheme of arrangement. The remit of the proxies was to vote for the members at the meeting or adjourned meeting either for or against the scheme. It was held that the duly appointed proxies were not restricted to voting either for or against the scheme of arrangement and that the proxies were entitled to vote on an amendment that consideration of the scheme should be deferred. A large number of members had appointed the chairman to vote as their proxy in favour of the scheme but the proxies had not given specific instructions in relation to their voting intentions in relation to a resolution to amend. On the amendment resolution the chairman cast the proxies that he held against the resolution, and the court decided that he was entitled to do so. The decision in *Re Waxed Papers Ltd* was followed in *Re BTR plc* [1999] 2 BCLC 675 (Jonathan Parker J); leave to appeal from the decision of Jonathan Parker J was refused—see [2000] 1 BCLC 740 (CA).

2007 Regulations—Private companies

Paragraph 12 of the 2007 Regulations provides as follows:

> 12. (1) Regulation 61 of Table A is amended as follows.
> (2) After the words 'our behalf at the' omit the words 'annual/extraordinary'.

This amendment applies only to a private company limited by shares.

The effect of the amendment: the 2007 form (private companies only)

> **REGULATION 61**
>
> Where it is desired to afford members an opportunity of instructing the proxy how he shall act the appointment of a proxy shall be in the following form (or in a form as near thereto as circumstances allow or in any other form which is usual or which the directors may approve)—
>
> ' PLC/Limited
>
> ____________ I/We, ____________, of being a member/members of the above-named company, hereby appoint ____________ of ____________, or failing him, of ____________, as my/our proxy to vote in my/our name[s] and on my/our behalf at the general meeting of the company to be held on ____________ 19 ____________, and at any adjournment thereof.
>
> This form is to be used in respect of the resolutions mentioned below as follows:
> Resolution No 1 *for *against
> Resolution No 2 *for *against.
> *Strike out whichever is not desired.
> Unless otherwise instructed, the proxy may vote as he thinks fit or abstain from voting. Signed this ____________ day of ____________ 19 ____________.'

2007 Regulations—public companies

Paragraph 22 of the 2007 Regulations provides as follows:

> 22. (1) Regulation 61 of Table A is amended as follows.
> (2) After the words 'our behalf at the annual' omit the words 'extraordinary' and insert the words 'any other'.

The effect of the amendment: the 2007 form (public companies only):

REGULATION 61

Where it is desired to afford members an opportunity of instructing the proxy how he shall act the appointment of a proxy shall be in the following form (or in a form as near thereto as circumstances allow or in any other form which is usual or which the directors may approve)—

'____________________________PLC/Limited

_____________ I/We, _____________, of being a member/members of the above-named company, hereby appoint _____________ of _____________, or failing him, of _____________, as my/our proxy to vote in my/our name[s] and on my/our behalf at the annual/ any other general meeting of the company to be held on _____________19 _____________, and at any adjournment thereof.

This form is to be used in respect of the resolutions mentioned below as follows:

Resolution No 1 *for *against

Resolution No 2 *for *against.

*Strike out whichever is not desired.

Unless otherwise instructed, the proxy may vote as he thinks fit or abstain from voting. Signed this _____________day of _____________ 19 _____________.'

This amendment applies only to a public company limited by shares.

REGULATION 62

The appointment of a proxy and any authority under which it is executed or a copy of such authority certified notarially or in some other way approved by the directors may—

(a) in the case of an instrument in writing be deposited at the office or at such other place within the United Kingdom as is specified in the notice convening the meeting or in any instrument of proxy sent out by the company in relation to the meeting not less than 48 hours before the time for holding the meeting or adjourned meeting at which the person named in the instrument proposes to vote; or

(aa) in the case of an appointment contained in an electronic communication, where an address has been specified for the purpose of receiving electronic communications—

(i) in the notice convening the meeting, or

(ii) in any instrument of proxy sent out by the company in relation to the meeting, or

(iii) in any invitation contained in an electronic communication to appoint a proxy issued by the company in relation to the meeting,

be received at such address not less than 48 hours before the time for holding the meeting or adjourned meeting at which the person named in the appointment proposes to vote;

(b) in the case of a poll taken more than 48 hours after it is demanded, be deposited or received as aforesaid after the poll has been demanded and not less than 24 hours before the time appointed for the taking of the poll; or

(c) where the poll is not taken forthwith but is taken not more than 48 hours after it was demanded, be delivered at the meeting at which the poll was demanded to the chairman or to the secretary or to any director; and an appointment of proxy which is not deposited, delivered or received in a manner so permitted shall be invalid.

In this regulation and the next, 'address', in relation to electronic communications, includes any number or address used for the purposes of such communications.

COMMENTARY: REGULATION 62

Regulation 62 contains amendments that were first introduced by the Companies Act (Electronic Communications) Order 2000, SI 2000/3373 with effect from 22 December 2000. These provisions are now to be found in CA 2006, s 333.[26] It is permissible for a member to appoint a proxy by electronic means. **23.101**

It is not lawful for a company to stipulate in its articles of association that an appointment of a proxy must be received more than 48 hours before a meeting or an adjourned meeting.[27] Such a provision is void. Similarly it is not lawful for articles to require in the case of a poll taken more than 48 hours after it was demanded, for documents to be received by the company earlier than 24 hours before the time appointed for taking the poll.[28] **23.102**

In calculating these time periods in reg 62 and CA 2006, s 327(3) no account shall be taken of any part of any day that is not a working day. A working day is defined in CA 2006, s 1173 as a day which is not a Saturday or Sunday, Christmas Day, Good Friday or any day that is a bank holiday in the part of the United Kingdom where the company is registered.[29] **23.103**

Accordingly, reg 62 must now be construed in accordance with CA 2006. It is to be noted that CA 2006, s 327(2)(c) has deliberately not been brought into force with the remainder of s 327.[30] **23.104**

REGULATION 63

A vote given or poll demanded by proxy or by the duly authorised representative of a corporation shall be valid notwithstanding the previous determination of the authority of the person voting or demanding a poll unless notice of the determination was received by the company at the office or at such other place at which the instrument of proxy was duly deposited or, where the appointment of the proxy was contained in an electronic communication, at the address at which such appointment was duly received before the commencement of the meeting or adjourned meeting at which the vote is given or the poll demanded or (in the case of a poll taken otherwise than on the same day as the meeting or adjourned meeting) the time appointed for taking the poll.

26 See Ch 8; see Ch 17.
27 See CA 2006, s 327(2)(a).
28 See CA 2006, s 327(2)(b).
29 Bank holidays vary in different parts of the United Kingdom.
30 See Commencement Order No 3, art 2(1)(f). See the commentary on this section in Part 3.

COMMENTARY: REGULATION 63

23.105 The area covered by reg 63 is now governed by CA 2006, s 330 and the regulation must be construed in the light of the requirements of that section. By CA 2006, s 330(2) the termination of the authority of a proxy does not affect whether he counts as part of the quorum, the validity of anything done by him as chairman or the validity of any poll demanded by him, unless the company receives notice of termination before the commencement of the meeting. Similarly, by CA 2006, s 330(3) the termination does not affect the validity of any vote given by that person unless the company receives notice before the commencement of the meeting or adjourned meeting or, in the case of a poll taken more than 48 hours after it is demanded, before the time for the poll.

23.106 In common with the previous three provisions of Table A the text of reg 63 was amended by the Companies Act (Electronic Communications) Order 2000, SI 2000/3373, as from 22 December 2000. Notice of termination may be given by electronic means.

23.107 The mere action of a shareholder appointing a proxy does not operate as an absolute impediment to that shareholder attending at the general meeting and casting the votes attached to the shares in person—see *Cousins v International Brick Co* [1931] 2 Ch 90 (CA). In such circumstances, it would be incorrect for a company to accept the vote of the member's proxy because the member's conduct in attending and voting personally has had the effect of making the proxy's role superfluous. It is important to note that the mere attendance of the member at a meeting does not have the effect of countermanding a valid proxy.

23.108 The purpose of reg 63 and CA 2006, s 330 is to afford a modicum of protection to a company in circumstances where a member has determined the authority of a proxy, but the determination of the proxy's authority has not been received by the company in due time and the proxy's vote has been accepted as a valid vote at a meeting or at an adjourned meeting. In order for a member to end the authority of the duly appointed proxy, it is incumbent on the member to ensure that due notice of the determination of the proxy's authority is received by the company before the start of the meeting or of the adjourned meeting.

1985 Table A—Regulations Affecting Meetings of Directors

Introduction

Directors

23.109 Regulations 88 to 98 (inclusive) of the 1985 Table A regulate the conduct of meetings of directors. The power to manage the affairs of a company is delegated to the directors. From time to time the directors of a company will have to meet in order to consider a plethora of issues affecting the business of the company. Just as with meetings of members, it is important to ensure that board meetings are held in accordance with the prescribed rules and regulations that are set out in a company's articles of association. The basic fundamentals regulating any meeting, such as ensuring that it is quorate and conducted in an orderly manner, apply equally to meetings of directors. Regulation 99 deals with the appointment by the directors of the company secretary.

Minutes

It is important that proper minutes of meetings of members and directors are kept so that there is an accurate record of the business that has been transacted at meetings. A statutory duty is imposed on directors by CA 2006, s 248 to maintain minutes of their meetings. These records must be kept for at least 10 years from the date of the meetings. [31] A similar statutory duty regarding minutes of meetings of members is found in CA 2006, s 355. [32] This is a very important procedural aspect of good corporate governance. The 1985 Table A contains a provision (reg 100) relating to the maintenance of proper minutes. In view of the importance of this requirement affecting meetings of members and directors, reg 100 is set out below and commented upon. **23.110**

REGULATION 88

Subject to the provisions of the articles, the directors may regulate their proceedings as they think fit. A director may, and the secretary at the request of a director shall, call a meeting of the directors. It shall not be necessary to give notice of a meeting to a director who is absent from the United Kingdom. Questions arising at a meeting shall be decided by a majority of votes. In the case of an equality of votes, the chairman shall have a second or casting vote. A director who is also an alternate director shall be entitled in the absence of his appointor to a separate vote on behalf of his appointor in addition to his own vote.

COMMENTARY: REGULATION 88

Under reg 88 the directors are empowered to regulate the conduct of their own proceedings. Such a provision is sensible in that it recognizes that the directors may, and it is hoped will, have developed good working practices and procedures for the effective and efficient management of the business for which they have responsibility. The articles of association of a company should be checked for any departures (small or large) from the standard form provisions of whichever version of Table A is applicable to a company. **23.111**

---

[31] See CA 2006, s 248(2). See Ch 21 and the Commentary in Part 3.

[32] See Ch 16 and the Commentary in Part 3.

23.112 It will be customary for directors to have a formal agenda for their meetings. The directors are entitled at their meetings to take their business in whatever order they consider to be appropriate. Routine board meetings will usually be convened by the company secretary but reg 88 empowers a director to call a meeting of the board. This is a very important power of real practical importance, as it enables a representative of minority shareholders to insist on the convening of a board meeting. It is to be noted that under CA 2006, s 270[33] a private company will no longer be required to have a company secretary. It remains to be seen whether existing private companies will dispense with the services of their appointed secretaries as they fulfil an important role in the due administration of a company.

23.113 Directors who are abroad need not be given notice of board meetings. This provision must not be abused by the simple expedient of convening a board meeting to consider controversial matters at a time when directors are overseas. Further, in this modern era of good and instantaneous communication, when it is often possible to participate easily in a meeting by telephonic or audio visual means, great care should be taken in excluding directors from the decision making process.

23.114 Articles of association that have been specifically drafted for a company may include a provision enabling members of a board to participate in board meetings by telephone or by audio visual means. If such a provision is included care should be taken in relation to the giving of notice to directors who are abroad because it could be said that such an article clearly contemplates the participation of directors in board meetings wherever they happen to be located.

23.115 Directors take decisions by voting upon properly formulated resolutions. Normally the voting will be done on a simple majority basis unless there are some enhanced voting provisions in the articles or in a shareholders' agreement or in an investment agreement. Again, subject to any special provisions in the articles, the chairman of the board may have a casting vote in order to resolve deadlocked situations. In the absence of a specific provision conferring a casting vote on a chairman there is no inherent right for the chairman to exercise such a power. The power is a fiduciary power and should not be misused or abused. Regulation 91 (below), deals with the appointment by the board of a director to hold office as the chairman of the board.

23.116 Under regs 65–69 of the 1985 Table A a director is able to appoint an alternate director, who is effectively a person who will be his 'alter ego' at a properly convened board meeting. Usually the articles of association of a company will provide that a director may appoint another member of the board to be his alternate. In this instance, an article in the form of reg 88 permits the member of the board who has been appointed as the alternate of another board member to have an additional vote on behalf of that person in addition to his own vote.

[33] This section came into force on 6 April 2008—Fifth Commencement Order, SI 2007/3494.

REGULATION 89

The quorum for the transaction of the business of the directors may be fixed by the directors and unless so fixed at any other number shall be two. A person who holds office only as an alternate director shall, if his appointor is not present, be counted in the quorum.

COMMENTARY: REGULATION 89

In order to hold a regular and valid board meeting it must transact business only when it is quorate. The stipulated quorum is the minimum number of participants required to render a meeting valid. In the absence of any prescribed requirement that may be contained in a company's articles of association, or in an applicable shareholders' agreement, or in an investment agreement, the minimum number of directors required for a valid board meeting is two. Plainly, a provision in this standard form must be excluded if a private company has a sole director. **23.117**

For the avoidance of doubt, it is sensible to have a provision making it clear that an alternate director will be counted in determining the quorum if the director who appointed him as an alternate is absent. **23.118**

REGULATION 90

The continuing directors or a sole continuing director may act notwithstanding any vacancies in their number, but, if the number of directors is less than the number fixed as the quorum, the continuing directors or director may act only for the purpose of filling vacancies or of calling a general meeting.

COMMENTARY: REGULATION 90

Regulation 90 permits directors to act even though there may be vacancies to fill on the board. It is important to note that reg 90 does not authorize a board of directors to transact lawful business if the number of directors is less than the minimum prescribed by the articles of association to constitute a quorum. In *Re Sly, Spink & Co* [1911] 2 Ch 430 (Neville J) held the articles of association fixed the minimum number of directors at four and the quorum for a board meeting at two. The articles also provide that the continuing directors might act notwithstanding any vacancies. In these circumstances, Neville J held that below the minimum number of four directors there was no board at all. Where the articles specify such a minimum number of directors (say four) but a lower number for a quorum of the board (say two) the presence of the minimum number of directors to form a quorum does not make legitimate the business carried out by a board consisting of fewer than four members. However, the conduct of two directors in filling the two casual vacancies was valid.[34] Under reg 90 if the number **23.119**

[34] See *In Re Scottish Petroleum Co* (1883) 23 Ch D 413 (CA).

of directors falls below the number required to constitute a valid quorum for a board meeting the only acts which can be undertaken by the remaining director or directors are to fill vacancies on the board or to convene a meeting of members.

REGULATION 91

The directors may appoint one of their number to be the chairman of the board of directors and may at any time remove him from that office. Unless he is unwilling to do so, the director so appointed shall preside at every meeting of directors at which he is present. But if there is no director holding that office, or if the director holding it is unwilling to preside or is not present within five minutes after the time appointed for the meeting, the directors present may appoint one of their number to be chairman of the meeting.

COMMENTARY: REGULATION 91

23.120 Very commonly a company's articles of association will contain a provision that empowers the board of directors to elect one of their number to act as the chairman of the board.[35] Such an election will be for an indefinite period of time but an appointment under a provision in this format could be for a prescribed duration or even for a specific meeting. Those who make the appointment also have the power to remove a chairman from his position. Appointment and removal will be effected by a vote of the board of directors and unless there is a provision to the contrary such a vote will be passed by a simple majority. Clearly, if the elected chairman is replaced that person does not cease to be a director.

REGULATION 92

All acts done by a meeting of directors, or of a committee of directors, or by a person acting as a director shall, notwithstanding that it be afterwards discovered that there was a defect in the appointment of any director or that any of them were disqualified from holding office, or had vacated office, or were not entitled to vote, be as valid as if every such person had been duly appointed and was qualified and had continued to be a director and had been entitled to vote.

COMMENTARY: REGULATION 92

23.121 The purpose of an article in the form of reg 92, which is now covered by CA 2006, s 161,[36] is to ensure that once transactions have been decided upon by the directors the discovery of a defect relating to the appointment or qualification of a director will not vitiate the decision that has been made. The intention of such a provision is not to disregard the fundamental requirements for the effective appointment of directors—see *Morris v Kanssen* [1946] AC 459 (HL).

---

[35] See Ch 20.

[36] Formerly CA 1985, s 285.

Circumstances may arise where a defect is discovered in the appointment of a member of the board of directors. The 'defect' in the appointment may be because the person in question was not qualified to hold office as a director, or was not entitled to vote on a resolution or had resigned as a director or for some other reason. In the event that such a director has participated in a board meeting that has transacted business the subsequent discovery of the defect does not render nugatory the business that has been transacted. The saving provision contained in reg 92 applies to board meetings and to meetings of committees of directors. **23.122**

REGULATION 93

A resolution in writing signed by all the directors entitled to receive notice of a meeting of directors or of a committee of directors shall be as valid and effectual as if it had been passed at a meeting of directors or (as the case may be) a committee of directors duly convened and held and may consist of several documents in the like form each signed by one or more directors; but a resolution signed by an alternate director need not also be signed by his appointor and, if it is signed by a director who has appointed an alternate director, it need not be signed by the alternate director in that capacity.

COMMENTARY: REGULATION 93

Regulation 93 has to be read in the context of the provisions that apply to board meetings and in particular having regard to reg 89. Regulation 93 applies to meetings of boards of directors and to meetings of committees of directors. Further, alternate directors fall within the ambit of the provision. The regulation permits informal decision making in circumstances where all the directors who are entitled to receive notice of a meeting sign a written resolution. The written resolution that is signed need not be comprised in a single document but may be made up of a number of documents which may individually be signed by one or more of the directors. The key requirement under reg 93 is that of unanimous consent of the directors who are entitled to receive notice of the meeting. **23.123**

The decisions in *Davidson & Begg Antiques Ltd v Davidson* [1997] BCC 77 (Court of Session) and *Hood Sailmakers v Axford* [1997] 1 BCLC 721 (Carnworth J) are authority for the proposition that a written resolution of directors must be signed by all the directors entitled to receive notice of a board meeting and by the number of directors that are required to form a quorum. In those cases the number of directors required to sign an effective resolution was two, even though one of the two directors was absent from the United Kingdom and not entitled to notice of the meeting under reg 88. The courts emphasized that the object of reg 93 was to avoid the need for there to be a meeting where it would be a superfluous event. It is not directed towards making a fundamental change to the quorum requirements, which are set out in reg 89. **23.124**

REGULATION 94

Save as otherwise provided by the articles, a director shall not vote at a meeting of directors or of a committee of directors on any resolution concerning a matter in which he has, directly or indirectly, an interest or duty which is material and which conflicts or may conflict with the interests of the company unless his interest or duty arises only because the case falls within one or more of the following paragraphs

(a) the resolution relates to the giving to him of a guarantee, security, or indemnity in respect of money lent to, or an obligation incurred by him for the benefit of, the company or any of its subsidiaries;

(b) the resolution relates to the giving to a third party of a guarantee, security, or indemnity in respect of an obligation of the company or any of its subsidiaries for which the director has assumed responsibility in whole or part and whether alone or jointly with others under a guarantee or indemnity or by the giving of security;

(c) his interest arises by virtue of his subscribing or agreeing to subscribe for any shares, debentures or other securities of the company or any of its subsidiaries, or by virtue of his being, or intending to become, a participant in the underwriting or sub-underwriting of an offer of any such shares, debentures, or other securities by the company or any of its subsidiaries for subscription, purchase or exchange;

(d) the resolution relates in any way to a retirement benefits scheme which has been approved, or is conditional upon approval, by the Board of Inland Revenue for taxation purposes.

For the purposes of this regulation, an interest of a person who is, for any purpose of the Act (excluding any statutory modification thereof not in force when this regulation becomes binding on the company), connected with a director shall be treated as an interest of the director and, in relation to an alternate director, an interest of his appointor shall be treated as an interest of the alternate director without prejudice to any interest which the alternate director has otherwise.

COMMENTARY: REGULATION 94

23.125 Directors occupy a fiduciary position in relation to their companies and are subject to important duties regulating their conduct. These duties have been developed and refined since the nineteenth century. The duties of directors are now codified in CA 2006, Part 10, Chapter 2 (ss 170–181). A detailed examination of these important statutory duties is beyond the scope of this book.[37] At common law a director was under a duty to disclose to the shareholders in general meeting the nature of his interest, whether direct or indirect, in any contract or transaction to which the company is a party. Under CA 2006, s 175[38] a director is under a general duty to avoid any situation in which he has or can have a direct or indirect interest that conflicts or may conflict with the interests of the company. This rule

[37] See Ch 18.

[38] CA 2006, s 175 is due to come into force on 1 October 2008.

applies generally but is of particular significance in relation to the exploitation of any property, information or opportunity.

In addition, duties have been imposed on directors by statute requiring the disclosure to the board of directors of a director's interest in any contract or proposed contract with the company, such disclosure to be declared at a meeting of the directors. CA 2006, s 177[39] applies in relation to any proposed transaction or arrangement. This replaces CA 1985, s 317. Any director who is in any way directly or indirectly interested in a proposed transaction or arrangement with the company is required to declare the nature and extent of his interest to the other directors either at a board meeting or in writing in the form of a written notice under CA 2006, s 184 or a general notice under CA 2006, s 185.[40] In addition, where a director has an interest, direct or indirect, in a transaction or arrangement that has been entered into by the company he must declare the nature and extent of that interest to the other directors under CA 2006, s 182. Once again, that declaration must be made at a board meeting or by a written notice under CA 2006, s 184 or a general notice under CA 2006, s 185. **23.126**

Modern articles of association frequently contain provisions which release directors from their common law obligation to make disclosure to the company in general meeting,[41] but insist that the relevant director who is interested in a contract should not vote at any board meeting on any resolution to approve such a contract. Regulation 94 is an example of such a provision. **23.127**

The opening phrase, 'Save as otherwise provided by the articles…' acknowledges the fact that the regulations contained in Table A are often subject to specific modification in a company's articles of association. Accordingly, when considering whether a director is entitled to vote at a board meeting on a matter in which he may have any interest, care should be taken to determine whether the articles of association contain any modification or amendment of reg 94. **23.128**

The aim of reg 94, when combined with reg 95 (see below), is to ensure that the director who is interested in a contract does not participate in the decision whether or not to approve the contract. Under reg 95 the director in question is not permitted to form part of the quorum at a relevant board meeting at which he is not entitled to vote. That is an extension of the rule in reg 94 that the director cannot vote on any resolution concerning a matter in which he has, directly or indirectly, an interest or a duty which is material and which conflicts or may conflict with the interests of the company. It is to be noted that reg 94 is concerned only with interests that are material, and not with those which are negligible or too remote. The test of **23.129**

---

39 CA 2006, s 177 is due to come into force on 1 October 2008.

40 Both CA 2006, ss 184 and 185 are due to come into force on 1 October 2008.

41 See, for example, Regulations 85 and 86, 1985 Table A.

materiality is not set out in reg 94, but is a matter of fact and degree which has to be determined by the chairman of the board meeting under reg 98 (see below).

23.130 Regulation 94 is concerned with material interests and duties which not only conflict but *may conflict* with the interests of the company. This wording widens the scope of the regulation to areas in which there may be some doubt as to the nature and extent of the potential conflict. This aspect arises because it is one of the key principles of company law that directors may not place themselves in a position where their personal interests conflict, or may conflict, with their duties to the company.[42] Materiality is always a question of degree and must be assessed in relation to the all the relevant facts of a particular situation. The decision in *Cowan de Groot Properties Ltd v Eagle Trust plc* [1991] BCLC 1045 at 1115 e–g (Knox J) indicates that there may be a conflict of interest between a person's duty as trustee on the one hand and a duty as a director or the other. This may be just as significant a conflict of interest as a conflict between a personal interest and a duty as a director. However, that principle only applies where the trusteeship carries duties and there will be no conflict where all that is concerned is a bare trusteeship.

Four specific exemptions

23.131 Regulation 94 contains four specific exceptions that are commonly found in articles of association in respect of which the director retains the right to vote. The first concerns a resolution for the approval of a grant to him of a guarantee, security or indemnity in respect of a loan to the company or an obligation assumed by a director for the benefit of the company or any of its subsidiaries (sub-para (a)). The second arises in a similar situation but the resolution relates to the giving to a third party of a guarantee, security or indemnity in respect of a company obligation for which the director has assumed responsibility in whole or in part (sub-para (b)). A further exception arises where the director's interest is in connection with his subscribing for shares, debentures or other securities of the company or his participation in an underwriting arrangement. The fourth exception concerns a resolution that relates in any way to an Inland Revenue approved pension scheme or one that is conditional upon such approval.

REGULATION 95

A director shall not be counted in the quorum present at a meeting in relation to a resolution on which he is not entitled to vote.

---

[42] See *In Plus Group Ltd v Pyke* [2002] 2 BCLC 201 (CA); *Bhullar v Bhullar* [2003] 2 BCLC 241 (CA).

COMMENTARY: REGULATION 95

Where a director is disenfranchised by reason of the provisions that are contained in reg 94 in relation to a particular resolution, it is not permitted to include that director in calculating the quorum at the board meeting for the passing of that resolution. This provision is of considerable importance in that it seeks to ensure that the director who is interested in the transaction does not participate in the decision whether to approve the resolution. The law does not require the interested director to leave the meeting. However, as a matter of good judgment the director concerned may choose to do so. The effect of reg 95 is that a resolution of this type requires to be passed at a board meeting at which there is a quorum of disinterested directors. If such a quorum cannot be obtained the resolution to approve the contract cannot be considered. **23.132**

Regulation 95 reflects the established principle that where a director is prohibited from voting he cannot be taken into account for the purpose of ascertaining whether a quorum of directors is present—see *Re Greymouth-Point Elizabeth Rly and Coal Co* [1904] 1 Ch 32 (Farwell J). In that case a resolution was passed at a meeting of three directors, two of whom were interested in the subject matter of the resolution and under the articles of association of that company could not vote. The court held that as the articles of association required two directors to form a quorum for the transaction of business, that meant two directors who were capable of voting on the business before the board. There was only one independent director present and therefore there was no quorum.[43] Accordingly, if the quorum for a board meeting is set at two and the business to be transacted is business on which two directors cannot vote the presence of a third director who is capable of voting will not form the requisite quorum. **23.133**

REGULATION 96

The company may by ordinary resolution suspend or relax to any extent, either generally or in respect of any particular matter, any provision of the articles prohibiting a director from voting at a meeting of directors or of a committee of directors.

COMMENTARY: REGULATION 96

Under this provision it is possible for a company by means of an ordinary resolution of the members in general meeting (which resolution requires the support of only a simple majority) to suspend or relax any other provisions in the articles of association which prohibit a director from voting at a meeting of directors or of a committee of directors. Provisions that can be suspended in this way include regs 94 and 95. **23.134**

---

[43] See also *Colin Guyer & Associates Ltd v London Wharf (Limehouse) Ltd* [2003] 2 BCLC 153.

23.135 The effect of reg 96 is that an interested director may be permitted to vote at a board meeting provided that the restriction in the articles of association has been suspended in advance by the shareholders in general meeting.

23.136 By virtue of the new provisions for written resolutions that are applicable to private companies only in CA 2006, Part 13, Chapter 2 such an ordinary resolution may take the form of a resolution in writing, signed by each member who would have been entitled to vote on it on the circulation date if it had been proposed at a general meeting. [44]

23.137 To the extent that the resolution suspends or relaxes these provisions of the articles that suspension or relaxation operates in effect as an amendment to the articles of association procured by ordinary resolution rather than by the more usual mechanism of a special resolution. An ordinary resolution passed for the purposes of reg 96 must meet the test of being a resolution that is passed in good faith in the best interests of the company as a whole—*Allen v Gold Reefs of West Africa* [1900] 1 Ch 656 at 671 (CA). However, notwithstanding the broad wording of reg 96, if such an ordinary resolution is passed by a majority for an improper purpose or in a manner which constitutes conduct of the affairs of the company that is unfairly prejudicial to the interests of certain members the minority may seek redress under CA 2006, s 994.

REGULATION 97

Where proposals are under consideration concerning the appointment of two or more directors to offices or employments with the company or any body corporate in which the company is interested the proposals may be divided and considered in relation to each director separately and (provided he is not for another reason precluded from voting) each of the directors concerned shall be entitled to vote and be counted in the quorum in respect of each resolution except that concerning his own appointment.

COMMENTARY: REGULATION 97

23.138 Circumstances may arise where a board meeting has to consider appointment of two or more directors with the company or another company in which the company is interested. It is legitimate to divide the resolutions into two separate resolutions. The director personally concerned in relation to a particular resolution is prohibited from voting and will not be counted in the quorum on that resolution. The text in parentheses indicates that due consideration must be given to the provisions of reg 94.

23.139 Resolutions of a board of directors that are passed without a disinterested quorum will not be valid—see *Re North Eastern Insurance Co* [1919] 1 Ch 198 (Lawrence J). In *Victors, Limited (In Liquidation) v Lingard* [1927] 1 Ch 323 (Romer J) the articles of a company provided that no director should be disqualified from

[44] See CA 2006, s 288(4). See Ch 15.

entering into contracts or arrangements with the company, but no director should vote in relation to any arrangement or dealing in which he was interested. It was held that all the directors were 'interested' in an arrangement that had been concluded with the company's bank concerning the issue of the debentures as security for the company's overdraft, because they were personal guarantors for that overdraft. As the directors had voted in favour of the board resolution relating to the issue of the debentures, those debentures had been invalidly issued.[45]

REGULATION 98

If a question arises at a meeting of directors or of a committee of directors as to the right of a director to vote, the question may, before the conclusion of the meeting, be referred to the chairman of the meeting and his ruling in relation to any director other than himself shall be final and conclusive.

COMMENTARY: REGULATION 98

Under reg 98 the chairman of the board is given jurisdiction to make rulings on questions that may arise at a board meeting concerning the right of a director to vote. This will include questions of whether a director has a material interest in a proposed contract or a material duty which conflicts or may conflict with the interests of the company under reg 94. **23.140**

Regulation 98 creates and confers a fiduciary power which must be exercised by the chairman in a regular manner and for the proper purposes of the company, taking account of all relevant considerations. If this power is exercised dishonestly or in bad faith it may be open to legal challenge. It is to be noted that reg 98 does not declare the chairman's ruling to be final and conclusive where it relates to the chairman himself. In those circumstances a capricious or improper exercise of the power by the chairman may be more readily open to legal challenge. **23.141**

REGULATION 99

Subject to the provisions of the Act, the secretary shall be appointed by the directors for such term, at such remuneration and upon such conditions as they may think fit; and any secretary so appointed may be removed by them.

COMMENTARY: REGULATION 99

The directors of a company are empowered to appoint a secretary to hold office for such period and on such terms and conditions as they see fit. The directors are also given jurisdiction to remove the company secretary from office. Under CA **23.142**

[45] However, in the light of the evidence before the court concerning the subsequent proceedings between the company and the bank, the company was estopped from alleging the invalidity of the debentures.

2006, s 270 a private company is no longer required to have a company secretary. However, the role of a company secretary in many large companies, whether private or public, remains an important one as he or she will be responsible for virtually all matters of internal corporate administration and the maintenance of statutory records. For the significance of the role of a company secretary see the decision in *Panorama Developments (Guildford) v Fidelis Furnishing Fabrics Ltd* [1971] 2 QB 711 (CA).

REGULATION 100

The directors shall cause minutes to be made in books kept for the purpose

(a) of all appointments of officers made by the directors; and

(b) of all proceedings at meetings of the company, of the holders of any class of shares in the company, and of the directors, and of committees of directors, including the names of the directors present at each such meeting.

COMMENTARY: REGULATION 100

23.143 CA 2006, ss 248 and 355 impose statutory duties on directors to maintain proper minutes of their meetings and of the meetings of members. The Transitional Provisions in the Third Commencement Order 2007[46] stipulate that CA 1985, s 382 continues to apply to meetings of directors held before 1 October 2007. Such records must be retained for at least 10 years.[47]

23.144 With regard to board meetings, it is important that directors comply with these legislative requirements because if minutes are made in accordance with s 248, by s 249 the board meeting is deemed to have been duly held and convened, all proceedings are deemed to have duly taken place and all appointments made at the meeting are deemed valid unless the contrary is proved. Similar provisions are to be found in ss 355 and 356 with regard to the records of resolutions of members and general meetings.

23.145 Directors may be the subject of a fine under CA 2006, ss 248(4) and 353(4) if they fail to comply with these important statutory duties.

23.146 Reflecting the requirements of the statute, reg 100 requires directors to maintain minutes of their meetings, of meetings of members, of class meetings and of the appointments of officers of the company.

23.147 Under CA 2006, s 358 members of a company are entitled (without charge) to inspect the records of proceedings of general meetings and resolutions required to be kept by s 355. If a member requires a copy of the minutes of a general meeting

[46] S1 2009/2194.

[47] See CA 2006, ss 248(2) (directors' meetings) and 355(2) (resolutions of members). See Ch 16 and Ch 21.

or other records the company is under a duty to provide a copy. The company is entitled to charge the member a fee for the provision of such a copy.[48] Directors must not impede the right of a member both to inspect and take copies of these records. Where directors refuse to comply with the duties imposed on them by CA 2006, s 358 they may become liable to a fine under s 358(6). A member is entitled to enforce his statutory rights by means of an application to the court under s 383(7). These statutory provisions apply also to class meetings and class resolutions by virtue of CA 2006, s 359.

Members are not entitled to inspect board minutes unless the articles of a company specifically provide. The 1985 Table A makes no such provision. Board minutes are therefore treated for all purposes as private documents which may be inspected only by the directors themselves,[49] the company secretary and the company's auditors for the purpose of carrying out their audit function.[50] However, in the event of legal proceedings being taken against the company by a shareholder the board records may be required to be disclosed under CPR Part 31.[51] **23.148**

[48] See CA 2006, s 358(4).

[49] See *Conway v Petronius Clothing Co* [1978] 1 WLR 72 (Slade J); *McCusker v McRae* 1966 SC 253.

[50] See CA 2006, s 499(1)(a).

[51] See *CAS (Nominees) Ltd v Nottingham Forest plc* [2001] 1 All ER 954 (Evans-Lombe J); *Arrow Trading and Investments v Edwardian Group Ltd* [2005] 1 BCLC 696 (Blackburne J).

Appendix

COMMENTARY ON THE DRAFT MODEL ARTICLES

APPENDIX

COMMENTARY ON THE DRAFT MODEL ARTICLES

Under CA 2006 new standard form articles of association for private companies limited by shares, private companies limited by guarantee and public companies referred to as 'model articles' have been proposed. These model articles have been produced in draft form on a number of occasions and at the time of writing the proposed versions of the model articles are contained in a Draft Statutory Instrument which is entitled 'Companies (Model Articles) Regulations 2008'. On 24 October 2008 the Department for Business, Enterprise and Regulatory Reform announced that the model articles, which were due to be published in December 2008, would contain changes to the provisions dealing with directors' indemnities, directors' and officers' insurance and decision making by directors. In addition, it had been planned to amend the model articles for public companies in relation to proxy forms. At the date of writing none of these proposed changes has been published. The existing Draft Statutory Instrument contains three schedules. Schedule 1 contains the Draft Model Articles for Private Companies Limited by shares. Schedule 2 contains the Draft Model Articles for Private Companies Limited by Guarantee. Schedule 3 contains the Draft Model Articles for Public Companies. It is not compulsory for companies to adopt the provisions that are contained in the model articles and there is much to be said for having articles that are drafted to meet the particular requirements of individual companies. It seems unlikely that many public companies will choose to adopt the Model Articles for Public Companies. **APP 1**

The Draft Statutory Instrument contains three schedules. Schedule 1 contains the Draft Model Articles for Private Companies Limited by shares. Schedule 2 contains the Draft Model Articles for Private Companies Limited by Guarantee. Schedule 3 contains the Draft Model Articles for Public Companies. It is not compulsory for companies to adopt the provisions that are contained in the model **APP 2** articles and there is much to be said for having articles that are drafted to meet the particular requirements of individual companies.

APP 3 It is anticipated that the model articles will take effect from 1 October 2009. This date is now the backstop date on which it is anticipated that all of the provisions of CA 2006 will come into legal force.

APP 4 Set out below are the provisions contained in the model articles that relate to meetings of members and of directors of private companies limited by shares and of public companies. As with the commentary that is found in Part 4 of this book on the provisions of the 1985 Table A that relate to meetings of members and directors, each such provision of the model articles has been annotated. The provisions relating to private companies limited by shares are considered first.

Draft Model Articles Relating to Private Companies Limited by Shares

DECISION-MAKING BY DIRECTORS

7 Directors to take decisions collectively

(1) The general rule about decision-making by directors is that any decision of the directors must be either a unanimous decision under article 8 or a majority decision at a meeting.

(2) If—

(a) the company only has one director, and

(b) no provision of the articles requires it to have more than one director (either generally or for the purposes of taking decisions other than majority decisions), the general rule does not apply, and the director may take decisions without regard to any of the provisions of the articles relating to directors' decision-making.

(3) Subject to the articles, decisions of the directors must be taken—

(a) at a directors' meeting, or

(b) in the form of a directors' written resolution.

COMMENTARY: 7 Directors to take decisions collectively

APP 5 The article contemplates that as a general rule the board of directors may reach a decision by unanimous agreement (to which art 8 applies) or by means of the views of the majority at a meeting. As companies vary in a myriad of ways from one to another it is very common for specific provisions to be inserted in the articles of association to meet the particular needs of different businesses. Subject to the articles of a private company, decisions of directors can be taken at a meeting of the directors or in the form of a written resolution of the directors.

APP 6 Recording decisions taken by directors is very important for the efficient running of a company. If the directors hold a meeting they are under a duty to have minutes of that meeting taken and recorded under CA 2006, s 248. Article 15 (below) deals with the important subject of recording decisions that are taken at board meetings.

In the case of a private company with only one director *and* where the constitution of that company does not require any other director to hold office, the general rules about decision-making by directors do not apply. **APP 7**

8 Unanimous decisions

(1) The directors take a unanimous decision when they all indicate to each other by any means that they share a common view on a matter.
(2) A unanimous decision may take the form of a resolution in writing, copies of which have been signed by each director or to which each director has otherwise indicated agreement in writing.

COMMENTARY: 8 Unanimous decisions

Article 8 governs decisions of directors that are taken unanimously. Such a decision need not be taken at a formal board meeting, provided that all of the members of the board indicate to each other that they are in agreement on a particular matter. This may prove to be a recipe for uncertainty and subsequent dispute over what was decided upon. The reference in art 8(2) to such a unanimous decision being the subject of a resolution in writing is to be welcomed as it seems to be a prudent precaution. However, it is surprising that this is not a mandatory requirement and it is to be contrasted with the duty under CA 2006, s 248 to keep minutes of meetings of directors. However, under art 15 (see below) the directors must ensure that the company keeps a record, in writing, for at least 10 years from the date of the decision recorded, of every unanimous or majority decision taken by them. **APP 8**

It is to be noted that the wording of art 8 is somewhat imprecise. Very often where articles of association permit the directors to take decisions by way of written resolutions the article also makes it clear that a resolution in writing signed or approved by fax or in electronic form, and subsequently confirmed in writing or by fax or in electronic form, by all the directors entitled to receive notice of a meeting of the board shall be as valid and effective as a resolution passed at a meeting of the board, and that such written resolution may be contained in one document or in several documents in like form each signed by one or more of the directors concerned. **APP 9**

9 Calling a directors' meeting

(1) Any director may call a directors' meeting by giving notice of the meeting to the directors or by authorising the company secretary (if any) to give such notice.
(2) Notice of any directors' meeting must indicate—
  (a) its proposed date and time;
  (b) where it is to take place; and
  (c) if it is anticipated that directors participating in the meeting will not be in the same place, how it is proposed that they should communicate with each other during the meeting.

(3) Notice of a directors' meeting must be given to each director, but need not be in writing.
(4) Notice of a directors' meeting need not be given to directors who waive their entitlement to notice of that meeting, by giving notice to that effect to the company not more than 7 days after the date on which the meeting is held. Where such notice is given after the meeting has been held, that does not affect the validity of the meeting, or of any business conducted at it.

COMMENTARY: 9 Calling a directors' meeting

APP 10 Article 9 governs the calling of a meeting of directors. All directors have the power to give notice of a board meeting. Alternatively, where the private company still has a company secretary and has not taken advantage of CA 2006, s 270 (dispensation to a private company from the requirement to have a company secretary), a director can authorize that person to convene the board meeting.

APP 11 As with all meetings it is a fundamental requirement for a valid notice to state the date, time and venue of the proposed meeting. Where it is not possible for all the directors to meet together in the same place the notice must state how the directors are going to communicate with each other at the board meeting. For example, if a company's articles permit the holding of board meetings by telephone or video conference, it would be necessary to give details in the notice of the conference call facilities, such as any dial-in number and any relevant password. Care should be taken to fix a time that is convenient to all of the directors, especially where some of the participants may be in different time zones.

APP 12 All of the directors are entitled to receive notice of a board meeting but a notice does not have to be in writing. The word 'writing' is defined in Article 1 as '... the representation or reproduction of words, symbols or other information in a visible form by any method or combination of methods, whether sent or supplied in electronic form or otherwise'.

APP 13 If notice of the meeting is not given in writing disputes can occur as to whether all of the directors were given notice. If notice of a board meeting is given orally in person or by telephone it may be prudent for the company secretary or director who has convened the notice to prepare a memorandum that records how and to whom the notice was given. The final phrase of art 9(3) is permissive not mandatory and best practice dictates the notice of a board meeting should in normal circumstances be given in writing. Of course, there may be occasions when a board meeting has to be convened at short notice to deal with an emergency or other unforeseen event. In such circumstances it may prove to be convenient that the notice does not have to be given in writing.

APP 14 Article 9(4) permits directors to waive their entitlement to receive notice for a period of not more than seven days after the date on which the board meeting is held. If such a retrospective notice is given by a director, the business that is transacted at the board meeting is not rendered invalid. This provision is predicated on there being a quorate board meeting without that particular director being present.

10 Participation in directors' meetings

(1) Subject to the articles, directors participate in directors' meeting, or part of a directors' meeting, when—
  (a) the meeting has been called and takes place in accordance with the articles, and
  (b) they can each communicate to the others any information or opinions they have on any particular item of the business of the meeting.

(2) In determining whether directors are participating in a directors' meeting, it is irrelevant where any director is or how they communicate with each other.

(3) If all the directors participating in a meeting, are not in the same place, they may decide that the meeting is to be treated as taking place wherever any of them is.

COMMENTARY: 10 Participation in directors' meetings

A company's articles are permitted to make separate provision for the holding of board meetings. Article 10 reflects the fact that meetings of directors may be held by modern methods of communication where participants may not be physically present in the same room. The article is designed to produce a wide degree of flexibility. The law now has no problem with the concept that a meeting can be duly held and proceed to transact lawful business even if participants are situated in different places and participate in the meeting by telephone or video conferencing facilities. The important factor for effective participation is the ability for members of the board to be able to communicate simultaneously with others in the sense that all participants can be heard. The Canadian decision in *Re Associated Color Laboratories Ltd* (1970) 12 DLR (3d) 388 to the effect that two persons cannot hold a valid meeting by telephone is no longer good law. **APP 15**

It is suggested that art 10 could have been drafted in clearer terms to emphasize that all or any of the members of the board may participate in a board meeting by means of a conference telephone or any other form of communication equipment which allows all persons participating in the board meeting to hear and speak to each other. Article 10 has also failed to make clear in unequivocal terms that a director participating by conference telephone or other form of communication shall be deemed to be present in person at the meeting and shall be entitled to vote or be counted in a quorum. **APP 16**

Under art 10(3) the directors are empowered to decide where the board meeting shall be deemed to have taken place if the directors participate in different venues. Although this provision affords the directors a degree of flexibility it could prove to be problematic in the event that the directors cannot reach agreement on this issue. Very often articles of association contain a provision to the effect that when members of the board participate in a meeting by electronic means the board meeting **APP 17** shall be deemed to take place where the largest group of those participating is assembled or, if there is no such group, where the chairman of the meeting is located.

11 Quorum for directors' meeting

(1) At a directors' meeting, unless a quorum is participating, no proposal is to be voted on, except a proposal to call another meeting.
(2) The quorum for directors' meetings may be fixed from time to time by a decision of the directors, but it must never be less than two, and unless otherwise fixed it is two.
(3) If the total number of directors for the time being is less than the quorum required, the directors must not take any decision other than a decision—
 (a) to appoint further directors, or
 (b) to call a general meeting so as to enable the shareholders to appoint further directors.

COMMENTARY: 11 Quorum for directors' meeting

APP 18 Every meeting has to be properly constituted in accordance with its applicable constitutional requirements and the meetings of the board are no exception to this basic rule. As a matter of general law, in order to transact lawful business a board meeting must be quorate. This principle is not quite reflected in this article, which (in a literal sense) merely restricts voting on any proposal at an inquorate meeting. If the board meeting is not quorate the only proposal that can be voted on is to call another board meeting.

APP 19 Directors can decide what the quorum provision is for board meetings but it cannot be less than two. Where the number of directors falls below the stipulated quorum the directors can only take two decisions. First, to appoint further directors and secondly to a call a general meeting of the members to as to enable them to appoint additional directors.

12 Chairing of directors' meetings

(1) The directors may appoint a director to chair their meetings.
(2) The person so appointed for the time being is known as the chairman.
(3) The directors may terminate the chairman's appointment at any time.
(4) If the chairman is not participating in a directors' meeting within ten minutes of the time at which it was to start, the participating directors must appoint one of themselves to chair it.

COMMENTARY: 12 Chairing of directors' meetings

APP 20 The directors are empowered, but not obliged, to appoint a member of the board to act as the chairman of the board meeting. Where such an appointment is made the director will be designated as 'the chairman'. The members of the board also have power to determine the chairman's appointment. The power of appointment and removal of the chairman are fiduciary powers and must not be used for improper or collateral purposes. In the event that the chairman does not arrive at the board meeting within ten minutes of the time specified for the start of the meeting, the directors who are in attendance must appoint another chairman to fulfil the role of the absentee chairman. The role of the chairman in relation to meetings of directors is considered in detail in Chapter 20.

13 Casting vote

(1) If the numbers of votes for and against a proposal are equal, the chairman or other director chairing the meeting has a casting vote.
(2) But this does not apply if, in accordance with the articles, the chairman or other director is not to be counted as participating in the decision-making process for quorum, voting or agreement purposes.

COMMENTARY: 13 Casting vote

In order to avoid a situation where the board of a private company cannot reach a decision because there is an equality of votes this provision will have the effect of breaking the deadlock by conferring on the chairman a casting or second vote. It is not axiomatic that a chairman will have a casting vote at all or in specific situations and close attention must be paid to the provisions that are contained in a company's articles of association. In many cases where the company constitutes in law a quasi-partnership the chairman may not have a casting vote, as the parties may have intended that in certain circumstances there is an intentional deadlock. **APP 21**

The chairman will only have this casting vote if under the articles of the company the chairman, or other director who happens to be chairing the meeting, is counted in the calculation that constitutes the quorum, or for voting or 'agreement purposes'. This latter imprecise phrase is not defined in the articles. **APP 22**

14 Conflicts of interest

(1) If a proposed decision of the directors is concerned with an actual or proposed transaction or arrangement with the company in which a director is interested, that director is not to be counted as participating in the decision-making process for quorum, voting or agreement purposes.
(2) But if paragraph (3) applies, a director who is interested in an actual or proposed transaction or arrangement with the company—
    (a) is to be counted as participating in the decision-making process, and
    (b) is entitled to vote on or agree to a proposal relating to it.
(3) This paragraph applies when—
    (a) the company by ordinary resolution disapplies the provision of the articles which would otherwise prevent a director from being counted as participating in the decision-making process;
    (b) the director's interest cannot reasonably be regarded as likely to give rise to a conflict of interest; or
    (c) the director's conflict of interest arises from a permitted cause.
(4) For the purposes of this article, the following are permitted causes—
    (a) a guarantee given, or to be given, by or to a director in respect of an obligation incurred by or on behalf of the company or any of its subsidiaries;

(b) subscription, or an agreement to subscribe, for shares or other securities of the company or any of its subsidiaries, or to underwrite, sub-underwrite, or guarantee subscription for any such shares or securities; and
(c) arrangements pursuant to which benefits are made available to employees and directors or former employees and directors of the company or any of its subsidiaries which do not provide special benefits for directors or former directors.

(5) For the purposes of this article, references to proposed decisions and decision-making processes include any directors' meeting or part of a directors' meeting.

(6) Subject to paragraph (7), if a question arises at a meeting of directors or of a committee as to the right of a director to vote, the question may, before the conclusion of the meeting, be referred to the chairman of the meeting whose ruling in relation to any director other than the chairman is to be final and conclusive.

(7) If any question as to the right to participate in the meeting (or part of the meeting) should arise in respect of the chairman of the meeting, the question is to be decided by a decision of the directors at that meeting, for which purpose the chairman of the meeting is not to be counted as participating in the meeting (or that part of the meeting) for voting or quorum purposes.

COMMENTARY: 14 Conflicts of interest

APP 23 This article reflects the important provisions against self-dealing that are imposed on directors by CA 2006, ss 175 (duty to avoid conflicts of interest) and 177 (duty to declare interest in proposed transaction or arrangement).

APP 24 Article 14(1) disables a director from taking part in any way in a decision if that director is interested in an actual or proposed transaction or arrangement with the company. However this general inability on the part of a director to participate in the decision-making process does not take effect if any of the provisions of art 14(3) applies. Under this latter provision a company is permitted by an ordinary resolution of the members to disapply the provision of the articles which would otherwise prevent a director from being counted as participating in the decision-making process and where such a decision has been made the director can participate in the board meeting. In addition, if the director's interest cannot reasonably be regarded as likely to give rise to a conflict of interest he can participate in the board decision. This will be a question of fact in each case. Finally art 14(3)(c) permits a director's participation in a board meeting if the director's conflict of interest arises from any of the three 'permitted causes' which are defined and described in art 14(4).

APP 25 Questions that arise at a board meeting as to the right of a director to vote can be referred to the chairman whose decision in relation to any director other than himself shall be final and conclusive. Where a question arises as to the capacity of the chairman to participate in the meeting this issue has to be determined by all the other directors excluding the chairman. It is apparent from art 14(6) that those restrictions apply not only to board meetings but also to meetings of committees of the board.

15 Records of decisions to be kept

The directors must ensure that the company keeps a record, in writing, for at least 10 years from the date of the decision recorded, of every unanimous or majority decision taken by the directors.

COMMENTARY: 15 Records of decisions to be kept

This provision in part reflects the requirements of CA 2006, s 248 which imposes a statutory duty on directors to keep records of board meetings for a period of 10 years. The reference in this article to keeping the record in writing does not imply that the record must be made in manuscript only. Article 1 defines the word 'writing' as '... the representation or reproduction of words, symbols or other information in a visible form by any method or combination of methods, whether sent or supplied in electronic form or otherwise'. A record of a meeting or a decision will be within this definition if it is typed and accessible by electronic means. The danger with keeping records on a computer system is that the record must be legible for at least 10 years. In the event that a computer file became corrupted and unreadable after a short period of time, this could lead to problems if the file was not adequately backed up or maintained in hard copy format. **APP 26**

16 Directors' discretion to make further rules

Subject to the articles, the directors may make any rule which they think fit about how they take decisions, and about how such rules are to be recorded or communicated to directors.

COMMENTARY: 16 Directors' discretion to make further rules

This wide provision makes it clear that, subject to a company's articles of association, directors have the ability to regulate the conduct of their meetings and proceedings as they see fit. This capacity is subject to express provisions that are contained in a company's articles of association. In an era of great advances in technology it is prudent for directors to make express provision in the articles that directors can participate in board meetings by advanced and diverse forms of electronic means. **APP 27**

DECISION-MAKING BY SHAREHOLDERS ORGANISATION OF GENERAL MEETINGS

38 Attendance and speaking at general meetings

(1) A person is able to exercise the right to speak at a general meeting when that person is in a position to communicate to all those attending the meeting, during the meeting, any information or opinions which that person has on the business of the meeting.

(2) A person is able to exercise the right to vote at a general meeting when—

(a) that person is able to vote, during the meeting, on resolutions put to the vote at the meeting, and

(b) that person's vote can be taken into account in determining whether or not such resolutions are passed at the same time as the votes of all the other persons attending the meeting.

(3) The directors may make whatever arrangements they consider appropriate to enable those attending a general meeting to exercise their rights to speak or vote at it.

(4) In determining attendance at a general meeting, it is immaterial whether any two or more members attending it are in the same place as each other.

(5) Two or more persons who are not in the same place as each other attend a general meeting if their circumstances are such that if they have (or were to have) rights to speak and vote at that meeting, they are (or would be) able to exercise them.

COMMENTARY: 38 Attendance and speaking at general meetings

APP 28 Article 38(1) and (4) are designed to ensure that members can participate at general meetings whether or not they are physically present at the meeting. It is to be regretted that the language that is used in art 38(1) is not as clear as it might have been.

APP 29 The directors are given authority by art 38(3) to make appropriate arrangements for members to participate in a general meeting. It is now well established that a general meeting can take place in a regular manner even if the members are in two venues that are linked together by audio-visual means. The important criteria are that members in each of the meeting rooms can see and hear and see and be seen by the members in the other venue.

APP 30 Article 38(4) reflects the fact that modern methods of communication permit members to take part in meetings when they may be located in different venues. The essence of a meeting in the eyes of the law is no longer the physical presence of the members in the same venue, but the ability of the participants in a meeting to take part and contribute simultaneously in the proceedings of the meeting. Modern technology has made concurrent participation in meetings possible even though the participants may be in different locations. The essential ingredient is the ability to communicate with everyone.

39 Quorum for general meetings

No business other than the appointment of the chairman of the meeting is to be transacted at a general meeting if the persons attending it do not constitute a quorum.

COMMENTARY: 39 Quorum for general meetings

APP 31 General meetings must be quorate, that is to say attended by at least the minimum number of participants in order to be able to proceed to transact lawful business. Chapter 1 discusses the concept of the quorum of a general meeting in detail.

APP 32 Article 39 contemplates that even if a general meeting is not quorate a valid decision can be taken to appoint a chairman of the meeting. This is to be contrasted with the provision in reg 40 of the 1985 Table A which provides that no business shall be transacted unless a quorum is present. A chairman so appointed will have only a limited role, namely that of closing the meeting for lack of a quorum.

40 Chairing general meetings

(1) If the directors have appointed a chairman, the chairman shall chair general meetings if present and willing to do so.
(2) If the directors have not appointed a chairman, or if the chairman is unwilling to chair the meeting or is not present within ten minutes of the time at which a meeting was due to start
    (a) the directors present, or
    (b) (if no directors are present), the meeting,
must appoint a director or shareholder to chair the meeting, and the appointment of the chairman of the meeting must be the first business of the meeting.
(3) The person chairing a meeting in accordance with this article is referred to as 'the chairman of the meeting'.

COMMENTARY: 40 Chairing general meetings

Where a board of directors has appointed one of their number to hold office as chairman that person will take the role as chairman of a general meeting of members provided that he is present and willing to perform this role. If there is no chairman of the board of directors, or if this individual is either absent or unwilling to act as chairman of the general meeting, the directors must appoint a director or a member to act as chairman. Where no directors are present the members themselves are empowered to appoint a chairman of the meeting. This must be the first matter to be dealt with at the start of any meeting. **APP 33**

41 Attendance and speaking by directors and non-shareholders

(1) Directors may attend and speak at general meetings, whether or not they are shareholders.
(2) The chairman of the meeting may permit other persons who are not
    (a) shareholders of the company, or
    (b) otherwise entitled to exercise the rights of shareholders in relation to general meetings,
to attend and speak at a general meeting.

COMMENTARY: 41 Attendance and speaking by directors and non-shareholders

Under CA 2006, s 310(1)(b) directors have a statutory right to receive notice of a general meeting even if they are not registered members of the company concerned. Having been given notice of a general meeting it would be odd if a director who was not also a member was unable to address the general meeting. Article 41(1) enables non-shareholding directors to attend and speak at a general meeting. The ability of other non-members, including persons who are entitled to exercise rights of members, both to attend and speak at a general meeting is a matter that is left to the discretionary jurisdiction of the chairman of the general meeting. The article links attendance with the right to speak. This is not always appropriate. For instance, a member's solicitor **APP 34** may be permitted to attend a general meeting but the board or the chairman may not be prepared to permit him to address the meeting or ask questions.

42 Adjournment

(1) If the persons attending a general meeting within half an hour of the time at which the meeting was due to start do not constitute a quorum, or if during a meeting a quorum ceases to be present, the chairman of the meeting must adjourn it.
(2) The chairman of the meeting may adjourn a general meeting at which a quorum is present if
  (a) the meeting consents to an adjournment, or
  (b) it appears to the chairman of the meeting that an adjournment is necessary to protect the safety of any person attending the meeting or ensure that the business of the meeting is conducted in an orderly manner.
(3) The chairman of the meeting must adjourn a general meeting if directed to do so by the meeting.
(4) When adjourning a general meeting, the chairman of the meeting must
  (a) either specify the time and place to which it is adjourned or state that it is to continue at a time and place to be fixed by the directors, and
  (b) have regard to any directions as to the time and place of any adjournment which have been given by the meeting.
(5) If the continuation of an adjourned meeting is to take place more than 14 days after it was adjourned, the company must give at least 7 clear days' notice of it (that is, excluding the day of the adjourned meeting and the day on which the notice is given)
  (a) to the same persons to whom notice of the company's general meetings is required to be given, and
  (b) containing the same information which such notice is required to contain.
(6) No business may be transacted at an adjourned general meeting which could not properly have been transacted at the meeting if the adjournment had not taken place.

COMMENTARY: 42 Adjournment

APP 35 Many issues can arise in relation to the adjournment of a general meeting of a company and this subject is discussed in detail in Chapter 12. Under art 42(1) the chairman of the meeting must adjourn a general meeting in two prescribed situations. First, if the general meeting is not quorate within 30 minutes of the time specified for the start of the meeting, and secondly, if during the general meeting it ceases to be quorate. The chairman has a discretion to adjourn a general meeting under art 42(2). The discretion to adjourn the general meeting arises where the members authorize this course of action or where the chairman has to maintain order or the safety of the participants. Under art 42(3) the chairman must adjourn the meeting if he is directed to do so by the members. This provision does not articulate how the instruction to the chairman is to be given or indeed how the members proceed to take such a decision. It must be assumed that the direction will have been resolved upon by a majority of the members.

The practicalities of the adjourned meeting are dealt with in art 42(4). When adjourning a general meeting, the chairman of the meeting must either specify the time and place to which it is adjourned or state that it is to continue at a time and place to be fixed by the directors. The new provision is silent as to how this is to be communicated to the members. In addition the chairman must take account of any directions as to date, time and venue that are given by the general meeting itself. **APP 36**

Where an adjourned meeting is to take place more than 14 days after it was adjourned, the company must give at least seven clear days' notice of it. Article 1 does not offer a definition of the phrase '... clear days' hence the need for the words of explanation that are contained in the parenthesis in art 48(5). Where a further notice is required it must be given to the same persons to whom notice of the company's general meetings is required to be given under CA 2006, s 310 and the articles. The notice must also contain the same information which such notice is required to contain under CA 2006, s 311. **APP 37**

An adjourned meeting is limited to, and cannot depart from, transacting the business that was contemplated by the original meeting and this rule is enshrined in art 48(6). **APP 38**

VOTING AT GENERAL MEETINGS

43 Voting: general

A resolution put to the vote of a general meeting must be decided on a show of hands unless a poll is duly demanded in accordance with the articles.

COMMENTARY: 43 Voting: general

Article 43 reflects the position that voting at general meetings will either be by a vote taken on a show of hands, where each member has one vote irrespective of the number of shares that he holds, or on a vote on a poll where the precise numbers of shares held are the decisive factor. Detailed consideration of the subject of voting by members at general meetings is found in Chapter 9. The default option is always a vote on a show of hands. **APP 39**

44 Errors and disputes

(1) No objection may be raised to the qualification of any person voting at a general meeting except at the meeting or adjourned meeting at which the vote objected to is tendered, and every vote not disallowed at the meeting is valid.
(2) Any such objection must be referred to the chairman of the meeting, whose decision is final.

COMMENTARY: 44 Errors and disputes

If an issue arises as to the capacity of a person to cast a vote at a general meeting that matter must be raised and dealt with at the general meeting. The chairman is empowered to deal with all such objections and his decision on such a matter is final. An article in this form requires the issue to be raised and resolved at the general meeting **APP 40** where it arises, and in the absence of special circumstances it is difficult to mount a successful challenge to this type of issue if it had not been raised at the general meeting. The chairman's power in this respect is a fiduciary power which must not be abused.

45 Poll votes

(1) A poll on a resolution may be demanded—
  (a) in advance of the general meeting where it is to be put to the vote, or
  (b) at a general meeting, either before a show of hands on that resolution or
  (c) immediately after the result of a show of hands on that resolution is declared.

(2) A poll may be demanded by—
  (a) the chairman of the meeting;
  (b) the directors;
  (c) two or more persons having the right to vote on the resolution; or
  (d) a person or persons representing not less than one tenth of the total voting rights of all the shareholders having the right to vote on the resolution.

(3) A demand for a poll may be withdrawn if—
  (a) the poll has not yet been taken, and
  (b) the chairman of the meeting consents to the withdrawal.

(4) Polls must be taken immediately and in such manner as the chairman of the meeting directs.

COMMENTARY: 45 Poll votes

APP 41 Article 45(1) regulates the occasions when a vote on a poll may be demanded. A poll can be demanded in advance of the general meeting at which the resolution will come up for decision, or at the general meeting before a vote is taken on a show of hands or immediately after the result of the vote on a show of hands has been declared. The right to demand a poll in advance of the meeting is a new and valuable right.

APP 42 Article 45(2) designates the four categories of person who have the capacity to demand a poll. These comprise the chairman of the meeting, the directors, two or more persons who are able to vote on the resolution, and a person or persons representing not less than one-tenth of the total voting rights of all the shareholders who have the right to vote on the resolution. It is not clear whether the reference in art 45(2)(b) allows a single director to demand a poll. It is to be presumed that the provision covers a demand by a single director, as the provision cannot be construed as requiring a board decision for this purpose.

APP 43 Two conditions are prescribed in art 45(3) for the effective withdrawal of a demand for a poll. First, the poll must not have been taken and secondly the chairman of the meeting must agree to the poll being withdrawn. Again, this is a fiduciary power which must be exercised by the chairman for proper purposes.

APP 44 Under art 45(4) a poll is required to be taken immediately and in the manner that is decided upon by the chairman. In a private company it is important for the chairman to have a degree of discretion as to the manner in which a poll shall be conducted.

As with the discretionary powers that are conferred upon the chairman of a meeting, this power must be exercised in a regular manner for proper purposes.

46 Content of proxy notices

(1) Proxies may only validly be appointed by a notice in writing (a 'proxy notice') which
  (a) states the name and address of the shareholder appointing the proxy;
  (b) identifies the person appointed to be that shareholder's proxy and the general meeting in relation to which that person is appointed;
  (c) is signed by or on behalf of the member appointing the proxy, or is authenticated in such manner as the directors may determine; and
  (d) is delivered to the company in accordance with the articles and any instructions contained in the notice of the general meeting to which they relate.
(2) The company may require proxy notices to be delivered in a particular form, and may specify different forms for different purposes.
(3) Proxy notices may specify how the proxy appointed under them is to vote (or that the proxy is to abstain from voting) on one or more resolutions.
(4) Unless a proxy notice indicates otherwise, it must be treated as
  (a) allowing the person appointed under it as a proxy discretion as to how to vote on any ancillary or procedural resolutions put to the meeting, and
  (b) appointing that person as a proxy in relation to any adjournment of the general meeting to which it relates as well as the meeting itself.

COMMENTARY: 46 Content of proxy notices

The ability of a member to appoint a proxy is a fundamental tenet of company law **APP 45**
that is now enshrined in CA 2006, s 324. This important subject is considered in detail in Chapter 8. In addition, CA 2006, s 325 requires the notice of a meeting to contain a statement informing the members of their statutory rights under s 324 or any more extensive rights that may apply under a company's articles. Apart from the provision in s 327 as to the timing of lodging proxies the legislation does not impose any specific requirements as to the form of proxy. Article 46 contains important provisions relating to the content of proxy notices and departs from the practice that was adopted in Table A of setting out the actual form of the proxy notice. Article 46(1)(a)–(c) (inclusive) stipulates the content of the proxy notice and provides that this information must be contained in the relevant document. In practice the vast majority of companies will adopt the sensible precaution of sending out a pre-printed proxy card which the member has to complete and return within the prescribed time limit in the articles or under CA 2006, s 327.

A private company is empowered by art 46(2) to prescribe the form of the proxy **APP 46**
notice and to have different types of notice, for example different colours for different classes of shares.

Under art 46(3) the member can direct the proxy to vote for or against a resolution **APP 47**
or to abstain from voting altogether. Sometimes unexpected procedural matters may arise for consideration at a general meeting. The provisions in art 46(4) are to

be welcomed in that they make clear that unless the proxy notice indicates otherwise, it must be treated as allowing the person appointed under it a discretion as to how to vote on any ancillary or procedural resolutions that may arise for consideration and decision by the meeting. This will include how to vote on an adjournment resolution. In addition, unless the proxy notice indicates to the contrary, the proxy notice is treated as appointing the nominated person as a proxy in relation to any adjournment of the general meeting as well as at the meeting itself.

47 **Delivery of proxy notices**

(1) A person who is entitled to attend, speak or vote (either on a show of hands or on a poll) at a general meeting remains so entitled in respect of that meeting or any adjournment of it, even though a valid proxy notice has been delivered to the company by or on behalf of that person.
(2) An appointment under a proxy notice may be revoked by delivering to the company a notice given by or on behalf of the person by whom or on whose behalf the proxy notice was given.
(3) A notice revoking a proxy appointment only takes effect if it is delivered before the start of the meeting or adjourned meeting to which it relates.
(4) If a proxy notice is not executed by the person appointing the proxy, it must be accompanied by written evidence of the authority of the person who executed it to execute it on the appointor's behalf.

COMMENTARY: 47 **Delivery of proxy notices**

APP 48 Where a proxy form has been completed and lodged this does not prevent the appointor from attending, speaking and voting at the general meeting. This general principle of law is enshrined in art 47(1). Where the appointor of the proxy has a change of mind it is permissible to send to the company a notice of revocation. For such a notice to be valid and take effect it must be delivered to the company before the start of the general meeting or adjourned meeting to which it relates.

APP 49 Under art 47(4) where a proxy notice is not executed by the person appointing the proxy, it is a mandatory requirement that it must be accompanied by written evidence of the authority of the person who executed it to execute it on the appointor's behalf. This will include a power of attorney as proof of authority.

48 **Amendments to resolutions**

(1) An ordinary resolution to be proposed at a general meeting may be amended by ordinary resolution if
   (a) notice of the proposed amendment is given to the company in writing by a person entitled to vote at the general meeting at which it is to be proposed not less than 48 hours before the meeting is to take place (or such later time as the chairman of the meeting may determine), and
   (b) the proposed amendment does not, in the reasonable opinion of the chairman of the meeting, materially alter the scope of the resolution.

(2) A special resolution to be proposed at a general meeting may be amended by ordinary resolution, if
   (a) the chairman of the meeting proposes the amendment at the general meeting at which the resolution is to be proposed, and
   (b) the amendment does not go beyond what is necessary to correct a grammatical or other non-substantive error in the resolution.

(3) If the chairman of the meeting, acting in good faith, wrongly decides that an amendment to a resolution is out of order, the chairman's error does not invalidate the vote on that resolution.

COMMENTARY: 48 Amendments to resolutions

Article 48 addresses the important subject of the amendment of resolutions. Table A in its various forms has never made specific reference to the amendment of resolutions. Companies that have not adopted the provisions of Table A have sometimes inserted specific provisions regulating the amendment of resolutions but the practice has not been universal. As the amendment of resolutions can give rise to controversy a clear statement of the circumstances where amendments are permitted is to be welcomed. The subject of amendment of resolutions is considered in Chapter 11. **APP 50**

Article 48(1) permits amendments to an ordinary resolution provided that two conditions are satisfied. First that notice of the proposed amendment is given to the company in writing by a person entitled to vote at the general meeting at which it is to be proposed not less than 48 hours before the meeting is to take place (or at such later time as the chairman of the meeting may determine). The second requirement is that the proposed amendment does not, in the reasonable opinion of the chairman of the meeting, materially alter the scope of the ordinary resolution. **APP 51**

In some ways this new provision is quite restrictive. It strengthens the power of the board to control the business of a general meeting. The chairman's power to reject an amendment is subject to a test of reasonableness and therefore open to legal challenge. For the reasons explained in Chapter 11, if an amendment is wrongly rejected the resolution would be invalidated at common law. Article 48(3) attempts to reverse this rule by providing that the chairman's error does not invalidate the resolution. **APP 52**

ADMINISTRATIVE ARRANGEMENTS

49 Means of communication to be used

(1) Subject to the articles, anything sent or supplied by or to the company under the articles may be sent or supplied in any way in which the Companies Act 2006 provides for documents or information which are authorised or required by any provision of that Act to be sent or supplied by or to the company.

(2) Subject to the articles, any notice or document to be sent or supplied to a director in connection with the taking of decisions by directors may also be sent or supplied by the means by which that director has asked to be sent or supplied with such notices or documents for the time being.

(3) A director may agree with the company that notices or documents sent to that director in a particular way are to be deemed to have been received within a specified time of their being sent, and for the specified time to be less than 48 hours.

COMMENTARY: 49 Means of communication to be used

APP 53 Under CA 2006 there are extensive provisions (CA 2006, ss 1144–1148 and Schs 4 and 5) dealing with the sending and receipt of documents by and to a company by electronic means. The Company Communication Provisions are discussed in Chapter 17. Article 49(1) acknowledges the existence of the Company Communications Provisions. Article 49(2) applies only to directors. A director is entitled to stipulate a particular method of communication for the receipt by him of any notices or documents.

APP 54 Under CA 2006, s 1168 where a company sends or supplies documents or information provision is made for the deemed delivery of such documents or information. Where the postal system is used as the method of delivery, s 1168(2) provides that there will be deemed receipt by the recipient 48 hours after they were sent. Where documents or information have been sent or supplied by electronic means there is deemed receipt under CA 2006, s 1168(3) 48 hours after they were sent. Under art 49(3) it is permissible for the company and its directors to agree a time period for deemed receipt that is less than 48 hours.

Draft Model Articles for Public Companies

APP 55 Schedule 3 of the Draft Statutory Instrument contains draft model articles for a public company. In practice most public listed companies will have articles of association that are specifically drafted to meet the special circumstances of how they operate their businesses and it is highly unusual for such a company to rely on standard form provisions provided for in the legislation. It remains to be seen whether significant numbers of public companies will adopt the provisions of Sch 3 of the Draft Statutory Instrument.

DRAFT MODEL ARTICLES FOR PUBLIC COMPANIES
DECISION-MAKING BY DIRECTORS

7 Directors to take decisions collectively

Subject to the articles, decisions of the directors must be taken—

(a) at a directors' meeting, or
(b) in the form of a directors' written resolution.

COMMENTARY: 7 Directors to take decisions collectively

This provision is identical to art 7(3) of the draft model articles relating to private companies limited by shares. In the absence of specific provisions in the articles of a public company there are two methods by which directors may take decisions. First, decisions can be taken at a duly convened board meeting. Secondly, the directors may take a decision by means of a written resolution (see further arts 17 and 18 (below)). Public companies vary enormously in size. Where the board of a public company is comprised of many individuals it is doubtful whether recourse will be had to taking decisions by means of a written resolution where unanimity is required. The decisions of directors must be recorded accurately. Written resolutions must be retained for at least 10 years in accordance with art 18(4) (below) and CA 2006, s 248. **APP 56**

8 Calling a directors' meeting

(1) Any director may call a directors' meeting.
(2) The company secretary must call a directors' meeting if a director so requests.
(3) A directors' meeting is called by giving notice of the meeting to the directors.
(4) Notice of any directors' meeting must indicate
  (a) its proposed date and time;
  (b) where it is to take place; and
  (c) if it is anticipated that directors participating in the meeting will not be in the same place, how it is proposed that they should communicate with each other during the meeting.
(5) Notice of a directors' meeting must be given to each director, but need not be in writing.
(6) Notice of a directors' meeting need not be given to directors who waive their entitlement to notice of that meeting, by giving notice to that effect to the company not more than 7 days after the date on which the meeting is held. Where such notice is given after the meeting has been held, that does not affect the validity of the meeting, or of any business conducted at it.

COMMENTARY: 8 Calling a directors' meeting

Article 8 regulates how a board meeting of a public company should be convened. It may be compared with art 9 for private companies. Any director (defined in art 1, which mirrors CA 2006, s 250, as '... a director of the company, and includes any person occupying the position of director, by whatever name called...') has capacity to call a board meeting. When the company secretary of a public company is asked by a director to convene a board meeting, he must respond in a positive and timely manner to such a request. It is not stated how the director must make the request to the company secretary but it is suggested that an oral or written request will be sufficient. **APP 57**

The notice of the board meeting, in common with a valid notice for all meetings, must state the date, time and location. In addition, where the board meeting is to be held with some directors participating by telephone details must be supplied of how the directors will communicate with each other during the board meeting. It is not a **APP 58** mandatory requirement to give the notice of the board meeting in writing (see art 8(5)), but it is suggested that such a notice is more desirable than a notice that is given orally. The word 'writing' is defined in art 1 as '... the representation or reproduction of words, symbols or other information in a visible form by any method or combination of methods, whether sent or supplied in electronic form or otherwise'.

APP 59 Article 8(6) permits directors to waive their entitlement to receive notice for a period of not more than seven days after the date on which the board meeting is held. If such a retrospective notice is given by a director, the business that is transacted at the board meeting is not rendered invalid. This provision is predicated on there being a quorate board meeting without that particular director being present.

9 Participation in directors' meetings

(1) Subject to the articles, directors participate in a directors' meeting, or part of a directors' meeting, when
  (a) the meeting has been called and takes place in accordance with the articles, and
  (b) they can each communicate to the others any information or opinions they have on any particular item of the business of the meeting.

(2) In determining whether directors are participating in a directors' meeting, it is irrelevant where any director is or how they communicate with each other.

(3) If all the directors participating in a meeting are not in the same place, they may decide that the meeting is to be treated as taking place wherever any of them is.

COMMENTARY: 9 Participation in directors' meetings

APP 60 This provision is the same as Sch 1, art 10 which operates in relation to private companies. It is of cardinal importance that board meetings are held and conducted in accordance with the specific requirements that are set out in a company's articles of association. Article 9 permits board meetings of public companies to be held by modern means of communication and acknowledges that the essence of a valid meeting is no longer physical presence of all of the participants in the same venue but the ability of participants to communicate with each other. The directors can decide for themselves where the board meeting will be deemed to have been held. It would appear that in the event of dispute on this latter point the matter will have to be put to a vote of the directors. Many listed public companies have had provisions in their articles to permit directors to participate in board meetings by telephone and such provisions have been drafted in clearer and simpler terms that the tortuous and opaque language of art 9.

APP 61 Article 9(3) preserves the rule that a board meeting must be held at a precise location even when all the participants attend the meeting by telephone.

10 Quorum for directors' meetings

(1) At a directors' meeting, unless a quorum is participating, no proposal shall be voted on, except a proposal to call another meeting.

(2) The quorum for directors' meetings may be fixed from time to time by a decision of the directors, but it must never be less than two, and unless otherwise fixed it is two.

COMMENTARY: 10 Quorum for directors' meetings

This provision may be compared with Sch 1, art 11 for private companies limited by shares. Article 10 stipulates that no business can be transacted at a board meeting of a public company unless a valid quorum is present. If there is no quorum the only matter that can be voted on is a proposal to call another board meeting. The statutory draft articles provide that the directors may determine what the quorum provision is to be for their meetings but sets the default number at two. **APP 62**

11 Meetings where total number of directors less than quorum

(1) This article applies where the total number of directors for the time being is less than the quorum for directors' meetings.
(2) If there is only one director, that director may appoint sufficient directors to make up a quorum or call a general meeting to do so.
(3) If there is more than one director
    (a) a directors' meeting may take place, if it is called in accordance with the articles and at least two directors participate in it, with a view to appointing sufficient directors to make up a quorum or calling a general meeting to do so, and
    (b) if a directors' meeting is called but only one director attends at the appointed date and time to participate in it, that director may appoint sufficient directors to make up a quorum or call a general meeting to do so.

COMMENTARY: 11 Meetings where total number of directors less than quorum

This provision is the equivalent of Sch 1, art 11 for private companies. Where the number of directors falls below the number that is required to constitute a quorum for a board meeting (under art 10 this number is two) and there is only one director, that director may appoint an additional director so as to be able to comply with the quorum provision or convene a general meeting to appoint additional directors. **APP 63**

Article 11(3) makes provision for the situation where there is more than one director but a quorum still cannot be formed. In this case a board meeting can take place to appoint further directors provided that at least two directors participate in such a meeting. However, if only one director attends the board meeting that director may appoint additional directors in order to satisfy the quorum requirement or convene a general meeting for this purpose. **APP 64**

12 Chairing directors' meetings

(1) The directors may appoint a director to chair their meetings.
(2) The person so appointed for the time being is known as the chairman.
(3) The directors may appoint other directors as deputy or assistant chairmen to chair directors' meetings in the chairman's absence.
(4) The directors may terminate the chairman's appointment at any time.

(5) If neither the chairman nor any director appointed generally to chair directors' meetings in the chairman's absence is participating in a meeting within ten minutes of the time at which it was to start, the participating directors must appoint one of themselves to chair it.

COMMENTARY: 12 Chairing directors' meetings

APP 65 The equivalent of this provision for private companies is to be found in Sch 1, art 12. Directors are empowered, but not obliged to appoint one of their number to hold office as chairman. They also have the jurisdiction to remove a chairman from this appointment. The role of the chairman in a public company may well be a more important position than in a private company and as a consequence under art 12(3) the directors may also appoint other directors to hold office as deputies or assistants to the chairman. In the event that the chairman or his deputy are not present within 10 minutes of the appointed starting time the directors may make an ad hoc appointment as chairman from one of their number for that specific board meeting.

13 Voting at directors' meetings: general rules

(1) Subject to the articles, a decision is taken at a directors' meeting by a majority of the votes of the participating directors.

(2) Subject to the articles, each director participating in a directors' meeting has one vote.

(3) Subject to the articles, if a director has an interest in an actual or proposed transaction or arrangement with the company—

(a) that director and that director's alternate may not vote on any proposal relating to it, but

(b) this does not preclude the alternate from voting in relation to that transaction or arrangement on behalf of another appointor who does not have such an interest.

COMMENTARY: 13 Voting at directors' meetings: general rules

APP 66 Article 13 acknowledges that decisions at board meetings will be taken by means of the directors voting. Subject to the articles of association which may confer on directors weighted voting rights in certain circumstances, each director shall have one vote. Directors or their duly appointed alternates (see art 15 (below)) may not vote where the director (ie the appointor of the alternate) has an interest in an actual or proposed transaction or arrangement with the company. The use of the word 'arrangement' denotes that non-contractual situations fall within the ambit of this provision. However, if an alternate has been appointed by two of the directors the restriction on the alternate in relating to voting will only operate in relation to the director who has the conflict of interest.

14 Chairman's casting vote at directors' meetings

(1) If the numbers of votes for and against a proposal are equal, the chairman or other director chairing the meeting has a casting vote.

(2) But this does not apply if, in accordance with the articles, the chairman or other director is not to be counted as participating in the decision-making process for quorum, voting or agreement purposes.

COMMENTARY: 14 Chairman's casting vote at directors' meetings

Matching Sch 1, art 13 for private companies provision is made by art 14(1) for the chairman or other director who happens to be chairing a board meeting to have a second or casting vote in the case of an equality of votes. This is a prudent precaution in order to avoid a situation where the board is in a state of deadlock and cannot make a decision. However, the chairman does not have a casting vote where the company's articles provide that the chairman or other director acting as chairman is not counted in the calculation of the quorum or for voting or for agreement purposes. **APP 67**

15 Alternates voting at directors' meetings

A director who is also an alternate director has an additional vote on behalf of each appointor who is

(a) not participating in a directors' meeting, and
(b) would have been entitled to vote if they were participating in it.

COMMENTARY: 15 Alternates voting at directors' meetings

Under Sch 3, art 25 provision is made for directors of a public company to appoint another director, or any other person approved by the board as his alternate. Such an appointment permits the alternate in the absence of the director to exercise the powers of that director and to carry out his responsibilities. If a director has been appointed to be an alternate for another director, art 15 makes it clear that a director in such a position has a second vote on behalf of the absent appointor provided that such a person would have been entitled to vote had they been present. **APP 68**

16 Conflicts of interest

(1) If a directors' meeting, or part of a directors' meeting, is concerned with an actual or proposed transaction or arrangement with the company in which a director is interested, that director is not to be counted as participating in that meeting, or part of a meeting, for voting or quorum purposes.
(2) But if paragraph (3) applies, a director who is interested in an actual or proposed transaction or arrangement with the company—
  (a) is to be counted as participating in a decision at a directors' meeting, or part of a directors' meeting, relating to it, and
  (b) is entitled to vote on a proposal relating to it.
(3) This paragraph applies when—
  (a) the company by ordinary resolution disapplies the provision of the articles which would otherwise prevent a director from being counted as participating in, or voting at, a directors' meeting;

(b) the director's interest cannot reasonably be regarded as likely to give rise to a conflict of interest; or
(c) the director's conflict of interest arises from a permitted cause.

(4) For the purposes of this article, the following are permitted causes—
(a) a guarantee given, or to be given, by or to a director in respect of an obligation incurred by or on behalf of the company or any of its subsidiaries;
(b) subscription, or an agreement to subscribe, for shares or other securities of the company or any of its subsidiaries, or to underwrite, sub-underwrite, or guarantee subscription for any such shares or securities; and
(c) arrangements pursuant to which benefits are made available to employees and directors or former employees and directors of the company or any of its subsidiaries which do not provide special benefits for directors or former directors.

(5) Subject to paragraph (6), if a question arises at a meeting of directors or of a committee as to the right of a director to vote, the question may, before the conclusion of the meeting, be referred to the chairman of the meeting whose ruling in relation to any director other than the chairman is to be final and conclusive.

(6) If any question as to the right to participate in the meeting (or part of the meeting) should arise in respect of the chairman of the meeting, the question is to be decided by a decision of the directors at that meeting, for which purpose the chairman of the meeting is not to be counted as participating in the meeting (or that part of the meeting) for voting or quorum purposes.

COMMENTARY: 16 Conflicts of interest

APP 69 The terms of art 16(1)–(4) (inclusive) are identical to wording that is found in art 14(1)–(4) (inclusive) of Sch 1 which is applicable to private limited companies. The reader is referred to the commentary on that provision. Article 16 omits the provision that is found in art 14(5)—the reason for this omission is unclear. The wording of art 16(5) and (6) is once again identical to the wording found in art 14(6) and (7) respectively.

17 Proposing directors' written resolutions

(1) Any director may propose a directors' written resolution.
(2) The company secretary must propose a directors' written resolution if a director so requests.
(3) A directors' written resolution is proposed by giving notice of the proposed resolution to the directors.
(4) Notice of a proposed directors' written resolution must indicate—
(a) the proposed resolution, and
(b) the time by which it is proposed that the directors should adopt it.
(5) Notice of a proposed directors' written resolution must be given in writing to each director.
(6) Any decision which a person giving notice of a proposed directors' written resolution takes regarding the process of adopting that resolution must be taken reasonably in good faith.

COMMENTARY: 17 Proposing directors' written resolutions

Article 17 provides that any director may propose a written resolution to the board. If asked by a director to do so the company secretary must propose a written resolution. All of the members of the board must be given due notice of the written board resolution. The notice must be in writing and must set out the text of the written resolution and indicate the time by which it is proposed that the resolution should be adopted. The word 'writing' is defined in Sch 3, art 1 as '… the representation or reproduction of words, symbols or other information in a visible form by any method or combination of methods, whether sent or supplied in electronic form or otherwise'. **APP 70**

The crepuscular wording of art 17(6) appears to be a reference to the duty of a director to act reasonably and in good faith in relation to the procedure to be adopted proposing a written resolution. **APP 71**

18 Adoption of directors' written resolutions

(1) A proposed directors' written resolution is adopted when all the directors have signed one or more copies of it.
(2) It is immaterial whether any director signs the resolution before or after the time by which the notice proposed that it should be adopted.
(3) Once a directors' written resolution has been adopted, it must be treated as if it had been a decision taken at a directors' meeting in accordance with the articles.
(4) The company secretary must ensure that the company keeps a record, in writing, of all directors' written resolutions for at least ten years from the date of their adoption.

COMMENTARY: 18 Adoption of directors' written resolutions

Under art 18(1) a written resolution of directors will only take effect if the board is in unanimous agreement with the proposal and the board members have signed the resolution. It is not necessary for all the directors to sign the same document as art 18 permits agreement to be given by the directors by signing copies of the written resolution. **APP 72**

The written resolution of the directors is declared to take effect when all of the directors have signed the resolution. Under art 18(2) it is immaterial whether any director signs the written resolution before or after the time by which the notice proposed that it should be adopted. This link back to art 17(4)(b), which provides that the notice of a written resolution must indicate this 'deadline'. In reality, it is only a guide. **APP 73**

No provision is made in art 18 for the company secretary or other officer of the company to send out notification to the board that the resolution has received the required unanimous consent. A decision that is taken by means of a written resolution has the same effect as if it had been taken at a duly convened board meeting. **APP 74**

APP 75 Article 18(4) reflects the statutory duty imposed on the directors by CA 2006, s 248 that proper records must be kept of all of their decisions for a period of 10 years. In relation to written resolutions it is the company secretary who is charged with the responsibility for proper record-keeping.

> **19 Directors' discretion to make further rules**
>
> Subject to the articles, the directors may make any rule which they think fit about how they take decisions, and about how such rules are to be recorded or communicated to directors.

COMMENTARY: 19 Directors' discretion to make further rules

APP 76 The members of the board are entitled to make further rules about their decision-making and how those rules are set and are made known to the members of the board. This is equivalent to Sch 1, art 16 for private companies limited by shares.

DECISION-MAKING BY MEMBERS
ORGANISATION OF GENERAL MEETINGS

> **28 Members can call general meeting if not enough directors**
>
> If—
>
> (a) the company has fewer than two directors, and
> (b) the director (if any) is unable or unwilling to appoint sufficient directors to make up a quorum or to call a general meeting to do so,
>
> then two or more members may call a general meeting (or instruct the company secretary to do so) for the purpose of appointing one or more directors.

COMMENTARY: 28 Members can call general meeting if not enough directors

APP 77 In normal circumstances the decision when to call a general meeting will lie with the board of directors. Of course, directors must respond positively in response to a lawful request from members for a meeting under CA 2006, s 303—see Chapter 5. The purpose of art 28 is to prevent a situation from arising where a company is unable to function by reason of a dearth of directors. Where a public company is in a situation where it has fewer than two directors and the remaining director (if any) cannot, or will not appoint sufficient directors in order to form the required quorum, two or more members of a public company are given capacity either to instruct the company secretary to convene a general meeting or to proceed to convene a general meeting themselves. It seems that the only business that such a general meeting will be able to transact is the appointment of additional directors. A provision in this form is to be welcomed as without it the situation may arise that it was 'impracticable' to convene a general meeting, thus requiring an application to the court under the provisions of CA 2006, s 305—see Chapter 6.

29 Attendance and speaking at general meetings

(1) A person is able to exercise the right to speak at a general meeting when that person is in a position to communicate to all those attending the meeting, during the meeting, any information or opinions which that person has on the business of the meeting.

(2) A person is able to exercise the right to vote at a general meeting when—

(a) that person is able to vote, during the meeting, on resolutions put to the vote at the meeting, and

(b) that person's vote can be taken into account in determining whether or not such resolutions are passed at the same time as the votes of all the other persons attending the meeting.

(3) The directors may make whatever arrangements they consider appropriate to enable those attending a general meeting to exercise their rights to speak or vote at it.

(4) In determining attendance at a general meeting, it is immaterial whether any two or more members attending it are in the same place as each other.

(5) Two or more persons who are not in the same place as each other attend a general meeting if their circumstances are such that if they have (or were to have) rights to speak and vote at that meeting, they are (or would be) able to exercise them.

COMMENTARY: 29 Attendance and speaking at general meetings

The wording of Sch 3, art 29 is identical to the wording of Sch 1, art 38 and the reader is referred to the commentary on that provision. **APP 78**

30 Quorum for general meetings

No business other than the appointment of the chairman of the meeting is to be transacted at a general meeting if the persons attending it do not constitute a quorum.

COMMENTARY: 30 Quorum for general meetings

The wording of Sch 3, art 30 is identical to the wording of Sch 1, art 39 and the reader is referred to the commentary on that provision. **APP 79**

31 Chairing general meetings

(1) The chairman (if any) of the board of directors shall chair general meetings if present and willing to do so.

(2) If the chairman is unwilling to chair the meeting or is not present within ten minutes of the time at which a meeting was due to start

(a) the directors present, or

(b) (if no directors are present), the meeting, must appoint a director or member to chair the meeting, and the appointment of the chairman of the meeting must be the first business of the meeting.

(3) The person chairing a meeting in accordance with this article is referred to as 'the chairman of the meeting'.

COMMENTARY: 31 Chairing general meetings

APP 80 With minor linguistic changes the wording of Sch 3, art 31 is identical to the wording of Sch 1, art 40 and the reader is referred to the commentary on that provision.

32 Attendance and speaking by directors and non-members

(1) Directors may attend and speak at general meetings, whether or not they are members.

(2) The chairman of the meeting may permit other persons who are not

(a) members of the company, or

(b) otherwise entitled to exercise the rights of members in relation to general meetings, to attend and speak at a general meeting.

COMMENTARY: 32 Attendance and speaking by directors and non-members

APP 81 Save for the use of the word 'members' rather than 'shareholders' the wording of Sch 3, art 31 is identical to the wording of Sch 1, art 41 and the reader is referred to the commentary on that provision. In relation to public companies with large numbers of members it may be a harder decision for the chairman to decide whether non-members in general should be permitted to speak at a general meeting.

33 Adjournment

(1) If the persons attending a general meeting within half an hour of the time at which the meeting was due to start do not constitute a quorum, or if during a meeting a quorum ceases to be present, the chairman of the meeting must adjourn it.

(2) The chairman of the meeting may adjourn a general meeting at which a quorum is present if—

(a) the meeting consents to an adjournment, or

(b) it appears to the chairman of the meeting that an adjournment is necessary to protect the safety of any person attending the meeting or ensure that the business of the meeting is conducted in an orderly manner.

(3) The chairman of the meeting must adjourn a general meeting if directed to do so by the meeting.

(4) When adjourning a general meeting, the chairman of the meeting must—

(a) either specify the time and place to which it is adjourned or state that it is to continue at a time and place to be fixed by the directors, and

(b) have regard to any directions as to the time and place of any adjournment which have been given by the meeting.

(5) If the continuation of an adjourned meeting is to take place more than 14 days after it was adjourned, the company must give at least 7 clear days' notice of it (that is, excluding the day of the adjourned meeting and the day on which the notice is given)—

(a) to the same persons to whom notice of the company's general meetings is required to be given, and

(b) containing the same information which such notice is required to contain.

(6) No business may be transacted at an adjourned general meeting which could not properly have been transacted at the meeting if the adjournment had not taken place.

COMMENTARY: 33 Adjournment

The wording of Sch 3, art 33 is identical to the wording of Sch 1, art 42 and the reader is referred to the commentary on that provision. **APP 82**

34 Voting: general

A resolution put to the vote of a general meeting must be decided on a show of hands unless a poll is duly demanded in accordance with the articles.

COMMENTARY: 34 Voting: general

Article 37 is declaratory of the position with regard to voting that is enshrined in CA 2006, s 284. The wording of Sch 3, art 34 is identical to the wording of Sch 1, art 43 and the reader is referred to the commentary on that provision. **APP 83**

35 Errors and disputes

(1) No objection may be raised to the qualification of any person voting at a general meeting except at the meeting or adjourned meeting at which the vote objected to is tendered, and every vote not disallowed at the meeting is valid.

(2) Any such objection must be referred to the chairman of the meeting whose decision is final.

COMMENTARY: 35 Errors and disputes

The wording of Sch 3, art 35 is identical to the wording of Sch 1, art 44 and the reader is referred to the commentary on that provision. **APP 84**

36 Demanding a poll

(1) A poll on a resolution may be demanded—
  (a) in advance of the general meeting where it is to be put to the vote, or
  (b) at a general meeting, either before a show of hands on that resolution or immediately after the result of a show of hands on that resolution is declared.

(2) A poll may be demanded by—
  (a) the chairman of the meeting;
  (b) the directors;
  (c) two or more persons having the right to vote on the resolution; or
  (d) a person or persons representing not less than one tenth of the total voting rights of all the members having the right to vote on the resolution.

(3) A demand for a poll may be withdrawn if—
  (a) the poll has not yet been taken, and
  (b) the chairman of the meeting consents to the withdrawal.

COMMENTARY: 36 Demanding a poll

APP 85 Apart from a difference in the wording of the heading, the substance of Sch 3, art 36 is identical to the wording of Sch 1, art 45(1)–(3) (Poll Votes) and the reader is referred to the commentary on that provision. Article 37 (below) deals in detail with the manner of taking a poll in a public company, which for a private company is dealt with by the sentence comprising Sch 1, art 45(4).

37 Procedure on a poll

(1) Subject to the articles, polls at general meetings must be taken as and when the chairman of the meeting directs.

(2) The chairman of the meeting may appoint scrutineers (who need not be members) and decide how and when the result of the poll is to be declared.

(3) The result of a poll shall be the decision of the meeting in respect of the resolution on which the poll was demanded.

(4) A poll on

(a) the election of the chairman of the meeting, or

(b) a question of adjournment,

must be taken immediately.

(5) Other polls must be taken within 30 days of their being demanded.

(6) A demand for a poll does not prevent a general meeting from continuing, except as regards the question on which the poll was demanded.

(7) No notice need be given of a poll not taken immediately if the time and place at which it is to be taken are announced at the meeting at which it is demanded.

(8) In any other case, at least 7 days' notice must be given specifying the time and place at which the poll is to be taken.

COMMENTARY: 37 Procedure on a poll

APP 86 Article 37 contains detailed provisions for the taking of a poll at a general meeting of a public company. Voting by way of a poll at a general meeting of a listed public company is commonplace with voting on a show of hands being very much an exceptional and rare event. The manner of taking the poll and its timing are issues that fall within the competence of the chairman of the general meeting. These important powers are fiduciary in nature and must not be misused or abused. It is desirable that the chairman of the meeting is given express power to appoint scrutineers who will assist in the counting of the votes cast on a poll. In addition, the chairman will decide how and when to declare the result of voting on a poll. When the result of the poll is declared, that will constitute the result of the general meeting on that particular matter.

APP 87 With the exception of the poll votes on the two important issues that are specified by art 37(4) which must be taken at once, all other polls must be taken within a period of 30 days of being demanded. The demand for a poll which is taken at a later time does not operate as any form of restraint on the business of the general meeting other than that to which the poll relates.

Where notification of the time and place of the poll is given at the general meeting at which it was demanded there is no need for the company to issue notice of the poll. However, where notification is not given at the general meeting, art 37(8) requires that at least seven days' notice is given specifying the time and place at which the poll is to be taken. **APP 88**

38 Content of proxy notices

(1) Proxies may only validly be appointed by a notice in writing (a 'proxy notice') which—
 (a) states the name and address of the member appointing the proxy;
 (b) identifies the person appointed to be that member's proxy and the general meeting in relation to which that person is appointed;
 (c) is signed by or on behalf of the member appointing the proxy, or is authenticated in such manner as the directors may determine; and
 (d) is delivered to the company in accordance with the articles and any instructions contained in the notice of the general meeting to which they relate.

(2) The company may require proxy notices to be delivered in a particular form, and may specify different forms for different purposes.

(3) Proxy notices may specify how the proxy appointed under them is to vote (or that the proxy is to abstain from voting) on one or more resolutions.

(4) Unless a proxy notice indicates otherwise, it must be treated as—
 (a) allowing the person appointed under it as a proxy discretion as to how to vote on any ancillary or procedural resolutions put to the meeting, and
 (b) appointing that person as a proxy in relation to any adjournment of the general meeting to which it relates as well as the meeting itself.

COMMENTARY: 38 Content of proxy notices

The wording of Sch 3, art 38 is identical to the wording of Sch 1, art 46 and the reader is referred to the commentary on that provision. **APP 89**

39 Delivery of proxy notices

(1) Any notice of a general meeting must specify the address or addresses ('proxy notification address') at which the company or its agents will receive proxy notices relating to that meeting, or any adjournment of it, delivered in hard copy or electronic form.

(2) A person who is entitled to attend, speak or vote (either on a show of hands or on a poll) at a general meeting remains so entitled in respect of that meeting or any adjournment of it, even though a valid proxy notice has been delivered to the company by or on behalf of that person.

(3) Subject to paragraphs (4) and (5), a proxy notice must be delivered to a proxy notification address not less than 48 hours before the general meeting or adjourned meeting to which it relates.

(4) In the case of a poll taken more than 48 hours after it is demanded, the notice must be delivered to a proxy notification address not less than 24 hours before the time appointed for the taking of the poll.

(5) In the case of a poll not taken during the meeting but taken not more than 48 hours after it was demanded, the proxy notice must be delivered at the meeting at which the poll was demanded to the chairman, secretary or any director.

(6) An appointment under a proxy notice may be revoked by delivering a notice given by or on behalf of the person by whom or on whose behalf the proxy notice was given to a proxy notification address.
(7) A notice revoking a proxy appointment only takes effect if it is delivered before—
(a) the start of the meeting or adjourned meeting to which it relates, or
(b) (in the case of a poll not taken on the same day as the meeting or adjourned meeting) the time appointed for taking the poll to which it relates.
(8) If a proxy notice is not signed by the person appointing the proxy, it must be accompanied by written evidence of the authority of the person who executed it to execute it on the appointor's behalf.

COMMENTARY: 39 Delivery of proxy notices

APP 90 Article 39(1) designates the place specified in a notice of meeting for the receipt of proxies as the proxy notification address. No such provision appears in Sch 1, art 47 which is applicable to private companies.

APP 91 Schedule 3, art 39(2) is identical to the wording of Sch 1, art 47(1) and the reader is referred to the commentary above in respect of that provision.

APP 92 Article 39(3)–(5) (inclusive) deals with the timing of the delivery of proxies. The general rule is stated in art 39(3).

APP 93 Article 39(5) would appear to permit the late delivery of proxies which may be used on a poll if delivered at the general meeting and the poll takes place within 48 hours thereafter. This is a somewhat surprising provision in view of the fact that CA 2006, s 327(2)(c) dealing with the same issue has not been brought into force.

APP 94 Article 39(6) and (7) permits the revocation of a proxy in respect of a public company in the same manner as Sch 1, art 47 in respect of private companies. It is to be noted that art 39(7)(b) makes it clear when notice of revocation takes effect in respect of a poll that is not held on the same day as the general meeting.

APP 95 With the exception of the use of the word 'signed' in lieu of 'executed', art 39(8) is in identical terms to the provisions of Sch 1, art 47 and the reader is referred to the commentary on that provision.

40 Amendments to resolutions

(1) An ordinary resolution to be proposed at a general meeting may be amended by ordinary resolution if—
(a) notice of the proposed amendment is given to the company secretary in writing by a person entitled to vote at the general meeting at which it is to be proposed not less than 48 hours before the meeting is to take place (or such later time as the. chairman of the meeting may determine), and
(b) the proposed amendment does not, in the reasonable opinion of the chairman of the meeting, materially alter the scope of the resolution.
(2) A special resolution to be proposed at a general meeting may be amended by ordinary resolution, if—

(a) the chairman of the meeting proposes the amendment at the general meeting at which the resolution is to be proposed, and
(b) the amendment does not go beyond what is necessary to correct a grammatical or other non-substantive error in the resolution.

(3) If the chairman of the meeting, acting in good faith, wrongly decides that an amendment to a resolution is out of order, the chairman's error does not invalidate the vote on that resolution.

COMMENTARY: 40 Amendments to resolutions

The wording of Sch 3, art 40 is identical to the wording of Sch 1, art 48 and the reader is referred to the commentary on that provision. **APP 96**

RESTRICTIONS ON MEMBERS' RIGHTS

41 No voting of shares on which money owed to company

No voting rights attached to a share may be exercised at any general meeting, at any adjournment of it, or on any poll called at or in relation to it, unless all amounts payable to the company in respect of that share have been paid.

COMMENTARY: 41 No voting of shares on which money owed to company

Article 41 disenfranchises a member unless all amounts that are due to the company in respect of the share have been paid. A provision in this form is commonly found in a company's articles. The provision is designed to ensure that the right to vote is attached only to shares where the member is not indebted to the company in respect of his shareholding. **APP 97**

APPLICATION OF RULES TO CLASS MEETINGS

42 Class meetings

The provisions of the articles relating to general meetings apply, with any necessary modifications, to meetings of the holders of any class of shares.

COMMENTARY: 42 Class meetings

Article 42 acknowledges the fact that very often the share capital of a public company may be divided into shares of different classes. From time to time class meetings will have to be convened and conducted and such meetings will adopt the procedure that is employed at general meetings with suitable modification. The model articles in Sch 1 which are applicable to private companies do not contain a similar provision in relation to class meetings. **APP 98**

MISCELLANEOUS PROVISIONS
COMMUNICATIONS

79 Means of communication to be used

(1) Subject to the articles, anything sent or supplied by or to the company under the articles may be sent or supplied in any way in which the Companies Act

2006 provides for documents or information which are authorised or required by any provision of that Act to be sent or supplied by or to the company.

(2) Subject to the articles, any notice or document to be sent or supplied to a director in connection with the taking of decisions by directors may also be sent or supplied by the means by which that director has asked to be sent or supplied with such notices or documents for the time being.

(3) A director may agree with the company that notices or documents sent to that director in a particular way are to be deemed to have been received within a specified time of their being sent, and for the specified time to be less than 48 hours.

COMMENTARY: 79 Means of communication to be used

APP 99 The wording of Sch 3, art 79 is identical to the wording of Sch 1, art 49 and the reader is referred to the commentary on that provision.

80 Failure to notify contact details

(1) If—
 (a) the company sends two consecutive documents to a member over a period of at least 12 months, and
 (b) each of those documents is returned undelivered, or the company receives notification that is has not been delivered

that member ceases to be entitled to receive notices from the company.

(2) A member who has ceased to be entitled to receive notices from the company becomes entitled to receive such notices again by sending the company—
 (a) a new address to be recorded in the register of members, or
 (b) if the member has agreed that the company should use a means of communication other than sending things to such an address, the information that the company needs to use that means of communication effectively.

COMMENTARY: 80 Failure to notify contact details

APP 100 The costs that have to be incurred by a public company with a large number of registered members in sending out notices and other documents should not be underestimated. Against this background it is prudent to make provision in the articles for the company to cease to be under an obligation to send out notices and other documentation where there is cogent evidence that the member has not been receiving such material. The decision to exclude a member from the receipt of corporate information may have far-reaching consequences, hence the dual requirements of art 80(1).

APP 101 An article in this form does not contravene the mandatory requirements of CA 2006, s 310(1)(a) which provides that notice of a general meeting must be sent to every member. Section 310(4)(b) provides that the mandatory requirement to give notice to all members is subject to 'any provision in the company's articles'.

APP 102 It is important to note that a member is not excluded from receiving documentation and notice forever, but can submit a new address or other method by which he can be contacted to the company under art 80(2).

INDEX